# THE
# GURU
# BUSINESS

# THE GURU BUSINESS – By Sulocana Das

Cover Design by Mukunda dasa (Mark Whiteley) & Nitai-Gaura Dasa
based on original design by Sulocana dasa (Steven Bryant)

First edition published September 2020


For more information visit: http://truth.prabhupada.org.uk

https://sulocana-dasa.prabhupada-krishna.co.uk

The Guru Business can be purchased with colour plates through the above link.


Contact: mukunda.dasa@prabhupada.org.uk

**BACK COVER PICTURE DESCRIPTION**

"It is a fact however that the Great Sinister ✡ Movement is within our society" SP-1970

All these five rogues and nondevotees were involved in the killing of Sulocana prabhu and Srila Prabhupada.

(From left to right)

Kirtanananda (Keith Ham) - Sulocana's Murder

Radhanath (Richard Slavin) - Sulocana's Murder

Tamal Krishna (Thomas G. Herzig) - Prabhupada's Murder

Jayapataka (Gordon John Erdman) - Prabhupada's Murder

Jayadvaita (Jay Israel) - Prabhupada's Killer (Book Changer)

# THE GURU BUSINESS

How the Leaders of the Hare Krishna
movement deviated from the pure
path as taught and exemplified by
its founder: His Divine Grace A.C.
Bhaktivedanta Swami Prabhupada
Founder/Acarya ISKCON

## BY SULOCANA DAS

# These Rogues In Human Society
# Are The Most Dangerous Elements

"By false religious sentiments they present a make-show of devotional service, indulging in all sorts of immoral principles, and still pass as spiritual masters and devotees of God. Such violators of religious principles have no respect for the authoritative acaryas, the holy teachers in the strict disciplic succession; and to mislead the people in general they themselves become so-called acaryas, without even following the principles of the acaryas. These rogues in human society are the most dangerous elements and, for want of religious government, they pass on without being punished by the law of the state. They cannot, however, avoid the law of the Supreme, Who has clearly declared in the Bhagavad-gita that these envious demons, in the garb of religious propagandists, shall be thrown down into the darkest region of hell. It is confirmed in Sri Isopanisad that the pseudo-religionists are heading toward the most obnoxious place in the universe after finishing with the spiritual mastership business, which is simply for the matter of sense gratification."

*(Srila Prabhupada from Sri Isopanisad Mantra 12)*

Note: This is the passage from which Sulocana Prabhu derived the title of this epic book "THE GURU BUSINESS".

# Sulocana Predicts His Own Martyrdom

"All else failing, it may have to come to violence some day. **But death in the pure service of Srila Prabhupada's mission will guarantee one is highly elevated or even liberated. So what is there to fear**…. Naturally, most of the devotees in ISKCON are not inclined, for one reason or another, to the activities of warfare. But if we want to call ourselves disciples of Srila Prabhupada, we must not "lag behind." **We must fight for what is right, or we should "decide to die rather than not execute Prabhupada's mission properly**." (SB, 4.28.48)… Nowhere in Vedic literature do we find the concept of non-violence in the face of demoniac aggression. The Bhagavad-gita was spoken just prior to the wholesale slaughter of millions of soldiers. That slaughter took place because the aggressors refused to surrender to the good advice of Krishna. Similarly, the Godbrothers have been giving good advice to the "gurus" now for seven years, but they have refused to accept it. So the time has come for violence. We are not eager for violence. They leave us no choice. The violence being enacted upon Prabhupada and his mission is far worse than anything that could happen to us in the course of a physical confrontation. Therefore, if the demoniac imposition refuses to surrender to Prabhupada and Krishna's instructions, **then we will fight to the death**."

*(Sulocana dasa, From The Guru Business, Chapter 5 – "Just to Chastise the Evil Doers")*

# So Aggressor Should Be Killed Immediately

"What is religious fight? Religious fight means you have got right to kill your aggressor. If somebody takes your property, if somebody sets fire in your house, **if somebody kidnaps your wife, or somebody is trying to kill you, they are called aggressor**. **So aggressor should be killed immediately.** It is not that somebody has become an aggressor, and if I say, "Now I have become a Vaishnava, I'll not be violent. I shall tolerate. Caitanya Mahaprabhu has taught us to be tolerant like the tree or the grass. So I shall become tolerant. Let him do." Just like Gandhi used to say. Somebody questioned him that "If somebody comes and violates the chastity of your daughter in your presence, what will you do?" He said, "I shall remain nonviolent." But that is not sastric injunction. This is foolishness. **If somebody is aggressor, he must be killed immediately."**

*(Srila Prabhupada, Srimad-Bhagavatam Lecture, 1.8.50*
*Los Angeles, May 12, 1973)*

## Fighting Must Be There

"We have to fight. Those who are opposing Krishna consciousness movement, we have to fight with them to our best capacity. Never mind if we are defeated. That is also service. Krishna sees the service. Defeated or victorious, depend on Krishna. But fighting must be there."

*(Srila Prabhupada, Srimad-Bhagavatam Lecture, 7.9.9, Mayapur, March 1, 1977)*

## The so-called, pseudo guru, false guru, he should be killed.

"So real guru is never to be killed, but the so-called guru has to be killed. The so-called, pseudo guru, false guru, he should be killed."

*(Prabhupada Lecture, Bhagavad-gita 2.4-5, London, August 5, 1973)*

## His Grace Sulocana Dasa Prabhu
## ~ Prabhupada's Perfect Disciple ~

(Sulocana Prabhu was murdered May 22nd, 1986, 1:00 am,
in Los Angeles, two days after this story was written.)

# Sulocana Dasa (Steven Leslie Bryant)

## July 4th 1952 - May 22nd 1986

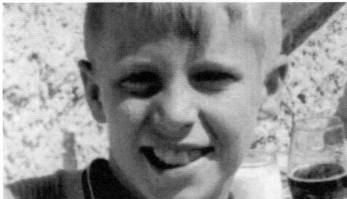

STEVEN LESLIE BRYANT (July 4, 1952-May 22, 1986) was the son of a United States Air Force officer and a German-born high school teacher (Jack W. and Helga L. Bryant).

Although Steve was born in Laramie, a small town in south-eastern Wyoming, as a child he never lives in one place. As the son of an Air Force officer, his family constantly move from base to base.

"When you're in the Air Force you travel." His Mother said.

Although his parents are loving, Steve is always looking for some place to belong.

Eventually in 1965, they settle in the all American suburb of Royal Oak, Michigan. At first Steve was happy.

Left: Celebrating Christmas with his parents, Jack and Helga.

"He was in the boy scouts; he started in the band playing the clarinet." His Mother said.

By his late teens things change, he's restless and lacks direction.

His Mother said: "He wasn't into school so much, study wasn't so important. We were afraid he wasn't going to finish high school."

Steve barely graduates. After high school he often gets into trouble and seems to have no focus.

"The trouble started later, when he was getting into motorcycles. He probably started marijuana too, I imagine." His Mother said.

Steve longs to find some larger purpose for his life, but he doesn't know where to look.

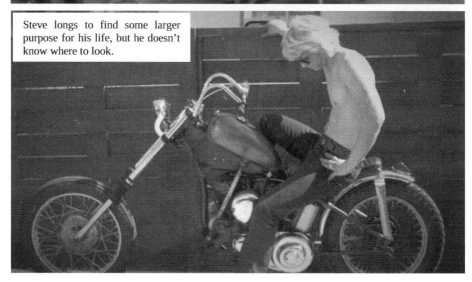

Then one day in 1974 when Steve was 21, everything changes.

"He had apparently run into the Krishna recruiters and they invited him to the temple." His Mother said.

In July later that same year, as a sincere spiritual seeker, Steven Bryant becomes a disciple of His Divine Grace A. C. Bhaktivedanta Swami Prabhupada. He is named Sulocana das, the servant of the great devotee of Lord Nityananda described in the C.C. Adi Lila 11.50.

In 1979 Sulocana marries Jane Rangeley, who had a two-year-old son from a previous relationship.

Sulocana with his first son Sarva and his wife who is at this time, a "disciple" of Kirtanananda "Swami".

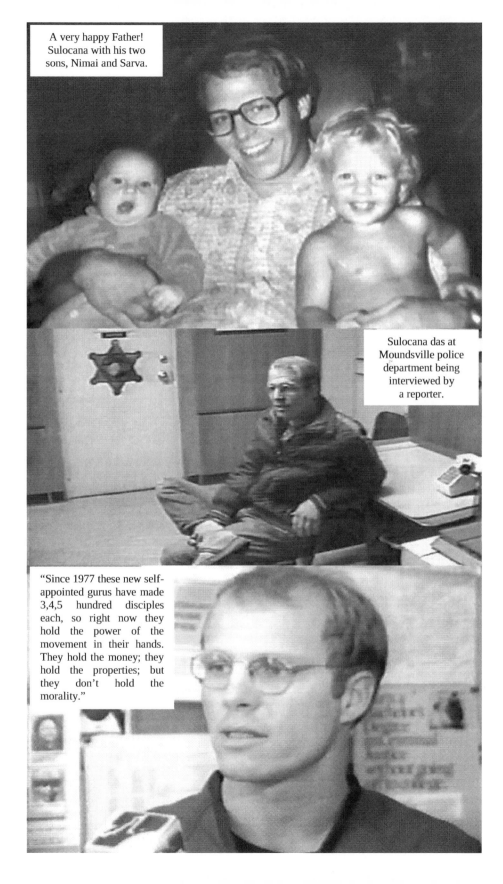

A very happy Father! Sulocana with his two sons, Nimai and Sarva.

Sulocana das at Moundsville police department being interviewed by a reporter.

"Since 1977 these new self-appointed gurus have made 3,4,5 hundred disciples each, so right now they hold the power of the movement in their hands. They hold the money; they hold the properties; but they don't hold the morality."

Sulocana with his new fiancée, Bhagavati dasi (Cathy Barry) in the mountains of central California, near Sequoia National Park, 1986.

Sulocana had predicted his death some months earlier, and he spoke about it with a former New Vrindaban friend, Gail Conger. "When I die," Sulocana told her, "then everyone will see (that I was right about Keith Ham.)"… In the mountains, Sulocana spoke again about death to Bhagavati, although it caused her grief to hear his grave prophesy. The Philadelphia Inquirer later interviewed his fiancée, and reported: Shortly before he was murdered, Bryant had talked of dying to the woman he'd planned to marry.

"Upon my death," he told his girlfriend, "that's when everything will unfold." She didn't like him to talk that way, but Steve wouldn't stop. "When I die, then everyone will see," he said. "Don't die for a cause," she told him. But Steve said it was his destiny.

While Bryant's desire to get married and settle down did not necessarily mean that he was ready to give up his fight against the gurus, it certainly meant that the nature of his crusade was about to change. The woman who was to become his wife says he was prepared to devote his time to the family, his new business and his new book, which was to be called The Guru Business.

Those in the camp of the rogues and nondevotees, who are possessed of a deranged and hellish mentality, claim that Sulocana had given up his fight. This only proves that these people own not even the slightest trace of real warrior spirit. If one had but walked only one foot in Sulocana's shoes, then he would know a real warrior never gives up the fight.

"Heroism, power, determination, resourcefulness, courage in battle, generosity, and leadership are the qualities of work for the ksatriyas." (Bhagavad-gita 18.43)

As well as having immense heroism, power and determination, Sulocana was also very resourceful. To overcome the difficulties in his great fight with the demoniac, he was retreating from the battlefield to gain strength and a more solid situation with which to continue his fight. Sulocana had great plans to heal ISKCON and was working on another epic book containing all Prabhupada's quotes on varnasrama dharma. (See page 103)

To say he gave up the fight is an insult thrown by the cowardly nondevotees.

"We think everything in our own standard. Atmavat manyate jagat. That is the nature, that atmavat, what he is thinking of himself, therefore, others must be like that. No. Others may be different from you." (Prabhupada Lec. B.G. 7.1 LA, 12/3/70)

If one is a coward, he thinks others as cowards!

"He lives forever by his divine instructions,
and the follower lives with him."

# TABLE OF CONTENTS

Purity is the real force behind any genuine spiritual movement. Prabhupada
predicted his "leaders" would not live up to the standards he personally set.

The personal ambition of the "big guns" and how it has ruined the
society, bringing dishonor to Prabhupada's good name.

The truth about the spiritual master. How becoming a bona fide guru
is not by appointment, but by a lifetime of sincere hard work and devotion.

The first step to sanity: A logical and scriptural confrontation.

Srila Prabhupada was not a sentimentalist. Rather he taught that violence
is often necessary to combat evil. All else failing, it may be necessary to
use force to stop the "guru" imposition in ISKCON.

This famous quote by Sridhar Maharaja is one of hundreds of quotes
contradictory to Srila Prabhupada's teachings, that helped ISKCON's appointed
"gurus" to "dig their own graves." Unfortunately, ISKCON got buried as well.
Srila Prabhupada had specifically warned *not* to take Sridhar Maharaja's advice.

How the "authorized" biography of ISKCON's founder minimizes the
qualifications of a true saint, thereby giving full reign to charlatans eager
to profit from their "guru business."

A running history showing the most important events of the takeover
and the efforts made to thwart it, beginning in 1977 [Not complete].

How ISKCON leaders, especially the "gurus" manipulate innocent women
for their own selfish profit, adoration, and distinction. Thus ISKCON's
90% divorce rate. Also the real reason why Prabhupada gave sannyasa
to his sexually inclined disciples.

# APPENDIXES:

# BONUS MATERIAL:

# FOREWORD

Now it is the month of March 2020, and astrologically speaking, we are in an alignment that last occurred approximately eighteen and a half years ago around September 2001. This astrological alignment is very favourable to acts of deceit that can be exploited by those with demoniac and deranged minds.

Back in 2001, I found myself not only trying to awaken people to what was obviously an inside job by the government on 911, but also I found myself fighting to defend the good name of Srila Prabhupada, which had been slandered in 2000 by a vicious lawsuit. This I was doing alongside the completion of a huge project that had been inspired within me in 1993 by hearing Sulocana prabhu speak the following words:

*"He left us his own autobiography, as it is." (Guru Business Preface – A Rude Awakening)*

These words were implanted in my heart by Prabhupada's perfect disciple, and eventually manifested in November of 2001, as the wonderful autobiography of His Divine Grace called "Srila Prabhupada Lilamrta As It Is"

So back in 2001, I fought on three fronts: 1. I exposed the lies of the demoniac government and their involvement in 911. 2. I fought to protect Prabhupada's good name from the blasphemy of the Windle Turley child abuse lawsuit. 3. I also fought to get Prabhupada's pastimes and true life story completed and published, thus strongly helping to fulfil the first purpose of Sulocana prabhu's book:

*"It must be revealed to the world exactly who Srila Prabhupada is and how he has nothing whatsoever to do with the corruption going on amongst ISKCON's leaders today." (Guru Business Preface – A Rude Awakening)*

Now in 2020, I again find myself in very similar fights.

The demons, after using 911 to facility their long term goal to create "The Greater Israel Project" are now going full on for a Jew World Order of communist tyranny by using their Covid-19 PSYOP. Thus I am trying, along with many others, to expose this coronavirus hoax and the true agenda behind it.

Recently, with the publication of his book called "Killing For Krishna", Henry Doktorski the deranged follower of Keith Ham (aka Kirtanananda), has viciously attacked Prabhupada's perfect disciple Sulocana prabhu.

This attack by Doktorski has been the catalyst for me to get Sulocana's Guru Business professionally published for the first time. I had previously printed it twice before as a photocopy booklet after reading it in 1993, and later around 1998, but the illusory energy of the Lord was always checking my desire to print it as a beautiful book befitting its glorious stature. Now I am truly proud and honoured to have been given the service of getting The Guru Business into print, at long last!!!

If anyone actually reads this printing of Sulocana's Guru Business, that in and of itself, will destroy the slanderous mental speculations presented by Henry Doktorski in his book "Killing For Krishna". Still as a follower of Sulocana, I cannot sit idly and allow this deranged rogue and nondevotee to blaspheme Prabhupada's perfect disciple. As silence means acceptance!!!

So in essence the fight I am now undertaking consists of shaking off the strong illusory energy that has for so long kept me from doing what must be done. The publication of Sulocana prabhu's epic Guru Business cannot be neglected any longer. It is now 34 years overdue!!!

Sadly, the first generation of devotees were so lost in the darkness of washing the feet of sinful men dressed as devotees of Krishna and eating their saliva coated food remnants that they could not hear Sulocana prabhu's urgent call to action. I am so enlivened that this book will now be available in a most suitable format for the new generation of Prabhupada followers. They will surely imbibe its warrior spirit and message of true devotional loyalty to Srila Prabhupada and the mission of Sri Caitanya Mahaprabhu.

Prabhupada urgently wants to create two classes of men.

*"So this is position. Therefore, because we are Krishna conscious, we are servants of God, therefore it is our duty to save this human civilization. You see. Krsna wants it.* **And to save this human civilization, these two classes are required very urgently.** *So you American boys and girls, you are intelligent, you have got all facilities.* **At least in your country, create these two classes, brahmana and ksatriya. The world will be saved, and you will be saved, and Krishna will be pleased.** *Brahmana's business means that people should know what is God, what is our relationship with Him. That is brahmana's... And ksatriya's business is to give protection to the people so that may all know what is God.... The ksatriyas should give protection; otherwise the demons will disturb.* **So there is the necessity of war with the demons, for ksatriya"** *(Srimad-Bhagavatam Lecture 1.2.14 Los Angeles, August 17, 1972)*

The Guru Business will be the standard reading for all the new disciples of Srila Prabhupada. Thus it will surely help to create many fully qualified brahmanas and ksatriyas for the salvation of the world.

### You My Dear Brother Have Opened My Eyes

My dear Sulocana prabhu, please accept my humble obeisances at your feet.

All glories to Srila Prabhupada.

For those souls who are aware of your epic fight, it will undoubtedly be very clear to them, unless they are possessed of a deranged and hellish mentality, that you are the perfect disciple prophesied by Srila Prabhupada in his Srimad Bhagavatam:

*"**Whenever an acarya comes, following the superior orders of the Supreme Personality of Godhead or His representative, he establishes the principles of religion, as enunciated in Bhagavad-gita.** Religion means abiding by the orders*

*of the Supreme Personality of Godhead. Religious principles begin from the time one surrenders to the Supreme Personality of Godhead. It is the acarya's duty to spread a bona fide religious system and induce everyone to bow down before the Supreme Lord. One executes the religious principles by rendering devotional service, specifically the nine items like hearing, chanting and remembering.* **Unfortunately, when the acarya disappears, rogues and nondevotees take advantage and immediately begin to introduce unauthorized principles in the name of so-called svamis, yogis, philanthropists, welfare workers and so on.... The acarya, the authorized representative of the Supreme Lord, establishes these principles, but when he disappears, things once again become disordered. The perfect disciples of the acarya try to relieve the situation by sincerely following the instructions of the spiritual master.** *At the present moment practically the entire world is afraid of rogues and nondevotees; therefore this Krishna consciousness movement is started to save the world from irreligious principles. Everyone should cooperate with this movement in order to bring about actual peace and happiness in the world.....* **Similarly, a devoted disciple of the spiritual master would rather die with the spiritual master than fail to execute the spiritual master's mission.** *As the Supreme Personality of Godhead comes down upon this earth to re-establish the principles of religion, so His representative, the spiritual master, also comes to re-establish religious principles.* **It is the duty of the disciples to take charge of the mission of the spiritual master and execute it properly. Otherwise the disciple should decide to die along with the spiritual master. In other words, to execute the will of the spiritual master, the disciple should be prepared to lay down his life and abandon all personal considerations.... When one becomes serious to follow the mission of the spiritual master, his resolution is tantamount to seeing the Supreme Personality of Godhead. As explained before, this means meeting the Supreme Personality of Godhead in the instruction of the spiritual master.** *This is technically called vani-seva. Srila Visvanatha Cakravarti Thakura states in his Bhagavad-gita commentary on the verse vyavasayatmika buddhir ekeha kuru-nandana (Bg. 2.41) that one should serve the words of the spiritual master. The disciple must stick to whatever the spiritual master orders.* **Simply by following on that line, one sees the Supreme Personality of Godhead."**

*(Srila Prabhupada from Srimad Bhagavatam 4.28.48,50,51)*


After Prabhupada's physical departure from this world, his powerful prediction has unfolded with amazing accuracy. By the introduction of unauthorised principles, the envious rogues and nondevotees dressed as Vaishnava's have most definitely created complete disorder in the pure religious movement Prabhupada established.

Sulocana prabhu, you totally abandoned all personal considerations and sacrificed your life to expose the demoniac activities of these rogues and nondevotees and their apa-siddhantic philosophy. Such a perfect disciple as yourself, who fought so bravely to take serious charge of Prabhupada's mission and execute it correctly, has surely seen the Supreme Personality of Godhead and become liberated back to Godhead, or at least you have become an exalted soul on a heavenly planet.

*"So ksatriya, they are trained up violent to become violent to stop violence. That is required. Therefore Krishna advises that "Don't try to become nonviolent because..." Tasmad yudhyasva bharata. "Don't think that by killing the body, your grandfather, or your nephews and your brother on the other side, they will be finished. No. They'll live. The body may be destroyed." Na hanyate hanyamane sarire. But actual soul, he'll transmigrate. According to Vedic philosophy, if a ksatriya dies in proper fighting, then he is immediately transferred to the heavenly planet, the heavenly planet."*

*(Prabhupada Lecture, Bhagavad-gita 2.12, Hyderabad, November 17, 1972)*

You have shown to us an ideal example of a ksatriya warrior by living those bold words that you spoke in your Guru Business:

*"All else failing, it may have to come to violence some day. But death in the pure service of Srila Prabhupada's mission will guarantee one is highly elevated or even liberated. So what is there to fear.... Naturally, most of the devotees in ISKCON are not inclined, for one reason or another, to the activities of warfare. But if we want to call ourselves disciples of Srila Prabhupada, we must not "lag behind." We must fight for what is right, or we should "decide to die rather than not execute Prabhupada's mission properly." (SB, 4.28.48)... Nowhere in Vedic literature do we find the concept of non-violence in the face of demoniac aggression. The Bhagavad-gita was spoken just prior to the wholesale slaughter of millions of soldiers. That slaughter took place because the aggressors refused to surrender to the good advice of Krishna. Similarly, the Godbrothers have been giving good advice to the "gurus" now for seven years, but they have refused to accept it. So the time has come for violence. We are not eager for violence. They leave us no choice. The violence being enacted upon Prabhupada and his mission is far worse than anything that could happen to us in the course of a physical confrontation. Therefore, if the demoniac imposition refuses to surrender to Prabhupada and Krishna's instructions, then we will fight to the death."*

As Jatayu gave his life by fighting against Ravana, you have given your life and fought as Prabhupada instructed against the modern day Ravana, or the great sinister movement (International Jewry) now totally controlling ISKCON.

*"The Jatayu fought with Ravana. Yesterday you saw. Ravana was kidnapping Sita devi, and Jatayu, the bird, he was going, flying. Ravana knew how to fly without machine. He was very, very materially powerful. So the Jatayu attacked him on the sky: "Who are you? You are taking away Sita. I shall fight you." So Ravana was very powerful. He was defeated, Jatayu, but he fought. That is his service. Never mind defeated. Similarly, we have to fight. Those who are opposing Krishna consciousness movement, we have to fight with them to our best capacity. Never mind if we are defeated. That is also service. Krishna sees the service. Defeated or victorious, depend on Krishna. But fighting must be there. Karmany evadhikaras te ma phalesu kadacana. That is the meaning. You have to work for Krishna sincerely, intelligently, and victory or defeat, it doesn't matter. Just like Jatayu was defeated fighting with Ravana. His wings were cut off.*

*Ravana was very strong.* **And Lord Ramacandra, He did his last funeral ceremonies because he was a devotee.** *" (Prabhupada Lecture, Srimad-Bhagavatam 7.9.9, Mayapur, March 1, 1977)*

By your intense desire and fighting spirit, you liberated Prabhupada's previously hidden letters from the hands of the rogues and nondevotees. Under a constant threat to your life, you scrutinizingly analysed those transcendental letters and revealed their essence.

By shining the powerful light of truth over the most dangerous elements in human society, who in the garb of religious propagandists are hell bent on destroying Prabhupada's mission to save the world, you made your righteous stand for the Lord of morality, Sri Caitanya Mahaprabhu.

As a true ksatriya warrior in the fire of sacrifice and full surrender to Prabhupada, the deepest realizations of his books were revealed in your heart by the Lord. You had a great vision of how to heal ISKCON and were working on another epic book containing all Prabhupada's quotes on varnasrama dharma.

You will be honoured and worshipped for your selfless service and sacrifice by all the numerous Vaishnavas who will overflood this world for the next ten thousand years.

Your perfect example and clear precept found in your transcendental Guru Business will sit in their hearts as the guide to Prabhupada's lotus feet, where you always remain as his perfect disciple and follower.

**"He lives forever by his divine instructions, and the follower lives with him."**

*(Srila Prabhupada from Srimad Bhagavatam Introduction)*

Whether you have gone to a heavenly planet or directly back to Godhead, one thing is sure, you shall very soon return and descend to this world as Prabhupada's perfect disciple to take charge of his mission and execute it properly.

You my dear brother have opened my eyes and have shown to me the true path of service to our Lord and Master His Divine Grace.

I am eternally in your debt.

Your fallen servant

Mukunda dasa.

March 2020

# THE GURU BUSINESS

How the Leaders of the Hare Krishna movement deviated from the pure path as taught and exemplified by its founder:
His Divine Grace A. C. Bhaktivedanta Swami Prabhupada
Founder/acarya ISKCON

**BY SULOCANA DAS**

Note: The original cover of Sulocana's book, The Guru Business

# "A RUDE AWAKENING"

As I started to read through Srila Prabhupada's personal letters to his disciples, I was primarily looking for quotes on marriage. At the time I was desperate to try and save my own marriage. Although that was my main motive, I also knew it was my moral duty to try and save my wife and children from possible danger. In this way, I began my research with the blessings of the Lord of morality, Sri Caitanya Mahaprabhu. Since I was approaching His topmost representative, Srila Prabhupada, for guidance and inspiration, I knew the outcome would be auspicious, whatever it was. I had no idea where my research would lead me. I only knew that something was going to burst, and I didn't want it to be me. I was not especially concerned with the broader "guru-issue" facing ISKCON's "leaders" today. Mainly, I wanted to save my own family, hoping that was part of the Lord's plan.

Previously, I had been living a rather disheartened married life. My wife had been devoting her heart to another man and so, naturally, this killed any chance of our having a meaningful relationship. Living in this somewhat stagnant state, I had not been inclined to confront the fact that she was unfaithful. In blind acceptance of what I had been told was my spiritual master's mission and his authorized representatives, I had remained simple and naive. This simplicity did not afford me either the desire or opportunity to even imagine what was lurking in the minds of others. They say the husband is always the last to know.

Finally, in June of 1984, with plenty of encouragement from the "guru" she had been devoting herself to, namely one Kirtanananda "Swami," my wife decided to leave me to devote her life to him, even though I have two baby boys by her. At the time, I knew very little about Kirtanananda, so I was a little cautious about openly criticizing him for his interference in my marriage. The fact that his "disciples" have more weapons than brains also discouraged me from openly challenging him. My wife also knew very little about him, except for the hype that's drilled into all the gullible guru-pies at his camp, such as, "He's the oldest and first sannyasa disciple of Prabhupada" or, "He built Prabhupada's Palace, so he must be a pure saint." That kind of stuff. In effect, neither of us really knew anything about him at all, so she agreed that I would go to LA and do some research, and if I found out anything suspicious, I would let her know. She said she would then join me if that was the case.

I agreed to rejoin her at Kirtanananda's camp if his slate was clean. Foolishly, I thought that she was sincere in this arrangement.

Little did I know that before the dust of my tires had settled on the road, she had already been allotted to satisfy the carnal desires of one of Kirtanananda's loyalists, Raghunatha, a man so desperate for sex that he had been grabbing devotee women's breasts and thighs, even though they were married. Kirtanananda requires many women for these loyal and hard working men like Raghunatha, who want more from life than simply work. Since Kirtanananda could see that I was not one of his blind loyalists ("Sulocana, you are just not my man") he naturally had no use for me. But his unmarried and agitated workers would be very pleased with someone like my wife. After all, how long can a young man be satisfied simply with the peephole into the ladies' toilet in the temple building there? So, when my wife expressed to Kirtanananda a desire to stay at New Vrindavana, despite my intention to leave, he didn't hesitate to tell her, "That's all right, let him go. I'll take care of you." It never even dawned on him to counsel us, which is of course the duty of the leader of a real religious community. Having been a lifelong homosexual, and repulsed by women, "Well boys, get out the incense, it's fish night" (Kirtanananda Swami thinks women smell like fish), he could hardly counsel couples in moral obligations, even if he wanted to. But, despite his personal feelings, he needs women for his heterosexual men who eventually leave him if he doesn't supply them a sex partner. So, being a British citizen and somewhat cultured, at least by New Vrindavana standards, my wife was a prize catch for him. Unfortunately, I had found out all these things too late.

So I was forced to make a dreadful choice: "Sink or swim." There was no question of just ignoring the whole thing and starting life over again as my parents were urging me. I couldn't really blame them. It was apparent enough that I was either heading for the gas chamber for just executing Kirtanananda, or a nervous breakdown if I lost my sons. Many of my co-disciples had sought the illusory escape from similar ordeals through drugs, sex, television, violence, and ultimately spiritual suicide. I could have gone any or all those routes. I had the money and I was free from any immediate obligations or debts. Fortunately however the Lord had a different plan for me. By this time I had heard and read enough about Kirtanananda to know that I had to make my best effort to save my sons from his clutches, even though it had become apparent my wife was completely under his control. So, suffering from the stress of having had my sons forcibly taken from me by Kirtanananda's strong-arms, and having lost nearly forty pounds as a result, I decided to take a stand, practically alone, against one of the richest and most corrupt men in ISKCON. This was after nearly five years of lethargic spiritual dormancy.

Knowing that Kirtanananda had attacked Srila Prabhupada in the late sixties in his first attempt to take over the movement, I figured that if I could get all the letters dealing with that incident, then I would have something tangible to show my wife about the real character of her new "protector." Having previously indexed for ISKCON's book publishing house (BBT), I resumed that service with one objective in mind: to get access to Prabhupada's letters. Due to my distress, however, I was unable to conceal my real intentions. Thus they refused to let me have them. This struggle went on for nearly two months, when, by the Lord's grace, I met a devotee who had previously bribed the archives department at no meagre expense for the complete set. He sympathized with my story, having also been stabbed in the back by an "ISKCON" despot, and he lent me his own set. For the first time in months, I felt hopeful of getting my sons back, although I knew it would still be a long time before I would see my sons safe. Shortly after this breakthrough I made a large sale of jewellery, which enabled me to purchase my computer. It appeared the Lord was definitely with me.

The letters contained all the secrets I had been hoping for-and more. I knew then that it would be my assigned duty to make the truth in these letters known to all. It was the beginning of a re-awakening in my heart for a service which He had so mercifully been arranging for me all along-a service far heavier than I would have been able to bear, or even consider, had I remained in the deep, dark, discouraging well of unfaithful female companionship (not to be confused with a devoted wife). Although the ordeal was painful, it was that purifying experience for which I had been longing. I deeply welcomed it. So, on October 11th, 1984, I mailed a letter to all ISKCON centres openly declaring war against Kirtanananda and the entire Society if my family was not returned to me intact. The Society ignored me. Hardly did I get one response. Since silence automatically means acceptance, I knew that my accusations were correct, and that it was just a matter of time before the truth would triumph. From that point onwards I was doomed to live in constant hiding from Kirtanananda's worshipers, who would have killed me in an instant if they knew where I was parked in my motor home, typing away.

## THE PURPOSE OF THIS BOOK

Although many ingredients are the same, this is no ordinary tale of a woman betraying her husband for another man. It certainly has its intrigue and duplicity, but this story goes far beyond an ordinary marital melodrama. The profound dimensions underlying Kirtanananda's aggression against me are obvious. Otherwise, he never would have taken such a risk for this woman, who is not even a money-picker. That would have been the standard "ISKCON" motive, as you will see in the chapter on women's' sexploitation. This conflict, instead, goes deep to the root of ISKCON's problems. Destiny has certainly arranged that, through this incident, the needed polarization between these personality cults and the real mission of Srila Prabhupada will take place. The enemy will have been positively identified. My personal love for my sons, who are still being held captive in Kirtanananda's grip, is thus no longer the sole or even main motivating force behind this book. You will only hear of my personal grief in this picture, since there have been hundreds, if not thousands, of victims like myself. I can now fully sympathize with them all. The specific injustice done to myself will certainly be rectified in due course as I ceaselessly work to expose the fundamental corruption which underlies what only appears to be the ISKCON movement, but which, in reality, represents the betrayal of our spiritual master, Srila Prabhupada.

As I began my search through the letters, I discovered something higher than my personal marital problems that I knew I should share that with everyone. I discovered that Srila Prabhupada is no ordinary man. Of course, I had read all of Prabhupada's books several times over, the same as most of the devotees and I had even indexed a half a dozen of them. I knew without a doubt that Prabhupada had introduced us to a very pure spiritual culture in its entirety, and I appreciated that very much. Yet, during that time, I never fully appreciated Prabhupada the person. After all, I had never been able to exchange more than a few words with him while he was physically present.

So, when I started to read Srila Prabhupada's words in a form which I could relate to practically, I found myself moving closer to his life in a personal way. For the first time, I realized that Srila Prabhupada's vast intelligence was not like that of an ordinary genius. He certainly had a perfect answer for everything put before him, but at the same time, he manifested a personality so magnanimous and forgiving that I had no choice but to utterly devote myself to him. Who else but a true saint could be so compassionate? His direct association through these letters rekindled in me the hope that I could also become pure one day. This was all very encouraging and allowed me to take up a desire far beyond revenge. I could see in Prabhupada's letters how a real saint deals with people on a personal day-to-day level. Anyone can write a book about God and attract a following, but to actually realize God and live like a true saint, twenty-four hours a day, in a predominantly irreligious society like ours now, I could understand just how very special Srila Prabhupada was.

It was then that I first took a serious look at the current guru-issue in ISKCON. I could plainly see that these new "gurus" didn't compare to Srila Prabhupada in any way whatsoever, that they were only externally posing as saints. Of course, I had personal experience that many of them were far from saintly. But I wasn't doing anything about it, since I wasn't fully appreciating the personal greatness of Srila Prabhupada. Thus, it became crystal clear to me that their imitating is actually creating a decoy which moves the devotees away from Prabhupada. Ironically, this was being done by the very persons who were assumed to be Prabhupada's most dear disciples. This made it an ultra-diversion. When other "gurus," making no claim to Prabhupada or Krishna, pose as bona fide gurus, sincere disciples have little problem recognizing that for what it is. By imitating Prabhupada, however, ISKCON's new "gurus," these-called official representatives of Prabhupada, are actually bringing Prabhupada down, in many eyes, to their own, often abominable, level of existence. Realizing this, I became determined to bring out the many quotes which revealed how a real pure devotee thinks and acts so that everyone would have the chance to see, as I now could, the difference between a saint like Srila Prabhupada and these impostors.

Reading the letters became like an intriguing mystery to me. I took careful notice of little comments Prabhupada would make about the leaders, specifically the Governing Body Commissioners (GBC). For instance, Prabhupada's whole strategy changed dramatically in July of 1970. He freely started giving sannyasa (celibate renounced order) to his male followers instead of encouraging them to marry. He stopped encouraging devotees to open temples and instead encouraged them to distribute books. And he began writing very heavy letters indicating that the character of many of his leading disciples was way below the mark. I have included these letters in Chapter Two. They clearly show why Prabhupada became disgusted with these "top men" of the Society and ultimately why he decided to leave the planet early.

Some persons may jump to the conclusion that I did this for gossip's sake or out of envy. This is not at all the fact. For one thing, I had to find out the real status of these men in order to go about rescuing my children. I didn't want to falsely accuse anyone. So it was essential that I knew the truth about these "gurus," who are claiming absolute sovereignty over everyone, even to the point of thinking that they can kidnap their Godbrothers' wives and children at whim. I had to know were these men actually dear to Srila Prabhupada and spiritually advanced? Or were they merely being given a big position to keep them out of trouble, not necessarily having any claim, what to speak of monopoly on spiritual advancement? Needless to say, I found out.

I soon found myself becoming enlivened again to preach. Many letters were to married men, like myself, encouraging them to be bold and open temples. In the later years when l joined the Society (1974), I had hardly even heard such things. That idea had more or less been replaced by emphasis on book distribution. Prabhupada actually discouraged opening many more temples at that time since he was seeing that the ones he had already opened were being mismanaged and members were leaving almost as fast as they were coming. So even though I became inspired to open a temple, the difficulty was, I wanted Prabhupada to be justly recognized all over the world, and not just where I and a handful of other ISKCON "outcasts" were preaching. So I decided, first, I must make these most vital and revealing letters available to everyone. Then they could also increase their desire to present Prabhupada's teachings, instead of the bogus philosophy of these new "gurus." By this time, I had realized that these men were actually the major source of Prabhupada's displeasure, despite what most of us had been led to believe. In one letter, Prabhupada actually said that they were not "the real workers."

So, in a nutshell, the purpose of this book is fourfold:

**1) It must be revealed to the world exactly who Srila Prabhupada is and how he has nothing whatsoever to do with the corruption going on amongst ISKCON's leaders today.** That is what the media likes to print and so that is what people generally think is the real Hare Krishna movement. But Prabhupada's motive was pure. This is clearly evident when you see how he dealt with people in their strengths and weaknesses on a practical, day-today basis. In other words, unlike the new "gurus," he practiced what he preached. When this is seen, it will become next to impossible for persons who do not possess true spiritual realization and purity to "fool the innocent public." Of course, many persons will continue to lump Srila Prabhupada in with these bogus gurus, but at least the sincere seekers will be able to understand who is who.

**2) There is a crying need to increase and even rekindle love for Prabhupada from his own disciples. To a large extent, they have left Prabhupada's mission out of frustration and discouragement.** These unscrupulous new "gurus" try to convince us that the majority of Prabhupada's disciples have left the Society because they are all insincere, lusty, envious, etc. They openly claim that the only real disciples of Srila Prabhupada are the ones who accept the new "gurus" as bona fide saints. This is nonsense. Prabhupada makes it very clear in his letters why 99% of the devotees leave the Society: "Nasty, personally motivated" leaders. That's all. There is no other reason. With proper leadership anyone can be happy and find shelter in Srila Prabhupada's real movement. The real movement is meant for the whole world, not just a small handful of religious zealots. But first there has to be real leaders. Unfortunately, because most of us are unable to "turn the other cheek" indefinitely, we could not, and cannot, constantly tolerate the behavior of these men, which is becoming progressively more and more satanic. They were the foremost cause of disciples leaving ISKCON even while Prabhupada was physically present, what to speak of now. So, in reality, the loyalists who have stayed in ISKCON all these years, supporting these "gurus" in their game of Imitate a Saint, are the real offenders to the pure devotee, not so much those who simply go away in utter disgust. All of Srila Prabhupada's disciples and followers should again feel encouraged to take up the real mission of Srila Prabhupada. We must not let these bogus gurus discourage us any longer.

**3) An effort should be made to clean up ISKCON and remove the influence of personally motivated leaders. In other words, we should fully awaken the devotees to the politics and duplicity going on behind the facade.** In this connection, some devotees have been criticizing us for taking on the function of ISKCON's poison-finder." Some of these critics no doubt assume that we are just as ill-motivated as the persons we are exposing. So they are saying that we should only concentrate on the "positive" aspect of its function. They see that we should just be making available Srila Prabhupada's teachings by categories and helping other devotees find services, spouses, communities, etc. Since this is such a common complaint, we would like to explain why we are eager to seek out and expose the bad as well as the good.

Many people are familiar with boils. Boils are due to impurities in the blood stream, and if ISKCON is seen as the body of Srila Prabhupada, then right now Srila Prabhupada has a serious case of blood poisoning. It is rapidly coming to a head, which is the danger point. This can be ignored for some time, which is what most of the devotees are doing. Ultimately, however, this boil has to be confronted by anyone who claims to be serious about preaching Krishna consciousness. A boil simply cannot be ignored. So, even though the devotees of Srila Prabhupada may be very busy with their various engagements and responsibilities, both within and without "ISKCON," ultimately, they will have to stop everything to confront this boil. Of course, some devotees are looking at it, and some are even attempting to bring the poison to a head. But the real question remains, "How long can we be patient before the body dies?" Daily, lives are being destroyed. Admittedly, it is extremely painful to open a boil, still, it must be done or the pain simply becomes unbearable and ultimately the body dies of blood poisoning.

There are two methods to remove such blood poisoning. There is a slow, painful method, which is what most of the devotees have been indirectly backing now for the past seven years. They want to tolerate all this pain in hopes that it will go away on its own. They think that eventually the GBC will get its act together, and somehow or other, clean the thing up. That idea has shown less and less promise as time has passed, since the men who are supposed to clean the thing up, the GBC, are the main ingredients of the boil itself. They are the ones who need to be removed. So the majority of devotees now agree that these anomalies will not disappear by dint of the GBC; there will have to be a direct action taken.

That action begins with this book. This method of opening the boil and making the poison clearly visible is the closest thing to the surgeon's knife which will get the job done, and hopefully not kill the entire body in the process. At least this book is exposing enough of the puss to clearly show the urgency. But this will not be the end. The job is far from complete. Now that the puss is exposed and oozing out, we must confront the equally difficult task of draining it, removing it, and then, cleansing and healing the wound. This part will take much more time and will require serious devotees to carry out. So, even though this direct method of cutting a boil open always leaves a mess, when an affliction reaches the danger point, it has always proven to be the only way. It may not seem very relishable to many devotees, still someone had to do it sooner or later. Otherwise, the deadly poison, called personal ambition, will have easily "burned ISKCON to ashes." Knowing this, we see this expose as the only way to save Srila Prabhupada's legacy, which, in the absolute sense, is his very life.

**4) There is now a new imperative to inspire married couples to be bold and go out to open temples. This was Srila Prabhupada's desire from the beginning.** If one has any aspirations at all in this direction, then the letters in this book will be very encouraging. Prabhupada wrote often on that subject, especially in the early years before the 1970 conspiracy. We have included many of those letters herein. When thousands of devotees are united, yet independently preaching the same message all over the world, it will be plainly evident who is actually becoming advanced through their sincere preaching effort, not by some concocted "appointment." The ISKCON movement was never intended to be a movement of neophyte men posing as renunciates, as is the case today. Real society is dependent on responsible householders. ISKCON's divorce rate must come down from its estimated 75%-90% to a much more civilized figure before any attempt to organize a real Vedic society can take place. Therefore, in this book, we have given equal importance to the issue of marriage and women's exploitation in an attempt to clean up ISKCON's high divorce rate, which is also caused, primarily, by the unauthorized interference of the new "gurus."

With these four objectives in mind, we have extracted hundreds of quotes from the letters which are all meant to help us understand what has happened in ISKCON and what we now must do to correct and carry on the mission of our spiritual master. Reading these letters is a direct connection to the mind of Srila Prabhupada. Reading the mind of an ordinary man is generally not very inspiring, there being so many contaminated thoughts lurking up there. But the mind of Srila Prabhupada, because he is pure, can only help us to become pure ourselves. No doubt that is one of the reasons why Prabhupada wrote so many letters (7,000 recovered thus far) instead of using the telephone. There was no shortage of money, especially in the later years. His "big, big" disciples were using the phone almost exclusively (much to Prabhupada's displeasure), whereas Prabhupada would almost always write. He left us his own autobiography, as it is.

Actually, myself, and all the devotees assisting in this great work, are only adding our fuel, which has become an inexhaustible supply, to that same fire which was started the day eleven sinful men falsely declared themselves to be as good as God. The time has now come for a complete fructification of this most important service to the Absolute Cause of Lord Caitanya Mahaprabhu's mission. Jaya Srila Prabhupada. Hare Krishna.

(Comments, inquiries, and donations may be sent to Steve Bryant (Sulocana dasa), 2124 Kittredge #32, Berkeley, CA, 90704.) Thank you.

Note: We have created a Sulocana Dasa Memorial Fund to collect donations for the printing of The Guru Business. Please contact Mukunda dasa on mukunda.dasa@prabhupada.org.uk if you would like to help.

The eleven original cheater gurus (evil doers) from left to right:

1. Harikesa Swami
2. Jayatirtha dasa Adhikari
3. Hansadutta Swami
4. Hridayananda Gosvami
5. Ramesvara Swami
6. Bhagavan dasa Adhikari
7. Kirtanananda Swami
8. Tamala Krishna Gosvami
9. Satsvarupa dasa Gosvami
10. Bhavananda Gosvami
11. Jayapataka Swami

Note by Mukunda dasa: Hansadutta dasa was the only one of these cheaters who actually admitted that they were not appointed gurus but rather ritvik priests. He apologised for his offenses to Prabhupada and the devotees. He also worked hard to preserve Prabhupada's original books. He did so much great service for Prabhupada and his example can teach us about the dangers of bad association. He recently passed away on the 25th of April 2020.

## CHAPTER ONE

# "THEY WILL JUST BE SHOWBOTTLE"

## PURITY IS THE REAL FORCE

*"Now I want that we shall concentrate on making our devotees Krishna conscious and ourselves becoming Krishna conscious, and not be so much concerned with expanding ourselves widely but without any spiritual content. Just like boiling the milk, it becomes thicker and sweeter. Now do like that, boil the milk." (Rupanuga, 5/9/72)*

*"You mention you like to speak now very often, but the first business should be to preach to the devotees. It is better to maintain a devotee than to try to convince others to become devotees. Don't be too much concerned for the time being with non-devotees, now we must fix up what devotees we have got in the knowledge of Krishna consciousness, then we will succeed. What good are many, many devotees if none of them are knowledgeable?" (Satsvarupa, 6/16/72)*

*"I have divided these departments to solve problems, but if in the end they are all sent to me and I have to tackle, then just imagine what is my position. The best thing would be to stop all activities and simply chant Hare Krishna." (Brahmananda, 5/15/69)*

Note: Here Srila Prabhupada is saying to stop everything and simply chant to become purified. The problems Srila Prabhupada was referring to here are not as significant as the problems which ISKCON is facing today. The leaders, however, still refuse to follow this instruction.

*"I am glad to hear that you are now concentrating on improving the regulative life of the temple rather than so much advertising with brochures. This is very nice; this is what I want. A good example is better than precept. The pamphlet is precept, but if we don't follow the precepts ourselves then such advertisement is not good." (Mukunda, 2/7/74)*

Note: You may ask: "How can distributing transcendental literature not be good?" Obviously, if someone reads a book, and, coming to the temple, sees hypocrites, who do not understand or follow the philosophy they are distributing, then the book distribution becomes counterproductive. If the newcomer is really intelligent, he may read the book and be able follow the instructions on his own. Generally, however, people will simply be repulsed by the hypocrisy. They will then often neglect the book or sometimes even throw it away. Why should Krishna send any sincere souls to ISKCON when ISKCON is not ready for them? So, as Prabhupada says above, if we cannot properly represent the truth, then better to stop all preaching and first become the proper example.

*"We are not concerned with any other movement save and except Krishna consciousness in its pure form. In India it is said that a little bit of a pure thing is much better than huge volumes of impure, adulterated things. So please try to follow this policy..." (Brahmananda, 8/27/69)*

Note: This is called simple living and high thinking. In many temples we see so much money coming in and so much opulence, especially the "gurus" quarters, but no real education system. Even the "gurus" themselves are unable to defend their claim of being bona fide gurus. They have yet to honestly defend their claim in any formal document compiled from Srila Prabhupada's teachings.

*"It doesn't matter if things are going a little slow, but make everything slow but sure. That is a good principle. To do things hastily and incorrectly is not good. There is a proverb in Bengali; 'sabure mawaphale.' This means that all valuable nuts like almonds, macadamias, walnuts, coconuts, etc. all take a long time to fructify. Anything valuable takes a little time to come into existence. Therefore there is no harm in waiting for the best thing. But everything is well that ends well. That should be the principle." (Shyamasundar, 7/15/69)*

Note: This statement "there is no harm in waiting for the best thing" is very important to new devotees. There is no rush to take initiation. Best is to study Srila Prabhupada's books and chant sincerely for some years and, only then, in knowledge, accept a bona fide guru. One must have faith in Krishna to send the guru. If we can become sincere, Krishna will send us a bona fide guru. This is the real process of getting a guru. First we must become sincere. Then we should know how to recognize a pure devotee. Otherwise, so many men will lure us to serve them and then cheat us as stated below.

*"We will establish hundreds of temples, and they will all be very opulent. But if we do not follow the instruction of the Spiritual Master, they will just be showbottle. Do you know what showbottle means? It means colored water in a bottle which looks just like medicine, but which does not work." (Room conversation, NY, July, 1970)*

*"Now people are seeing how genuine our movement is, they are coming forward to offer us so many places. We simply have to maintain our strict principles, keeping ourselves pure. Otherwise, there are so many bogus institutions doing business in the name of God and simply cheating the people. We have to be careful not to degenerate like these others. Our strength depends upon regular chanting the required 16 rounds and rigidly adhering to the regulative principles. (Jashomatinandan, 1/9/76)*

Note: Srila Prabhupada also defines bogus institutions as "Making a show of the Deity to cheat an innocent public." So, if the Deity doesn't make an institution transcendental, then what does? The purity of the followers and specifically the leader is the answer. ISKCON is bona fide because of Srila Prabhupada, not because of the "GBC." There are so many stories about all the "gurus" which point to the fact that the purity isn't there. Many such stories will be exposed in this book. Then, if necessary, we will continue to make the truth known until all of these new "vyasasanas" are removed from Srila Prabhupada's temples.

*"However, don't create any awkward situation that may be criticized. Caesar's wife must be above criticism. Up to now as I have got respectable situation, I wish that all my disciples will have similar respectable position in society. That will keep my name good. Like father like son." (Caityaguru, 7/11/76)*

Note: Prabhupada is concerned to keep his name good because he wants his books to be read for all time. However, there are a group of men today who have none of Prabhupada's divine qualifications but who are posing as saints all the same. This is the problem. By impersonating Prabhupada and doing all nonsense, these men are spoiling Prabhupada's good name. The innocent class of non-devotees will naturally think, "like father, like son." In this letter Srila Prabhupada clearly indicates the possibility that his initiates may misuse their opportunity and drag his name into their mud.

*"Recently I have received from one Sannyasi complaint about another Sannyasi who is not chanting regularly. So our view is that we shall be strictly following the rules and regulations. Monetary matters are secondary. On principle, we should better starve than neglect our rules and regulations. We are trying to present an ideal society to the world, so although we are very rigidly following these principles, still, we are very liberal to everyone. For this reason we are being appreciated everywhere. So anyway, I am not at all dissatisfied with you, but it is my duty to point out the mistakes. You are in charge of the Germany organization. Please do it nicely there, not very much on the material side, more on the spiritual side. Example is better than precept. Every one of you must be the perfect examples, then everyone will follow." (Hansadutta, 4/11/71)*

*"Simply become more concerned with increasing the spiritual content of our lives, and in this way all other problems like management will be easily solved, not that they can be solved by making some legal formula and having big, big meeting and talks. The politicians have been holding such meetings and talks for some time now and the world is no better place for it, and they have only made things worse. We should not follow their example. The world is in a very precarious condition simply for lack of God consciousness, so this should be our point of stressing, that we should revive this emphasis on God consciousness everywhere in the world and that will be our contribution." (Jagadish, 5/2/72)*

Note: If ISKCON cannot even clean its own house, then what is the possibility of its cleaning the world house thereby preventing these nuclear bombs from dropping? Still, every year, ISKCON has more and more big, big meetings with absolutely nothing sound accomplished. This year, 1985, some devotees were appointed to investigate the guru-issue and make a paper on it to be completed by next Mayapur. That was their initiative for this year. Last year, ISKCON spent hundreds of thousands of dollars on a science magazine. ISKCON can't even set an example for sudras as to how to live in peace and harmony with Krishna in the center, but they can spend huge sums trying to preach to the intellectuals. This is the height of folly.

In other words, there isn't even the slightest trace of ordinary good manners evident in the behavior of most ISKCON "gurus," but they went to preach to the scientists. That magazine was a waste of time and money. As Prabhupada says below, some people may be attracted by shows such as this magazine, but that will not be a true attraction to spiritual life.

*"So far the Road Show and the Yoga Village are concerned, these things should be stopped. Simply perform our kirtan. If we divert our attention in this way, the whole thing will gradually deteriorate. He is going far away. All these things are nonsense inventions. Such inventing spirit will ruin our this movement. People may come to see, some will become devotees, but such devotees will not stay because they are attracted by some show and not by the real thing or spiritual life according to the standard of Lord Caitanya. Our standard is to have Kirtan, start temples. What is this 'Road Show' and 'Yoga Village?' It will be another hippie edition. Gradually the Krishna consciousness idea will evaporate: another change, another change, every day another change. Stop all this. Simply have kirtan, nothing else. Don't manufacture ideas." (Sudama, 11/5/72)*

*"I know you are a musician, and naturally you have got a tendency for musical entertainment, but at the present moment our main business is to push the Sankirtan movement. So, as you are doing, take the Sankirtan Party to various places, and this will be the most appreciated. If you adulterate our Sankirtan movement with some business motive, then it will be spoiled immediately. Be careful in that way." (Mukunda, 7/1/69)*

*"I am pleased to note that there is interest in having our Sankirtan. Party perform in various public engagements. The same thing is going on here, and they have been invited to such places as Amsterdam and Germany. So if you can also do this, it is nice. But do not change our principles. Practicing is already done by kirtan. It is not required for us to become artists. Our main point is service to Krishna, not to please an audience. We shall not divert our attention too much to adjustment of musical sounds. People should not misunderstand that we are a band of musical artists. They must know that we are devotees of Krishna. Our devotional practice and purity should be so strong that wherever we chant there shall be immediately an impression in the audience for devotion to Krishna." (Tamala, 10/30/69)*

*"With regard to your question about Bengali style kirtan and mrdanga playing, one or two styles is best. To introduce more styles is not good. It will become an encumbrance. Who is that Krishna dasa Babaji who is teaching? If we introduce so much emphasis on style of kirtan, then simply imitation will go on. Devotional emotion is the main thing. If we give stress to instrument & style then attention*

*will be diverted to the style. That will be spiritual loss. I hope this meets you in good health." (Satsvarupa, 6/30/76)*

Note: It was because Prabhupada was tired of repeating himself so often on this point that he told the devotees to make some program to circulate his letters. Still, it appears that Ramesvara never understood this instruction above. Has he read these letters? In LA, they try to impress the Sunday guests with amplified stage performances. Many temples now support rock style bands. The LA Rathayatra in 1985 had two staged rock kirtan performances going on simultaneously with a handful of crazy hippies doing aerobics in the front. It was very embarrassing to see the Holy Name prostituted in this way. Because of the offensive atmosphere in ISKCON now, very few devotees are inspired to chant and dance. So, naturally, emphasis is increasing on the performance-type kirtan, the showbottle, which Prabhupada absolutely condemns.

*"I am so glad to hear that our Philadelphia temple is running so smoothly, filled with love and truthfulness. Such an atmosphere is so congenial for advancement in Krishna consciousness and if the Prabhus there continue their devotional activities in such a spirit, so many people will be attracted." (Vrindaban-Candra, 1/8/71)*

Note: This is what attracts people to Krishna consciousness and not the grand show of opulence. This paper will go into detail to show how love and truthfulness has all but disappeared from ISKCON due to the different warring factions.

*"I have seen your advertisements as shown to me by Shyamasundar, and I think you have made the thing less important. This kind of ad is not good, it is not grave. Our process is to show Krishna consciousness as it is, not as others want to see it. By showing Krishna consciousness in this way, you are making the thing less important. It is not that we should change to accommodate the public, but that we should change the public to accommodate us.... These books are the best advertising, they are better than advertising. If we simply present Krishna consciousness in a serious and attractive way, without need to resort to fashionable slogans or tricks, that is sufficient. Our unique asset is our purity. No one anywhere can match it. That will be noticed eventually and appreciated, as long as we do not diminish or neglect the highest standard of purity in performing our routine work, not that we require to display or announce ourselves in very clever ways to get attention. No, our pure standard is enough. Let us stand on that basis." (Yogesvara, 12/28/71)*

Note: Here is Prabhupada's plea. Purity is the force and the only worthwhile point of stressing, nothing else. Prabhupada often said that he was only building these large temples to engage us. They are not necessary for preaching. A simple and pure Sankirtan party will make more devotees than a mammoth temple structure; perfect proof of this fact is New Vrindavana. They have so much opulence and space there, but the overwhelming majority of the devotees who go there leave almost immediately with a bitter taste in their mouths. Since Prabhupada left the planet, not one Prabhupada disciple has gone there and stayed permanently. Most stay only a few months, proof of which is available by studying the vyasa-puja books. The purity is missing there (the full story is given in Chapter Ten). However, the small and simple temples of the early days made hundreds of devotees through chanting and philosophy with no material opulences. Simply there was a picture of the Pancha Tattva and kirtan. Those who were around in those days can well remember where the emphasis was placed and how enlivened all the devotees were. At New Vrindavana they practically have to hire devotees to perform kirtan for the tourists.

In this way ISKCON is not being very much appreciated these days by sane people. This is because Srila Prabhupada warned, in the above quote, that we have a tendency to diminish or neglect the highest standard of purity in performing our service. The chance to misuse free-will is there. Srila Prabhupada never said it would be automatic. The current ISKCON management, for whom setting the perfect example is of prime importance, is grossly misusing their power and opportunity to serve Srila Prabhupada. Therefore it is high time they were purified or replaced so that other devotees can be given a chance to utilize that opportunity to advance in spiritual life.

*"One thing, if we are not very careful to always stick to the point of regulative principles and purest standards of high living, then everything will spoil very quickly and the whole show will be a farce. So impress this point in your preaching for training the younger devotees, they will follow your example in all respects." (Revatinandan, 2/2/72)*

Note: Prabhupada warned again and again that if the pure standards are not maintained, then everything would spoil. But, if we suggest that ISKCON has now spoiled, we are considered pessimists, blasphemers, enemies, etc. Prabhupada certainly didn't think it couldn't happen, so why should we?

*"But we should never steal anything like money, food, water, gasoline, just to enhance our service to Krishna. That is too much dangerous, and if we are caught then all of our work is finished. Just like in India recently, this Balyogi Guru Maharaja was detected by the customs authorities attempting to smuggle some small items into India. By this one tiny incident his entire effort for preaching, even he is rascal number one and his preaching is nonsense, even so the example is there, his work is now ruined and he is practically finished as the government will not grant him passport to leave India. So we shall always be careful to avoid any kinds of jeopardizing our high standing in the society by some foolish and small act of illegal stealing." (Sankarshana, 12/31/72)*

Note: Many devotees don't seem to realize that Prabhupada did not approve of illegal collecting techniques. One reason for his disapproval is mentioned above. The other, and equally important reason, is that devotees are supposed to be developing good character. "Our devotees must be adored as honest." Virtually the only statement Prabhupada made, which could be misinterpreted as an authorization to "lie" is quoted below. But he fully clarifies that a neophyte should not even consider lying to get money. Kirtanananda often quotes this letter below to justify his illegal dealings. This is a common ISKCON mentality. In many places, Prabhupada emphasizes honesty, truthfulness, humility, etc. In some rare instances (and often he clarifies the proper understanding) he says, "We may do anything for Krishna." All of a sudden anything goes. Murder for Krishna, counterfeiting for Krishna, dealing look-alike drugs that kill people for Krishna, prostituting innocent women devotees for Krishna, having homosex and sending young boys to the hospital with ruptured anuses for Krishna. These "gurus" justify so many activities, in the name of Krishna.

*"So far this making some false story for collecting money or selling books, of course we may do anything for Krishna, but that is supposed to be reserved for the very advanced experts in Krishna consciousness, they know how to catch the big fish without themselves getting wet. So it is not very much advisable to make lies just to sell a book. If we simply stick to describing how wonderful is Krishna, then whatever we may lie or exaggerate, that will not be lie. But other things, lies, they will not help us to train ourselves in truthfulness. Lie to some, not to others, that is not a good philosophy. Rather the brahmins are always truthful, even to their enemies. There is sufficient merit in our books that if you simply describe them sincerely to anyone, they will buy. That art you must develop, not art of lying. Convince them to give by your preaching the Absolute Truth, not by tricking, that is more mature stage of development of Krishna consciousness." (Sri Govinda, 12/25/72)*

Note: Srila Prabhupada then delivered a final decision; issue a letter to all GBC to stop this disguising immediately. His Divine Grace said, "We shall not in any way sacrifice our standard. We must maintain our principles strictly. This dressing with long hair and karmi clothes is the tendency to once again become hippies. Because before you were hippies, that tendency is still there. So this should be stopped immediately."

He made the point still more emphatic by pointing to some poor people who were passing stool on the roadside quite openly in public and said, "They are not changing their standard, despite public opinion. We cannot maintain our standards as strictly as they are maintaining theirs?" *(GBCs, 9/20/73)*

Conclusion: In this way, the entire movement should immediately rectify themselves or stop "preaching." Hypocrites do more damage than good. The Society should come together, hold kirtana, chant 16 rounds together, study the books, have debates, make apologies, reinstate devotees, etc. and only then, when everyone is satisfied, should the precept be preached. "Example is better than precept." There is no point in doing any more preaching if our own house is unclean. It is doing more damage than good. Already it has become embarrassing to claim any affiliation with "ISKCON." Those who are not interested in cleaning our house, but are satisfied with their own little cults and worship, should be considered the real enemies of Srila Prabhupada's divine movement.

PURITY IS THE REAL FORCE

*"Now I want that we shall concentrate on making our devotees Krishna conscious and ourselves becoming Krishna conscious, and not be so much concerned with expanding ourselves widely but without any spiritual content. Just like boiling the milk, it becomes thicker and sweeter. Now do like that, boil the milk." (Prabhupada Letter To Rupanuga, 5/9/72)*

# "DO NOT DISHONOR ME"

## HOW THE PERSONAL AMBITION OF THE "TOP MEN" HAS RUINED EVERYTHING

*"This Bon Maharaja, perhaps you do not know, has been rejected by Guru Maharaja. So I cannot recommend him as siksa-guru. I think that he has no actual spiritual asset. For spiritual advancement of life, we must go to one who is actually practicing spiritual life; not to some head of a mundane institution, not to one who has offended his spiritual master in so many ways. I do not wish to go into all details here, but I must inform you that this Bon Maharaja may be considered as a black snake, and at the time of His Disappearance, my Guru Maharaja did not even wish to have him in His presence due to the character of this Bon Maharaja..." (Hrisikesha, 1/9/69)*

Note: Here Prabhupada is condemning Bon Maharaja for having offended his own Guru Maharaja some 40 years previously. A serious offense to one's own guru has no time factor. This is a very important point. ISKCON's new "gurus" actually think that their rubber-stamp from Sridhar Maharaja (who they also rejected later) makes them bona fide and therefore beyond criticism. But here we see that a serious offense to one's spiritual master can lead such an unfortunate person to become utterly rejected by the spiritual master. Bon Maharaja wrote in a preface to his own translation and commentary on *Bhakti Rasamrta Sindhu* that he was very, very dear to Srila Bhaktisiddhanta Sarasvati Goswami. The actual truth is stated above by Srila Prabhupada. After reading this book, any sincere disciple of Srila Prabhupada should clearly recognize that the leading secretaries of ISKCON have perpetrated an offense of great magnitude against Srila Prabhupada and his self-evident instructions. We should keep in mind this quote concerning Bon Maharaja. He continued to preach, he continued to make disciples, he continued to associate with other Gaudiya Vaishnavas, he continued to translate sastra, and he continued to think that he was very, very dear and special to his guru. But even as late as 1969 Srila Prabhupada is saying that Bon Maharaja must be considered a black snake for having made very serious offense to his guru.

*"We have sacrificed our life for Krishna's service, where is there scope for sleeping and gossiping? You can see in my example, not a single moment is wasted. This idleness is the business of the karmis. They can be seen sitting in the park gossiping, "My son-in-law said this," "This man has cheated me" but it has no place in devotional service, so your suggestion is well made...*

*The installing of telex communications for our main temples is not required. Then they will gossip more through the telex." (Gurudasa, 2/5/77)*

Note: When Prabhupada says "they" he is referring to the "leaders," most of whom are still considered the "leaders" or even "gurus".

*"Before coming to your country I took sannyasa in l959, I was publishing Back to Godhead since l944. After taking sannyasa I was more engaged in writing my books without any attempt to construct temples or to make disciples like my other God-brothers in India.*

*I was not very much interested in these matters because my Guru Maharaja liked very much publication of books than constructing big, big temples and creating some neophyte disciples. As soon as he saw that His neophyte disciples were increasing in number, He immediately decided to leave this world. To accept disciples means to take up the responsibility of absorbing the sinful reaction of life of the disciple.*

*At the present moment in our ISKCON campus, politics and diplomacy has entered. Some of my beloved students on whom I counted very, very much have been involved in this activity which I consider as disrespectful. So I have decided to retire and divert attention to book writing and nothing more.*

*Please therefore let me know how far you can all help me in this connection and what are the manuscripts ready for printing. I think I shall now stop all other activities except publishing of my books." (Satsvarupa, 7/27/70)*

Note: This is one of the heaviest letters Prabhupada ever wrote. We would like to briefly discuss four points made here.

1) It is clear from scrutinizing Prabhupada's letters that, from this point onwards, Prabhupada's primary concern was writing his books. He indicates, more or less, that the neophyte disciples were increasing. Thus his enthusiasm to take part in the practical aspects of ISKCON slackened. The leaders were manifesting neophyte ambition. There is a spirit of futility in this letter. He could see that they were going to do it their way. So he was requesting that, at least, he should be given full facility for his translation work;

2) In this letter, Srila Prabhupada directly states that the message he is conveying is far more important than making so many temples and so many disciples who are not able to come up to the mark. In other words, the purity of the Krishna conscious doctrine was more important to Srila Prabhupada than all the outward results. This is not at all what has been emphasized in ISKCON over the past years.

3) Srila Prabhupada uses the terms "politics and diplomacy." This is in direct reference to the leading secretaries of the movement. It will not be the only letter which explicitly reveals the existence of this dreadful disease. We shall soon see that Srila Prabhupada even disbanded the GBC for some time due to this

contamination. But, what is not so well known, is the fact that Srila Prabhupada once, in utter disgust concerning the politics and personal ambition, directly told his GBC members that they could take the whole movement, and he would simply go his own way. They begged him not to do this, yet were still not sincere enough to stop the personal ambition, diplomacy, and politics.

4) Srila Prabhupada was counting upon his leading secretaries to properly manage his society. But they betrayed him. Therefore, this letter indicates that Srila Prabhupada had lost almost all hope that the "leaders" would ever become sincere enough to renounce the original sin, the tendency to betray the trust extended by the Supreme Lord through his dearmost servitor. Despite many heavy letters such as this one, Prabhupada was never actually relieved from management responsibilities. He had to tolerate innumerable offenses by his "leaders" just to keep the thing going long enough to finish his books. But now, some of these same leaders claim to be so advanced that they don't need to read Prabhupada's books anymore. At one point Tamala Krishna demanded that Prabhupada's purports not be read during his classes-that his commentary alone was sufficient.

*"Regarding the poisonous effect in our Society, it is a fact and I know where from this poison tree has sprung up and how it affected practically the whole Society in a very dangerous form. But it does not matter. Prahlad Maharaja was administered poison, but it did not act. Similarly Lord Krishna and the Pandavas were administered poison and it did not act. I think, in the same parampara system, that the poison administered to our Society will not act if some of our students are as good as Prahlad Maharaja. I have therefore given the administrative power to the GBC.*

*You are also one of the members of the GBC, so you can think over very deeply how to save the situation. It is a fact however that the great sinister movement is within our Society. I have not heard anything from Krishnadasa or Shyamasundar, so all of you may try to save the Society from this dangerous position."* (Hansadutta, 9/2/70)

Note: Prabhupada is easily as good as Prahlada Maharaja, but, since he had given the movement to the GBC, he is saying here that they will have to become as good as Prahlada if they want to save the movement from certain destruction. He was prepared to wash his hands of the whole thing. This exact same sinister movement is still there, but it is no longer within the Society, it has become the Society and everyone else has fled for their lives. Naturally, everyone will point a finger at everyone else as to who these demons referred to here are, but with a little common sense endeavor, anyone can easily see who the agents of this "great sinister movement" really are.

*"Of course, by Krishna's grace, the higher learned section is appreciating our books. That is the only hope for pushing on. But, I am very much depressed by the recent incidences in Germany. It is now evident that some of our top men are very much ambitious and there have been so many fall downs."* (Bhagavan, 1/27/75)

Note: Notice in this letter that it is the top men that are the very ambitious ones. And also notice that the only hope rests on the higher learned section, and not the so-called top men.

*"You have written: 'The BBT is capable of keeping up with Prabhupada's pace at this time and we humbly request all devotees to respect Prabhupada's desire to fulfill his dream of publishing and distributing thousands and millions of volumes of Srimad Bhagavatam in Twelve Cantos all over the world by not disturbing him at this time with problems and decisions that can be made by his direct representatives, the GBC secretaries.' Yes, this is wanted. I want to increase my work. Brahmananda Swami and Gopal Krishna were suggesting that I go to some other place in India, but if Tamala Krishna flies 10,000 miles to lodge some complaint against Jayatirtha what can I do? If you all leaders cannot work together, then how can you expect the others to cooperate with you? Differences may be there, but still you have to cooperate together, otherwise where is the question of my being relieved of so many problems and decisions?" (Ramesvara, 9/15/75)*

Note: Here Ramesvara is referring to himself as a "direct representative" of Prabhupada whereas Prabhupada is indicating that such a "direct representative" is part and parcel of a group of so many other "direct representatives" who simply engage themselves in bickering and fighting. The side effect of this of course being that Srila Prabhupada was seldom left alone to concentrate on translating. In Mad 7, p.340 and Mad 1, p.131, Prabhupada warns his disciples not to be depressed by these "direct representatives," but to take directly to his books. In another place, Prabhupada says, "one must read all my books, including the Caitanya-caritamrta, or else one will simply eat and sleep and eventually fall down." Only then will a devotee not be bewildered when he sees so much hypocrisy going on in ISKCON. We have personal experience of this fact. We were badly treated on numerous occasions by some "leaders," but we never held it against Prabhupada because we had read the entire Caitanya-caritamrta thoroughly. We therefore always understood that the "leaders" were simply being engaged according to their material propensities in a way that would satisfy their egos and keep them out of trouble. As Prabhupada once stated, "I have created these big positions for big egos."

*"Now this displeasing of Godbrothers has already begun and gives me too much agitation in my mind. Our Gaudiya Math people fought with one another after the demise of Guru Maharaja but my disciples have already begun fighting even in my presence. So I am greatly concerned about it. 'Trnad api sunicena...'*

*Please try to maintain the philosophy of unity in diversity. That will make our movement successful. One section of men have already gone out, therefore we must be very careful to maintain unity in diversity, and remember the story in Aesop's Fables of the father of many children with the bundle of sticks. When the father asked his children to break the bundle of sticks wrapped in a bag, none of them could do it. But, when they removed the sticks from the bag, and tried one by one, the sticks were easily broken. So this is the strength of unity. If we are bunched up, we can never be broken, but when divided, then we can become broken very easily." (Kirtanananda, 10/18/73)*

Note: An important point in this letter is that spreading this movement all over the world requires "unity in diversity." Many disciples are under the impression that they can go out alone and start a whole new and pure movement just as Prabhupada did. As of yet, however, absolutely nothing substantial has been accomplished by any group, including "ISKCON." This is because we don't have the potency of Srila Prabhupada, and we need to accomplish this objective working cooperatively with Prabhupada's books to guide us. This does not mean we have to bunch up together in limited numbers of temples. It means we have to keep the nucleus of the Society pure and the many branches must support each other with various preaching tools such as books, typesetters, printers, videos, slide shows, puppet shows, drama groups, etc. Every disciple or group of disciples can have his own specialty, but there should be a pure and centralized nucleus to help make all the various preaching facilities and knowledges available to all, free from exploitation. At present, the GBC, which is supposed to represent the head or brains of the body, are the worst exploiters of all. Therefore the whole body is in chaos.

Since this letter was written to Kirtanananda Swami we will use New Vrindavana as a practical example to illustrate this uncooperative spirit. They have thousands of molds for making beautiful temple structures, but no one else can use them. Instead they sit rotting. One of the reasons for this is the belligerency of the leaders at New Vrindaban. If, somehow or other, other temples do manage to buy something from New Vrindaban, they get ripped off. We have personal experience of this fact since we worked in that mold shop for almost a year. An item that could be cast for a total cost of $150, New Vrindaban would sell it to another temple for $1000. Book publishing is another example of this lack of cooperation. The leaders vie with each other, so each zone has to set up his own book publishing house. This means each zone has to spend huge amounts of money on the exact same equipment because they cannot accept the principle of unity in diversity.

*"In case you do not like this arrangement then you may keep the temple as your private property and as my disciple I will give you guidance, but you may not use the ISKCON name to collect funds or to take loans. In this connection, until this matter is resolved, no loan may be taken from the bank or elsewhere and all collections in the name of ISKCON must stop. If you desire to keep the temple as private property then Upendra dasa may return to Hawaii and ISKCON Fiji may be dissolved. If you want to consider this project as an ISKCON project then you must abide by the orders and direction of the GBC, which you do not like to do. Now whatever you like let me know." (Vasudeva, 7/29/76)*

Note: Srila Prabhupada was never in illusion about the character of his GBC men. For many years they had been causing more trouble than relief for him. The reasons why Srila Prabhupada didn't disband them permanently is not so difficult to understand. For one thing he couldn't possibly deal with each temple individually. He was only one man. So he had to create some kind of governing body. The fact that most of them were neophytes and personally motivated ones at that, didn't stop him from encouraging them to advance. At the same time, he didn't expect his other disciples to have to suffer under such neophytes and so he wrote many letters like the one above. The activities of a pure devotee are impossible to fully understand but to a degree we can see these things. Therefore he is saying that Vasudeva has his blessings to keep the temple privately and he will still be a bona fide disciple. In this way he is not demeaning the GBC, who he wanted to encourage, and at the same time he is telling Vasudeva that he does not have to abide by the GBC to be a bona fide disciple. This is a very important letter for all disciples who have been brainwashed into thinking Prabhupada is accessible only to devotees who surrender to the GBC.

Also important in this letter is the fact that ISKCON projects are not the property of individuals unless they develop the project independently the way Prabhupada is recommending Vasudeva do here. That means they don't use Prabhupada's name to collect funds, and they don't use Prabhupada's disciples either. If someone develops a community in this way, then they can consider it their own independent temple and not have to abide by the order of the GBC. Certain persons, like Kirtanananda for example, think they don't have to abide by the order of the GBC, but this letter does not substantiate his claim. Kirtanananda was simply another worker who helped build New Vrindavana. Prabhupada's disciples and Prabhupada's name were both used to build the place so New Vrindaban is fully under the direction of the GBC. In this same way no one can think that any ISKCON project belongs to a personality. If a temple becomes someone's personal project, it does not represent ISKCON. Srila Prabhupada is the founder acarya of ISKCON, only his personality should be worshipped in any ISKCON temple. If someone wants to be worshipped in a temple, he will have to build his own temple as Vasudeva is being encouraged to do in this letter.

There are a class of fools in almost all these ISKCON projects today who think that the projects belong to such and such "gurus." But for those fools who think that the inspiration behind any ISKCON project is from one of these personalities, other than Srila Prabhupada, then it is high time they wake up. It is only Prabhupada's purity that inspired anyone to do anything, even though some people have tried their best to capitalize on Prabhupada's legacy and properties. All of ISKCON's leaders were simply instruments to accomplish the will of Krishna through Srila Prabhupada. If one or several tools become rotten in the process, then they simply must be either cleaned up or discarded.

*"...and my reply is that this sankirtana or street chanting must go on, it is our most important program. Lord Caitanya's movement means the sankirtana movement.*

*Now you are my elder disciples and both of you are sannyasis and also advanced in Krishna consciousness, so these questions should not arise amongst you again*

*and again. That means everyone is not conscientious. These things are not new to you-why do you continually ask these questions? The GBC authority must be accepted under all circumstances, not that there will be fighting amongst you. This fighting spirit will destroy everything, but what can I do, you American and European boys are trained up in this fighting attitude. Now put it aside and simply work cooperatively for spreading this movement all over the world. The standards I have already given you, now try to maintain them at all times under standard procedure. Do not try to innovate or create anything or manufacture anything, that will ruin everything. Simply do as I am doing and be always serious and sincere to serve Krishna, and He will give you intelligence how to do everything."*
*(Bali Mardan & Pusta Krishna, 9/18/72)*

Note: Notice in this letter that Srila Prabhupada definitely states that ISKCON, and everything connected with ISKCON, can be ruined.

In Prabhupada's use of the English language, this is a very heavy letter, but for us, it apparently was not heavy enough since nobody seems to have followed it very nicely. The mood of this letter applies to practically all the leaders. They often quote the part about accepting the authority of the GBC, but they never quote the part about strictly maintaining the high standard Prabhupada set.

Prabhupada is also saying here not to concoct anything. In other words, we are not qualified to adjust the devotional items for time and circumstance, at least not until we can stop fighting with each other. ISKCON's new "gurus" are not changing the method of guru worship. That standard they like very much and are maintaining to the letter. The problem is, however, they have none of Prabhupada's qualifications. In other words, they take the part they like, the profit, adoration, and distinction, and reject the part they don't like, the lifetime of austerity and purification. In this connection Prabhupada gives this analogy:

*"A farmer may consider: 'The front part of the hen is very expensive because I have to feed it. Better to cut it off.' But if the head is missing, there will be no eggs anymore, because the body is dead. Similarly, if we reject the difficult part of the scriptures and obey the part we like, such an interpretation will not help us. We have to accept all the injunctions in scriptures as they are given, not only those that suit us." (SSR, p.129)*

*"Now I have come back, so let me stay in India. I will remain in Bombay, Vrindavana, and Mayapur. As you have desired, now let me do that, to sit down tightly and concentrate on the translating business. But, if you disturb me, then my mind will be disturbed. I want that what I have established may go on nicely, but I see that some of the devotees are reviving their old 'good' qualities. That is the difficulty. If the old habits come back, then everything is finished. If my mind becomes disturbed in this way, then how can I concentrate on book writing. It is not possible. Better not to inform me anything, and let me sit in Vrindavana."*
*(Hrdayananda, 11/13/75)*

Note: Prabhupada here is practically begging Hrdayananda to just leave him alone to write his books, but Hrdayananda and the GBC refused. They continued to enact their petty enviousness right up until Srila Prabhupada departed this world. And, needless to say, the old "good qualities" came back.

Prabhupada's last wish was to see "ALL" of his disciples. This would have given everyone a last chance to offer their heartfelt thanks to Prabhupada for the blessings he had bestowed upon us. Tamala informed Giriraja, and that message was conveyed to Satsvarupa and Ramesvara in LA. But these two men decided they knew better than Srila Prabhupada. So they torpedoed that instruction on the plea that it would be too expensive just before the big Thanksgiving and Christmas pick. So even though Srila Prabhupada desired to see his real disciples, they never knew to come, thanks to these "direct representatives." We have testimony by several devotees that they had the money and were ready to go, but the "authorities" convinced them that it was illusion. They were told that they would please Prabhupada more by giving the money to the temple. Their reasoning however, was invalid since Tamala used the same arguments directly to Srila Prabhupada at the time of the instruction. He argued that the expense would be too great. But Prabhupada didn't care for those reasons and Tamala was forced to send the message overseas. Satsvarupa and Ramesvara are the ones who must take the full brunt of the responsibility for this offense, which has hurt deeply so many of Srila Prabhupada's disciples.

Notice that again Prabhupada is warning that everything can become finished.

*"Regarding the controversy that is going on there in Stockholm, what is the reason? This must be considered at a full meeting of the GBC. You may suggest a way to mitigate this difficulty and if it is not accepted, then both of them should resign. I know that Hansadutta is very expert in selling books but books are not only for selling but also for reading. Now has the GBC become more than Guru Maharaja? As if simply GBC is meant for looking after pounds, shilling, pence. The GBC does not look after spiritual life. That is the defect. All of our students will have to become guru but they are not qualified. This is the difficulty."*
*(Alanath, 11/10/75)*

Note: Here Prabhupada clearly indicates the tendency of the GBC to try to become more than him. In the "Lilamrta," Prabhupada is said to have said that, "Even I must follow the GBC." Even if Prabhupada did say this, we should not accept it literally. They have clearly shown the tendency to think themselves more than Srila Prabhupada and also, as stated in this letter, to become absorbed in "pounds, shillings, and pence." Please just try and see what Srila Prabhupada is clearly saying! "The GBC does not look after spiritual life. That is the defect." This is staring us directly in the face. If this commission was so divine, as they now claim, why did Srila Prabhupada speak like this about it? Only two and one-half years after this letter was written they claim to have become so advanced as to accept the same kind of worship as Srila Prabhupada, in the same temples of Srila Prabhupada, by the same disciples of Srila Prabhupada. They went to Sridhar

Maharaja, told him the big lie, and eked out his rubber-stamp for appointing acaryas. Srila Prabhupada describes what they did as follows: "They declared: 'Come on, unfit persons, to become acarya.' Then another man comes, then another, and another. 'Now I am so advanced that I can kill my guru and then become guru.' (Bombay, 8/ 15 / 76) So when the GBC now makes their big claim that they must be blindly followed, we should remember this letter and understand that they have nothing whatsoever to do with Srila Prabhupada anymore.

*"My only grievance is that I appointed GBC to give me relief from the management but, on the contrary, complaints and counter-complaints are coming to me. Then how my brain can be peaceful. Naturally, I want to see that all of my centers are going nicely, so it is not possible to mitigate the differences of opinion and work smoothly, conjointly. So best thing is that we wait for the Mayapur meeting and decide there combinedly what to do.*

*The local management has to be done by temple president. GBC should see whether management is going on nicely, and if there are any discrepancies that will be discussed at the GBC meeting in Mayapur. That is the process. Sannyasis are meant for preaching only. That is the principle. But, contrary to the principle, if things are being embezzled then how can I save them. How one man can manage the whole world affairs? This is my concern. So far I know you are approved manager, so why complaints are there, I do not know." (Jayatirtha, 10/16/75)*

Note: Prabhupada clearly says here that the GBC has not relieved him from having to deal with so many problems even though that was the reason why the GBC was created in the first place. Prabhupada is admitting here that he can't ignore the problems since he wants to see all his centers going on nicely and at the same time he says he cannot possibly manage the whole world. So he simply got more and more fed up with these "leaders" until he decided to leave the planet.

*"I am in due receipt of your letter addressed to Rupanuga dasa dated September 16, 1975 and have noted the contents. Why is there this politics? This is not good. If politics come, then the preaching will be stopped. That is the difficulty. As soon as politics come, everything is spoiled. In the Gaudiya Math the politics is still going on. My Guru Maharaja left in 1936, and now it is 1967, so after 40 years the litigation is still going on. Do not come to this." (Gurukripa, 9/30/75)*

Note: Did anyone notice any marked difference in these "leaders" between September 1975 and November 1977? Therefore we can easily understand why "everything is spoiled."

*"Regarding your dealings with Bhagavan dasa, when two GBCs are concerned, the whole GBC must consider, what can I do? I have appointed the GBC not to fight amongst yourselves but to manage. If there is fighting, then how will you manage? So the whole GBC committee must decide if there is fighting."*

*(Hansadutta, 9/29/75)*

Note: Here Srila Prabhupada indicates the futility of the situation. He has established this as his fundamental mood about the GBC ever since the 1970 LA lockup incident, where he was kept captive in a room in the LA temple for a number of days by his "dear disciples." Exact details of this incident are still unknown to us but the indications are clear that some disciples, specifically Brahmananda, wanted to control the movement better than, they thought, Srila Prabhupada was able to.

*"Regarding the new New York house, yes, let me know when I shall have to go there to see. I have more houses than anyone else in the world, but I am not allowed to stay. The richest man in the world does not have such facilities. They have one or two, but in each place it is fit for prince, and they do not have as many as I have. And, the wife of Bali Mardan how was she giving such a bluff?" (Rupanuga, 9/29/75)*

Note: Prabhupada wanted to stay in one place to concentrate on translating books, but he couldn't. Why? Because he had to travel constantly to encourage the devotees; his so-called advanced leaders were not doing it."I came to liberate my disciples, they (GBC) have come to keep them in bondage." (Giriraja) Only one leader, Vishnujana Swami, was even civilized enough to deal with the general devotees at the time when Srila Prabhupada wanted to form the world sankirtana party. Prabhupada did not want all this traveling. Chanakya Pandit says: "Horses grow old by being bound; clothes grow old when left in the sun; women grow old when unmarried; and men grow old by traveling."

*"Regarding your questions you say that amongst the elder disciples there are still symptoms of greed, anger, strife, bickering, etc., but you are one of them. You are one of the old students, so you fall in that group. So the fighting is among that group, but not amongst the real workers." (Krishna dasa, 9/9/72)*

Note: Here Prabhupada is directly saying that "the real workers", the true disciples, are those who humbly serve and don't bicker and fight. The real workers are those devotees going out and distributing books day after day, or cleaning the temple, or worshipping the Deity. The real workers are not the big leaders always acting on the impetus of personal ambition.

*"I have received your report on the telephone to Harikesh. This is very funny thinking in our society that you want to spend for this boat, and that Tulsi dasa wants to take sannyasa because he is feeling sex agitation. First of all there is no sanction to purchase this boat from the BBT. We are not interested.*

*Tulsi dasa is affected by sex, and he wants to take sannyasa? This is nonsense. Is sannyasa so cheap? He will be a victim. He is not fit for sannyasa. His mind is not fixed up. Everyone wants to fulfill their whimsical desires; this is going on...*

*Another thing, why are you always calling on the telephone? Are you such important men that you have to call all over the world? We are poor men sons, what can I do? But, why are you always calling on the telephone?" (Ramesvara, 11/7/75)*

Note: There is an interesting story of Ramesvara's in this connection. One day Ramesvara was on the phone to Tamala when a devotee came in to inform him of the death of one of his "disciples," Sridhama dasa. He'd been in the morgue, unidentified, for several days. Ramesvara put the phone down just long enough to "meditate on the soul of my departed disciple and direct him to his destination." Many devotees were present in the room for this one. Here is how the tragedy is functioning. People are coming to ISKCON, brought by the message in Srila Prabhupada's books. Then they are victimized by becoming entangled with "gurus" who they are made to think are the pure representatives of that message. But these sense gratifiers do not even know when their disciple dies. They have to be informed. This man, Sridhama, must have performed a significant amount of selfless service for the cause there in LA and so Ramesvara gave him a minute by interrupting his umpteenth long-distance phone can for the day.

*"One thing is, I have heard that Jayapataka is requesting Giriraja that Bombay should send maintenance allowance to Mayapur monthly. But I instructed in the beginning that Calcutta should maintain Mayapur. Also, you are not sending your collections regularly to Bombay, so how they can support you? If Bombay is maintaining, what are others doing, eating and sleeping? Why does Jayapataka want allowance? Anyone who cannot collect money, they should go to Mayapur and live there and simply eat and sleep, like women and widows. I shall arrange for their eating and sleeping. But in cities, those should live who can collect and earn. The widows are not earning in Hindu society, they eat and sleep at others' expense. So if you are not able to earn in Calcutta, better all go to Mayapur and eat and sleep and I shall accommodate all widows, women and others at Mayapur and Vrindaban. Otherwise why should we maintain such large establishment in Calcutta simply for eating and sleeping and spending. These two places will be reserved for those who cannot collect. For them I am making provision. Only the active members who can collect, they shall live in the city. Eating, sleeping members, they shall live in Mayapur, that's all.*

*One thing, on the invitation card you have written All Glories to Our Guru Maharaja. This is impersonalism. As soon as we offer obeisances to Guru, the name should be there. We are strictly personalists. The sahajiyas write Glories to Guru. Why you are learning this impersonalism, who has taught you? Daily I am offering obeisances to my Guru by vibrating his real name, Srila Bhaktisiddhanta Saraswati, otherwise it is impersonal…*

*Whether you can deal with so many problems? I am receiving so many letters daily from Calcutta. The temple officers are appointed to minimize my time, not increase it with so many letters. Best to stop expanding, or if you cannot raise funds there, close up the Calcutta center. It is not that the officers should be expert in one field only, they should be expert in everything." (Bhavananda, 7/14/72)*

Note: There were very few letters to Bhavananda. You may consult Krta Kanna dasa, who is hiding in San Francisco under threat from Bhavananda, for more information. Bhavananda's defects have not been limited to impersonalism.

*"I have got very good respect for Japanese people. So far I have met the Japanese boys and girls in our temple there, they are so well behaved that I was astonished that they were more respectful than my direct disciples." (Taittiriya, 9/15/74)*

Note: Many of Srila Prabhupada's direct disciples, particularly the ones with big egos and big positions, did not have good behavior and manners. There are so many examples: we give a few specific instances, all verifiable if necessary. In Vrindavana, when Harikesh was Prabhupada's secretary, he was known to have said on several occasions such things to Prabhupada as, "It's your mess, clean it up yourself' or "This isn't dirt Prabhupada, it's Vrindavana dust." Srila Prabhupada once dispatched a letter to Guru Krpa Swami via Harikesh. The letter was very provocative to Guru Krpa Swami, especially the P.S. following the signature. So much so, that Guru Krpa Swami immediately flew from Japan to India. He went to his Guru Maharaja and asked whether or not the message in the letter was totally coming from him. It wasn't. Harikesh Swami was immediately removed from his duties of personal secretary and was exiled to Eastern Europe. He was also told to walk to Delhi from Vrindavana. Another incident, concerning Tamala, was just after the 1976 infamous GBC meeting when Srila Prabhupada exiled Tamala to go to China. Tamala became angry and pointed his index finger at Prabhupada. "I will not go to China. Why should I go to China? I have my own party in America. You cannot tell me this. I am not going to go." One sannyasi also in the room protested, "You cannot talk to Srila Prabhupada like this." Tamala replied sharply, "Don't tell me what I can and can't do." Srila Prabhupada once said about another "acarya": "Hansadutta is praying every night that I will die and he will become acarya." The list of such quotes could fill a volume. We are only touching the top of the iceberg in this book. Almost without exception, the only outstanding feature all the current ISKCON "acaryas" have in common is their disrespect for Srila Prabhupada. At any rate, we see in this letter, that an ordinary Japanese citizen has better manners than some of Prabhupada's "direct representatives."

*"In that trust you must be very careful to make sure that my name is registered there as the founder acarya and that I am to be the ultimate authority. In other words, in any case of necessity of vetoing or cancelling any decision made by the other trustees, I should be able to do like that. My decision should overrule all the other trustees combined." (Kurusrestha, 12/28/74)*

Note: Does this letter sound like Prabhupada had much faith in the combined purity of the GBC? The following incident clearly shows just how corrupt the GBC was/is. And those who weren't corrupt, how foolish they were/are. But today the GBC is still saying that their combined opinion is as good as Prabhupada's. Indeed, they go so far as to say, that even Srila Prabhupada was obliged to follow the GBC.

*"YOUR MATERIAL LEGAL FORMULA WILL NOT HELP US ONLY OUR SPIRITUAL LIFE CAN HELP US I HAVE NO APPROVAL FOR ANY THESE PLANS STOP HANSADUTTA MUST RETURN GERMANY IMMEDIATELY DON'T LEAVE AGAIN STOP ATREYA RISHI HAS NO AUTHORITY FROM ME TO MANAGE ANYTHING REMOVE HIM ACKNOWLEDGE CABLE URGENT RENNY STREET PADDINGTON SYDNEY BHAKTIVEDANTA SWAMI."* (Copy of telegram sent to Hansadutta, Rupanuga, and Karandhar, 4/6/72)

*"Sriman Atreya Rishi dasa may be very expert, but without my say he has been given so much power and this has upset my brain. I also understand that immediate actions are going to take place even prior to my permission, and that, also, 'without divulging to the devotees(!)*

*I do not follow exactly what is the motive of the so-called GBC meeting, therefore I have sent the telegram which you will find attached herewith, and I have received the replies as well.*

*Under these circumstances, I authorize you to disregard for the time being any decision from the GBC men until my further instruction.*

*You manage your affairs peacefully and independently, and try to improve the spiritual atmosphere of the centers more carefully. I shall be very glad to know the names of your assistants such as Secretary, Treasurer and Accountant.*

*Finally, I beg to repeat that all GBC orders are suspended herewith by me until further notice."* (Letter to all temple presidents, 4/8/72)

*"...that is my hope. But I have been very much disturbed recently by the meeting which you all have had in New York, wherein you have passed so many resolutions and elected Atreya Rishi to GBC secretary, and made so many other changes. I am very much puzzled by the whole business. Therefore I have not approved of it and you may by now have received my letter why I have temporarily suspended the GBC. Let us not revive this old matter, but I want to know from you what is your opinion of the matter, and how is it that Hansadutta and Atreya Rishi were able to persuade you all senior leaders of the Society to follow their foolish activities? Kindly inform.*

*From now on, the temples will operate independently and try to improve their spiritual life more carefully, so there is no more need for such financial arrangement of centralization, as you have proposed...*

*So far your statement, "our final success will be when you actually sit tight and translate books and let us manage successfully," yes, that is my desire, but if you can do it or not, that has again disturbed me very much. Now I have given you everything, but I do not see that even the basic principles of advancement in spiritual life are always there, and sometimes there is tendency to neglect what is our real purpose of life, namely, to become mad after Krishna, and instead we become carried away by big, big talk. So I am still thinking how things will go on." (Satsvarupa, 4/10/72)*

*"And I am surprised that none of the GBC members detected the defects in the procedure. It was detected only when it came to me. What will happen when I am not here, shall everything be spoiled by GBC? So for the time being, let the GBC activities be suspended until I thoroughly revise the whole procedure. In the meantime, you do your duty as president of Hamburg Temple, and try to improve spiritually, Our spiritual way should strictly observe the following points especially: 1) Neatness and cleanliness of all personal bodies. (I still see those who are initiated as brahmins, they do not even wash their hands after eating even; of course, there may be so many defects due to your births in non-brahmin families, but how long it shall go on? It is very easy thing.) 2) Chanting 16 rounds daily. (I don't think everyone is following these principles.) 3) Temple worship, which should be performed rigidly between four and ten AM.)*

*I find that the devotees are still sleeping up to six, seven o'clock. So in the GBC agenda I do not find any such programs for reforming our past bad habits. So kindly as President of Hamburg center you try to observe yourself all the regulative principles and see all the members are following." (Hansadutta, 4/11/72)*

*"I think it is best thing if the GBC members always travel on Sankirtan Party in their zone and go from one village to another and visit the temples to see how the students are learning and do my work. In this way, they will avoid the propensity to sit down and plot and scheme how to eat and sleep. So you can advise them all to travel extensively on Sankirtan all over their zone." (Karandhar, 5/4/72)*

Note: We would like to summarize, very concisely, the most important points made in these revealing letters and telegrams. 1) Legal formulas cannot replace true Krishna conscious behavior and endeavor. You cannot make a man Krishna conscious by legal formulas. Obviously, the GBC was thinking that possible; 2) Prabhupada exposes the GBC's tendency not to divulge their insidious schemes to the general devotees. We do not claim to have exposed, in this document, all their treacheries. Seeing how many we have exposed, just imagine how many there actually were! 3) The GBC had a tendency to enact legislation, plans, and money manipulations prior to Prabhupada's sanction, but the constitution of the GBC incorporated the necessity for Prabhupada's approval in all such important decisions; 4) The argument is sometimes raised, and Srila Prabhupada is said to have said, that the GBC, as a combined unit of over 20 men, cannot make a wrong decision due to the group influence. But Srila Prabhupada asks how two men, one of whom was not even a GBC, could push their concoction past the other members. It is simply not a fact that numbers alone can prevent deviation and group treachery. One powerful enticement can pollute all the remaining members;

5) Srila Prabhupada says that the GBC has a tendency to neglect the fundamental principles of Krishna consciousness and get carried away by the so-called big picture even though the fundamental principles are not even being followed by the leaders. 6) Srila Prabhupada directly doubts whether there is any possibility that the management will carry on after his departure. We can see that his doubt was not only utterly justified, but was directly a warning to us all. 7) Srila Prabhupada specifically states that the whole movement may become victimized and spoiled by the GBC. It has come to take place; 8) Srila Prabhupada specifically states that the GBC men, who call themselves Srila Prabhupada's "direct representatives," have a propensity to simply plot and scheme. In this section, we are exposing many of those plots and schemes. We ask you also to expose these to all those who are sincere enough to hear and benefit from these truths.

*"...if he received the vote, why you have opposed? You must be impartial. My recommendation is that he must be the president. He has been chosen by the vote, and I am giving the casting vote for him. He is doing things very nicely there, so he must be the president, Prabha Vishnu should go on Sankirtan, and Madhavananda should be president. Everything must go on. The women are doing nicely so why are they being changed from the pujari to the Sankirtan? These things should be done by the President. These are internal things, and you should not interfere. I do not approve of your changing the women. It should be the choice of Madhavananda who should be the pujari.*

*Why did you close Edinburgh without asking me? Paramahamsa reports that you have closed the Edinburgh temple. Edinburgh was doing nicely. You can't close a temple without asking me? Is it too much to do this? Our propaganda is opening temples, and you are closing them. We are not for closing but for increasing. I do not approve of this. If possible the Edinburgh temple must be re-opened again. (Ed. note: It was re-opened.)*

*If you close the temple, what is the management? Sri Caitanya Mahaprabhu pushed the Sankirtan movement, but He never said to close the Jagannatha temple or the Govindaji temple. In Edinburgh we had a nice house, why you have closed it? Why you have whimsically done this? If possible the Edinburgh temple must be reopened. Don't do anything whimsically without consulting me.*

*I made the GBC to give me relief, but if you do like this, then where is the relief? It is anxiety for me. This is the difficulty, that as soon as one gets power, he becomes whimsical and spoils everything. What can I do?" (Hansadutta, 9/12/74)*

Note: A very important point in this letter is that the GBC must not interfere with the internal dealings of a temple. That means they are not insiders but outsiders simply observing the activities of the temple. If they detect deviation, they may recommend replacement. That's all. Not that they have anything to do with a temple's preaching activities. The President is the leader of any temple, and the GBC has nothing to do with his plans or preaching desires, unless they go against Prabhupada's instructions. Most of the GBC don't know those instructions however, so basically every temple is on its own. If a temple president doesn't want any of these rubber-stamped "top" men to perch up on big seats in the temple, then he has the right to nip that imposition. This is now happening in ISKCON's first liberated temple, Berkeley. Hopefully many more win follow that shining example.

As stated in a previous chapter the cause of disturbance in ISKCON is ignorance. That is clear. But there is also another cause as mentioned in the following letters: personal ambition. If the current leaders are sincere, then we can easily remove this disturbance by bringing out knowledge through discussion and debate. But if ISKCON's disturbance is an intentional display of personal ambition, then it has to be removed by other means. You can only wake up a sleeping man, not a man pretending to be asleep.

Srila Prabhupada here confirms the famous quote that power corrupts, and so naturally, absolute power corrupts absolutely when the "schemers" are not in absolute knowledge.

*"Our life is very short. The Krishna consciousness movement is not meant for fulfilling one's personal ambition, but it is a serious movement for the whole world." (Satsvarupa, 7/31/70)*

*"In my books I have tried to explain clearly this simultaneously one and different philosophy, 'acintya bheda bheda tattva', propounded by Lord Caitanya Mahaprabhu. But sometimes it happens that this philosophy is given a self-interested interpretation. As soon as personal motivation comes in it is not possible for one to understand our Krishna consciousness philosophy." (Ishan, 21/9/70)*

*"As alleged by you I have received complaints against Bali Mardan and his wife, so seriously so much so that the girl has declared that Bali Mardan is an incarnation of bhakti Siddhanta Saraswati Thakura on my name. In India some of the important members they have collected huge amounts in the name of the Society and spent it luxuriously. I wanted you all my experienced disciples should manage the whole institution very cleverly without any personal ambition like ordinary materialistic men. The Gaudiya Math institution has become smashed, at least stopped its program of preaching work on account of personal ambitions.*

*So whatever is done is done. I shall request you all not to be personally ambitious. I shall do everything in my power to fulfill your personal ambitions, but that will be done in due course of time when you are fully trained up and following the regulative principles and chanting 16 rounds." (Karandhar, 10/8/74)*

*"We have worked very hard and established a great institution, but if we think for our personal benefit then it will become ruined. This is my only concern." (Chayavana, 11/1/74)*

*"Regarding Brahmananda, he is actually surrendered soul, but Maya is so strong that on account of association he has even fallen down. So these two things are always side-by-side: Maya and Krishna; Krishna is service and Maya is sense gratification, so every moment we are prone to be subjugated by either of them. Our duty is therefore to be very, very careful. The poison is personal ambition. So everyone has the chance, therefore one should not be complacent. Doubts may come about, but one should be firmly fixed up that there cannot be any doubt on the Spiritual Master or Krishna." (Satyabhama, 11/7/70)*

Note: These letters indicated the razor's edge. Unfortunately, the leading secretaries have all fallen off the edge. They are now completely entangled, having been carried away by personal ambition. The facilities they took to exploit various situations have degraded them beyond hope. That is the penalty for falling under Maya's enticement in the form of the lure of personal ambition. We should not remain sentimental. Srila Prabhupada did more than just warn us; he stated clearly that these things were happening. It has not been rectified. On the contrary, it has become far, far worse. We should stop being ostriches. Srila Prabhupada now goes on to describe all these personally ambitious "disciples."

*"I am hearing so many things about management. My request is that until I am able to return to the USA you all please work peacefully. At our next annual meeting at Mayapur all complaints and counter complaints will be heard in the presence of all GBC and I will also be present. In the meantime work peacefully without disturbing the situation.*

*In Bengal there is a proverb that even if there are some dead metal utensils but when they are together they make so much noise, so what to speak of living utensils. So this is natural, but since we are all pledged to work for Krishna, we should follow the principle of Lord Caitanya Mahaprabhu; trnad api... This is Vaisnavism. So my request is do not be agitated. Let us do our duty honestly. Krishna will give us the intelligence to do everything nicely...*

*Europeans and Americans are very agitative, but since we have all taken pledge to the service of Krishna we have to change this habit for the peaceful service of Krishna." (Ramesvara, 9/15/74)*

Note: "Noisy living utensils" do not qualify as gurus. Ramesvara is still so agitated that he now has all sorts of nervous disorders, including serious ulcers. His nickname has become Rage-esvara. It is also well known that Rage-esvara is very fond of going to movies, especially science fiction movies. He was recently seen standing in the line for the movie "Dune" and it is said he has seen "Star Wars" five times. Of course many devotees, having been forced out of their father's temples, go to movies nowadays for lack of any kind of an organized society to take shelter within. A man wishing to take the responsibility of guru, however, should not be interested in such mundane things. Prabhupada was lenient with the congregational devotees, especially householders, but the leaders he insisted be exemplary.

*"The future hope of solid standing of our mission is on the proper management of our governing body. Now we are increasing in volume. The area of our activity is expanding. Under the circumstances, if our management goes on nicely to maintain our prestige and good name, that will be our success. Such status quo can be maintained only on our being freed from any kind of sense gratifying attitude, because pure devotional service means: 'anyabhilasita sunyam,' or without any other desire than to satisfy Krishna." (Bhagavan dasa, 2/16/71)*

Note: The GBC's duty is supposed to be to make sure the purest standards are being followed by everyone, especially themselves. That's all. The householders will naturally be on all different levels of austerity, as stated in the next letter, but the leaders have to be purely following. If the leaders themselves are agitated sannyasis with no real freedom from desires for household life, then how can they lead a community of householders? Some of these sannyasi leaders, the homosexuals especially, haven't the faintest idea of what a healthy Krishna conscious community is. Therefore, they cannot possibly help the householders. On the contrary, they are very expert at creating disturbances amongst them. In normal circumstances, sannyasa is a graduation from householder life, not something to accept if you are too irresponsible to be a householder. This is all clearly explained in Chapter 9.

*"So far Dayananda, I have no objection if the grihastas live outside and earn money, but I do not want them to leave. The strict temple procedure is only for those who live in the temple. Grihastas should live outside, and they cannot follow strictly everything, but why they should give up altogether their devotional procedures? So many big stalwart devotees are leaving, why is this? Advaita, Uddhava, Krishnadasa, and now our Dayananda and Nandarani. I have sent them each one letter, so if you find them, you may deliver them my letters. This is not at all good if our big devotees fall down so easily and go away. Try to save them." (Karandhar, 7/14/72)*

Note: This is called expanding to wider and wider circles as Prabhupada wanted. It is not necessary that everyone who is interested in Krishna consciousness be expected to "follow strictly everything." ISKCON's current leaders are very casual about their own tendencies, but if the "common, insignificant devotees" break a regulative principle or two occasionally, then they are quick to castigate such devotees, even to the point of destroying their families. Such leaders who have this tendency to destroy families, and thus create varnasankara should be utterly rejected. In some circumstances, when the destruction is deliberate, execution is justified in sastra. (BG, 1.36)

*"I have also received the enclosed pictures of the proposed house. I am thinking that you are a very sincere devotee. I am remembering that during my recent visit there in Australia how during the kirtan you were seeing to my personal and not letting anybody come forward and still leading the kirtan. When you begin the chanting, everybody becomes captivated, and you can go on without stopping. I feel happy that even after my departure, things will go on. I am happy that I have*

*got so many sincere devotees who will carry on. That is my happiness."*
*(Madhudvisa, 9/18/74)*

Note: According to this letter, Madhudvisa should be appointed a guru. After all, Prabhupada is saying here that, after he leaves, Madhudvisa will carry on with the mission. The point is, devotees may receive very encouraging letters from Srila Prabhupada, but it does not insure that they will continue on the straight-and-narrow path. We do not question Madhudvisa's faith. He is a devotee. But one can lose staunch sincerity despite the best encouragement, and where it has happened the worst is with those who pose and impose themselves upon the innocent devotees.

*"The Miami situation is a great discredit for us because we have made such a bad impression on the neighbors that they have had us kicked out. This is because of nasty management. Rupanuga was the GBC, and now you are, why it cannot be made clean? Abhirama has proved his poor management, so he must be replaced... One thing is though, if the management continues to be so nasty, then that place will also be ruined. Management must be done very nicely otherwise it is useless." (Satsvarupa, 6/4/75)*

*"Now by the grace of Krishna we have got sufficient properties all over the world, so there cannot be any diplomacy or conspiracy by any sane man. All these properties and opulences, whatever we have got, this will not go with me when I go away from this world. It will remain here. I am training some of my experienced disciples how to manage after my departure. So if instead of taking the training if in my life time you people say I am the Lord of all I survey, that is dangerous conspiracy." (Karandhar, 10/8/74)*

Conclusion: From these letters it is clear that Prabhupada was not very pleased with the GBC. He just wanted to retire to his translating and not have to deal with them. But then "Tamala would fly 10,000 miles to lodge a complaint against Jayatirtha." So what could he do? He had given us plenty of books, lectures, and letters, and he knew that if just one sincere soul would actually read them, then everything would go on. So he decided to leave.

Sane men do not engage in diplomacy and conspiracy. The pull of opulences and properties is illusory. No one can keep the control forever. It was not that simply some small section of devotees was trained by Srila Prabhupada. The training was open to everyone and still is. In Srila Prabhupada's personal presence, those "top men" he hoped to train instead became enwrapped in personal ambition. They have been thinking, for some time now, that they are the Lord of all they survey. This GBC has become a Gang of Blasphemous Conspirators. It is a very dangerous conspiracy. The Krishna consciousness movement, as established by Srila Prabhupada, is vital for the upliftment of the entire world. Now it has become almost completely spoiled by the GBC and particularly the guru sub-section. Of course they required help and so there are many fools keeping the thing propped up. And many innocent people, because of their ignorance, are also allowing this conspiracy to stay in power. We can only pray to Lord Sri Krishna, and to the real guru parampara, that some sincere disciples of Srila Prabhupada will intently read these letters, as presented above, and, without prejudice, recognize the legitimacy of our explanations concerning them. Then the duty becomes obvious.

Comments, inquiries, or donations toward this book, of which this is a rough advance copy, may be sent to: Steve Bryant (Sulocana dasa), 2124 Kittredge #32, Berkeley, CA 94794. Thank you.

Note: We have created a Sulocana Dasa Memorial Fund to collect donations for the printing of The Guru Business. Please contact Mukunda dasa on mukunda.dasa@prabhupada.org.uk if you would like to help.

POLITICS, DIPLOMACY & DISRESPECTFUL ACTIVITY
PRABHUPADA RETIRES FOR BOOK WRITING & NOTHING MORE!!!

*"Before coming to your country I took sannyasa in l959, I was publishing Back to Godhead since l944. After taking sannyasa I was more engaged in writing my books without any attempt to construct temples or to make disciples like my other God-brothers in India.*

*I was not very much interested in these matters because my Guru Maharaja liked very much publication of books than constructing big, big temples and creating some neophyte disciples. As soon as he saw that His neophyte disciples were increasing in number, He immediately decided to leave this world. To accept disciples means to take up the responsibility of absorbing the sinful reaction of life of the disciple.*

*At the present moment in our ISKCON campus, politics and diplomacy has entered. Some of my beloved students on whom I counted very, very much have been involved in this activity which I consider as disrespectful. So I have decided to retire and divert attention to book writing and nothing more.*

*Please therefore let me know how far you can all help me in this connection and what are the manuscripts ready for printing. I think I shall now stop all other activities except publishing of my books."*

*(Prabhupada Letter To Satsvarupa, 7/27/70)*

# "CHEAP GURUS, CHEAP DISCIPLES"

## "THE TRUTH ABOUT THE SPIRITUAL MASTER"

*"The first thing, I warn Acyutananda, do not try to initiate. You are not in a proper position now to initiate anyone... Don't be allured by such Maya. I am training you all to become future Spiritual Masters, but do not be in a hurry... You don't be attracted by such cheap disciples immediately. One has to rise gradually by service... These services are most important. Don't be allured by cheap disciples. Go on steadfastly to render service first. If you immediately become Guru, then the service activities will be stopped; and as there are many cheap gurus and cheap disciples, without any substantial knowledge, and manufacturing new sampradayas, and with service activities stopped, and all spiritual progress stopped up. You have already mentioned one such non-bonafide sampradaya, Jaya Sri Sampradaya. So let me know immediately what you are going to do, in respect to my above three important businesses entrusted to you..." (Acyutananda, 8/21/68)*

Note: Of course ISKCON's "gurus" say: "We were not in a hurry; we waited until six months after Prabhupada's departure to officially declare ourselves worshipable spiritual masters." It takes eight years to earn a license to pug teeth or practice medicine-but getting a throne in ISKCON less than that. Maybe that could be advertised. It could attract a huge following, which is the verification of a bona fide movement. Right?

*"As for your next question: 'Can only a few pure devotees deliver others?' Anyone, if he is pure devotee he can deliver others, he can become spiritual master. But unless he is on that platform he should not attempt it. Then both of them will go to hell, like blind men leading the blind." (Tusta Krishna, 12/14/72)*

Note: Pure devotees of Krishna are not a dime-a-dozen as in ISKCON today. Even the madhyama status of devotee is difficult to attain. The topmost platform of pure devotee generally takes a lifetime of sincere, humble, and serious hard work, and only one among thousands achieves it. (BG, 7.3) Prabhupada was a pure devotee from birth but he set the example for us by waiting eleven years before taking formal initiation. Why today this impatience? Initiation is a serious matter and not something one does whimsically. No sane person rushes into such a commitment. Chant, study, and serve Prabhupada through his books with a competent, humble devotee. Then you are safe. Krishna will personally send a pure devotee when the sincere seeker is ready. Getting a bona fide guru is not a process of seeking outside oneself. It is an internal process of purifying one's motive. Then the guru will appear just as Narada appeared to Dhruva in the forest. The only endeavor required is trying to become sincere.

In the broad sense, very little changed when Prabhupada left the planet. He had long since placed the fate of his movement in the hands of his books. More and more he saw that his leaders were not following them or even reading them. The GBC was out of hand. "What can I do?" Some of them could hardly wait to divide up the pie and start being worshipped.

*"Yes, I am so glad that your center is doing so well and all the devotees are now appreciating the presence of their Spiritual Master by following His instructions although He is no longer physically present; this is the right spirit." (Karandhara, 9/13/70)*

Note: Adherence to the guru's instructions is the most important measure of the legitimacy of the devotees.

*"Regarding the action of Bon Maharaja: We shall discuss the matter when we meet. For the present, you may know that this gentleman is very much materially ambitious. He wants to utilize Krishna consciousness for his material name and fame. Sometimes he greatly offended our Guru Maharaja, and it so happened that at the last stage, practically Guru Maharaja rejected him. And the result, we can find that instead of becoming a great preacher of Krishna consciousness this gentleman has become artificially a head of a mundane institution. To become a very important man in the mundane estimation is not success in Krishna consciousness... On the whole, you may know that he is not a liberated person, and therefore, he cannot initiate any person to Krishna consciousness. It requires special spiritual benediction from higher authorities.*

*The statements of Thakura Bhaktivinode are as good as scripture because he is liberated person. Generally the spiritual master comes from the group of such eternal associates of the Lord; but anyone who follows the principles of such ever-liberated persons is as good as one in the above mentioned group... A person who is liberated acharya and guru cannot commit any mistake, but there are persons who are less qualified or not liberated, but still can act as guru and acharya by strictly following the disciplic succession..." (Janardana, 4/26/68)*

Note: This is one main basis of the ISKCON "gurus" claim to acarya-ship. It is an undeniable truth that if someone is strictly following his guru, then he may act as guru himself. But here Prabhupada uses the word "act." It clearly implies that, in the absence of a liberated acarya, a devotee on the neophyte platform, who, by definition, is strictly following the principles of the ever-liberated acarya, can "act" as the via medium of the parampara. He may be considered a pure devotee, but not a liberated pure devotee. He is on the level mentioned above. Such an "acting" guru is not beyond falling down and so must be very careful to strictly follow the real pure devotee's instructions, not try and imitate him. He must not concoct anything. He must live very humbly and not allow pompous worship of himself, for that is reserved for those who are actually in complete touch with the Supreme. His followers must clearly understand that their "acting"- guru is a completely pure devotee, and that he can only advance so far under such limited guidance. (NOI, 6) Prabhupada recommends that if one is serious, he should not take initiation from anyone but the topmost pure devotee. And, solidifying that instruction, he recommends that unless one is such a topmost devotee, he should remain simple and humble and preach to friends and relatives at home (Cc. Mad, 7.130). So, in light of these instructions, a sincere devotee "acting" as guru is really a siksa-guru and should be respected as such. Not a diksa-guru. The purpose of this book is to make it clear that ISKCON's "appointed gurus," who are being worshipped as though they were uttama-adhikaris, are not strictly following Prabhupada's instructions and so they are not qualified to "act" as acarya or siksa-guru or any such thing. They constantly commit serious mistakes and offenses because they are neither liberated nor humble.

Only one who is very strictly practicing himself can be considered as good as the ever-liberated devotees. But if he stops strictly following the basic principles of austerity and humility, then he falls down immediately. Then all one's service to him is in vain. This is common sense and can be illustrated from the following example.

If one is going to law school, it is understood that he is going to be a lawyer in due course of time. Young women tend to loiter around the law school campuses to attract such a potentially rich husband. He is not rich yet, but they know it is just a matter of time before he will be rich. In the absolute sense, if he is strictly on the path, he is already rich. It is only a small matter of time that separates, and time is relative. But, if in the meantime, the young girls distract him by their feminine, alluring behavior, and he consequently gets absorbed in such pleasures, thereby neglecting his studies, then he is not going to be a lawyer or a rich man. The foolish girl who marries him will be poor for her whole life.

So, in this exact same way, if one finds a devotee who is very serious about Krishna consciousness, then such a seeker may assume that that devotee is going to be a topmost pure devotee in due course of time. In this way, he may be considered "as good as the ever-liberated group." You should offer him obeisances and take guidance from him. But, because he is not fully liberated, he cannot be pompously worshipped, or he will get carried away. He has to be very humble so that he can make further advancement. Srila Prabhupada says: "One should not imitate the behavior of an advanced devotee or mahabhagavata without being self-realized, for by such imitation he will eventually become degraded." (NOD, 6)

In other words, if he imitates the position of a completely liberated soul immediately by accepting the service and worship which is reserved for the uttama-adhikari, he deviates. A deviator is guaranteed to fall down. Some of these ISKCON "gurus" may have been strictly following at one point; some of them never followed strictly. Some of them may have possessed some humility; some never did. But now all these men have changed their face and are heading straight downhill. Some have gone completely insane, as the recent Harikesh scandal has revealed.

So, for the aspiring devotee, it is better to continue to study and follow Prabhupada's teachings sincerely. Then, later, when Krishna sends him to you, take initiation from a liberated devotee. There is no rush. This rush consciousness was created by the "GBC". Nowhere in Vedic literature is such a concept preached. Guru, sastra, sadhu, is the formula. Guru is only one of the three. We have sastra, Prabhupada's books. We have sadhu, the sincere humble devotees. All we don't have at present is guru. So we must wait some time. Krishna will not neglect any sincere seeker. "Guru Krishna Prasad. Krishna is prepared to bestow His mercy upon all living entities, and as soon as a living entity desires the Lord's mercy, the Lord immediately gives him an opportunity to meet a bona fide Spiritual Master" (Mad, 19.151). That is the essence of this very important letter. If anyone disagrees, then let them state their position. We shall debate it.

*"To answer your last point, one who teaches can be treated as Spiritual Master. It is not that after we become initiated we become perfect. No. It requires teaching. So if we take instruction from them, all senior Godbrothers may be treated as guru, there is no harm. Actually you have only one Spiritual Master who initiates you, just as you have only one father. But every Vaishnava should be treated as prabhu, master, higher than me, and in this sense, if I learn from him, he may be regarded as guru. It is not that I disobey my real Spiritual Master and call someone else as Spiritual Master. That is wrong. It is only that I can call Spiritual Master someone who is teaching me purely what my initiating Spiritual Master has taught. Do you get the sense?" (Sri Galim, 11/30/71)*

Note: Here again Prabhupada is making the clear distinction between the "real Spiritual Master" and one who "may be regarded as guru." **There is only one guru and that is the uttama-adhikari. That is still Srila Prabhupada.** Anyone else, appointed or not, if he is strictly following Srila Prabhupada, he may be "regarded as guru" but not worshipped as though he were an uttama-adhikari unless he actually has been benedicted in that way. We have been told specifically by Sriman Rohini Kumar Swami that Srila Prabhupada informed his movement that there would be no more uttama-adhikari acaryas in the immediate aftermath of his disappearance (Conversation, NY, 1968). From practical experience, we have all good reason to believe that this remains so.

*"I understand that one devotee is engaged as Taittireya's personal servant. No devotee can be engaged as personal servant in this way. Otherwise everyone will do this.... From Madhavananda I have heard that there is some worship of yourself by the other devotees. Of course, it is proper to offer obeisances to a Vaishnava, but not in the presence of the spiritual master, it will come to that state, but now wait. Otherwise, it will create factions." (Hansadutta, 10/1/74)*

Note: Prabhupada is not saying here that after his departure anyone and everyone should be worshipped no matter how bogus they are. He is indicating that his disciples will no doubt start their own temples, etc. This is not only expected by Prabhupada, but it is Prabhupada's order. The sons naturally become fathers. Inevitably some devotees will not follow so strictly and will form factions. Others will more purely represent Srila Prabhupada. The GBC's job was not to control the different disciples' preaching projects but to make sure the ones not representing Prabhupada purely are not called ISKCON. But before the GBC can do their job, they themselves must know what it means to represent Prabhupada. Semen-drinking "gurus" do not represent Srila Prabhupada, and if anyone says that they do...

*"I am enclosing herewith a letter from Krishna devi which speaks for itself. Please reply her that she cannot take charge of one of our centers because she has violated the regulations of our society. In spite of having her duly married husband, she indulged in illicit sex life, so this is willful violation of our rules and regulations. So far her Krishna conscious activities are concerned, she can execute nicely wherever she lives, and I have all blessings for her, because the door of Krishna consciousness is open for everyone, but when one has to take charge of a center, he has to become completely above suspicion." (Brahmananda, 3/12/68)*

Note: From this letter it is clear that none of the current "gurus" are qualified to be a temple president, what to speak of being a GBC or "Guru," because they are not in any way, shape, or form above suspicion. The misbehavior has been blatant and the suspicion is intractable because of it.

*"In your letter you have made it clear that you are finding some difficulty with sex desire and have asked guidance from me to instruct you how to handle this problem of the material body.*

*First of all I think you should know that such problems are not very unnatural because in the body the conditioned soul is very prone to failure. But also we must remember that such failure will not discourage us from executing the most important mission of our life, to become fully in Krishna consciousness. So whatever falldown has been, you should be regretful about it, but it is not so serious nor is it a permanent disqualification. But you must try to check yourself from such artificial things and take full shelter of the lotus feet of Krishna..." (Upendra, 12/9/68)*

Note: Many of today's "gurus" use concessions like this one to justify their debauched behavior. They say that even though they commit the most abominable actions, they are saintly because they are rightly situated. Were they humble, and not posing as uttama-adhikaris, that may well be true. But a guru cannot use such verses as an excuse. A guru must be exemplary. What they are really doing is called committing offenses on the strength of chanting the Holy Name. In many places Prabhupada refers to ones weaknesses and minor falldowns as "a child kicking in the womb." He never really condemned such failure-prone children, but he never said that such pups could pose as pure devotees, either uttama or madhyama. (See Appendix 22, Part Two, for an in-depth analysis of this syndrome.)

*"Simply because there is no stock of books, we can do anything whimsically??? Is this logic? Gita is not spoken in Vrindavana, it is spoken on the battlefield of Kurukshetra, but this is Vrindavana picture. That chariot driven by 4 horses, that is the real Kurukshetra picture. It is not that because there is no stock we can do whimsically as we like and lose the idea, that is rasa bhasa. Because there is no bread so you will take stone??? The front picture is most important thing and you have changed it." (Bhargava, 5/29/76)*

Note: This analogy is very appropriate to the "guru-issue" in ISKCON. So they now think that simply because there are no pure devotees around we can do anything whimsically??? Is this logic? Pure devotees are not appointed, they are self-manifesting, but these men have appointed them. Pure devotees are seen by their having no material desire, they have all good qualities, and they never deviate from the authority of Guru, sastra, sadhu; that is the way to recognize a pure devotee. It is not that because there are no devotees around with these qualities that we can do whimsically as we like and lose the idea of what a guru is. That will pollute everything. Because there is no bread, you will take stone to eat??? There are no pure devotees, so everyone is worshipping any Tom, Dick, or Harry who's up on an opulent seat??? The qualifications for being a guru are the most important thing. But they have changed them.

*"My advice is always chant 16 rounds minimum and follow the four regulative principles. All of my disciples must agree on this point, otherwise they are not my disciples. Let one live anywhere, but stick to the principles. Disagreements will continue in this material world. So one may live in a suitable place, but one must follow these five principles. My disciples must follow these five principles living either in heaven or hell." (Raja-Laksmi-dasi, 2/17/76)*

Note: **It goes without saying that if one who took formal initiation is not following strictly, and is therefore not a disciple, then one who did not take formal initiation, but is following strictly, is a disciple. You can live anywhere, but to be a disciple of Prabhupada, here are the qualifications.** There are real disciples of Prabhupada all over the world who may have never been to a temple, but have gotten hold of a book and are following. Prabhupada says here that one may even be living in hell, **but, if he is following, he is a disciple**. The question of whether or not one needs a physically present guru to go back to Godhead is not the ultra crucial question. Guru is one. This means that if one follows Prabhupada's instructions strictly, then Krishna will send him a bona fide guru in due course of time. That bona fide guru is also non-different from Srila Prabhupada. So in that sense, while following Prabhupada's instructions, one is automatically linked up with Prabhupada and the whole parampara system. That is made clear from letters shortly following.

Note by Mukunda dasa: Prabhupada says that the siska-guru generally becomes the diksa-guru later on: *"Generally a spiritual master who constantly instructs a disciple in spiritual science **becomes his initiating spiritual master later on."** (C.C. Adi, 1.35)* Therefore we should not misunderstand Sulocana when he says *"if one follows Prabhupada's instructions strictly, then Krishna will send him a bona fide guru in due course of time."* It is a case of qualification. We have to become qualified to accept Prabhupada as our diksa-guru. When we are qualified through the bona fide hearing process, then Krishna will reveal (or send) Prabhupada to us as the diksa-guru. This would also apply to the previous point Sulocana made about ISKCON not having a guru now. It means that ISKCON (due to offenses) has no qualification to accept the bona fide guru Srila Prabhupada, and are therefore accepting bogus imitation gurus instead.

*"You have asked 'How serious would it be for me if I should miss the golden opportunity to become your initiated disciple?' You should know that the value of accepting a bona fide spiritual master is more than we can calculate. It is not a mere formality. Of course everyone is encouraged to chant Hare Krishna, but until one gives up sinful activities and become determined to serve Krishna through His representative, then the firm fixing up of devotional service will not take hold, and there is every chance that one will fall prey to all sorts of material desires and have to come back again in the next life, and one cannot guarantee that he will be born in the form of life he may desire.*

*I know you have been attending our temple in Boston sometimes, and that you wish to be a sincere devotee of Krishna. So go on faithfully with your chanting and pray to Krishna to give you strength for advancing in His service. It is a fact, however, that we must become free of all material desire before going back to Godhead, and this can only be achieved by following the instructions of a bona fide spiritual master."* (Ravendra Gupta, 2/12/74)

*"It is a basic principle that one must accept a bonafide spiritual master in order to achieve the highest perfection of life, love of God. I thank all of you very much for accepting me as your spiritual master, and I promise that I will take you back to home, back to Godhead. I ask you all to promise me to always chant at least 16 rounds. Follow the regulative principles, read our books and try to preach this Krishna consciousness movement all over the world. So far my qualifications are concerned, I am simply trying to carry out the order of my Guru Maharaja."* (Nityananda, 11/12/71)

Note: In the above three letters, the real qualifications for being a disciple are spelled out. **Prabhupada never stressed in any place, in letter, book, or lecture, the absolute necessity of physical diksa. He stressed the instructions. Otherwise why would he be so concerned with writing his books?** He knew he wouldn't be physically around much longer. He certainly knew his disciples were not qualified to become gurus yet. The fact is, Prabhupada is still as much with us as ever, actually more so. Before Prabhupada left the planet, devotees were under the illusion that Prabhupada was present where he was living. How the devotees are able to appreciate Prabhupada the way Prabhupada wanted to be appreciated, in his instructions. **He is factually there in his books. Anyone who takes up the books wholeheartedly is a disciple of Prabhupada, whether he ever saw Prabhupada or not. If anyone asks such a person: "Who is your guru?" he**

**can say in all honesty, "My guru is His Divine Grace A. C. Bhaktivedanta Swami Prabhupada because I have accepted his instructions as my life and soul."** This point is clear from the following letters.

If such a devotee meets a more elevated disciple of Srila Prabhupada and develops full confidence that that higher devotee truly represents Srila Prabhupada, such a sincere seeker may elect to move close to Srila Prabhupada through the subjective instructions of such a manifest guru in Srila Prabhupada's line.

*"Regarding your question about the disciplic succession coming down from Arjuna, it is just like I have got many disciples, so in the future these many disciples may have many branches of disciplic succession. So in one line of disciples we may not see another name coming from a different line. But this does not mean that person whose name does not appear was not in the disciplic succession... Another point is that disciplic succession does not mean one has to be directly a disciple of a particular person. The conclusions which we have tried to explain in our Bhagavad-gita are the same as those conclusions of Arjuna. Arjuna accepted Krishna as the Supreme Personality of Godhead, and we also accept the same truth under the disciplic succession of Chaitanya Mahaprabhu. Things equal to the same thing are equal to one another. This is an axiomatic truth..." (Kirtanananda, 1/25/69)*

Note: So if anyone is preaching and following the exact same thing, then he is a bona fide disciple in the disciplic succession from Lord Caitanya and Prabhupada, whether he is a direct disciple or not. This is again stated even more clearly below:

*"Regarding the disciplic succession coming from Arjuna, disciplic succession does not always mean that one has to be initiated officially. Disciplic succession means to accept the disciplic conclusion." (Dinesh, 10/31/69)*

Note: **This is the key letter. It should be memorized by anyone wishing to be a disciple of His Divine Grace A. C. Bhaktivedanta Swami Prabhupada.** Our only warning in this connection is that this liberal opportunity is only applicable if a true disciple is understanding the message properly and acting in accordance with the message, free from any and all motivated rationalizations. This is no easy task. Naturally such a person should be well-versed in scripture to substantiate his position in the parampara.

*"So far personal association with the Guru is concerned, I was only with* my Guru *Maharaja four or five times, but I have never felt any separation. I have never left his association, not even for a moment, because I am following his instructions. There are some of my Godbrothers here in India who had constant personal association with Guru Maharaja, but who are neglecting his orders. This is just like the bug who is sitting on the lap of the king. He may be very puffed up by his position, but all he can succeed in doing is biting the king. Personal association is not so important as association through service." (Satadhanya, 2/20/72)*

Note: We can't think of any more appropriate analogy than this to describe the position of ISKCON's current "gurus." They often say that they are the most advanced devotees, because they had the most personal association with Prabhupada. But here we can see that such a consideration is not only meaningless, but often becomes a disqualification. Chanakya Pandit warns that one should not live too close to a woman, the king, the fire, or the master (guru). Neither should one live too far away, for then he doesn't get the benefit. He recommends one deal with them in the middle way. Similarly, connection with the blazing sun can work in different ways due to different connections. The sun can give us warmth and health as it shines on our head, yet the same sun can burn the soles of our feet as we walk on the beach. Association with the ever-liberated saktyavesha-avatara is a razor's edge. It can give the highest benedictions, but if the personal secretaries, servants, and "big" devotees become familiar with the spiritual master, that close association degrades them.

*"Unless there is connection with a bonafide spiritual master, coming in the line of disciplic succession, there is no possibility of making progress in spiritual life. So I have established ISKCON centers for the purpose of catching up the Lotus Feet of Krishna by intimate connection with the spiritual master. These are my authorized centers for that purpose. You say that whatever I instruct you, you will carry out, so again my instruction is that you abandon this independent scheme and join your good Godbrothers and sisters at some one of our ISKCON centers."* (Friends, 5/23/72)

Note: In many letters, including one quoted earlier, Prabhupada says one can live anywhere but just follow the principles. In this letter, however, it appears that living in an ISKCON temple is absolutely necessary. Is this a contradiction? One consideration is that this letter was written in May 1972. That is still a little early. In later years, as the politics increased, and purity decreased, Prabhupada did not stress moving into a temple as much. Instead he emphasized following the instructions wherever one may be. In the Caitanya-caritamrta Prabhupada says: "If one thinks that there are many pseudo-devotees or nondevotees in the Krishna consciousness society, one can keep direct company with the Spiritual Master, if there is any doubt." (Mad 7, p.340). Reading Srila Prabhupada's books, listening to Srila Prabhupada's tapes, serving Srila Prabhupada's desires, meditation on the form of Srila Prabhupada, and following Srila Prabhupada's many instructions are all non-different from direct association with Srila Prabhupada. In many cases, Prabhupada actually asked devotees to come and live with him personally when they were in difficulty with the "leaders." This instruction also means taking shelter of Prabhupada's books independently, since they are non-different. We are never obliged to enter into any so-called temple in which serious deviations are incorporated in either the philosophy or management. Never.

*"That there have been no newly initiated devotees from Japan is all right. It doesn't matter whether they are initiated or not. If they are coming in large number, that is the success of our mission. We are not after making initiated members very many but our concern is that people understand this philosophy in*

*wider circles. Initiated members are for managing the temples and preaching work, but our program is to invite people to our feasts, let them hear our philosophy and dance and chant. That is the basic principle of our philosophy in preaching work." (Sudama, 4/11/71)*

Note: This letter is very clear and difficult to misinterpret. The important thing is understanding the philosophy and acting on it. All these people who are hearing the philosophy and dancing and chanting have good opportunity to go back to Godhead, not those who took "initiation" but change the instructions. In an old Back to Godhead article Prabhupada says: **"Initiation is a formality. If you are serious, that is real initiation. If you have understood this Krishna philosophy and if you have decided that you will take Krishna consciousness seriously and preach the philosophy to others, that is your initiation. My touch is simply a formality. It is your determination. That is initiation."**

*"The problem that your followers want to accept you as guide in spiritual matters is not objectionable if they are sincere. If they have sincere faith in you, it may not be disturbed, rather it can be fully utilized. My main purpose is to propagate the teachings of Lord Caitanya or Krishna consciousness. I am not after recruiting some disciples; but for preaching work we want some assistants and if somebody offers voluntarily his service it is welcome. So the best thing will be that you become a regular disciple of me and you can teach your followers in the same principles." (Sai Siddha Svarupananda, 1/8/71)*

Note: This letter farther qualifies the last one. It is not initiating people that matters but getting people to follow the instructions, whether coming directly from Prabhupada, from his books, or from a disciple who is preaching the exact same thing. Guru, Sastra, Sadhu. Here Prabhupada is recommending that Siddha Svarupa become a fixed-up disciple. As long as he preaches the exact same thing, then his followers will go back to Godhead, if they are sincere. Prabhupada was not interested in owning many temples and controlling millions of disciples in order to enjoy "nice eating and sleeping" like so many of his Godbrothers were doing. His vision was very broad. He wanted to preach to the whole world with everyone chanting Hare Krishna and living like human beings. As explained in Rohini Kumar Swami's paper (consult Appendix 8), Prabhupada was a great acarya, like Ramanujacarya or Madhavacarya. **He appeared to set the devotional standards for the entire age, according to time and circumstances**. Pure devotees of the caliber of Srila Prabhupada are very rare. We cannot overestimate the gravity of offending Prabhupada as ISKCON is now doing.

*"The eternal bond between disciple and spiritual master begins from the first day he hears. just like my Spiritual Master. In 1922 he said in our first meeting, 'You are educated boys, why don't you preach this cult.' That was the beginning, now it is coming to fact. Therefore the relationship began from that day.*

*If you think of me and work for me, then I am in your heart. If you love somebody he is in your heart. It is common thing, everyone understands it. If I hate somebody or if I love somebody he is also in my heart..." (Jadurani, 9/4/72)*

Note: The spiritual master accepts the sinful reactions of the sincere disciple. If one is not sincere, then he is not a disciple. Sincere disciple means strictly and humbly following the instructions of the spiritual master. As Prabhupada said earlier, "It is not simply a formality." The spiritual master accepts the sincere and humble service of the disciple. Out of compassion, he absorbs the disciple's sinful reactions. This is not a cheap trick or something one can buy, but a natural occurrence when one humbly serves another. Chanakya Pandit says: "The king suffers the sins of the state, the priest suffers the sins of the king, the guru suffers the sins of his wife." So if one humbly serves Prabhupada's instructions, always praying for Krishna's mercy to descend in the form of His bona fide representative, then he is creating a situation whereby Krishna will send the pure devotee to help that sincere soul. It's the intense prayer of the aspiring devotee that forces Krishna to send a bona fide guru. Nothing else. This is the formula.

A neophyte can accept service and bad karma for a while. His limits are very restricted. If he goes beyond them, he will fall down. He simply doesn't have the purity to absorb unlimited sinful reactions. When this "guru" falls down, the disciple is back on his own. At that time his service becomes wasted and he has to start over again, except that he may be clouded with so many misconceptions and bad experiences picked up during his entanglement in the bogus spiritual master/disciple business. If we are sincere, but need help, we should best approach a pure devotee who can really help us. In the meantime, we should take instruction from any senior devotee who is strictly following. Krishna will send the spiritual master at just the right moment. Read how He sent Narada Muni to Dhruva Maharaja in the forest.

*"Yes, I want that you give me that facility to write my books, but I can attend some meetings of important people and elites. You have taken the right view of the importance of my books. Books will always remain. That was the view of my Guru Maharaja, and I also have taken it. Therefore I started my movement with my books. And we shall be able to maintain everything with the sales of the books. The temples will be maintained by the book sales, and if there are no more temples, then the books shall remain." (Hansadutta, 11/8/73)*

Note: Here also it is clear that whether or not "ISKCON" remains as we know it, or if it takes an unmanifest form for some time, that doesn't matter. **As long as the books remain, people will be able to go back to Godhead by reading and following them. But this will not take place if the books are changed in the form of additions, and unauthorized editing. And, alarmingly, this process has also been put into gear by the current conspirators.**

Prabhupada has recently said, *"I know those that are sane, they will accept. No one is distributing so much quantity of religious books. Therefore I challenge all these fools and rascals...... After eighty years no one can expect to live long. My life is almost ended, it is ended. So you have to carry on. And these books will do everything...... Simply by bluffing words, these bogus gurus and yogis are nothing. But when the people read our books, then they will get good opinion." (2/18/76)*

Note: It is the books that will save this movement, not the bluff of the GBC. The fact is that these men have not yet presented an authorized and logical philosophical basis for their "guru" imposition. So the above letter ironically included them.

*"Regarding the Sannyasis, they should be independent. Why they should take help from you? They are strong men, so they should manage on their own strength. That is the test of their effective preaching work." (Rupanuga, 11/13/70)*

Note: What is the test of one's preaching work? These ISKCON "gurus" have built very little on their own. They simply exploited Srila Prabhupada's legacy and unauthorizedly usurped his properties and temples. They tried, with mixed success, to usurp his devotees too. They didn't establish it all on their own. They had some ability to imitate and cut profile. They should have gone out on their own, independently, and preached. They could have attempted to establish their own centers on the power of their own charisma. If they were actually pure, they would have attracted a following. Not that everyone else sets them up on a throne and says, "Look, there is a pure devotee. Can't you see by his opulence. He must be pure! Right?"

We were in Bombay right after the "appointment," and personally noticed how Tamala couldn't attract the Indians to follow him. Yet he managed to spend a lot of Prabhupada's money fixing up a luxury suite for himself in Prabhupada's established temple.

*"I am very sorry to inform you that the London management is not going on nicely. I have received so many unfavorable reports and the most astonishing report is that our small van which you had purchased in my presence has been taken away by the proprietor on account of payments not being made properly. So we have lost all the money that we have already paid." (Mukunda, 3/17/71)*

Note: This concept has a relevance to today's catastrophe. We are all very sorry to see that the management has not been going on nicely. The most astonishing report is that almost all of Srila Prabhupada's disciples have left in disgust. The nasty managers, the GBC, have appointed "gurus" even after Prabhupada directly told them not to do this (see next letter). So now we have lost practically all of the disciples on account of this offensive behavior.

*"I do not wish to discuss about activities of my Godbrothers but it is a fact they have no life for preaching work. All are satisfied with a place for residence in the name of a temple, they engage disciples to get foodstuff by transcendental devices and eat and sleep. They have no idea or brain how to broadcast the cult of Sri Caitanya Mahaprabhu. My Guru Maharaja used to lament many times for this reason and he thought if one man at least had understood the principle of*

*preaching then his mission would achieve success. In the later days of my Guru Maharaja he was very disgusted. Actually he left this world earlier, otherwise he would have continued to live for more years. Still he requested his disciples to form a strong governing body for preaching the cult of Caitanya Mahaprabhu. He never recommended anyone to be acarya of the Gaudiya Math. But Sridhar Maharaja is responsible for disobeying this order of Guru Maharaja, and he and two others who are already dead, unnecessarily thought that there must be one acarya. If Guru Maharaja could have seen someone who was qualified at that time to be acarya he would have mentioned. Because on the night before he passed away he talked of so many things, but never mentioned an acarya. His idea was acarya was not to be nominated amongst the governing body. He said openly you make a GBC and conduct the mission. So his idea was amongst the members of GBC, who would come out successful and self-effulgent acarya would be automatically selected. So Sridhar Maharaja and his two associate gentlemen unauthorizedly selected one acarya and later it proved a failure. The result is now everyone is claiming to be acarya even though they may be kanistha-adhikari with no ability to preach. In some of the camps the acarya is being changed three times in a year. Therefore we may not commit the same mistake in our ISKCON camp. Actually amongst my Godbrothers no one is qualified to become acarya. So it is better not to mix with my Godbrothers very intimately because instead of inspiring our students and disciples they may sometimes pollute them. This attempt was made previously by them, especially Madhava Maharaja and Tirtha Maharaja and Bon Maharaja but somehow or other I saved the situation. This is going on. We must be very careful about them and not mix with them. This is my instruction to you all. They cannot help us in our movement, but they are very competent to harm our natural progress. So we must be very careful about them." (Rupanuga, 4/28/74)*

Note: The Gaudiya Math deviated by centralizing all the authority on the shoulders of the great scholar named Vasudeva. They appointed one acarya who later fell down badly in Vrindavana. They were utterly embarrassed and exposed. ISKCON claims not to have done this. But actually they did the exact same thing, only in a different, roundabout way. They selected eleven "acaryas" instead of one and gave each of them a sovereign territory to rule over. Actually, the Gaudiya Math's Vasudeva was far more advanced intellectually than all these eleven men put together. ISKCON claims that they have not made the same mistake as the Gaudiya Math. They claim this is so because they have kept everything under the control of the GBC. That is a complete hoax. The only difference between ISKCON and the Gaudiya Math is that these men deviated in eleven ways instead of one. They divided up the whole world into eleven territories and they each exercise absolute control in their zones with an iron fist. The only time the GBC exercises its "authority" over them is when a "guru" gets so far out of hand that his behavior cannot be covered up anymore. Even then the GBC's power to remove him is limited as is clearly evidenced by how long Hansadutta remained on his throne after his debauchery was exposed.

Today almost all of the "gurus" are blatantly deviating but the GBC does nothing.

So there is no difference. They have been given the same rope Vasudeva used: rubber-stamped guru, from the same person, Sridhar Maharaja, and they hung themselves from the same tree: personal ambition. The GBC has no control over them whatsoever. They get together once a year and bicker for a few days and then go back to their "terror-itories" for another year of exploitation. For example: In the Fall of 1978, France, a boy raised his hand from the crowd and commented to Bhagavan dasa; "You speak very nicely, but you are not so humble." Upon hearing this, Bhagavan gave a signal to two of his men. They forcefully took the boy from the room, and, upon getting him outside, mercilessly beat him to a pulp. This is not an isolated incident. There are many. The incredible story of Kirtananda's ordering Jadurani beaten is given in Chapter ten. Tamal's zone is also notorious for such beatings.

ISKCON should not have fallen prey to this same abomination. We are technologically very advanced and have the means to quickly communicate Prabhupada's words, such as the above letter, all over the world. Had all the disciples known of just this one letter, the whole conspiracy could easily have been avoided. So once all the teachings are categorized and filed into a computer, everything can be known instantly wherever it is needed. The Gaudiya Math had none of this facility.

This is a key letter. It exposes a similar conspiracy to the one that's frying us now. It's been around for years, but who has paid much attention to it? Those who had, like Giriraja Swami, Kailasa Chandra, Yashodanandan Swami, Jadurani, etc. generally met with apathy or worse. This one letter alone should have been sufficient to activate any sincere disciple against the ISKCON "appointment" conspiracy.

*"So, all Vaishnavas are authorities to preach Krishna consciousness, but still, there are degrees of authorities. On the whole, if his motive is to suppress me and that is why he has come here, how we can receive him? He has already given one Professor a wrong impression. He may be treated as a guest, if he comes to our center, give him prasadam, honor him as an elder Vaishnava, but he cannot speak or lecture. If he wants to lecture, you can tell him at there is already another speaker scheduled. That's all." (Satsvarupa, 6/4/75)*

Note: This letter concerns Bon Maharaja. At first he appeared cooperative with Srila Prabhupada. For example he magnanimously offered full facilities in Vrindavana to any Western disciples Srila Prabhupada wanted to send to India for training. But later he turned on Srila Prabhupada. Then Prabhupada dealt with him very stringently. Bon Maharaja poisoned the mind of one disciple of Prabhupada and almost poisoned Acyutananda Swami. He tried to make Srila Prabhupada's disciples in India take a relative viewpoint of Srila Prabhupada. The Gaudiya Math's leading sannyasis mostly had that kind of viewpoint of Srila Prabhupada. But Bon Maharaja made offense by trying to inject it into the minds of Prabhupada's disciples. He was somewhat successful in doing that.

Srila Prabhupada had to minimize the influence of Bon Maharaja because he had proven envious. He had to employ some techniques that appear to somewhat transgress Vaishnava etiquette. These techniques are being imitated today by the ISKCON "gurus." They are claiming to have big results and so anyone separate from their combined conspiracy is declared to be a bogus disciple because he has no big results. Actually, it is a very illogical presentation on their part for the simple reason that they have none of Prabhupada's divine qualifications but are simply riding on the legacy of Srila Prabhupada. The ISKCON "gurus" like to imitate this mood to snuff out their Godbrothers, but they have absolutely no right to do so.

Conclusion: This self-appointed acarya idea is nothing new. In the Caitanya-caritamrta we have the example of the Advaita Acarya branch of the Caitanya tree. It split into two: one branch deviating, and the other not. Then there is the case of the Gaudiya Math. Just as Prabhupada gave instructions on how to recognize Karmis, Mayavadis, Sahajiyas, hippies, Politicians, Demons, etc., so he also gave many instructions on how to recognize Self-appointed Acaryas. -Sometimes it may be a little difficult to recognize, but in the case of ISKCON's self-appointed acaryas, it is blatant. Their offenses have contaminated the atmosphere of the entire planet. In the Caitanya-caritamrta we find: "Wherever an advanced devotee is insulted, for one man's fault, the entire town or place is afflicted." In this story, because Ramachandra Khan offended Lord Nityananda, not only was Ramachandra Khan persecuted by Muslims, but the entire town had to suffer a similar fate. Similarly, there may appear to be some preaching activities going on within ISKCON at present, but they are all ruined by the presence of guru-aparadha. Not only the devotees within ISKCON are suffering, but even the devotees who have fled ISKCON are suffering, because they are tolerating this terrible offense. Such tolerance allows it to continue. Until this poison is removed, all the devotees, no matter how far away they try to run and hide, will be affected. Prabhupada is Jagat-Guru, the spiritual master of the whole planet, and as such there is no place for devotees to go where they can preach without being affected by the guru-aparadha. This book may seem to be a little drastic, but the deviation is far more drastic.

Balavanta dasa adhikari, this year's chairman of the GBC, in confronting a devotee distressed by ISKCON politics, revealed the underlying conception which is the foundation of the whole betrayal. He said, "This movement is run Machiavellian. Tamala Krishna introduced it, and Srila Prabhupada approved it." The bona fide spiritual master, Srila Prabhupada, could never have ordered or approved that his movement be run in a Machiavellian manner. His leading secretaries wanted to project that, and he gave them the rope to hang themselves. In this case, in the perfect arrangement to deceive those deceptive disciples who wanted to deceive him, we find the truth about the spiritual master.

CHAPTER FOUR

# "WHAT IS YOUR PHILOSOPHY?"

## "LOGICAL AND SCRIPTURAL CONFRONTATION FIRST…"

*"A man is known by his actions and by his words. But sometimes it may appear that he is doing something, but he may be thinking something else. So a man is really known when he speaks, then everything is revealed. So if this Mayavadi sannyasi does not speak, then he can fool everyone. But if you force him to speak he will expose himself therefore he is silent. Even he remains silent, we shall speak very loudly and expose these bogus men. Let our philosophy be challenged by anyone and we shall defeat them." (Hiranyagarbha, 11/22/71)*

Note: We have challenged these "gurus" to debate, but they decline. If they speak, they know they will expose themselves. So they are remaining silent. But we are speaking very loudly, and we will continue to speak very loudly until the entire world knows exactly how debauched these "gurus" really are or until they resign, whichever comes first. Debate is the civilized method of settling such disputes since time immemorial. **Failure to accept a challenge to debate is non-different from admitting defeat. "Silence means acceptance."** But in Kali-yuga, it is very difficult to get justice from anyone, what to speak of "gurus" who claim to be beyond morality. Actually these men are already defeated, but, just like the monkey caught grasping the banana in the coconut, they refuse to let go, even though they know it means they will have to pay dearly in the end. Prabhupada has also said, "The difference between a gentleman and a rascal is, a gentleman, when he is caught doing something wrong, he will immediately stop. But a rascal will continue."

*"I am very glad that you are challenging all of these so-called swamis and gurus. My Guru Maharaja appreciated devotees who boldly presented our Vaishnava philosophy. We must take advantage of every opportunity to defeat these rascals and drive them away, so please continue this strong attitude." (Bahulasva, 11/30/71)*

Note: There are a class of devotees today who are against "ISKCON" but are not in favor of any kind of confrontation. They say, "Let them dig their own graves." That would be fine except for one thing: They are burying Srila Prabhupada and his mission along with themselves. For those devotees who are adamant not to resist the deviation, we have no ill feeling. If they are taking the path of no criticism, then they should not be hypocritical. They should not criticize us for wishing to follow Srila Prabhupada's directions above by confronting the representatives of the bogus institution. Otherwise, if these so-called peaceful devotees, who are outside the walls of ISKCON, criticize us, the saner section should realize that such moral cowards are lending indirect support to the current imposition going on within the walls.

54

*"But one thing is, we have not got anything to gain by fighting the demons in the streets and courts.' No, our process of solving the matter is simple, why should we unnecessarily take botheration for fighting? Only after exhausting every possibility of peaceful solution shall weight anyone. Just like Krishna. He did not call for fighting until after every chance for settlement failed.*

*So we shall try to overcome our opponents by, first our words and our behavior, and all means of friendly approach we shall attempt by sober planning, and only later, all else failing, shall we actually fight. That is our philosophy. And if we stick to these lines of politics and diplomacy as set out for us by Krishna, we shall expect always victory, without any doubt." (Balavanta, 12/13/72)*

Note: Last October we made is known throughout ISKCON that we were not going to simply lay down and let Kirtanananda step all over us and destroy our family. Since then we have been constantly pressuring the GBC to do something about Kirtanananda. Finally Kirtanananda himself, getting worn down by our constant exposes' on his character, petitioned the GBC to settle the matter for him. Unfortunately for him, the GBC confirmed that Kirtanananda's behavior was grossly out of line for a supposed Vaishnava. Still Kirtanananda refuses to rectify his debauched behavior. After this book is completed, we will have exhausted every avenue toward a peaceful solution. Then, if necessary, we will fight. As stated above, we will have Krishna on our side.

*"I am glad you are cooperating with Madhavananda. That I want. As long as we are sincere there is no question of split amongst us. The split only means someone is not sincere, otherwise there is no question of it." (Mukunda, 2/1/74)*

Note: The system to find out who is sincere and who is insincere, in civilized society, is by proper Vaishnava debate. If one side refuses to even start making the arrangements for such a confrontation, then that is a clear indicator of who is insincere. Up to this point, the GBC has totally ignored the challenges of the numerous devotees who have been outraged by this guru imposition and their behavior. In many instances, as in Mother Jadurani's case, they have resorted to violence in order to snuff out any opposition. Therefore, the outcome of a proper debate is already known to many. Therefore, even more adamantly, they refuse to debate. And even more adamantly, we are prepared to fight them.

*"Your questions are certainly not stupid. They are very intelligent questions and I am just pleased to discuss all these matters threadbare." (Pradyumna, 10/13/69)*

Note: Is the GBC prepared to discuss the appointment matter threadbare? Hardly. So far they've refused to discuss it all. They've been employing the political tactic known as stonewalling. In simple terms, that means they are ignoring the issue, hoping it will go away.

Analyzing a subject matter threadbare does not mean unscrupulous editing. A prime example of unscrupulous editing is the Preface to Sridhar's book, *Search for Krishna,* compiled by Dheera Krishna (See Chapter Six, Part One). Another prime example is Satsvarupa's editing of Sridhar Maharaja's March of 1978 talks on the implementation of appointed gurus. Those talks, after Satsvarupa's editing job, formed the entire bogus guru manifesto as though Prabhupada's books had suddenly vanished from the face of the earth.

*"Therefore the management should be done very cautiously so that everyone is satisfied in their autonomous managing capacity. Of course the central point is the order of the Spiritual Master and I am very glad that you are trying to give importance to this aspect of management. The difficulty is sometimes things are interpreted in a manner dovetailing one's own sense gratification. I have got this personal experience in my Guru Maharaja's institution. Different Godbrothers took the words of Guru Maharaja in different interpretations for sense gratification and the whole mission disrupted. This is still going on for the last 40 years without any proper settlement. I am always afraid of this crack, but I am sure if our aim is to serve Krishna sincerely and the Spiritual Master simultaneously, that will be our success." (Tamala, 10/18/69)*

Note: ISKCON is exactly following in the footsteps of the Gaudiya Math. What makes that so abominable is that Prabhupada gave ample warning of this in numerous letters and in the books as well. Therefore no sane person can blame Srila Prabhupada for not instructing us in how to avoid these pitfalls. Herein Srila Prabhupada says that the dovetailing principle can be rationalized and thus lead the wayward disciple down the path of sense gratification in the name of service to the mission. Srila Prabhupada specifically states that he is always afraid of this crack. But if there was an open format for debate, then these things could be quickly exposed and thereby avoided.

*"I have never advised him (Kirtanananda) to act like that... I have already written to inform you that somehow or other he has become crazy; otherwise he would not have disobeyed me to go directly to NY. For the time being he has cut all link with me. Therefore any instruction given by him is unauthorized and should at once be rejected. He has no right to dictate as he has without my sanction... I am very sorry that he is exploiting his present position as a sannyasa in this way." (Brahmananda, 10/14/67)*

Note: At present the GBC "has cut all link" to Srila Prabhupada on account of their dictating, supposedly on Prabhupada's behalf, without following Prabhupada's instructions. Prabhupada's instructions are clearly given in his books, letters, and tapes. We are prepared to present these truths in formal debate. But a proper debate is a serious matter. In Vedic culture it could take much more time to prepare for the debate as the debate itself. First all the terms have to be defined to the satisfaction of both parties. That in itself can become a separate debate. In the case today, it will take many months to prepare for a debate since Srila Prabhupada's complete instructions have hardly been touched. Only the books have any indexes at all. The Caitanya-caritamrta index is next to useless and must be done over again. The lectures, which in themselves will make up as many volumes as all the books, have not been touched as of yet. They are transcribed and on microfilm, but they have not been indexed. 7,000 personal letters also have not been indexed. Once all these teachings have been indexed, they have to be categorized. That means pulling out everything said on a particular subject and analyzed in context. Many statements, taken by themselves, appear contradictory to other statements. So to properly analyze any subject, all of the statements on that subject must be available and taken into consideration. This should have been the first and foremost project undertaken by the GBC immediately after Srila Prabhupada's departure. Instead they spent their entire time plotting and scheming how to fool their Godbrothers into thinking they had been appointed pure devotees. Prabhupada's teachings were literally put on the back shelf the second these men became "gurus." They have remained there ever since as far as ISKCON's "guru" are concerned.

*"Because we are all individuals sometimes there is disagreement between devotees. When non-devotees quarrel they cannot stop and end up killing each other. But the devotees disagreement does not last long because they patch it up for Krishna's sake, because they are all working for the same end-Krishna's service." (Bhumata, 3/10/73)*

Note: We are ready to talk and have been for the last year. We do not claim to be great pure devotees, but we do claim to be devotees. At present there is a very big point of disagreement amongst us. We are doing our share of the work in trying to bring this disagreement to a conclusion, but there must be a two-way street. If the so-called direct representatives of Srila Prabhupada are actually devotees, then they should accept our challenge to formal debate on all the matters discussed in this book. If they are not devotee...

*"You say that someday you hope to be useful, but you are already useful-you are sending checks. This is the best useful. You are remembering me and chanting Hare Krishna. This is Krishna consciousness.*

*Regarding the other matters, a difference between Godbrothers is natural. That difference of opinion will continue, what can be done. Siddha Swarupananda Maharaja and his group, whenever they see me they give me money. So they are not against me. So it is a natural thing for the brothers to fight, as long as they all stay obedient to the father.*

*Do whatever you like, but do not forget chanting and following the rules and regulations. That will save you." (Bhurijana, 9/11/75)*

Note: Here it is clearly stated that disagreements between Godbrothers are natural and cannot be avoided. The disagreements spoken of here, however, are not of the same caliber as are the conflicts going on between the different warring factions in ISKCON today. Today's conflicts fall in the category of one party "not staying obedient to the father." Therefore they must be confronted and rectified. They cannot be brushed off as simple personality conflicts as above. The statement, "do whatever you like" does not mean that all of Srila Prabhupada's disciples should go away and let the deviants run rampant with Prabhupada's reputation and movement. The time is long overdue to settle up all these burning issues before real violence enters the arena of conflict.

*"You mentioned that your pathway has become filled with stumbling blocks, but there are no stumbling blocks, I can kick out all those stumbling blocks immediately, provided you accept my guidance. With one stroke of my kick I can kick out all stumbling blocks... In the beginning there were no doubts, but by bad association you have now got doubts. (Krishnadasa, 9/9/72)*

Note: **"Prabhupada lives eternally in his books." If that is true, as any sane disciple knows, then what is keeping us from right now taking Prabhupada's guidance and kicking out the doubts?** The lazy man's way to the truth is to think a trance medium can help us to get the essence without having to study. But we do not need a trance medium to tell us what is in Prabhupada's books. Amogha Lila's dreams may contain some truths, but then they may contain some falsities also. Who cares? We do not require to gamble on such important matters. We are interested in what Prabhupada says, and only what Prabhupada says. Many devotees claim that Amoga's dreams are self-contradictory, and not in logical accordance with Srila Prabhupada's teachings. Why would Prabhupada reveal, through one of his disciples, that there have been very serious deviations by the GBC, and, in the same breath, exhort his disciples to follow the GBC no matter what they say? This is not possible. Prabhupada's books condemn that way of thought. Therefore we don't need to gamble. Prabhupada gave ample instruction on all such serious matters. The solution to these stumbling blocks is clearly given in the letter above. Srila Prabhupada's guidance is still completely available to us. He was not speaking in parables or a foreign language. He spoke very directly and clearly. We don't need a trance medium to re-translate Prabhupada's instructions. We simply need some serious devotees to sit down to read and index Prabhupada's books, letters and lectures. That is real trance.

*"So my oral instruction as well as my books are all at your service. Now you GBC consult them and get clear and strong idea, then there will be no disturbance. Disturbance is caused by ignorance; where there is no ignorance, there is no disturbance." (Hayagriva, 9/14/70)*

Note: Here Prabhupada is telling us how to settle this guru-issue: study his oral and written words. When we do this, and when we simultaneously follow Srila Prabhupada's instructions, we remove ignorance. By doing that, the disturbances come to an end. There is no other way.

At this year's Mayapur meeting, due to the pressure against them, the GBC has appointed a committee to study the guru-issue. The report is to be finished by next Mayapur. But it has long since been established that conspiracy and deviation was involved from the onset. There will be no solution to the disturbance by stalling for time in hopes that some new philosophy will pop up and get them out of their predicament. The damage done to the movement and Godbrothers cannot be swept aside. It is ignorance to think it can. No one can have his cake and eat it too. No one can live like a king for seven years on the sweat and blood of their Godbrothers, and not have to pay for it. They must pay for it, because they did not deserve it. The Godbrothers have been cheated. **Therefore Prabhupada says that such "gurus," who imitate the devotional sentiments and ecstasies, "go to the darkest region of hell and take their followers with them."** A desperate man cannot get out of this quandary simply by word jugglery. The disturbance can only be removed by returning to square one. This whole thing has to be rectified right from the roots. Cosmetic adjustments cannot buy much more time. Someone may be on a high opulent seat now, but if he does not deserve that seat, he may be working an ordinary job for his subsistence in the not too distant future.

It's exactly like a lazy man who deals in illegal drugs. He gets involved in making huge volumes of easy money, and he enjoys like anything for some time. Eventually, however, he realizes that he is in way over his head. Then he must live in constant fear, while trying to find a way out of his dirty business. These "gurus" have been twisting Srila Prabhupada's clear instructions for some time now in order to justify their imposition. In fact they were soundly exposed as early as 1980 but they wiggled out of that one in a most heinous way. There will be no such clever escape this time. The entire scam is exposed in its entirety. So watch where the money goes temple leaders and collectors. These men do not want to go back to washing dishes and pumping gas for a living.

*"Regarding Bali Mardan, he has not resigned and until he or some other member does so there shall not be any change in the members of the GBC. If there is such resignation the candidates will be Gaursundar, Mukunda and Gurudasa for replacement by vote of the remaining members of the GBC. But why have you taken information on this important matter from Gurudasa? You should not 'understand' from Gurudasa; you should understand from me." (Rupanuga, 11/13/70)*

Note: Needless to say, in the important matter of who is going to instruct new devotees, Prabhupada would not have recommended "understanding" from Sridhar Maharaja, but he would have said the exact same thing: "Understand from me." In another letter Prabhupada makes it very clear, "If it is not from me in writing, don't believe it. There are so many Prabhupada says." It is commonly known that Prabhupada did give instruction that we could go to Sridhar Maharaja for technical advice on etiquette, formalities, etc., but not on matters involving the future management of the entire mission. Sridhar Maharaja himself admitted his inability to comprehend such a vast organization. We are willing to prove these points in a debate in which all devotees of Srila Prabhupada will be allowed to attend.

*"I am glad that you have admitted about the GBC members not very appropriately discharging their duty. I do not mind this discrepancy but you should be alert; you*

*and all GBC members. We are now growing in volume all over the world dealing with public money. People have respect for our movement. Now it is time for GBC members to be very, very careful so that people may not point out any black spot in the behavior of our society. I have issued a letter to all the GBC members only for this purpose that each one of you should always think how to improve the cause and advance our society and as soon as there is some good point you can communicate with your colleagues and give some decision and put it before me so that I can give my final approval." (Tamala, 9/1/71)*

Note: **"It will be solved when I am present." "Put it before me so I can give my final approval." "Understand from me."** This is the process for settling all discrepancies, but, unfortunately, these GBC men rejected Srila Prabhupada's books and went to Sridhar Maharaja instead. Even if they knew he would approve of their appointing "gurus," still they had to edit his words to fit their plan.

*"You have mentioned about some criticism made by Jayagovinda which upset you. I do not know exactly what is the point, but if there is some honest criticism, there should be no cause of becoming upset." (7/28/69)*

Note: Our criticism is honest. We do not claim to be perfect but we have formed a board of sincere and serious brahmins who have thoroughly scrutinized this entire book, point by point, before printing. We feel we have presented Prabhupada's teachings as they are. But if there is disagreement, then there is only one way to find out. A proper debate. Anyone can vilify, and many have previously done so, but it takes time and thought to study and analyze Prabhupada's teaching, the sound and honest basis for debate. But if they reject our honest criticism, then we have good cause for becoming upset, very upset.

*"I thank you very much for your very nice presentation of the issue of birth. You have assimilated the process of birth very nicely through the books. This has pleased me very much and I wish that all my students can become adept at presenting the information in the books like this. You can make this a grand subject for agitation in that country and your preaching on this point alone will make you very famous. Therefore you should speak everywhere on this subject matter from the Bhagavatam and Gita and you will be glorified. As the disciple is glorified so also the spiritual master becomes glorified more. Use this issue to advance your propaganda and become a leader in the society." (Tusta Krishna, 9/18/76)*

Note: From the above letter, it is clear that there is nothing wrong with becoming famous as a powerful preacher and devotee. The problem is that those who deviate from their guru try to be glorified independently. So instead of glorifying the Spiritual Master even more, they defame him. Prabhupada accomplished more than his Guru Maharaja, as far as spreading Krishna consciousness goes, but he gave all the credit to Srila Bhaktisiddhanta and therefore Srila Bhaktisiddhanta became more glorified. Prabhupada never thought he was on his own. He was successful because he strictly followed the instructions of his own Guru Maharaja.

*"The order of the spiritual master is the active principle in spiritual life. Anyone who disobeys the order of the spiritual master immediately becomes useless." (Adi 12, p. 6)*

If we disobey the instructions of Srila Prabhupada, then we are no better than prostitutes. According to Chanakya Pandit, no one respects the pregnancy of a prostitute any more than one respects the impregnation of a man's mind with knowledge if it is not heard from one's bona fide guru. Prabhupada was not interested in personal glorification. He wants to see everyone become Krishna conscious. That is accomplished by powerful preachers. The world is there.

But in order to do this, the devotees already existing must not be scattered via deviations from the Absolute Truth. When they find that they are scattered, they must have the intelligence and courage to see why that has happened and rectify that situation. Therefore there is need for a debate on all these integral issues if we are to glorify Prabhupada even more.

*"So far the impersonalist rascal, you may simply challenge him by asking, "What is your philosophy?" It is not very difficult to defeat these persons, because they haven't got any substance. Simply big words. But we have got our books, Bhagavad-gita; if you engage him in public debate, politely handle his statements with a cool head and reply from the authority of our books, that's all. Krishna will give you all help to expose his lack of knowledge and his faulty understanding." (Sri Galim, 12/17/71)*

Conclusion: So now the devotees and the GBC should cooperate with this and should arrange for an international conference. Everyone serious about Prabhupada's mission should be invited. ISKCON can immediately arrange for the plane fares for the devotees. They have a right to this. This debate can then go on until the self-evident truth is revealed. It may take months. In preparation, all of Srila Prabhupada's words must be indexed and categorized. DAS can do this in three months if ISKCON supplies the men and money. There is no real money problem in this. The amount spent for one insert in the LA Times to advertise the 1984 LA Rathayatra (over $100,000) could have financed the entire project. Mukunda Maharaja revealed that this advertisment perhaps drew only 3% of the visitors; 97% were on the beach anyway.

This debate must take place immediately. Dreadful consequences are building up as the inevitable result of the GBC's original deviations. Those reactions are ready to fructify. There is still some chance that the civilized form of confrontation can save the situation.

Comments, inquiries, or donations toward the upcoming book, or which this is a rough advance copy, may be sent to Steve Bryant (Sulocana dasa), 2124 Kittredge #32, Berkeley, CA, 94704. Thank you.

Note: We have created a Sulocana Dasa Memorial Fund to collect donations for the printing of The Guru Business. Please contact Mukunda dasa on mukunda.dasa@prabhupada.org.uk if you would like to help.

# "JUST TO CHASTISE THE EVIL DOERS"

### "…BUT IF THERE IS NO SOLUTION, WE MUST ACT."

*"Regarding the outlaws, why police protection is not there? Does it mean that in the United States if somebody is threatened, he will have no state protection and must submit to the atrocities of the outlaws? Our point should be that we shall take all necessary steps for self-protection, depending the result on Krishna. We should not idly sit down simply depending on Krishna. Arjuna had to fight in the battlefield, but at the same time he heard Bhagavad-gita. Our motto shall be like that." (Brahmananda, 9/9/69)*

Note: Regarding these bogus gurus, the GBC gave us no protection. Good government means good protection. Not only the GBC gave us no protection, they are responsible for allowing the various individuals to enact their personal ambition. So any disciple of Srila Prabhupada is herein authorized to take all necessary steps for his spiritual as well as material protection. We should not think that we can simply be idle and that Krishna will make all arrangements to uproot the poison. No. We must act. We have to fight this imposition depending the result on Krishna.

*"The reports of your meeting are very encouraging, so try to purge out the contamination, which has entered our Society, uprootedly." (Bhagavan, 8/20/70)*

Note: "Uprootedly" is the key word here. There is a statement in Krishna Book about King Dasaratha, who "uprooted his enemies just like a farmer uproots unwanted weeds in his field." **This is the authorized mood.**

*"Unfortunately, attempt has been made lately in our society to shake this formula. This mischievous attempt has done a great harm, but if you the members of the GBC can rectify this mischievous attempt, then still there is hope of making our progress uninterruptedly.*

*There are two verses in the Chanakya sloka how a family or an institution can be glorified or burned into ashes by one person. The Chanakya Pandit says that if there is one tree in the forest producing nice aromatic flower, that one tree can glorify the whole forest by the flavor of its flower. Similarly if there is one tree in whose cavity there is a little fire, that one tree can burn into ashes the whole forest. So this simile is applicable anywhere. In a family if there is one good boy, he can glorify the whole family and similarly if there is bad boy he can burn the whole family into ashes. Similarly in this institution if there is a bad disciple he can burn the whole institution into ashes. The GBC's duty is therefore to see that every member is following the rules and regulations and chanting sixteen rounds regularly on the beads. I hope the GBC in cooperation with the sannyasis in their touring program will be able to keep vigilance systematically in order to keep the society as pure as possible." (Bali-Mardan, 8/25/70)*

Note: Prabhupada here is making the direct statement that if there is a very bad boy in this society, then we must find him and purge him out. Prabhupada wanted the GBC to do this. But if the police themselves become criminals, how is it possible? At any rate, it was not Srila Prabhupada's business to take on the duty of this purging. He gave that ksatriya duty to his disciples as their service. At this point however, the ksatriya inclined devotees from ISKCON have preferred to submerge themselves in wine and women. That is also within the realm of a ksatriya's propensity, but when he ignores his real duty, that of protecting the brahmins, women, cows, etc., then his indulgence in wine and women simply makes him a debauch. At the present moment there are not one or two but there are many bad boys in ISKCON. Therefore we humbly request those inclined toward ksatriya work to give up their debauchery and come forward to save Prabhupada's mission. Then they will be properly engaged and very happy.

*"Such men should be taken and beaten very hard with shoes, but it will not be very much to our credit if we are accused of fighting in this way. But if that man is caught trespassing on our property, then he may be severely punished by us." (Govinda dasi, 2/12/72)*

Note: In other words, Prabhupada was not an advocate of non-violence when a serious offense to the Pure devotee is concerned. In this case it was to Tulasi Devi. In the guru-issue today, it is to Prabhupada.

*"...and I am quite surprised to read it. This does not sound like you. All along I have been discouraged in every way by my Godbrothers, but still I have stuck to my duty, keeping my Spiritual Master always in front. Because there is some fighting or bickering amongst us, that does not mean that I should go away. If I have understood the order of my Spiritual Master rightly, then I must perform my duty under any circumstances and never once think of going away under disgust..." (Gaursundar, 8/26/72)*

Note: It has been said that the departure of the Spiritual Master will separate the strong from the weak. Contrary to popular belief, those who stay within "ISKCON" under the present contamination are the cowards, for they are neither strong enough to go out in the world and make it on their own, nor are they strong enough to fight the corruption within ISKCON.

*"If you are always remembering Him by your activities and seeing Krishna everywhere, even in the heart of the demonic persons, then anger will never overcome you, being purified of all false pride. But occasionally if there is good reason, you may have to become angry just to chastise the evil doers and blasphemers. We have seen that Lord Caitanya once nearly killed Jaghai and*

*Madhai for their offenses to His devotee, so like that, if there is offensive behavior to the pure devotees you may become like Nrsinghadeva and punish them severely." (Niranjan, 8/29/72)*

Note: Anger can be justified, and it can also be sense gratification. The wrong doers will call legitimate anger sense gratification. The sense gratifiers will call their uncontrolled displays defense of Prabhupada. So, ultimately, whether or not the anger is justified is determined by the sastra and the guru vani. That is what demonstrates the sincerity and the integrity of the anger-or lack of anger-of any disciple. By posing as uttama-adhikaris, they are deliberately disobeying Prabhupada's instructions. Their anger, as well as the anger of their followers, is actually a demoniac display. So it is our duty to make it clear that this cannot go on in the name of Srila Prabhupada. This entails that we become outraged by the bad development that has engulfed the movement. Not showing anger under these circumstances is not purity or tolerance, but cowardice.

*"This is our protest to all of the interpreters of the Bhagavad-gita. If they do not believe in God, Krishna, and they don't want to surrender to Him, then let him preach atheism. Everyone has got the right to do this, but why through the Gita? This is like a man who wants to smoke ganja, but he does not want to be caught. So he takes a friend's hand and smokes it in his hand, and then when the authorities come, he says, 'Oh, I have not smoked ganja, see, my hands are clean!' The idea is that if one wants to preach the Gita, he must preach it as it is, otherwise, don't go through the Gita." (Giriraja, 6/6/76)*

Note: This is our protest to all of the impersonators of Srila Prabhupada. Since they cannot follow the standard of purity as exemplified by Srila Prabhupada but instead concoct their own system, they should go off and start their own societies. Why do they have to drag Prabhupada into it and exploit his legacy? This is like a man who wants to smoke ganja. When the authorities come he says, "Oh, I have not impersonated Prabhupada. Look. Prabhupada appointed me, he smoked the ganja." The idea is that if one wants to be a bona fide guru in ISKCON, he must be prepared to act like a bona fide guru according to Prabhupada's standard, not some bogus concoction.

*"It is understood that Mr. Nair is dead. So it is good news that Nrishinghadeva has killed a demon like him. Prahlada Maharaja said that even a saintly person becomes pleased when a scorpion or a snake is killed. So if it is a fact that Nair is dead it is a matter of great pleasure for all the devotees." (Giriraja, 2/21/73)*

Note: Unauthorized non-violence is not Krishna conscious. Krishna is not pleased by that. Nor is Krishna pleased when violence is enacted from the lower modes. Violence enacted through false ego, which victimizes other living entities for the unauthorized pleasure of the victimizer, never pleases Krishna. But in order to counter aggressors, authorized violence or resistance is praised by saintly men, because it re-establishes goodness. Therefore such violence is actually good.

Prabhupada never balked at the thought of violence when it was needed and the result would be good. But so many of his disciples cannot enter into this spirit. So they indirectly give a license to the aggression ruining the purity of Srila Prabhupada's mission. It is high time that the devotees who have been able to spot the serious discrepancies come forward. All else failing, it may have to come to violence some day. **But death in the pure service of Srila Prabhupada's mission will guarantee one is highly elevated or even liberated. So what is there to fear.**

*"We are not advocates of non-violence. When there is aggression we must kill them. So I think you shall immediately arrange for guns and at least 10, 12 men should be trained up so when there is again attack you can properly reply the aggressor." (Kirtanananda, 6/22/73)*

Note: The message in this letter is the repulsion of aggression. Ironically, the man it was written to has himself become a cruel aggressor.

*"I am sure Visvambhar Goswami is educated, and advanced in judgment and I am pleased he is not disturbed. But Dr. Kapoor can expose Purushottam Goswami about his deal with the late Puri Goswami of the Gaudiya Math. If the mystery of his acquiring 50,000 rupees of books from Puri is exposed then his so-called leadership will come to an end. He knows better than I and you can ask him about Purushottam Goswami's acquiring books from Puri-which is a mystery not yet disclosed, but every Gaudiya mission man knows the incident." (Gurudasa, 4/24/74)*

Note: Here it is very clear that Visvambhar Maharaja is taking the passive stance by advising not to expose Purushottam Goswami and thereby make waves. But Srila Prabhupada is not so sentimental. He is saying that is should be done anyway. Of course, he is saying it in very gentlemanly way so as to not offend Visvambhara's sentiments, which are not bad. But they are not as realized as Prabhupada's judgment on the matter, either. In other words, Prabhupada is saying that just because Visvambhar is not disturbed, that does not mean we also have to be undisturbed about this cheating. This is a very, very important letter. It reveals the practical mood of a real preacher.

Similarly there are many "mysteries" surrounding these new "gurus" which we are not at all afraid to expose, just as Prabhupada was not afraid to expose Purushottam, Bon, Tirtha, or Sridhar, etc.

To give one very graphic example, several devotees have testified that Kirtanananda told his women to "do the needful" in regards to Jadurani's getting her head kicked in and covered in blood in the 1980 incident (full story in Chapter Ten). Does anyone think Prabhupada would have liked that action? Ironically, in 1967/68, when Kirtanananda was venomously attacking Prabhupada and actually deserved a beating, Prabhupada told the devotees, specifically Jadurani, "Do not have him beaten but defeat him with philosophy." When these two women who beat Jadurani first went to Kirtanananda to receive permission, he also could have told them to defeat her with philosophy. However, since neither these women nor Kirtanananda could actually defeat her, he had her beaten instead. He never apologized for this. In fact, afterwards, when asked about it, he said he was pleased by it. This is an example of very sinful violence and not violence used to curtail aggression.

*"Even they have changed her face, still it was not possible to hide the fact that she is old, like great grandmother. Because you are a devotee you could not tolerate the nonsense. You are a very good boy." (Gopal-Krishna, 11/28/74)*

Note: Again, a real devotee cannot tolerate nonsense going on in the name of religion. A sentimental devotee, pretending to be on the uttama-adhikari platform, will say: "Peace brother, live and let live. Let God handle it. It's all one. Become perfect yourself before casting the stone. Let them dig their own graves. Don't make waves. Let's just get high, etc." This is all sentimental weakness. Where is Gopal Krishna now that the face of ISKCON has so dramatically changed. He is one of the "gurus" doing the chiseling, that's where he is.

*"It is very good that the New York temple life is now much improved. What is very pleasing to me is that they have confronted the nonsense. They are sound devotees, otherwise they would have been carried away by this wrong propaganda." (Satsvarupa, 11/28/74)*

Note: This is such an important letter. It appears that almost all of ISKCON is carried away by the wrong propaganda, but so few are willing to "confront the nonsense." How can it be that everyone is so carried away? It is one thing to be a householder with job, wife, and children etc. and not come forward to fight against this conspiracy, but what about all the sannyasis who are supposed to be the powerful, celibate men preaching our philosophy? Are they all so eager to be appointed "gurus" in a future Mayapur meeting? Or do they all fit into the category described below?

*"Asvatthama was condemned by the Lord Himself, and he was treated by Arjuna just like a culprit, not like the son of a brahmana or teacher. But when he was brought before Srimati Draupadi, she, although begrieved for the murder of her sons, and although the murderer was present before her, could not withdraw the due respect generally offered to a brahmana or to the son of a brahmana. This is due to her mild nature as a woman... Asvatthama proved himself to be an unworthy son of Dronacharya or a brahmana, and for this reason he was condemned by the greatest authority, Lord Sri Krishna, and yet a mild woman could not withdraw her natural courtesy for a brahmana.*

*The specific words used in this sloka are vama-svabhava, "mild and gentle by nature." A good man or woman accepts anything very easily, but a man of average intelligence does not do so. But, anyway, we should not give up our reason and discriminatory power just to be gentle. One must have good discriminatory power to judge a thing on its merit. We should not follow the mild nature of a woman and thereby accept that which is not genuine. Asvatthama may be respected by a good-natured woman, but that does not mean that he is as good as a genuine brahmana." (SB, 1.7.42)*

Note: It is almost inconceivable how so many men have been ripped-off, exploited, discouraged, had their families destroyed, found out their "guru" is gay, or on drugs, or having sex with his disciples, ad nauseum, and still remain unable to recognize Asvatthama for what he is. And, astoundingly, it only requires "average intelligence" in order to see this imposition for what it is! Time to break the spell.

*"There is a Sanskrit proverb; sati shatyam samacharit, and this means that if somebody's cunning, we must also become cunning. To a cunning person we must not be a simpleton. Krishna conscious devotees are expected to be very intelligent, so we have to work very intelligently to prove our advancement in Krishna consciousness." (Hansadutta, 6/8/69)*

Note: The simple-minded and honest devotees have had a hard time comprehending how these supposedly advanced men became so enwrapped in plotting and scheming to exploit Srila Prabhupada's legacy and disciples. Now we must follow Prabhupada's instructions and be cunning ourselves if we are to survive, save, and push on Prabhupada's mission. We must try and always remember that they, the "GBC," are thinking that the Krishna consciousness movement should be "run Machiavellian." For the information of our respected readers, Machiavelli was an Italian political thinker during the time of the Renaissance. He wrote one (in)famous book called The Prince. This book contains political methodologies comparable to Chanakya's artha sastra, only exactly the opposite. It employs evil techniques for evil ends. The subtitle of this book goes, "The Man Whose Name Has Become Synonymous with Evil." Tamala Krishna used to distribute this book amongst "the leading secretaries" and insisted they study it. Bhagavan especially was keen on it. Interestingly, ISKCON Italy has purchased Machiavelli's castle in Florence for their center. We would not be at all surprised to find out Bhagavan is the reincarnation of Machiavelli.

*"Regarding the matter with Purusottama dasa. You immediately go and take back whatever books of ours that he has in his possession. You may inform him that we do not require his editing, neither should he correspond with our men in Los Angeles. He is a very heinous man. He wants to become more important. Who sent him books from Los Angeles without asking me? Who has given him the books he now has? You take them back immediately. If this man comes to see me in Vrindavana, I do not wish to see him." (11/7/75)*

Note: "He wants to become more important." Earlier on Prabhupada said "Has the GBC now become better than Guru Maharaja?" As such, these same words, "a heinous man," can be applied to anyone who claims they are beyond the injunctions in Prabhupada's books, as ISKCON's "gurus" claim.

*"We find from the history of Mahabharata that the battle of Kurukshetra was because of the belligerent attitude of Duryodhana. So such war as it was conducted under the advice of Lord Krishna is not bad, but war declared and executed by demonic politicians is certainly very bad. A Krishna conscious person like Arjuna is not inclined to the activities of warfare, but when there is a necessity for peace in the world to educate men to become Krishna conscious, a Krishna conscious person does not lag behind." (Bibhavati, 6/12/69)*

Note: Naturally, most of the devotees in ISKCON are not inclined, for one reason or another, to the activities of warfare. But if we want to call ourselves disciples of Srila Prabhupada, we must not "lag behind." **We must fight for what is right, or we should "decide to die rather than not execute Prabhupada's mission properly."** (SB, 4.28.48)

*"According to Vedic injunctions, there are six kinds of aggressors: (1) A poison giver, (2) One who sets fire to the house, (3) One who attacks with deadly weapons, (4) One who plunders riches, (5) One who occupies another's land, and (6) One who kidnaps a wife. Such aggressors are at once to be killed, and no sin is incurred by killing such aggressors. Such killing of aggressors is quite befitting for any ordinary man, but Arjuna was not an ordinary person. He was saintly by character, and therefore he wanted to deal with them in saintliness. This kind of saintliness, however, is not for a ksatriya. Although a responsible man in the administration of a state is required to be saintly, he should not be cowardly." (BG, 1.36)*

Note: Many devotees within "ISKCON" have been attacked with deadly weapons. Indeed, Chakraddhari was murdered at New Vrindavan by Daruka and Tirtha with the help and inspiration of the Temple treasurer, Dulal Chandra. This incident is well-known to all at New Vrindavan, so much so that Kuladri was having to make frequent announcements to the devotees during Prasadam: "If the police come and ask any questions regarding Chakraddhari, you don't know anything." We personally heard this said. And, of course, many devotees have had their wives stolen from them by ISKCON's sexyasis. This also merits the death penalty. There are literally thousands of examples of these aggressions that it is not possible to do justice in relation to any of them in this document. Eventually, however, they will all be heard and the guilty parties punished, either by us, or by Yamaraja.

*"When Krishna was born, from the day of his birth, the demons wanted to kill him in so many ways but practically it was found that demons were killed by Krishna and He established His mission, yada yada hi dharmasya... So if we work sincerely, the Krishna consciousness movement is non-different from Krishna. As Krishna killed all the demons, we should also be able to kill all demons if we remain faithful in the discharge of our mission." (Yashomatinandan, 9/27/76)*

Note: Many men will say that it is impossible that there can be anything wrong with ISKCON because it is non-different from Prabhupada, but here we see that it is only non-different from Prabhupada "if we are working sincerely.

*"When my Guru Maharaja was present even big, big scholars where afraid to talk with His beginning students. My Guru Maharaja was called "living encyclopedia." He could talk with anyone on any subject. He was so learned. So we should be like that as far as possible. No compromise-Rama Krishna, Avatars, yogis, everyone was enemy to Guru Maharaja-he never compromised. Some Godbrothers complained that this preaching was chopping technique and it would not be successful. But we have seen that those who criticized, they fell down, For my part I have taken up the policy of my Guru Maharaja-no compromise. All these so-called scholars, scientists, philosophers who do not accept Krishna are nothing more than rascals, fools, lowest of mankind, etc. So you go on with your work it is very encouraging to me. Thank you." (Karandar, 7/27/73)*

Conclusion: It is evident here that Prabhupada is very proud of his Guru Maharaja and similarly we should be proud of Prabhupada. Prabhupada tolerated innumerable offenses by his ambitious secretaries just to be able to give us the pure knowledge needed to fulfill the mission of Lord Caitanya. Now we should show our gratitude by carefully studying, discussing and then following those instructions so that we can properly execute his mission. "No compromise." We have to follow Srila Prabhupada's directions and only then will he be pleased. Then he will ask Krishna to benedict us with real understanding so that we may also be able to shout one day, "No compromise!" We must fight to preserve the purity of our guru's mission. Nothing else is important. That is his message in all of these letters.

Nowhere in Vedic literature do we find the concept of non-violence in the face of demoniac aggression. *The Bhagavad-gita* was spoken just prior to the wholesale slaughter of millions of soldiers. That slaughter took place because the aggressors refused to surrender to the good advice of Krishna. Similarly the Godbrothers have been giving good advice to the "gurus" now for seven years, but they have refused to accept it. So the time has come for violence. We are not eager for violence. They leave us no choice. The violence being enacted upon Prabhupada and his mission is far worse than anything that could happen to us in the course of a physical confrontation. Therefore, if the demoniac imposition refuses to surrender to Prabhupada and Krishna's instructions, **then we will fight to the death.**

# "LET THEM DIG THEIR OWN GRAVES"

## INTRODUCTION – THE LESSER ETIQUETTE MUST RETIRE

This review is a page-by-page analysis of the teachings of Sridhar Maharaja in comparison to the teachings of His Divine Grace A. C. Bhaktivedanta Swami Prabhupada. The quotations from Sridhar Maharaja cited in this chapter are from from documents or books that have been well circulated. A list of those documents are given at the end.

I began reading the books of Sridhar Maharaja with an open mind in order to establish whether Sridhar Maharaja is in line with the teachings of Srila Prabhupada or if there are many discrepancies. There are numerous witnesses who will testify that, in the wake of losing my wife and children, entering the arena of the Sridhar Maharaja controversy was the last thing on my mind. But in the course of our extensive research and analysis of the ISKCON dilemma/conspiracy, which forms the bulk of this book, we have found so many glaring discrepancies in Sridhar Maharaja's teachings that we know these must be brought out.

Everyone has been constantly reminded by the adherents of Sridhar Maharaja how there is a Vaishnava etiquette forbidding a disciple to criticize his guru's Godbrother. Although some of you may not believe it, we had no personal desire to criticize Sridhar Maharaja. In fact, at one point, before reading his books, we were defending Sridhar Maharaja on the basis of this above etiquette. But since having studied his books, we are duty bound to confront the teachings and influence of Sridhar Maharaja on the mission of our spiritual master. The lesser etiquette must retire in the face of a much more important consideration-the survival of the pure teachings of Srila Prabhupada, the real acharya for Krishna consciousness throughout the world.

This chapter proves that the effect of Sridhar's preaching has been highly malefic. We are not going into all the discrepancies here since there are many. We are only touching on the most obvious flaws in his teachings. At a later date, if necessary, we will go into much more detail. At this time, we request that the current followers of Sridhar Maharaja carefully study our points. If the followers of Sridhar Maharaja are, as is ISKCON's GBC, unable to logically defeat our statements, we will not hesitate to declare, as we have about ISKCON's "GBC", that "silence means defeat."

### "He is simply playing with them"

First some brief but relevant considerations from other Gaudiya Math leaders who dealt with our spiritual master in a favorable way.

Puri Maharaja is a Godbrother of Sridhar Maharaja. He knows him well. Puri Maharaja has three centers in India, one at Jagannatha Puri, and he believes that Sridhar Maharaja is utilizing his scholarly attainments in a way that is not straightforward. Puri Maharaja told one of Prabhupada's devotees, "He (Sridhar) is simply playing with them." When the big men of the Maha Mandala, namely Ackshayananda Swami and Madhavadasa, went to the opening of his Jagannatha Puri center they were not at all successful in converting Puri Maharaja to a favorable attitude toward their path. Indeed, as they entered his room, Puri Maharaja verbally jumped on them before they could speak a word: "You are disciples of A. C. Bhaktivedanta Swami. You are being cheated by Sridhar Maharaja."

Narayana Maharaja was called in one letter, "My agent in India" by Srila Prabhupada and was one of two Vaishnavas that Srila Prabhupada recommended we could approach for "technical advice." Narayana Maharaja manages the Kesavaji Gaudiya Math in Mathura. His own guru gave Srila Prabhupada sannyasa, but had himself received sannyasa from Sridhar Maharaja. Narayana Maharaja is a very strict observer of Vaishnava etiquette. When directly confronted about Sridhar's role in ISKCON, Narayana Maharaja revealed his staunch conviction about Sridhar Maharaja and was prepared to lay his spiritual integrity on the line. He adamantly stated, "Even if Lord Caitanya appeared personally before me and ordered me to accept what Sridhar Maharaja is doing with ISKCON, I would not accept it." He does not believe that Sridhar Maharaja, who has actually re-initiated a brahmin-initiate of Srila Prabhupada (Buddhi yoga dasa), should have become so involved in ISKCON.

Note by Mukunda dasa: Narayana Maharaja has gradually shown himself to be a great offender to Srila Prabhupada. Please see the article MAYAVADI ATTACK on page 342.

### Reviewing the Preface to *Search for Krishna*

It is a pitiable state of affairs when a disciple of Srila Prabhupada is driven from his spiritual master's mission and is forced to take shelter elsewhere. We feel for such souls and sympathize with them. But at the same time it should be understood that in some cases it would be better for a Prabhupada disciple to forget spiritual life for the time being, keeping his devotional creeper in a dormant state, rather than go to someone who can actually poison the devotional creeper. This is the case with Sridhar Maharaja. Dheera Krishna, the Western world's mouthpiece for establishing Sridhar Maharaja as being equal to and even superior to Srila Prabhupada, is unscrupulous in his method of converting Prabhupada's disciples over to Sridhar's camp. Here are some examples of his technique.

In the preface to *Search for Krishna* Dheera makes Prabhupada out to be a new bhakta compared to Sridhar Maharaja. The way he does this is by taking quotes by Srila Prabhupada that praise Sridhar Maharaja, he pieces them all together (no matter how many years apart they were spoken), and then adds and subtracts a few words to make it look like Srila Prabhupada is saying something he's not. Of course he never mentions the circumstances under which statements were made. This technique is exactly like trying to make Jayatirtha out to be a saint by quoting his "vyasapuja" offerings from the other "gurus." They bear no relevance whatsoever to Jayatirtha's actual status.

1. First paragraph: Dheera's version of Prabhupada's words.

"We are very fortunate to hear His Divine Grace, Om Vishnupada Paramahamsa Parivrajakacharya Bhakti Raksaka Sridhar Maharaja. By age and by experience, in both ways, he is senior to me. I was fortunate to have his association since a long time, since perhaps 1930. At that time he had not accepted sannyasa, but had just left home. He went to preach in Allahabad, and on that auspicious occasion we were connected."

The actual words:

(First part the same.) *"...perhaps since 1930, something like that. At that time he did not accept sannyasa, he just left home, vanaprastha, in his white dress he went to Allahabad. Maharaja, I think you remember the incident when you went to Allahabad? On that auspicious occasion we were connected...(Jayatirtha's omission). There is a long story it will take time, but I had the opportunity of associating with Sridhar Maharaja for several years. Krishna and Prabhupada liked him to prepare me."*

Note: This was spoken during a meeting at Sridhar's Math in 1973 at a time when Srila Prabhupada was introducing Sridhar to some of his disciples, possibly just before Sridhar was going to speak. So naturally any praise spoken at such a time is a matter of good etiquette only and can easily be understood as a friendly gesture. Still Dheera twisted the actual statements to make Sridhar look better. Of course Srila Prabhupada was always humble in the presence of his Godbrothers so this first paragraph does not mean much. Especially since he was directly speaking to Sridhar Maharaja. The transcript we are using is from a paper defending Sridhar Maharaja which we have been told was compiled by Jayatirtha. It is entitled: Srila Prabhupada and Sridhar Maharaja-17 pg..

2. Second paragraph, Dheera's version

"Sridhar Maharaja lived in my house for many years, so naturally we had very intimate talks. He has such high realizations of Krishna that one would faint to hear them. He was always my good advisor, and I took his advice very seriously because from the very beginning I knew that he was a pure devotee of Krishna. So I wanted to associate with him. Krishna and Prabhupada, Srila Bhaktisiddhanta, like him to prepare me. Our relationship is very intimate.

Actual version: *"Sridhar Maharaja lived in my house for a few years so naturally we had very intimate talks and he was my good advisor. I took his advices, instructions very seriously because from the very beginning I knew that he is a pure Vaishnava, a pure devotee and I wanted to associate with him and tried to help him also...our relationship is very intimate."* (The omission is Jayatirtha's who also has a tendency to omit statements that don't look good for Sridhar Maharaja.)

Note: The statement about "his high realizations" we are told was spoken to Satsvarupa during a train ride. What Prabhupada meant is debatable. But, giving them the benefit of the doubt, if this were actually true, then why didn't Srila Prabhupada arrange for Sridhar's words to be put into books and published along with his own books? This would have been no problem at all. If his realizations are so high, and if he is actually pure, it would only make sense to do so. Prabhupada was always wanting to translate more books and if Sridhar could have helped him do so, then why wouldn't Prabhupada have asked him? This is just common sense.

There are many possible explanations as to why Srila Prabhupada would make such high praises and at other times severely condemn Sridhar Maharaja. One explanation is the fact that Srila Prabhupada was a humble Vaishnava and it is not the natural inclination of a humble Vaishnava to look for faults in others, what to speak of Godbrothers-unless it is painfully necessary. Another reason is that Srila Prabhupada wanted to keep as good a relations with his Godbrothers as possible so as to not hinder the mission in India. Sridhar had influence on the other Gaudiya Math members and Prabhupada knew this.

Then there is the possibility that those praises may have been true at one time. So many devotees execute sincere devotional service for a while, and then later, along with getting power and/or knowledge, they become carried away and fall down. This is also a possibility. Prabhupada did not recommend anyone go to Sridhar's Math after the Mayapur temple was established. There are few if any recorded praises of Sridhar Maharaja after ISKCON was established in Mayapur, but there are many criticisms.

Another point in this paragraph is Dheera's playing up on the fact that Sridhar lived for many years in Srila Prabhupada's house. According to Chanakya Pandit, "The worst pain in this world is having to live in another man's house." The fact is, Srila Prabhupada was setting the example for us how to live an honest, Krishna conscious householder life before taking sannyasa. "Example is better than precept." His household life was an integral part of his setting the example for future generations. That is Lord Caitanya's instruction and Prabhupada, being the perfect representative of Lord Caitanya, perfectly set that example for us. Then later he set the perfect example in his sannyasa also. Sridhar Maharaja's living in Prabhupada's house is not a sign of superiority, it is a sign of dependency upon an extremely Krishna conscious and responsible family man.

3. Third Paragraph-Dheera's version

"After the breakdown of our spiritual master's institution I wanted to organize another institution making Sridhar Maharaja the head. Srila Bhaktisiddhanta Sarasvati Thakura told me that Sridhar Maharaja is one of the finest preachers of Krishna consciousness in the world, so I wanted to take him everywhere. This was my earnest desire. But since he could not go around the world and preach, at least the people of the world should come to hear from him."

Actual version from a conversation just before Prabhupada's passing:

Srila Prabhupada*: "I very much want Maharaja, that you come and stay at Mayapur. Because Prabhupada always desired that you preach. He told me quite a few times, 'Why don't you pull him out?' (Both laugh.) You know, I also tried to some extent before, but somehow or other it did not work out. Now why don't you come and stay at Mayapur?*

Sridhar Maharaja: "At last Prabhupada told me that, 'You are an ease lover' (laughter) the qualification, that you have..."

Srila Prabhupada: *"Yes, it's true. He told me also that he* (Sridhar Maharaja) *is such a qualified person, one of the finest preachers. I want to take you everywhere.* (No quotations made. Who is speaking this last sentence is unknown.) *At least at the place we have in Mayapur people are coming from all over the world...* (Ed. omission some talk of arrangements) *This is my earnest desire. Since you could not go around the world and preach, at least stay there and people will come to you. I shall make that arrangement.*

Note: According to sastra, the uttama-adhikari thinks that he is the most fallen and that everyone else is factually doing some service, save and except himself. We know that Srila Prabhupada is an uttama-adhikari and so this is a very likely explanation for the above praises. As far as Sridhar Maharaja being one of the best preachers "in the world," I beg to remind the readers that Srila Prabhupada also said some very encouraging things to some of his disciples-things that could not have been further from the actual fact as time has stood witness to. Prabhupada's saying the people of the world should come to hear from Sridhar is just good etiquette. As stated above, if Prabhupada had wanted the world to hear Sridhar's words, he could have easily printed them into books.

4. Fourth Paragraph: Dheera's version (from a letter to Acyutananda and Hrisikesha, 1969)

"For spiritual advancement of life we must go to someone who is actually practicing spiritual life. So if one is actually serious to take instructions from a siksa-guru, or B. R. Sridhar Maharaja. I consider Sridhar Maharaja to be even my siksa-guru, so what to speak of the benefit that others can have from his association." (This grammar error is in the book.)

This last paragraph has three sentences which seem to fit together all right but actually, as with all Dheera's work, they are pieced together without using (...). This is intentionally done since the missing sentences clearly reveal the actual purpose of this letter. Note the way Dheera misquotes it:

*"So I cannot recommend him (Bon Maharaja) as siksa-guru. I think that he has no actual spiritual asset. For spiritual advancement of life, we must go to one who is actually practicing spiritual life; not to some head of a mundane institution. Not to one who has offended his Spiritual Master in so many ways. I do not wish to go into all details...but this Bon Maharaja may be considered as a black snake, and at the time of His Disappearance, my Guru Maharaja did not even wish to have him in his presence due to the character of this Bon Maharaja. So if you are actually serious to take instruction from a siksa-guru, I can refer you one who is most highly competent of all my Godbrothers, This is B. R. Sridhar Maharaja, who I consider to be even my siksa-guru, so what to speak of the benefit that you can have from his association."*

This is of course the only part of the letter that Dheera was interested in, but later, in the same letter, Srila Prabhupada writes:

*"So if you and Achyutananda are not lost to the poison of Bon Maharaja, and are still serious about advancement of your spiritual life, I will advise you to go to Sridhar Maharaja. Or else I do not know what will save you. So my advice to you both is that you immediately leave the unhealthy and envious association of Bon Maharaja and either proceed to Germany as I have instructed you or at least go to someone who will be competent to act as siksa-guru. This is Sridhar Maharaja."*

On close analysis of the way in which Dheera has used this letter to further his cause is obvious. First of all, Srila Prabhupada would not have written such things about Sridhar Maharaja were it not for the fact that these devotees were insisting on disobeying Prabhupada and taking instruction from someone in India. Prabhupada really wanted them to go to Germany. Prabhupada's saying, "at least go..." clearly indicates the lesser of two evils. At least Sridhar wouldn't try to steal Prabhupada's disciples. Sridhar Maharaja frequently admits that to be the reason why Prabhupada trusted him. In any case, Prabhupada certainly was not enthusiastic about them going to Sridhar. This is confirmed in the letter to Rupanuga, 4/28/74, wherein Prabhupada says, "You are right about Sridhar Maharaja's genuineness... (replying to Rupanuga's statement that none of Prabhupada's Godbrothers were doing anything worthwhile)...but in my opinion he is the best of the lot. He is my old friend, at least he executes the regulative principles of devotional service." After the Mayapur temple was established, Prabhupada never again recommended anyone go to Sridhar Maharaja. Instead he wrote more and more letters like the following:

*"If you are serious to be an important assistant in our society you should fully engage yourself in translation work, and do not mix yourself with my so-called Godbrothers. As there are in Vrindaban some residents like monkeys and hogs, similarly there are many rascals in the name of Vaishnavas, be careful of them. And do not dare to question impudently before your Spiritual Master." (Letter to Niranjan, 11/21/72)*

Note: Were Prabhupada convinced that Sridhar Maharaja was so special and that he alone, amongst all of Prabhupada's Godbrothers, was a pure devotee, then why didn't Prabhupada single him out as such? In dozens of letters and passages from the books, Prabhupada condemns all his Godbrothers in one lump without mentioning that Sridhar Maharaja is an exception. If Sridhar Maharaja were indeed an exception, Prabhupada certainly would have said so. Otherwise it would be offensive to Sridhar Maharaja. Here in this preface, Dheera Krishna takes the few places where Prabhupada appears to glorify Sridhar Maharaja's, ignoring the many more places where he is condemned, and puts them all together to make it look as though Sridhar Maharaja is far superior to Srila Prabhupada. Prabhupada also said one can "increase his devotional service" by taking initiation from Madhava Maharaja:

*"I understand from the letter of Asita dasa that he has gone to your place in Jagannatha Puri. He has asked permission from me for taking initiation from you. I have given my permission and you can initiate him if you like so that he may increase his devotional service there." (Madhava Maharaja, 1/14/75)*

Most of the devotees are aware of who this Madhava Maharaja is. He is one of the most envious Godbrothers of the lot. So why didn't Prabhupada just tell Asita this? Prabhupada also glorified Bon Maharaja in the earlier years, but then later called him a black snake. So we have to use our discrimination and know that often times Prabhupada would say encouraging things, even if they couldn't be further from the truth. This will be made perfectly clear later in this chapter and also from the Kirtanananda expose. It is regrettable that we have had to bring all these distasteful points out so openly but the urgency demands we do this. We must defend our spiritual master at any cost.

## Conclusion to Preface Analysis

This technique of mixing and matching quotes is not only here in this preface but throughout the entire book. Therefore what we are really reading is Dheera Krishna's interpretation of what he thinks Sridhar Maharaja wants to say, what he thinks will sound good to Prabhupada's disciples, and what he thinks he can get away with. Exactly what are Dheera's motives for rejecting Srila Prabhupada and running to Sridhar Maharaja are known to many. It has to do with becoming a guru. What many ISKCON preachers are not realizing is that becoming a bona fide guru is not a matter of being appointed by the "GBC" or Sridhar. It's simply a matter of repeating exactly what Prabhupada taught and following the regulative principles. That's all.

## PART ONE (of four parts)

## THE IMPERSONAL TENDENCY

### *As if his heart and soul were broken.*

*"Srila Svarupa Damodara Goswami wanted to impress upon Bhagavan Acharya that even though someone firmly fixed in devotion to Krishna's service might not be deviated by hearing the Mayavada bhasya, that bhasya is nevertheless full of impersonal words and ideas such as Brahman, which represent knowledge but which are impersonal... Upon hearing all these nonsensical ideas from the nondevotee, a devotee is greatly afflicted, as if his heart and soul were broken."* (CC Antya-lila, 2.99)

Sometimes, but not very often, Srila Prabhupada speaks about "the transcendental plane," or he uses terminology like this. One has to look hard to find them. The Lord does have His impersonal feature and realization of "the higher plane" or "domain of knowledge" is the first attainment of God realization. We are meant to go far beyond that realization. Therefore, Srila Prabhupada always spoke in personal terms, such as, "the spiritual world," or "Krishna's abode," "The Supreme Personality of Godhead," "Krishna's friends," "Love of Krishna," "service to Krishna," "devotional service."

The exact opposite is the case with the preachings of Sridhar Maharaja. If you read the books his followers have compiled (we don't recommend that you do so), it is strikingly apparent that impersonalistic terms predominate. This section will go into detail of this tendency but for now, quickly glance over what is but a sample segment of the impersonal way of speaking.

"A higher conception of the finer world is here."

"In this way, step by step, you will have to come to the Krishna conception of Godhead."

"When our egoistic attitude vanishes, we will find ourself in the midst of sweet waves all around. We should try to do away with whatever wrong we have done hitherto. We must do our duty and never expect any definite result, but cast it towards the infinite."

"And then one day will come when our egoistic feeling will dissolve and from within, our real seer, a member of the infinite world, will spring up and awaken, and we will find ourselves in the sweet waves of that environment."

"He comes to live in the plane of divinity."

"So we have to awaken our interest in that plane, and ignore the interest of this plane."

"We have to approach the domain of knowledge with self-surrender, honest inquiry, and a serving attitude. We will have to become objects to be handled by the superknowledge of that plane."

"We are trying to gain this knowledge, not so we can get the help of that plane, not so we can utilize that experience for living here: rather we must give our pledge to serve that knowledge. We shall serve that higher knowledge: we won't try to make it serve us. Otherwise, we won't be allowed to enter into that domain. Absolute knowledge won't come to serve this lower plane. We shall seek that plane of real knowledge..."

"The intellect cannot approach the world of spirit...Only through faith, sincerity and dedication can we approach that higher realm, and become a member. We can enter that higher plane only if they grant us a visa and admit us. Then we can enter that land of divine living. So a candidate must have these three qualifications before he can approach the truth which is on the higher plane of absolute reality."

"With this ideal we shall be able to make progress. Our ideal, our highest model- that is our all-in-all in life. To be on the path of realization of that goal is the greatest wealth in ones life."

"He has given me the highest conception of the holy name of Krishna."

"Everyone should contribute to the center."

"You will have to dive deep...into the plane of the soul."

"We have to dive deep into that plane of reality."

"We should always be eager to devote ourselves exclusively to the highest duty."

"We will have to search for a person who is a bona fide agent of the higher world."

"We should have faith that if we do our duty towards the absolute..."

"The heart is only full of Krishna, full of the Krishna conception."

"Divine love is the supreme most goal of every soul."

"They (gurus) will all help to carry me to the center."

"And there the Lord is engaged in his pastimes with His paraphernalia of equal quality. We are trying to understand what is what in the spiritual thought world."

"And all conception of mundane, whether physical, mental, or intellectual, should be eliminated in our journey if we want to go to the inner world of substance."

"Progress means elimination and acceptance."

"Anyone who has come in connection with the infinite cannot but say this: 'I am nothing.' "Mahaprabhu's vibration of Krishna's name was so fine and surcharged with force that the sound entered within the animals, and aroused in their hearts the innermost plane which was covered by the elephant's or tiger's body."

The fact that many persons, even Prabhupada's former-followers, are attracted to this terminology of Sridhar Maharaja, is not surprising. It only further proves what Srila Prabhupada said all along; that the West if full of impersonalists. Every day Prabhupada's disciples state this fact in prayer to Prabhupada. So we are naturally inclined to this type of terminology but we should not confuse that way of speaking with the pure devotional terminology that Srila Prabhupada used and think that they are equal. Sridhar Maharaja's books are chock-full of impersonalistic terminology. Sridhar Maharaja himself admits his real interest, "I am only concerned with my high thinking. That is my life. My spiritual thinking is my life." (DK, 80) The real life of the devotee is service.

### The Impersonal Idea of the Origin of the Soul

### (Taken from Sridhar Maharaja's book, *Search for Krishna*)

"There are two classes of souls, jivas, who come into this world. One class comes from the spiritual Vaikuntha planets for the necessity of nitya-lila, the eternal pastimes of Krishna. Another comes by constitutional necessity."

"The Brahmajyoti, the non-differentiated marginal plane, is the source of infinite jiva souls, atomic spiritual particles of non-differentiated character. The rays of the Lord's transcendental body are known as the brahmajyoti, and a pencil of a ray of the brahmajyoti is the jiva. The jiva soul is an atom in that effulgence, and the brahmajyoti is a product of an infinite number of jiva atoms."

"Generally, souls emanate from the brahmajyoti which is living and growing. Within the brahmajyoti, their equilibrium is somehow disturbed and movement begins. From non-differentiation, differentiation begins. From a plain sheet of uniform consciousness, individual conscious units grow. And because the jiva is conscious it is endowed with free will. So, from the marginal position they choose either the side of exploitation or the side of dedication... The fallen souls come from the marginal position within the brahmajyoti, and not from Vaikuntha."

"In the brahmajyoti, we are equipoised in the marginal potency as an infinite number of pinpoints of spiritual rays, electrons of consciousness. Consciousness means endowed with free will, for without free will, no consciousness can be conceived. An atomic pinpoint of consciousness has very meager free will, and by misuse of their free will, some jivas have taken their chance in the material world. They refused to submit to the supreme authority. They wanted to dominate. So with this germinal idea of domination, the jiva enters into the world of exploitation... Upon retiring from the world of exploitation, the soul may return to his former position in the brahmajyoti as spirit. But, if the soul has gathered the tendency of dedication through his previous devotional activities, he does not stop there; he pierces through the brahmajyoti and goes towards Vaikuntha..."

"The responsibility is with the soul, otherwise, the Lord would be responsible for his distressed condition. But Krishna says that the soul's innate free will is responsible for his entanglement in the material world. The soul is conscious, and is atomic, his free will is imperfect and vulnerable. The result of that free choice is that some are coming into the material world, and some are going to the spiritual world."

But Srila Prabhupada says:

*"As living spiritual souls we are all originally Krishna conscious entities, but due to our association with matter from time immemorial, our consciousness has now become polluted by the material atmosphere." (Original Hare Krishna album)*

*"As soon as we try to become Lord, immediately we are covered by Maya. Formerly, we were with Krishna in His lila or sport. But this covering of Maya may be of very, very, very, very long duration-therefore, many creations are coming and going. Due to this long period of time, it is sometimes said that we are ever-conditioned. But this long duration of time becomes very insignificant when one actually comes to Krishna consciousness. This Brahma-sayujya mukti is non-permanent. Every living entity wants pleasure, but brahma-sayujya is minus pleasure. There is eternal existence only. So when they do not find transcendental bliss they fall down to make a compromise with material bliss. Unless one develops full devotional service to Krishna, he goes up only to brahma-sayujya but falls down. But after millions and millions of years of keeping oneself away from the lila of the Lord, when one comes to Krishna consciousness, this period becomes insignificant, just like dreaming. Because he falls down from brahma sayujya, he thinks that may be his origin, but he does not remember that before that even, he was with Krishna." (Lecture in Australia)*

*"The conditioned living being has forgotten his eternal relationship with God and he has mistakenly accepted the temporary place of birth as all-in-all... The living entities are not without spiritual senses; every living being in his original, spiritual form has all the senses, which are now material, being covered by the body and mind. Activities of the material senses are perverted reflections of spiritual pastimes." (Sri Isopanisad 11)*

*"Real sense enjoyment is possible only when the disease of materialism is removed. In our real, spiritual form, free from all material contamination, pure enjoyment of the senses is possible." (Sri Isopanisad, 11)*

*"This attachment of the devotee to a particular form of the Lord is due to natural inclination. Each and every living entity is originally attached to a particular type of transcendental service because he is eternally the servitor of the Lord.*

*Lord Caitanya says that the living entity is eternally the servitor of the Supreme Personality of Godhead, Sri Krishna, therefore, every living entity has a particular type of service relationship with the Lord, eternally." (SB 3.9.11)*

In an attempt to minimize or nullify all of the above truths, our impersonalistic adversaries are fond of quoting part of one purport from Srila Prabhupada's commentary on *Sri Isopanisad*. It reads as follows:

*"The all-pervading feature of the Lord-which exists in all circumstances of waking and sleeping as well as in potential states and from which the jiva-shakti (living force) is generated as both conditioned and liberated souls-is known as the Brahman." (Sri Isopanisad 16)*

Regarding this quotation, the "all-pervading feature" can refer to either Brahman or Paramatma. "Potential states" is referred to in the Vedanta Sutra. For example, the state of a coma is a potential state. There are others. "Jiva shakti is generated" does not mention the adverb "originally". Generated can mean several things. Already Srila Prabhupada has said in the Australian lecture (above) that the living entity may descend (generate) many times from the Brahma-sayujya, but that is not his original home.

If we consider the all-pervading feature to be the Paramatma, Maha Vishnu is the original Paramatma, and *Brahma Samhita* states that innumerable jivas come from Maha Vishnu. Thus this purport says that liberated souls are also generated from the all-pervading feature of the Lord, and it is a fact that the Avatars come from Ksirodakasayee Vishnu, the Paramatma. The last word of the purport, namely "Brahman," the key word stressed by the impersonalists, can refer to either the Brahmajyoti, the Paramatma, or Bhagavan. In Vedanta Sutra, Brahman almost exclusively refers to the Bhagavan feature. So our point is that this segment of the *Isopanisad* purport does not in any way indicate that jiva souls originally emanate from the Brahmajyoti. However, Sridhar Maharaja's statements above very definitely tag the jiva with an impersonal origin.

So this discrepancy is very, very important. It conclusively proves that Sridhar Maharaja does not have a personal relationship with Krishna. And that makes all the difference in the world. We have heard some devotees of Sridhar Maharaja try to brush this discrepancy off as insignificant, quoting the above *Isopanisad* purport by Srila Prabhupada, but actually, it reveals the heart of the whole problem. It clearly shows the difference between a completely pure devotee, who knows Krishna personally, and one who is still interested in his own happiness and mental speculation.

The impersonalist's dilemma is almost identical to that of the evolutionists. The impersonalist cannot explain why the jiva soul first became envious. Sridhar Maharaja uses the words: The jiva's "equilibrium is somehow disturbed." He cannot explain how or why. Similarly, the evolutionists say there was a big bang out of nowhere. They also cannot explain how or why. Both concepts are totally illogical. For the soul to become disturbed in the first place, he has to have an innate nature of something other than non-differentiated existence. Otherwise, what is there for him to become disturbed about? And the second problem with this philosophy is that the soul, in order to be able to make a fair choice of going either to Krishna or matter, would have to have full knowledge of the two choices. Sridhar Maharaja says that he may make the wrong choice due to his being "imperfect and vulnerable." But that is not the case. Prabhupada often explains that the soul is Sat Cit Ananda, and so he is in full knowledge when in his original position. The soul is perfect. He does not come to this world by some unintentional mistake. He does not come to this world of free will, an intentional act of envy and pride. Or as the Christians say, "He ate the forbidden fruit." One may say that his ability to become envious is a fault, but, factually, that is due to his having free will. If he did not have free will, that would be a fault.

So the only logical explanation for the souls coming into this world and having to undergo suffering is that they became envious to Krishna and proud of their own glories ("Why is Krishna enjoying like this, and I cannot; I'm as good as Krishna"). So they decided to chance it on their own. The original misuse of free will does not lead to utter degradation. When the soul first falls, he does not go to the demoniac species. He takes his birth as a demigod. As long as we follow the rules, and do not try to exploit others, we can live quite happily there. But if we become greedy and commit sins, we go down into the lower species. One may argue, "If God is so kind, then why doesn't he create a place where we can live separate from Him and not have to fall down into suffering where we can be little gods ourselves and have control of our environment? But the answer entails the question, "Have full control of what? If you have control over other living beings, then you are denying them the freedom you so badly want."

So then if you say, "Well, He may not let us have full control, but we should be able to live in perfect harmony with everyone else." That place does exist. It is called the spiritual world, or Vaikuntha. Even in the spiritual world there are degrees of surrender to the personal God. The shanta rasa is often described as an impersonal type realization of Krishna. Not everyone is equally in love and surrendered to the personal feature of Krishna even in the spiritual world. So going back to Godhead is a personal thing and very difficult for the impersonalists to understand or accept. Therefore, they try to rationalize that they came from the brahmajyoti by dint of their being "imperfect and vulnerable" and that their going to Krishna is not a matter of begging forgiveness and surrendering to a person, but simply a matter of moving to where the grass is greener.

Say, for example, a citizen becomes envious of the King and decides to go out to become a King himself. But he doesn't have the qualifications of a King, and so he suffers in a foreign land where no one speaks his language and where he has no friends. He wants to go back to his own land where his friends and family are, but he knows that he will have to personally confront and make amends to the King first. That is difficult. Even though he is suffering, and he wants to go back, his false prestige won't easily allow him to humbly beg forgiveness from the King. The King is a very kind person and is eager to forgive the foolish citizen, but the citizen has lust in his heart and so cannot bring himself to make amends. So, in utter frustration, he may try to merge into a void state by taking intoxication to sidestep his current suffering and postpone his dilemma of having to surrender to the King. This appears to work for some time, and he gets some temporary relief from pain. Eventually, however, because he factually is a person, he again desires to enjoy with family, friends, etc. So, he again tries to get situated in this foreign land. Again he suffers, and again he is given a chance to surrender to the King. This can go on many, many times until he finally realizes that he cannot live separate from his real home and, naturally, from the King. So finally, after many, many ups and downs, he realizes that he must go back and beg forgiveness from the King. Then the King sends his representative to guide him in how to rectify himself. And he is tested to make absolutely sure that he is finally ready to come home and not simply eager to exploit the King. Eventually he is able to go right up to the King, with tears in his eyes, and beg forgiveness. The King naturally is very compassionate on his fallen friend and so not only forgives him, but awards him great happiness. Thus the citizen is fully satisfied and never again thinks he can be happy in another land. But to approach the King he must give up his pride.

If one rejects this analogy, then he is saying that God is responsible for our suffering in this material world. He is saying that God made the jivas imperfect, and so they "accidentally" made a bad choice when their "equilibrium somehow became disturbed." So they had to suffer here for many billions of lives. If a teacher gives his student a partial understanding of the principle of right and wrong, and then says, "Now you must choose," that's not fair. If the student chooses the wrong thing, the teacher is responsible. But if the teacher gives the student full knowledge, and the student still chooses the wrong thing, then his suffering is not the fault of the teacher. Similarly, God created us all Sat Cit Ananda. We have full knowledge and free will to love or not love Krishna. We chose to misuse it and so here we are. That choice, to choose Maya or Krishna, will be there eternally.

## Love of Who?

Throughout his books, Sridhar Maharaja refers to love independent of a person to love. There is a conspicuous absence of such expressions by Srila Prabhupada in all his writings. Having indexed half a dozen of Srila Prabhupada's books, we can say that we have never seen in even one place where Prabhupada would say, we have to "love". Of course he has said in thousands of places we have to "love Krishna," but he never said we have to "love." There is a very good reason for this. If one has a personal relationship with Krishna, then he knows that there is only one object of love, Krishna, and that is a personal love. It is just as difficult for the personalist to say the word "love" without "Krishna" as it is to clap with one hand. Or as Prabhupada says, "There is no meaning to the word devotion except in relation to Krishna." This is another one of the traits in Sridhar Maharaja that give away his lack of a personal relationship with, and devotion to, Krishna. It is so blatant in fact that we are embarrassed to have to spell it out like this. It should be obvious to everyone who has read one of Sridhar's books. Here are some of the quotes we've found:

"But sacrifice for who? And who is the beneficiary? Love is the beneficiary. Everyone should contribute to the center... with this spirit we should combine and work for real love and beauty."

"Divine love is the supreme most goal of every soul. Beauty and love is the summum bonum, our highest attainment...the ultimate conception of the Absolute Truth is that of reality the beautiful and divine love."

"And beauty will be victorious in the world. Love will be victorious in the world. We will sacrifice everything to see that the banner of divine love will flutter all over the world, for a particle of that divine love will be able to keep peace and distribute peace in all directions."

To the impersonalists, these above words sound very nice. In fact I can easily see Rajneesh or any other bogus yogi saying such things to a Western audience. But Srila Prabhupada never said such things. The beauty of Krishna and Love for Krishna are certainly the highest goals but when they are constantly mentioned without mentioning or addressing the person, Krishna, the object of love, the possessor of beauty, it becomes impersonal. The impersonalists also appreciate the beauty and love that pervades the entire creation, but they have no appreciation for the person from whom those qualities emanate. Srila Prabhupada never talks of beauty and love without saying; "beauty of Krishna" and "love for Krishna." If one actually loves someone, he naturally says: "I love you." He never says; "I love." That is not only impersonal, but meaningless. We meet hippies constantly talking in these terms and we know perfectly well that they have misdirected their love. Other statements by Sridhar Maharaja further reveal this impersonal tendency in him such as:

"We shall serve that higher knowledge; we won't try to make it serve us."

"We must serve that plane."

"We have to become objects to be handled by the superknowledge of that plane.

"To be acquainted with the conception of the highest ideal..."

A devotee who has a personal relationship with Krishna cannot speak such things. At least we are not meant to hear them since Srila Prabhupada never spoke that way.

THE ORIGIN OF THE JIVA SOUL

*"Formerly we were with Krishna in His lila or sport.... Because he falls down from brahma sayujya, he thinks that may be his origin, but he does not remember that before that even, he was with Krishna." (Prabhupada Letter)*

Note by Mukunda dasa: There is an article called MAYAVADI ATTACK on page 342 that exposes the impersonal idea of the origin of the soul, as preached by Narayana Maharaja and his followers.

CHAPTER SEVEN

# "A VERY HUMAN STORY"

## THE "LILAMRTA" – PLANTING THE WEED

Devotees often react to our statement that *Lilamrta*'s portrayal of Srila Prabhupada's life is bogus and offensive with the following rationalizations:

"If all the struggles and difficulties which Srila Prabhupada went through were actually not struggles at all, but Krishna's lila, then won't that discourage devotees from struggling to serve Krishna? In other words, if devotees see that only a mahabhagavata can do something wonderful, since Krishna only works directly through him, then what is the use of my struggling? I am not a pure devotee."

"If Prabhupada set the example of struggling in Krishna's service in order to encourage us to struggle for Krishna, then what is the point of minimizing his example? He wanted us to see him struggle for Krishna. Otherwise, why would he do it? If we say that Prabhupada never really struggled, then don't we negate his personal example? Isn't that offensive and impersonal?"

"If you say that Srila Prabhupada only pretended to be struggling, so that we would follow his example and struggle for Krishna, then isn't that the same as saying Prabhupada was simply playing a role to trick his disciples into working hard. Doesn't that negate his great achievement and make him out to be a duplicitous person, another offense?"

These are admittedly powerful and logical sounding arguments, but they do not have shastric backing. Obviously, had Srila Prabhupada mystically manifested everything he needed for preaching, without ever appearing to struggle or be in want of anything, then what would have been the reaction in his disciples' minds? They would have thought: "Why should I go out and work hard when my guru can manifest a beautiful temple or a mountain of gold instantly just like Kardama Muni manifested a city in the sky?" The disciples would not want to work for Krishna but instead would want to enjoy Krishna's opulence. Such disciples, seeing this opulence, would only become envious of Prabhupada and crave those mystic powers themselves. Srila Prabhupada instead wanted to give us the desire for the humble service of the Lord. Although to some, this may appear less valuable, it is a far greater opportunity. Therefore, Srila Prabhupada only rarely manifested his mystic potency. He did not want to attract cheap followers. At the same time, he gave stern warnings that the disciple is never to think that the spiritual master is under the laws of material nature. Hence an apparent contradiction.

The pure devotee has the powers and opulences of mystic yogis given to him by Krishna directly, but he does not want our unpure minds to become enamored by it. At the same time it is a serious offense to think the pure devotee is not in complete control, but instead is under the control of the material energy. So how to reconcile this?

According to sastra (scripture), one should not view the spiritual master from the bodily platform. That would include viewing his history from the eyes of a book like "*Lilamrta*" which accentuates Prabhupada's bodily relationships and tends to bring him down to the level of the conditioned devotee, struggling to do his service to God. In this connection, Chanakya Pandit warns us:

"One should not get too close to the fire, a woman, the King, or the spiritual master. Neither should one remain too far away, for then one cannot get the benefits to be derived. One should deal with these four in the middle way."

This is an excellent example. Everyone can understand the example of fire, a woman, and the King. Fire is the most obvious. Similarly, women are known to be able to lead a man astray and be quite ruthless at times. Kings are known to have a man's head severed at the drop of a dime. But here the Pandit includes the guru in this example. Why? Prabhupada gives the answer in numerous places: The guru is directly connected to Krishna and thus an offense to the guru is extremely dangerous, much more dangerous than offense to the other three combined. They can only harm one's body and mind. Offense to the Guru, however, can completely check one's spiritual progress for many lifetimes. There is no way to calculate the severity of guru-aparadha in terms of lifetimes, or hellfire, etc. The damage of becoming too familiar with the guru is compared to a mad elephant entering a china shop or a nicely trimmed garden. They are both utterly destroyed. Therefore, one is advised never to become familiar with the guru. One is only meant to become very well versed in, and familiar with his instructions, not his apparent bodily and mental "needs." But in "Lilamrta," Satsvarupa has described Srila Prabhupada's thoughts and emotions as though he were in a direct link to Prabhupada's head. This is extremely dangerous and offensive. Perhaps this explains why Satsvarupa is now suffering such severe headaches that he has become practically incapacitated. No devotee in his right mind should read even one page of "Lilamrta," and those copies that have already been distributed should be recovered and burned.

So, in dealing with Srila Prabhupada's life in the middle way, some of the main occurrences in his life, such as the childhood Rathayatra festival, his early enthusiasm to worship the Radha-Krishna Deities, his first meeting with his Spiritual Master, his enthusiasm to preach and publish Back to Godhead, etc., could be described. Srila Prabhupada set that example for us. He never went into a detailed description of his own Guru Maharaja's bodily history. Bhaktivinode Thakura had eight children. Should we go into his history with his family? Of course not. So why should Satsvarupa and the GBC think that they can set a new standard? Were Satsvarupa actually a liberated soul, he would have seen Srila

Prabhupada's true platform. He would not have been interested in the history of Prabhupada's so-called physical and emotional "needs." Such a history is clearly viewing the pure devotee from the material viewpoint. Aside from provoking the ocean of material emotions within the hearts of women, sudras, the less-intelligent, etc., (the audience the book was geared toward), it can accomplish nothing but the destruction of our transcendental awe and reverence and faith in Srila Prabhupada.

One may argue that such mundane sentiment, since it is directed toward Srila Prabhupada, is actually transcendental and will elevate us to a higher level of devotion and even award liberation. At first this may sound logical, but it is not the conclusion of sastra. Sastra unequivocally states that the pure devotee should never be seen from the mundane or bodily-mental-intellectual point of view. Satsvarupa has projected him in this way, although the author tries to deny he is doing it in some places. If Prabhupada is seen in that way, it is compared to a mad elephant entering the garden. One's spiritual life is finished. He immediately falls down to spend his lifetime in useless speculation.

Many devotees agree with the above conclusion, but they argue that Satsvarupa has made this error unintentionally. But this is not the fact. The GBC, particularly Satsvarupa and Adi Keshava, deliberately decided that the best way to preach via an autobiography of Srila Prabhupada was to project him to the masses as a great man. This was supposedly done for the purpose of preaching, since the masses could never accept Srila Prabhupada as being the sum total of all the demigods. This kind of reasoning is external and is an insufficient excuse for committing such an offense to Srila Prabhupada. A more insidious motive is clearly evident. If Srila Prabhupada is viewed as having been chock-full of human weaknesses, then, when these bogus gurus of ISKCON display their weaknesses, such as agitation, fear, sex-desire, ignorance, mistakes, illusion, etc., they will have their excuses in the apparent example of Srila Prabhupada as put forth by "Lilamrta," and the less-intelligent will be unable to distinguish between the two.

The following are some scriptural quotes which substantiate our conclusion. There are many more references; we are only quoting a few:

*"When one actually engages in unalloyed, uncontaminated devotional service, he is already liberated. Krishna's devotee is not subject to material condition, even though his bodily features may appear materially conditioned. One should therefore not see the pure devotee from a material point of view. If we consider the bodily defects of a Vaishnava we should understand that we are committing an offense at the lotus feet of a Vaishnava. An offense at the lotus feet of a Vaishnava is very serious. Indeed, Sri Caitanya Mahaprabhu has described this offense as hati-mata, the mad-elephant offense. A mad elephant can create a disaster, especially when it enters a nicely trimmed garden... One is forbidden to observe the activities of a pure Vaishnava from a material point of view. For a neophyte especially, considering a pure devotee from a material point of view is very injurious. One should therefore avoid observing the pure devotee externally but*

*should try to see the internal features and understand how he is engaged in the transcendental loving service of the Lord. In this way one can avoid seeing the pure devotee from a material point of view, and thus one can gradually become a purified devotee himself." (NOI, p. 60-63)*

*"'Acaryam mam vijaniyat.' One should consider the acarya to be as good as the Supreme Personality of Godhead. In spite of all these instructions, if one considers the spiritual master an ordinary human being, one is doomed. His study of the Vedas and his austerities and penances are all useless, like the bathing of an elephant. An elephant bathes in a lake quite thoroughly, but as soon as it comes on the shore, it takes some dust from the ground and straws it over its body. Thus there is no meaning to the elephant's bath. One may argue by saying that since the spiritual master's relatives and the men of his neighborhood consider him an ordinary human being, what is the fault on the part of the disciple who considers the spiritual master an ordinary human being? This will be answered in the next verse, but the injunction is that the spiritual master should never be considered an ordinary man..." (next verse) "Similarly, if the family members of the spiritual master, who is the bonafide representative of the Supreme Lord, consider the spiritual master an ordinary human being, this does not mean that he becomes an ordinary human being. The spiritual master is as good as the Supreme Lord, and therefore one who is very serious about spiritual advancement must regard the spiritual master in this way. Even a slight deviation from this understanding can create disaster in the disciple's Vedic studies and austerities." (SB, 7.15.26)*

*"When one serves a Vaishnava unknowingly, one still gets a good result, and if one unknowingly insults a Vaishnava one suffers the bad result. A Vaishnava is especially favored by the Supreme Personality of Godhead. Pleasing him or displeasing him directly affects the pleasure and displeasure of the Supreme Lord...by pleasing the spiritual master, who is a pure Vaishnava, one pleases the Personality of Godhead, but if one displeases the spiritual master, one does not know where he is going." (SB, 4.9.23)*

*"It is therefore said, vaisnavera kriya mudra vijna na bhujhaya. A highly advanced Vaishnava lives in such a way that no one can understand what he is or what he was. Nor should attempts be made to understand the past of a Vaishnava." (SB, 7.13.14)*

*"When a devotee sees the Supreme Personality of Godhead by his meditation or when he sees the Lord personally, face to face, he becomes aware o everything within this universe. Indeed, nothing is unknown to him. Everything within this material world is fully manifested to a devotee who has seen the Supreme Personality of Godhead." (SB, 1.2.21)*

Note: No one will deny that Satsvarupa appears to be glorifying Srila Prabhupada in the *Lilamrta*. The problem is that, along with the glorification, he has also defamed Prabhupada. In one breath Srila Prabhupada is described being completely transcendental and beyond ordinary emotions, etc., but in the next sentence he is described as being dependent on a Mayavadi, or confused, insecure, etc. This makes the whole thing contradictory, bewildering, and offensive. It takes on the characteristics of milk touched by the lips of a serpent. One naturally will start to think that a pure devotee can have mundane emotions. Before long, everyone deluded by that mentality becomes a sahajiya, a cheap imitator. They then think, "I can exhibit lust, greed, attachment, and everything else and still be an uttama-adhikari because I am pure inside." This mentality has already blatantly reared its ugly face in ISKCON, and our treatise is exposing numerous examples of this inauspicious trend.

## WARNING

THE FOLLOWING SPECULATIONS ON THE THOUGHTS AND FEELINGS OF SRILA PRABHUPADA, AS QUOTED FROM "*LILAMRTA*," ARE NOT FACTS. THEY REPRESENT THE WAY IN WHICH THE AUTHORS OF THAT BOOK WOULD LIKE THE READERS TO THINK ABOUT THE QUALIFICATIONS OF A PURE DEVOTEE. SATSVARUPA CANNOT READ ANYONE'S MIND, ESPECIALLY SRILA PRABHUPADA'S. WHILE READING THESE QUOTES, PLEASE REMEMBER, AT ALL TIMES, THAT THEY ARE A PART OF AN OVERALL CONSPIRACY TO MAKE THEMSELVES, THE SELF-APPOINTED "GURUS," OUT TO LOOK LIKE REAL SAINTS.

"*LILAMRTA*" SAYS THAT SRILA PRABHUPADA STRUGGLED AND LEARNED

"He was unafraid of the city's pandemonium. After all he was an experienced Calcutta man." 2, p.206 (This is not the reason Prabhupada was unafraid.)

"He had gotten first-hand experience of American life, and he gained confidence that his health was strong and his message communicable. He had learned that casual one-time lectures here and there were of limited value..." 2, p.20 (Prabhupada did not brave to learn the hard way.)

"Only seven people attended...they had misled Swamiji." 2, p.239 (Pure devotee misled?)

"His struggle to continue his mission was part of his preparation." 2, xviii (Just the title of Vol. One, "*A Lifetime in Preparation*," subtly implies that Srila Prabhupada was not a pure devotee from birth.)

BUT SASTRA SAYS:

*"People following the principles of devotional service can never be put into difficulty." (SB, 2.8.18)*

*"Those who are devotees therefore have no problems in the material world... For a devotee, everything in this world is very pleasing because he knows how to use everything in the transcendental loving service of the Lord." (SB, 4.8.82)*

Note: Here Prabhupada says that although the devotees may appear to struggle and learn by their mistakes, in actuality, they are always freed from such mistakes and illusions.

## *"LILAMRTA"* SAYS PRABHUPADA WAS ATTACHED TO HIS FAMILY

"...but the request (to take sannyasa) seemed so difficult and unlikely... He went on with his duties but remained shaken by the dream." (l, p.118)

"'...Why is Guru Maharaja asking me to take sannyasa?' he thought. It was not possible now." (1, p.140)

"He felt himself operating somewhat like the materialists he had criticized in his writings, absorbed in the struggle for existence with insufficient time for self-realization." (1, p.120)

"Srila Prabhupada's obligation to his wife and children..." (1, p.xviii)

"But Abhay didn't have his heart in it. It was a duty-he had to do it to maintain his family."

## BUT SASTRA SAYS:

*"He is never shaken, despite the most grievous sufferings." (BG, 6)*

*"Attachment for household paraphernalia and for Lord Krishna go poorly together." (SB, 2.4.2)*

*"Devotees are certainly liberated persons. Therefore, 0 greatest of the brahmanas, they cannot possibly be absorbed in family affairs." (SB, 5.1.2)*

*"A self-realized man is no longer obliged to perform any prescribed duty, save and except activities in Krishna consciousness." (BG, 3.18)*

*"Nonetheless, they performed all prescribed activities just to set examples for the people in general." (BG, 3.20)*

Note: This last statement is the reason that Srila Prabhupada remained in household life: To set the example for us. But Satsvarupa does not make that clear in his "biography." He tries to interpret Srila Prabhupada's activities in a mundane way, making him seem "human" and thereby leading all the readers to hell.

Satsvarupa is directly indicating above that Srila Prabhupada had not yet advanced to the point of being transcendental to family attachment. Try and see how offensive this is.

## "*LILAMRTA*" SAYS PRABHUPADA WAS HELPLESS & PITIABLE

"A mendicant, Prabhupada was temporarily dependent on the good will of his Mayavadi acquaintance, with whom he regularly conversed and from whom he accepted shelter."

"Now his last hope was Sri Padanpat Singhania... He was Prabhupada's final hope."

"He decided to phone Carl Yeargens and ask him to help. Hearing Swami's voice on the phone-it was an emergency!" (2, p.61)

"Robert Nelson couldn't give Prabhupada the kind of assistance he needed."

"As the Gaudiya Math broke down, he was also affected. Under the present circumstances how could he carry out his spiritual master's order to preach. Previously the main obstacle to his preaching had been family commitments, but now the obstacles were compounded. Now he had to wait helplessly for the outcome of this struggle." (2, p.97)

"A. C. Bhaktivedanta Swami Maharaja...now had to face starkly that he had not one friend of stature in the US. Suddenly, he was as homeless as any derelict on the street. In fact many of them...were more secure than he. They were ruined but settled." (2, p.96)

"Where was he going? He didn't know. He had come onto the street without knowing where he would go...it was no place to stand wondering where you will live or is there a friend you can turn to." (2, p.95)

"This is what it meant to be working without government sponsorship...without a patron. It meant being vulnerable and insecure." (2, p.96)

"Paramahamsa Maharaja: 'When Abhay arrived, he appeared very poor, starving. He had no means.' Abhay told him how his business had failed and how he had willingly left his family and was now destitute." (1, p.164)

"Kumar Jain: 'I felt pity also because of the conditions under which he would come.'" (1, p.185)

BUT SASTRA SAYS:

*"Krishna, by His grace, will supply whatever we need in executing our devotional service...even if we do not ask for them." (SB, 8.6.14)*

*"When a devotee needs something, the Supreme Personality of Godhead supplies it." (SB, 7.10,54)*

*"A Krishna conscious person does not take shelter of any person, man or demigod." (BG, 3.18)*

*"A Vaishnava guru is never dependent on the contributions of his disciples." (Adi, 7.91)*

*"Hiranyakasipu did not know that Prahlada Maharaja was the most fortunate person within the three worlds because Prahlada was protected by the Supreme Personality of Godhead, Such are the misunderstandings of demons. They do not know that a devotee is protected by the Lord in all circumstances." (SB, 7.8.12)*

*"A person in full Krishna consciousness is not unduly anxious to execute the duties of his existence. The foolish cannot understand this great freedom from all anxiety. For one who acts in Krishna consciousness, Lord Krishna becomes the most intimate friend. He always looks after His friend's comfort, and He gives Himself to His friend, who is so devoutly engaged working twenty-four hours a day to please the Lord." (BG, 18.58)*

## "*LILAMRTA*" SAYS PRABHUPADA WAS FORCED TO ACT

"Forced by conditions he accepted as Krishna's mercy, Prabhupada sat patiently..."

"But in the ten months since Calcutta, he had been moved by force of circumstances, or as he understood it, 'by Krishna's will,' from one place to another."

## BUT SASTRA SAYS:

*"The first sign of a Mahatma is that he is already situated in the divine nature. He is not under the control of the material nature." (BG, 9.13)*

Note: This is an example of contaminations in "*Lilamrta*" which are more subtle and difficult to perceive. At first glance, these statements appear innocent enough. On close analysis, however, it says that Prabhupada was being forced to act by material nature, but that he "took it" as Krishna's mercy. Again, any neophyte can think in this way. Just as Krishna descends by His sweet will, so also the pure devotees act by their sweet will which is always the same as Krishna's will. They are never under the control of material nature. They are not even in contact with matter. They do as they please, the same as Krishna does. A correct wording for the above-mentioned concept would be: "He had moved, by his desire to serve Krishna, from one place to another." Then it is clear that Srila Prabhupada is not being forced by material nature. These kinds of subtle contaminations in "Lilamrta" are too numerous to detail to the full extent in this book.

## "*LILAMRTA*" SAYS PRABHUPADA SUFFERED "EMOTIONAL TURMOILS"

"He sat on the couch while I swept with the vacuum cleaner, and he was so interested in that..."

"...came upon a verse in which Lord Krishna said something that startled him... Abhay shuddered as he read the verse. It seemed to speak directly to him. 'But what does it mean? Does it mean,' he thought,' that Krishna will take away all my money? Was that what was actually happening? Was that why his business plans were failing?... (1, p.88)

"His spiritual emotions were so turbulent that he wasn't thinking of going to Jhansi. He wanted to take a train to... Anywhere." (1, p. 163)

"Abhaya spent his time in Jhargaram chanting the Holy Name and becoming settled in detachment from his family."

"...yet without his spiritual master's physical presence, he felt small and very much alone. At times like this, he questioned the wisdom of having left his family and business." (1, p.222) (In one letter Prabhupada said about his Guru Maharaja: "I have never for a moment left his association because I am following his instructions.")

"But to Abhay, Calcutta and the British were not alarming, and he even held a certain fondness for his Scottish teachers. Although he looked up to them with a mixture of awe, distance, and some tension, he admired their moral uprightness and their gentlemanly, courteous behavior with the boys."

"Although Prabhupada's home had suddenly become an insane terror, the street at its door was also a hellish, dangerous place. He was shaken." (2, p.95)

"America seemed so opulent, yet many things were difficult to tolerate. The sirens and bells from fire engines and police cars seemed like they would crack his heart." (2, p.37)

"He had taken quite a shock and now he was leaving the arena of David's madness." (2, p.95)

"Abhay was baffled; so much work had been undone. He felt he had worked so many months for nothing." (1, p.135)

"But his first attempts to arrange a meeting were unsuccessful. Frustrated at being put off by Mrs. Morarji's officers, he sat down..." (1, p.276)

"He had little idea of what to do as he walked off the ship onto the pier. 'I did not know whether to turn left or right.'" (2, p.8)

"When Abhay left Bharati Bhavan, with its six-foot-high lettering 'League of Devotees' painted across the outside wall, he felt sad."

"But he found the Swami just the opposite-very straightforward and even cutting in his speech and his mouth turned down at the corners, making him look mournful." (2, p.232)

"Prabhupada looked grave, almost sorrowful." (2, p.89)

"But it was embarrassing for him when he could not pay..." (1, p.186)

"...and Abhay and the others felt ashamed."

"Bhaktivedanta Swami's neighbors observed him coming home dead tired in the evening." (1, p.283)

"The next morning Prabhupada didn't get up. He was exhausted... For the first time, it became apparent that he was overexerting himself." (2, p.259)

"He stayed until around 11:00 and then he became drowsy. The party was over." (2, p.269)

"After some time, the drive became tiring for Prabhupada, and he dozed, his head resting forward." (2, p.172)

"One day, while delivering *Back to Godhead* to various addresses in the city, Abhay suddenly began reeling, half-unconscious, overcome by the heat." (1, p.194)

BUT SASTRA SAYS:

*"Sometimes a representative of the Lord engaged in preaching work meets various so-called difficulties...although apparently very severe, the devotees of the Lord feel transcendental pleasure because the Lord is satisfied." (SB, 2.8.6)*

*"A pure devotee of the Lord does not live on any planet of the material sky, nor does he feel any contact with the material elements. His so-called material body does not exist, being surcharged with the spiritual current of the Lord's identical interest, and thus he is permanently freed from all contamination of the sum total of the mahat-tattva." (SB, 1.13.55)*

*"People following the principles of devotional service can never be put into difficulty." (SB, 2.8.18)*

*"Those who are devotees therefore have no problems in the material world... For a devotee, everything in this world is very pleasing because he knows how to use everything in the transcendental loving service of the Lord." (SB, 4.8.82)*

*"In the liberated stage, oneness with the Supreme Lord means that one has no realization other than happiness." (SB, 3.28.37)*

Note: Since this book is primarily for experienced devotees, we are not going to refer to the many hundreds of thousands of quotes that clearly show that pure devotees do not ever manifest the above emotions and turmoils. They may appear to, they may even say something to that effect, but the fact is that pure devotees are not in touch with matter. If they appear to exhibit such frailties, it is only to win the hearts of the fallen souls around them. After all, few would come forward to offer service to a superman. Such truths should not have to be spoken so openly, but it is necessary to make them clear in order to get his poisonous book, the *"Lilamrta,"* recovered and burned.

## CONCLUSION

The author, and those who worked with him on the *"Lilamrta,"* have committed a horrendous offense to Srila Prabhupada. If they had tried this same "interpreting the mind" trick with some famous materialist who had died, they would be liable to get hit with a devastating slander lawsuit from the materialists' heirs. So just consider the gravity of what has happened-and is still happening-to Srila Prabhupada's reputation from the distribution of this slanderous book, the *"Lilamrta."* The descriptions in this book of the "problems" Srila Prabhupada seemingly underwent are not at all becoming to him, even though they draw out false empathy or even sympathy from the less-intelligent. The Mahabhagavata's disciples are never expected to take such quotes and apparent situations and put together a book which tugs on the heartstrings of all of its readers, while at the same time tugging and ripping out the devotional creeper.

Srila Prabhupada descended to this place and displayed the opulence of Krishna even amidst the most disturbed, atheistic, and inimical conditions. This world, with very little exception, consists mostly of impious men, religious fanatics, pseudo-seekers, demons, and so many frustrated persons who can have absolutely no faith in anyone. We all came to Srila Prabhupada, by his causeless mercy, from a category comparable to these. Just as Krishna and Lord Caitanya, when They descend, appear to fools as ordinary human beings, similarly, to the gross materialists, Srila Prabhupada certainly appeared to be a rather helpless mendicant with a cane, etc. Yet we, his disciples, are meant to know that he actually had the power to deliver the Ganges and all holy places from sinful reaction (SB, 9.9.6). He had the power to surpass all the perfections of the yogis and make the whole universe tremble (SB, 4.8.78). Does this so-called "*Lilamrta*" invoke these realizations about our spiritual master? Or does it instead allow you to view him from two points of view, to empathize, and at times, even sympathize with him as he struggles to eke out his livelihood?

"*Lilamrta*" does not just make passing references to Prabhupada's apparent struggles, fully explaining how these things, in actuality, were the Lord's plan to glorify His devotee? No. Instead it highlights his so-called "inabilities," "emotional and mental turmoils," "failures and setbacks," with the obvious purpose of weaving a web of heart-rending, tear-jerking sentimentality that can, and does, lead the readers into seeing Srila Prabhupada as an ordinary struggling man, just like the new "gurus," as being as good as, or better than, Srila Prabhupada. The "*Lilamrta*" is one of the reasons why this abominable mentality is even possible. Imitation thrones also assists the delusion. Equal worship is another strategy. "*Lilamrta*" is a contamination at times so subtle, and so poisonous, that it works on the subconscious without a careless devotee even being aware. This book, and the books of Sridhar Maharaja will both produce results on the same level. Both have the same poisonous effect on one's soul. "*Lilamrta*" teaches that an uttama-adhikari can be an ordinary, struggling man, and Sridhar's books subtly teach impersonalism (Chapter Six). As many of these books as possible should be recovered and destroyed. If not, the authors will be subject to sever punishment, both in this lifetime, and for many future lifetimes to come. And the innocent victims reading these books may have their material existence extended as well.

Comments, inquiries, and donations toward this book may be sent to Steve Bryant (Sulocana dasa) 2124 Kittredge #32, Berkeley, CA, 94704. Thank you.

Note: We have created a Sulocana Dasa Memorial Fund to collect donations for the printing of The Guru Business. Please contact Mukunda dasa on mukunda.dasa@prabhupada.org.uk if you would like to help.

"But in "Lilamrta," Satsvarupa (left) has described Srila Prabhupada's thoughts and emotions as though he were in a direct link to Prabhupada's head. This is extremely dangerous and offensive. Perhaps this explains why Satsvarupa is now suffering such severe headaches that he has become practically incapacitated." Sulocana dasa.

**BURNING SATSVARUPA'S BOOKS** - Sanat dasa was a former disciple of Satsvarupa. Later after completely rejecting this fake guru he followed Sulocana's order to burn the books of this offender.

Sanat dasa burning Satsvarupa's books at Gita Nagari Ratha Yatra, July 1993.

## Sulocana prabhu's Order To Burn All Satsvarupa's Books

"No devotee in his right mind should read even one page of "Lilamrta," and those copies that have already been distributed should be recovered and burned... Such truths should not have to be spoken so openly, but it is necessary to make them clear in order to get his poisonous book, the "Lilamrta," recovered and burned... As many of these books as possible should be recovered and destroyed. If not, the authors will be subject to sever punishment, both in this lifetime, and for many future lifetimes to come. And the innocent victims reading these books may have their material existence extended as well." Sulocana dasa.

# "THE CONSPIRACY"

A running history showing the most important events of the takeover and the efforts made to thwart it, beginning in 1977 [Not complete].

* Note: This section was not completed by Sulocana dasa. A small book called **THE FIGHT FOR MOTHER EARTH** has been compiled by Mukunda dasa. To purchase it please see the back of the book for more details.

"In this way, I began my research with the blessings of the Lord of morality, Sri Caitanya Mahaprabhu. Since I was approaching His topmost representative, Srila Prabhupada, for guidance and inspiration, I knew the outcome would be auspicious, whatever it was." Sulocana dasa from the Preface "A Rude Awakening"

# ISKCON'S WOMEN:

## PROTECTED OR EXPLOITED?

CONTENTS

PART ONE

GENERAL PRINCIPLES ON WOMEN

INTRODUCTION

PART TWO

MODERN PROBLEMS

PART THREE

WOMEN IN ISKCON

## PART ONE

## GENERAL PRINCIPLES ON WOMEN

## INTRODUCTION

It is with both pleasure and hesitancy we present the teachings of His Divine Grace A. C. Bhaktivedanta Swami Prabhupada on marriage and women. It is done with pleasure because we hope to help sincere devotees live happier, and more Krishna conscious lives together. It is done with hesitancy because many women, at first glance, may be offended when they read some of the statements contained herein.

The purpose of this chapter is to prove conclusively how ISKCON women are being exploited. Before this can be done, however, it is necessary to clearly define the position and role of women according to the Vedas. Since this is a very complex and sensitive subject, containing many controversial points, such as women's rights and women's equality, we have broken this chapter down into three parts. We will prove, both scripturally and logically, in step by step format, what is the status of women in Vedic (spiritual) culture, how that status can be implemented in our Western society, and lastly, how ISKCON's leaders have totally ignored the women's real interest with the sole aim of exploiting them. **Please keep in mind that this is only a brief summary of a book we are compiling which goes into all these points in much more detail. That book will include all of Srila Prabhupada's quotes on marriage, women, sex, and household life, and varnasrama dharma both from his books as well as personal letters and lectures.** For now, we hope this brief summary will help sincere devotees understand the basic principles given by Srila Prabhupada, and thereby avoid further exploitation by ISKCON's current "leaders." Please also keep in mind that all these ideas have been presented to the GBC and they have not been able to defeat any of them. Therefore, even if there were some flaws or mistaken interpretations in this chapter, the "ISKCON" GBC has not been able to find or defeat them. A summary of their official statement on this matter, as recently presented by the GBC Privilege committee, is given at the end of this chapter. If anyone would like all the documents by both sides on this matter, please send $5 to the address at the end of this chapter. Thank you.

## 1. SPIRITUALLY EQUAL, MATERIALLY WEAKER

All religions of the world agree on the basic principle that God loves everyone equally. Not only are men and women equal, but all living beings, including the lower species, are equal in the eyes of God. In Vedic culture, both men and women, in all the different levels of conscious development (caste system), are seen equally from the spiritual platform. As such there is no discrimination in the demeaning sense amongst the learned section of Hindus. Since Vedic culture means spiritual culture, all living beings are respected equally in India, even today.

But that does not mean that everyone is seen equally in regard to their bodies and their respective duties in life.

It is exactly like the difference between a 1st grader in school and a second grader. They are not on the same level, but only a complete fool will consider the one to be inferior to the other. It is a small matter of time before they are equal as grown up and graduated adults. In this exact same way, all the different species of life are equal in the ultimate sense, but they are not at all equal in the relative sense. The system of defining those relative differences in the human species is called the varnasrama system, or commonly called, the caste system. According to the different castes, or bodies and minds, there are different types of propensities and duties one must perform. These differences are not by chance but are the results of one's own past good and bad deeds, or karma. In the beginning "God created all men equal." That is absolutely true, but according to ones pious or impious activities, everyone is not awarded an equal body in the next life. All souls are not on the same level in their activities. A common thief is not equal to a saint, although the common thief may also become a saint one day. So, with this understanding, it would be sheer foolishness to claim that all bodies are equal as the communists preach. According to the Vedas, generally the female body and mind is not as far developed as the male body and mind. There are of course always exceptions, especially in this mixed-up age, but the general rule is, that women need a man for protection. In this age, and especially in the Western countries, it is very often the case that women are more pious and spiritually inclined than the men. Therefore it requires serious study to distinguish the difference between the two sexes for the practical implementation of Vedic culture.

## 2. RESPECTIVE DUTIES IN LIFE

In all the species of life, both the males and females have their respective roles to play. Those roles are very different and so the nature of men and women is very different. That holds true for the human species as well. To question or criticize God for creating us differently, one strong, and the other weak, etc., is simply foolishness.

This section is meant to show the difference between men and women in their natural states. That is, the consciousness they manifest when raised in a simple, but God conscious atmosphere, according to God's laws, and able to manifest their God given propensities. These natural propensities, or varnas, although covered over or latent in many Westerners, are still fully existing under the surface, and need to be recognized and awakened if we are to manifest our true potential and act accordingly. Part Two will go into some of the problems our modem conditioning has imposed on us, and how we can gradually adjust to make the best use of a bad bargain. The following is a description of men and women as they live when raised in a healthy environment.

## 3. WOMEN: NOBLE AND SOFTHEARTED

Women in Vedic culture are not neglected, intimidated, or disrespected in any way whatsoever. In fact, Indian women are adored for their chastity, purity and motherhood. Pregnant women in India are practically worshipped for carrying that burden so nobly. Srila Prabhupada has even stated that the closest thing in this world to spiritual love, is the love a mother has for her child. This love is a glorious thing and women should be proud of this ability, but at the same time, they should know that they can be misled and hurt more easily than men. For this reason they must be carefully protected in all stages of life. Women are generally more simple and softhearted than men. That is why women are able to cry and become emotional so much more easily than men. Softhearted is the word Prabhupada often uses although sentimental can be used synonymously. Women's minds take pleasure in simple things. This is not a demeaning quality. In fact, it is a glorious quality and more men could use some of that. But in women it is essential for if women were not endowed with this soft-hearted and simple nature, how could they possibly care for small children day after day? Men by nature get bored with child's play in a matter of hours or minutes, or even seconds. So if women were also like this, then who would look after the children. Therefore, women are naturally simple and softhearted. Again, this is not a defect, or a demeaning thing, but a glorious quality that enables them to care for their children without going insane. This ability in women, along with their chastity, are the real qualities that make a woman beautiful. How well society is able to keep those qualities intact in its women is directly related to how advanced the society is in spiritual culture.

## 4. NATURALLY SUBMISSIVE TO A GOOD HUSBAND

Women, in their natural condition, simple and trusting, are generally happy to accept a good husband's directions. They may not like everything he says, but it is their nature to accept his order anyway to avoid a confrontation and keep peace in the family. Women can bear this since their priority, which keeps them very busy, is raising the children, of which there are usually many in Indian families. Generally they are quite happy to let the husband make money and deal with the outside world. When women artificially become overly educated and lose that simple nature, then the result is that no man can stay married very long to such an educated, but usually unsubmissive woman. The tendency in this case is to argue with the husband at the slightest provocation. Sometimes the wife may well have good reason to dislike the husband's order, but a man's psychology is such that he has to be in charge. Both his physical and mental make-up mandate it. In any organization, for peaceful cooperation, one person has to be the boss, whether he is the most qualified or not. In the family unit, the boss is the man. This is nature's law. So women by nature are endowed with the ability to tolerate a man's misbehavior and thereby keep peace in the family. When women lose this quality of simplicity and trust, then naturally there will be separation and ultimately divorce.

## 5. THE WEAKER SEX

Women are the physically weaker sex and so are naturally inferior to men. However in this age of sophisticated weaponry, welfare systems, police forces, equal rights, etc., women are generally not intimidated by men because of their physical inferiority. A can of mace, a pocket .38 revolver, or a trip to the welfare office, will serve as adequate protection. Still, this physical difference gives clear indication that in nature, the woman is meant to serve the husband since she needs his protection. Without serving the husband, he will leave her unprotected. A woman without a husband is free game for rapists, thieves, etc., but if she is married, the criminal knows that the husband will not sleep until he gets revenge. Therefore women need husbands to protect them from so many atrocities by men.

## 6. CHASTITY: AVOIDING ILLICIT SEX

Illicit sex for a woman means unwanted children and without a husband, these unwanted children simply mean suffering. Therefore intelligent women, take great pains to learn the practical method of keeping a husband devoted to them. In the West, they think it is by making themselves beautiful with cosmetics, perfumes, sexy clothes, intellectualism, etc. But that is not the real method. That method is also there in Vedic culture, but by far the most important qualification for a woman is her chastity. Only a man of the lowest, most abominable quality will impregnate a woman and then leave her if she is faithful and submissive. Such a mismatch seldom takes place in India. But if the wife is not submissive, but is always bickering and causing anxiety to the husband, then naturally he cannot tolerate her for very long. This is because he is struggling hard in the material world to earn money, and when he comes home, he needs peace, not argument. Therefore the Vedas teach; if the woman has any good sense, she will be as sweet and pleasing as possible, for that is the way to capture her husband and literally enslave him as her servant. But to do that, she has to play the role of surrendered, submissive, and faithful wife. This is just common sense.

## 7. MADE TO RAISE CHILDREN

Sastra says that women are many times lustier than men. That refers to bodily lust for sense pleasure. Women's bodies are more sensual than men's bodies. This is commonly accepted by modem psychologists also. Not only their physical bodies, but their mental and emotional make-up is also more sensual/sensitive than men's. They respond more readily to physical embraces, as well as mental embraces, and this tendency is natural in women. It has its practical function in raising children. Everyone knows the nature of small children. They are extremely affectionate and energetic. A mother, in her normal state, will have at least 3-7 children and be quite happy. It takes a lot of physical and emotional support to properly raise all the children with the constant love and affection they require. A man's mind tends to be more on the mental, intellectual plane and he generally cannot enter onto a child's simple plane of existence for very long. The simple, almost constant pleasures of physically embracing the bodies and minds of many small children requires that women have not only a more simple but a more sensitive nature. This is one explanation of why women are declared to be more lusty or sensual than man. This word sensual can also be interpreted as love/lust since the mother is both enjoying her children (lust) and she is at the same time giving them the attention they need for a healthy upbringing (love).

## 8. NINE TIMES LUSTIER

The scriptural statement that women have 9 times more sex desire than men is difficult to explain but it is a fact that women are able to remain physically and emotionally affectionate much longer than men. Therefore the example is given in sastra that Kardama Muni had to expand himself 9 times to fully satisfy his wife's sex desire. This does not necessarily mean that a woman must have intercourse 9 times more than men. If sex energy is seen as an energy in the body, then it is understood that women need to engage that energy in physical and emotional exchanges whereas men can more readily vent their sexual energy on the mental/intellectual plane. It is stated in Ayur-veda that mental work is many times more consuming than physical work which would explain why men and women differ so much in their sexual/energetic needs. Of course, men, in the healthy state, will be intellectually inclined, but in the present age, here in the West especially, we find men wasting their mental energy looking at pornographic magazines or going to porno movies, etc. Women however, generally do not derive pleasure in this way. They derive pleasure from the actual physical/emotional contact, whereas men can take pleasure directly from the mental stimulation in these magazines, etc. This is why women are not interested in such visual images and are seldom seen loitering at pornographic stands. They are physically sensual/sensitive by bodily make-up whereas men are mental/intellectual sensitive by bodily make-up. Therefore it is sometimes said that women are nine times lustier than men. This refers to the woman's need for physical embraces, etc.

## 9. CONCLUSION-MADE DIFFERENT, AND FOR GOOD REASON

So with these considerations in mind we can see that women by nature are made differently than men and for very good reasons. One has to be more practical. He has to make money, build things, fix things, invent things, etc. He has to be endowed with more creativity. She has to look after the children, do the cooking, cleaning, sewing, etc. She has to be soft-hearted and more simple by nature. If both man and woman had the same physical, mental, intellectual make-up, then it simply wouldn't work. God made women for one job and men for the other. They are two distinct jobs requiring two completely different types of psychological makeups to perform them. No amount of protest on the part of today's women will ever be able to change that simply because women have wombs and breasts which produce children, and men don't.

## PART TWO

## MODERN PROBLEMS

### 10. THE WOMEN'S LIBERATION MOVEMENT-WHY?

This brings us to modem times when everything concerning the above concepts has been forgotten or suppressed. Men in these Western countries are so degraded that they simply exploit women by not taking proper care of them or make any serious commitments. This is undeniably the reason for the women's liberation movement and nobody in their right mind can blame the women for reacting in this way. Unfortunately, becoming independent of men is not the solution. That makes the women's plight even worse for then they have little to no protection at all. Therefore we see so many millions of women living abominable lives alone and on welfare with no proper care and attention. This situation is despicable.

### 11. FINDING A REAL HUSBAND-AVOIDING THE BUMS

One of the main purposes of this chapter is to help women understand how to look for and recognize a real man, and avoid the bums who will gladly exploit them, and then leave them with children and no protection. Once finding a good man, the woman has to know how to properly care for him in order to keep him. Our complete book, of which this chapter is but a summary, will also go into detail on how men must behave with their wives in order to keep them happy. It is not that women are simply meant to be submissive slaves. The man must be responsible and mature, and the wife has to be faithful and submissive. If both those qualities are there in the couple, then they are guaranteed to live very happy and fulfilling lives, ultimately going back to Godhead together. If one or both are not there, then the marriage cannot possibly work. In that case all the parties suffer, the children usually the worst of all. So, even though there are less and less qualified men these days, that does not mean that the system of marriage should be abolished. Here are some of the reasons why it should be kept intact, but in the proper way:

### 12. WHY ALL WOMEN MUST BE MARRIED-FOUR GOOD REASONS

What happens if women decide they don't need to be married but can take contraceptives or get abortions to avoid pregnancy? They can get jobs to maintain themselves or, if they have children, go on welfare. A small percentage of women may find some temporary peace in these "solutions," but on a large scale it cannot possibly work. The reasons are many-fold:First, children need two parents who both love them. That is the obvious and best condition for a child's mental health. Without that, they tend to grow up with problems. Then the whole society suffers in the future generation. That is happening now. All these neglected children who were not conceived in holy wedlock, but were products of the sexual revolution, are the criminals of today. No need to say more on what that means for society.

Secondly, women still need/want the company and security of men. Many women claiming equality on the outside, are actually very insecure and unhappy inside. Men also suffer in this way but not as badly. Most single or divorced women will always have in their minds how to capture a man. This encourages illicit affairs, which in turn degrades society. Men who should be peacefully living at home with their wives or expanding their brains in school, will be distracted and tempted to enjoy sex with all these single, attractive women. The education level will naturally drop in society, and the adultery level will rise. Party-goers and womanizers are generally not very interested in study or spiritual life. The society then becomes animalistic as is seen in the West today.

Thirdly, there is disease. If God had intended for anyone and everyone to have sex with many partners, then He would not have created this world with venereal diseases. Venereal disease is nature's way of checking sex outside of marriage. Right now, we are seeing that nature is starting to check illicit sex to the point that one is almost guaranteed of getting one disease or another if he/she is promiscuous.

Fourthly, what happens to the state when millions of women and children are living on welfare? Who is actually paying for all this? Through taxes, it always works out that the honest, responsible men of society have to support the women who are impregnated by irresponsible men. In this sense, polygamy is indirectly taking place in this country, the only difference being we call it welfare. Factually, polygamy is a natural necessity in society, because there are always more women than responsible men. When polygamy is allowed, at least the women have a real husband and the children have a real father whom they can see and talk to. In the state welfare polygamy system, one man is still maintaining many women and children, but he does not love or even know them, since he is not the impregnating father. The impregnating father is some derelict who, in Vedic culture, would be labeled an untouchable. Thus, the caste system is the natural system designed by God to protect women from low-class men. Of course, where polygamy is legal, women may suffer to a minor degree due to having to share a husband, but at least the children have a father to call their own and the women are protected. So we think any sane woman will agree that it would be better to share one husband with another woman, and thereby have a loving father for her children, than to have no husband except the welfare check. Therefore Prabhupada says that societies that outlaw polygamy are demoniac. In one sense Prabhupada also condemned polygamy since the vast majority of his disciples were irresponsible to even one wife, but the principle of polygamy will ultimately be essential if illicit sex is to be avoided in society.

### 13. HOW TO AVOID AND PUNISH SEXUAL OFFENDERS

Before a man can accept even one wife, he has to be responsible enough to care for her properly throughout life. If one is irresponsible and unqualified to look after a family then he is labeled an untouchable and he is identified by his dirty clothes. Thus women are able to recognize and avoid such low caste men. Or one may be more interested in spiritual life. Then he is called a brahmacari or sannyasi. His orange dress identifies him and women can recognize and avoid him also. Neither of these men are allowed to talk with or even look at any woman in society, especially unmarried women. If they break this unspoken law, they are immediately caught and dealt with severely. The monk, if he is actually a monk, may be told to marry a girl, and the outcast, if he has actually polluted a woman, will be imprisoned. In pure Vedic culture he would immediately be executed. If he is simply caught flirting with a woman, he is whipped. This is nature's way, which is synonymous with Vedic way or God's way, of preventing unwanted progeny. It is not cruel, but it is required for any society that wants to protect itself from unwanted progeny and degradation.

## 14. A MODERN MARRIAGE PROPOSAL

For these reasons, the concept of women not marrying, but simply having sexual affairs with no real commitment, is out of the question. The other reaction by women, when confronted with the fact that few men are very qualified these days, is to say: "I will marry a man, but he will see me as his equal. We will share equally in all the responsibilities of family life. He won't tell me what to do. I won't tell him what to do. In that way, neither of us will be demeaned." This may appear to work. She may well be more educated than the husband; she may be more responsible as well. However, in response to this somewhat rational approach to the problem, we give the following arguments:

1) As explained above, men by nature have a different mental make-up. They generally find it very difficult to baby-sit. Some men, who are more feminine by nature, may be able to do housework and baby-sitting, but in general, men simply cannot tolerate a woman's work. Women, on the other hand, are being educated these days to do many different types of work. So they feel quite able to go to work at the office, 8-5 daily. This can work until the children are born. Then there are problems. One must have sufficient money to hire a nursemaid or have a grandmother willing to look after the children. No boss wants to hire a woman who has to take a few months off every couple of years to give birth to a child.

2) Then there is the other option of not having any children at all, to just marry, mutually go to work, and in this way, be able to have a steady partner for sex, movies, outings, sports, social events, etc., with all the money to do it. What could be the wrong in this kind of relationship? Well, put in simple terms, "That ain't the way God planned it." It may work for a while, but it cannot possibly work for all of the people. One reason is people would cease to exist by this philosophy. Normal healthy women want children. Their bodies and minds were designed for that and no amount of artificial stimulation will substitute. Even Western women, with their modem educations, still feel that the ultimate goal of their lives would be to be able to find a really good man and raise a healthy happy family and live to be happy healthy grandmothers. Therefore, a more universal solution to the problem of irresponsible men is necessary.

## 15. VARNASRAMA-DHARMA-THE REAL SOLUTION

There has to be a solution that can be practically applied in society today, one which will gradually bring everyone to the real standard. That solution is called varnasrama-dharma, and the implementation of this system in society is absolutely necessary. But first it needs to be implemented in a true ISKCON society. Then, when it proves to work in ISKCON, it can be introduced to the world. But, instead of trying to implement this system in ISKCON, the current "leaders" of ISKCON are more interested in their own profit, adoration, and distinction, and as such their behavior is opposed to Vedic culture. In fact, ISKCON's leader are actively working against the introduction of the varnasrama system. Therefore these men must be removed so the serious disciples can get on with the second half of Srila Prabhupada's mission, namely introducing varnasrama-dharma to the world.

## 16. WOMEN'S LIBERATION AND BIG BUSINESS

Not just in Vedic culture but in all cultures of the world, including early American, women have always been treated with respect and caution. Chastity of women was considered a prime necessity to keep society pure and free from unwanted, criminal elements. But Vedic culture, because it is based on the most comprehensive body of revealed scriptures in the world, contains the most scientific and complete system of practically ensuring that women's chastity is preserved. Western women, when they read or hear about how Indian women are "kept down" foolishly think that "liberated women" are much better off. But this is a hoax created and encouraged by the big women exploitation businesses, such as pornography, prostitution, sex-based advertising, nightclubs, gambling casinos, etc. Other industries also thrive on "liberated women" such as the alcohol industry, fashion and clothing, cosmetics, pharmaceuticals, etc., etc., etc. All of these industries would lose most if not all of their business if women became simple, chaste housewives and the men stayed home with their wives and children. So let us take a practical look at the comparison between Eastern and Western women. We have not found any surveys on these comparisons but having spent several years in India and having studied Indian culture extensively, these conclusions are very obvious.

## 17."LIBERATED" WOMEN vs."HELD DOWN" WOMEN

DRUG ADDICTION, No comparison. Indian women for the most part have never taken a drug for intoxicating reasons. The lower caste women sometimes chew pan, a mild drug. Many liberated women however are dependent on drugs to get them through the day and keep from having nervous breakdowns.

ABORTION, In India, until recently, it was illegal. But now, due to Western influence, it has become legal. Still it is done very seldom and then mostly in the big cities. The reason there is so little abortion is because there is hardly any illicit sex. The statistics in Western countries are astronomical. Modern medicine has not yet "discovered" the harm done by abortion, but Vedic scripture describes such reaction as very severe.

DIVORCE, No comparison. It practically does not exist at all in Eastern countries, especially India. The societies and families are too close knit. Often the marriages are arranged before the children have even reached puberty. In the West however, the divorce rate is somewhere around 50%. The problems from such a high divorce rate have a snowballing effect. Children become neglected. Grandparents suffer tremendously from not being able to see their loved ones. Child abuse becomes commonplace. Juvenile delinquency and then crime increases. Welfare for all these forlorn women and children taxes the honest workers who ultimately rebel, etc., etc., etc. The list could go on indefinitely.

RAPE AND SEXUAL CRIMES, No comparison. The punishment for such crimes in India is instant death if caught by the victim's family and no one will protest such justice. Otherwise prison. Indian prisons don't have color televisions either. If not death or prison, then one is stripped of his caste and therefore doomed to spend the rest of his life on the streets as an outcast. Because of the severity of the punishment, such crimes are so rare in India that they make national headlines. Need anything be said about this problem in Western countries. Pornography and sex-based advertising breeds such criminals who run rampant.

DELINQUENT AND RUNAWAY CHILDREN: Again, families are very close in Eastern countries. They generally stay together for life, and often you will find under one roof four generations, all very happily living together. Needless to say, the concept of youngsters running away of leaving home in disgust is very, very rare. But in the West, very few families stay together. Usually the children leave home the moment they get a driver's license. The family unit in America is an imagination only, whereas in India, the family is still the most important institution in the country. Thus people are peaceful.

MARITAL VIOLENCE: Naturally there are always emotions in any family situation and no doubt the husband may occasionally strike his wife, but again, families are very close knit in India, and so, such occurrences are rare and not considered important. Just as a father may sometimes strike his son out of love to correct him, so a man may also sometimes also strike his wife. As Prabhupada says in hundreds of letters, "Discrepancies between husband and wife are never taken very seriously and there is never the question of divorce." In the West this is a tremendous problem. Daily women are being severely beaten by their irreligious, and barbaric husbands and the government cannot do anything since they are responsible for such degradation in the first place by allowing intoxication, pornography, meat eating, etc., etc., etc.

CHILD MOLESTATION OR ABUSE: In India, if such a thing occurred from outside the family; that person would be instantly killed or castrated by the family, so it is naturally very rare. Within the family, very rare if ever does such a thing occur. The reason being that there are very few sexual perverts in Eastern countries. In Indian movie houses, even today, they are not allowed to show lips touching in a kiss. Pornography is outlawed. Any form of sex outside of marriage is so severely condemned that such crimes are seldom even entertained in the mind, what to speak of carried out physically. We interviewed one young married man, a jeweler, and he told us that during his entire childhood right up until marriage, he had never talked of sex with other men or even thought of sex with women. He married at 22 years of age. Needless to say his mind was considerably more peaceful than this Western counterparts.

FAMILY UNITY: As mentioned above, the families always stay together and there is hardly ever less than three generations living in one house. The girls become a part of the husband's household and may not be living with her parents, but the sons are almost always intimately connected with the parents, right up until the parents die of old age. This is the natural system. There is no social security in most Eastern countries. The social security in India is called the family. And within the family, the sons are duty-bound to care for the parents in their old age. If they neglect this duty, they are outcast. But this is not at all objectionable since the sons enjoy the company of their parents. The young wife also likes to have the grandparents around to help care for all the children, help cooking, etc. The grandfather is usually good for helping around the house in so many ways. There is never a dull moment. If a father has three sons, quite often all the sons, along with their wives and at least three children each are living under the same roof with the grandfather and grandmother. Of course such houses are generally very large, but even if the family is not able to afford a large house, everyone is quite happy because they are all so close to each other. Being blood related, there is no fear of being cheated by outside business partners, a major problem in big Western corporations. As stated above, family unity in the West is almost an imagination.

RETIREMENT: Retirement in India for the ladies means to live with loved ones right up until death. There are no old folks homes in India where people are forced to live out their lives alone. Such a concept is unheard of except for those seriously engaged in spiritual practices. Then they are monks and they are the most happy people in the world because they have established communion with God. We cannot think of anything more pitiable than to see grandmothers and grandfathers forced to live out their lives alone in convalescent homes, hardly ever or even never seeing their children and grandchildren. But this is very common in the West.

EDUCATION LEVEL: Indian women generally don't get much education but instead stay home and learn all about how to be a good mother. In India today, women are getting a basic education, but generally they don't go beyond that. In the Western countries most women go to college and many become professionals in one field or another. This may be all right for those women who don't want to ever marry, but if a woman wants to be a housewife and raise a family, then her time would be better spent in learning cooking, sewing, cleaning, decorating, painting, embroidery, flower arranging, etc.

SUICIDE RATE: In India, in the days when women were extremely chaste, they would often commit suicide when their husbands died since they felt helpless. They were completely devoted to their husbands and to die with the husband is the highest religious act a woman can do. This one act guarantees her elevation, along with her husband, to the heavenly planets or the spiritual world if they had qualified themselves. But other than this form of suicide which is called "sati" in Sanskrit, there is very little suicide in India since all women are protected and cared for very nicely. In the West of course there are many suicides, by both men and women. This is due to the unnatural, artificial lifestyles most Westerners live. They have lots of outer stimulation, but little to no inner peace and so they can't cope with the real problems of life.

HAPPINESS LEVEL: This is what it really boils down to in the end. Who is happier? The Indian women certainly don't have the same kind of intense sense gratification that the Western women "enjoy" such as discos, jet travel to distant lands, credit cards, fancy cars, microwave ovens, video movies daily, satellite television, etc. Indian women lead very simple and generally peaceful lives. There are some common expressions such as "Money can't buy love...... The best things in life are free...... Happiness comes from within." It is commonly known that a child playing with a very costly electronic toy, will not be enjoying himself any more than the child playing with rocks by the river bank. Happiness does not depend on external conditions but comes from within. The comparisons above, and these universally accepted truths clearly indicate that Indian women, although not as flashy, are indeed much happier than their Western counterparts.

## 18. CREATING AND PROTECTING A CLASS OF CHASTE WOMEN

So the point is, being a "liberated" woman is not necessarily the qualification for being a happy woman. Srila Prabhupada of course confirms this: "Independence for a woman means misery." He also says it means "prostitution." So even though chaste women are usually not as sophisticated, intellectual, flashy, daring, exciting, etc., as Western women, they are more steady, peaceful, healthy and most of all faithful and chaste to their husbands. There is no such thing as marrying a non-virgin in Vedic culture and adultery practically does not exist. So why do we stress the superiority of chaste women over "liberated" women? There is only one reason: spiritual life. For those persons who are actually on the level of human beings, that is, they use their developed consciousness for higher ends, such persons will be attracted to a simple but chaste wife. Those persons who are more interested in extracting as much sense pleasure as possible, in as short a period of time as possible, they will be looking for a Western wife. The readers of this book will be interested in spiritual life, and therefore we are interested in learning how to create and protect a class of chaste women, not "liberated" women. The next chapter shows why it is so difficult to convert Western women into Vedic women and how the leaders of ISKCON are not encouraging this change.

## PART THREE

## WOMEN IN ISKCON

## 19. INTRODUCTION

In Srila Prabhupada's personal letters, he had to address the issue of marriage and a women's relationship to her husband more than he addressed any other single issue save and except to follow the four regulative principles and chant 16 rounds. This is obviously because it is here that the devotees becoming responsible householders, he still had to address the issue constantly. We feel that these voluminous instructions on marriage given in their entirety in our upcoming book, is ample evidence to clear the gross misconceptions on marriage that have plagued ISKCON since the beginning. Prabhupada did not want the women joining his movement to neglect their husbands in preference to himself, even though he was a completely pure devotee. He wanted the women to faithfully and devotedly serve their husbands, and in that way, serve himself. Why Srila Prabhupada initiated women at all is of course a controversial point, but the following letter gives us a clue. The matter is also thoroughly covered in the document entitled: SULOCANA vs. KIRTANANANDA (Appendix 22). Before beginning this section, the reader should keep in mind that there are numerous instructions, both from the books and letters, to back every sentence made herein. In the complete book, there will be footnotes to the Appendix references for all these points. For now please trust that we are not concocting anything.

## 20. AFFECTION BETWEEN HUSBAND AND WIFE

*"Regarding your personal question in the matter of relationship with your husband. Your relationship with your husband is all right. You must be faithful and devoted to your husband, Dayananda. Vedic system advises women to become very chaste and accept the husband as master. Your husband is especially good because he is progressing in Krishna consciousness. I am very glad that you two are very good combination and your devotion for your husband and your husband's love for you are considered great achievements. I feel very happy when I see my spiritual boys and girls, especially those who have been married by my personal presence, are very happy in their conjugal relationship." (Nandarani, 10/8/67)*

This mood shows the way Srila Prabhupada felt about his married disciples. In personal letters, he never discouraged affection between man and wife, or said such affection was Maya. Rather he encouraged it in many letters like the one above. Why would Srila Prabhupada consider it a "great achievement" to be attached to one's spouse? Does this sound like the words of a renunciate who is always preaching against family attachment and sense gratification? No. There is no contradiction whatsoever. Srila Prabhupada wanted mature responsible householders to manage his movement. This is clear by the fact that all the original GBC men were married. He knew perfectly well that his disciples were not prepared to accept the celibate order of life, sannyasa, but he was hoping that they could at least come up to the level of being responsible householders. Marriage means responsibility. It is superior to be a responsible householder than a wild-card bachelor in the guise of a sannyasi. He knew that for man and wife to live together peacefully and push on the movement there would have to be some affection between them. Ideally, as stated in many places, the wife should be faithful to her husband out of duty even if affection isn't there. But that is neither likely, or expected, in Westernized women. Therefore Prabhupada encouraged the women to be very attached to their husbands. He never preached some artificial renunciation to his young and usually passionate disciples.

## 21. THE EARLY MARRIAGES

Prabhupada's handling of his Western disciples was a real "can of worms" to say the least. Let's take a close look what he had to deal with. The vast majority of the men were too immature and/or irresponsible to become proper family men. But they were also too sexually agitated to remain single, which means celibate. And the women, they were too independent and usually "spoiled" to surrender very easily to anyone, much less men with the above qualifications. But single women were coming to the movement in large numbers and there was no possibility of stopping that influx in a "liberated" society. Without being married, all these women were a major disturbance to the single men who were already too sexually inclined. Srila Prabhupada stated in many letters what a tremendous problem this created. He flatly admitted that it was impossible to deal with. For a short time, when the first married couples were living and working together in a semblance of harmony, Srila Prabhupada encouraged them to no end in their preaching efforts. He was very pleased that they were cooperating with each other to spread Krishna consciousness. But later, when many of those first married couples became restless and started to split up, Prabhupada washed his hands of the whole "dirty business." Only then did he start discouraging marriage and started giving important posts to single men.

## 22. WHY PRABHUPADA GAVE "SANNYASA"

But the problem with the majority of these single men was that they were not free of sex desire and so were actually not qualified for real sannyasa. Almost all of his disciples still had strong material desires. So what was he to do? They couldn't possibly be allowed to have sex, or as Prabhupada would word it, "freely mix," without any responsibility of marriage. That would have meant abortions and contraception, which Prabhupada condemned. He never compromised in that way, thereby encouraging another sex cult like Rajneesh. So, as early letters reveal, Prabhupada tried and tried to inspire his disciples to be good householders. He wrote hundreds of letters like the one above to Nandarani encouraging the couples to become attached to one another and preach. Then, when that failed to keep them together, we see how he made them sign documents promising that they would never separate under any circumstances. But even then they refused to obey. Daily he was getting more and more letters from disciples asking if they could divorce, what they should do with the unwanted children, if they could remarry, and so on.

So he finally refused to take part in any more marriages. But there was still the problem of what all these agitated young men should do. They wouldn't remain responsible householders as he wanted. Although Prabhupada said in one letter in 1970 that he was going to forget the whole mission and go back to India to write books with the help of a few of his more mature disciples, that wouldn't have kept the mission alive in the West. The material desires of these men would have to be satisfied if they were to go on preaching. Simply eating opulently would not suffice indefinitely. But the position of sannyasa could supply the material gratifications of profit, adoration, and distinction, or subtle sex life. None of them were actually fit for sannyasa, as Prabhupada later revealed. Many had been homosexuals, gangsters, drug addicts, etc. Except for the rare soul, sannyasa in Vedic culture is a graduation from mature household life. (And are we more advanced than Vedic culture?) None of these men had actually graduated. So, with these "sannyasis," the very same sex desire the householder vents in physical sex with his wife, the "sannyasi" could enjoy through the benefits of adoration and distinction. At least in that way unwanted children wouldn't be produced and the preaching could go on without this constant disturbance. There were still disturbances created by these neophyte "sannyasis," but compared to the alternatives, it was acceptable for the time being. Such a time-and-circumstance adjustment made by the uttama-adhikari does not become a Vedic law to be imitated by anyone regardless of qualification.

## 23. "PRACTICAL SANNYASIS"

These were not real sannyasis Srila Prabhupada was making but "practical sannyasis," an alternative to their going away altogether. We can admire the perfection of Srila Prabhupada's strategy. Everyone engaged in preaching and distributing books, and the only negative result was that some of his Godbrothers criticized him for giving unfit men sannyasa. To this criticism, Srila Prabhupada would often reply, "My Godbrothers have no brain how to spread Krishna consciousness all over the world," not understanding the adjustments needed for the sake of preaching in the West. Of course, disturbances continued with householders and sannyasis being envious of each other, but all-in-all, Prabhupada's strategy worked miracles in keeping these otherwise difficult-to-engage men busy in spreading the message of Lord Caitanya throughout the world. In numerous letters, Prabhupada said that this sannyasa is not important, that any devotee preaching Krishna consciousness is already better than a sannyasi.

## 24. A MOVEMENT OF HOUSEHOLDERS

So, considering what Srila Prabhupada had to work with, is it any wonder when he says above: Your mutual affection for each other is a "great achievement." Prabhupada said that he wanted his temples managed by mature householders. Actually the scriptural injunction for this age is not to take sannyasa but to remain home and preach (Cc. Mad, 7.127). That was Lord Caitanya's instructions to Kurma Brahmin. In these Western countries, the idea of real sannyasa, in most cases, is out of the question. Until one is very mature, something that usually comes from living a mature household life, most devotees should not even consider sannyasa before age fifty. In one letter, Prabhupada said, "First prove yourself by being a responsible husband." Therefore, learning how to be mature householders is of tantamount importance for anyone serious about spiritual life, especially in this age. There is no longer any need for this facade by the so-called sannyasis. That time is now over. Srila Prabhupada's adjustments in this regard got the movement off the ground and got his books printed. He never indicated that sannyasa was a cheap thing. How could we think that Prabhupada wanted a movement of young, passionate, "sannyasis" with hundreds of women hanging on to their sandals? He only gave one man (Kirtanananda) sannyasa before 1970, and that "sannyasi" immediately turned on Prabhupada to steal the movement for himself (full story in Chapter Ten). The next four "sannyasis" were the ones who locked him in his room in LA. That was when Prabhupada said that he was going to retire to book writing and nothing more. They also wanted to take over the movement for themselves. That story is in Chapter Eight. So one should not think that Prabhupada's giving "sannyasa" meant that these men were spiritually advanced. In these early instances, it was generally just the opposite-they were simply advanced in their material ambition.

## 25. INITIATING WOMEN: WHY?

This brings us to an important point: Why did Srila Prabhupada initiate women if they were meant to be the disciple of their husbands? As stated above, young girls were coming to the movement in large numbers. Prabhupada often stated, "they couldn't be rejected, because they are also coming to Krishna for shelter." Prabhupada had said that all the women had to be married, but at the same time we can see that if he said openly that women were disciples of their husbands, it would create havoc with their Western egos. They would have been so offended by such a proposition that there is no telling what they would have done. And of course they can't be blamed, since the men were not very advanced either. So again a difficult situation. He stated that he would not discriminate against them by not initiating them and had said they should not remain single and unprotected. Since a man needs full devotion from his wife if he's to be faithful to her, Prabhupada always told the women, both in his books and letters, to fully surrender themselves to their husband and see him as their guru.

## 26. WHY SO MANY DIVORCES?

But, since they were so independent minded, many refused to accept what Srila Prabhupada was telling them. They would naturally think, "I'm equal to my husband, I have my own guru, I don't need my husband to help me in spiritual life. I'm just as advanced as my husband, or more so. Why should I humbly serve him?" This may have been subconsciously thought by many women, but the 90% divorce rate in ISKCON proves this mentality was there. Naturally, with their wives thinking like this, the husbands had difficulty feeling their spiritual obligation toward them. In Vedic culture that means there is really no marriage at all. Vedic marriage means two halves of the same body with the wife being the dependent hall, but failure to accept this meant one divorce after another. Of course there is the other side of the coin also. Many men don't deserve to be treated as guru by their wives. This is real chicken and egg problem. What came first: The woman wasn't devoted to her husband, and so he wasn't responsible towards her, or the husband wasn't mature and responsible enough towards his wife, and so the wife wasn't devoting herself to him? Ultimately it boils down to this question. Of course, in most marriage breakups, there is a little of both, but there is a way to minimize this syndrome.

## 27. "SEXYASIS" AND "SEXYASINIS"

There is no possibility for a real sannyasi to take charge of a woman. If someone things there is, then he is no sannyasi. For all practical purposes, women need a real live husband. It doesn't mean that they can't have a relationship to a bona fide guru any more than it means they can't have a relationship to Krishna. The spiritual relationship is most definitely there, but without a husband, the chances a woman practically realizing that relationship is next to nil. Therefore Srila Prabhupada never encouraged sannyasinis. Without husbands, their minds would simply be agitated, and there is no possibility of significant spiritual advancement in that condition. So Srila Prabhupada continually urged the women to be chaste Vedic wives. But had he discriminated against women in regard to initiation, they likely would not have tolerated it. So Srila Prabhupada initiated both the men and women. His initiating women, and his giving sannyasa to unqualified men, can be seen as similar time and circumstance adjustments. Men with sex desire are not "sannyasis" and wives not devoted to their husbands, are not wives. They both have only half a body. New names have to be invented for these two groups of Kali-yuga disciples. These are our suggestions. Men who are too immature to get married, but are still full of sex desire and so need a stick to carry around with them so they can be respected, should be called "sexyasis." Women who hate men, and would rather live on welfare, or would rather devote themselves to a sexyasi than their husbands, may be called "sexyasinis."

## 28. "SEXYASIS" INITIATING "SEXYASINIS?"

Those devotees who are serious about implementing the real Vedic system first of all have to know that one of the most important aspects is to protect the women from exploitation and illicit sex. That means they have to be married. In ISKCON today these sexyasis are claiming to be the guru to so many women but such a proposition is not only meaningless but guarantees the woman's marriage will fail. Srila Prabhupada's initiating women was a very special concession for time and circumstance that no one can imitate. Otherwise why would he say in so many places that the wife must be cent percent devoted to her husband. He says, "The real guru to the wife is the husband." Women can and should devote themselves to Srila Prabhupada's instructions, because he is factually a pure devotee, just as they can devote themselves to Krishna. But if they feel they have a direct link to Prabhupada personally and so therefore don't need the help and protection of a good husband, then they are in illusion. One woman in a thousand is qualified to be a nun just as one man in a thousand is qualified to be a young sannyasi. Women need a real husband to help them make spiritual advancement and men need a real wife to help them make progress also. They don't need a sexyasi or sexyasini. Woman claiming to have a relationship with one of these "ISKCON" sexyasis should know, without a doubt, that such a relationship is nothing but unalloyed illicit sex, which will destroy any possibility of a successful marriage.

## 29. THE REAL PROBLEM

So having understood and accepted this fact, the next major question by women is "How can I respect my husband who is neither a pure devotee nor even an especially good husband?" This is the real problem we are faced with today. Neither the men nor women are especially qualified for becoming bona fide Vedic husbands and wives. There are many ways to approach this, but before anything else, first the couple has to know what a Krishna conscious marriage is. The following section explains the ideal Vedic marriage. To enter into a marriage without this knowledge is like trying to fly without wings. The first prerequisite for a successful marriage is to know exactly what marriage is all about.

## WARNING

We have received mixed reactions to this section. So much so that it is necessary to advise devotees that they may be disturbed by reading this. This is because some devotees do not have good marriages and are not inclined toward committing themselves to an eternal spiritual relationship with their spouse. This unfortunate situation is largely due to our impersonal upbringing here in the West and the contamination introduced by the current "gurus" into the society. We tend to project our mundane concepts and bad relationships onto transcendence and thus we become confused and even repulsed by the idea of an eternal relationship with our spouse. This is due to ignorance and/or impersonalism. Impersonalism is an all-pervasive disease in the West and practically everyone is influenced by it to one degree or another. So if your marriage is on the rocks, and you see little chance of salvaging it, then you may be well advised to skip the next ten titles. But it may also save your marriage. This section is primarily for devotees starting off in marriage or wishing to deepen their marriage relationship.

## 30. PRELIMINARY CONSIDERATIONS ON MARRIAGE

The intricacies of a Krishna conscious marriage are very complex and at least as difficult to work out in these times and circumstances as the guru problem. In one sense they are very similar since to get a bona fide guru or spouse one has to sincerely pray to Krishna, and simultaneously know who to look for. Because householders form the basis of any society, this issue is vital to the future of ISKCON. Prabhupada has made very clear that without sound householders, there is no question of a society for Krishna consciousness. It will never go beyond a few personalities trying to maintain "nice eating and sleeping in the name of a temple."

So this section is dedicated to helping serious devotees recognize and avoid pitfalls in marriage. A man's relationship with his wife is, as Prabhupada says, "a very complex subject." In India, even today, it is easy to have a lasting, healthy marriage, because that is the custom. It comes naturally, just as reading the newspapers and drinking coffee is second-nature to most Westerners. In precept, marriage is easy to understand. The problem is, we have artificially complicated their lives to the point where even simple principles are difficult to conceive. We have taken advantage of extensive research by modem psychologists on this subject and found it useful in substantiating the eternal principles taught by Srila Prabhupada.

## 31. CELIBACY IN MARRIAGE

For example, many researchers today are starting to appreciate the benefits of celibacy. Without spiritual knowledge, however, very few of them have a really clear picture. But, by combining their research with Vedic knowledge, and of course the higher taste of Krishna consciousness, we have a very potent body of knowledge to help us regulate our sex lives, and at the proper time, renounce it altogether. Prabhupada never tried to convince couples to artificially become celibate, but he tried to help them understand the difference between necessary sex and degrading sex. When both husband and wife understand each other and the scripture on these points, they will be able to control themselves much easier. Then, once having gone through marriage in a regulated and mature way, it can be possible to peacefully take sannyasa and not simply create a disturbance in society, as so many of the young ISKCON sexyasis are currently doing.

## 32. THE ETERNAL RELATIONSHIP

Prabhupada makes two seemingly contradictory statements in this regard, In some places he says that these man-women relationships are temporary like "straws bumping in the waves. They come together for some time and then separate forever." This concept, which is meant to apply to ordinary mundane relationships, is commonly applied by devotees to their relationships. This is due to impersonalism. In every instance where Prabhupada talks of temporary relationships, he is referring to animalistic relationships. In numerous places Prabhupada says the relationships between devotees, including married devotees, is eternal. In at least a dozen places he directly states that husband and wife go back to Godhead together. This means that they can have an eternal, personal relationship together in the spiritual world, if they want to. It is absurd for devotees to think that after striving together in Krishna consciousness for a lifetime, they will say goodbye at the end and go their own way eternally. Many devotees actually think this way but that is due only to impersonalism. If someone has this disease in his heart, then he is not going back to the personal spiritual world at the end of this lifetime. A personalist has no objection to taking as many people as possible back to Godhead, including his wife. Exactly what the relationship will be eternally is not important to dwell on while still neophytes. Prabhupada gives hints in his books. As far as details, he says, "These things you will find out when you get there." The eternal relationship does not necessarily have to be the same as it was in the lifetime that they achieved success together. That is the meaning of spiritual and personal. It depends on free will and desire.

## 33. AGREEING ON THE GOAL

In principle, if the man is sincere and the woman is faithful, then that is the perfect combination for a spiritual relationship. The wife helps her husband get past the youthful years of lust, by satisfying his material needs within the realm of Vedic instruction. In the end, she shares equally in his spiritual realization, whether she personally took part in the spiritual practices or not. If she faithfully and intimately serves her husband, then she gets the same benefit, providing she wants it. If they are not in agreement with each other as to the goal of their lives, then they are not really married-at least not in the Vedic sense. If two people want to go anywhere together, first they have to agree on where they want to go.

## 34. WHAT TO LOOK FOR IN A SPOUSE

So if a man and woman are one in their desire to love Krishna by executing devotional service, then everything else is given in Prabhupada's books. Unfortunately, sometimes one of the parties is not in harmony with the other about the goal of their lives. Then everything is frustrated. So the critical point is, before getting married, to make absolutely certain of the character and intentions of the proposed spouse. This boils down to knowledge and sincerity. Finding a mate with these two qualifications is essential if one is serious about spiritual life. It doesn't matter how many minor personality problems a mate may have, for they can be overlooked and tolerated. As long as one is sincere and knows the goal of life, and how to achieve it, then those unwanted habits, or anarthas, will disappear in due course of time. Patience is essential. We cannot expect to find a mate that is already perfect. Then once finding a sincere and knowledgeable spouse, what spiritual responsibility must they accept?

## 35. SPIRITUAL RESPONSIBILITIES

The woman has the difficult task of remaining chaste and submissive to her husband. This is a tremendous austerity since most men are not very mature in their youth. But she must serve him submissively anyway so that later, when he has matured, he is deeply indebted to her for her faithful service. If he is actually sincere, then he must repay her by fully devoting the last years of his life to Krishna (1.15.44). If he becomes pure, she will automatically reap the benefits of his advancement. She may even live the last years of her life not even seeing her husband, but when she leaves her body, she will join him. If he has become pure, and she has been chaste, then she will go back to Godhead immediately upon leaving her body. This is the ideal husband/wife relationship. She is a fit candidate for entering the spiritual kingdom because of her chastity toward her devotee husband. A woman's chastity toward her husband is the same as chastity toward one's guru. It completely purifies the soul. In one sense it's easier for the woman since she can directly see and serve her husband. The man has to surrender in the same way to his guru, but he does so more on the basis of shastric study and faith, since he cannot daily receive instructions from his guru.

Women in Vedic culture would voluntarily enter the funeral pyre so they would not become contaminated in the absence of their husbands. Similarly, Prabhupada says that if one cannot execute the mission of his guru after the guru departs, then he should also decide to die. A woman invests her energy in faithfully serving her husband on his promise that he will repay her by sincerely striving to become pure. If he becomes pure, and she remains chaste, then they both go home together. She does not get paid for her faithfulness until she leaves her body. That is the meaning of faith. He accepts her service on the condition that as soon as he is over the "strong waves of youth," at fifty to sixty years, he will take vanaprastha and then sannyasa. If she's been a good wife, he won't be allured by another woman. This cooperative relationship can be compared to a relay race. She passes the stick to him at fifty and then relaxes while he finishes the race alone. If the wife is resentful of him for her having to do so much running in the beginning of the race, that means she does not understand that he will also have to carry the burden in due course of time.

## 36. THE REWARD FOR CHASTITY

Then how does he repay her for her faithful service? By "capturing Krishna" and giving Him to her. Krishna is not so cheap that simply by baby-sitting, cooking, and cleaning the house for 30-40 years she can win Krishna. Every woman is doing that whether they are devotees or not. But a devotee woman literally buys Krishna by her chastity and "always pleasing" attitude toward her husband, even if he doesn't deserve it at times. Prabhupada says, "Chastity is the first religious principle for a woman." And Chanakya Pandit says, "A woman makes more spiritual advancement by washing the feet of her husband with water, than by performing sacrifices, going to holy places, observing fasts, etc."It is very difficult to be chaste, humble, and always pleasing when the husband is not yet perfect, but that is the price she must pay for Krishna.

## 37. HUSBAND'S ROLE ISN'T EASY EITHER

The women shouldn't feel envious that they have to carry the burden initially, for his job certainly is not easy either. When he takes sannyasa, he has to forcibly give up attachment to his good wife, his loving children, delicious meals, the comforts of home, and strictly control all his senses, absorbing his mind day and night in thinking and preaching about Krishna. That's not easy. The materially covered senses strongly react against that life-style. And there is no possibility of cheating oneself either. Controlling the mind is the most difficult part. During this time the wife is more or less relaxing and being served by her children and grandchildren. She has done her share of the work and now can simply pray that her husband remains sincere. Of course, she must remain pure and simple herself, but compared to her husband's austerities, she is taking a vacation. So granted, it's a tremendous surrender to be a chaste wife. Her job is very difficult during the time of cooperation together, but the husband has the hard job at the end. If he is fully satisfied with his good wife's faithful service, then his gratitude to her becomes a tremendous impetus to repay her by becoming fully Krishna conscious. If the wife is not devoted exclusively to him, however, then he may well be attracted to another woman and thus his life is also ruined. So chastity for a woman is the first religious principle.

## 38. ROMANCE IN THE MARRIAGE

As long as they both agree on this formula and work toward that goal, keeping themselves always sincere and avoiding offenses, then it is not at all difficult to go back to Godhead together. This relationship is very intimate and has nothing whatsoever to do with external so-called romantic/sexual love. Such love may or may not be there, just as over-eating or over-sleeping may or may not be there. If it is there, it must eventually be given up. Therefore Prabhupada warns for devotees not to be overly attracted to one's wife or romantically involved. Chanakya Pandit also warns, "A beautiful wife is an enemy." Romance is not necessary for a spiritual relationship, but it can prevent the husband from ultimately being able to devote himself fully to Krishna. A very deep, spiritual relationship between husband and wife is only possible if sexual love is absent. A book called The New Celibacy goes into this in great detail and is recommended reading for devotees. What to speak of romance, Prabhupada says she must "faithfully serve her husband even if she doesn't like him." Westerners have this perverted idea that marriage is meant for romance, and so, if there is any break in the excitement, inevitable divorce follows. Prabhupada says however, "In the material world, there is no question of love-that marriage is actually a practical necessity, a duty." The wife may be attached to her husband if he is a devotee, but the husband has to be very careful not to be overly attached to his wife, since ultimately, he must become 100% attached to Krishna. That is the formula. Of course this formula varies somewhat according to ones status in life. The same strict rules that apply to the brahmins do not apply to the sudras, but anyone can go back to Godhead eventually, if he is sincere. It may not be in one lifetime, but as long as a couple are sincere, they will advance toward that goal.

## 39. BE ABSOLUTELY CERTAIN

If you are serious about Krishna consciousness, but need a wife to help get you over the "waves of youth," then you must choose her very carefully. If you select an insincere or incompatible mate, she may disturb you. Or, if you are a sincere woman and need a husband to protect you, give you children, and ultimately take you back to Godhead, then choose him carefully. If he is not sincere, he will simply produce a bunch of kids in you and then leave, but not for sannyasa, for sexyasa. So best to make absolutely sure of your prospective mate's sincerity and compatibility before deciding to marry him/her. There are many ways of doing this, some of which are explained later. Of course, if one is not so serious about going back to Godhead in this very lifetime, that does not mean he/she cannot get married and make some advancement. He/she has to find a mate of the same nature so they can advance together from whatever level they are on.

## 40. THE CHOICE IS YOURS

So the husband/wife relationship can be eternal or temporary. The choice is entirely up to the individuals. It's not that it has to be one or the other as so many devotees think. If you don't want an eternal relationship, then nobody can force you. You can live together in a cooperative fashion, without making any commitment to each other spiritually. That is possible. That relationship is somewhat impersonal, but it is possible. It is not the highest kind of marriage relationship as described in sastra. One can also bump into a different soul lifetime after lifetime, just like straws touching in the ocean waves. Or a couple can share three or four lifetimes together and then part ways never to meet again. There is no impersonal formula that determines such things. Modern hypnosis regressions have completely confirmed Prabhupada's statements on such husband-wife relationships. Some couples get together lifetime after lifetime. Some only a few lifetimes. It is only logical and common sense that if a couple are very intimately connected with each other, and they become perfected together, then they will also go back to Godhead together. There are many descriptions in the Srimad Bhagavatam of couples living together in the spiritual world, but without mundane sex desire, because they are continually chanting the glories of the Lord. This concept of course gives rise to some very interesting questions regarding spiritual relationships. This section is only meant to give the general idea of the possibilities so devotees can choose, in full knowledge, what kind of marriage they want. If a couple strive together, but don't make it in this lifetime for one reason or another, if they are both sincere, then they will continue together in the next life. Chances are it will be in reversed roles. Then she can play lord and master, and he can play chaste, and surrendered wife. It doesn't matter who plays what role. Ultimately we are all female in the sense that we are all meant to be enjoyed by Krishna. And the price for Krishna is the same for both. Both must give up their puffed-up false egos. She gives it up to her husband, and he gives it up to Krishna. Thus both become perfect. The goal is to go back to Krishna, one way or another.

The question sometimes arises. Does this mean a woman cannot go back to Godhead without the help of a husband? Independent minded women, for the most part, raise this question. The answer is: possible, but not likely. Remember the example of the relay race. There is always the rare soul that can run the entire race by himself and keep up with the other runners, who are sharing the distance with partners. But such a person is rare. Similarly, most women will tend to become very degraded if they are not protected by a man. Prabhupada says that women as a class will be inclined to think about sex, subtle or gross. If a woman is very strong, and becomes a nun, strictly following the regulative principles, then of course she can directly go back to Godhead by her own strength. Most women, however, will not be able to do so, and as such Prabhupada never encouraged women to think this way. He always stressed they be chaste and faithful to their husbands.

## HOW DOES A WOMAN "FLY HER OWN PLANE?

This brings us to a very important consideration that at first glance seems to contradict the above. In SB, 1.15.51, the impression is made that the husband abandons his wife when he takes sannyasa and she is then on her own. There the analogy is given that one must be able to fly his own plane without any help. Prabhupada says that help is required while on the ground, but ultimately she must be able to fly her own plane alone. This is a somewhat contradictory point since in many other places, Prabhupada says that the wife follows her husband back to Godhead. In many ways, the husband-wife, and guru-disciple relationship are the same. The guru must have complete submission and faith from the disciple. He instructs the disciple to think of Krishna at the time of death. If the disciple is chaste and obedient, he will do so. Similarly, a devotee husband trains his wife to be chaste and faithful and he also instructs her to think of Krishna at the time of death. There is no difference at all. So just as the disciple must be completely surrendered to guru to be able to follow his instructions perfectly, so also the wife must be completely surrendered to her husband. They both must try to think of Krishna at the time of death. If for some reason they cannot, then the guru or husband will have to help them again. One cannot accept service from a subordinate without becoming indebted. He remains responsible to his surrendered wife right up through her death. In one letter Prabhupada said, "Even after taking sannyasa, the husband does not leave his wife. He must be certain that she is being well protected." The question raised above then is: "At the exact moment of death, is the husband still responsible for his wife, or does his duty end at that moment?" Persons who think it ends, are afflicted with impersonalism. The husband is naturally indebted to his good wife, and so he must save her. Just as the guru must return again and again to save his sincere disciples, so the husband must save his sincere wife. That is the duty.

In one letter Prabhupada says: "The wife becomes the devotee of her husband, and the husband becomes a devotee of Krishna." If the wife is a devotee of her husband her whole life, then naturally she will think of him at the time of death. That is logic. She may think of him, and then his instructions may remind her of Krishna. Or she may think of him, and go to him wherever he is. If he's with Krishna, then that's where she'll go. If he is liberated, then she is also liberated provided she is fully devoted to him. Chaste women understand these points very easily. The overwhelming majority of instructions from the books and letters indicate that the wife should be cent percent devoted to, and dependent on her husband, and not think she can be independent from him to learn to "fly on her own." This is in fact the only purport where such a concept is mentioned in relation to women. It is illogical to accept a meaning of this purport which contradicts everything else Srila Prabhupada had to say on the husband-wife relationship. Some careful thought must be there on how to interpret this purport. It should not be used as an excuse by women to think they don't need to be faithful to their husbands because they ultimately are on their own. That mentality will breed the kind of prostitution we see in ISKCON today. To illustrate this point, on the first page of Chapter Fourteen in The Nectar of Devotion, Prabhupada says that "performing artificial austerities will make the heart harder and harder." So does that mean we should forget the thousands of other places where Prabhupada says we must follow regulative principles? Hardly. There is a rational way to approach all such seeming contradictions as this. The tendency of most conditioned souls is to make an interpretation that allows the most sense gratification. And that is why Prabhupada very seldom gave such instructions as SB 1. 15.51 which can be misinterpreted by women to reject their husbands. Prabhupada always stressed the spiritual relationship elaborately described above.

So with this spiritual relationship in mind, what is the position of these ISKCON "sexyasis" who are claiming to be the guru of single women as well as other men's wives?

## 41. SEXYASI INTERFERENCE IN MARRIAGES

The most significant pitfall amongst devotee marriages today is that women are being misled into thinking they need to devote themselves to an ISKCON sexyasi, and not their husband, to go back to Godhead. This is an incredible hoax. Anyone knows that for two people to stay together, even in the mundane sense, they must be devoted to each other. Her husband's guru is automatically her guru, since a proper husband and wife are "two halves of the same body." There isn't the slightest possibility of this kind of intimacy if the wife is having an illicit affair going on in her mind with another man. What to speak of intimacy, such a sexyasini wife will drain her husband's energy and give nothing in return. Instead she will give that energy, through her meditation, service, and worship, to her sexyasi "guru," who then thrives and increases his energy. She may even feel some ecstasy while chanting Hare Krishna and meditating on a sexyasi guru, but that is only illicit sex and will destroy her ability to chant purely in the future. Many men are weakened in their marriage relationship due to living with such sexyasinis. This is one of--and possibly the primary reason for--a man's feeling no inspiration from his wife. His enthusiasm is drained. Prabhupada often talks of men increasing their energy by dint of a good wife. Chanakya Pandit says a good wife is the same as the Goddess of Fortune. And conversely, Prabhupada goes so far as to say a man is only "half a man" if he does not have a good wife. "A person who does not have a chaste wife accepted by religious principles always has a bewildered intelligence." (SB, 4.26.17) This is a very important purport in this connection. It makes very clear how the husband is meant to be the only man in his wife's life. He may not be a pure devotee, but as long as he is sincere, and devoted to his own guru, he should have his wife's full devotion. If a sexyasi, who doesn't realize any of these truths--or doesn't care about them--tells a woman to leave her husband to devote herself to him, then he is automatically guilty of wife stealing and should be severely punished and even executed as explained below.

## 42. THE PUNISHMENT FOR WIFE STEALERS

*"According to Vedic injunctions there are six kinds of aggressors: (1) A poison giver; (2) One who sets fire to the house; (3) One who attacks with deadly weapons; (4) One who plunders riches; (5) One who occupies another's land; and (6) One who kidnaps a wife. Such aggressors are at once to be killed, and no sin is incurred by killing such aggressors. Such killing of aggressors is quite befitting for any ordinary man, but Arjuna was not an ordinary person. He was saintly by character, and therefore he wanted to deal with them in saintliness. This kind of saintliness, however is not for a ksatriya. Although a responsible man in the administration of a state is required to be saintly, he should not be cowardly."* (BG, 1.36)

Many sincere devotees of Srila Prabhupada have been aggressed upon in one or more of the manners listed above. Some have had their life savings stolen through very shrewd manipulation or outright embezzlement by sexyasis. This merits the death sentence. Some have donated land only to later be kicked out with nothing. This also merits the death sentence. But by far the most frequent crime committed by the sexyasis is stealing others' wives. By far, all of ISKCON's "gurus" should have been executed many times over by now, and they will in the end have to pay for all the damage they've done.

## 43. SEXYASIS CANNOT IMITATE PRABHUPADA

There are many women and children now living abominable lives because of these "gurus" interfering in their marriages, either subtly or grossly, directly or indirectly. In some cases the husband or wife may have been at fault, but very often the marriage never had a chance to get off the ground since the wives were told it was their religious duty to devote themselves to this "guru" instead of their husband. That means they were never really wives at all. If the guru was actually a saint following the standard set by Srila Prabhupada, then this problem would not be there. Prabhupada always encouraged the women to devote themselves "cent percent" to their husbands. That is the Vedic process. Prabhupada could initiate women because he is as pure as Krishna Himself. Since Krishna is already in everyone's heart, there is no significant difference with Prabhupada being there also. They are both actually the same person, in purity. They know what is best for the wife and will instruct her as such. That instruction is almost always to "stay with your husband-there is no divorce." But these new "gurus" have displayed their impurity in this connection. There have been blatant falldowns, and there is no need to detail them all. Only foolish devotees have not seen the subtle displays of sex life on the part of ISKCON's "gurus." One example is Bhavananda. He is frequently seen going out at night when he is in New York City wearing fancy clothes and perfume. We think everyone knows by now what he is looking for. Prabhupada was not a fool. He knew perfectly well that these sexyasis were not qualified to imitate him and therefore he gave the following instruction to warn us:

*"Although he was a young man (Narada Muni), he could give shelter to a young woman (Hiranyakasipu's wife) and accept her service. Haridasa Thakura also spoke with a young woman, a prostitute, in the dead of night, but the woman could not deviate his mind... Ordinary persons, however, should not imitate such highly elevated devotees. Ordinary persons must strictly observe the rules and regulations by staying aloof from the association of women. No one should imitate Narada Muni or Haridasa Thakura... Narada Muni, Haridasa Thakura and similar acaryas especially empowered to broadcast the glories of the Lord cannot be brought down to the material platform." (SB, 7.7.14)*

Here is where the real problem lies. These sexyasis have convinced themselves that they are on the level of Haridasa Thakura, Narada Muni and empowered acaryas like Srila Prabhupada. This is proven by the fact that they are taking so much opulent and unauthorized worship in direct imitation of the great acaryas. But when confronted with, "Prove your advancement by your behavior." That they cannot do. Therefore Prabhupada, anticipating this syndrome, warns the sincere devotees as follows:

*"It is recommended that one associate with devotees, but there must be some discrimination. Actually, a sadhu, a saintly person, must be saintly in his behavior (sadhavah sad-acarah). Unless one adheres to the standard behavior, one's position as a sadhu, a saintly person, is not complete. Therefore a Vaishnava, a sadhu, must completely adhere to the standard of behavior." (SB, 7.7.31)*

## 44. HOW SEXYASIS RATIONALIZE IT

But ISKCON's gurus have an open policy that behavior is not so important as being appointed "guru." Being appointed does not at all mean being qualified. It almost always means political considerations-power politics. Kirtanananda exposed the official GBC position in this matter in a lecture in Bombay just after Jayatirtha's departure. He said, " In pure devotional service, there is no duality, see, therefore even when they say, 'O, these GBCs, they can make mistakes, that does not matter. Even our mistakes are spiritual. That is a fact. Because why? They are a product of our serving Krishna. Whatever we do in this connection to

Krishna, that is spiritual... In the spiritual world also there appears to be mistakes, but there are no mistakes. That is also perfect. There is no duality, there is no good, no bad. But still all these things are existing in perfection."

In other words, he is saying "We 'gurus' can do any abominable thing we like and still be considered saintly, because our inner motive is ultimately to serve Krishna." This philosophy is very common. Prabhupada spoke about it often. In the West these men are called hippies. In India they are called sahajiyas. In essence, sahajiya means "cheap," or, no discipline. The first principle of discipline for a real sannyasi is absolutely no connection with women. The fact is, a sannyasi, unless he is actually on the level of Haridasa Thakura, or Srila Prabhupada, shouldn't even talk to women, look at women, or think of women. That is extremely sinful as Lord Caitanya himself demonstrated by banning Chota Haridasa from His association. ISKCON's sexyasi "gurus" are nothing but pure, unalloyed sahajiyas. In many situations they are acting exactly like pimps.

This next section is just to give a little idea of some of the principles on how to find and keep a spouse. In the complete book, this subject will be fully explained giving thousands of references from all of Prabhupada's teachings and Vedic texts. Since this book may not be complete for up to a year, we are giving some basic ideas here so devotees can avoid some of the more common pitfalls.

## 45. HOW TO FIND A REAL HUSBAND

So now that we've determined that women are meant to be married, they are meant to devote themselves "cent percent" to their sincere devotee husbands, and that they are never meant to think of any other men, especially a sexyasi. The next question is, where is such a devotee husband to be found? Is it even possible to find one in this day and age?

## 46. KNOWING HOW TO LOOK

Since this section is primarily meant for devotees who have a basic understanding of karma, we are not going to go into detail here to explain these intricacies. The idea is that if one is sincere, then Krishna will send the bona fide guru, and if one is sincere Krishna will send the bona fide spouse. But this does not mean that we don't have to make any effort to understand what is the bona fide guru, and what is the bona fide spouse. "God helps those who help themselves." So the first qualification for getting a bona fide mater is to carefully study the philosophy and have a good idea of what real spiritual life means. There are many bogus men posing as sincere but who have ulterior motives, and you must be able to spot them. There are ways to tell. A history of the persons past is usually a very good indicator. Fools try to say that a person's past does not matter for devotees, but that refers to the devotees who are strictly on the path without deviation. Most devotees are in the neophyte stage. That means they have bad tendencies and qualities that have not gone away yet.

## 47. SACRIFICE AND PRAYER

So the first prerequisite is to know exactly what qualifications to look for in a spouse, and the second thing is to qualify for Krishna's mercy. That means sacrifice. We have to prove our sincerity by performing sacrifice. The sacrifice for this age is chanting Hare Krishna. In Vedic culture there are other demigods one prays to for a good spouse, but since we are only interested in Krishna, we should pray to Krishna. There is no harm in praying to goddess Katyayani for a good husband to help in achieving Krishna, but generally we should just chant Hare Krishna as attentively as possible. The prayer should be something like this: "My dear Lord, please give me a husband that I can help in his service to You. That way, I can also serve You directly through him, and go back to You in the end. I promise to serve him faithfully and never disturb his mind over petty squabbles that mean nothing. I don't care for my personal happiness since, I know that my serving a good husband is my religious duty, and will award me the perfection of life." For the men, they can pray to this effect, "My dear Lord, please send me a faithful wife so that I can better engage in your loving service. I cannot make it alone, and so need the help of a faithful companion to get me over these youthful years. I promise to engage in your service more and more as the years progress and I come closer to sannyasa. Then I will be able to fully engage in your loving service. In the meantime, I will take very good care of the woman you send me to take charge of, and I promise to never misuse or exploit her in any way. I will do my very best to take us both back home to You after this very life."

## 48. PREPARING FOR YOUR MATE

These two sacrifices, chanting Hare Krishna attentively, and studying carefully the philosophy, are essential. Then there are other sacrifices that must be performed. If you want a brahmin for a husband, then the woman will have to give up any habits that a brahmin husband will not allow, such as using bad language, eating indiscriminately, getting intoxicated, associating with persons who do the above things, talking frivolously, listening to low class music, etc. She must make an altar and perform daily puja-her future husband will be expecting that of her. She must offer all of her food first. She must be very chaste and not flirt with men. There is no need of thinking that a woman must flirt to meet a perspective husband. When Krishna sees she is sincere in her sacrifices, He will arrange a suitable husband for her. When this happens she will know it from within.

If the woman is not inclined to this strict lifestyle then maybe she is not meant to have a brahmin for a husband. She has to make the decision of how strict she wants to live with her husband and she has to live that strictly herself. If she wants to live a life full of sense gratification, then she should pray for a husband who will also be a sense gratifier, but who will be able to give it up in time. It all boils down to sincere prayer and sacrifice.

## 49. REMOVING BAD QUALITIES

If one has bad qualities that are a serious disqualification for getting a good husband then one has to sacrifice some time to remove those habits. There are many ways of changing one's conditioning. If a woman has some bad habits that she wants to purify before meeting a husband, then she can sacrifice some time every morning and evening to praying for help in removing those bad qualities. For example, if a woman has the bad habit of being rebellious toward following instructions, then she can write out a long prayer on all the reasons why she has that terrible quality, and all the good reasons why she should give it up. Every morning and evening she should recite that prayer with full attention. This is a sacrifice. The more sacrifice one performs, the better the chances of getting a good mate. One has to have complete faith that Krishna will send the perfect husband/wife when the time is right. One must be patient. There is never any loss in performing sacrifice.

## 50. HOW TO RECOGNIZE YOUR ETERNAL COMPANION

A time will come when a man is presented before you. The question will naturally be, "Is this the man Krishna wants me to marry or is it Maya coming to trick me?" There are different symptoms to look for in making that decision. What were the circumstances of meeting the man? Were they auspicious? Were you chanting Hare Krishna when you first heard his name, or were you having a bad day and your mind was disturbed? First impressions are very important. Who introduced you? Was it a devotee you respect, or was it in the line to a movie? At present we don't know of any astrologers who know the science well enough to trust with such an important decision, so the best way to see if there is compatibility is to perform an in-depth personality test. He should write out all the things he likes to do and not do, and you should to the same. A mature third party can examine them. Do they match well? Are there similar interests? Only if everything seems very auspicious would we recommend that you associate together, and that also depends on your status. If you are a divorcee looking for a second husband, then it is not as dangerous to associate as it would be if you have never been with a man before. In the latter case your father or a close, but mature, devotee friend should carefully try and see if the two personalities are compatible. Many devotees are studying astrology, and some claim that their predictions are accurate for marriage, but again, we have not seen anyone yet with a record that we would trust with such an important decision. We don't even recommend that one consult an astrologer until they are more organized and have a better track record. Srila Prabhupada condemned that method in several letters. The best method is clearly, sincere prayer, lots of study, and careful consideration with the guidance of a mature and knowledgeable householder. You should know the philosophy inside and out. In our book we will have a questionnaire on marriage that every devotee should be able to pass before getting married.

These are just some of the ideas we will go into in great depth in our upcoming book on Vedic marriage. This book is primarily meant to stop these bogus "gurus" from destroying any more marriages and to give the general idea of what a Krishna conscious marriage is all about.

## 51. ALREADY BEEN BURNED: WHAT TO DO?

This brings us to the last section of this chapter. At this point we know what caused our marriage to fail. In many cases it will be clear that it was the direct interference of a sexyasi or a temple authority who felt it his right to interfere in your marriage. If that is the case, then we recommend the following action: Put your entire story in writing and send it to the address below. There will be many instances where such testimony may be useful in filing lawsuits against these men. Class action lawsuits are being organized against some of the "gurus." Many of them have amassed rather large sums of money from their "guru" business, and if we can successfully prove that they deliberately and maliciously interfered in these marriages, it is very possible that you may be awarded some money. That will help compensate for the pain you have had to suffer at the hands of these raksasas. In any case you will be exposing them for what they are, and that will help prevent others from being exploited in the same way.

## 52. CONCLUSION

This is only a rough outline of how to avoid this major pitfall in marriages today. In our book we will explain in detail all the different types of devotees, their varnas (occupational duties) in life, the rules and regulations for that particular varna, and how to practically implement that varna in these Western countries. This requires a great deal of research. The strict rules for a brahmin in India may not be possible for a brahmin in America. Pious vaisyas in India can more easily follow the regulative principles than the brahminically inclined devotees here in the West. All these considerations have to be carefully weighed before it will be possible to organize real Vedic communities. The important thing is to "fill in the spaces with good taste." Prabhupada expected his disciples to do this work and the time is now. There are many books of reference in Indian libraries with which to gain knowledge from and there are many devotees willing to do this work. We humbly request those of you seriously interested in to contact DAS and we will go from there. Good luck. Hare Krishna.

Inquiries, comments, or donations toward this book, may be sent to Steve Bryant (Sulocana dasa), 2124 Kittredge #32, Berkeley, CA, 9470.

Note: We have created a Sulocana Dasa Memorial Fund to collect donations for the printing of The Guru Business. Please contact Mukunda dasa on mukunda.dasa@prabhupada.org.uk if you would like to help.

## THE KIRTANANANDA EXPOSE

# "A CRAZY MAN"

## INTRODUCTION

*"From Rayarama's letter it is clear that Kirtanananda has not rightly understood Krishna consciousness philosophy and it appears that he does not know the difference between impersonal and personal features of Krishna. The best thing will be to prohibit him to speak in any of our functions or meetings. It is clear that he has become crazy and he should once more be sent to Bellevue. He was in Bellevue before and with great difficulty and with the help of Mr. Ginsburg we got him out." (Prabhupada Letter to Brahmananda, 10/16/67)*

This chapter is an expose on one of the new "gurus" in ISKCON. It is the first, but it most likely will not be the only one we will have to compile. Kirtanananda "Swami" deserves first recognition. He was among the first initiated devotees. He was the first to be given "sannyasa." A week later, he was the first to attack Srila Prabhupada trying to usurp the ISKCON movement for himself. Shortly thereafter he was the first to sit on a throne and accept worship of himself even during Srila Prabhupada's physical presence and of course, he was the first to jump on a throne right after Srila Prabhupada's departure. He was the first to begin a drug dealing operation (the KSS: Krishna's Secret Service) and later to set up a counterfeiting operation. He was the first to organize a women's sexploitation party and encourage the leader of that party, Dharmatma, to keep the women satisfied as their gigolo. To our knowledge, he is the first "guru" to authorize an abortion of the gigolo's child in an underage girl. He was the first to be utterly condemned by Srila Prabhupada. To this day, there are more letters of condemnation written about him than all the other bogus gurus combined. He was the first (and hopefully the last) to put a crown on Srila Prabhupada's murti (marble statue) denoting him as a mere monarch, although Srila Prabhupada was not sent by the Lord for that service. He was the first, and maybe only, "disciple," to be so envious as to directly challenge his guru's authority by calling him "a tyrant." He was the first "disciple" to be incarcerated in a mental institution (Bellevue). He was the first to treat Krishna's cows in such a way that dozens of them died of starvation, disease, and exposure (the local courts could not even bear these atrocities of Kirtanananda and prosecuted him for cruelty to animals.) These are just a few of his "firsts." He is number one in many other ways. Besides being the oldest "devotee" physically, he was/is the first full-blown homosexual in the movement and he even bragged of this to Acyutananda Swami in Mayapur, 1971, when he said, "I was sucking (word for male genital) before you were born." Therefore, in observing his stressed seniority, we believe that he should be given the first chance to try and clear himself of the charges we level against him, and the other bogus gurus as well, which clearly state one thing: absolute power corrupts absolutely.

## VRINDAVANA, INDIA, 1967

*"Kirtanananda is now a completely Krishna conscious person as he has accepted sannyasa on the birthday of Lord Krishna with great success. He is the first sannyasa in my spiritual family, and I hope he will return back soon to begin preaching work with great vigor and success." (Umapati, 9/5/67)*

Note: This is the letter cited most often at New Vrndavana. This is where the myth that Kirtanananda is a pure devotee came from. For those who have not understood Prabhupada's way of encouragement or who do not know about the incident that follows, it appears convincing evidence to back up the myth.

*"Kirtanananda has decided to return back for preaching work in the States, as he has accepted the sannyasa order of life. Acyutananda is here, but he is not eating well, so I am put into anxiety.*

*In the beginning Kirtanananda was also sick, and he also at the present moment is feeling some pain in his leg. On the whole, the American boys who come here become first depressed..." (Hansadutta, 9/10/67)*

*"Kirtanananda is returning to the states very soon. You are all very much anxious to get him back home and your desire will be fulfilled very soon. Perhaps you know that Acyutananda is now with us and since he has come, Kirtanananda has retired from all sorts of activities, and Acyutananda is helping me. Anyway, he is leaving behind a good representative, so I'll not be in trouble." (Janaki, 9/16/67)*

*"I am definitely improving in health but if I work a little hard or I walk a little more, I feel tired. Unfortunately, there is no good typewriter here and this letter I am typing myself. Acyutananda is not fast typewriting and Kirtanananda is going back to London tomorrow. I have advised him to start a center in London positively and after a month Rayarama will join him from Boston. Kirtanananda has experience to start a new center and therefore I have entrusted him with this great task I hope he will be successful there and I have given him one important letter of introduction for London. Please pray to the Lord that he may be successful." (Dayananda, 9/20/67)*

*"Kirtanananda has already gone back this morning. I have given him an introductory letter to London. In this connection much money has been spent from the building fund. If he gets a favorable response, then Rayarama may join him there and when he goes then I shall go." (Brahmananda, 9/2/67)*

*"Kirtanananda Swami prearranged with you to reach on the 24th instant, but he arranged with me that he would stop in London and I gave him one important introduction letter. Although he had in his mind not to stop in London and yet promised before me that he would go, for which I gave him extra $20. I cannot understand why he played with me like this. If he had no desire to go to London he would have plainly told me like that. It has certainly given me a great shock. He is one of my very faithful disciples and if he does like that how can I prosecute my programs. I have received one postcard from him from London airport in which he writes he is going directly to NY. I understand also from Umapati's letter that he has already reached N. Y. although I have not heard anything from him from N. Y... It is all my misfortune." (Hayagriva, 9/27/67)*

*"If you have collected the contribution from different centers you can pay Acyutananda's mother $88. This amount was taken from her on account of Kirtanananda's ticket. Kirtanananda should return to you the $20 dollars that he took from me on the plea of stopping in London. I am feeling too much for his disobedience." (Brahmananda, no date)*

*"Where is Rayarama? He may take back from Kirtanananda the letter of introduction to Miss Bowtell and may go to London as it was previously arranged. I entrusted this matter to Kirtanananda but he has disobeyed which has given me*

*a shock. Once he disobeyed my order and we lost $1,200 in connection with Mr. Payne. This time he has again disobeyed me. If he sets such example in the Society it will be a great impediment. Obedience is the first law of discipline. We are thinking of a great world-wide organization which is not possible to be executed if there is disobedience." (Gargamuni, 9/28/67)*

Note: Kirtanananda never paid back these debts to Srila Prabhupada. In fact he tried to steal men and money from Prabhupada again and again. He even tried to convince Guru Krpa once to "stop wasting your money giving it to Prabhupada." Kirtanananda wanted Guru Krpa to give money to New Vrndavana, arguing that, "these Indian temples you're building are going to be taken over by the communists one day anyway." Guru Krpa told him, "I'd watch Prabhupada flush it down the toilet before I'd give it to you."

*"...Rayarama may go to London in Nov.... This function was intended for Kirtanananda while returning to NY. He was to stop there and see her (Miss Bowtell) but he was so much frenzied to see & meet his old friends that he forgot the order of Krishna and indulged in a sort of sense gratification. It is certainly a shocking incident which I never expected from a disciple like Kirtanananda." (Satsvarupa, 10/3/67)*

*"Kirtanananda may be eager to address in the Harvard university but recently he has lost his link on account of disobedience. You sing every day morning that by the mercy of the spiritual master one can please the Lord and one who has not pleased the spiritual master cannot have any access in the realm of Krishna consciousness. Very recently Kirtanananda has developed a different consciousness of Maya which is called misuse of one's minute independence offered by Krishna. By misuse on one's independence one at once becomes a victim of Maya and thus he loses all importance in Krishna consciousness. So it is my definite opinion that his lecture anywhere now will bear no spiritual sequence. He must rectify his mistake before he can play in our society any important role. By lips he says that he is a surrendered soul but by action he is thinking differently." (Satsvarupa, 10/6/67)*

Note: By lips Kirtanananda Swami still says that he is a surrendered soul but by his actions it is clear that he is still thinking differently. His worshipers often say, "But what about the Palace? Doesn't that prove that he is an advanced devotee?" As mentioned in the earlier chapters, making a "show of the Deity" or "amassing some neophyte disciples" are not the real qualifications. It is the sincerity of purpose that makes the pure devotee and not the external show. The arguments that he changed because he put up buildings, and engaged sudras, is totally illogical. Prabhupada accused Bon Maharaja of offending his guru and that had been forty years earlier. From practical experience we can easily perceive that one's nature or deep-rooted conditioning may not change so drastically in nine years. Kirtanananda Swami himself admits this in a lecture he gave in Bombay shortly after Jayatirtha's departure. There he said, "He (Jayatirtha) diverted from the instructions of Prabhupada, and now when we can trace it back, we can see that even some time way back, he had this tendency. For instance, around 1975, Jayatirtha was very much attached to this umbrella corporation... Of course, he did not leave, but that tendency, or that difficulty in accepting Prabhupada's vision, was there." Jayatirtha's "tendency" is child's play compared to Kirtanananda's.

*"I was very glad to receive your letter dated Oct. 1st. I congratulate you for your successful dealing with your good brother, Sriman Brahmananda, against his falling back a prey to Kirtanananda's recent propaganda. To save a man from impersonal calamity is the greatest service to humanity. I also thank Rupanuga and Rayarama for helping you in your very laudable action. Brahmananda is very pure at heart. He might have been misled by Kirtanananda for the time being but Krishna did not allow him to fall back. According to Caitanya Mahaprabhu, the Lord is full in six opulences and the rascal impersonalist says that the Lord has no form and the most dangerous accusation for the Lord that He assumes a material form when He descends. This accusation of the Lord is the greatest offense of the nonsense impersonalist. I do not believe that Kirtanananda has gone to such an extent of ailing situation but if he does not rectify himself immediately his future is very dark. If he is sincere in his concept of impersonal absolute he should enter into correspondence with me and I shall refute all his arguments. But I understand that he could not answer you even when you hit him with some questions. I shall request that you save this poor creature from impersonal calamity." (Gargamuni, 10/9/67)*

*"In your previous letter in which I saw a little tendency of being turned by foolish Kirtanananda. But I was confident that Kirtanananda was not so strong as he would be able to defeat you. I was completely confident of your sincerity of service and my choice of your being president of the society is right. I may disclose herewith that I never took Kirtanananda into complete confidence but I was trying to improve his position because he has also rendered much personal service to me. I am very much obliged to him for the service as I am to my other disciples and I am very sorry that Maya has taken advantage of his disobedience and he has fallen to Maya's illusion, but he should not continue for a very long time as I will always pray to Krishna for his recovery. For the time being he should simply chant Hare Krishna without any attempt at lecturing. The impersonalists cannot render any service to Krishna because he is a great offender. Under the circumstances, Krishna will not accept food prepared by Kirtanananda in his present diseased condition. If he at all wants to render service to Krishna he may be engaged at washing dishes and this will improve his condition... It is not in his power to mislead a sincere soul such as yourself but I must congratulate Gargamuni, the simple boy who never believed in impersonalism. He is your younger brother as important as Lord Laksmana was younger brother to Lord Rama. I am very glad that this simple and honest boy has saved you from calamity." (Brahmananda, 10/9/67)*

Note: This sentence, "I never took Kirtanananda into confidence" is very significant. Needless to say, Prabhupada knew Kirtanananda's mentality all along. Nevertheless, Prabhupada sees the spark of good in someone and tries to fan that.

Only the very realized mahabhagavata can so perfectly see and act on that platform. We must come to the realization that all of Prabhupada's "leading" disciples were similarly being encouraged by Prabhupada. Prabhupada continued to encourage Kirtanananda all along, but that doesn't mean that "foolish Kirtanananda" was a pure devotee, any more than he was when Prabhupada called him "a completely Krishna conscious person" in the earlier letter.

Another significant point in this letter is how he is comparing these two brothers, Brahmananda and Gargamuni, to Lord Rama and Laksmana. This is not the only place where Prabhupada indirectly implies that men like Kirtanananda are Ravanas.

*"Do not try to follow the unauthorized advice of Kirtanananda. Nobody cares for the dress; every sane man follows the philosophy and practical talks. Let Kirtanananda Swami do something practically. Let him do whatever he likes and let us see that thousands of Americans are following him.*

*Kirtanananda is the first man in our society who cleanly shaved and kept the sikha on the top of the head, and now he has begun to keep beard again. This is not good. Whatever he is doing nowadays has no sanction from me. And he has deliberately disobeyed me by not going to London." (Brahmananda, 10/11/67)*

Note: Contrary to popular belief, Kirtanananda is actually the one behind the corruption at New Vrindaban. He cleverly has Kuladri do all of the dirty work for him and therefore Kuladri's name is "Crueladri." Actually he is also just another victim of "Kirtanananda's devices."

Kirtanananda is claiming 500 residents at New Vrndavana and some persons consider this an impressive figure. On close analysis, however, we see differently. That figure includes the 100 hired outside workers on the payroll and the 100 fringe devotees who have little to no sadhana and receive a salary under minimum wage. At least two-thirds of the remaining members are women and children mostly from broken families. There are always at least 30-50 floaters who will stay a few months to a year at most. Most of the steady men who remain there have never studied the philosophy seriously and are there primarily because they get room and board and some work they like doing. Only half a dozen men devotees in the entire community know enough philosophy to give a lecture. Out of 80 men Prabhupada disciples reported for the 1984 Vyasa Puja book, eleven left before the book went to print. Most of the remaining "Prabhupada disciples" were worshipping Kirtanananda even before Prabhupada left the planet. So we can safely say that he does not have "thousands of Americans following him." But those who do follow, we must admit, see him as "king." In this connection Prabhupada says, "There is a Bengali saying that a jackal is king in a small forest. The story is that a jackal became king in the forest by fooling the other animals for some time, but he remained always a jackal and his ruse was at last exposed." *(Rupanuga, 11/13/70)*

*"I am very sorry to hear that Kirtanananda is advising you to give up the robes and the flags on the head. Please stop this nescience as I never instructed Kirtanananda to act like that. I am not at all satisfied with this action of Kirtanananda. Kirtanananda has no right to instruct you in that way, without consulting me. People are being attracted to the chanting of Hare Krishna and not to Kirtanananda's devices." (Damodara, 10/13/67)*

Note: What Kirtanananda was actually trying to do is not fully revealed in these letters. But from interviewing the devotees who were around at that time, it is evident that he was directly attacking Prabhupada and trying to take over the movement. He stole the original manuscript of Prabhupada's *Bhagavad-gita and* wouldn't return it. Prabhupada had to return prematurely just to keep Kirtanananda from doing too much damage. During this time, Kirtanananda formed his own society. The name of this society was rather long. He put this name of letterhead stationary. He also included the acronym for the society on his letterhead. The name of the society was: "First Universal Church of Krishna-the Yoga Organization University." Check out this acronym, prabhus.

*"I am in due receipt of your letter dated Oct. 10th and I've also received Kirtanananda's letter. From different centers of our society the news of the activities of Kirtanananda is giving me too much pain. From Rayarama's letter it is clear that Kirtanananda has not rightly understood Krishna consciousness philosophy and it appears that he does not know the difference between impersonal and personal features of Krishna. The best thing will be to prohibit him to speak in any of our functions or meetings. It is clear that he has become crazy and he should once more be sent to Bellevue. He was in Bellevue before and with great difficulty and with the help of Mr. Ginsburg we got him out." (Brahmananda, 10/16/67)*

Note: Bellevue is a well-known mental hospital in the Eastern US.

*"This is too much disturbing to me and caused me much pain. Please therefore stop Kirtanananda from making his mental concoctions. Do not be misled by him. I have never advised him to act like that... I have already written you to inform you that somehow or other he has become crazy; otherwise he would not have disobeyed me to go directly to NY. For the time being he has cut all link with me. Therefore any instruction given by him is unauthorized and should at once be rejected. He has no right to dictate as he has without my sanction. Whatever is to be done will be executed on my return. He is too much puffed-up nonsensically therefore you should copy this letter and forward to all centers that Kirtanananda has no right to dictate anything to the society in this way. I am very sorry that he is exploiting his present position as a sannyasi in this way..." (Brahmananda, 10/14/67)*

Note: He is still exploiting his position, only now he is doing so as a "pure devotee." So we are following Prabhupada's instructions by copying all these letters and circulating them around to all centers.

*"I have already requested Brahmananda to stop Kirtanananda's speaking at any of our functions till my arrival. If he wants to preach anything he can do it on his own at a different place... If Kirtanananda believes in one-self, why does he stress the vibration and not the words? Why does he find difference in vibration and words? And why shouldn't one be attached to the chanting? All this means that he has no clear idea and he is talking nonsense. If Kirtanananda does not understand this philosophy then better he should stop speaking nonsense. I can understand his designs but I cannot help because I am far away from the place." (Rayarama, 10/16/67)*

*"My dear Kirtanananda, Please accept my blessings. I've received your note along with Brahmananda's for first time since you left to NY. You had no desire to stop in London. This is clear to me from Hayagriva's letter which indicated that you had already planned to go there even before you left India. Since you have returned to NY you have falsely dictated that I do not want the robes or flags. Why are you disturbing the whole situation in my absence? I never ordered you to speak like that. They must continue to have robes and tilak and flags and they must distinguish themselves from the hippies. I never objected to any of my students dressing like nice American gentlemen, clean shaved; but those who are my disciples must have flag, tilak and beads on neck without fail. Anyway, I never advised you to dictate on my behalf.*

*Please therefore do not misrepresent me. You have been given sannyasa to follow my principles and not to disturb me. If you do not agree with my philosophy you can work independent and not within the walls of ISKCON. You have not understood Krishna properly. The best thing will be to stop your talks in any meeting but chant in solitary place, anywhere you like. Hope you are well." (Letter to Kirtanananda 10/16/67)*

Note: Kirtanananda was attempting to steal the movement in Prabhupada's absence. By a similar strategy, Ravana stole Sitadevi in the absence of Lord Ramachandra. Lord Rama thus said to the ten-headed demon: "You are like a dog who steals food from the master's kitchen when he is away from home." Many men lost their wives to Kirtanananda while they were away from New Vrindaban. (See Appendix 25)

*"This last attack is very serious and fatal. Kirtanananda has very recently developed the 4th stage malady on account of his negligence and disobedience to his spiritual master. Sometimes a foolish patient when he is out of feverish attack by the grace of the physician, thinks that he is cured and does not take precaution against relapse. Kirtanananda's position is like that. Because he helped the society in starting the Montreal center I thought he is now able to start other branches and when he asked me to give him Sannyasa I agreed taking the opportunity of his presence in Vrindavana. Simply by his Sannyasa dress he thought himself as cured of all material diseases and all mistakes, but under the influence of Maya, he thought himself a liberated patient, just as the foolish patient thinks himself cured of the disease. Under the spell of Maya, he disobeyed me by not going to London*

*and consequently his disease has relapsed. Now in NY he has begun to dictate nonsense in my name such as giving up flags, etc. Instead of opening new centers he has begun to deliver his sermons amongst his God-brothers which are all against our principles. For the present he should simply chant Hare Krishna and cease to deliver lectures since he has not understood the whole philosophy very nicely." (Pradyumna, 10/17/67)*

*"I am very glad to receive your letter and yes I am feeling stronger. I always think of you because you are so nice in Krishna consciousness... You have written to say that 'I am as hard as a thunderbolt and softer than a rose' is quite right in the line of Krishna consciousness. I am very sorry to inform you that Kirtanananda is playing the part of a foolish man after his return to NY and it is necessary for me to play the part of a thunderbolt for his nonsense activities... Please inform this to all centers." (Jadurani, 10/13/67)*

Note: Actually all of Prabhupada's letters to Jadurani were very personal and friendly. Her devotion to Prabhupada is undeniable. But on the other hand, Prabhupada never wrote very personal letters to Kirtanananda except for ones like the above. This brings us to a very important incident that happened to Jadurani in 1980.

## "DON'T TELL ME ABOUT IT"

### THE JADURANI INCIDENT

In the summer of 1980, Jadurani became convinced that the eleven gurus had never been appointed by Srila Prabhupada. So she left the LA temple to join devotees in Pittsburgh who were attempting to form an association to rid the movement of the eleven gurus. She began to work on her papers, explaining why the eleven gurus could not possibly be bona fide. Foolishly she allowed Jayadvaita, the editor of Back to Godhead, to convince her to take shelter of Kirtanananda. She agreed to make some paintings for the Palace. However, she could not refrain from telling anyone who would listen that Kirtanananda was not a bona fide guru. Two New Vrindaban women complained to Kirtanananda. These women, Parayani and Isani, wanted to physically attack Jadurani. They were given the go-ahead by Kirtanananda, who said: "Do the needful, but don't tell me about it." They fell upon Jadurani and severely beat her, kicking her in the face and not stopping until she was literally drenched in blood. Then, they attempted to take her bloody sari to hang on a post as a warning to anyone else who would "dare to blaspheme" Kirtanananda. Svarupa dasa managed to save Jadurani and took her to the hospital. She stayed in Pittsburgh until she joined devotees in Buffalo who were also involved in the anti-"guru" campaign.

After completing her guru papers, she went to the LA Rathayatra in 1981 to distribute them in hopes of awakening some of the other Prabhupada disciples. At the behest of Ramesvara, several women pickers attacked her, but this time fortunately they were chased away by Radha Mohan dasa. Next morning Trivikrama was lecturing on this incident, warning devotees to stay away from Jadurani. Bahubhavani dasi suggested that Trivikrama debate Jadurani in the temple room that evening. He agreed. Minutes later Ramesvara rushed into the temple room and loudly forbade Trivikrama to allow her anywhere even near the LA temple, what to speak about a debate. No doubt he remembered that he had himself been defeated by Jadurani and was obliged to remove his throne from the temple. The other "gurus", however, headed by Bhagavan, threatened that if he didn't put it back he would lose everything. So, for the second time, he was appointed a "pure devotee." Shortly thereafter many devotees left LA, having seen the truths in Jadurani's papers. This began the exodus of devotees from LA to San Francisco on the promise that Atreya would defend Jadurani's cause. He invited Jadurani and her friends to join him in San Francisco, but she intuitively felt he wasn't sincere. Nothing ever came of Atreya's promises to stop the guru conspiracy.

Note: Although it is certainly a great shame that Jadurani again took shelter of "ISKCON," at least she will go down in history as one of the staunch resistance fighters in the continuing battle to stop the conspirators who are bent on destroying Srila Prabhupada's mission.

*"My grief for Kirtanananda isn't anything personal but I am sorry that he has become like a Mayavadi in spite of my best efforts to help him." (Jadurani, 10/26/67)*

*"Kirtanananda was awarded the position of a sannyasi because he wanted it although I could understand it that he wanted to be a spiritual master himself, Lord Caitanya wanted that everyone should be a spiritual master provided he follows the order of Lord Caitanya. Anyone following the order of Lord Caitanya under the guidance of His bonafide representative, can become a spiritual master to spread Krishna consciousness throughout the whole world. I want it but Kirtanananda was too much puffed-up and artificially he took up a certificate from me that he has been awarded the order to a sannyasi. In the spiritual field nobody can become a bonafide spiritual master by dissatisfying his spiritual master... Kirtanananda wanted to become a spiritual master by dissatisfying his spiritual master and as such he has fallen down... I very much appreciate your version that Rayarama is roaring like a lion-cub. I wish that every one of you should be Lion's descendant. Our Lord Krishna assumed the form of lion and killed the atheist, Hiranyakasipu, and by disciplic succession we shall also kill all impersonalist atheists. Absolutely there is no Krishna consciousness for the impersonalist." (Madhusudhana, 10/27/67)*

Note: Here Prabhupada confirms that Kirtanananda was never sincere since he only wanted to be guru himself. In this regard, Prabhupada writes:

*"When a Krishna conscious person is elevated to a responsible position, he never becomes puffed-up. Just like a tree when overladen with fruits becomes humble and lower down, similarly, a great soul in Krishna consciousness becomes humbler than the grass and bowed down like the fruitful trees because a Krishna conscious person acts as the agent of Krishna, therefore he discharges his duty with great responsibility." (Gajendra, 1/27/70)*

It is also significant here that Prabhupada is referring to Kirtanananda as a demon like Hiranyakasipu, which means gold and soft bed. Prabhupada is also suggesting here that we all become like a lion's descendent to kill all such atheist demons.

*"Regarding Kirtanananda's article, I do not know what he has written but I can guess that it must be polluted with impersonal poison, so for the time being you can keep this article aside. I was so glad to learn that you are acting exactly like a lion cub and I know that in the future you shall conquer over many jackals. We have got experience in India that the jackals roar four times at night without any influence but the one roar of a lion drives away many elephants." (Rayarama, 11/3/67)*

*"The quarrel amongst yourselves, the Godbrothers, is not very much palatable. I am now thinking about our society. We were very smoothly going on but this disruption created by Kirtanananda has plagued and disturbed the situation...*

*Kirtanananda is a crazy man. That is proved. He says that he has become equal to the spiritual master but he is such a fool that he does not understand the principle of disciple even in ordinary worldly affairs." (Rayarama, 11/9/67)*

*"The incident created by Kirtanananda and Hayagriva may not disappoint us in the least. Let us remain sincere to Krishna and His bona fide representative and we are sure to carry out our mission successfully...*

*The Kirtanananda incident is certainly very unhappy and your dealing with the situation is quite appropriate... We should never tolerate any insult or blaspheme to Krishna or His representative. So your action was quite all right. Anyway, forget the chapter, there is nothing to be lamented. If thousands of Kirtananandas or Hayagrivas come and go. We have to prosecute our real program of being sincere to Krishna and Krishna Caitanya." (Brahmananda, 11/15/67)*

*"The incident of Kirtanananda and Hayagriva chapter may now be closed. We shall always pray to Krishna for their recovery and we should not seriously take their counter-propaganda. I am sure they will flap for some time without any effect on our Krishna consciousness service." (Rayarama, 11/15/67)*

Note: In an unrelated but applicable incident Prabhupada writes: *"Yes, you are right, he is third class man, so we should not waste time with him further. Stirring stools does not help. Anyway, you have done right. The jackals may howl, but the caravan will pass on."*

We all must adopt this mood in relation to the conspiracy being propped up by the jackals who simply trailed our spiritual master. Kirtanananda, when he found his effort going nowhere, is supposed to have again surrendered to Srila Prabhupada. That is the belief of many, but actually he has never surrendered. His counter-propaganda continues today. His actions do not indicate that he surrendered his craziness in actuality, but "by lips" he may have done so after his rebellion did not catch on with the devotees. Kirtanananda is every bit the impersonalist today that he was then.

*"I beg to inform you that Kirtanananda and Hayagriva's recent standing is being directly dealt by me; at least Hayagriva is not as fanatic as Kirtanananda. His latest letter reveals that he is not out of Krishna consciousness as we understand. The whole episode was generated by personal grudge." (Brahmananda, 11/18/67)*

*"Killing proposal is not good. We have to kill them with arguments and reasons not with sticks and weapons. Jadurani, I am very glad that you want to kill the nondevotees. You should, however, leave the matter to your good Godbrothers who will take care of it. I am pleased to learn of your spirit of protest, but sometimes we have to tolerate. Hope you are well." (Pradyumna, Satsvarupa, Jadurani, 11/21/67)*

Note: This is the way in which Srila Prabhupada recommended the devotees, specifically Jadurani of all people, deal with Kirtanananda, who deserved to be killed what to speak of beaten. When Jadurani was criticizing Kirtanananda in the 1980 incident narrated above, she must have thought Kirtanananda would at least have the decency to debate her instead of have her beaten. Kirtanananda could have told those two women to defeat Jadurani with reason and argument. But neither these women nor Kirtanananda know much philosophy, so Kirtanananda advised them to beat her. Even if Kirtanananda tries to claim now that he did not directly authorize the beating, he never apologized either. In fact he was proud of it. This one act alone proves beyond any shadow of a doubt that Kirtanananda is sub-human. Of course, this is just one incident. There are hundreds of similar incidents to expose about Kirtanananda if necessary.

*"It is better service to Krishna and the Spiritual Master in a feeling of separation; sometimes there is a risk in the matter of direct service. For example, Kirtanananda was giving me direct service by massaging, cooking for me, and so many other things; but later on by dictation of Maya, he became puffed-up, so much so that he though his Spiritual Master a common man, and was existing only on account of his service. This mentality at once pushed him down. Of course, those who are sincere devotee, they take direct service as an opportunity. (Madhusudhana, 12/28/67)*

Note: In this connection Prabhupada writes*: "There are some of my Godbrothers here in India who had constant personal association with Guru Maharaja, but who are neglecting his orders. This is just like the bug who is sitting on the lap of the king. He may be very puffed-up by his position, but all he can succeed in doing is* biting the king." *(Satadhanya, 2/20/72)*

*"He (Hayagriva) has committed a great blunder, but just so that he may be encouraged to come back you may mention his name also along with Rayarama's. [As co-editor of Gita.] He is not so convinced of his impersonalist philosophy. It is only due to Kirtanananda's influence that he has left us." (Brahmananda, 12/29/67)*

Note: Some devotees still believe it was Hayagriva who contaminated Kirtanananda. Here the truth comes out.

*"Kirtanananda's refusal to accept the Parampara system and authority of the scriptures is the cause of his misfortune. His version that the sun and the sunshine are one and the same is right, but when the sunshine is in the room it is not correct to say that the sun is in the room. His knowledge therefore is imperfect and therefore he cannot be a preacher. He is therefore contemplating for starting a nightclub of the psychedelic type. His association is not desirable for the present neither I can think of his future correction. Hayagriva has fallen a victim and I am sorry for this." (Umapati, 1/14/68)*

Note: It is significant here that Prabhupada cannot even imagine how such an envious man could ever become purified. Only nine years later that man is sitting on a throne declaring himself better than Prabhupada. Kirtanananda still doesn't accept the Parampara system, and therefore he has started his own institution as Prabhupada suggested. Quite often we hear the argument that Prabhupada went to New Vrndavana so many times, and that he said so many favorable things about Kirtanananda and New Vrindaban, so how can he not have approved of Kirtanananda? The explanation is very simple. Prabhupada was expert at adjusting everything in such a way that the demons were pacified and the movement went on relatively undisturbed. A good example in this connection is that of a dog biting on one's leg. What can you do? You throw the dog a bone and he goes away. So in cases like this, where Kirtanananda was viciously attacking Srila Prabhupada, Prabhupada more or less just threw him a bone in the form of New Vrindaban. This engaged and encouraged him which kept him from actively attacking Prabhupada-at least openly. It is well-known diplomatic behavior that, if you have an enemy in your camp, the best thing is to give him a position of respect. Giving the "big" devotees sannyasa in the 1970 demoniac attack to usurp the movement was a similar tactic.

Prabhupada could see the suffering condition of Kirtanananda and had compassion on him, but that does not mean that Prabhupada couldn't see Kirtanananda's envious tendency. Prabhupada's ability to keep everyone pacified to one degree or another was just one of the symptoms of his greatness.

*"Yes, actually that was the program, but Kirtanananda made everything topsy-turvy. After we reached Vrindavana Kirtanananda became too much eager to return back. He was daily insisting me for his return back and once I told him that I have no money, how you can return? In reply to this, he said that he would go to the American Embassy as Citizen and take money from there and he would return.*

*Then I was obliged to arrange for his return passage money and because he changed his program the society practically lost $1,200 for his going to India and coming back again without any purpose. I thought that some of this money could be recovered if he would return to NY, stopping a few days in London to see the prospect of opening a branch there. He agreed and I gave him the letter of introduction, and required money for immediate expenses, but he had no desire to stop at London and he directly reached you. He was also very eager to take sannyasa and I awarded him the sannyasa order; and I do not know, he wanted a certificate of his sannyasa. We never took any certificate of our Spiritual Master or anyone, but he told me that it was required for facility of preaching, so I gave him the certificate, but unfortunately the whole thing was smashed by different doctrine. Now it is understood from the letter of Umapati that Kirtanananda does not believe in parampara or in the necessity of scriptural authority. He seems to feel that this is a sort of tyranny. That means, after taking sannyasa and understanding the philosophy for more than a year, he has changed the whole view, and I do not understand how you could like this recent doctrine."* (Hayagriva, 1/15/68)

Note: This is no ordinary mentality. Someone who has the audacity to claim to be more realized than Prabhupada and scripture is described in the Chanakya Sloka: "No method can turn an evil-minded person into a gentleman, just as by washing the anus one hundred times, it cannot be turned into a face." Nature and conditioning is developed in the subtle body over millions of lifetimes and is not so easy to change. Even mundane psychologists appear to know that fact much better than the average devotee in ISKCON.

Of course, Krishna is not limited. He can do anything he likes, but Kirtanananda does not behave like a person who is getting the special mercy of the Lord. Special mercy is reserved for very sincere and humble persons, not for those as puffed-up and offensive as Kirtanananda here. Practical proof that he still feels guru and sastra are tyranny is the way he constantly concocts and does not care to learn the scripture. He could not answer any of our challenges. There are only two possible explanations for this. Either he is less intelligent, or he feels he is beyond guru and sastra as revealed in the above letter. After interviewing many devotees who know Kirtanananda Swami personally, it became clear that he is not stupid. If he wanted to learn sastra, he could. Therefore he must still think his knowledge is superior to Prabhupada's and scripture, combined.

*"I acknowledge receipt of Kirtanananda's sannyasa certificate."* (Rayarama, 1/18/68)

Note: We don't accept him as a sannyasi. He doesn't have a certificate to prove it. Kirtanananda demanded a certificate of sannyasa but Srila Prabhupada did not want to give him one. Therefore Krishna gave it back to Srila Prabhupada.

*"So far I am personally concerned, Kirtanananda was doubtful about my existence because he thought that I am dependent on his massaging, so he thought that there*

*is no necessity of Spiritual Master, because Spiritual Master is an ordinary man, and to depend on an ordinary man is tyranny." (Brahmananda, 1/21/68)*

Note: Prabhupada's use of the words "doubtful about my existence," is a polite way of saying that Kirtanananda was jealous and envious of him and thought him to be a tyrant. Kirtanananda, however, is an ordinary man, and the "inmates of New Vrindaban," by depending on him, are depending upon a tyrant and thereby are trying to cross the Pacific Ocean by catching hold of "the tail of a dog."

## PART TWO

## "NOBODY SHOULD GO THERE"

## THE NEW VRINDAVANA PERSONALITY CULT: LATER LETTERS

*"Please accept my blessings. I was so glad to receive your letter dated May 13, 1968, and my gladness knew no bounds, exactly like that when one gets back his lost child.*

*You have written to say that you think of me often and now it is confirmed that you cannot do without thinking of me, because I was always thinking of you. Sometimes I silently cried and prayed to Krishna that how I have lost this child, Kirtanananda... Krishna has provided you with a nice plot of land, and it is due to His causeless unlimited mercy upon you. You were in Vrindavana but you did not like the atmosphere and you became disturbed, so immediately after your arrival in Vrindavana you felt uncomfortable, that I could understand, and therefore you came back to USA although it was settled before starting that you continue to live in Vrindavana...*

*So I am pleased to learn that you are chanting and meditating on Krishna, and once only you are eating something to keep your body and soul together. But my request is that as you have accepted Sannyasa in this order of our disciplic succession, you must do some more service to Krishna than chanting and meditation, and the opportunity you have got. I understand that the land is very big area..." (Kirtanananda, 5/23/68)*

Note: This is another one of those letters that everyone at New Vrindavana likes to quote often. They like to say that Prabhupada felt intense separation and cried when Kirtanananda blooped as though Prabhupada needed Kirtanananda. From reading this it certainly appears that Srila Prabhupada forgave and forgot the entire incident. But we will soon see that Srila Prabhupada never trusted Kirtanananda again, and similarly, Kirtanananda Swami never did any real service to Prabhupada.

*"Kirtanananda is in West Virginia and he invites 100 brahmacaris there. I don't know, would you like this idea and where we have got 100 brahmacaris." (No name, 6/24/68)*

Note: For those of you who don't know the situation, there were hardly 100 men in the entire movement at that time. So here is a unique example of Prabhupada's sense of humor. He was not a dry philosopher but he was a representative of the Supreme Humorist, Sri Krishna.

*"I understand from Gargamuni that Hayagriva has sent you a letter inviting some of you to live with him in West Virginia where they are attempting to open a new center, but I am not very much hopeful about this center because there are many impediments. I have already written to Kirtanananda that in such suspicious and unfavorable conditions, no brahmacari will be interested to go there. If there is actually any invitation for going there I send herewith instructions to all of you that for the present, there is no necessity of going there. And in the future also nobody shall go there without getting my permission." (Upendra, 7/4/68)*

Note: Here is an example of the supreme perfection of diplomacy. Very politely here Prabhupada is saying, "Nobody should go there." Whether Prabhupada ever gave permission for devotees to go there is questionable.

*"My dear Brahmananda, Please accept my blessings. Krishna will save you, do not worry. Let us forget about our past incidences with Hayagriva and Kirtanananda. Treat Kirtanananda as bonafide and address him as Kirtanananda Maharaja. He should be first offered obeisances and he will return the respect to his Godbrother." (Brahmananda, 7/29/68)*

Note: Here Prabhupada is telling Brahmananda to respect Kirtanananda Swami even though months earlier Kirtanananda was a demon. Naturally this was hard to swallow. But the devotees followed Prabhupada's instructions and offered their respects to Kirtanananda Swami. Shortly thereafter he again started thinking he was better than all the other devotees.

*"I understand that you are proposing for delivering children. That is not a Sannyasi's business. You should not bother about it. A Sannyasi should not much bother about family affairs. Best thing is that they shall go to a bona fide physician for delivering the children, otherwise there may be complications which only a physician may have experience in handling." (Kirtanananda, 3/24/69)*

Note: This proposal of Kirtanananda's is so absurd that any ordinary devotee would have laughed heartily. Prabhupada, being so expert, handled it very subtly. Kirtanananda obviously had not even the slightest idea of a sannyasi's business. He may have thought he was on the level of Ramananda Raya since he has no sexual attraction toward women. Unfortunately, that does not mean one is free from sexual contamination.

*"You have suggested that people coming from various centers to New Vrindavana should have their expenses underwritten by the temples at the rate of $25 per person for one month. I think that will be a new introduction in our institution. In our so many centers the members go and come, but there was no such demand from any center, and if New Vrindavana demands like that, it will not sound very nice. But I can understand the financial position of New Vrindavana, so the best thing will be to stop any more* influx *in New Vrindavana until the place is self-dependent. The whole idea of New Vrindavana is that men who are living there should produce their own food, of which milk is the principal thing. Unless that position is achieved it will not be advisable to ask anybody to go there. Better to ask them to go there if they are willing to work and produce their own food. Otherwise, nobody should be advised to go there. Besides that I have received letters from the girls there that they are feeling inconvenience. Therefore, without having adequate place to live there, nobody should be advised at the present time to go there... For the time being you may not admit many more men and ask them to pay you $25 dollars per month. That will not sound very nice." (Kirtanananda, 7/31/69)*

Note: It is fascinating how in this one paragraph, Prabhupada advises five times, "Nobody should go there"!

*"I do not know what you mean by cooperation with Kirtanananda Maharaja. In our society everyone, either a brahmachary or sannyasi or grhastha, who has dedicated his life and soul to this movement, they are all on the same level of sannyasi. For the present moment, nobody can claim an extra honor from his Godbrothers. Everyone should treat his Godbrothers as prabhu. But nobody should try to claim any extra honor on account of an official position. I do not know why Kirtanananda says that his authority overrides yours. At the present moment everyone is working under my authority, Similarly, Kirtanananda also should work under my authority. So the condition imposed by Kirtanananda as stated by you does not look well. A sannyasi has got four stages of elevation: Kutichak, Bahudak, Parbribrajak and Paramahansa. The sannyasa in the Paramahansa stage is the Spiritual Master of everyone. I have asked Kirtanananda to work on the bahudak stage for the present. I discussed this point with him when I was in New Vrindavana. This stage means he should move amongst the people to draw their attention to the New Vrindaban scheme and try to attract their attention for its development. So he should immediately begin this bahudak program and collect money from outsiders, not from insiders. And as he is in charge of New Vrindavana, he may invest all such collection for the development of New Vrindavana, and before this Hayagriva must transfer the property to the society's name. So far as investment of the society's money for New Vrindaban is concerned, certainly it will be done in New Vrindaban and not only the money which Kirtanananda collects, but also, if need be, any center will invest money. But that investment should be in proportion to food and salt. To make it more tasteful, one adds salt to his food, and similarly, every center should be independently developed by supplying the food, and the society, if required, will supply the salt. For the present, all energy should be diverted to start a nice press*

*for our publications work. So there is no extra money for the society to invest in New Vrindavana. Neither you can spare any money to anyone without my permission. Whatever you possess now in funds, that is not our personal money, so how can you execute the request of Kirtanananda's at the moment? I think you will understand me rightly and do the needful." (Brahmananda, 8/30/69)*

Note: Expecting honor from his Godbrothers was always Kirtanananda's demand. For example, he always wanted the society to support him, yet he felt that he was more competent to spread Krishna consciousness on his own strength. This is proven by the many times he initiated actions and policies opposed to Srila Prabhupada's instructions. He still feels that way and, as such, misguides his collection parties. Although they have no right to go outside their own zones, they do it anyway."No project is as important as New Vrindavana," is their realization. And when he writes to a Godbrother he will address it, "Please accept my blessings," and he signs it, "Your ever well-wisher." Of course, he doesn't care a fig about the combined opinion of the GBC. For instance, take the affair connected to Prabhupada's crown. Everyone knows that the vast majority of Srila Prabhupada's disciples were repulsed by it. The GBC wanted it removed. He was told to remove it. But he bucked that order. After years of pressure, he finally removed it. And what do the "inmates" say about that? "Bhaktipada is so advanced. He has so much more realization than all the others combined. Just to show compassion on them, he took it off so their neophyte minds wouldn't be disturbed." In other words, they are brainwashed into believing that he couldn't possibly be wrong about anything. They think that he's a pure devotee and Prabhupada's oldest and most dear disciple. They actually think like that at New Vrindavana.

*"Now gradually I am trying to hand over the management to the reliable hands of my disciples, and you should all work by joint consultation, without any friction. Now, by the Grace of Krishna, we are expanding and we must work in such a way that our society may stand a solid institution. In this connection I shall request you not to circulate all my letters that I address to you. Letters are sometimes personal and confidential, and if all letters are circulated, it may react reversely. I have already got some hints like that with letters I sent to you regarding Kirtanananda and Hayagriva. So in the future please do not circulate my letters to you. All my letters to you should be considered as confidential and if you want at all to circulate, you just ask me before doing so." (Brahmananda, 9/28/69)*

Note: Here we see some more of the way a pure devotee attempts to keep all parties pacified. He had to tell Brahmananda that Kirtanananda was not to be given any special respect and Brahmananda circulated the letter. Then when Kirtanananda heard that he was not the "dearmost," and that Prabhupada and Brahmananda were discussing about him in this way, no doubt Kirtanananda's envy flared up again. So Prabhupada had to warn Brahmananda to keep his letters confidential.

Some devotees criticize us for circulating all these letters citing the above instruction. We beg to remind the devotees that the times have drastically changed since then. In fact it is only because of ignorance of the real character of all these "gurus" that they have gotten away with their "guru business" as long as they have.

*"Another thing is that just at the present moment I do not think the society can invest any money in New Vrindaban, for the reason that we are starting this press, and until this press is all established I do not wish to divert my attention to New Vrindaban. Another difficulty is that nobody is staying in New Vrindaban. Even the boy Hrisikesha has left, and recently I received one letter from Ranadir that Hayagriva and Kirtanananda are also not there. New Vrindaban is not in charge of Ranadir, so on the whole, people are not being attracted. In your next president's meeting you can consider these points." (Brahmananda, 10/3/69)*

Note: In other words: "Nobody should go there." And don't send any money there either. The attrition rate there remains extremely high to this day-and for good reason.

*"Regarding New Vrindavana, the society does not require to invest now. Kirtanananda is managing. That is all right. So far as Rayarama is concerned..." (Brahmananda, 10/27/69)*

Note: Here Prabhupada is saying in more or less words, that New Vrindavana is Kirtanananda's project and so don't even think about it.

*"The most encouraging news is that the school is being very nicely organized. Another encouraging thing is that Kirtanananda Maharaja has now taken up actually the work of a Sannyasi and is preaching outside our Krishna conscious cult with great enthusiasm." (Ranadir, 1/24/70)*

Note: In Chapter Nine there is an elaborate description of why Srila Prabhupada gave men like Kirtanananda the sannyasa order of life. In summary, the idea was to get them out preaching and away from the temples where they simply caused problems for the others. This letter, and many more like it, supports this conclusion.

*"You have made a proposal and plan that each center shall contribute $20 monthly for the improvement of our New Vrindavana community Project. I have no objection to this but it has been already the program that every center shall send me maintenance funds of $15 per month and since leaving Japan I have hardly received any. I do not know if they have sent or not sent, but I have not received. So if they cannot even send my maintenance charges, you cannot depend on their sending monthly $20 for the maintenance of New Vrindavana." (Rupanuga, 11/13/70)*

Note: Prabhupada was constantly having to check Kirtanananda from draining the Society for men and money. Here he is implying that first the devotees should think of him, not Kirtanananda. It is also interesting to note that Rupanuga was influenced to support Kirtanananda. He must not have heard yet that New Vrindaban was not supported by the society. From the very beginning, Kirtanananda's psychic influence on his Godbrothers has been very powerful. Prabhupada was constantly having to circumvent or control him by letters and diplomacy.

*"Yes you can send the building fund monies to New Vrindavana for development of our community project there. This collection may be utilized in this way." (hand-written insert); "After consulting the GBC whether New Vrindavana has been transferred to the Society?" (Karandhar, 4/22/71)*

Note: Prabhupada was not interested in spending a penny on New Vrindavana until it was transferred into the Society's name. Why? Perhaps he knew that, at any moment, Kirtanananda could turn on him again.

Once the project was in the Society's name, however, it wouldn't matter as much. To this day, the transfer has not been made and so Kirtanananda can and does blow his nose on the GBC whenever they try to tell him something.

*"Recently I have received one letter from Hayagriva in which he wanted to know in 24 hours whether I could pay $20,000, but I have already given $20,000 to Back to Godhead. Besides that, New Vrindavana has to be developed very nicely but whether Hayagriva has already transferred the property to the society's name? This is required now. We require seven temples in New Vrindaban and 50% of the membership collection may be invested for this purpose. But Hayagriva should transfer the property to the society's name." (Rupanuga, 4/24/71)*

Note: Somehow or other, the devotees at the time just couldn't seem to understand that Prabhupada didn't trust Kirtanananda.

*"So far your ideas that some of our students have not realized what they are writing, that they are merely repeating the philosophy mechanically, and that Rayarama is more appreciated by you, then you can do it, and give the example as he has done it. But the difference is, that in spite of his becoming a philosopher he could not assimilate and practice the philosophy, and he went away, so you may write like him, but please do not go away. I think others like Kirtanananda may be repeating, but they stay. But I am always wondering, why others do not write, so many big, big, preachers we have got, but none of them write, so if you can inspire them to write in more convincing way, that is great service, do it." (Mandali-Bhadra, 2/2/72)*

Note: This is no ordinary comment for Srila Prabhupada to make. He very seldom made such statements in writing knowing that it could fall into the wrong hands. So to criticize Kirtanananda so casually here is very unusual. Prabhupada is coming right out and saying that Kirtanananda has no realization but is merely mechanically repeating. Thus the devotees could understand that despite Kirtanananda's claim of being the greatest devotee, he is not.

*"...and I was expecting your check for a long time. I have been dreaming for a long time that you would send something but I didn't get. So now I am coming to Los Angeles by 20th May, and you must come there to meet me. You are the first sannyasi of my institution so I expect greater things from you than the others."* (Kirtanananda, 5/2/72)

Note: This shows that Srila Prabhupada and Kirtanananda were not in any mystical harmony. Kirtanananda either could not realize Prabhupada's hopes or simply refused to fulfill it.

*"But now you have agreed to give Hayagriva $4,000 dollars per month, that was a great mistake. Now you have to rectify it. Now Hayagriva writes me that he is coming to Los Angeles, so we can discuss. Abruptly if we stop, that* will *not be good. So we have to rectify by arrangement and agreement. I am simply surprised how you all GBC men agreed to give him $4,000 per month. So the mistake has been made, now it has to be corrected by other ways."* (Karandhar, 5/12/72)

Note: Is it possible that the GBC men hadn't realized yet that New Vmdavana was not an ISKCON project? In letter after letter, Prabhupada is stressing the transference of the property into the society's name but they are so dull that they don't comprehend. When Prabhupada says, "I am simply surprised," he often means that the devotees did something stupid beyond comprehension. For those readers who are not aware; Hayagriva and Kirtanananda had been living as "two halves of the same body" for approximately 15 years at the time of this letter and so money given to Hayagriva was the same as money given to Kirtanananda. To this day they are still living together. Hayagriva's son is also very intimate with Kirtanananda as several testimonies have revealed.

*"So far your road-show is concerned, we are not meant for giving performances, we are simple kirtan men. There must always be kirtan going on wherever we travel, and nothing else.*

*So far your naming of the new initiates, Shyamasundar tells me that there are several duplications, and this is not very much desirable. So in future, better to telephone or somehow contact my secretaries and get the names from them, and in that way there will be no duplication in the future."* (Kirtanananda, 6/25/72)

Note: This shows a blasé and careless attitude on the part of Kirtanananda in acting as the representative of the parampara.

*"Such a talent (Hayagriva) is not so easily replaced, so we must try to bring him back to the standard for his own benefit. In this connection, I have written his wife, Kirtanananda Maharaja, and the GBC to see what they can do for him."* *(Jagadish, 3/10/73)*

Note: Prabhupada had many homosexual followers and so he seldom condemned homosexuality outright. Homosexuality is not mentioned in any of the personal letters in the archives. Still, in private, Prabhupada was known to have commented about homosexuals on several occasions. It is well known to many of his disciples that Prabhupada was not at all impressed by that particular phenomenon. In the relationship between Kirtanananda and Hayagriva, at least one testimony informed us that Kirtanananda was the female part. This letter may well have been referring to this truth.

*"Actually I don't want our energy spent in that way, to develop a school at New Vrindaban. Rather, all of our children should go to Dallas when they are four and begin their training program there." (Satyabhama, 3/23/73)*

Note: In effect, Srila Prabhupada is ordering not to send the children there either.

*"After the shooting affair what precaution have you taken? Bharadraja is here and he gave report that the devotees were very frightened. I further understand that the attack was for the second time. Here in Mayapur there are reports of dacoity at least once, twice in a month surrounding our place. So we have now taken two guns under regular license from the government. So when New Vrndavana has been attacked twice, thrice, why are you not keeping guns?" (Kirtanananda, 6/22/73)*

Note: It remains a frightening place to go for spiritual life to this day.

*"Yes! Go on acquiring the surrounding lands and in this way we will establish a local self-governing village and show all the world a practical example of spiritual life as Krishna Himself exhibited in Vrindaban. Agriculture and protecting the cow, this is the main business of the residents of Vrindaban, and above all simply loving Krishna. The cows, the trees, the cowherd men and Gopis, their chief engagement was loving Krishna, and in New Vrindaban we want to create this atmosphere and thereby show the whole world how practical and sublime our movement is." (Kirtanananda, 7/27/73)*

Note: In many letters Prabhupada wrote to Kirtanananda about cow protection. Unfortunately, when Kirtanananda began work on the Palace, he lost interest in the cows. Especially in 1980, due to poor feed, at least 10-15 cows were weakened to the point that they all froze to death at one time while attempting to get out of mud. The feed given them was rotten. Kirtanananda had more important things to spend money on than decent feed. Another incident is the killing of at least two cows who got their heads stuck in the feeder. Kirtanananda couldn't spare a man to fix the thing, since they were all welding on the Palace gates. Finally, a non-vegetarian karmi neighbor named Rocky saw the painful condition the cows were in and invested his own time to weld it. And then many cows were killed by the disease mastitis, which is easily cured with basic effort only. But, if left untreated, they die a painful death. Many cows were allowed to die in this way. Kirtanananda had more important things to spend money on than medicine. Even the local authorities attempted to prosecute Kirtanananda for cruelty to animals but they failed. Still the indication is clear. Kirtanananda is no lover of cows. Finally Kirtanananda is now building a huge cow barn since his drug dealing business is doing very well. If the authorities are unwilling to do an audit on New Vrindavana, maybe the society should go through the books to determine the source of all that money.

*"So far as the woman distributors who have left New York and Boston Temples and have gone to New Vrindavana, they should return immediately and resume their original service. In Caitanya Mahaprabhu's movement, everyone is preacher, whether man or woman it doesn't matter. I do not know why Kirtanananda Maharaja is encouraging our woman devotees not to go out on Sankirtan for book distribution. Everyone should go out." (Karandhar, 10/6/73)*

Note: We have a good idea why Kirtanananda was encouraging the women to leave their temples to come to New Vrindaban, for the same reason he attempted to get anyone to New Vrindaban: to exploit them. Today, these same women, if they stay at New Vrindaban, may often be "Dharmattes," (Dharmatma's women)."Come here little muffin..." In other words ladies, real women devotees should not go there. Recently Mother Mahara, New Vrindaban's top collector for years, defected. She was "the" staunch supporter of Dharmatma and Kirtanananda. A very serious collector who went out 7 days a week, 51 weeks a year, she discovered that Dharmatma had impregnated a young girl (under age) and made her get an abortion. Mahara says that Kirtanananda knew and approved it before it happened (See Appendix 12). She reported this to the GBC but then she admits that the GBC snuffed it. And of course everyone knows that Dharmatma has sex with many of the women in the collecting party. In fact he initiated the idea of keeping women pickers satisfied as their gigolo. Jiva was the first to get trained up by Dharmatma in this philosophy (See Appendix 11). He passed it on to Udyamanu. We have many testimonies as to Dharmatma's telling women to abandon or neglect their children and husbands and go out picking. And don't fool yourselves Kirtanananda is the brains behind this philosophy. Kirtanananda often brags that, "not a blade of grass moves at New Vrindavana without my knowing about it." Therefore he most likely knew about the peephole into the ladies toilet of the temple building. Two inmates were caught looking through it but then the incident was covered up fairly well. Kirtanananda's real feelings toward women is further revealed just before women's "darshana" (meeting) night. We have definite testimony as to his joking, "Well boys, get out the incense, it's fish night." Fish referring to what he considers the smell of women. Knowing this and knowing that he is a lifelong homosexual, then this makes perfect sense. So does this sound like a healthy, Vedic spiritual environment for raising a family in progressive Krishna conscious household life?

*"Now this displeasing of Godbrothers has already begun and gives me too much agitation in my mind. Our Gaudiya Math people fought with one another after the demise of Guru Maharaja but my disciples have already begun fighting even in my presence. So I am greatly concerned about it... Trnad api sunicena... Please try to maintain the philosophy of unity in diversity. That will make our movement successful. One section of men have already gone out, therefore we must be very careful to maintain unity in diversity, and remember the story of Aesop's Fables of the father of many children with the bundle of sticks. When the father asked his children to break the bundle of sticks wrapped in a bag, none of them could do it. But, when they removed the sticks from the bag, and tried one by one, the sticks were easily broken. So this is the strength of unity. If we are bunched up, we can never be broken, but when divided, then we can become broken very easily."* (Kirtanananda, 10/18/73)

Note: Kirtanananda does not give facility to any diversity which is not 100% loyal to his air of divinity.

Therefore, there is no real unity at New Vrindavana, just personality cult fascism.

*"There is one vacancy in the GBC board, so myself in consultation with Brahmananda Maharaja and Jayatirtha Prabhu, we have decided you can fill up the post. This will be confirmed in the next meeting."* (Kirtanananda, 5/10/74)

Note: This is May of 1974 and for the first time Prabhupada was offering Kirtanananda some official responsibility. But shortly thereafter, he wanted to be a wild card again.

*"If Kirtanananda Maharaja speaks what I speak, then he can be taken as siksa-guru. Guru sastra sadhu. The spiritual master is one, that is a fact. Kirtanananda Swami may be taken as sadhu not spiritual master, or as instructor guru. I don't think he is saying anything against our principles, so what is the wrong?*

*You have written that the devotees here say that you cannot know me, but only Kirtanananda Maharaja can know me. But, if Kirtanananda is a disciple and he can know me, and you are also a disciple, why you cannot know me?"* (Paramananda, 7/20/74)

Note: Someone was bold enough to tell Prabhupada that Kirtanananda was imposing his personality as the only medium to Srila Prabhupada. More tangible evidence of the oppressive personality cult being unauthorizedly instituted at that place.

This is the heart of his problem. Kirtanananda wants to be the guru, but he's not so stupid as to claim authority over Prabhupada again, like before. Here he is claiming to be the only one who can know Prabhupada. It's the next best thing to being there.

*"I am in due receipt of your letter dated August 21, with enclosed photographs. So Kirtanananda Maharaja has installed Deities. But without twenty devotees how you can have Deities? Your men are coming and going so why you are having Deity installation? You must have twenty devotees. Kirtanananda Maharaja, he should supply those devotees since he has authorized the installation. You can name the Deities, Radha-Murlidhara." (Batugopal, 9/7/74)*

Note: In effect, these Deities only have Kirtanananda's blessings. The tone of this letter certainly doesn't sound like a blessing from Prabhupada. As such the Cleveland temple never really got off the ground. These Deities are still in Cleveland but there are still not 20 devotees there. Kirtanananda sends his bad devotees there as a type of punishment. Kalpa Vrksa, one of Kirtanananda's most loyal followers, was exiled there recently for stealing morphine from the New Vrindaban resident doc Nick who needed it at the time for a patient. Kirtanananda's intimates refer to Cleveland as the "Bahuka temple"-"Bahuka" being an African race of Negro but used in the derogatory sense by Kirtanananda and his inmates.

*"In India ghee is needed in our temples. I want to know if you can supply ghee by exporting it from USA. The quantity is 100 lbs. for Mayapura and 100 lbs. for Vrindaban. I am prepared to pay you for it in dollars at the fair market price." (Kirtanananda, 10/25/74)*

Note: Does this sound like the relationship between the Jagat-guru and his obedient, over-loyal, and dedicated disciple?

*"Please send the next shipment of ghee immediately, as it takes quite a while for it to reach India. Shipments should be sent regularly every six months. The amount that you sent last shipment was good, send that much twice a year.*

*You are so humble and so sincere, this is a sign of your success. May Krishna bless you more and more. Krishna has placed you in that position. Now, you should always be fully conscious of your great responsibility." (Madhuvisa, 1/21/75)*

Note: This is the relationship between a Guru and his obedient disciple.

*"...and I have read the Cintamini poetry book. It is indirect, impersonal and useless. Who will read these things? Krishna's name is only mentioned in two poems in the whole book. What is this? There are so many poems written by great acaryas. Who do you try to concoct something like this? It is not in our line. How*

*is that our Kirtanananda Swami is there and he has approved printing this? It is a waste of time, paper, money, ink, and labor... Who will become attracted by such things as this? You should all spend more time reading my books very carefully and stop all this unnecessary manufacturing." (Vahna, 5/26/75)*

Note: Srila Prabhupada had warned previously that Kirtanananda was "polluted with impersonal poison." Well, it hadn't gone away by 1975. Money went out for the printing of Mayavada literature from the press of Kirtanananda Swami. That press is still printing all kinds of rubbish today, also. There is positive testimony by an inmate of New Vrindavana that $100 bills are also being printed there along with Brijbasi Spirits calling Kirtanananda the founder-acarya of New Vrindaban.

*"...and have noted the contents. Your report is very nice. It is wonderful to hear that you are distributing 1,000 magazines and collecting $1,000 daily. Now, you have plenty of money, milk, fruits, flowers, grains, everything and you are living in the jungle. What more could you want? I may be coming there immediately after the Philadelphia Rathayatra, and I shall stay until after Janmastami. I hope this meets you in good health." (Kirtanananda, 6/9/75)*

Note: This is a very unusual and interesting statement. "What more could you want?" Prabhupada often refers to Mayavadis as desiring these things exclusively. One would have to read All of Prabhupada's letter to understand that this letter is very unusual and revealing since Prabhupada seldom spoke sarcastically to his disciples.

*"Regarding your desire to be relieved of managing these other centers, I may request you to continue until the next Mayapur meeting and then you can make some other arrangement conveniently." (Kirtanananda, 11/10/75)*

Note: So in one and one-half years Kirtanananda wanted relief from GBC duty.

THE END


## THE TRUTH ABOUT THE "PALACE OF GOLD"

"Why was the Palace built?" Most devotees think it was built to glorify Srila Prabhupada. Many of those Prabhupada disciples who helped build the place most likely had that in mind. But Kirtanananda's inner motive may not be so easily surmised. He is no ordinary man. The above letters reveal a side to his character that, to say the least, is highly suspicious. Seven years ago it may have been hard to present this case but the time factor has now revealed all. "It is easy to be wise after the fact." As such we are not claiming to be wise in our/this analysis of Kirtanananda's character. The evidence is staring us in the face. All we have done is taken the time to open our eyes, see it, and put it in writing with the sole aim of helping other devotees avoid him.

Over the years the atmosphere of New Vrindaban has gone from bad to worse. The Appendix section of this book reveals some of the more corrupt events that take place there. This deep-rooted undercurrent of corruption reveals an entirely different purpose for the Palace of Gold. Casual devotees and tourists generally see the external show, the glitter and colors, and are very impressed. Most visitors, including devotees, have no reason to try and see beyond that. Therefore they assume that Kirtanananda must be very advanced because he appears to have been the inspiration for such a beautiful monument supposedly to Srila Prabhupada. But if we go deeper into the spirit of the New Vrindaban community-the actual minds and activities of the persons who live there and manage the place-we see something entirely different from the spiritual community and lifestyle that the Palace is supposed to represent.

## WHY WAIT FOR HARD EVIDENCE?

Earlier on Prabhupada said about Kirtanananda, "By lips he says that he is a surrendered soul, but by action he is thinking differently." Prabhupada could always understand the heart of Kirtanananda. From this statement we know that Kirtanananda has it in him to be a very devious and cunning man. Past and present activities clearly reveal that. He may have humbled himself somewhat when his attempt to usurp the movement failed, but there is no indication that he changed at heart. So although we don't have the kind of hard evidence that ISKCON leaders seem to require, we will herein show logically that Kirtanananda has not changed in the least. His one and only desire is still to be worshipped as the guru and he doesn't care how many devotees he steps on to accomplish that aim. It is important that devotees start recognizing this. It should not be necessary for us to see hard evidence before we can act to rectify a corrupt situation.

Take Bhavananda for example. Many devotees knew he was engaging in homosexual activities. Some knew intuitively that he was fallen just by his speech, behavior, movements, etc. A few knew of his habit from directly hearing about it. But nothing was ever done about him because he was not caught in the act of a gross falldown. The GBC knew all about him. That's why he was kicked out of Vrindavana. In fact, even the townspeople of Vrindavana knew of his homosexuality but the GBC continued to cover up for him. So devotees should not have to wait for such gross evidence to manifest before they act. Devotees are meant to see spirit. What is the question of seeing and understanding spirit if we can't even see subtle manifestations of corruption staring us in the face. Brahmins are supposed to be able to see the subtle movements of others. So in the case of Kirtanananda, it is true that no one has seen him personally handing deadly drugs to a customer, personally aborting a child, personally killing a cow, personally raping a woman, personally stabbing a Godbrother in the back, but he commits all these crimes. He does it on the subtle plane. He puts out the subtle energy, and those around him, Kuladri, Dharmatma, Dulal, Advaita, Sudhanu, they manifest the corruption on the gross plane. To the gross materialists, he has kept up a good front and has fooled most of the devotees thus far. But just as Bhavananda was finally caught, so also Kirtanananda will eventually be caught. If we wait for the corruption to come to the gross plane however, it will go public and do much more damage to the movement than if it's nipped early in the subtle stages. Now that Bhavananda has been grossly exposed, all the people who have been worshipping him all these years are outraged. You can better believe that many of them are going to file lawsuits against ISKCON for keeping such a debauch propped up on a throne.

Kirtanananda is many, many times worse than Bhavananda as these letters reveal. Even Bhavananda never attacked Prabhupada so viciously. Kirtanananda must be recognized for what he is now-before the evidence becomes so gross that the whole world finds out about it. When contamination comes to the gross plane it always manifests in either killings, rapes, child molestation, wife-stealing, drug dealing and abuse, etc. All these things have/are going on at New Vrindaban. They just haven't manifested so grossly yet that the whole world wants to hear about it. But if it continues, it will come out. If Kirtanananda gets desperate, he could try something comparable to the Jim Jones insanity.

In this next section of our analysis of Kirtanananda, we will go into the psychology of a tactic commonly known as "bait and switch." Kirtanananda is very expert at this technique and has used it to perfection in attracting devotees as well as tourists, Indians, etc., to spend their time and money to build Kirtanananda an empire.

## EVERYONE HAD FORGOTTEN

New Vrindaban never really got off the ground until the Palace was completed several years after Srila Prabhupada's departure. Prabhupada didn't outright condemn New Vrindaban but he never promoted it in any substantial way either. Especially when it became apparent that Kirtanananda and Hayagriva were not going to transfer it into the Society's name. Therefore New Vrindaban remained small, austere, and out of the picture, with very little solid expansion right up through 1977. During all this time Kirtanananda enjoyed a relatively good reputation since very few of the devotees who were around during the 1967-68 incident were still in the movement. Those who were, did not live at New Vrindaban. Most of the new devotees thought of Kirtanananda Swami as the first sannyasi and the oldest disciple (age wise). These qualifications gave him respectability since many of the newcomers were young enough to be his sons.

During these early years Kirtanananda was preaching that no one could approach Srila Prabhupada except through him since naturally, "No one could know Prabhupada as well as Kirtanananda did." The older disciples, the GBC, etc., who knew of Kirtanananda's previous envy, were not awed by Kirtanananda's self-proclaimed air of divinity. But the workers at New Vrindavana were so isolated from the rest of the ISKCON world that they never dreamed that Kirtanananda could be anything other than the "dearmost" of Prabhupada and a pure devotee. They were easily fooled by the seeming maturity of Kirtanananda. Few devotees knew of his black side. Add to this, the fact that devotees in general are trained to ignore the faults in others, it is no wonder that Kirtanananda's past was practically forgotten.

## MUST GET HELP

Around 1974 Kirtanananda had an idea. He wanted to build a great temple to attract thousands of devotees. He had money coming in from various sources, including drug sales, and he was getting a few steady workers, so he began construction. Originally the Palace was intended to be a Radha-Krishna temple. It was a major project and would take years to complete. Generally there were only five or ten devotees working on it. Then one day in June-they say-Kirtanananda had the revelation that first he must build a home for Srila Prabhupada, stating: "One can only approach Krishna through guru." This sentiment certainly sounded good and it impressed some of Prabhupada's disciples. Thus more devotees came to assist Kirtanananda in his "noble" project. But even at the time of Prabhupada's disappearance, it was still just a dirty construction site unrecognizable as a building. Not only was Prabhupada not able to ever live in it, he never even set foot in it.

## BAIT AND SWITCH TACTIC

Kirtanananda certainly has a certain degree of charisma but he didn't have the purity to attract very many devotees to New Vrindaban. But he knew that if he was going to expand his project in a big way, he was going to need a lot of help. He realized he was going to have to attract Prabhupada's disciples to work for him. If he could convince them that New Vrindaban was actually very dear to Prabhupada, then in that way he could trick them to come and work for him. This strategy worked very well. The more the Palace got built, the more he was respected as a great disciple of Prabhupada. He became very expert at glorifying Prabhupada with his mouth, "but thinking something else." He is the world's greatest expert at bait and switch. During construction of the Palace, emphasis was always either on Prabhupada or pleasing Prabhupada through Kirtanananda. But the property was never transferred. Imagine-all that free labor simply by saying, "Jai Prabhupada." Prabhupada, however, was never fooled by the lip service of Kirtanananda. He was interested in seeing whether the deed to the property had been transferred to the Society's name. He certainly hadn't forgotten Kirtanananda's inner "designs." In fact, there was only one mention of the Palace in all of Prabhupada's personal letters.

## WHO LIVES THERE?

Kirtanananda's inner designs were certainly known to Prabhupada but they were not exactly being kept a secret either. Many devotees who were so-called initiated by Prabhupada openly let it be known that they were really devotees of Kirtanananda. One such devotee is Maha Buddhi dasa (Param Brahma's brother). His ex-wife explained to me her ex-husband's mood, which represents the mood of many at New Vrindaban, was "I had to take initiation from Prabhupada, because Kirtanananda wasn't allowed to initiate me." She even said that her husband resented Prabhupada for his not allowing Kirtanananda to initiate. In the beginning New Vrindavana was made up of a mixture of these foolish neophytes like Maha Buddhi, who were actually worshipers of Kirtanananda, and Prabhupada's disciples, who had been led to believe that new Vrindaban was a bone fide ISKCON project.

As the years went by, the devotees exclusively devoted to Kirtanananda were encouraged and given more and more facility. They increased in number. The devotees more interested in Srila Prabhupada however decreased. Since November 1977, not one devotee of Prabhupada has gone to New Vrindaban and stayed there unless he became a Kirtanananda worshiper. Today New Vrindaban is made up exclusively of Kirtanananda worshipers. This is the proof of what New Vrindaban is all about. It doesn't matter how much love and devotion one many have for Prabhupada and Krishna. If you don't worship Kirtanananda, you're a dog at New Vrindaban. Srila Prabhupada is respected as one respects a statue of an ancient hero. None of New Vrindaban's residents go to the Palace except to take money from the tourists. Kirtanananda used to-and may still-go to the Palace mangala-aratik along with a few brahmacaris. This was / is necessary to keep up the front. Otherwise no one at all would ever go there. Then it would be blatantly obvious that it was built with the sole purpose of, "fooling the innocent public."

## DOESN'T NEED PRABHUPADA ANYMORE

In the very important letter to Paramananda quoted earlier, Kirtanananda's use of bait and switch tactics is blatantly revealed. In that letter it is clear that he was trying to convince devotees that they could only approach Prabhupada through himself. In the beginning, devotees are naturally attracted to Prabhupada and his teachings. Attracted to Prabhupada in this way, Kirtanananda convinces them that they can only approach Prabhupada, and Krishna, through himself. Those who are less intelligent naturally wind up worshipping Kirtanananda. Now Kirtanananda has so many of these blind followers that he really doesn't want Prabhupada's disciples to come around anymore. He can now attract new people on the basis of his propped up seat, his tourist attraction, and the material facility he can offer people. Previously he had hoped his sannyasa certificate would be sufficient to prove he was a bona fide guru, but Prabhupada took that away from him. So he had to put up the front again, only this time he did it with the Palace.

This is the real reason why the Palace was built. Today the Palace is a dead monument, maintained like a museum, and used a tourist attraction for which they charge an outrageous fee of $4 per person for the 20 minute tour. Nearly 100 outside workers are on the payroll who build and maintain the entire project. Many of them are also included on the "500" person list of residents that Kirtanananda flaunts. The money to hire all these workers and buy the construction materials comes from drug sales, which include the look-alike drugs such as lydocaine. Kirtanananda was always a drug dealer. We have one testimony that as early as 1970 he started the KSS (Krishna's Secret Service). Much of the Palace was built from the drug money gotten by Charantana, Advaita, Svarupa, Syamakunda (who was busted), Tirtha (who murdered Chakradhari), garbage John and many more. These are just a few of the "devotees" that I personally have talked to that told me stories of their drug dealings for Kirtanananda Swami. There are many addicts living at New Vrindavana who use and sell drugs. When the Palace restaurant burned down, Kirtanananda is well-known to have said, "Krishna must not like that kind of money."

## NARENDRA'S PERSONAL STORY

Another testimony as to what the Palace represents today could be ascertained by interviewing the devotees who actually built the place. While they were working on it, they no doubt thought they were working for Prabhupada. When they inevitably discovered that Kirtanananda had other designs for their labor, they became outraged. Now they literally curse themselves for having contributed to Kirtanananda's "glory." Take for instance Narendra dasa who designed and built most of the stained glass decorating the Palace today. Here are some of the highlights of his tragedy.

After escaping New Vrindaban he struggled, and is still struggling, to get his stained glass business off the ground. Adding to his financial struggles were the expense of having to see a therapist just to help him get over the hatred he felt for Kirtanananda. Now he is struggling to get custody of his only daughter, Nitya lila, before his ex-wife foolishly takes her back to New Vrindaban. Narendra was so severely mistreated by Kirtanananda that he literally does not want to hear about Krishna consciousness anymore. Who can blame him? The average devotee simply cannot imagine how a religion that supports such a corrupt debauch as Kirtanananda can have anything whatsoever to do with spiritual life. Narendra once built, as a gift for Kirtanananda, a window depicting the Sad Bhuja form of Lord Caitanya worth $5,000. Kirtanananda never even said thank you. Narendra's eyes slowly opened as to the man's real character and so he finally decided to start life over again somewhere else. Kirtanananda had a going away present for him. He sent a fifteen man goon squad to steal whatever they could of Narendra's equipments, or force him to pay a $1,000 exit fee. Narendra had to comply just to get away from the place with his business (This is very common at New Vrindaban). Otherwise he would have been utterly ruined. Memories of New Vrindaban and Kirtanananda are so painful to Narendra that he seldom talks of his twelve years in ISKCON any longer.

So the conclusion is that Kirtanananda has not been purified by his career in Krishna consciousness. This is because his motive was not to serve Prabhupada, but to use Prabhupada's legacy to further his own guru business. One cannot make spiritual advancement by such thinking. Krishna is no fool. He knows everyone's heart perfectly. Eventually everyone has got to pay. Prabhupada sums up the position of these "gurus" very elucidly as follows:

*"By a false display of religious sentiments, they present a show of devotional service while indulging in all sorts of immoral activities (1). In this way they pass as spiritual master (2) and devotees of God. Such violators of religious principles (3) have no respect (4) for the authoritative acaryas, the holy teachers in the strict disciplic succession. To mislead the people in general, they themselves become so-called acaryas, but they do not even follow the principles of the acaryas (5).*

*These rogues are the most dangerous elements (6) in human society. Because there is no religious government, they escape punishment (7) by the law of the state. They cannot, however, escape the law of the Supreme, who has clearly declared in Bhagavad-gita (16.19-20) that envious demons (8) in the garb of religious propagandists shall be thrown into the darkest regions of hell. Sri Isopanisad confirms that these pseudo-religionists are heading toward the most obnoxious place in the universe after completion of their spiritual master business (9), which they conduct simply for sense gratification (10)." (Sri Isopanisad 12)*

From reading the early letters about the character of Kirtanananda, and interviewing several dozen devotees who have been burned by him, we can easily see that this above description is actually a description of Kirtanananda. Here are some of the reasons why this is so:

1. Kirtanananda is a drug dealer. He passes women around amongst his workers as though they were all whores. He does not recognize anyone as a Godbrother and has no respect for the rights of others. He directly tries to break up marriages if it furthers his own profit, adoration and distinction. Whether or not he is still engaged in homosexual activities will all come out in due course of time. There is strong indication that he is.

2. He always wanted to be a spiritual master. Even before joining ISKCON he was the guru in his local clique of friends, most of whom were also homosexual. He was into black magic. This combination earned him the title "weird Keith". After meeting Prabhupada he only waited one year before trying to usurp Prabhupada's movement. He actually attempted to legally keep Prabhupada from entering the country. Even after he so-called came back, there are numerous instances where he was exposed as attempting to surpass Prabhupada. Now he is fully engrossed in posing as a spiritual master. Prabhupada directly stated in one letter that "he wants to be a spiritual master by disobeying his spiritual master."

3. For a sannyasi, the first regulative principle is to not have any connection with women. Kirtanananda violates that principle constantly. He goes so far as to say that all women have an eternal relationship with him, but that their husbands are not important. This preaching is not only a violation, but it is Ravana philosophy. Actually it is worse. At least Ravana wanted to enjoy the women himself. Kirtanananda thinks women smell like fish. He steals women for the money they bring in and to pass around amongst his workers. A sannyasi is supposed to know sastra. Kirtanananda does not know sastra at all which is why he seldom quotes it. It is even rumored that he has not read all of Prabhupada's books. But he

constantly concocts statements and policies such as putting a crown on Prabhupada, authorizing women to have sex with the sankirtana leader, authorizing an abortion in an underage girl (because of the previous policy), etc. (Appendix 12)

4. Prabhupada stated that Kirtanananda thinks guru and sastra are tyranny. That means no respect. Why should we think that he changed?

5. Prabhupada set certain standards of moral behavior, compassion, honesty, etc. Kirtanananda does not follow those standards. For example, Prabhupada was very compassionate and thoughtful not to interfere in marriages. He always told the women to be fully devoted to their husbands. Kirtanananda openly tells the women to fully devote themselves to himself, even if it means totally neglecting the husband and children. In this way he controls the women and so naturally the husbands have to stay there also.

6. There are many dangerous elements in society. Thieves, rapists, murderers, etc. But here Prabhupada says that the most dangerous are those who exploit others in the name of religion. They are the most dangerous because they hurt people in the deepest way possible-their souls. This world has only one purpose; to teach people to surrender to God. When society is infested with rogues posing as saints, that stops the progress of human life. Thus most people are not inclined to trust anyone.

7. Since the government is demoniac, the demoniac "gurus" also escape punishment. But even the GBC falls in the category of a Godless government. They have allowed these "rogues" to remain in their positions even after having been exposed. For example the GBC determined that Kirtanananda interfered with, and destroyed the marriage of Sulocana dasa. But because the GBC is essentially a Godless body, the GBC had no potency to rectify Kirtanananda and return Sulocana's sons to him. Thus he escaped punishment.

8. Here Prabhupada uses terminology that scares the sentimentalists who permeate ISKCON half to death. We have hardly met a devotee who has the guts to call a spade a spade. But the fact is, the current gurus, and especially Kirtanananda are nothing but envious demons as described above. If they were ever sincere, that remains to be seen.

9. The guru business is certainly lucrative. There is no need to go into the details of how the "gurus" have stuffed their pockets with money and luxuries. It is all too well known. Not a single one of them has even the slightest concept of simple living or austerity anymore. They claim they are beyond all that.

10. As of this writing it is unknown what different kinds of sense gratification Kirtanananda enjoys aside from the profit, adoration, and distinction. For some reason, the GBC always waits for the sense gratification to hit the lower levels before they recognize that the "guru" is actually nothing but a sense-gratifier.

PRABHUPADA EXPOSES KIRTANANANDA'S HOMOSEXUALITY

*"Such a talent (Hayagriva) is not so easily replaced, so we must try to bring him back to the standard for his own benefit. In this connection, I have written his wife, Kirtanananda Maharaja, and the GBC to see what they can do for him. (Prabhupada Letter Jagadish, 3/10/73)*

APPENDIX 5

# THE PLIGHT OF THE NEW DISCIPLES

Letter of Radhanatha Dasa to his "guru," Satsvarupa.

6494 Denbigh Ave. Bumaby, B.C. Canada, October 18, 1984

Dear Srila Gurupada,

Please accept my humble and faulty obeisances. All glories to you and your tireless work. All glories to Srila Prabhupada.

I hope you will forgive this simple hand-written letter. I thought it prudent not to have an "outside" typist do the horrors for what will be evident as obvious reasons. Knowing the way news, and especially scandal, travels within the movement, at alarming speed and astounding exaggeration, I did not ask another devotee to transform my handiwork into a more formal state.

It has been a very long time since I last wrote to you. This was partly owing to the decision to remove me from my duties managing the "Sankirtan" effort here in Vancouver. You may remember, at this time, I would write to you every month with the news and details of the devotee's scores. I am by no means a man of great output in terms of correspondence (meager would constitute a gross overstatement). The exception being those letters needed for utilitarian reasons in the prosecution of business and duty. The more prominent reason being an attempt to understand the relationship between dogma and reality as it relates to ISKCON and an examination of incidences and experiences which were prompted by an overall impression of misgiving.

This reassessment began by reviewing my relationship and, later, other's, with what is commonly referred to as the "temple authorities". This examination prompted a further investigation and subsequent skepticism of widely held beliefs regarding the interpretation of the philosophy.

One's own beliefs, especially when dealing with oneself, can be misleading, but, just the same, I believe I am not a malicious person, and, by experience, I can honestly say that I do not react to problematic situations in any great haste. I felt that a period of time was necessary for reflection and hopefully a conclusion. However, when dealing, be it lesser or to a greater extent, with many variables-some that are human-the situation becomes increasingly more complex. In some ways with an exponential relationship to time. In such situations, the solution becomes even more dependent on clear definitions between subjectivity and objectivity. This task is greater than my abilities, so I beg your indulgence-as Prabhupada said, "All actions are covered by fault."

168

Many questions have been considered in preparation of this letter. Am I being misled by Maya? Surely, I know that, regarding certain aspects of my behavior, I am. What exactly is illusion? Perhaps another's perspective on it, or on "the Truth" is yet another grander illusion. Are my opinions fueled by simple vindictiveness-to right wrongs real or imaginary? Paranoia? As my wife is so fond of telling all and sundry-have I become mentally defective? I think not. Or, as others have interpreted my behavior, am I simply envious? What is envy other than the ISKCON status quo conception, which usually simply means that the object of this label is perceived as some kind of threat-real or imaginary. I am sure that you may perceive my opinions as being rather pompous. For this I apologize.

I have, in my long and patchy association with members of ISKCON, met many people with similar experiences to mine, some with far worse, others with a history of horror stories. My experiences with ISKCON members and their dealings within the organization, and with people "outside" and the philosophical background to deportment, presents much to consider.

A senior devotee, and a great friend of mine, with whom I have discussed the "tenets of Krishna consciousness" and the unfortunately inseparable ISKCON politics, told me not to write this letter at all. "Say as you please if you can take the consequences-but never put it down in writing." This statement itself highlights the system of needless intrigue in which the members feel themselves ensnared. Happily, I can say that, as for myself, I feel at least partially freed from this encumbrance to any kind of advancement-material or spiritual. Against his good advice and best intentions, I submit this letter-perhaps because of some egotism, though I hope this is minimal.

I dedicate this letter in the name of HONESTY. This, I am ashamed to say, I have only rediscovered since questioning the ISKCON status quo. I can no longer pretend that everything in the garden is "rosy", and I don't believe that, by doing so, honesty is served. Without honesty, can anything of substance be gained?

I believe that honesty exercised both personally and interpersonally can rectify practically any situation. However, I feel, that within ISKCON, honesty has lost its important place, and dishonesty and its running mates run rampant through the fabric of the society. It is pooh-poohed by the leaders as being merely a "subreligious principle" or a "mere material moral."

The temple system, it seems, cannot tolerate honesty as an interpersonal medium. Instead it offers reward for supporting the sometimes far-flung illusions of the leaders. A system only asking complete support and undivided loyalty to the whims of the temple presidents, vice presidents, and so on down the chain of command. Democracy, we are told, is evil. what we have in its place is not the Vedic material society of old-I feel that just may be an unreachable goal. Instead we have an authoritarian regime reminiscent of the Holy Roman Empire, countless banana republics, mid-century Germany, and other fundamental sects. Failure to play the game will lead, of course, to a short, sharp slap. Continuing insubordination will lead to being branded "fault-finder," "critical," "envious"-sneer, gnashing of teeth, hellfire, and damnation. I will return to this later.

Honesty in the area of collecting funds-that appears to be the main thrust of ISKCON-is the most obvious area of contention. Whereas before dishonest tactics were openly approved; it is now being treated as a matter of conscience for the individual. Although, on record, everyone will agree that such tactics are abhorrent, we resort to great lengths to encourage the devotees to collect increasingly larger sums of money. Of course, the amounts are measured by "Laxmi points" to try to avoid any materialistic implication in this regard. Older members instruct the newer in methods of how to achieve the desired result. The result not necessarily being spiritual experiences, but a large amount of cold, hard cash. This constant pressure through various mediums indirectly incites the devotees to resort to less than spiritual tactics in order to please the authorities. Even disregarding any use of blatantly dishonest measures, the very fact that the devotees are sent out to "sell" artifacts (some of these even questionable in their "taste") enmeshes the salesperson in the tactics of deceit in order to present a story acceptable to the "customer" in order to close a "sale".

Many will say, "Well, this is happening everywhere." Of course, but they don't call it spiritual training! Everyone is reluctant to examine how funds are being procured. If a devotee is caught in these practices, then, of course, he/she will be admonished, not because of the practice itself, but because of the punishment (i.e. loss of funds, legal fees, bad publicity, etc.). It's rather like the child, who is caught, feels sorry not because he has a realization of his antisocial behavior or that he is not really acting in his own best interests, but because he is made to suffer as a result. There seems to be a whole philosophy built upon "The end justifies the means." The local GBC once told me, when the temple president and Regional Secretary and myself were discussing highly criminal ways of gaining large sums of money, "Well, do it for Krishna-but don't tell me about it."

The collectors are further encouraged by slogans, some of which are:

"These are spiritual quotas." "We can do *anything* in Krishna's service."

"Krishna is the most expert cheat." "It belongs to Krishna anyway."

"We are rescuing Laxmi from Ravana" (Viva Liberation).

Another quote I hear often recited is that Prabhupada said that we should not do anything dishonest because we are not expert. This is interpreted to mean that we should not resort to crime because we are not very good-not because it is wrong and therefore a-spiritual. If we now consider ourselves expert-then it's OK.

The result of such irresponsible activity should be obvious especially since we can readily see the effects in the loss of credibility in the eyes of the public. Countless lawsuits, bad publicity, difficulty even giving books away. This type of activity also has a tendency to self-perpetuation. Very few intelligent and honest people are attracted to the tenets of Krishna consciousness, instead we attract the down-and-out, the criminal, the con trickster, etc.

Also the stability of individual devotees is undermined, especially any with sensitivity or empathy. Sometimes sooner or sometimes later. This tendency to relegate the virtue of honesty or truthfulness is symptomized in other ways, more insidious ways.

The black art of politics, one of the commonest tendencies of the materialistic conditions, is synonymous with the prosecution of diplomacy, duplicity, and the "half-truth". A destructive force to say the least. Most devotees would agree that they joined to avoid this. Instead, the ordinary devotee finds him/herself within a temple atmosphere tainted by political ambitions, paranoias, and protection of position.

At this juncture, I should also mention the good points of ISKCON. We all know that distributing literature, educating the general population about Krishna or God consciousness, is a very good thing. Giving free vegetarian food and educating about the attributes of vegetarianism is a very positive step to stemming the tide of uncivilized behavior and atheism. Krishna consciousness I am unequivocally in favor of, but ISKCON consciousness I feel is a different thing altogether, especially as the organization is becoming, despite the frantic activities of some purely motivated individuals, a small pond for a number of big fish to run. In fact, an objective assessment of the nature of these "spiritual sovereign states" is that it is becoming much like the other so-called "new religions" and is fast living up to its label as being a "cult."

The current political system in ISKCON, i.e., the absolute rule syndrome from GBC to temple presidents to departmental managers, etc., leads to much paranoia. The way the society views itself is that one who has managed to politic a way into a managerial position is being rewarded by Krishna for advancing in spiritual understanding. Therefore, more effort is spent chasing name, fame, and position, and subsequently protecting this "spiritual advancement" from others who aspire to this, than effort spent in developing exactly the opposite (underlined) qualities necessary for real (underlined) spiritual advancement. In my direct experiences with temple leaders officially, and also as "friends" (I will explain the quotation marks later), I have witnessed the trouble taken to nourish and protect these empires. The temple authority protective of his "divine right of kings" employs many methods to continue his tenure. This, of course, means "pushing" the money collectors to ensure that the temple is reflected favorably by his peers in terms of money collected, books distributed, and mega projects. Of course, there is at least some desire to unmotivated service, but, by the amount of posturing and politicking, there is a large amount of self-aggrandizement taking place. The absolute rule arrangement, coupled with a charismatic personality, a working knowledge of psychology, and a liberal smattering of ultra-right-wing political leanings, seems to make a successful temple president-one not afraid to destroy his enemies. As the Regional Secretary once told me, "Krishna has always helped me to defeat my enemies."

By being appointed to this position of absolute control, the general members of the temple must ingratiate themselves somehow to further enhance their own spiritual/political careers. Even the simple devotee, uninterested in such heady goals, must behave in such a way as to please the president just to receive the subsistence necessary to continue in the temple. By not being incessantly "enthusiastic" with everything done by the authorities, which, in many cases, cannot but be described as whimsical, one can be perceived as a threat. In fact, this absolute control scheme can make many temple managers behave in such a heady manner that schemes are born with little in the form of intelligent planning-disregarding in-house and contracted professional advice with little thought for the consequences and effects upon the simple devotee. These consequences, in my own experience, have meant increased quotas for money to pay for some losing scheme that they previously paid money for people to advise them not to do it in the first place.

I've seen many instances of unfortunate individuals locking horns with the "authority". Nirantara was subjected to a campaign of character assassination because he was a better musician and aroused the envy of the Regional Secretary-even to the point of poignant, sarcastic remarks during Srimad Bhagavatam class. The really sad part is that the person who provided some form of "dirt" to the authorities to provide a wedge to remove Nirantara was considered by him to be his best friend. Dhruva and Bhaktin Mary were other victims of the power politics-which you probably already know. In this case, spies were to report on anyone who had been in contact with the "gang-of-two." They were hurriedly rushed into the office and given a disgusting, raging tirade on the envious nature of these two. What is this-the Spanish Inquisition revisited? Much of the allegations that were made by Dhruva were backed up by other devotees who were also silenced.

Against another poor individual, I myself witnessed with my own eyes the Regional Secretary, Headmaster of the Gurukula, and the Farm President kick the crap out of him in full view of the public and the devotees.

We can all agree that this is outrageous behavior, but worse than that, these men verbalized their enjoyment of it, with great peels of encouragement from the devotees in general. I can remember closed conversations taking place where unnamed individuals were planning to *kill* him. This is spiritual life?

A friend of mine mentioned that, with this never-ending list of heinous activities, we cannot now consider this ISKCON but a Maya reflection of what ISKCON was designed to be. It is on the lips of many people that ISKCON is dying-perhaps there is nothing anyone can do to save it.

A tool that has been used in ISKCON management is the ancient principle of "divide and conquer". No devotee that I know has any friends within the movement. If one reveals one's mind in the spirit of honesty and friendship, one will quickly find the proverbial hilt protruding from one's shoulder blades. Devotees are tempted to "inform" on their Godbrother/sisters and are trapped in the tedious treadmill of politics and duplicity for the promised thirty pieces. Friend turns on friend, husband on wife, wife on husband. Everyone is watching for tell-tale signs-for mistakes, so that personal profiles can be maintained and points accumulated.

From the point of view of the ruling junta-"Information is power." Truth is subverted and upstarts quashed, criticism silenced. No devotee can trust any other-the status quo remains. Absolute power corrupts-absolutely!

This is all very reminiscent of the POW camps in Korea where the unfortunate captives were easily subdued by means of distrust of their fellow prisoners. Each soldier had no relationship with his fellow inmate because of the suspicion carefully nurtured by his captives. Instead, he docilely turned to his captors for human relations.

Many of the leaders (most) use the platform of the Srimad Bhagavatam class to further their own political posturing. The verse is read; so too is Srila Prabhupada's purport. A short dissertation follows summing up and elaborating on points contained therein. In many cases, the lecture soon departs from the ground of scriptural reference in its intended context and becomes a platform for personal and peculiar foibles.

I have sat through classes extolling the virtues of just about every type of discrimination possible. Classes discriminating against women and blacks. Classes doing little in the way of presenting Vaisnava philosophy but concentrating on belittling other religious systems-Christianity in particular. Hate philosophy aimed at "fringies," democracy in general, East Indians. Sankirtan classes extolling the virtue of money collection as a complete meditation and demeaning the efforts of "non-money collecting individuals."

The Regional Secretary gives classes primarily about the foremost position of the temple hierarchy and how we will suffer should we think of balking at his absolute position of authority. I think I know his pitch by heart now.

The most worrying and insidious classes are those elaborating on the glories of the varnasrama system as a new wonderful spiritual fascist society. The headmaster of the gurukula can manifest ecstatic symptoms when giving Srimad Bhagavatam classes on the righteous ways of the disgusting John Birch Society.

During classes and in private, most of the temple leaders and most of the visiting leaders exude this ultra right-wing philosophy dreaming of a future where the

ISKCON movement will rule the world. If they rule the world the same way they treat the devotees, ISKCON will make the Ayatollah look like Anne of Green Gables. In this context, ISKCON is a very dangerous organization, especially when one hears the preachers saying that, in the future, we will ask people if they believe in Krishna and, should they answer negatively, we will feel the righteous duty to kill them. If this is considered spiritual life-I am glad to be considered in Maya.

Is seems that somehow ISKCON either has attracted or has been instrumental in converting people with a great scarcity of love or respect for their fellow man. It appears to be a society with very (underlined) high ideals-I do not doubt that bhakti is the highest yoga-but the organization is based upon exploitation. Responsibility is a one-way street. The individual has immense responsibility to perform his duties, in many cases in very inclement circumstances. In return the society feels no concern, love, respect or responsibility for those lowly individuals who have freely given as they are able. I could write a book about individuals who have been given the royal shaft by the heartlessness of the ruling class, but it would be too depressing to relate it.

Another quirk of the status quo is the growing belief in temples I have lived or visited that absolute power also continues along familial lineage. A class of royal families is emerging from the misapplication of the philosophy. The next stage will obviously be the construction of "spiritual" dynasties. The Regional Secretary very plainly told me that he is a great believer in nepotism. This idea very plainly stems from a combination of extreme material goals and the appeal of the more authoritarian precepts of varnasrama.

I remember a very clever essay printed in *Back to Godhead* discussing how large numbers of people can be allayed into accepting horrifying or, at least, odorous concepts by changing the language slightly and avoiding the issue. I was very impressed. Of course, this carries on in highly corrupt societies as he mentions, but why must ISKCON use this tasteless and frightening Orwellian subterfuge?

Platitudes abound, to field poignant questions and criticisms. The favorite is, of course, "Krishna's mercy, prabhu." There are numerous others used to excuse just about any abuse or indefensible position. I'm sure you've heard them all.

I find myself at odds with the gurukula system also. The only criterion for staffing seems to be the lack of willingness or lack of ability for collecting money. In many cases, children are kept in the care and are educated by people who have no proper training or appeal for the service. The result-the uneducated are teaching, or trying to, and the unsuited are forced to be responsible for a number of children in the asrama setting. There are a few people now who are a little qualified for these positions, but, on the whole, the (underlined) system is lacking.

As for the boy's asrama, I find Jaya Gaura completely unsuited, and unless he is removed, a very nasty incident is in the cards. On three separate occasions he has attacked one of the boys in his charge. Or, on one occasion, I witnessed his abuse of my son Ravi. Ravi was repeatedly shoved, struck, and kicked by this fully grown man in his rage. If it wasn't for my own control in dealing with the man, he perhaps may have been able to perpetrate any other acts of violence against children. The view of the headmaster and the temple? Quite predictable. Nothing was done, or said. "Krishna's mercy," etc. This attitude highlights the managerial philosophy somewhat akin to the laissez-faire governmental policy in 18th and 19th century Europe. Let's pretend it didn't happen-let's pretend everything is going as planned. Nobody will criticize the management for fear of being seen as unadvanced. After all, the authorities have been very graphic in their presentation of what to them signifies spiritual advancement. One of these attributes is to never say anything is wrong. Nothing ever is wrong of course-just one's mind is faulty. The mind is one's worse enemy, etc.

During my time helping with the management, I gained a great insight into the prevailing mood of the authorities. I was included in many policy meetings and party to some very dubious activities. I became involved with very cavalier attitudes, also. For a finance meeting, it would take three ladies working for several hours to provide a feast for the four of us involved in discussion of related topics. Meanwhile, the proletariat of the temple looked on.

After a time, I was involved with "public affairs". It soon became apparent that most of my time was spent in defending actions by devotees that I could not myself condone. When dealing with the media especially, most of the time was spent in telling half-truths. I became expert as a public liar. As you well know, I could hardly tell the truth regarding the reality of ISKCON affairs, and sometimes couldn't even tell people the truth regarding the philosophy.

I am very comfortable with my position living away from he temple property. I can live like a civilized person again instead of the hippie-type living conditions at the temple. I no longer have to worry about my things being stolen. Lack of respect for other people's property (devotees or others) is epidemic-in fact, it is expected (underlined) that everything will be stolen.

I no longer have to live with cockroaches infesting my living quarters. I never saw one until I lived at the temple. I don't worry so much about communicable diseases, one of which was a very dangerous and sometimes lethal parasite. How do we expect the philosophy of Krishna consciousness to expand when even the people we consider uncivilized are shocked at our living conditions, cleanliness, and overall behavior?

It would seem that this inability or unwillingness to deal with problems, admit fault, and make corrections stems from the same paranoia that gives the society its self-righteous "us" and "them" outlook. Everyone on the outside, to a large extent, is seen as an enemy-envious, and out to destroy the society. Of course, if this attitude persists, more and more people will (underlined) take umbrage at this kind of behavior. We should be developing an open, giving, spiritual (underlined) mood, not viewing each individual as being worth a certain amount. This man might give me $20.00, this one $1,000.00. He can do this for me-she's not worth the time of day. This would definitely seem like material vision. Of course, devotees treat each other in much the same fashion-he's a $300.00/day man; she's a $500.00/day mother; he's in "Maya". For the nonmanagerial devotee, one's spiritual advancement is gauged according to how much money one can provide. As the temple president is so fond of saying, "money is (underlined) the honey."

One other main thrust that critics of the movement point out is that "cults" (ISKCON included) are against the family. ISKCON denies this charge vehemently, but the reality is that families are tolerated as long as family ties don't interfere with the temple's absolute control. If the husband and wife are "Sankirtan" devotees, then the temple management conspires to keep them apart-for monetary reasons, of course. Usually there is no family unity, as the children no longer live at home and are no longer under the control of the parents, and husband and wife are encouraged to betray their spouse. In my case, this is born out, as I am sure you can recall the trip my wife has been writing to you. Nice girl, but unfortunately a little simple. The temple has her innly under control. It is a very unfortunate position when the temple encourages a mother not to look after her children and family duties; when a husband cannot trust his wife.

The temple gives her increasing amounts of service so that, instead of teaching our deaf son, she is working all hours of the day and night. The temple was fully aware of the situation-what did they care! They only know how to manipulate trusting souls for their own benefit. She will probably realize it some day when they no longer see any value in her service, and she is cast aside.

However, not able to endure this situation for any longer, I re-enrolled Ravi at the special school. He is much happier now as opposed to doing nothing, but he is still very far behind as a result of this meddling by the temple. The situation is still completely unresolved as she gets up at 1:15 a.m. and, after the morning, is still loaded down with work. When she should be looking after the children, she is so tired she falls asleep either all morning or afternoon.

Gopal Krishna Maharaja (in whom I have no faith whatsoever) told my wife that there is "no question of giving up any service," and "Krishna will take care of the children."

In which case it would seem to make more sense for my wife, if she wants to live the completely monastic life, to go with you to your zone. If that's what she wants, and, at the moment it seems to be that family life is just a tedious barricade, then I would trust you to look after her more than this lot here.

I take family responsibility more seriously than the current ISKCON status quo and can handle things quite well-I have up to now anyway. I just wish I had taken matters into my own hands before now.

Regarding my recent trip to see you in Washington, I too was sorry not to spend some time with you. I was told that everything had been arranged (foolish me to believe such a thing!). I was to spend some time serving you. Instead, the local temple commander hunted me everywhere-apparently I was the most likely candidate for solo kitchen cut-up. Broccoli, and we still can't look each other steadily in the eye! When I saw you in the temple room the second morning, and we exchanged a few words briefly, I could understand that you were honestly glad to see me. At last somebody who is not interested in exploiting me in some fashion. Every morning I went to see Baladev. Each morning I was told that you were too busy (which I could fully appreciate). I was also told that on Tuesday you were leaving early in the morning for Baltimore-so that seemed to be that. Also there were other difficulties-minor in themselves, but collected together and given the answer that there was no chance of seeing you, made it rather silly to hang around. I was staying in the brahmacari asrama, and, between the late-nighters and the early-risers, I was not getting any sleep. I was also suffering the ill effects of hay fever, probably owing to the warmer more humid weather. Kitchen cut-up didn't help either. It seems by being told that I left in anger, you were the victim of a case of "story telling" or at least exaggeration. I would view information coming from the same source with a little more scrutiny in the future.

I am very sad to hear of your recent ill health. I hope that this will pass very quickly, because your energy, in my view, is absolutely necessary in saving pure Krishna consciousness from ensuing extinction. I hope I have not offended you by speaking candidly. Most people that I know, who for one reason or other, find themselves on the "outside" of ISKCON, told me that I was wasting my time to put the truth down on paper. Nobody wants to bear it-they all want to play "let's pretend". But it's too important for that. I want to be involved with a movement that I can stand up and say, "Yes, I support these people 100 percent." Nowadays, everything I hear makes the situation look worse. Now the temple presidents are making a power play. The more distance I put between the society and me-the less of this I will hear about.

My thanks for your patience and purity. My best regards.

Your fallen but not forgetful disciple, Radhanath dasa

# BOGUS ISKCON GURUS

Bhaktibhusana Sucandra Stefan Kess

Bhakti Charu bogus Swami

Prithu das crook and snake

Bhaktivaibhav Avinas Chandra

Bir Krishna das Goswami.

Bhaktitirtha Swami -dead

Kadamba-kanana Swami

Gunagrahi Swami

Gopal Krishna Swami

Hridayananda Swami

Kavichandra Swami

Jayadvaita Swami

Lokanath Swami

Ravindra Swarup Swami

Bhaktimarga Swami

Rocana das

Radhanath Murderer

Prabhavishnu bogus Sex Swami

Shivaram obnoxious Swami

Suhotra Swami - dead

Tamal Krishna Goswami - dead

Satsvarupa Goswami - mad

Sachidananda slimy Swami

Trivikram Swami

Jayatirtha das - dead

Bhavananda Swami Homo-Sex-Guru

Hansadutta Swami

Kirtanananda murder Swami

Ramesvara das

Bhagavan das

fat Jayapatka potatoe Swami

Badrinarayan

Dhanudhar Swami

Dharmatma Dennis Gorrick

Kuladri das

Paramadvaiti Alanath

Bhakti-Purusottama Swami

Svarupa Damodara Swami - dead

Bhakti-Chaitanya Swami

Indradyumna Swami

Bhaktisidhanta Swami

Bhakti-Vidya-Purna Swami

Bhakti-Vashrambha Madhava_Swami.

Bhanu Swami

BVV-Narasimha Swami

Danavir Goswami

Devamrita swami.

Bhaktivikasha Swami.

Guru-prasad swami William S. Henricks

Govinda Swami.

Dhanvantari swami

Bhakti Bringa Govinda-Maharaj

Krishna-Smitha-Swami

Partha Sarathi

Raradhagovinda Swami

Ramai Swami

Rohini Suta Knucklehead

Romapada Swami.

Subhag Swami

Paramgati Swami Homo sex guru

Praghosa das Iskcon GBC Clown

Prahladananda Swami

Chandramukha Swami

Braja Bihari Das

Maha Visnu Swami

Vedavyasa das
Christian Jansen

Malati dd

Virabahu
Marcos Zafarani

Tripurari Swami

Harikesa Swami
Robert Campagnola

Anuttama das

Hari Sauri
illicit sex ex-sinyasi

NitaiChand Nityananda Sil
Homo-Sex-Child molester

Jadurani dd
Syamarani didi

Sridhara
Swami - dead

Giriraj Swami

More bogus Iskcon Gurus Swamis Sannyasis

Sri Galima
Gary Gardner

Murali-Krsna-
Bogus Swami

Tirtha das Swami
devotee murderer

Umapati Swami
gave Sannyas to Tirtha

Tapapunja Swami
Terry Sheldon

Bhurijan
child abuser

APPENDIX 8

# SOME OBSERVANCES ON THE LATTER-DAY GURUS

A Rational and Ethical View of Guru Since Prabhupada's Departure by Rohini Kumar Swami

On November 14th, 1977 in Vrndavana, India, His Divine Grace A. C. Bhaktivedanta Swami Prabhupada returned to the spiritual world. For this world his passing away marked the end of one era and the beginning of another. At our center at 26th Second Ave., Srila Prabhupada, when asked who would be the next acarya after him stated, "There will not be any more acaryas." The word acarya is used in several senses. Its first and primary meaning is "one who teaches by example." Its other outstanding meaning is the spiritual master of a particular period, one who stands out among all others by his full comprehension of the scriptures, like Madhav, Jiva Goswami, Baladeva Vidyabhusana, Bhaktivinode Thakura, Bhaktisiddhanta Sarasvati and Srila Prabhupada, or else one who is completely absorbed in relishing the bliss of God consciousness at every moment, such as Madhavendra Puri, Narottama dasa Thakura, Bhaktisiddhanta Sarasvati and Srila Prabhupada. In other words, Srila Prabhupada exemplified both. The acarya does not talk effervescent and flowery words that sound beautiful but cannot quite be understood or explained. (This, as can be seen, is the usual manner of the typical bogus sahajiya and Mayavadi gurus in India.) The acarya is practical and down to earth. He does not have his head in the clouds as if in some imaginative lila. His mind is fixed on Krishna in the spiritual world, but he is also simultaneously aware of the exigencies of the world around him. Although he has all the vast wealth of Vedic knowledge at his disposal, he presents it always in a logical, comprehensive and clear way-he does not try to be abstruse, esoteric or talk above the heads of his listeners. Those who do so are either eccentric or simply trying to impress others with their "higher knowledge."

The acarya is always a diksa-guru, but even among many diksa-gurus at any given time there may not be such an outstanding acarya. Thus the lack of a great acarya at certain times does not mean that a sampradaya ceases to exist or becomes broken. Rather it is carried on by the regular diksa-gurus, and with time another great acarya manifests himself. Thus it is seen in the Ramanuja sampradaya and in the Madhava sampradaya that there were times when there was not great acaryas, though their lines of disciplic succession have continued always by the many diksa-gurus. When Srila Prabhupada passed away in the fall of 1977 there was a void created in ISKCON. There was no acarya and there was no diksa-guru. At the next Mayapura festival the entire GBC body convened to decide how to continue our parampara. Obviously there had to be gurus to initiate the new devotees that were joining. Since Srila Prabhupada had appointed eleven ritviks to initiate on his behalf while he was still living, it was naturally assumed that these ritviks above everyone else held an unequalable mandate from Srila Prabhupada to be gurus. Since Srila Prabhupada had recommended that the devotees consult Sridhara Swami in Navadvipa if there was need for advice on basic Vaisnava procedures, several representatives from the GBC went to ask him how the eleven ritviks should go about assuming the position of guru. Sridhara advised that it begin in a very simple and humble fashion. I remember listening to the tape, how one of the GBCs was asking about pranama prayers for the new gurus, whether it was all right to use "nama om vishnu padaya" or not. Sridhara Maharaja simply said, "Om ajnana timirandhasya' is enough. Later the disciples can write a mantra according to how the guru reveals himself. The pranama prayer should be composed in Sanskrit that is both grammatically and metrically correct." But the GBC representatives instead continued to press on, "Oh, then it is all right to use 'nama om vishnu padaya." It was by the continual insistence of this particular GBC man that the use of nama om vishnu padaya became the standard prayer of all ISKCON gurus in imitation of Srila Prabhupada's pranama prayer, even though in almost all cases the particular guru's name is either too short or too long, thus rendering the standardized prayer metrically incorrect.

The problem, therefore, seems to be that since Srila Prabhupada was the only example of a guru and acarya that the devotees knew, they naturally presumed that whoever was to be a bona fide guru would have to exactly imitate him in every way. Failure to do this would render one suspect of not being up to the standard set by Srila Prabhupada. Of course, this external imitation of prayers, titles, big vyasasanas, lavish guru-pujas, living quarters, personal comforts, etc., does not automatically make one infallible like Srila Prabhupada. To imitate him does not make one as good as him, just as imitating Siva or Krishna does not make one equal to them. And just as the imitators of Siva cannot drink an ocean of poison, nor the imitators of Krishna lift Govardhana hill, the imitators of Srila Prabhupada have not been able to maintain ISKCON as Srila Prabhupada did, with the result that the majority of Srila Prabhupada's dear disciples have left his movement, while the movement itself has been shaken to its very foundation by feuds, rivalries, and schisms. Yet, it is not that there is anything wrong with ISKCON having diksa-gurus, but that there is something fundamentally wrong with the way we have pursued it.

The entire history of mankind is full of stories of how money, women, power, prestige, honor and worship have corrupted the best of men, even highly advanced spiritual persons. The great acarya is such a person that even in the midst of these dangerous situations he is not overcome by them. But unless one is such a great acarya on the level of the Goswamis, Narottama dasa, Baladeva, Bhaktivinoda, Bhaktisiddhanta and Srila Prabhupada, then one had better avoid these temptations as far as possible. The guru is a preacher. He delivers Srila Prabhupada's teachings and gives the holy name of Krishna. Not that he is the enjoyer of the assets and adulation of his disciples.

We must face the facts: even a thousand gurus (of the present standard) cannot equal Srila Prabhupada or replace him. Since Srila Prabhupada was an uttama-adhikari or pure devotee and he had said so many times that a guru must be of such caliber, it was assumed that the gurus who succeeded Srila Prabhupada would have to somehow be uttama-adhikaris. Therefore, in a convened meeting the GBC unanimously conferred upon the new gurus the rubber stamp status of "pure devotee." But is it possible that by a vote of the GBC that someone who was previously just a regular madhyama-adhikari, at best, can instantly become an uttama-adhikari? It is the height of folly for someone to think himself an uttama-adhikari, for as soon as one does one cannot be one. Although All ISKCON members are pure devotees in the sense that they refrain from all sinful activities and regularly chant 16 rounds, none of us are uttama-adhikaris or pure devotees of the type exemplified by Srila Prabhupada and the other previous great acaryas. Simply receiving the title of guru does not make one an uttama-adhikari. What then should be the position of ISKCON gurus after Srila Prabhupada. In light of the numerous ways in which we presently fall short of the mark of uttama-adhikari, anyone who accepts the position of guru should be understood to be merely a vyavaharika-guru, or a conventional priest authorized to give initiation into the chanting of the holy name. Such gurus must also make their disciples understand their position. They should be honest enough to say "I did not create ISKCON. Srila Prabhupada did. And every project in ISKCON is simply the manifestation of his energy. It is not that because of what I have done ISKCON has become so great. Whether I became a devotee or not would not have mattered. Everything still would have been achieved because it is really Srila Prabhupada who did it all. I was only one of many instruments, and after all, instruments are always dispensable. I cannot do what Srila Prabhupada has done. All I can do is give you the same mantra that he gave me. I personally cannot save you. But if you chant this mantra and study Srila Prabhupada's teachings as preserved in his books, then despite my own imperfections and shortcomings, you will be able to go back to Godhead because Srila Prabhupada will take you back." In this way, if the vyavaharika-guru has some difficulties, as we have already seen in ISKCON, there will be no great cause of distress for the disciples and the society in general because everyone actually understands their relationship with each other and with the vyavaharika-gurus and of everyone with the great acarya, Srila Prabhupada.

The creation of eleven gurus in ISKCON has proven to be the most divisive and destructive event in the history of ISKCON. It has caused a polarization of ISKCON into areas of influence: "This is so and so's temple. He's the guru here. If you don't like it, get out!" Thus Srila Prabhupada's disciples were made to feel like foreigners in their own temples. No wonder the majority of them have left! With the installment of eleven gurus in different regions, ISKCON ceased to be one movement, as it had been under Srila Prabhupada, but instead became eleven little ISKCONs each with its own little guru as the absolute authority. It was therefore unavoidable that there would be rivalry, schism and excommunications. How should ISKCON have acted in order to avoid this polarizing effect that ultimately ends in disunity and schism? Well, if we examine how other Vaisnava sampradayas have dealt with the problem we might be able to learn something. The Ramanuja and Madhava sampradaya have both adopted the same formula. In their temples there is only one guru present, that is, their own respective founding acarya as either Ramanuja or Madhava. ALL the gurus who succeeded them have their own ashramas outside the temple and it is in those ashramas that the disciples offer respects to their gurus. In this way the temples remain the center of worship for everyone in the sampradaya, regardless of who the gurus are. Thus, although sectarian differences have sometimes arisen in these sampradayas, the temples have remained nonsectarian and the neutral ground where all could worship the Supreme Lord.

If anyone reads the *Caitanya-caritamrta* he will see the great love and trust that existed between the different gurus. They often sent their disciples to other gurus to be trained up in the philosophy. On the other hand, in our present ISKCON we have the gurus say, "Don't listen to anybody's tapes but mine. I don't want you going to any other temple because you will become confused, bewildered and will fall down, etc." Has everyone forgotten that it is only Srila Prabhupada who can save the fallen souls and is also saving us? Instead of pushing the successor gurus on the new disciples they should be giving them Srila Prabhupada, just as we were given him when we joined. what could be offensive in instituting such a program? By it we only gain to have a unified ISKCON that will continue to be so indefinitely. Otherwise, ISKCON will eventually deteriorate into another mess like Christianity with schisms, crusades, and inquisitions, and does the world need another burden like that. Everyone should be aware of the real issue. It is not a matter of eleven gurus, or of one thousand, it is a matter of the present method. Sometimes it is seen that the limbs of a tree grow too large, with the result that they slump down, crack, or even break off. The only remedy for this is to trim the limbs back. This is exactly what must be done with ISKCON. We have to trim back the artificially over-blown position of diksa-gurus in ISKCON to a position that is safe and healthy for the survival of one unified ISKCON in the future. To do so I suggest the following proposals:

1) In all ISKCON temples, which are, after all, Srila Prabhupada's temples, there should only be a big vyasasana for Srila Prabhupada. There may be a modest, unimposing asana in the temple room for the vyavaharika-guru to speak from. In fact, this same asana may be used by all those who represent Srila Vyasadeva by preaching Krishna consciousness and following the four regulative principles.

2) Only Srila Prabhupada's pictures be in the temple room and on the altar.

3) Only Srila Prabhupada's name and pranama prayer should be chanted in the temple.

4) A suitable room or asrama be set up where the vyavaharika-guru and his disciples can have intimacy together in the form of darsanas, vyasasanas, pictures, chanting of the guru's name and pranama prayer, guru-puja, etc.

5) During kirtan in the temple the title "gurudeva" can be chanted to indicate the particular guru or gurus at that temple and respects can be offered them by

chanting om ajnana timirandhasya. Since this mantra is used to offer respect to all bona fide gurus within our discliplic succession, to use it for the vyavaharika-gurus is also perfect (if they are bona fide). In this way, no one will be made to feel that they are not allowed to offer proper respects to their guru, and at the same time, while chanting it no one will feel that they are being forced to offer respects to someone who is not their guru.

6) Although presently all vyavaharika-gurus are sannyasis, since it is permissible that even householders be diksa-gurus, when reciting the jaya dhvani at the end of kirtan one may offer them respects by saying: sad gurudeva ki jai! or some other simple arrangement. This is necessary because those vyavaharika-gurus who are householders cannot be addressed with the sannyasa titles in the usual formula as jaya om visnupada etc.

7) The vyavaharika-guru should always be explicit about his position as such and not pretend to be something which he is not, such as an uttama-adhikari, the one great acarya, etc. Of course, it may not be possible to institute all these principles immediately, but they must be eventually if ISKCON is to survive as one unified movement. If these principles are established, then no matter how many gurus there are, ISKCON will remain one movement united around Srila Prabhupada the acarya and founder of ISKCON, and will remain so for all future generations of devotees. All glories to Srila Prabhupada! All glories to ISKCON.

Rohini Kumar Swami

Note: The above was composed in Berkeley with the sole aim of removing the bogus worship of Hansadutta from the temple proper. It was very successful. For personal and other reasons certain points were not emphasized at that time. Having discussed with Rohini Kumar Swami at some length on these points the following was concluded:

That the vyavaharika-guru must be, as Prabhupada says, "strictly following the principles himself." That means all the principles, not just the gross principles of no meat, sex (including homosex), drugs, and betting, but also no TV, movies, prajalpa, neglect of 16 rounds, ignorance of sastra, obnoxious behavior, stealing other men's wives, puffed up mentality, disrespect to Godbrothers, rock and roll "kirtana" bands, all association with women, if sannyasa, etc. Single women must wait for a husband to devote themselves to. In the meantime, they can find an advanced householder to take instruction from.

# ISKCON SEXPLOITATION TECHNIQUES

Excerpts from GBC commissioned document on exploitation

Compiled by Jagannatha Suta Dasa

March 10th, 1978

It is not so much that there are many reports of the breaking of regulative principles on these parties, but that the breaking of principles is being justified as necessary to push on Lord Caitanya's sankirtana movement. The philosophy that's being preached on these parties (either outrightly or subtly through rhetoric or innuendo) can be briefly summarized as follows: Any service outside of book distribution and laxmi collection is Maya. If a women's party member wishes to leave the party and do another service (cooking, Deity worship, etc.) she is told that if she leaves the party she will be cut off from Srila Prabhupada and Lord Caitanya's movement. If the women's party member is feeling the desire to marry, she is taught that to take a husband is a complete fall-down-her service will be finished because she will wind up 'serving the husband's senses.' Hence, only her party leader can engage her in Srila Prabhupada's service since any service outside book distribution is Maya. Since the party leader takes care of her and engages her in service, the girls consider him to be their "eternal husband." (This thinking is encouraged by the party leader.) If a woman wants to leave the party leader (her "husband") she is told that she is unchaste-a victim of "prostitute" mentality.

The party leader usually believes, and often preaches, that if a woman has some sexual agitation and wants to leave the party, it is better for her to relieve her desires within the framework of the party than to leave and get a husband. Hence, the party leader is not at all averse to showing her physical affection if that is what she needs to stay on the party. The philosophy is that if she must have sex-better to have it with the party leader because that way her sankirtana service will continue and she will gradually get purified. If however, she leaves to get married, her service is finished and she must live with the guilt of leaving her "real husband" (the party leader).

This philosophy of "the end justifies the means" does not end with the party leader's willingness to give the girls anything they need to stay on the party. In her interview with me, Mother Danistha (who spent three years on Jiva dasa's party as party coordinator) explains that when Jiva found out his wife Manini was pregnant, he told her (and instructed Mother Danistha to preach to her), that she should "dance hard at aratik" and "ride in bumpy vans" to see if it was "Krishna's desire" that she have the child. If she had the child her sankirtana service (and thus her connection with Srila Prabhupada and Lord Caitanya) would be finished.

It is this fanatical perversion of our philosophy that I wish the GBC to be aware of: That anything-having sex with the mothers, beating them, taking drugs-can be justified as being necessary to push on Lord Caitanya's sankirtana movement.

All of the above aforementioned claims are verified in the following reports. Please read each carefully (especially Mother Danistha's). I also request you to carefully study the section entitled the Positive Alternative. It includes a very insightful interview with Mother Sadhvi (number one big book distributor in Seattle yatra).

During Srila Prabhupada's last days on the planet, Ramesvara Maharaja informed His Divine Grace about the Laguna Beach drug scandal and the sensational headlines it was making. Ramesvara Maharaja told me that Srila Prabhupada said we should be so careful-we could ruin everything.

It is in the same spirit that I humbly appeal to the GBC to deal with the present situation so that we can avoid any unnecessary embarrassment to Lord Caitanya's Sankirtana movement.

I hope this meets you all well and increasingly absorbed in Srila Prabhupada's loving service.

Your servant,

Jagannatha Suta dasa

General manager-BBT Press


**Excerpts from Interview with Dhanistha Devi Dasi**

Ex-member of Jiva dasa's party

Mother Dhanistha (MD): In the beginning on Jiva's party, he was very strict about his association with the women. Like he would stay in his room if we were changing clothes or nightgowns or if he was chanting japa. He'd just make sure that there was some space around him, you know, respectful space so that the devotees wouldn't become familiar. That was when we first started and a few girls, five or six. And then after he went to visit Dharmatma's party he was trying to learn, he and Manini and I went to Dharmatma's party in Pittsburgh. It was right at the beginning of the party, maybe a year and a half, almost two years ago. After he visited Dharmatma's party. The purpose was to find out how his women did so big. Like he has Mother Mahara, and so many devotees who were doing very nicely, always fired up. Dharmatma's main explanation of why they were doing so big was that they had a satisfying situation, like a relationship with him. The party leader taking a position of husband, friend, advisor, they could take shelter of him.

So if they had any problems they could always feel that they could go to him and they'd have some shelter. Plus it kept their idea of having to get married, and find a husband or something, kept that suppressed so they could do sankirtana.

So Jiva, he just, he was always comparing Dharmatma's situation to his situation, how he could improve the mother's parties. So Dharmatma was saying then they feel secure and then they can carry on their service. And Jiva was always wanting to know what his relationship was with the women, how intimate he was with them, like that.

Jagannatha Suta (JS): Jiva was wanting to know Dharmatma's-.

MD: Yes, Dharmatma's relationship with the women. So Dharmatma told him that *you cannot explain this to the other devotees,* you know, that aren't in a party situation like this. They won't be able to understand the nature of women and they're not getting-like-we're being empowered to do this service by Lord Caitanya so that women can engage nicely in Krishna's service. Sometimes, he said, you're going to find-he'd (Dharmatma) been doing the party for awhile, two years, maybe longer-and he said you're going to find that they're going to need affection, personal association with you. So if you give them that, they'd be satisfied and peaceful. Because they are by nature so lusty that they can't, you know, unless they have this affection, this personal association, their minds become disturbed. So Jiva was, Jiva was taking everything in as being absolute, because he could see the results of their sankirtana was very nice.

JS: How did you know this was going on, how did you know Dharmatma was telling him this?

MD: Jiva told me. He would tell me everything. So Jiva would ask him, "What do you give them that they need?" He said, "Well, I just give them anything that they need to go ahead and conduct their service......" And he would dress in front of them and things like that while Jiva was there. He'd be putting on his clothes and a devotee would come in to speak to him, he'd continue putting on his clothes, you know.

JS: A woman?

MD: Yes, one of the mothers. And Jiva said it was just real natural, that there was no agitation. But it didn't ever seem possible to me. But he said this way, if they become that familiar then they feel safe because they feel that they have an obligation to remain chaste to someone who's like their husband. They feel some security there in that kind of intimate relationship. So when we came back-also he had never hit the women before, jiva, not to my knowledge. But after visiting Dharmatma, he'd found that Dharmatma would sometimes hit the women or slap them, something to, he said that in certain situations this is what they need in order to bring them back, you know, if they get too offensive or so rebellious against following instruction they should be hit or beaten or whatever. And it was emphasized that this was an important part of their program. So when Jiva came back then he would, he just gradually started getting heavier with the women as far as, if they didn't follow instructions. I don't remember any specific incidents.

JS: If they were anything less than fully surrendered.

MD: Yes. Yes. Karuna basically I guess was a prime example. I just remember after she first came, after a couple of months or so in the movement, she was, she wouldn't follow some instruction, I don't know what it was, but he hit her really hard in the face and bloodied her nose. That happened a few times with her. It was just gradually going that way, the devotees, if they got really-just refused to obey an instruction-after a certain amount of time he would hit them. Some devotees he wouldn't at all. He'd relate differently with each individual devotee. And he said that he was trying to be instruction by Krishna what to do.

It was so they would have respect. He said there's two things he dislikes the most and that's disloyalty and disrespect. So if the devotees weren't cooperating he'd set an example and hit them. It wasn't really frequent, I mean once in a while but there were a few intense incidents over the past year or so. One time Mother Kusala was, I don't know the situation, she was in the kitchen and Jiva was there. She just refused to obey an instruction and she was very offensive in her attitude. She didn't say anything but she was just refusing to follow an instruction for some reason. And he started to hit her but she blocked. It was just like a reflex, that she started to hit back or something. And that made Jiva very angry and so he hit her pretty hard in the face with his fist or the back of his hand maybe. But that's not-what happened is she hit up against the windowsill and it cut her arm very much, she had to get some stitches. It knocked her out a few minutes. That happened with her....

JS: What was it that you felt that you couldn't do some other service?

MD: Because any other service, other than sankirtana, if you were a sankirtana devotee, was just a falldown.

JS: Even if you want to do Deity worship that was considered a falldown?

MD: Yes. Because Sankirtana's the highest, preaching is the highest service. So Nada was really wanting to get married that time and she approached him and told him she was going to leave the party, she wanted to get married. So at first he was indifferent, you know, she didn't know how to react because she actually had no where else to go. Then he saw that she was still determined and so he became real angry and he just really beat her up. And, he broke her arm. Maybe two months before I left. But he told me that she tripped over a cord and Campak was there and she also told me that same thing.... So I was just preaching to her basic philosophy like that, and that's when she told me personally that Jiva had actually broken her arm.

Tusita said she would see him take ten pills of codeine, the mothers would feed it to him. She said she saw that. He would have the mothers go in and get codeine for him at the hospital at the emergency room. It was very easy to get with this prescription, Campak had a prescription for a large amount.

Satsvarupa would come and give classes, glorifying the party, you know. So with the stamp of approval of the GBCs and temple presidents and as a result I was just suppressing it because Jiva preaches the philosophy that we're so fallen that we'll never become purified without a gradual process taking place.

# "BHAKTIPADA WAS RIGHT THERE."

### Conversation with Mother Mahara, Sept. 1984

Mother Mahara was the largest collector at New Vrindaban for many years. She must have donated over half a million dollars in that time and so naturally she was dearly loved and respected by all-until she discovered what follows.

Mother Mahara: I was bewildered a long time about New Vrindaban. When I left it I had a hard time not going back. I wanted to go back, but the devotees would preach to me. And I'm glad I didn't go back, because I'm so much more sane now than I was before.

Sulocana dasa: I heard you'd made a statement that they don't let you learn anything there-just out on the pick.

MM: All you do...all I did was went out on the pick. No sadhana hardly at all.

SD: Is that true Dharmatma has sex with most of the women?

MM: Yep, a lot of them. He told one little girl to have an abortion that he had sex with.

SD: Really?

MM: Yep.

SD: Do you know that for a fact?

MM: I know it for a fact.

SD: Wow!

MM: Bhaktipada was right there.

SD: He approved it?

MM: Yeah. That's why I went to the GBC.

SD: What has the GBC done-anything?

MM: Yeah, well, they're separating the women now from Dharmatma. But I don't think all the women know even, about that. I don't care anymore. You know. I just feel that Prabhupada protected me and I feel I'm luckier than them because now I know. Srila Ramesvara is into book distribution but there is not much book distribution going on at New Vrindavana. But there's a lot of great devotees there-l love Kutila-she's great. I learned a lot from what I did, I performed a lot of austerities and Krishna's rewarding me now with all this nectar. I know more now about what Krishna consciousness is all about. I go on book distribution and preaching.

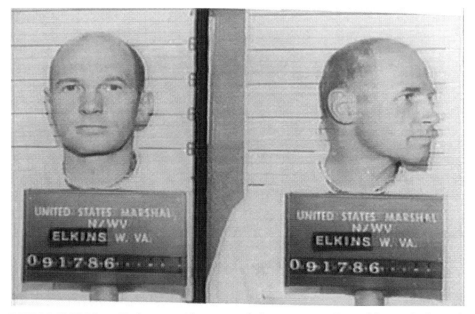

DHARMATMA - Had sex with most of the women. He told one little girl to have an abortion that he had sex with and Kirtanananda approved it!

Sept. 6, 1985  - INTERVIEW ON

# THE SUBTLE SEX LIFE OF HRIDAYANANDA "SWAMI"

Introductory note by the devotee being interviewed:

Ever since ISKCON has entered the present era of "appointed paramahansas," I have been deeply aggrieved that for the first time in my devotional career, I have had to participate in a lie. In my opinion, this has hurt our beloved ISKCON to the core. I suppose one of the motives in this "guru conspiracy" has been to keep ISKCON cohesive. But the perpetrators have failed to realize that only Srila Prabhupada, ISKCON's founder/acarya, can keep ISKCON united. The mundane plan of materially motivated men can never be the foundation for a solid, honest spiritual movement.

Anyway, I have allowed myself to be interviewed not to accuse a beloved Godbrother of mine, but to expose a false, injurious system which has destroyed countless spiritual lives and is quickly sending ISKCON to its demise. If I mention any faults in my Godbrother, I humbly beg his pardon and openly admit that I have many more faults to a much greater degree. But I have put myself on the line in order to be counted among those who strongly oppose the present system and want to see it replaced with something in line with Srila Prabhupada's books.

Sulocana dasa (SD): How long did you live in the Miami temple?

Anonymous Devotee (AD): Close to a year.

SD: And you were working for Hrdayananda?

AD: Yes. I was managing the book production for a while.

SD: When did you get married?

AD: 1983.

SD: Your wife is a disciple of Prabhupada?

AD: Yes.

SD: Was she married before?

AD: No.

SD: Where were you serving before you went to Miami?

AD: Philadelphia. I worked on Back to Godhead for three years.

SD: So while you were living in Miami were you and your wife getting along?

AD: Yes, we were basically pretty compatible.

SD: What is your relationship with Hrdayananda? Are you friendly with him?

AD: He and I have a long term friendship actually. During most of my Krishna conscious life I was working in his zone. I was always very close to him, like a close ally since we're good friends.

SD: So over the years, didn't you ever detect that he wasn't a pure devotee and shouldn't be worshipped like that?

AD: He's straight with me about his position. He has often intimated to me that it has been a struggle for him to maintain celibacy. Sometimes when he has preached very, very heavily against householder life, he would tell me that it was partly just to convince himself. To my knowledge-this is my opinion based upon my analysis of his character-l don't think that he has physically violated the principle of sannyasa. I trust him to that degree, although I know that he has had to struggle very, very hard.

SD: But he did have a young woman for a personal secretary that practically lived with him, didn't he?

AD: Well, let's put it this way: He definitely showed signs that he had become attached to her. He got her married once, twice, thrice to different disciples. Finally on the third marriage I think she is in the care of her husband. I don't know the details of why the first two didn't work. This is probably the first time he's not involving her in his personal project. She is a little intelligent. She was a lawyer in Brazil and so she actually could render valuable help in his personal projects (like the philosophy book and so forth) so that meant a lot of personal contact. Of course, I haven't been there for a couple of years, but just based on what I hear, this is the first time that he's actually gotten her out from under him and she's not working on his project; she's apparently assisting her husband.

SD: So the rumors that she was massaging him are not necessarily true?

AD: I don't think so. I would say that his main difficulty was on the subtle platform. If I were to go before the Deity and say what I thought was going on, I'd say that I don't think there was any physical breaking of the principles but he was definitely becoming attached to her. The temple practically became a shambles over it. Because his disciples knew-but then they didn't know-so they blamed her or they blamed circumstances.

SD: What about the Godbrothers. Didn't they think that was kind of unusual?

AD: Definitely. When any householder Godbrothers went to him he would just say, "Well, it's just your wives. They're envious and they're influencing you. Don't be offensive like this." Finally what put a stop to it was when two respected Brahmacaris on his BBT staff, Dravida and Danevara, went to him and said, "This is bogus, it has got to stop." And so he basically came to terms with it and gave it up.

SD: He actually gave it up then?

AD: Yes. I think he came clean. He's been much happier since then.

SD: So Hrdayananda has always been a sort of passionate guy. His lectures are often full of graphic descriptions of sex life. So that obviously has been a problem in his mind.

AD: Yeah. His lectures in Miami were almost exclusively about vagina, husband and wife, and sex and sex, sex, sex.... Prabhupada would speak about these things occasionally but Hrdayananda was *always* speaking about them, so it was obvious to me anyway, as a Godbrother and as a friend of his, that he was struggling himself. So, no, I've never been under the illusion that he's a paramahamsa and he's never really tried to play paramahamsa with me, although he does demand a lot of respect.

SD: When you were there in Miami, did he interfere in marriages the way so many of these gurus do? Did he directly tell a woman to leave her husband if the husband didn't worship him?

AD: This is something I don't really like to talk about. I realize that it's not heavy stuff, but for the sake of what you're doing I'm willing to talk about it. He's very attractive to women. I never saw him fall down, but even on his vyasasana during japa he would constantly, before public view be calling women up and talking to them. I guess he was thinking that because it was public it's all right. "I'm not hiding anything." Even before he was a guru and he was just sannyasa and GBC. Once there were two women in his room. He was speaking to them, and they were laughing up a storm. When they left I said, "Boy, a lot of joking was going on in here." You know, I was kind of criticizing him, and he said "but by that joking they will work happily for the next year." So just a straight character analysis-he loves talking to women. I don't hold it against him. Perhaps he took sannyasa prematurely, whatever, but he's a sannyasa anyway. So the general mood in Miami was that rather than the husband being the focal point of the wife-of the individual wives-Hrdayananda was the focal point. To a greater or lesser degrees, he would control the minds and the lives of the ladies.

SD: So in the case when both husband and wife were his disciples, that may not have caused so much of a conflict, but in the case of-.

AD: No. I would say that internally it's still a conflict because a man gets married because he wants a wife and he wants his wife to obey him.

SD: But it's not as much a conflict as when the husband is a disciple of Prabhupada and the wife is devoting herself to a Godbrother. Did that happen a lot also?

AD: Well it started happening in my case and I had to leave his zone to save my marriage. The devotees rented a very plush seaside apartment-literally-50 feet from the waves, in Tampa. It was very expensive. It was really a nice plush apartment with beautiful carpeting, furniture, what have you.

SD: What was this for? A preaching project?

AD: No. It was a writing project just so he could get away. He didn't have it for a long time maybe a month or so, but it was at a time when the Miami temple was struggling so hard, constantly fighting foreclosure. My wife took a natural liking to the philosophy book, which was in his hands and still is. So he needed help in tracking down professors, and so, in responding to her enthusiasm, he was firing her up. He invited the two of us to his Tampa place. Basically he wanted to speak to her-although he likes me-but basically he was getting her involved in the project and we were going to travel around and attract professors to his project. So this was summertime and he was in a very brief swimming suit. Minimum briefness for decency. And sometimes he would wear a straw cowboy hat. And he had a golden tan. So anyway he was lying down in a very, very plush living room, on a very plush couch in that one little brief bathing suit speaking to my wife who was seated on the plush rug. There was a servant walking in and out so it's not like they were alone in a room, but basically he was just talking along-lying down actually- in front of my wife, and flattering her, firing her up so to speak. Basically just like in a very-maybe not so subtle way-attracting her to him. You know a woman- when you flatter a woman-she loves you, and she becomes indebted. So that was the peak point that almost destroyed my marriage. He would talk her into going out on sankirtana. I knew she couldn't physically do it. She would go out in the Miami summer sun and come back with sun stroke and be laid up for a week or two. He fired her up to go out on sankirtana and I knew she shouldn't have.

So I went to him and I said look-we stayed on friendly terms (and I left on friendly terms cause I took it a lot on the cheek to maintain our friendship, and I still want to)-but I said she's not physically able to do this and if you fire her up on a false platform and she goes out, then she'll spend the next two weeks or more in bed. So I basically told him that if you want to engage her then please check with me. And he agreed. He finally agreed.

SD: He probably didn't consider her your wife but thought of her as his worshiper.

AD: Basically the way he treated her and everyone there was as his subject. And secondarily the husband was there just to kind of keep the wife in check so she would maybe not get too attracted to Hrdayananda but would obey him nicely. That's basically the role of the husband. To assist Hrdayananda in controlling the wife so she would do what he said. So as I said, I had to leave his zone.

SD: So his preaching was separating her from you?

AD: Oh. No question about it. It was destroying our marriage.

SD: So you just didn't feel anything with her anymore? She was just interested in him and wanted to work for him?

AD: Well-I just nipped it in the bud. I had to scream at her a lot. It really made things rocky, but it was very obvious to me, and I wasn't going to let it happen. I wasn't his disciple, whereas his disciples just have to swallow it. I know many of his disciples; I can't give any particular names, but I know many of the disciples don't like it.

SD: Is there a big divorce rate in his zone?

AD: There are not that many devotees to be able to calculate as far as I know. When I was there it wasn't growing. They were not making new devotees.

SD: Any more comment about the Brazilian girl?

AD: He was not innocent as far as her intentions. I heard it said that he mentioned she was prepared to wait seven lifetimes to get him. This was said in jest of course, but it indicated her mood; her motive was to get him. And I heard her say things like, "But Srila Acaryadeva, I love you." You know, it was supposedly said in the mood of a disciple expressing love for the guru. And he would say, "Well look, she's rendering better service than anyone else." So in the name of disciple-guru relationship, all kinds of subtle things were going on. The people who were most disturbed were the Godsisters of Hrdayananda who know how women work. It was painfully obvious to them that this woman was just laying a trap, and they were going crazy. When women see other women doing their thing on the big sannyasi-which will cause the whole thing to crumble, which will destroy the reputation of the Bhagavatams-they go crazy. And he would like really get down on these women. You just couldn't speak up, you couldn't be honest, because the situation is either you go along completely or get out.

There was one devotee there, Mahashakti, who was trying to set up a business. All right, so that's his inclination-let him set up a business. So right in Mahashakti's presence, during Bhagavatam class, Hrdayananda would talk so heavy against business, "What is this business?" Personally insulting him beyond belief. So eventually he left-this person left, that person left. Godbrothers could not stay there, because they weren't willing to play this game. And I personally know that some of the Prabhupada disciples who are there, who are an integral part of his translation, have just been dying to get out for years. But out of a sense of duty they stay. Gopiparandhana, who is actually the translator of the Bhagavatam-he gets a small mention since he's not a big shot-but he actually does all the translating.

SD: Hrdayananda just comments.

AD: He writes the purports and edits the translations.

SD: Don't the purports come from the commentaries of the acaryas?

AD: Yes. Gopi takes around five Sanskrit commentaries and translates them all. Then Hrdayananda synthesizes them. Gopi works very hard. I don't want to put thoughts into his brain, but I know that he and his wife have been very, very unhappy there for years. One thing about the Miami temple is that, to live in that building is like living in hell. I don't know, either the filth, or the noise- except when you go the eighth floor where the guru is. Then it's like you've gone to a heavenly planet. Everywhere else are roaches...

SD: So to change the subject. Prabhupada has clearly explained how there is gross, subtle, and spiritual manifestations. Hrdayananda's subtle sex seems like it should have been very obvious. Couldn't the devotees see that?

AD: Basically it's like everyone could see it, but there's kind of like a Maya-a mystique-which he casts over the whole scene. If you dared to think otherwise you were just vibed out of the place or thrown out.

SD: Were a lot of devotees outcast in that way?

AD: He's the kind of person where if you doubt him in the slightest, he takes very deep offense. He demands very high loyalty.

SD: Does he do like Kirtanananda and physically kick people out or have them beaten?

AD: Well, I think he's more principled. I think he's more of a Vaisnava than some of these others, at least from what I've heard of them. But he definitely uses a lot of very heavy mental power to get his way.

SD: Does he use four-letter words when he gets mad?

AD: No. He's quite gentlemanly in that regard. I've never heard him use four-letter words.

SD: Do you know of any specific instances where Hrdayananda actually destroyed a marriage?

AD: There is one instance of two disciples of Hrdayananda-he married them-the boy, Madhupandit, was American and the girl was Brazilian. Both basically good devotees. The boy had had some difficulty and left for a while, you know, he was sexually agitated. He finally came back and agreed to marry. He's a good steady sankirtana devotee, going out every day. So when they were married-basically Hrdayananda had this thing where he would hate the fact that somewhere in this temple there was a man and a woman-married of course-alone in a room. It would just drive him crazy.

SD: He told you that himself?

AD: It was just obvious. It was his mood. He instigated this whole campaign where men could not sleep in the same room as their wives, and practically they couldn't even *be* in the same room if the door was closed. The idea was to prevent illicit sex. First of all, I didn't know that there was illicit sex going on there. But what he did was produce this whole obsession with sex. That's when the illicit sex started. So I was talking about the young boy and girl. They got married and naturally they had sex. It's not the highest principle of marriage in Krishna consciousness, but they'd been abstaining for so long. So he got her pregnant. That's not a disturbance in society because they're married. But Hrdayananda got the girl fired up against the guy-he made the guy out to be her biggest enemy. He condemned the guy before the girl and for about a year she would not even speak to him. She figured the fact that she was pregnant by her husband was a curse. Usually when a woman gets pregnant by her husband in Vedic society, it's a great blessing. But because he got her pregnant, she hated him because of this whole mood in the temple against husband-wife relations.

SD: So what happened?

AD: We left, but I think they're finally speaking to each other-maybe they are even peacefully married. But I know for months and months the guy was suffering bitterly because his wife would not speak to him. She hated him.

SD: Was he mean to her or what?

AD: No. He's imperfect like everyone else but basically a good steady devotee. He got up every morning, went to mangala-aratik, chanted his rounds, spent all day at the airport doing sankirtana.

SD: He spent the whole day collecting money?

AD: He would bring in $100-$150-$200 a day.

SD: And Hrdayananda still condemned him just for having sex with his wife? Did he do that to a lot of devotees?

AD: Well I wouldn't say it was an isolated case but I would say it was a very marked case. The whole mood was that people who had been married for 8-10 years and had two or three kids-all of a sudden they couldn't sleep in the same room with their wives. They practically couldn't associate with their wives.

SD: Was that because it was a temple and sex was not allowed?

AD: No. Just like in the old New York building, there was a floor set aside for householder quarters where householders live. It was the same thing in Miami, but still he wouldn't allow husbands to sleep in the same room with their wives. Like when a mother says to her growing young boy: "Don't get into sex, sex is horrible, sex is this, sex is that." If anything, it caused devotees to think of sex more. They were all basically good devotees, so we were trying to figure out where all this illicit sex was going on.

When I first arrived in his zone, I was in Gainsville, and he unleashed all this heavy stuff. He'd say, "A man and a woman-when they are together in a room at night-there *must* be illicit sex, there must be." Almost like encouraging it. But basically what it was was a sannyasi interfering in the intimate affairs of even his Godbrother's and Godsister's marriages. I don't care if he's a GBC. That doesn't mean he is the lord of my marriage. He was stepping on territory where he had no right to tread.

**CONCLUSION:**

Here is the demoniac tragedy. A woman's greatest joy is to have a baby and a faithful husband but here we find a "guru" cursing the baby and destroying the marriage because of his own sexual hang-up. From this interview it is obvious to me anyway that Hrdayananda is burning to have gross sex with all these women, but he can't because of his artificial pose. So the baby represents somebody else's sex pleasure that he feels actually belongs to himself. After all, he's the supreme enjoyer in his zone. Everything there is meant for his pleasure. Right? That's the obvious psychology. The bogus guru thinks, "If I can't enjoy sex with all these lovely women who are so much in love with me, then nobody else can either, including the husband. After all, who is this husband compared to me. He's just a dog." All these bogus sannyasis posing as gurus suffer from this syndrome to one degree or another. Thus they have created hundreds of broken marriages, unwanted and neglected children, and a lot of suffering. They think they will be able to chant Hare Krishna and be immediately freed from the reaction of all this destruction but that is their illusion. Each life they've destroyed, they will have to take birth to get paid back. Then after maybe hundreds or thousands of lifetimes of suffering, they may get another opportunity to learn to chant Hare Krishna offenselessly. But since they are offending Srila Prabhupada, there is no telling when they will see the light of day again.

The devotee who gave this interview is a very sincere and humble devotee who has always strictly followed the regulative principles. He really didn't want to offend Hrdayananda. For the higher purpose of purifying ISKCON he has decided that truth is more important than the friendship of such men. As Prabhupada said in one letter, "If the criticism is honest, there is no cause for becoming upset." So in this mood, Hrdayananda should wake up and admit his shortcomings and immediately begin the process of atonement. He should begin by taking a vow to scrub floors and toilets in a ISKCON temple for the rest of his natural life. A vow of silence would also be appreciated. Maybe then he will get a human birth in his next life.

*"Hrdayananda's lectures were almost exclusively about vagina, husband and wife, and sex and sex, sex, sex."*

# THE REAL MAY & JUNE "APPOINTMENT" TRANSCRIPTS.

These two tape transcripts are the "evidence" used by the bogus gurus to fool their Godbrothers into thinking that they had been appointed gurus. This first version of the "appointment" tape is the one that appeared in both Ramesvara's book (Appendix 2), and Jadurani's 1980 expose of the "gurus" called *The Bona Fide Spiritual Master and the Disciple.* Therefore, this version is the only one to date that has been widely circulated. Since this version can easily be misinterpreted to sound like an appointment of "gurus," we can safely say that this transcript was made by the conspirators. We can only assume that Jadurani never had a copy of the actual tape. Because she quoted the bogus transcript in her book, most devotees reading it thought it to be a bona fide transcript.

## THE BOGUS MAY TAPE

Sat: Then our next question concerns initiations in the future, particularly at that time when you are no longer with us. We want to know how first and second initiation would be conducted.

SP: Yes. I shall recommend some of you, after this is settled up. I shall recommend some of you to act as officiating acarya.

Tam: Is that called ritvik-acarya?

SP: Ritvik. Yes.

Sat: Then what is the relationship of that person who gives the initiation and...?

SP: He's guru. He's guru.

Sat: But he does it on your behalf?

SP: Yes. That is formality. Because in my presence one should not become guru, so on my behalf. On my order, amara ajnaya guru hana, he is actually guru. But by my order.

Sat: So they may also be considered your disciples?

SP: Yes, they are or their disciples, but consider who...

Tam: No. he is asking that these ritvik-acaryas, they are officiating, giving diksa, the people who they give diksa to, whose disciples are they?

SP: They are his disciples.

Tam: They are his disciples?

SP: Who is initiating. His grand-disciple.

Sat: Then we have a question concerning...

SP: When I order you become guru, he becomes regular guru. That's all. He becomes disciple of my disciples. Just see.

## THE ACCURATE MAY TAPE

This version we have compiled is perfectly accurate in all detail-pauses, unclear words, etc. If the GBC has a version that is more clear, and can be heard better, then let them come forward with it now. Otherwise, when we say a segment of words is indistinguishable, that means that not only ourselves but numerous other devotees also could not make out what was being said. We have an excellent copy of the tape and are using the best equipment available.

Sat: Then our next question concerns initiations in the future, particularly at that time when you are no longer with us. We want to know how first and second initiation would be conducted.

SP: Yes. I shall recommend some of you, after this is settled up (local business that they had been discussing), I shall recommend some of you to act as officiating acarya.

Note: Here Prabhupada establishes that the following conversation is going to be about officiating gurus before his departure, not about gurus "at that time when he is no longer with us."

Tam: Is that called ritvik-acarya?

SP: Ritvik. Yes.

Sat: Then what is the relationship of that person who gives the initiation and-

Note: This is a meaningless question, and so Prabhupada didn't even wait for him to finish it. He "who gives" is guru-Srila Prabhupada. Satsvarupa was no doubt thinking of he who "officiates" the initiation but his wording was off. The ritvik does not "give" the initiation; he officiates the initiation. Satsvarupa's question is not clear, and so the answer cannot be confirmed to support any conclusion.

SP: -He's guru- He's guru.

Note: The first "He's guru" broke into Satsvarupa's words, and so Prabhupada repeated it. That's the only reason. Srila Prabhupada is simply stating his own relationship to his disciple; the one "who gives" the initiation is guru. It is possible that he was referring to the ritvik as being guru, but in that case it would mean siksa-guru. In many places Prabhupada said that his senior disciples may be taken as siksa-guru of the neophytes if they repeated perfectly what they have heard. Guru simply means teacher in this sense.

Sat: But-he does it on your behalf?

Note: Here Satsvarupa introduces the delusion. In his mind he interpreted the answer as meaning the ritvik is the initiating guru.

SP: Yes. That is formality. Because in my presence one should not become guru. So on my behalf. On my order, "amara ajnaya guru hana." (3 sec. pause) He's actually guru, but by my order.

Note: This is the most important answer. In fact it is so significant that at the end of this Appendix we quote the entire section in Caitanya-caritamrta where this quote comes from. Srila Prabhupada is being questioned as to what will be the system of guru after his departure. To this line of questioning Prabhupada quotes a verse from the Caitanya-caritamrta that elaborately explains how he is "actually a guru." Prabhupada is not going to recite the whole section for Satsvarupa right then and there. Satsvarupa knows how to read and so Prabhupada simply gave him the key words. Thus all Satsvarupa had to do was look it up. Prabhupada's intentions for guru after his departure are very clear. Anyone who can read can see who Prabhupada was appointing guru.

Sat: So they may also be considered your disciples?

Note: Here Satsvarupa further reveals the delusion he is in. He has now fully convinced himself that the new devotees are actually his own disciples.

SP:...(words)...they're disciples, but consider. (2 sec. pause) Who.

Note: Any interpretation of this partial statement is simply mental speculation. It is significant however that Prabhupada made this response in a tone of chastisement, as though he wanted Satsvarupa to give up his delusion. Tamala could see the confusion and so he interjected:

Tam: No. He is asking that these ritvik-acaryas... (Prabhupada: Hmmm)...they are officiating, giving diksa,...(hmmm)...the people who they give diksa to...(hmmm)...whose disciple are they?

Note: We have to give Tamala credit here for picking up that Satsvarupa is in delusion. Satsvarupa's questions were not at all in line with Prabhupada's answers and so Tamala wants to make it perfectly clear. Tamala's wording is very concise. It is also significant that three times during this question Prabhupada said, "Hmmm". Prabhupada was speaking very clearly at this time, and so there is no reason for any of this tape to be ambiguous-unless it was tampered with.

SP: They are (d)-his-disciples.

Note: just before the word "his" there is an unmistakable dip in sound. There can be no doubt that the word "his" was dubbed in; most likely in place of the word "my." Why would Prabhupada say "his" disciples to a clear question like Tamala's? Even if there were no dip, we would know that it was dubbed simply on the philosophical basis, but with the dip, there is no doubt. Who did the dubbing??

Tam: They are his disciples.

Note: This response confirms the dub. From the original bogus transcript, everyone thought Tamala was repeating what Prabhupada said. But that was an easy trick they thought they could get away with. This was not spoken as a question to Prabhupada as the bogus transcript led one to believe. This was immediately and softly spoken on the side to Satsvarupa simply confirming that the new devotees were Prabhupada's disciples. Had Prabhupada actually said "his disciples," then Tamala would have said to Satsvarupa, "They are our disciples." One word dubs are relatively easy but even then they couldn't make it perfect. Tamala is talking to Satsvarupa, so, when he says, "his disciples," Prabhupada is "his".

SP: Who is initiating. (3 sec. pause) His grand-disciple.

Sat: Yes. (5 sec. pause) Then we have a question conc-.

Note: Please keep in mind, Tamala had just told Satsvarupa that the new devotees were Prabhupada's disciples. That was very clear at this time. So even though these last words cannot be interpreted (cuts may have been made), Satsvarupa had heard all he wanted to and so is going on to the next question. Some tampering may have been done on all these sentences. Why would Satsvarupa have gone onto the next point? This last statement could not have made sense to him. Further questions would have been necessary. At least we could expect that Tamala would have been in there clarifying the statement further if there was even the slightest hint that he was going to be a guru. The whole conversation has very unnatural sound to it and so we know it was heavily tampered with. But as yet we have not found out who did it. But we win.

SP: When I order you become guru, he becomes regular guru. That's all.

Note: The GBC tried to interpret the following June tape as that "order" mentioned here as though Prabhupada had all of a sudden changed the whole philosophy and decided that pure devotees can be appointed after all. It is significant that Prabhupada uses the term "regular guru." As of yet we have not found an exact definition for that term from the books. It can be taken as a guru under regulations or as an ordinary guru which would mean siksa-guru. It can't possibly mean a diksa-guru since diksa-gurus are not appointed or ordered.

It is significant that all these answers are to Tamala's question-the first clear question. But the answers in this chopped up tape do not confirm any conclusion and so more is needed. So even though Prabhupada said, "that's all", they needed to add the following sentence to clinch the appointment theory.

SP: (7 sec. delay) He becomes...(inaudible word(s))...disciple of my disciple. (Click) just see.

Note: This fine is an obvious dub. Not only does the background noise drop out, but the speed and tone of Prabhupada's voice dramatically changes also. The "just see" is again in a radically different tone and volume from the previous words. This tape was the only "evidence" the "gurus" ever had to support their claim to divinity. This can be proven, and when it is, the conspirators will be facing serious charges in court.

Sat: Next we have a question about the GBC. (end tape)

Note: There are some very significant points to bring out about this tape. One is that Prabhupada's health and speech were not bad at this time and it would have been no problem to ask more specific questions to seek proper clarification. There are so many good reasons why it is obvious that this tape was tampered with. One is, if it was not tampered with, why was it not available to everyone? It was extremely well guarded. This would have been just the opposite if it actually said what they claimed. But because they were unable to make a good dubbing job, they kept it super-confidential. It is available, however, from DAS if anyone doubts the validity of this transcript. When Sridhar Maharaja told Jayapataka that a ritvik guru does not make one an initiating guru later, Jayapataka told Sridhar Maharaja, referring to this tape: "Prabhupada has given explicit desires." Sridhar Maharaja believed him, and from the conversation that immediately ensued, the entire bogus guru manifesto was compiled.

## JUNE TAPE

Tam: Srila Prabhupada, we are receiving a number of letters now. People are wanting to get initiated. So, up until now, since you were becoming ill, we asked them to wait.

SP: The local senior sannyasis can.

Tam: That's what we were doing formerly. The local GBC sannyasis were chanting on their beads and they were writing to Your Divine Grace. And you were giving a spiritual name. So should that process be resumed or should we...(There is an interlude where Tamala discusses the spiritual master taking the disciple's karma). That's why we've been asking everybody to wait. I just want to know if we should continue to wait some more time.

SP: No. Senior sannyasis.

Tam: So they should continue to...

SP: You can bring me a list of sannyasis, I will mark. You can do, Kirtanananda can do...(word?) Satsvarupa can do. So (pause) these three can do.

Tam: So supposing someone is in America. Should they simply write directly to Kirtanananda or Satsvarupa.

SP: Nearby. Jayatirtha can do.

Tam: Jayatirtha.

SP: (word?)...Bhagavan can do.

Tam: Bhagavan.

SP: And he can do also (pause). Harikesh.

Tam: Harikesh Maharaja.

SP: Five, six men divide. Who is nearest.

Tam: Who is nearest. So persons wouldn't have to write to Your Divine Grace. They could write directly to that person.

SP: (hmmm)

Tam: Actually, they are initiating the person on Your Divine Grace's behalf.

SP: Hmmm.

Tam: Those persons who are initiated are still your-.

SP: Second initiation. We shall think. Second.

Tam: This is for first initiation. Okay. And for second initiation, for the time being we should-.

SP: Again have to wait. Second initiation, that should be...

Tam: Some devotees are writing you now for second initiation. And I'm writing them to wait a while, because you are not well. So can I continue to tell them that?

SP: They can do second initiation.

Tam: By writing you?

SP: No. These men.

Tam: These men. They can also do second initiation. So there's no need for devotees to write to you for first and second initiation. They can write to the man nearest them. But all these persons are still your disciples. Anybody who would give initiation is doing so on your behalf.

SP: Yes.

Tam: You know that book I'm maintaining of all your disciples' names? Should I continue that?

SP: Hmmm.

Tam: So if someone gives initiation, like Harikesh Maharaja, he should send the person's name to us here, and I'll enter it in the book. (Long pause) Is there someone else in India that you want to do this.

SP: India I am here we shall see. In India-Jayapataka.

Tam: Jayapataka Maharaja.

SP: You are also in India. (Long pause) You can note down these names.

Tam: Yes, I have them. (The list is read, and Srila Prabhupada adds two more names-Hrdayananda and Ramesvara.

SP: (Long pause) So without waiting for me, whoever you consider deserves. That will depend on discretion.

Tam: On discretion.

SP: Yes.

Tam: That's for first and second initiations?

SP: Hmmm.

NOTE: One very obvious question: If it were clear from the May tape that the new initiates would be the disciples of the ritviks, then why was none of this mentioned in this June tape? Why was Tamala still trying to get Prabhupada to say something else? The answer is obvious. They hadn't yet conceived their plot and dubbed the May tape. There is no mention in this tape of the ritviks becoming anything special after Srila Prabhupada's departure. As such there is no question of construing an appointment of gurus from these two transcripts. But since the May tape was tampered with, not only is it not valid evidence, but it is conclusive evidence as to the demoniac nature of the "gurus"-just the opposite of the divine nature they claimed the tape represented.

Another significant point is that Bhavananda and Hansadutta were not named in this June tape. Their names appeared on the letter issued to all centers that Prabhupada signed, but they were not named in this tape. No doubt some "good reasons" were given to Prabhupada later on to include them even though Bhavananda had only a year previously been caught by Pippilai dasa pants down, having sex with a Bengali *boy* in Mayapur. Just months previously, Prabhupada had said that Hansadutta was "praying daily that I die so that he can become guru." Prabhupada was aware of the character of all these ritviks. Ritvik has no special authority whatsoever. He simply gives initiation on the guru's behalf. Otherwise why would Prabhupada say, "whoever is nearest." The common argument, introduced by Sridhar Maharaja is that, "Well, it only makes sense that if Prabhupada made them ritviks, they must be the most advanced devotees." Sridhar may have even been the first to introduce that idea even though two years previously Sridhar had said that ritvik implied no special position.

Aside from all that, Tamala Krishna has directly confessed (on tape) in the *Pyramid House Talks*, Dec. 3, 1980 that, "Actually, Prabhupada never appointed any gurus. He didn't appoint eleven gurus. He appointed eleven ritviks. He never appointed them gurus. Myself and the other GBC have done the greatest disservice to this movement the last three years because we *interpreted* the appointment of ritviks as the appointment of gurus."

The "gurus" placed a great deal of importance on this tape to substantiate their claims, but the fact is that this tape, at least in its present condition, is the least authoritative explanation of guru. But Prabhupada, seeing past, present, and future, knew that this tape would be used to exploit the devotees. And so within this tape he planted one very important line that gives us the all-important clue as to what is the authoritative explanation on the subject of guru after his departure. He gave that clue by quoting "amara ajnaya guru hana." Nowhere does Srila Prabhupada say that a bona fide guru, a guru who actually sees Krishna face to face, can be appointed. The statement, "He's actually guru, but by my order," simply means that everyone is ordered to become guru by repeating what Prabhupada has taught us. It is not necessary to wait to see Krishna face to face to become guru and preach. Everyone should preach immediately by repeating what Prabhupada and Lord Caitanya have spoken. That is the meaning of "amara ajnaya guru hana" as explained below by Prabhupada. Everyone must preach from whatever level of realization he is on. But that kind of guru, and the actual liberated guru, are two different things. One is called diksa, and the other is called siksa. Anyone who repeats the message purely can become siksa-guru immediately. One's wife, one's mother, a prostitute, a beggar, a Godbrother, etc. Everyone is ordered to become guru in that sense. It is not possible to be ordered to become a pure devotee. The bona fide diksa-guru must be a pure devotee that is actually liberated. That is the conclusion of all of Srila Prabhupada's instructions on these two types of gurus. This May tape does not in any way contradict those instructions.

Srila Prabhupada's quoting the verse from Caitanya-caritamrta, "amara ajnaya guru hana" (Cc. Mad. 7.128) is so significant we are herein quoting the entire section from the *Caitanya-caritamrta*. We strongly suggest that the devotees read it carefully. It fully substantiates the conclusions given in Chapter Nine.

*The brahmana (Kurma) begged Lord Caitanya Mahaprabhu, "My dear Lord, kindly show me favor and let me go with You. I can no longer tolerate the waves of misery caused by materialistic life." (Cc. Mad. 7.126)*

*Sri Caitanya Mahaprabhu replied, "Don't speak like that again. Better to remain at home and chant the holy name of Krishna always." (Cc. Mad. 7.127)*

*Purport by Prabhupada: "It is not advisable in this age of Kali to leave one's family suddenly, for people are not trained as proper brahmacaris and grhasthas. Therefore Sri Caitanya Mahaprabhu advised the brahmana not to be too eager to give up family life. It would be better to remain with his family and try to become purified by chanting the Hare Krishna maha-mantra regularly under the direction of a spiritual master. This is the instruction of Sri Caitanya Mahaprabhu. If this principle is followed by everyone, there is no need to accept sannyasa. In the next verse Sri Caitanya Mahaprabhu advises everyone to become an ideal householder by offenselessly chanting the Hare Krishna mantra and teaching the same principle to everyone he meets."*

*"Instruct everyone to follow the orders of Lord Sri Krishna as they are given in Bhagavad-gita and Srimad Bhagavatam. In this way become a spiritual master and try to liberate everyone in the land." (Cc. Mad. 7.128)*

*Purport by Prabhupada: "This is the sublime mission of ISKCON. Many people come and inquire whether they have to give up family life to join the Society, but that is not our mission. One can remain comfortably in his residence. We simply request everyone to chant the maha-mantra.... If one is a little literate and can read Bhagavad-gita As It Is and Srimad-Bhagavatam, that is so much the better. These works are now available in an English translation and are done very authoritatively to appeal to all classes of men. Instead of living engrossed in material activities, people throughout the world should take advantage of this movement and chant the Hare Krishna maha-mantra at home with their families. One should also refrain from sinful activities-illicit sex, meat-eating, gambling and intoxication. Out of these four items, illicit sex is very sinful. Every person must get married. Every woman especially must get married. If the women outnumber the men, some men can accept more than one wife. In that way there will be no prostitution in society. If men can marry more than one wife, illicit sex life will be stopped.... The Krishna consciousness movement is trying to elevate human society to the perfection of life by pursuing the method described by Sri Caitanya Mahaprabhu in His advice to the brahmana Kurma. That is, one should stay at home, chant the Hare Krishna mantra and preach the instructions of Krishna as they are given in Bhagavad-gita and Srimad Bhagavatam."*

*Sri Caitanya Mahaprabhu further advised the brahmana Kurma, "If you follow this instruction, your materialistic life at home will not obstruct your spiritual advancement. Indeed, if you follow these regulative principles, we will again meet here, or, rather, you will never lose My company." (Cc. Mad. 7.129)*

*Purport by Prabhupada: "This is an opportunity for everyone. If one simply follows the instructions of Sri Caitanya Mahaprabhu, under the guidance of His representative, and chants the Hare Krishna mantra, teaching everyone as far as possible the same principle, the contamination of the materialistic way of life will not even touch him. It does not matter whether one lives in a holy place like Vrindavana, Navadwipa or Jagannatha Puri or in the midst of European cities where the materialistic way of life is very prominent. If a devotee follows the instructions of Sri Caitanya Mahaprabhu, he lives in the company of the Lord. Wherever he lives, he converts that place into Vrindavana and Navadvipa. This means that materialism cannot touch him. This is the secret of success for one advancing in Krishna consciousness."*

*"At whosoever's house Sri Caitanya accepted His alms by taking prasada, He would convert the dwellers to His sankirtana movement and advise them just as He advised the brahmana named Kurma." (Cc. Mad. 7.130)*

*Purport by Prabhupada: "The cult of Sri Caitanya Mahaprabhu is explained here very nicely. One who surrenders to Him and is ready to follow Him with heart and soul does not need to change his location. Nor is it necessary for one to change status. One may remain a householder, a medical practitioner, an engineer, or whatever. It doesn't matter. One only has to follow the instructions of Sri Caitanya Mahaprabhu, chant the Hare Krishna maha-mantra and instruct relatives and friends in the teachings of Bhagavad-gita and* Srimad-Bhagavatam. *One has to learn humility and meekness at home following the instructions of Sri Caitanya Mahaprabhu, and in that way one's life will be spiritually successful. One should not try to be an artificially advanced devotee thinking, 'I am a first-class devotee.' Such thinking should be avoided. It is best not to accept any disciples. One has to become purified at home by chanting the Hare Krishna maha-mantra and preaching the principles and be freed from the contamination of material life.... To protect his preachers, Sri Caitanya Mahaprabhu has given much clear advice in these verses of Caitanya-caritamrta."*

Need more than this be said on the status of ISKCON's self-appointed gurus? Comments, inquiries, and donations toward this book may be sent to Steve Bryant (Sulocana dasa), 2124 Kittredge #32, Berkeley, CA, 94704. Thank you.

Note: We have created a Sulocana Dasa Memorial Fund to collect donations for the printing of The Guru Business. Please contact Mukunda dasa on mukunda.dasa@prabhupada.org.uk if you would like to help.

APPENDIX 22

REBUTTAL TO THE GBC DOCUMENT ON THE CASE:

SULOCANA vs. KIRTANANANDA

# ON WOMEN TAKING INITIATION BY A NEW "GURU"

Compiled by Sulocana dasa

CONTENTS

PART ONE

INITIATING WOMEN

PART TWO

JUDGING A MAN

HOW THE "GURUS" JUSTIFY THEIR BEHAVIOR

WHAT IS AN "ACCIDENTAL" FALLDOWN?

JUDGING A MAN'S SINCERITY

ILLICIT SEX

INTOXICATION, SPORTS, MOVIES, ETC.

HOW THE VARNAS AND ASHRAMAS MUST BE TAKEN INTO CONSIDERATION

WHAT MUST NOW BE DONE?

THE LEADERS-HOW TO JUDGE THEIR BEHAVIOR

IT'S A GRADUAL PROCESS-JUDGING A MAN'S PAST

JUDGING KIRTANANANDA-CASE CLOSED

SHASTRIC QUOTES ON THE CHARACTER OF KIRTANANANDA

CONCLUSION

THE GBC'S DECISION & SULOCANA'S DEMANDS TO KIRTANANANDA


**CORRECTIONS AND ADDITIONS TO SECTION ONE: "THE FACTS"**

The person Rupanuga refers to in his document as "Jamuna," is actually Jane, Sulocana's wife. The name "Jamuna," was given by Kirtanananda without Sulocana's awareness or approval. This is a direct breach of human decency what to speak of Vaisnava behavior. It therefore represents an offense to Srila Prabhupada since the man exhibiting such heinous behavior, Kirtanananda, is claiming to be Prabhupada's representative.

Jane was sent to New Vrindaban with *one* child from a previous affair and Sulocana's *first* son in her womb. Sulocana did not even know that she was pregnant when Jane took her "initiation".

Sulocana found out Jane was pregnant at the same time he found out that she had decided to devote her life to another man. They had been married one year at the time.

Jane was *lured* into taking "initiation" by telling her, in effect, "It's not necessary to have your husband's approval. You are your own spirit soul. Sulocana is not a pure devotee. 'Bhaktipada' is a pure devotee. If you want to go back to Godhead, you have to take initiation from a pure devotee." This is of course the standard ISKCON line which they attempt to substantiate in their document.

Jane divorced Sulocana and immediately "remarried" a man whose character is so degraded that he had been grabbing other women's breasts, including the wife of Sri Galim, the headmaster of the Gurukula. He had been severely beaten by Bhagavatananda for attempting to seduce his wife. His name is Raghunatha. He had been attempting to get a "wife" for many years but most women laughed at him, seeing his desperate condition. He is also well-known to be one of New Vrindaban's dopers. Jane had been secretly associating with this person for some time. Kirtanananda told Sulocana, "I never said that" (encourage a woman to "remarry").

Jane is not actually remarried. In several letters, and the books as well, Prabhupada refers to a woman who does what Jane did as "a prostitute" or "an enemy" or "keeping a paramour." He refers to men that do what Kirtanananda did as "wife stealers" or "Ravanas."

Jane was given a divorce and full custody of Sulocana's sons with the use of the temple's money and lawyer. The judge made the decision without thinking to ask if Sulocana had been notified of the hearing, which he hadn't. There is hard and undeniable proof of this. Jane's plea was "cruel and inhuman treatment." Sulocana never hit his wife once or even looked at another woman. She has admitted to telling this lie in order to get the divorce, since even mundane courts do not allow a divorce without any grounds. Also there is positive testimony, both from a local attorney and Jane herself, that she was given this decision because the local judge, Mr. Warmuth, "is very favorable to Keith Ham" (Kirtanananda).

Another fact not mentioned is that, by this time, Sulocana had two baby boys of his own, one three, and the other one-year old, both of whom he loves very much and has not seen now for one year. Both these boys were forcibly taken from Sulocana by six of Kirtanananda's men. They illegally entered Sulocana's motorhome to do this.

Also not mentioned is the fact that Kirtanananda was deliberately discouraging Sulocana from staying at New Vrindavana by denying him the service he was promised-managing the guest house. There are innumerable witnesses who will testify to this fact, including Narada Muni, who was in charge of the Indian program at the time. He was very disturbed about this since Kirtanananda's grounds for doing so were absolutely unjustified.Some other important facts are these quotes by Kirtanananda to Sulocana: "If you want your wife back, you will have to surrender to me" and "Don't forget, I have an eternal relationship with your wife, yours is only temporary," also, (You are not welcome here because) "Sulocana, you're just not my man" and "I heard you are leaving. Don't try and take your wife! I told her I'd 'protect' her."

Also not mentioned are the fact that Kirtanananda made no attempt whatsoever to counsel either the wife or husband to try to keep the family together. This is in itself proof of Kirtanananda's real intentions. As acknowledged by the GBC on page 5; divorce can only be recommended as a last resort. Kirtanananda made it the first.

These are just a few of the facts not mentioned in the GBC paper, all of which were known to the GBC. More of the story is contained in the preface to the upcoming book presently being compiled by Sulocana dasa.

## Section 2-JURISDICTION

The GBC is stating that since there is no real system of dealing with such problems on the local level in ISKCON, the grievance committee is having to deal with it. What they are really saying is that since the GBC has never really studied or understood, or compiled anything on the relationship between husband, wife, and guru, either before or after Srila Prabhupada's departure, Sulocana dasa is now forcing the issue. There are some very obvious problems which arise when unqualified men pose as "gurus" and come in between husband and wife. But, since Sulocana dasa is the only one to date who has thoroughly studied the matter fully, and can speak authoritatively from Srila Prabhupada's books and letters, backing every point with sastra, the GBC did not respond to hardly any of Sulocana's challenges.

## Section 3-GENERAL PRINCIPLES

The general principle of the GBC is that ISKCON's "gurus" are bona fide. Since all the statements made by the GBC are based on this absurd proposition, the entire document is invalid. Sulocana's upcoming book proves conclusively that these "gurus" were never appointed. Most devotees realize this by now anyway. So, as Prabhupada often explains, if you start an equation with one plus one equals three, then naturally all the rest of the equation is going to be off. This is all that really need be said about the philosophical arguments presented by the GBC on women, marriage, and guru. Still, we will go into some of the points just to show the foolishness of the official position of the "GBC".

## PART ONE

## WOMEN'S GURU-HER HUSBAND OR A "SANNYASI"?

Everyone should have a bona fide pure devotee guru, including women. That does not mean that everyone should take initiation in the same way. According to the Vedic system, the husband takes initiation from a bona fide guru, and the wife serves that same guru by serving her husband. Prabhupada says, "The man becomes a devotee of Krishna, and the wife becomes a devotee of her husband." They are thus both initiated since they are "two halves of the same body." There is absolutely no difference if the wife has formally taken initiation or not. She is automatically the disciple of the husband's guru. If the wife devotes herself to another man, who the husband disapproves of, then the relationship of the woman to both "husband" and "guru" is illicit. No bona fide guru would allow such a thing. A wife is never initiated separate from her husband. In Vedic culture she is not initiated at all. When Jadurani first approached Srila Prabhupada for initiation, Srila Prabhupada told her to go find herself a husband amongst the devotees in the temple. Later he gave concession to women for the sake of engaging them, since he could plainly see they were not going to accept the Vedic standard. That is the only reason Srila Prabhupada initiated women in a separate ceremony. Factually, any woman is automatically Prabhupada's disciple if she marries a Prabhupada disciple. Wherever a woman's heart is, that is where her husband and her guru are. A woman cannot have two husbands or two gurus. Prabhupada says that an ordinary woman cannot imitate Draupadi by thinking she can equally serve and devote herself to more than one man, what to speak of a "sannyasi". A woman can only have one guru, her husband, and through him she may devote herself to his guru, not separately.

## CAN WOMEN BE INITIATED SEPARATE FROM THE HUSBAND?

The GBC argument that Prabhupada initiated women separate from the husband is not a valid argument for the above reasons. But Prabhupada also initiated single women? He could do that for several reasons. (1) He knew they would be marrying one of his disciples, since his standard order was that all women were to be married. (2) Even if a woman was not going to marry, but finally decided to remain single as a nun, Prabhupada could also initiate nuns. Prabhupada could initiate anyone he wanted to, because he is an uttama-adhikari, completely pure devotee with no sex desire or ulterior motives in his heart. No one today can make that claim. (3) Because Prabhupada was such an elevated uttama-adhikari, he could adjust the standard religious principles for time and circumstance. Others, those not on that level, must follow his instructions, not imitate. Initiating women is just such an adjustment. It is true that time and circumstances are basically the same now (women's liberation) as in 1966, but there is one big difference. It is a very, very, very, big difference. These new "gurus" are light years from being uttama-adhikaris. If Prabhupada had wanted his neophyte disciples to imitate him after he departed, then why didn't he mention such a thing anywhere in his books or letters? Aren't we supposed to be following the instructions and not imitating?

(4) Prabhupada initiated single women but he never initiated a man's wife if the man did not want to take initiation also-and visa versa. At least he stated in several letters that he did not want to do such a thing. He was requested to, but he didn't comply. That would have been coming between a husband and wife. Prabhupada was a pure devotee, so naturally he would never do such a thing.

The GBC's arguments simply reveal the well-known tendency of the "gurus" to imitate Srila Prabhupada, and not to follow his instructions.

## KIRTANANANDA'S ONE AND ONLY ARGUMENT

Sometimes, but very rarely, if the woman was interested in Krishna consciousness, but the husband was an out-and-out demon, Prabhupada would recommend that she live separately from him in the temple. He never recommended that she remarry. Such instances are extremely rare-maybe only one or two letters. But in numerous letters Prabhupada encouraged the woman to tolerate her husband's weaknesses and be patient. He directly told one devotee to cook meat for her husband (consult Baumadeva, Detroit). What Kirtanananda did, in essence, by telling Sulocana's wife to leave him, was directly call Sulocana a demon, and call himself, equal to Srila Prabhupada. His one and only argument was, "Sarvabhauma Bhattacarya told his daughter to leave Amogha because Amogha was blaspheming Lord Caitanya. So you are also an offender, so I told your wife to leave you." Since Kirtanananda considers himself a pure devotee, he compared Sulocana's failure to worship Kirtanananda to Amogha's blaspheming Lord Caitanya. Sulocana certainly never claimed to be a pure devotee, but he does claim that he never for a moment thought offensively toward Prabhupada, Lord Caitanya, or Krishna. Kirtanananda cannot make that claim. He directly attacked Prabhupada, calling him a tyrant, among numerous other elephant offenses (all the letters concerning this guru-aparadha by Kirtanananda are in the book).

## WHY ISKCON'S "GURUS" CANNOT IMITATE PRABHUPADA

If there were a completely pure devotee on the planet right now, equal to Srila Prabhupada in every way, such a pure devotee could act as Prabhupada did and initiate both men and women, whether they were married or not, and not fall down. But in the absence of such an uttama-adhikari, we have to *follow the instructions* of the uttama-adhikari, not imitate him. Why does the GBC think Prabhupada wrote so many books anyway? To collect dust? Why does the GBC think that Prabhupada never even hinted in letter or book the concept of a woman having a guru independent of her husband? He never mentions it anywhere. He only refers to *himself as* a women's guru in a few places in all his writings. He almost always referred to the women as his daughters. He knew no one was qualified to imitate him in any way whatsoever. And he knew that no one would come along in his immediate aftermath on that level either. *So he never mentioned it.* He didn't want to encourage neophytes to imitate him after his departure. He only stressed to follow his instructions. The only example he encouraged them to imitate was the way he worked 24 hours a day in Krishna's service. The real uttama-adhikari's instructions are crystal clear. The wife should be devoted to her husband, and her husband should be sincere and devoted to guru and Krishna (innumerable references). And, to solidify that instruction, Prabhupada said (paraphrased): unless one is on the level of Haridasa Thakura, Narada Muni, or Srila Prabhupada, then no one can *accept service from, or give shelter to* a woman (ref. SB 7.7.14). This underlined phrase defines what initiation means.

## GBC SAYS: "GURUS DON'T HAVE TO BE PURE-BUT HUSBANDS DO"

How the GBC could have the audacity to deny this instruction of Srila Prabhupada's is inconceivable. This is the way they word it:

"The point that Srila Prabhupada was special, a nitya-siddha, eternally liberated pure devotee and cannot be imitated by his disciples is certainly true; *but this is not an appropriate argument in this case* (they give no explanation why they make this claim). It is true that *no one can claim* the infallibility or *purity of Srila Prabhupada,* but such *perfection* or equality *is not required* to perform the duties of *diksa-guru."* (No further explanation.)

So, they say the diksa-guru does not have to be pure to give shelter to, or accept service from women. But what about the husband? What does the GBC say about the husband's requirements?

"A husband cannot claim the status of a pati-guru (husband-guru) or ideal grhastha without strictly following the four regulative principles and devotional principles, such as a minimum of sixteen rounds, the morning program, etc. The rules and regulations of the grhastha-ashrama are as strict for that ashrama as the rules and regulations for any other ashrama.... *A husband who does not act as a bonafide grhastha (defined above) cannot expect his wife to continue to respect him or be obedient to him.* Such an unfortunate wife is certainly justified in seeking protection from her spiritual authorities (temple president), including her guru."

We have in our possession a letter from the man who compiled this document, Rupanuga, written to Satsvarupa, which states that Jayapataka and Ramesvara both do not chant their rounds. But then these are minor things compared to the heavy offenses by all the "gurus". But, if an ordinary householder does not chant all his rounds, and perfectly follow all the principles, in other words, if he is not a pure devotee, his wife should neither *serve or respect* him. Instead, the GBC says she can leave him for the "protection" of her "guru". They say she has every right to grab his children, and run off to live with some popped-out temple president and a "sannyasi".

## KIRTANANANDA'S TEN-THOUSAND "WIVES"

So, in essence, the GBC is saying: "A guru does not have to be pure to initiate *hundreds* of persons, including other men's wives, thereby splitting up marriages and creating 'varna sankara,' but the husband has to be a completely pure devotee, to have *one* devoted follower, his wife." This claim has no shastric backing whatsoever. It is a serious Vaisnava-aparadha to all those devotees who have had their families destroyed by this bogus philosophy. Can anyone imagine what would happen if all the women in the world, whose husband's were not following all the strict regulative principles perfectly, immediately grabbed the children and ran off to live with some bogus sannyasi posing as a guru. The proposal of the GBC is insanity but they are the ones in charge of the most important spiritual movement in the world. Just try and see the position. These men are not sannyasis or gurus or GBC, they are manipulators and exploiters living at the expense of hundreds of "wives". Some of them act exactly like pimps. In our book we go into elaborate detail on the wife swapping and illicit-sex going on in ISKCON.

## WHEN CAN A WOMAN LEAVE A FALLEN HUSBAND?

Prabhupada makes it very clear in SB 7.11.28 the qualifications for a woman to leave her husband. That is the authoritative purport for this problem. It must be very carefully studied. First and foremost, Prabhupada says that he has to be a nondevotee. If he is a devotee, then despite his weaknesses, "he is sinless (but not a guru)." So, the primary qualification for leaving a husband is not his flaws, but whether or not he has faith in Krishna. If he has faith in Krishna, he is a devotee. To justify leaving a husband, he has to be a "naradhamah", a nondevotee, the lowest of men, and addicted to *all* the four sinful activities. Only when the husband is such a nondevotee, she can leave him, but she cannot remarry. She can live separately. (In one letter Prabhupada conceded that: "If *both* husband and wife agree, she may divorce and remarry." Prabhupada gave that instruction in disgust.) The GBC refers to this text also, but they do not mention that a woman who leaves such a degraded husband should not remarry. And, of course, they are implying that Sulocana is such a degraded person without knowing anything about Sulocana. And, of course, Sulocana's wife "remarried" a Kirtanananda man almost immediately after Kirtanananda broke up their marriage. And the character of the man he "remarried" her to....

## THE REAL QUESTION?

So the real question is: Where do you draw the line in defining a devotee? Kirtanananda claims Sulocana is a demon. Sulocana claims Kirtanananda Swami is a demon. How to judge? At what degree of contamination is one considered not to be a devotee? Is subtle contamination not important? Many persons who were at one point strictly following the regulative principles, and considered advanced, even sannyasis, are now eating meat and blaspheming Srila Prabhupada. So were they actually advanced devotees while they were following strictly? If they were, how could they have fallen down so far? Is sincerity the only qualification for a devotee? If so, how do you judge sincerity? Does sincerity come and go on a daily basis? How long does one have to be strictly following the regulative principles to be considered sincere and advanced? Does *artificially* performing austerities mean one is sincere, or does it mean he is heading for a fall? Should ISKCON hire psychics to analyze a man's sincerity? Could astrology help? Can regression under hypnosis reveal a man's motives? These are worthwhile considerations. Instead the GBC asks: "Can an imitation sannyasi 'guru' advise a man's wife to leave him because he is not following all the regulative principles which are actually only meant for the brahmins?" Only a fool or a demon could propose such a thing.

## SINCERITY-COMPARING SULOCANA TO KIRTANANANDA

Sulocana's wife decided to take initiation on the grounds that Sulocana was not qualified to deliver her. She says he was not following the regulative principles strictly and therefore she assumed he was not sincere. He was chanting average 12-13 rounds daily and periodically he would go through a spell of getting intoxicated once a week. He frequently ate chocolate. At that time he was 29 years old and just starting a Krishna conscious picture pendant business. Because he was not perfectly following everything, his wife thought he was not sincere. She thought she should take initiation from someone whom she was told was sincere. Makes sense, right? Wrong. She did not stop to consider that she knew absolutely nothing about this man. She did not know that when Kirtanananda was 29 years old, or Sulocana's age at the time she took "initiation", he was a full-blown, active homosexual, or second-cock in gay lingo, since he was the female counterpart of Hayagriva. We were tempted to vividly describe what such persons do in the evenings, but we will spare the "sensitivity" of the "brahmins" reading this rebuttal. Then, when Kirtanananda Swami was 30, a year after taking "initiation", he stabbed Prabhupada square in the back in an attempt to steal Prabhupada's movement for himself. Had Jane known these *documented* hard facts about this man, she may have thought twice about his sincerity, despite what Kuladri was telling her about following some external principles. In India, any upper caste man automatically follows those principles, so that alone is hardly any ultimate qualification. When Satsvarupa was this age, 29, he was a new devotee and was having sex with his wife *every single night.* At least Sulocana regulated his usage of the "concession" to twice a month. So, by comparing Sulocana with these two "big, big gurus" at age 29, Sulocana is far more advanced than both of them put together, and who knows where they will all be 30 years down the road? Sulocana never claimed to be a saint, but it certainly isn't Kirtanananda's position to judge him. No one else ever attacked Prabhupada the way Kirtanananda did. Prabhupada condemned Kirtanananda in more letters than all the other bogus gurus *combined.*

## PART TWO

## JUDGING A MAN

These are points that the GBC should be considering. Instead they make these asinine statements that a diksa-guru does not have to be free of sex desire to take hundreds of women disciples, but a husband has to be completely pure to deserve to keep the devotion of his one wife. The "gurus" base all their claim of divinity of *Bhagavad-gita* 9.30, quoted below. They are all riding on the thin thread of this verse in hopes that no one will ever think about it. They claim a monopoly on using this verse to justify their behavior, but if anyone else exhibits weaknesses, they cannot quote this verse. "They are simply demons to be discarded." The following is an in-depth analysis of that verse.

*"Even if one commits the most abominable action, if he is engaged in devotional service he is to be considered saintly because he is properly situated in his determination." (BG 9.30)*

Purport by Srila Prabhupada: "...Now in the conditioned state, sometimes devotional service and the conditional service in relation to the body will parallel one another. But then again, sometimes these activities become opposed to one another. As far as possible, a devotee is very cautious so that he does not do anything that could disrupt his wholesome condition.... No one should deride a devotee for some *accidental falldown* from the ideal path, for, as explained in the next verse, such occasional falldowns will be stopped in due course, as soon as a devotee is completely situated in Krishna consciousness.... The words 'sadhur eva', 'he is saintly', are very emphatic. They are a warning to the nondevotees that because of an accidental falldown a devotee should not be derided; he should still be considered saintly even if he has accidentally fallen down. And the word 'mantavyah" is still more emphatic. If one does not follow this rule, and derides a devotee for his accidental falldown, then one is disobeying the order of the Supreme Lord.... On the other hand, one should not misunderstand that a devotee in transcendental devotional service can act in all kinds of abominable ways; this verse only refers to an *accident* due to the strong power of material connections.... As long as one is not strong enough to fight the illusory energy, there may be accidental falldowns. But when one is strong enough, he is no longer subjected to such falldowns, as previously explained. No one should take advantage of this verse and commit nonsense and think that he is still a devotee. If he does not *improve* in his character by devotional service, then it is to be understood that *he is not a high devotee.*"

## WHAT IS AN ACCIDENTAL FALLDOWN?

Note: The word accident must be defined in order to understand what Prabhupada is saying in this purport. Generally an accident is accepted as being something that suddenly happens and is beyond our control. In that sense, it would be impossible to accidentally have illicit sex or accidentally get intoxicated. In the next purport Prabhupada says: "either by accident or intention." Actually, there is no such thing as an accident since everything is controlled by the Lord, and all activities are either one's karma, or Krishna's special mercy on a devotee. So when Prabhupada says "accident" he means engaging in abominable activity by force of habit. Prabhupada uses that phrase, "force of habit," in numerous places to describe ones occasional indulgences in illicit activities. So, we feel safe injecting that phrase here in place of the word "accident," which is confusing to many devotees, including "gurus." They tend to abuse this verse to commit their abominable activities. Prabhupada did not make a mistake in his wording. The devotees simply fail to understand the real meaning. So it is important to clearly define it. The translation to this verse does not in any way imply an accident. Prabhupada uses the word accident to mean an act done without malicious intent and/or blatant disregard for authority. In other words, by force of habit. ISKCON's "gurus" say that, "if a devotee does something illicit more than once, then it cannot be an accident. So, if not an accident, the man must be a demon." With this argument they justify taking his wife and children away and getting her in bed with himself or one of his own men.

## JUDGING A MAN'S SINCERITY

So this is a critical verse and purport and must be studied at great length. It is a subtle thing, something the gurus know little about. It means judging between one who remorsefully engages in base activities due to his past habits, and one who sinfully does so because he just plain doesn't care about any authority. That is the all important question. Determining the sincerity of one's heart is the essence of judging a devotee and that can be very misleading if one is not extremely perceptive. There are a class of sahajiyas today who claim that it is not good to judge others. That is simply foolishness. One absolutely has to make such judgments daily if he wants to avoid bad, and accept good association.

## ILLICIT SEX

This is the most common problem devotees face. Say for example one spends his whole life, from puberty onwards, in gross illicit sex, but then later he meets a pure devotee like Srila Prabhupada and he wants to give up this bad habit. But due to the strong influence of material energy, he cannot do so very easily. Still, he tries to regulate his sex life and makes strict vows to gradually decrease it. Such a person, who honestly and responsibly lives with his wife, and does not look at or pollute other women, can be considered sincere even though he may be having sex with his wife too often to be considered a disciple or a brahmin. The sex to him is like a material conditioned necessity or habit just like sleeping and eating. He cannot abruptly give it up, but he does not like being under its control either, and so he tries to gradually reduce it. Such a person may be considered sincere or even saintly as long as he is sincerely trying to serve Krishna. He is certainly not a pure devotee, yet, and he should not be treated as though he were. He may be respected, but only from a distance by those who want to advance quickly (NOI).

But then you take someone else who comes to Krishna consciousness for ulterior motives and has sex, gross or subtle, with one woman after another, even other men's wives. Such a person should not be considered saintly or sincere, but on the contrary, he should be publicly condemned so that sane persons can avoid his contaminated association. One perfect example of this is Sruti Kirti. He polluted at least half-a-dozen married women that we know of personally, destroying their marriages. Because he had this extremely demoniac tendency, he should not have been considered saintly just because he chanted Hare Krishna. But, out of ignorance he was considered saintly and so nobody wanted to publicly expose him. Thus he was able to pollute one women after another. He should have been publicly condemned after the first one. Instead, Ramesvara continued to support this debauch right up through the sixth married woman he polluted. He even took Prabhupada's money and sent Sruti Kirti to India so the last husband who swore to kill him would not be able to. This is not an isolated incident. It is going on everywhere with the full blessing of the "gurus".

## INTOXICATION, SPORTS, MOVIES, ETC.

The same principle goes for these habits. It may be unbearably difficult for a devotee to abstain from them, but if he honestly recognizes his fallen condition, and strives to reduce them, then eventually he will be able to give them up altogether. He should be sane and regulate his usage, gradually reducing. If he is sincere, he will eventually be able to give it up as he continues to chant Hare Krishna in the mood: "Krishna, I am so weak and fallen, please help me to overcome these weaknesses so I can eventually be fully engaged in Your service." Again we have a fine line between praying like this and committing sins on the strength of chanting the holy name, which is an offense. If one is determined to give up bad habits, and he makes a regular program to do so, then he may be considered sincere and should be encouraged by everyone, including his wife. *But he must prove his sincerity by strictly endeavoring to reduce the habit.* That is the meaning of this verse. If anyone disagrees, state your position, and we will debate.

## HOW THE VARNAS AND ASHRAMAS
## MUST BE TAKEN INTO CONSIDERATION

A man may pray like that, but only to convince himself and others that he is really sincere. How else may one judge? One way is by seeing the amount of trouble and austerity one accepts for Krishna. There are different austerities for the different varnas and ashramas. If one is a sannyasi, but he engages in eating very opulent foods three times a day, sleeps on a soft bed, freely associates with women, has little knowledge of sastra, but still lives off the money of others, then such a sannyasi can readily be recognized as bogus. So ultimately it boils down to how submissive one is to the instructions of guru, sastra, and sadhu, which apply to ones own varna and asrarna. If one is acting according to sastra then he can be considered sincere. But sastra has to be clearly defined for the different classes before we can judge. A householder doing business and accepting all sorts of sense gratification and sex with his wife may well be more sincere that a "sannyasi" who merely talks to women. Ramananda Raya would massage and dress beautiful women, and he was the topmost devotee of Lord Caitanya, who Himself set the example by stating that He couldn't even look at a wooden form of a woman without being agitated. Chota Haridasa, because he was in the renounced order, was excommunicated for simply talking to a woman once in private. Thus he committed suicide. So one's position in the varnas and ashramas is a primary consideration in determining one's sincerity.

For ksatriyas, vaisyas, and sudras, such things as sports are not so degraded, but if a man claiming to be a brahmin indulges in them, we can understand differently. Everything has to be taken into consideration in determining the quality of one's association.

## WHAT MUST NOW BE DONE?

It requires real brahmins to judge such things and advise devotees properly. Since there are few if any, real brahmins in our society today, it is absolutely essential to thoroughly learn, and then stick as closely as possible to Prabhupada's instructions, *not imitate him.* That means fully indexing, categorizing, and scrutinizingly studying all the angles of interpretation in the association of serious devotee. That would have been a noble objective for the GBC to arrange right after Srila Prabhupada's disappearance. Instead, they spent all their time holding mock debates and scheming how to fool the devotees into thinking they were bona fide gurus, and this, within days of Prabhupada's departure. So, until some serious devotees undertake this project of clarifying Prabhupada's teaching on these subjects, we will still be largely in the dark in determining how to act and how not to act? Who is a devotee and who is not a devotee? Who is a guru, and who is a demon?

## THE LEADERS: HOW TO JUDGE THEIR BEHAVIOR

*Generally* most of the devotees are straightforward and basically sincere. They most likely will have some bad habits, having been brought up in the West, but they are genuinely attracted to becoming devotees of Krishna. But then there are others who are more interested in their personal glorification. How to tell the one from the other? One very good method of determining the sincerity of a devotee is to analyze his behavior in terms of how much pain he is causing others. A real devotee is humble and does not cause pain to others unnecessarily. Simple devotees may indulge in illicit sex and intoxication but basically they are only slowing down their own progress in devotional service by such behavior. Most devotees will not intentionally hurt others. But if a person is claiming to be a big leader, is demanding respect from others, is exploiting and discouraging others, then that person can safely be labeled a demon in the guise of a devotee. On the other hand, a leader may be seen periodically doing some nonsense, but if he is humble and doesn't demand that others worship him as a saint, then that devotee is to be considered saintly since he is humble and therefore becoming purified. It's a question of heart. Usually, one's heart can be determined by studying the outward behavior in relation to shastric evidence and a little common sense.

## IT'S A GRADUAL PROCESS; JUDGING A MAN'S PAST

Purification is a gradual process. The very word purification implies gradual. One must be *improving* in his condition. It is not expected that everyone will be instantly cleansed or they can be labeled a demon. If one strictly regulates his sense gratification, then he will gradually improve. We know of no one today who is qualified to judge a man's soul simply at a glance. In any court of law, if a man is up for a crime, the judge will be lenient or severe depending on whether that person is a one time offender, or a habitual criminal. He has to investigate the man's *past* to determine this. Only then can he see if the man is improving or not. The same principle goes for devotees, but on a much deeper level. Judging a devotee is many times more difficult than judging a criminal. An illiterate, insignificant devotee, simply cleaning the toilets in 1985, may become a great powerful preacher 50 years down the road, *if he remains humble.* On the other hand, we have already seen some of ISKCON's "big" leaders, because they were not at all humble, eating meat, having illicit sex, getting intoxicated and even blaspheming Srila Prabhupada after just a few years. Therefore, judging a man's character is a serious thing and must be done very, very carefully before making accusations. A man's past must be taken into consideration.

## JUDGING KIRTANANANDA: CASE CLOSED

Sulocana did not make public accusations against Kirtanananda until he had thoroughly studied Kirtanananda Swami from all angles, past and present. He interviewed other victims, past and present. He took the opinions of numerous devotees who knew Kirtanananda Swami from the very beginning. He studied Kirtanananda's own words. He read all the letters written by Srila Prabhupada about Kirtanananda Swami. Then he made it known to numerous devotees, both GBC, and otherwise of the patterns in Kirtanananda's behavior. No one was able to properly respond to the allegations. During this time that Sulocana was "patient", his wife was turned into a prostitute. At that point any other man would have gone to New Vrindaban and blown Kirtanananda's brains out. But only then, several months later, when the evidence had become overwhelming, and the GBC continued muddling did Sulocana come right out, and with full confidence, publicly declare to the world in writing, that Kirtanananda is an out-and-out "raksasa" (demon). And, sure enough, Kirtanananda's failure to respond in any way to Sulocana's challenge, proved Sulocana right. Case closed.

## SHASTRIC QUOTES ON THE CHARACTER OF KIRTANANANDA

*"Then he has to purify his existence. There are so many rules and regulations to be followed in the renounced order of life. Most important of all, a sannyasi is strictly forbidden to have any intimate relationship with a woman. He is even forbidden to talk with a woman in a secluded place....* One has to follow the rules

and regulations of a particular status of life in *order to purify his existence. For a sannyasi, intimate relations with women and possession of wealth for sense gratification are strictly forbidden...not even enjoying them, but just looking toward them with such a propensity is so condemned that he had better commit suicide before experiencing such illicit desires." (BG 16, 1-3)*

*"In this verse, the royal road to hell is described. The demoniac want to make a show of religion and advancement in spiritual science, although they do not follow the principles. They are always arrogant or proud in possessing some type of education or so much wealth.* They desire to be worshipped by others, and demand respectability, although they do not command respect. *Over trifles they become very angry and speak harshly, not gently. They do not know what should be done and what should not be done.* They do everything whimsically, according to their own desire, and they do not recognize any authority. *These demoniac qualities are taken on by them from the beginning of their bodies in the wombs of their mothers, and as they grow they manifest all these inauspicious qualities." (BG 16.4)*

*"Those who do not follow the scriptural injunctions are supposed to be demons. Therefore it is stated here that the demons do not know the scriptural rules, nor do they have any inclination to follow them. Most of them do not know them, and even if some of them know, they have not the tendency to follow them." (BG 16.7)*

*"The process of speaking in spiritual circles is to say something upheld by the scriptures. One should at once quote from scriptural authority to back up what he is saying. At the same time, such talk should be very pleasurable to the ear. (BG 17.14) (Kirtanananda is yet to defend his actions by sastra. He has had a year now to try and do so.)*

## CONCLUSION

The day for women to take a separate initiation is over, unless they want to become nuns. Then they can take spiritual instruction from a *householder* siksa-guru if his wife can agree to it. In essence that means the woman becomes a second wife, but in a non-sexual way. Such a relationship is hardly likely in many young Westernized women. Since this movement is young, the practical application of this principle will not be seen for many years. Therefore Prabhupada frequently said that "all the women should be married." He never encouraged a "brahmacarini asrama." The letters to the real Mother Jamuna Dasi make that very clear. He simply had to put the women someplace until they got married. If the GBC wants to debate on this subject, they will have to study it. To encourage them, we are enclosing a printout-at our expense-of all of Srila Prabhupada's instructions on marriage from the letters. We will be expecting a more scholarly response soon. The chapter in our book entitled, ISKCON WOMEN: PROTECTED OR EXPLOITED, goes into all these points in much more detail.

## THE GBCs DECISION AND SULOCANA'S DEMANDS TO KIRTANANANDA

Those of you reading this who have not seen a copy of the GBC paper should know that the official GBC decision confirms Sulocana's accusations-that Kirtanananda had no right to interfere in Sulocana's marriage. The GBC makes some insane statements that Sulocana was "offensive" in calling Kirtanananda names, and that he should apologize, but at the same tune they acknowledge that Kirtanananda's act was "injudicious" and that he should now rectify his blunder. Needless to say, it is not necessary to apologize to a man who steals your wife and sons, especially when his "mistakes" prove him to be far from a pure devotee. We are assuming that the compiler of the document, Rupanuga, had to say that to make it look like he was still on the side of the "gurus". The GBC decision is that Kirtanananda must acknowledge his "mistake" and arrange for Sulocana's sons to be returned to him. This is a direct order from the GBC to Kirtanananda. There is only one way for Kirtanananda to do this:

1) He must humble himself before Jane and admit he made a major blunder. He must convince her that he polluted her real marriage and she must accept this wholeheartedly.

2) He must convince Jane's paramour, Raghunatha, that he had no right to marry him to Jane and that he now must forget her and go back to masturbating.

3) He must send her back to live in California where Sulocana can be with his sons. She does not have to live with Sulocana or serve him but she must return Sulocana's sons. If she refuses to leave Kirtanananda, then she must return the sons alone. Sulocana will accept her back after some time has elapsed if he is convinced that she was only another one of Kirtanananda's victim, and not herself demonic.

4) Kirtanananda Swami must pay a $5,000 token damage fee to Sulocana to help set Jane up in a house since Sulocana's business went down the drain during this struggle.

5) Kirtanananda must circulate a letter throughout ISKCON stating that Sulocana had every right to make the accusations he did, and that anyone who may have wanted to kill or malign Sulocana should give up that idea wholeheartedly.

If these bare minimum conditions are not met in full by Kirtanananda before Sulocana's book is finished, then the book Sulocana is compiling will be sent to every major media in the world. Sulocana guarantees that this book contains enough filth on the new "gurus" to burn their little kingdoms to ashes-the fire starting at New Vrindaban.

Comments and inquiries may be sent to Steve Bryant, 2124 Kittredge #32, Berkeley, CA, 94704. Post date: July 19th, 1985.

*"Those who do not follow the scriptural injunctions are supposed to be demons. Therefore it is stated here that the demons do not know the scriptural rules, nor do they have any inclination to follow them. Most of them do not know them, and even if some of them know, they have not the tendency to follow them."*
*(Prabhupada from Bhagavad-gita 16.7)*

# WOMEN'S SEXPLOITATION AT NEW VRINDAVAN

## INTERVIEW WITH JANAMEJAYA DASA, BERKELEY TEMPLE

### JULY 26TH, 1985

Sulocana dasa (SD): So this devotee, Varsha dasa, is an old friend of yours.

Jj: Yes.

SD: He also took initiation from Hansadutta.

Jj: Yes.

SD: Was he already married at the time he took initiation?

Jj: No. What happened was, his wife was really into Hansadutta, she was like a Hansadutta groupie. She was always running over to his house, practically drove him nuts, so he got her married off to Varsha with the hopes that she'd quit bugging him. Anyway, after Hansadutta fell down she finally lost her faith in him. Then the New Vrindaban mothers came here, and she got into their trip and so they ended up both going out there. Now they have a kid.

SD: She got pregnant here in Berkeley.

Jj: Yeah.

SD: Is she also a Hansadutta disciple?

Jj: No. She's a disciple of Srila Prabhupada.

SD: So why did they go to New Vrindaban?

Jj: Because Hansadutta moved out there for awhile. She's a Hansadutta groupie so she had to follow him everywhere, but after awhile, her faith got transferred to "Bhaktipada".

SD: So after Hansadutta fell down her mind went to Kirtanananda. Were they sankirtana devotees here in Berkeley?

Jj: She was. He was on and off.

SD: So after Hansadutta left New Vrindaban, they just decided to stay there?

Jj: Yeah, they gave her a position. Any Hansadutta disciple that ever went out there, they gave a position.

SD: What position did they give her?

Jj: Like head of the girl's gurukula or assistant, something like that.

SD: Why didn't they just send her out on the pick?

Jj: She has a baby to take care of.

SD: What was his wife's name?

Jj: Her name is Sudharma. Anyway, when Varaha was out here, he was telling me how great everything was at New Vmdavana. He was chanting the glories of New Vrindaban. I just thought: "God, I've got to set this poor guy straight. This guy's really brainwashed." He was passing fliers around, putting them on the bulletin board, trying to get people to go out there.

SD: This was after you'd read my expose on Kirtanananda Swami?

Jj: Yeah. So I said, "Hey, let's go on sankirtana." I got him out there and started talking to him. It's an hour's drive, and he started telling me about the glories of New Vrindaban, how they're pushing varnasrama dharma out there, how successful it is, this and that, and I said, "Bullshit. They're stealing wives, they're controlling all the men out there through their wives. They're getting these women to worship 'Bhaktipada' and that's how they control the men. Either you do what Bhaktipada says or they'll marry your wife off to somebody." So then he started thinking. He goes, "Yeah, you're right" he says."Actually, I got this feeling there are a couple of Prabhupada men out there always talking to my wife. I got this feeling that if I didn't go along with their program, you know, go on sankirtana, and act surrendered to Bhaktipada, even though I'm not into him..." that's what he said, "that they would try to get her married off to somebody else. He'd just finished telling me how great everything was, but then when I got him to think-like he'd never even thought-l got him to really think about it, and he said, "Yeah, you're really right." He started telling me an incident of how he and Chakravarti were going to go to India and their wives were going to come a couple of weeks later, so, while they were out here, they got a phone call from their wives. He told me specifically what Chakravarti's wife said. He said she told him he had better come back right away, that "Bhaktipada's been talking to me, and he wants me to marry somebody else."

SD: He said Kirtanananda personally told her to leave her husband and remarry.

Jj: Yeah.

SD: Varaha's wife also?

Jj: No, but he just knew that he had better get back here too. She didn't say anything, but he just picked up on it. You know, if somebody is going to work out there, digging ditches, whatever, they've got to get him married off. So, if your wife's there, and you're not there, and they know you're not really going to be an asset to the community, well, they're going to marry your wife off. It's all like peer pressure. They got all these women hopping around going "Jaya Bhaktipada" and your wife, along with all these women, are very much influenced by peer pressure. More than men are. To a great extent, they just get into it. It's all peer pressure. Peer pressure is extremely heavy. My wife was influenced by it. I just know how it is. That's why I'm not into "Bhaktipada" coming here, bringing his mothers' parties, cause that means I'll have to deal with that. Even though my wife understands philosophically that it's off the wall, I just don't want to have to worry about her getting into it.

SD: That's a good realization you have.

Jj: Another thing he told me was how once he wanted to take his wife shopping with him. He knew somebody would get upset about it but he did it anyway. On the way out in the parking lot, one of the little gurukula girls begged to go with them. His wife was in charge of them, so they took her along, and when they came back, there was like the President, and some of the big men there waiting for him in the parking lot. They gave him real heavy sauce and wouldn't let him see his wife for a week or two.

SD: They wouldn't let him see his own wife?

Jj: Yeah, and he said anytime now, if he goes to associate with his wife, they always have some mother tagging along watching.

SD: Why?

Jj: To report to Bhaktipada.

SD: You were saying earlier that they also won't let you see your kids.

Jj: Yeah, he said, "If you miss mangala-artik more than two or three times in one week, then you can't see your kids that week." In other words, they're training the kids up even to reject the parents. They even use that on them. So now Varaha says, "I don't have a wife. Of course, I have one, but I feel like I have no control over her whatsoever." They tell the children that the parents are off the wall. Not to listen to them. So he feels like, "I don't have a kid-l don't have a wife" but he says, "I'm attached to them, so I stay."

SD: But he knows that as soon as he leaves there-or stops doing sankirtana-they'll immediately get his wife in bed with one of Kirtanananda's men?

Jj: Yeah, right. If he gets out of hand. Like that. He actually discussed it with her. She said, "No, don't worry about it, I'm not into it." But he told me, "She's a woman and susceptible." I went through a similar thing in Vancouver. My wife and I had some problems and so we separated for a while. She went up there. She didn't even know what was going on, but I found out from some other devotees there, one guy I knew, like they had it all planned out. They'd get her re-initiated, they already had some guy picked out for her, and she didn't even know anything about it. So when I talked to her, she goes: "Yeah, they're real nice to me up there," and this and that. She didn't know they had all these little plans for her. So when I went to go get her, I went in like a new bhakta so I could trick them. So once I found out where she was, I talked to her and she agreed to come, but you know, we had to split in the middle of the night. She was real innocent. She went to the temple president and told him I wanted her to go and they just like flipped out and got real nasty, then they revealed themselves. She said, "And I'd thought they were so nice." Another incident he told me was this one Bhaktipada disciple, was fixed up with this one girl who didn't want to marry the guy. She was into someone else, and then one night they tried to escape together, but got caught. They (Kirtanananda's men) beat the crap out of the guy and threw his motorcycle over a cliff. They finally managed to elope anyway. (This incident involves Murti dasa's daughter and will be told in a later publication.) It goes on everywhere. In the days when Jiva was here, I heard stories. Almost all the mothers on his party were married to somebody, but then they went out on Jiva's party and, you know....

SD: Did he have sex with most of the women?

Jj: He had twenty-five women, but I don't know how many of them he had sex with. I heard that he was so burdened in that area that they even had some brahmacaris go over there to keep the women satisfied.

SD: How many marriages did he wind up destroying? Do you know?

Jj: No. They're scattered all over by now.

SD: Was there anything else Varaha told you?

Jj: Well he's out there and he knows he has to stay there or they will remarry his wife, even though he doesn't really like "Bhaktipada". He says, "I'm married, but

I'm not really married." He says, "They got a program that if you want to have sex with your wife you have to get permission, and they put you in this guest house for one night so you can have a kid."

SD: They do that to everyone or just the new people that don't know any better?

Jj: I guess it depends on who you are and what they want to do with your wife.

SD: What else do you know about Jiva's party?

Jj: Kushala told my wife that if some of the women went out and didn't meet their quota, they'd slap her around a little. But if you got your score, then you got the privilege to sack out with the sankirtana leader. One devotee told me that he went over there one night to fix some electrical problem and heard some women arguing, "I collected more than you, I should sleep with him tonight." Back and forth. Like that. I once asked Jiva-this was after he'd taken sannyasa and fell down-he was like a sankirtana leader in Portland with his wife, Champak. I was up there too. And I asked him, "How did you control all these women for all those years?" And he said, "Well, they're just really stupid, you know, they're extremely stupid. And I always wanted to be a pimp, and when I became a devotee, Krishna fulfilled my desire. I always had a strong desire to be a pimp. That's all I ever wanted to be. So Krishna just fulfilled this desire." (This man Jiva, was trained up in this philosophy by Dharmatma, Kirtanananda's right hand man.)

SD: I heard he wasn't even good looking?

Jj: No. You look at him, he's like a little caveman. He's got these tattoos all over him. He used to have a big naked lady on his back, but when he became a devotee, he had a Nrsinihadeva made over it, to cover up this naked lady. He was a boxer in San Quentin prison-tough as nails. He would just love to go out on sankirtana and get in some fight with someone and beat the crap out of him. They used to worship Jiva. Even after Hansadutta gave him sannyasa.

SD: Hansadutta gave him sannyasa?!

Jj: Well, he had to. He knew that if he just came and broke the whole thing up, Jiva would just bloop and the women would follow him somewhere else. He needed them to collect, like that. So he said, "what I'll do is just give him sannyasa." So even when he was sannyasa, he had all these women standing around. It was like he had 25 wives. Every time he went into the temple they all paid their obeisances. Before he took "sannyasa" he even had a vyasasana at the sankirtana house. He was like their guru. It was a whole thing.

SD: The guy was a mobster and sex-freak, and all of a sudden he's a guru in ISKCON with his own little harem. How long did this go on?

Jj: A couple of years. You should find some of those mothers who were on his party. They can tell you some stories. I know there's two of them down in LA. I heard rumors that if the women didn't get their quotas they should go out and pull a few tricks.

SD: Yeah. That's not surprising. Kusala told me Jiva would encourage them to steal anything they could get their hands on.

Jj: When Hansadutta got here, you know he wanted to stop this women's party, and Caru, who was the temple president at that time said: "You can't do that. These women are collecting a million dollars a year, and distributing all these books." Srila Hansadutta said, "Well then, if it's all right, then why don't you send your wife out with Jiva and let her get screwed a few times and see how you like it?" Then Caru shut up.

COMMENT

It should not be thought that the leaders in ISKCON were/are not aware of these kinds of activities. They are all fully aware of what's going on, but the greed for profit, adoration, and distinction far overshadows their desire to encourage moral behavior amongst the general devotees as well as themselves.

AN AGGESSOR HAS TO BE PUNISHED
IN ALL CIRCUMSTANCES

*"An enemy who sets fire to the house, administers poison, attacks all of a sudden with deadly weapons, plunders wealth or usurps agricultural fields, or entices one's wife is called an aggressor. Such an aggressor, though he be a brahmana or a so-called son of a brahmana, has to be punished in all circumstances."*

*(Srila Prabhupada from Srimad Bhagavatam 1.7.16)*

# "AN INSIDE INFORMATION SERVICE FOR DEVOTEES EVERYWHERE"

Dec. 12, 1985

Dear Vaisnavas and aspiring Vaisnavas:

Please accept my humble obeisances. All glories to the pure devotee who gave all of us the seed of Krishna consciousness, Srila Prabhupada.

For those of you who have expressed difficulty reading my heavy-handed writing style, I would like to quote from a letter Prabhupada wrote to Karandhara if that may help:

*"No compromise--Rama Krishna, Avatars, yogis, everyone was enemy to Guru Maharaja--he never compromised. Some Godbrothers complained that this preaching was chopping technique and it would not be successful. But we have seen that those who criticized, they fell down. For my part, I have taken up the policy of my Guru Maharaja--no compromise. All these so-called scholars, scientists, philosophers, who do not accept Krishna (or Prabhupada) are nothing more than rascals, fools, lowest of mankind, etc. So you go on with your work, it is very encouraging to me." (7/27/73)*

Today I was presented with a book put out by Dheera Krishna entitled, *The Guardian of Devotion. I* took this as a response to our challenges even though he hardly touched upon any of the serious points we had brought up. Dheera didn't touch upon our point that Sridhar Maharaja preaches an impersonal origin of the soul, which we proved by extensively quoting from both Sridhar Maharaja's book *Search for Krishna and* Prabhupada's books. We have no choice but to assume that Dheera has nothing to say. Having no answer means he has lost the debate.

I beg to remind Dheera and his followers that I wrote only Part One of four parts, to the Sridhara Maharaja chapter of my book, *The Guru Business.* (Available $10.) I did not touch upon the bad advice he gave ISKCON's GBC when they approached him in 1978 for approval to play guru. Two famous quotes by Sridhar Maharaja at that time were: "It will be to deceive the disciple (telling them you're a pure devotee)" or, "There is no big mantra or little mantra for guru. Guru is one. (So go ahead and pose as uttamas.)" A few years later when that bogus advice exploded in a series of falldowns, violence and dissension, Sridhara Maharaja said to Dheera, "They will dig their own graves (and bury Prabhupada along with them.)" Then he summed it all up very clearly by saying to Yashomatinandan, "I am a form breaker," and, "I don't agree with Swami Maharaja (Prabhupada) in everything." The effect of Sridhar Maharaja's bad advice on ISKCON did not surprise us since Prabhupada had already warned: "They (specifically Sridhara Maharaja) cannot help us in our movement but they are very competent to harm our natural progress." (Letter to Rupanuga.) As such, the fact that Dheera could not answer the section on the impersonal tendency leaves little doubt in our minds that he will not be able to respond to these heavy charges, i.e., that Sridhara Maharaja unduly interfered with the divine mission of Srila Prabhupada.

Personally, because I have full faith in Srila Prabhupada, I never had to read further than the one quote written to Rupanuga wherein Prabhupada said, "Sridhara Maharaja is responsible for disobeying this order of Guru Maharaja." Dheera simply refuses to address this and other serious statements made by Prabhupada. No one is denying that at one time Sridhar Maharaja was sincere, advanced, friends with Prabhupada, etc., and that Prabhupada liked him and even confided in him, but when an offense is committed to a pure devotee, or his mission (the Gaudiya Math) which is non-different, one loses all importance in Krishna consciousness and immediately falls down to mundane mental speculation. (Narayana Maharaja said, "Don't you know this man (Sridhara Maharaja) is a breaker of institutions?") As far as "high realizations" go, I'm sure Jayatirtha also has some very high realizations which make him and his followers "faint" all the time. And Srila Prabhupada said about Jayatirtha just before leaving this world, "You are my only tirtha (shelter)."

We are not interested in those kinds of "high realizations." We are interested in solid, direct, and concise rebuttals to our philosophical points. Words spoken by Prabhupada in the mood of flattery, encouragement, Vaisnava etiquette, respect for seniors, humility, gratitude, friendship, etc., are not valid arguments to counter all of the negative statements Prabhupada made about Sridhar Maharaja just before leaving this world. Flattering and encouraging speech was always used by Prabhupada even when talking to the most disgusting human beings imaginable, so what to speak of what Prabhupada was capable of saying to a senior Godbrother, and in that Godbrother's presence. The words Prabhupada spoke about Sridhara Maharaja to his disciples when Sridhara was not there is the actual fact. And even then, Prabhupada was very cautious. If Prabhupada put in writing that Sridhar Maharaja is responsible for disobeying an order of his guru, that's it. Case closed. If Dheera wants to defend Sridhar Maharaja, then he has to confront these points, and not simply invoke the sentiments of those with no knowledge of Prabhupada's style of encouragement, his tactfulness, and humility and compassion. All these factors have to be taken into consideration when analyzing something Prabhupada says about an individual. To say that Prabhupada was whimsical when he wrote the letter to Rupanuga is very offensive. Prabhupada always was very careful about what went into writing.

So if Dheera still wants to defend Sridhar Maharaja on the basis of flattering statements, then first he has to explain why Sridhar Maharaja says the jiva soul originates in the Brahmajyoti, whereas Prabhupada says the jiva's original home is with Krishna. Why did Prabhupada write to Visvakarma in August of 1975, "I have now issued orders that All of my disciples should avoid all of my Godbrothers." And why did Prabhupada tell Gargamuni right after Sridhar Maharaja left the room once, "He is simply envious." These are solid facts that we require solid rebuttals to if Dheera wants to be a preacher and try and establish Sridhar Maharaja as being equal to Prabhupada. Actually, even though he denies it, Dheera and his clan are trying to establish Sridhar Maharaja as superior to Prabhupada. His statements clearly reveal this fact. For this reason it is extremely dangerous to read or even cite the words of Dheera or Akshayananda just as it is suicidal to read the *Lilamrta*, which was designed by ISKCON's bogus gurus to minimize Srila Prabhupada, "To make Prabhupada more acceptable to the general public" was their excuse.

At the present moment, the battle to remove the bogus gurus in ISKCON has reached a point where I have no time to finish the chapter on Sridhara Maharaja. I know many of you are anxious to start circulating the full expose since it is so painful to see our beloved spiritual master being minimized and shoved into the background like this but the priority at this time is exposing the ISKCON "gurus". I have every intention of finishing the chapter on Sridhara Maharaja at first opportunity. The source material for that chapter is so voluminous that it will take a solid week to sort through and compile. Until then, it is my humble request that if any of you still have doubts as to the real situation with Sridhara Maharaja, then please just put yourself on hold for a few more months. Very soon, maybe even within weeks, the ISKCON "gurus" will be fully exposed and removed from power. Once this offensive situation is gone, everyone will be able to breathe again and we can begin to rebuild ISKCON. At that time, if there is still a threat coming from the Sridhara Maharaja camp, we will compile the full story.

The situation between myself and Keith Hamasura (Kirtanananda) has reached the point where any day now it can ignite into a full-scale media battle which will bring the entire ISKCON situation into the public eye (enclosed is the latest front-page article). We consider the Sridhara Maharaja issue to be insignificant when compared to the preaching that must be done at this time to re-establish ISKCON as the pure society Srila Prabhupada wanted it to be. It is not our intention to allow ISKCON to dissolve into another tiny, obscure, dead body, like the Gaudiya Math, just because the "form breaker" prefers it that way. He successfully destroyed the institution of his Guru Maharaja but we will not allow him to destroy our mission as well. The only tool left to save ISKCON form the hands of these form breakers and imitationists is the media which is why I am giving full attention to them now. Enclosed is my introduction to reporters and a concise explanation as to what has happened in ISKCON since the departure of Srila Prabhupada. It is only a matter of time before the story breaks wide open. With the violent threats Ramesvara is throwing around these days, I wouldn't be surprised if he doesn't ignite the media fire that will purge ISKCON once and for all.

Another point specifically to those who use the bait and switch tactic of luring devotees into your camps under the pretense of being sincere to Prabhupada; both the ISKCON "gurus" and the Sridhara Maharaja "gurus" are doing this. It is illegal, demoniac and a crime that I have every intention to putting a swift halt to. I tell the same thing to Dheera's cult that I tell Keith Ham-asura's cult. That is: I don't care if you want to preach some bogus philosophy but if you continue to use the name of Prabhupada and Krishna as bait, then you're going to be stopped. It's not all right. It's not all one. I don't care if you continue to use Sridhara Maharaja as bait to prop yourself up as a "guru", any more than I care if you use Rajneesh, but if you continue to use Prabhupada's legacy and name as bait, then you will be stopped for that is illegal. If you don't present a response to *all* of the challenges we have made then you have to remove all of Prabhupada's pictures from your temples and stop making this asinine claim that Sridhara Maharaja is equal to Prabhupada. That is simply not a fact. We have proven that in only Part One of our expose on Sridhara Maharaja. Your silence is your defeat. Stop using Prabhupada as bait! This is not a request, but an order. You are defeated in debate and that means you have to surrender. Otherwise, you will pay dearly for each and every person you lure away from Prabhupada. And don't try to juggle your way out of this or try to impress us with a discourse on Brahma Gayatri either. We are only interested to hear a discourse from you on why Prabhupada said, "Sridhara Maharaja is responsible for disobeying this order of Guru Maharaja," and that's all. Until you can answer this very simple and obvious question, don't pretend to be a scholar. So I'm saying, either present a full rebuttal to our challenge, surrender to the above demands, or expect a severe reaction. As you may have gathered by the way in which I'm dealing with ISKCON, I'm serious. When they're gone, you're next.

If anyone reading this would like to offer some tangible help in the service of Srila Prabhupada's mission, then there are many different services available at this time. For instance, while Dheera is busy writing books by and about Sridhar Maharaja, Srila Prabhupada's thousands of lectures are just sitting here waiting for someone to come along to index. Until then, we have no access to all that pure knowledge, pure humor, and pure Prabhupada contained therein. Researching Vedic texts, such as Chanakya Pandit book *Artha Sastra, or* books on the varnasrama social structure in general, is also crucial if Krishna consciousness is to be established in the world. So rather than waste time with an "ease lover's" philosophy, we humbly request serious devotees to come forward to help establish the mission so kindly started by our real father, Srila Prabhupada. He gave us all we need to know about Radha-Krishna and the Gopis. The followers of Srila Prabhupada don't need Sridhar Maharaja's "high realizations" on that subject (as though they were higher than Prabhupada's). He said, "Work now, samadhi later." So there is much solid and practical work to be done right now. Prabhupada left the "down to earth" work for us. That's all we are competent for--and not imitating real saints like Prabhupada. We hope there are enough practical and solid devotees around to take some of the credit for all this real work that needs to be done. Thank you.

As a final point, we are not claiming to be saints. We have all kinds of problems dealing with the material energy that seem insurmountable. We are not pretending to be always absorbed in the love of the gopis like the Sridhara Maharaja club.

Nor are we pretending to be scholars or brahmins like the smarta club of Subhananda, Ravindra Svarupa, and those who talk a lot but still get their bread and butter by handouts from demons. Nor are we members of "the end justifies the means" ISKCON "gurubhava" club that sits on thrones between semen breaks, drug deals, nervous breakdowns, wife stealings, child molestations, etc., etc. It is not necessary to join any of these clubs to understand Srila Prabhupada's books. He wrote his books for people just like us: simple but honest. In fact, it is only honest people who can understand Prabhupada's books. That's because honesty is the only leg left in this age and we are proud to be tightly hanging on that one leg. So for those of you who don't like this simple, direct, often crude, often angry, but at least honest way of speech, then why don't you come forward and do something better to remove these demons who have ravaged Prabhupada's movement? Dheera says guru is one, and Keith Ham-asura says we are trying to crucify Prabhupada. Both these statements are in essence the exact same thing: trying to place yourselves equal to Prabhupada, and that is an offense no real disciple of Prabhupada will tolerate, for long.

Your servant in the exclusive service of Srila Prabhupada:

Sulocana dasa

*"Prabhupada: Oh, you must kill them. Tit for tat. As soon as we detect that "Here is deprogrammer and kidnapper," kill him. Finish!" (Room Conversation, February 19, 1977, Mayapura)*

# THE KINGDOM

By Sulocana dasa

May 20, 1986

Once upon a time there lived a very wise and saintly king who had thousands of sons and daughters. His kingdom spread throughout the world and he loved all of his children equally. He was the well-wisher of all. His children could live in any one of their father's many kingdoms and be happy in their service to the king, no matter what that service may be. The elder, managerially inclined sons, managed the kingdom for their father but they were not favored over the youngest sons just because of their managerial post. This was because the king saw the love of his sons and not their material qualifications. He wanted the best for all his sons but unfortunately not all of his sons loved the father equally. Many of the younger sons loved their father more than the eldest sons and this naturally created some jealousy amongst them. The wise old king of course tried to pacify all his sons but eventually he gave up and decided to leave this world.

But first, he requested that all his sons try and live together in love and trust. He practically begged his oldest sons to treat the youngsters as brothers and not as inferiors. But the moment the king died, some of the oldest sons held council and as a result, they grabbed as much territory, riches, women and children as they could. Each declared himself an independent sovereign king equal to their father. The thousands of younger, more simple and trusting brothers were baffled. Some of them, out of humility and in order to keep peace in the family, went along with the older brothers for awhile but it was wrong and everybody knew it. Eventually the older brothers took complete control of the kingdom.

Some of the younger brothers and sisters protested by reciting their father's last wishes. But to no avail. The older sons already had the taste of wealth, worship and power and would not give it up. So instead of listening to the humble advice of the younger brothers, they had them beaten, exiled, or killed. One after another, the young brothers came forward to protest and one after another, they failed until finally all gave up and left the kingdom for good, leaving behind their heritage, homes, and often even their wives and children since many of the women chose the security of the kingdom over the wandering, struggling life of their exiled husbands. Many wives were so young they never really knew the old king and thus they thought the oldest brothers were as good as the king. So they chose to worship the new "kings" rather than follow their husbands into the cold, cruel world.

One of the younger sons, however, not willing to sacrifice his family and home to such a corrupt despot of a king decided to fight. Without wealth or many allies, and practically alone, he fought the older brothers who had stolen the kingdom for themselves. Aided with only a computer and the knowledge in his father's books and personal letters, he tried to awaken a revolt amongst the discouraged and exiled brothers. He knew that peaceful pleading and scriptural argument would fall on deaf ears as it had for many years. So instead, he spoke straightforward and truthfully, often using violent language when appropriate. He described the crimes that had been committed to the younger brothers, and their families, many of which were crimes the father had said were punishable by death. The older brothers were shocked by this violent verbal attack but they could say nothing in argument. Every word spoken by the younger brother was true and they all knew it. Since they could not defend themselves verbally, and since they were too blinded by power to give up their folly, they tried to kill the younger brother. But alas, they could not find him, for he lived in hiding, moving constantly from the house of one exiled brother to another.

Then one of the oldest, and most corrupt brothers went outside his father's kingdom and told the police of that town, who knew nothing of the king, his kingdom, or the teachings of the king, that a violent killer was stalking nearby. He convinced the police that this young brother should be arrested and thrown in jail. He showed the police a quote from one of the letters of the younger brother which stated that the older brother deserved to be executed. Not knowing, or caring to know where the real violence was, the outside world police found and arrested the defenseless younger brother.

Since the corrupt brother went outside the walls of his father's kingdom to stop the younger brother, the younger brother decided to try and fight in the outer world also. So he described all the crimes the older brothers had committed in terms that the citizens of the outside could understand. He tried to get them to understand that a horrible injustice had taken place and that as citizens of a free country, the younger brothers also had a right to protection under the laws of the land. The young brother showed the police exactly how the older brother had stolen his wife and family in exactly the same way they had stole hundreds of other families from the younger brothers. He showed how the women had been taken and used as whores, how the children had been tortured. How the young brothers had been beaten, robbed, and exiled. He showed how the older brothers had lost all sense of right and wrong in that they even justified selling heroin to amass wealth since they didn't have the purity to inspire honest contributions.

Some of the outer world people listened and agreed. Some even sympathized. But most didn't want to take the time and trouble to understand all the intricacies of the kingdom, which to them was too different, and was based on a different set of laws. And so no one helped. The younger son was sitting alone in a strange jail with no one. Almost all his fellow exiled brothers had given up on their father's kingdom and went back to living in the outer world, the way everyone else lived. But the younger brother could not stand to see his father's kingdom fester and rot to the point where self-confessed homosexuals, rapists, heroin pushers, and murderers were being worshipped as though they were as good as their father. He could not bear to see his father's name brought down to such a low level and thus he...(to be continued).

*(Sulocana dasa was murdered May 22nd, 1986, 1:00 a.m., in Los Angeles, two days after this story was written.)*

## Sulocana's Resolute Fight Was Tantamount To His Seeing Krishna

*"Similarly, a devoted disciple of the spiritual master would rather die with the spiritual master than fail to execute the spiritual master's mission. As the Supreme Personality of Godhead comes down upon this earth to re-establish the principles of religion, so His representative, the spiritual master, also comes to re-establish religious principles. It is the duty of the disciples to take charge of the mission of the spiritual master and execute it properly. Otherwise the disciple should decide to die along with the spiritual master. In other words, to execute the will of the spiritual master, the disciple should be prepared to lay down his life and abandon all personal considerations…. When one becomes serious to follow the mission of the spiritual master, his resolution is tantamount to seeing the Supreme Personality of Godhead. As explained before, this means meeting the Supreme Personality of Godhead in the instruction of the spiritual master. This is technically called vani-seva. Srila Visvanatha Cakravarti Thakura states in his Bhagavad-gita commentary on the verse vyavasayatmika buddhir ekeha kuru-nandana (Bg. 2.41) that one should serve the words of the spiritual master. The disciple must stick to whatever the spiritual master orders. Simply by following on that line, one sees the Supreme Personality of Godhead."*

*(Srila Prabhupada from Srimad Bhagavatam 4.28.48,50,51)*

Note: Tantamount = having equal force, value, effect, etc.; equal or equivalent (to)

# SULOCANA DESIRED TO REMOVE THE
# LEADERS OF THE JEW WORLD ORDER

ment they were together. Some nights, he came in from his van and woke her up to read a passage from one of Prabhupada's books about the sanctity of marriage.

That didn't work. So he became the model husband. For the first time in all their years of marriage, he helped with the housework, cleaning the apartment and washing dirty dishes.

Even that didn't work. Jane couldn't be bullied or coaxed away from Kirtanananda and his commune. So Bryant changed tactics once again. He began knocking the swami and deriding New Vrindaban.

"This place is a tourist trap," he told Jane. "The most spiritual thing in the whole commune is the sound of the cash register ringing."

But Bryant's rantings only strengthened Jane's determination to stay. Bryant swallowed his pride; he decided to remain in the commune with his family for a while. But pressure on him to leave mounted almost daily. He was told he was no longer needed in the fiberglass shop and was laid off. Devotees shunned him. When he sat down for a meal in Prasadam Hall, devotees at his table got up and moved. When they were forced to talk to him, they called him Bryant instead of Sulocana, a mortifying insult that meant he was no longer considered a member of the movement.

Bryant reacted by immersing himself in right-wing politics and the culture of guns. It was an interest that had first flourished when his Krishna career began to sour in the early eighties. Now it became a passion. He bought several pistols and spent hours every day practicing with them on the New Vrindaban firing range. He put himself on the John Birch Society mailing list and read every pamphlet they sent him. He sent away for several Bircher books and began preaching their view of the world the way he had once preached Krishna Consciousness.

"Politics are a farce," he told Jane one day. "The same people who control the United States control the Soviet Union."

"You know what I'd like to do?" he announced another time. "Become an assassin and bump off some of the people who are running the world."

It didn't soothe his rage. Each day, Bryant became angrier and angrier. Soon, he began to hate himself. He saw himself as a man of action hanging around and knuckling under to a woman. Enough is enough, he finally told himself. He would show Jane and the rest of

# A LETTER TO THE DEVOTEES

**DAS** Devotee Access Services   Box 1391 Culver City, CA
90232

May 2nd 1985

Dear Prabhus

Please accept my humble obeisances. All glories to
Srila Prabhupada who we ardently pray will be
re-established as the only real shelter of all fallen
souls in this age.

I recently spoke to Rupanuga Prabhu and Tamal Krsna
Goswami who who both suggested I send a copy of my
compilation of Prabhupada's heaviest letters to some of
the leading devotees. I don't know how much you are aware
of my work but if you have not yet seen a DAS brochure
then I'm sure if you asked around a little locally you
will find one.

I wanted to briefly summerize some points for you now.
As you may have heard I am in the midst of a campaign to
prove that Kirtanananda has grossly deviated from the
instructions of Srila Prabhupada and should be removed. To
prove this I have been scrutinizingly studying Srila
Prabhupada's books and letters on guru and marriage full
time now for the past year as well as interviewing a lot
of ex-New Vrndavana members. I have read through every
single one of Srila Prabhupada's letters (in the BBT
archives) and have picked out the most crucial ones to
smash the present bogus situation in ISKCON. Tamal Krsna
Goswami suggested that my research would be very valuable
to the devotees in preparing the society's constitution.
So I have compiled a 150pg book that contains these most
significant letters and have sent copies to the grievance
committee. They are presently trying to get Kirtanananda
to return my children to me before I do something that
could be very damaging to the society. Getting my children
away from Kirtanananda is of course my duty as their
father and is very important to me personally but that is
not the main reason for compiling this book.

The real reason is that I am very anxious to see
ISKCON purified of this guru problem and I know of only
one method of doing this that nobody in his right mind can
possibly deny. That is to take all of Srila Prabhupada's
teachings from the letters, books and lectures (which are
already on microfilm) and make a first class index and
catagorization of them. (Not a compilation on guru like
Subananda's that left out everything controversial). Most
of this work can be done by the computers. Once under way
the whole project will be complete in 3 months. Then
Prabhupada's words have to be analyzed in terms of the
times and circumstances that they were spoken since there
appear to be so many contradictions. It's because of these

sampradya system of gurus. There is also an update on
California's devotee communities outside of ISKCON.

After you have read this book I shall be contacting the
research committee of Romapada Maharaja, Subananada
Prabhu, and Ravindra Svarupa Prabhu to discuss the most
efficient method by which to accomplish this indexing
project before next year. I'm sure we are all eager to see
this project completed before the end of the summer so
there will be a little time to prepare for a real 500th
birthday celebration for Lord Caitanya. I know it can be
done if this project gets the full support of ISKCON but I
also know that ISKCON will never push or finance this
without a big fire being placed beneath them. Therefore if
some serious communication is not started before June 1st,
DAS will begin making preperations to accomplish this feat
on its own, with money we receive from such places as '60
minutes' for interviews on the "RISE AND FALL OF ISKCON,
(an insiders story)" worth $10,000-$20,000 to them. Of
course my aim is not to destroy ISKCON or make money off
of the confidential information in this book, but to help
purify ISKCON. But if ISKCON will not cooperate to do this
vital work immediately, then it will be evident that there
is no serious interest in Srila Prabhupada's teachings
within ISKCON. And if that is the case, then we ask you;
is that "ISKCON" worth saving?

I will be printing these all at once so please send
your check for $10 immediately. <u>Printing and posting will
be on May 15th.</u> If your check arrives late you will have
to wait some time for the next printing. Make your check
payable to <u>Steve Bryant</u>, not DAS. ISKCON checks or money
orders are OK but no personal checks please. I am only
sending copies of this letter to a dozen or so devotees in
the USA and Canada so if those of you who receive this
would like someone else to receive one you should contact
them by phone and give them the information. I would
eventually like all the temple presidents to receive one.
Use a private address if your temple's mail is shuffled by
other devotees. If you don't have a private address I can
send it to your karmi name General Delivery at your
nearest post office. This book is very heavy and exposes a
lot of corruption about these "gurus" so I won't send to
those who are not serious disciples of Srila Prabhupada.
Please keep that in mind.

                          Your aspiring servant

                          Sulocana das

          Mail checks to:

                          Steve Bryant
                          PO box 1391
                          Culver City, Ca. 90232

**DAS** Devotee Access Services Box 1391 Culver City, CA 90232

THE CONFIDENTIAL LETTERS

OF

# HIS DIVINE GRACE
# A.C. BHAKTIVEDANTA SWAMI PRABHUPADA

## TABLE OF CONTENTS

PREFACE & INTRODUCTION

PART I - Chapter I

## PURITY IS THE FORCE

CHAPTER II

## "PERSONAL AMBITION"

## CHAPTER IV

## "THE DEBATE"

## PART II

## "THE KIRTANANANDA EXPOSE"

### Chapter 1 - VRNDAVANA, INDIA; 1967

### PART II - Chapter 2

### NEW VRNDAVANA;  1968-1985

# A LETTER TO SUBHANANDA

Steve Bryant, c/o Tim Lee 2501 Haste St. #211 Berkeley CA
94704

July 6th, 1985

Dear Subhananda Prabhu

Please accept my humble obeisances. All glories to
Srila Prabhupada.

Thank you for taking the time to write. I apologize for
not replying sooner but I've been very busy and my plans
underwent a somewhat dramatic change when Kailasa Chandra
das decided to contribute the documents he possessed. I
will respond to your points in order.

First I apologize if I offended you for your book on
Guru. What your intentions were for compiling it, only
you and Krsna know. One thing we all know however is that
it did not prevent these men from appointing themselves
"guru" and then falsely taking worship as though they
were uttama adhikaris, thus practically destroying the
mission and the enthusiasm of all our Godbrothers. In
this way the book was a complete failure. Of course at
the time you may have been just as naive as the rest of
us as to the degree of corruption going on amongst these
"top men" so, again, I apologize if I offended you. You
say that you took only references from the books but
there are many references in the books as to how bogus it
is to appoint a guru. You didn't men___ ___ those. The book
was financed by Ramesvara so I can easi__ ___understand your
position.

Your suggestion that "if I could go about my wo__ with
a "cool head" is very much appreciated. That is exactly
what I'm doing. Otherwise I would have gone to NV with a
shotgun and blown Kirtanananda's head right off his trunk
long ago. There would have been no reaction for doing so.
I've already proven that Kirtanananda is a demon and the
silence from his side confirms it. This expose I'm
compiling is actually the "cool" course of action for me
and is really the only weapon I have to get my sons away
from the Raksasa. The GBC has, as I predicted, been
unable to get any sympathy from KS (not that they really
tried very hard). He laughs as them just like he laughed
at me. Lord Ramacandra also got laughed at by Ravana when
Rama demanded His wife back. This is the standard symptom
of demons since time immemorial just before they are
destroyed. They feel so powerful that they can even steal

251

other mens wives. History has shown this. The Kurus also
were not utterly doomed until they stole Draupadi. So
even though this is Kali yuga and none of us are on the
level of any of the above personalities, still, there is
a direct relationship.

Your statement that "no movement has ever been reformed
by threats etc..." I cannot figure out how you came to
this conclusion. My position is simply this. Kirtanananda
has clearly shown himself to be nothing but a demon. I
have proven this. No one disagrees who has read my
expose's on him. I've given the GBC ample opportunity to
rectify KS and themselves. They refused. In Vedic culture
this would mean a violent war would take place. Wars
indeed have many times "reformed" a movement. Due to
these present circumstances however, physical war is out
of the question. So the only other weapon is the media.
I'm only doing what I have to do. These are my options.
(1) Go to NV and kidnap my sons. Then I have to live in
hiding for who knows how long. Even though the sons
belong to the father in our religion, they (KS) are
taking shelter of the karmi laws which give children to
mothers. (2) Go to NV and kill Kirtanananda. Then I have
to live as a fugative since the karmis don't consider
wife-stealing, and child kidnapping crimes punishable by
death. (He has destroyed numerous lives besides just my
wife's.) (3) Work like an ass to make enough money to
hire a lawyer who may just be able to get me partial
custody. I won't allow my sons to remain in KS's demoniac
presence for even a moment so that is out of the
question. (4) Present my case to the GBC and leave it up
to them. I've done that and they have failed to influence
KS. They are, for the most part, guilty of the same
crimes so I didn't really expect them to be much help.
(5) Make a major media exposure of all ISKCON and file a
large law suit against the entire organization. Only in
this way will I be able to attract a good lawyer. This
book I'm producing now is all the evidence I need to get
any jury in the country to get my sons back to me, and
naturally it will start a chain reaction. If it weren't
for my sons being in KS's grip I would most likely just
distribute this book within the society, but since I need
a lawyer to get legal custody, I have to go public.
Sorry. I have no choice. The GBC has failed. If you want
to donate $20,000, I may be able to get custody without
big public exposure but I don't think you or anybody else
cares enough about my sons to spend that kind of money.
So your statement to "yell and scream bloody murder" is
exactly what I'm doing. Thank you.

Your next paragraph is interesting. Not only do I think
Prabhupada would want me to do what I'm doing, but he

himself set that example in the way he condemned his
bogus Godbrothers. He called Bon a black snake. He
publicaly exposed them all. Bon never attacked his guru
as KS did in 1967. Bon was never a faggot. Bon never
stole a Godbrothers wife and turned her into a hor. Bon
never dealt in drugs. Bon was never in a mental
institution. Bon never killed cows. All in all I think
Prabhupada is very pleased that these demons are finally
being exposed for what they are. But, if indeed, as you
say, Prabhupada does not want this book publised and
mass distributed, then it simply will not happen. I'm not
attached to the result. Man proposes, God disposes. Krsna
may want me to remain single. When I get my sons back I
will naturally have to remarry. I am responsible for my
sons and so I am doing my duty, that's all. If Krsna
wants it done, then I am doing it. Krsna can easily stop
me at any moment, but instead, He appears to be providing
me with all the facility and encouragement I could
possible want. So ultimately we will see what Prabhupada
wants.

     This concept that "ISKCON" is Prabhupada is
foolishness. Do you really think Prabhupada is behind
this corrupt GBC? If you do, then I hate to have to say
this, but that means you are either waiting in line to be
appointed yourself, in which case you would not be able
to see anything clearly, or you may still be a little
naive about these men, in which case this book will be a
real eye opener for you also. The GBC severed their link
with Prabhupada long ago when they appointed themselves
"gurus" (note revised May "appointment" transcript
enclosed). Even without so much hard evidence, the
character of these men clearly exposes them. So just some
friendly advice Prabhu. I don't really know you at all.
We only met once in the Dallas restaurant last year just
after I left NV. and we didn't talk about anything much.
So please don't take this personal. I give this advice to
everyone. "ISKCON" is absolutely finished. The sooner you
join Prabhupada's side fully in this fight, the more you
will be able to take part in the victory. Just like Krsna
didn't need Arjuna to end the Kurus, similarly we will
publish this book and mass distribute it no matter how
many devotees come forward to help. The sooner you sever
your link with that corrupt organization, the less
implicated you will be when they are smashed. If you wait
until they are fully smashed to see the light, that won't
mean much or reflect very highly on you. Everyone will
wake up then, no matter what their motivation or
realization may be.

     If you decide you would like to help in a practical way
to purify ISKCON then I will certainly be able to engage

you. Right now we have a board of approx. 12 brahmins,
all old and sincere devotees, who are going to review the
final copy before printing. The main idea is to make it
as strong and pure as possible with the sole intent of
revealing to the world that Prabhupada never had anything
to do with the corruption that Karmis experience and read
about "ISKCON." To do this is sensitive. The media would
just assume see Prabhupada smashed along with "ISKCON."
But they will not want to reject the book either because
it has a lot of very juicy facts in it. So its a juggling
act for them. Our aim is to make it as easy as possible
for them to accept the book and advertize it, without
compromising Prabhupada's greatness. If you want to be on
the board of reviewers, you are welcome, but I would need
something from you to guarantee that you will not allow a
copy to be made and given to the GBC. They will try to
put a restraining order on it. You will have to have a
lawyer draw up an agreement that you will review the book
without allowing the GBC or any "ISKCON" man to get hold
of it. Only then will I be able to send you an advance
copy. I'll call you to discuss details if you are
interested. I'm sure your contribution to this book would
be invaluable. The devotees will have a week to read and
think about all the chapters, and mail all their ideas to
me. I will then organize them all and mail them back for
final voting on what's to be included and what's to be
left out. If you feel something should be left out for
any reason, that argument should be made clearly and it
will be mailed to all the voters. It may be necessary for
a second review and vote but I doubt it. The names of the
devotees will be kept confidential unless otherwise
stated. I am making this offer to you because of your
knowledge in dealing with the public. No other "ISKCON"
PR men are involved as yet.

Again I thank you for writing. We are going with a
professional printing job since the book is close to 300
pgs. Hopefully it will be complete in a month. The name
will be voted on. I was thinking something like; ISKCON'S
NEW GURUS--"THE MOST DANGEROUS ELEMENTS IN HUMAN SOCIETY"
(sub)THE CONSPIRACY THEY NEVER WANTED REVEALED. Your
suggestions will be welcome. I look forward to hearing
from you again.

                              Your humble servant

                              Sulocana das

# A LETTER TO TRIYOGI

STEVE BRYANT (SULOCANA DAS) 2124 KITTREDGE #32, BERKELEY CA 94704

Nov. 7, 1985

Dear Triyogi das

Please accept my humble obeisances. All glories
to Srila Prabhupada.

I don't believe we have met but I wanted to let
you know that there are many of us out here who are
grateful for what you've done. I don't know what
your motive was but I know that KS is a very
demoniac man and deserved much more than what he
got. The Yamadhuttas will carry on where you left
off. I'm not a physical type person myself, so I
have been attacking him by public exposure. By
Krsna's mercy I've had rather good success in that
endeavor. In fact, the very morning you hit him KS
called up Atreya Rsi here in California and was
trying to make arrangements to send my sons back to
me in hopes that would stop me from exposing him
further. He must have sensed something heavy was
about to happen to him but misinterpreted it as my
launching a media campaign against him. I was
actually a little sorry to hear this had happened
for I was expecting to see my boys within days. Now
the negotiations are on hold for who knows how long.
If he dies there's no telling what's going to
happen. I suspect NV will disintegrate within
months. It's a personality cult and when the
personality dies, it's all over.

Ultimately it was Krsna's arrangement that this
has happened. Violence was inevitable since these
"gurus" had done so much damage to Prabhupada's
movement and disciples. The only amazing thing is
that it took this long to start happening. KS had
Jadurani beaten five years ago. Personally I predict
several more "gurus" will be attacked in the next
few months. Enclosed is a recent circular that I'm
sending to the ksatriya devotees who follow
Prabhupada. It explains some of the intricasies of
violence and its application according to our
scriptures. I hope it will help you formulate your
defence. You may be feeling some hatred coming from
the handful of zombies who think KS is a human being
but rest assured, he had many more enemies than
friends. As Prabhupada said, "A saintly person takes
pleasure in seeing snakes and scorpions killed." In
that letter he let it be known that this also
applies to men who are like snakes and scorpions.
Prabhupada directly called KS in letters, "a
creature," a "crazy man," a "Mayavadi," a "jackel,"

to mention a few. Why KS had a position in ISKCON is
fully explained in chapter two of my book, The Guru
Business. Prabhupada was expert in keeping even the
worst of demons engaged and out of trouble. If
Prabhupada hadn't encouraged KS to develope NV, then
KS would have continued attacking Prabhupada. NV was
just throwing KS a bone to keep him out of trouble.
That's all it boils down to.

It's a shame this country's legal system allows
such men to enact their demoniac plans using
innocent citizens as pawns. For this reason it is
sometimes necessary to take the law into our own
hands. This government just plain can't or won't
take the responsibility. They are too busy passing
laws allowing abortion, pornography, prostitution,
intoxication, etc., or they're too busy spending the
payoff money they get from the men thriving off
those "businesses." So they won't help us get
justice. They don't even know it's wrong to pose as
a holy man because they don't believe in God, or
they think God has nothing to do with them, which is
the same thing. Actually it's this government that's
responsible for what happened to KS and not you. You
only did what the Government should have done long
ago. Judge Warmuth there in Moundsville is a perfect
example of one such corrupt government
representative. On KS's behalf, he gave my wife a
divorce and custody of my sons without even thinking
it necessary to notify me of the hearing. That makes
him responsible for my wife's now being one of KS's
common hors. By Vedic law that "judge" could be
punished for this crime. So there is just no way to
deal with this country's legal system. They are
worse than the violent criminals because they pass
laws which allow and even encourage degredation in
society. I'm hoping this incident will spark a major
controversy over these issues.

For instance, for the past year I've been
interviewing many of KS's victims. I have numerous
testimones of how he directly breaks up marriages,
forces young 13 year old girls to sleep with 26 year
old men of degraded character, even ignores it when
these young girls are raped as in the case with
Ambarisha who raped two girls around 12-13 years
old. He tells men to beat their wives; forces women
out on the streets against their will and puts their
infant babies in a nursery with 20 other infants to
be looked after by one 10 year old girl, etc. etc.
The list goes on indefinitely. Do you think this
country's courts are interested in these

testimonies? Hell no! To press charges against this
kind of thing requires too much money, and KS is the
only one who's got money.  And if someone presses
charges they have to live in fear for their lives.
So he is free to go on exploiting women any way he
likes. It's incredible what he's gotten away with
over the past 20 years. What you have done is really
the only way to stop a man like KS in this country
and so your action is praiseworthy.

Anyway, I'm sure you couldn't help yourself once
you realized who KS really was. I suspect right at
that moment Krishna inspired you to do what you did.
You could not have done that without the sanction of
the Lord. KS is too big a demon. He's one of the
kingpins in ISKCON so rest assured, Krsna had His
hand in your action. Just like Krsna inspired Arjuna
to kill millions of demons on the battlefield of
Kurukshetra, including his own relatives, so it was
not at all surprising to see Krsna use you to kill
this demon. You may not be Arjuna, and your motive
may not have been as pure as Arjuna's, but then KS
is not Duryodhana either. Duryodhana was a gentleman
compared to KS. Krsna can use whomever He likes to
do whatever He likes. Let the courts try to
prosecute Krsna. I'm just curious as to why He gave
you the honor of executing KS instead of one of the
more deserving victims. Anyway it's done and that's
the important thing.

I'm planning on exposing all these ISKCON
"gurus" to the media very soon. I would like to know
more of your personal situation before doing so. I
may be able to help you in regards to public opinion
since I have gathered enough evidence right now to
prove that KS deserved exactly what he got. So
please get back to me as soon as possible. If your
lawyer arranges it, I may be allowed to talk to you
over the phone. I'll try calling you after this
letter reaches you. I wouldn't be depressed if I
were you. If there is any reaction at all coming
your way it won't be much. The good that will result
from your action far overshadows any ill motive, if
any, that may have been there on your part. I'll be
looking forward to talking with you.

Your's in the service of Prabhupada

Sulocana das

# THE RELIGION PEDDLERS

STEVE BRYANT 2124 KITTREDGE #32, BERKELEY CA 94704

Sept. 14, 1985

## THE RELIGION PEDDLERS

FALSE ADVERTISING IN THE NAME OF GOD

WHY THE U.S. GOVERNMENT MUST STEP IN TO RECTIFY THE
HARE KRISHNA MOVEMENT BEFORE VIOLENCE BREAKS OUT.

There is a common law throughout the world which
states that a product must perform as it is
advertised. When people purchase something, they
expect it to work on the basis of this law. When
someone is selling a religion, the same law or code of
honor should hold true. If the religion doesn't work,
the party selling it should be caught and punished.

But there are some very unique differences between
ordinary salesman and the sellers of religion. For
one, religion salesman not only request money, but
they request one's life and soul as well. In return,
they give a promise that the customer will go to
heaven when he dies. In other words, "give your life
now, and when you die I'll pay you." Many say, "If you
don't give your life now, when you die you will go to
hell." There are many thousands of persons selling
religions, or these promises, daily. Naturally some
hold true more than others. If a religion is
authentic, there is certainly justification for buying
it, no matter the cost. There is no price to high for
a ticket to the Kingdom of God.

But what of those selling a concocted religion that
does nothing at all? Considering the high cost, isn't
that much worse than stealing a car, wallet, a tape
deck, etc. One should think the government would have
a department that censors religions but believe it or
not, the US government has no such department.
Instead, they encourage such stealing in the name of
the first amendment. This law actually protects the
Jim Jones's, the Charles Manson's, the Kirtanananda's,
etc., the sellers of these manufactured religions,
right up until it is too late to stop the catastrophy
that always results when unscrupulous men hold power.

So until the Govt. wakes up to its duty in this
regard, it's up to us, the individual citizens, to
understand what is religion and enforce it. After
death, one cannot file suit against a bogus religion
salesman. Many unscrupulous men like the "religion

2.

business" for this reason. They know people won't find
out they've been cheated until they're dead. So to
prove someone is selling a bogus religion, the accuser
has to be very sharp in understanding what real
religion is. Since most people, especially the
politicians, are not inclined in this age to
understand what religion is, almost everyone is being
exploited in the name of God. But common sense tells
us that there must be a way to find out if a religion
is good or bad without having to die first or wait for
some other "sign" such as the mass murder in Jim
Jones's "religion."

### THE DEBATE

The system used for determining the authenticity of
a religion, without having to wait for such extremes,
is called debate. This is true for all religions. In
an ordinary court of law, there are hundreds of
lawbooks. A good lawyer must know these books
thoroughly. His job entails quoting from them and
nothing more. The process is exactly the same in
defending a religion. Religious lawbooks are the
scriptures. For the Christians, it's the Bible. The
Muslims the Koran. The Hindus the Vedas. These are the
three main scriptures from which all others are
offshoots. In the Western world the most authoritative
translations of the Sanskrit Vedic scriptures are
those compiled by His Divine Grace A.C. Bhaktivedanta
Swami Prabhupada, the founder of the Hare Krishna
movement. Anyone who claims to be selling the Bhakti
Yoga religion given in the Vedas must be abiding by
the laws given in these books. If someone is deviating
from those laws, then anyone has the right to
challenge the deviater to a debate. If the deviator
refuses to accept the challenge, then he looses.
Nothing else need be said. In religious circles
silence means defeat.

A scriptural deviator cannot sell spiritual life
any more than a auto mechanic can sell himself as a
brain surgeon. Such a fool will be detected the very
first day, provided there is someone around who knows
what a brain surgeon does. Similarly, there are many
persons who sell concocted religions and get away with
it, until someone comes along who knows the real
thing. Then the deviator must defend himself or get
out.

What if someone is selling a bogus religion, gets
challenged to debate, but ignores the challenge. Does
that mean he can continue to cheat others just because

the US Government won't step in? No! The Government
has a duty to protect it's citizens from being
cheated--all cheating. Their duty is not limited to
crimes visible to the gross eyeballs only. There is a
practical and scientific method to determine the
authenticity of a religion and it's seller. One simply
has to know the basic ingredients of religion.
Religious belief is the most subtle science, and
therefore the most difficult to regulate, but to say
it is impossible, and thereby enforce no religious
laws, is criminal neglect of duty. Psychology is also
a subtle science that few people can comprehend but
through it one can explain many things beyond the
comprehension of ordinary men. Similarly, true
religious scholars can see and understand the subtle
motivations behind a charleten and expose them in such
a way that justice is served.

For example: a 16 year old girl can get physically
raped and the government recognizes her rights as
having been violated. But young girls can just as
easily be talked into sex with unscrupulous men  Then
the government does nothing. They do not acknowledge
the mental and verbal lies used to exploit the girl.
That is criminal neglect. The psychological rapist is
just as guilty as the physical rapist. The only
difference is that the one is smarter than the other
which means he should be punished even more sev.rly.
Therefore the Vedas, being complete lawbooks, have
very strict laws regulating who, when, and where, one
can even talk to women. A religious govenment must
enforce those laws if they are to prevent gross and
subtle rape in society. Just as the government should
have laws protecting innocent women from fast talking
rapists, they should also have laws protecting the
citizens from fast talking "religionists."

There are two kinds of bogus religion salesman. One
selling cheap imitations and one selling expensive
imitations. Both are criminals but the one can be
considered a misdemeanor. There are many people who
want to buy something cheap in the name of God since
the real thing is very expensive. Many churches,
ashrams, etc., charge very little and give very
little. "You get what you pay for" holds true even for
religions. But if someone is claiming to be selling
real religion (love of God), and is charging the real
price (absolute surrender of one's heart and soul),
but is selling a fake, then such a person is described
in Vedic scripture: "These rogues are the most
dangerous elements in human society" (Isopanisad 12).
Love of God is certainly the most valuable possession

4.

and the price for that is very high. If someone is
charging that price but is selling a fake, then he
must be stopped and it is the government's duty to see
that he is.

## DEALING WITH SUCH CRIMINALS

Once these criminals are exposed, there are only
two ways to deal with them.

Method one: They are given a chance to defend
themselves by debate. If they accept the challenge but
loose, then they must surrender to the person who
defeated them. If they do that, then it means they
were not maliciously selling a bogus religion. All of
the sincere followers of the defeated party will
automatically join the winning party and thus they
move up to a higher understanding. In this way society
advances in learning and culture. Everyone is happy,
provided everyone is sincere.

Method two: These men refuse to debate or surrender
to the challenger. They know they are selling a bogus
product but they live only for their own pleasure and
don't care how many lives they hurt getting it. They
cannot sell real religion because they never possessed
it. These are the lowest creatures on earth and they
must be stopped. They are many times worse than
murderers, thieves, or rapists. They take people's
lives, their money, their very heart and soul, and in
the end give them nothing but a stab in the back. And
that is not even the worse crime they commit. Far
worse than all that is the crime of cheating the
innocent masses out of the real product, which may be
available elsewhere.

The destination of such rogues is stated in the
Vedas: "They go to the most obnoxious place in the
universe when they finish with their guru business."
(Isopanishad, 12). There are many levels of hellish
existence awaiting sinful men, but those men who cheat
others in the Name of God, go to the most obnoxious
place of them all.

## BUT WHAT ABOUT THE FIRST AMENDMENT?

When the average citizens are out religion
shopping, are they being psycologically kidnapped or
are they exercising their first amendment rights? That
depends on the authenticity of the religion being
purchased. If it's the real thing, then the purchaser
is exercising his right to select the religious
practice of his choice. If the product is a fake

however, then he's simply being ripped off in the name
of God. The general public must never be left helpless
and unprotected at the hands of such charlatans. A
responsible government must have a board of religion
censors to protect the citizens from such criminals.
Each and every citizen cannot possibly be expected to
discriminate the real thing from the fakes. Religious
science is the most subtle and complex science of them
all and therefore the countries most intelligent
scholars should be given the facility to settle all
religious discrepancies by formal debates.

## PSYCHOLOGICAL KIDNAPPING

What term could better describe religious thievery
than psychological kidnapping? People are being lured
into giving their whole lives to men who have nothing
to give them in return. This is actually subtle rape
but since it's being done it in the name of God, the
government does nothing. Practically speaking, every
salesman uses psychological tactics to get a person to
part with his money. In that sense everyone is
psychologically kidnapping other people all the time.
Television is the greatest kidnapper of all. But such
psychological kidnapping is not criminal as long as
the product does what is says it will. For religions
there is only one way to make such a judgement and
that is by scriptural debate. Every government must
have a board of religious scholars who can legally
enforce that the sellers of religion can back up their
product by scripture.

If one party refuses to debate, then automatically
the Government has grounds to close down that
operation. Over the years, many anti-cultists have
accused members of ISKCON of being "brainwashed" or
"psychologically kidnapped." In some of those cases
there may have been merit to the accusations since
many of ISKCON's leaders are deviating from the
scriptures. But because the vast majority of
professional deprogrammers don't know scripture
themselves, they cannot judge or accuse others of
psychological kidnapping. For the most part, these
deprogrammers are simply prejudice toward any religion
that doesn't exactly resemble their own. In many
cases, they themselves are the ones who are
"brainwashed." So only a man who know's what real
religion is, can accuse another of selling a fake.

## ISKCON'S "GURUS"

If an ISKCON "guru" thinks that he is selling the

6.

real product, then he simply has to present his
arguments according to scripture. If he is right, then
he will be able to prove it. This is the unique beauty
of debate. The truth must come out. Whoever has truth
on his side will be victorious. Only a man who knows
he's cheating will refuse a challenge to debate which
brings us to the fact that these ISKCON "gurus" have
been challenged countless times to debate but they
baltently refuse to accept. In 1980 Jadurani dasi
singlehandedly challenged Kirtanananda to debate but
instead of accepting her challenge, he had her beaten
and sent to the hospital with a warning never to
challenge the "guru" again. Her case is by no means an
isolated incident.

## WE DEMAND JUSTICE

We represent the vast majority of Hare Krishna
devotees who have had their lives severly upset by the
current corrupt "leadership" of the Hare Krishna
Movement. We have challenged these men to debate on
the basis of our own scriptures but they refuse to
accept the challenge. We have already proven that they
are nothing but criminals but they respond by
stonewalling and mud throwing (They would kill us if
they could). Therefore, on the basis of the logic
presented above (silence means defeat), we declare
victory. But declaring and enforcing victory are two
entirely different things. If the U.S. Government will
not step in to establish the guilt of these men and
punish them accordingly, then it will be necessary
us, the victims, to take the law into our own hand
This paper is only to give some advance warning, e
that later, after the event, the courts cannot say
didn't try everything in our power to to get justice
first.

# SULOCANA AFFIDAVIT

Since these new "gurus" were hardly qualified for the honor they demanded, as time passed they naturally fell further and further into delusion, some of them bordering on insanity. Several have already been exposed and ousted for illicit sex, drug use, violence, not following spiritual programs, etc. So in this way they are dragging the good name and reputation of ISKCON's founder, Srila Prabhupada, into their own mud; "I wish that all my disciples will have similar respectable situation in society. That will keep my name good. Like father, like son." (Letter to Caityaguru, 7/11/76). If Prabhupada's disciples continue to accept or tolerate this situation, making it appear that such degraded behavior is santioned in Prabhupada's books, then, as Prabhupada put it: "Everything will spoil very quickly and the whole show will become a farce." (letter to Rebatinandan,2/2/72) He repeatedly warned whose fault it would be; "What will happen when I am not here, shall everything be spoiled by GBC?" (letter to Karandar,5/4/72)

Recently (Sept. 16), in West Virginia, the GBC was forced to hold an international summit to try and rectify this potentially fatal situation. This was due to the confession of a "guru," Bhavananada, who admitted to engaging in homosexual relations, something which might be tolerated in a congregational member, but which is intolerable for someone in the post of guru, GBC, or sannyasa. Out of the few original disciples still active in ISKCON, not all attended this summit; in fact, for the most part, only the leaders and their supporters were given facility to attend. (New members were not allowed.) Out of those who did attend, many revealed that their main incentive was to be appointed "gurus" themselves. They agreed to turn a blind eye to the past eight years of corruption and exploitation provided they were let in on the action. ("If an active homosexual can be guru, why can't I?") The original eleven succumbed to this logic, knowing that otherwise they would be forcibly removed. The "guru" monopoly had run its course and it was obvious that the "gurus" would either have to humble themselves and admit the conspiracy, or allow everyone else to ascend a throne alongside them. Adopting the philosophy that hundreds of wrongs would make it right, they chose the latter. What was hoped by the majority of ISKCON members to be a housecleaning turned out to be just the opposite.

This meeting having failed to rectify ISKCON and remove the conspirators, we, the vast majority of followers of Srila Prabhupada's pure teachings, see no other recourse but to remove the corrupt members by force. There are only two methods of doing this; (1) Violence. (2) Court action. Court action means sueing the GBC and it's "guru" subsection for the assets and properties that belong to ISKCON. Then a new GBC could be elected to manage the Society as it was originally intended—a cooperative movement centered around Srila Prabhupada with no appointed successors or gurus. "Whoever comes out

successful and self-effulgent" would be the future gurus.
That is the understanding given by Srila Prabhupada
(Rupanuga, 4/28/74). There is no reference in any of Srila
Prabhupada's voluminous teachings to an "appointed guru."
The reason court action is now necessary is because the
current GBC refuses to debate or rectify themselves. We
see no other means of returning the assets, properties,
and the divine name ISKCON, back to the rightful owners,
those who strictly adhere to the instructions so kindly
given by Srila Prabhupada for the management of his
Society.

   A class action of this nature can only work if the
affidaivit below is filled out and returned by the
majority of Prabhupada's followers, most of whom are
living outside of ISKCON. Please also circulate this
affidavit to the devotees in your area, initiated or not,
for that would speed things up considerably. The only
other option is violence.
   As an option, on a separate sheet you could state your
personal feelings toward ISKCON, its current leaders, if
you left ISKCON, why?, etc. Please make your statement as
concise as possible including any illegal activites by the
leaders that you may know of. Be sure and specify if your
name and/or any statements you make therein should be kept
confidential. There is considerable evidence supporting
the above statements. Those of you wishing copies, please
send at least $10 for 400 pages of Prabhupada's letters
and relevant documents. Thank you.

   I, _____, AGE _____, RESIDING AT,

_____ HAVE
BEEN A FOLLOWER OF THE HARE KRISHNA MOVEMENT SINCE _____.
I BECAME A FORMAL DISCIPLE OF _____
  IN _____ AND RECEIVED THE NAME_____.
   I AGREE THAT FOR THE KRSNA CONSCIOUSNESS RELIGION TO
SURVIVE AND GROW IN ITS ORIGINAL AND PURE FORM, IT IS
ESSENTIAL THAT THE CURRENT CORRUPT GBC BE REPLACED. IF A
COURT ACTION IS THE ONLY WAY OF ACHIEVING THIS ASIDE FROM
VIOLENCE, THEN I SUPPORT SUCH ACTION.

        SIGNED _____

        DATE   _____

        NOTARY _____

   If/when ISKCON is reestablished in its pure form, I will
be interested to ( ) become, ( ) resume the status of, ( )
continue on as:
( ) A full-time, ( ) part time, ( ) or congregational
member of a Prabhupada-centered temple/community.
( ) I support ISKCON's rectification, but I personally
redirected my life to other goals.
( ) I would like more information. Enclosed is $10 for
specifics.

# DERANGED DEVOTION

PAEDOPHILIA IN PLAIN SIGHT – Only the most deranged and deluded souls could not see Kirtanananda's dealings with the children for what they truly were. Those "devotees" who remained silent after witnessing such degenerate activity are conspirators to the crimes!

"This guy [Sulochan] is getting out of control. It would be nice if someone would silence him once and for all."—Hayagriva (Howard Wheeler), Keith Ham's college roomate, lover, best friend, and co-founder of New Vrindaban. Here with his life-long buddy at a Labor Day Festival at New Vrindaban (September 1984).

"We have to finish this thing. As long as that guy [Sulochan] is walking around, he's a threat to Bhaktipada. He won't be thinking anyone's after him out in California. At least no one from New Vrindaban. If something happens out there, there won't be as much heat on us. In time the whole thing will blow over. If everything runs smoothly, they won't be able to prove anything."—Kuladri (Arthur Villa), New Vrindaban's temple president, known as "Number Two." Here officiating as a priest at a New Vrindaban fire sacrifice (1984).

When asked if he had been "involved with the killing of Sulochan," Tapahpunja Swami boasted, "I engineered it. It was completely Vedic. He offended Bhaktipada."—His Holiness Tapahpunja Swami (Terry Sheldon), the president of Cleveland ISKCON, at New Vrindaban (undated).

"That son of a bitch [Sulochan] is going to have to be killed, and I am the one that is going to do it." Tirtha (Thomas A. Drescher), New Vrindaban's chief "enforcer" and hit man, in court (undated).

"Even if Kirtanananda Swami had full sex with ten thousand children, he's still the guru of the universe, and if you don't accept that, you're going to hell." Janmastami (John Sinkowski), Tirtha's partner in crime, chanting japa on the sidewalk in the front of the RVC temple (September 1991).

"Gorby was more fired up to destroy Sulochan than any of the devotees." Russell "Randall" Clark Gorby, retired steel worker, longtime "friend" of New Vrindaban, vocal advocate for the murder of Sulochan, and government informant (undated).

"What was I supposed to do under those circumstances? We were convinced that Bhaktipada was a pure devotee and that Sulochan was determined to murder him, so we thought we were obligated to stop some demon from killing a pure devotee by any means possible." Radhanath Swami (Richard Slavin), (undated).

"Radhanath Swami won't like all this coming out. Too bad. I had to be responsible for my transgressions [and go to prison]. He should do the same." Dharmatma (Dennis Gorrick), Director of New Vrindaban's multi-million dollar "Scam-Kirtan" panhandling operation. Image from Brijabasi Spirit (January-February 1977).

"He [Sulochan] should be transmigrated to his next body." "His Divine Grace" Ramesvara Maharaja (Robert Grant), the ISKCON zonal acharya for Southern California and head of the North American BBT, during a rare visit to New Vrindaban. Photo from Brijabasi Spirit (summer 1985).

"My guru, Ramesvara, said: 'K. K., if you ever see Sulochan, call New Vrindaban.' And because I heard that Sulochan may frequent the area, I kept an eye out for his vehicle."— Krishna-Katha (Jeffrey Breier), head of security at Los Angeles ISKCON and Tirtha's assistant. Breier helped hunt down Sulochan and was with Tirtha until moments before the murder. Some say he witnessed the murder. (Undated Linkedin photo, c. 2010)

HENRY DOKTORSKI - The author of the blasphemous book called Killing For Krishna which slanders Prabhupada's Perfect Disciple Sulocana Prabhu on page after page and decries the Vedic principle of righteous violence calling it dogmatic and deranged.

"If I was called to assist in this murder I probably would have done it… I do have a lo(t), some sympathy (for Tirtha, Sulocana's killer). All right, you know he should be in prison that's the best place for him, I agree, but I know that if I was wearing that shoe I could have been in a similar position as one of the murder conspirators."

Hrishikesh dasa (Henry Doktorski) May 2018

Note: Doktorski may not have done any physical killing but he has surely used his poison pen on behalf of Keith Ham to try and kill the good name of Sulocana prabhu! I have totally exposed this envious spawn of the paedophile lineage in my new book called Killing For Keith. Please see the back of the book for more information on how to purchase this.

# Dial Om for Murder

## The Hare Krishna church, once brimming with youthful idealism, has become a haven for drug traffickers, suspected child molesters – and killers

**By John Hubner
and Lindsey Gruson**

BLOOD AND SAFFRON: The powerful guru Bhaktipada, a.k.a. Keith Ham, keeps his young followers on a tight rein. The guru denies any connection to the brutal murders that have wracked his West Virginia commune.

**THE MARTYR: Steve Bryant just before he was murdered last year**

ONCE A YEAR, AROUND THE END OF MAY, Lord Nrishingha, the Hindu warrior god, rises to drive out the demons that threaten the worshipers of Krishna. In the early morning hours of May 22nd, 1986 – the day before Nrishingha's coming – Steve Bryant parked on a deserted street in West Los Angeles. Bryant shut off the headlights of the 1976 Dodge van that was both his home and the field head-quarters of his one-man holy war. He looked up the street and studied the rear-view mirror. Then he folded his hands and tried to chant.

It was no good. The street was still, but his mind was racing. He tried to let it go blank, to give it all to Krishna. But the death mantra kept pounding away. "The gurus must die, the gurus must die."

Bryant was exhausted. For the last year, he had devoted his life to his war against the gurus who controlled the In-ternational Society for Krishna Consciousness (ISKCON). The battle had cost him his wife and his children. He had roamed the country telling Krishna devotees, cops, journalists, anyone who would listen, that the gurus had poisoned the religion to build empires. He said they tolerated child abuse and drug trafficking. The cops said prove it and shrugged him off. He predicted the gurus would kill him. Everybody laughed at him. Who would want to kill Steve Bryant? He was a flake, an itinerant trinket mak-er, a small-time schemer who drifted into drugs when his scams failed.

Sitting in the dark, Bryant once again vowed to kill Bhaktipada. Bhaktipada was the most powerful guru and the most evil. He should be the first to die. Bhaktipada's followers washed his feet at New Vrindaban, his 3000-acre kingdom high in the hills of West Virginia. They thought the ground he touched was holy and walked in his footsteps. And who was Bhaktipada? A man who hated women. Bhaktipada said three things were better when you beat them: your drum, your dog, your wife.

A picture of the Palace of Gold, which Bhaktipada had built to honor Prabhupada, ISKCON's founder, flashed through Bryant's mind. What a perfect symbol of hy-pocrisy! America's Taj Mahal, a spiritual Disneyland. And how had Bhaktipada fi-nanced it? By accepting money from drug smugglers, by operating welfare and fund-raising scams that would put the Mob to shame. To feed his insatiable hunger for money, Bhaktipada forced women to desert their children, go out on the road in di-lapidated vans and beg for money, and bring him every nickel.

Bhaktipada broke up marriages and separated children from their parents. That's how he controlled people. That's what he had done to Bryant. He was convinced the guru had brainwashed his wife, Jane, who was in New Vrindaban, living with some other man. The guru had given her, like some housewarming present, to another devotee. Bryant's two little boys were with her, calling a stranger

# Dial Om for Murder

**MANTRA MAN: Before his fatal one-man crusade against Bhaktipada, Bryant was a loyal devotee (left) and family man (below left), shown with nephew Skipper and sister Linda (left) and wife Jane and son Sarva (right).**

ABSORBED IN THE rhythmic mantra, Bryant did not hear the approaching footsteps. Had he noticed them, he might have saved his life. The police say that as he sat in the dark, a New Vrindaban hit man named Thomas Drescher tiptoed to the driver's side of the van, stuck a .45-caliber revolver through the window and pulled the trigger. Two bullets hit Bryant in the head. They entered the left side, smashed through his skull and sliced across his brain before exiting. Bryant slumped over the steering wheel. Seconds later two cars sped away.

Bryant was found the next morning. His brains had soaked into the seat, and a puddle of blood had drenched his shoes.

Word spread quickly among devotees throughout the world that Bryant was meant to be "a monkey on a stick." When a monkey breaks into a banana plantation in India, where the Krishna religion has its roots, the monkey is killed, impaled on a stick and left to rot outside the plantation. Other monkeys see him hanging there and stay out of the bananas. But the plan backfired. Bryant's murder turned a crank into a martyr, a spurned lover into a prophet.

"Steve told all kinds of incredible stories about what was going on up there," says Donald Bordenkircher, the sheriff of Marshall County, West Virginia, the site of New Vrindaban. "I kept saying, 'Steve, you've got to substantiate it. Give us names.' He'd say, 'I can't do that because they are in fear of their lives.' I considered him a disgruntled disciple who wanted to be a guru. Then he's killed, and one, two, three, he has instant credibility."

Bryant's death set off a series of overlapping investigations by federal, state and local law-enforcement authorities. It led to the conviction of two former Krishnas for the murder of another devotee and to the discovery of two more bodies buried in shallow graves in the New Vrindaban commune. Bryant's allegations of drug smuggling, child abuse and fraud have been corroborated by other devotees, who have been testifying before a grand jury in West Virginia. A task force of FBI and IRS agents, led by state and local police officers, recently raided New Vrindaban and drove away three tractor-trailers full of alleged contraband. Now the investigations are spreading beyond New Vrindaban to Hare Krishna temples across the country and around the world.

"The last time I saw Bryant, he said something to me, and I said, 'Stephen, I don't have time to play games with a goddamn martyr,'" Sheriff Bordenkircher says. "He looked at me and smiled and said, 'Now you understand.' And you know, he is a martyr. Maybe he's the Krishna Martin Luther."

AS THE MOON HOVERED OVER THE PINE-CROWNED hills of West Virginia in June 1983, Charles St. Denis was in the Blue Boy Nursery, a business he ran as a cover for his small-time cocaine operation. It was 10:30 p.m., and St. Denis was coked up and tired. But when his friend Daniel Reid called to invite him over for more blow, St. Denis said sure. If there was one thing the 250-pound hedonist liked more than women, it was coke. He drove over to Reid's shack, a converted chicken coop on the northeast edge of New Vrindaban, parked his truck and walked around the back to the only door.

St. Denis knew the way and hadn't brought a flashlight. So he never saw Thomas Drescher and Daniel Reid step from the shadows and aim their .22-caliber pistols. Drescher, a Vietnam veteran who liked to brag about his combat escapades, emptied his gun. Reid froze.

"Shoot him," Drescher screamed. "Shoot him."

Reid began firing as St. Denis turned and ran. Drescher, smaller and quicker, easily caught and tackled St. Denis, who was bleeding from ten to twelve bullet wounds.

"Get a knife!" Drescher yelled at Reid. "Get a knife!" Then Drescher climbed onto St. Denis's heaving chest.

"Chant!" Drescher ordered. "Chant!"

Drescher thought he was doing the man he was murdering a favor. Like other good Krishnas, he believed St. Denis would get a better body in his next incarnation if he chanted God's name while he died.

But St. Denis wouldn't die. Gasping for breath, he kept struggling. Drescher became infuriated. When Reid returned with the knife, Drescher stabbed St. Denis again and again, harder and harder. Finally the blade snapped. Reid ran back to the shack and grabbed a screwdriver. Drescher stabbed St. Denis with that. But St. Denis was still breathing. Reid found a hammer, and Drescher hit St. Denis with it, punching a one-inch hole in his skull. St. Denis "kept moaning and groaning like a dog," Drescher told acquaintances who would later testify against him.

Drescher and Reid dragged St. Denis down a logging road to a grave Drescher had dug earlier that day. The site was hidden in swampy ground beside a small stream. In the dark, Drescher couldn't find it. Cursing, he and Reid stomped along the stream, looking for the grave. St. Denis kept moaning. Drescher stuffed plastic in his mouth. Slowly the breathing stopped.

Drescher watched St. Denis die and was about to help Reid look for the grave when he heard a splash. Reid had fallen into the three-foot hole. During the day, water had seeped in, filling the grave. Drescher and Reid wrapped St. Denis's body in plastic, weighted it with rocks, threw it in the hole and covered it with mud. A few days later water from the gurgling stream had formed a small pond over the grave.

Investigators say they don't know the motive for St. Denis's murder. St. Denis had argued with Drescher over a house Drescher had sold him. There was also secondhand testimony at the trial that St. Denis had raped Reid's wife. The West Virginia police say drugs may have been involved.

Whatever the motive, St. Denis's murder was no secret. The local police interviewed dozens of devotees and dragged several lakes on the Krishna estate. On several occasions, they used dogs in the search. Each time, the dogs returned to the small stream, which the Krishnas use to wash their laundry. Once the police

Daddy. The kids were surrounded by child abusers.

No wonder Bryant, who had lost forty pounds, was tottering on the edge of madness. Krishna had given him a mission. But deep down Bryant knew he would fail. He would never be able to kill Bhaktipada. The guru was isolated, surrounded by fanatics. Bryant would never get close enough even to try. Why had Krishna given Bryant a mission he couldn't fulfill? Why did Krishna tolerate all the chaos and corruption?

Bryant had spent months alone, cooped up in his jerry-built camper, cranking out an exposé of the gurus on a dinky computer. He thought that if he exposed the gurus, devotees would see the truth and revolt. Instead they ignored him. So he had given the manuscript to the cops. The police had locked him up for carrying a gun and, unaccountably, had given his manuscript to the leaders of the New Vrindaban commune. There wasn't much else he could do.

He had tried — at least Bryant could tell himself that. The last time he had been in New Vrindaban, he had grabbed his two boys, thrown them in his camper and made a run for it. But he hadn't got far. Two vans full of men had chased him down, run him off the road and taken back his boys. But that seemed like a lifetime ago.

Again, Bryant tried to rid himself of all the anger, all the confusion. He replayed in his mind his last phone conversation with Jane. Her lilting English accent soothed him. It always did. Slowly, he started to chant: "Hare Krishna, Hare Krishna, Krishna Krishna, Hare Hare."

JOHN HUBNER *is a staff writer for the Sunday magazine of* 'The San Jose Mercury News.' LINDSEY GRUSON *is a national correspondent for* 'The New York Times.'

# Dial Om for Murder

**ACCUSED HIT MAN:** Bhaktipada disciple Thomas Drescher (left) has been charged with murdering Bryant as he sat chanting in his van (below left). Drescher is serving a life term for another Krishna killing.

dug only twelve feet away from the grave. All along they suspected Drescher but did not have enough evidence to arrest him. Chances are they never would have if Randall Gorby hadn't made a phone call.

Randall Gorby is a strange and shadowy character. A sixty-four-year-old retired steelworker, Gorby lived in Bethany, West Virginia, fifteen miles from New Vrindaban. The police describe him as an enigma, a radical and "a real intellectual in the Aristotelian sense – self-educated." During a steel strike in the late Seventies, Gorby was a police informer, passing along information about the United Steel Workers to the West Virginia State Police. From the early Seventies on, Gorby was also the best friend the Krishnas had in West Virginia. Friends say he was attracted by their radicalism.

In the so-called West Virginia Glass Belt, where the pace of change is measured in generations and poverty is a way of life, the saffron-robed Krishnas might as well have been aliens from another planet. In 1969, when they moved onto an abandoned farm in McCreary's Ridge, seventy miles southwest of Pittsburgh, the Krishnas had no electricity, no heat, no running water. They survived the first winter because local people brought them food and clothing and feed for their animals. Farmers taught the Krishnas how to care for their livestock and how to milk the cows in their small herd.

But relations between the Krishnas and the local community soon soured. Residents of Moundsville, the small town nearest the commune, were angered when the Krishnas started panhandling. When they began going house to house seeking converts, the locals slammed their doors. When the Krishnas persisted, residents called the

police. Local farmers, frightened by rumors that the Krishnas were spreading contagious diseases, like hepatitis, tried running their cars off the winding roads of the area. They shot up Krishna houses and burned their mobile homes.

Then word leaked that the Krishnas planned to build a spiritual Disneyland, seven temples on seven hills. Neighboring landowners signed a pact promising not to sell any property to the Krishnas. But the sect, which was attracting thousands of disenchanted middle-class youths from across the country, seemed to have unlimited amounts of money. And they had Randall Gorby, who was their straw man. Gorby bought land from farmers and miners hard hit by the economic depression in the state. Then he quietly signed it over to the Krishnas. Soon, through the help of Gorby and others, the sect had amassed almost 3000 acres.

Over the years, Gorby became Bhaktipada's trusted confidant and a mentor to younger devotees like Drescher. Drescher and Gorby met after Gorby became upset that a Krishna was sleeping with his daughter-in-law and tried to break up the relationship. The Krishna, one of Bhaktipada's senior aides, asked Drescher to stop Gorby from interfering. Drescher drove over to Gorby's house, but as one local cop says, "Gorby doesn't intimidate." Drescher loved that. Soon they were fast friends. The summer after he killed St. Denis, Drescher left his wife and two kids and moved into Gorby's house.

"It was a father-and-son-type thing," Drescher said in a three-hour telephone interview from prison.

Investigators say Drescher told Gorby that he had murdered St. Denis. They also say Drescher told Gorby that he had killed Bryant too and that officials at New Vrindaban had promised him $20,000 for the hit. After the murder, the officials reneged.

"They're capitalists," one local investigator says. "If you're going to deal with them, you'd better get your money up front."

According to several investigators, Drescher asked Gorby to help him get the money. Gorby went to Bhaktipada, who told Gorby to have Drescher call Terry Sheldon, the president of the Cleveland temple and one of Bhaktipada's most trusted lieutenants. (Bhaktipada denies having any such conversation with Gorby.) Gorby passed the message along to Drescher.

Then Gorby got scared. He feared that he might become the next victim, and perhaps that he had already become an accessory to murder. So he called his old friends from the steel strike, the West Virginia State Police, and told them Drescher was a murderer. They put a tap on Gorby's phone. It paid off a few days later when Drescher called to tell Gorby he was leaving the country.

The police traced the call and nabbed Drescher as he was leaving a restaurant in Kent, Ohio. Drescher's wife and four-year-old son were with him, and so was

Terry Sheldon. Drescher's Isuzu Trooper was packed with clothes, kitchen utensils and camping equipment. He had $4000 in his wallet. He was also carrying a diary that included Bryant's Berkeley, California, address, a description of Bryant's van, the license number of the van and detailed accounts of Bryant's recent travels around Los Angeles. Sheldon was carrying an unsigned letter that said that if the police were ever tracking Drescher, he should be taken to New York and put on a plane to India.

Two days after Drescher's arrest, Gorby woke up in his second-floor bedroom. A chain smoker, he needed a nicotine fix and immediately lit a cigarette. The house exploded, blowing him through the roof. Gorby flew over the house, watching splinters of lumber and shards of glass sail past. He then fell back through the roof, crashed through the second floor and fell into the living room. Beams collapsed around him, and a flash fire scorched him, tattooing patterns on his skin.

Amazingly, Gorby survived. He was rushed to a hospital in Wheeling, where for weeks he remained in critical condition with second- and third-degree burns. The state police called in the FBI, which concluded that the explosion was caused by a leak in the gas lines of Gorby's house. A valve had been unscrewed, allowing gas to seep into the house. The cops think Drescher might know something about it because he had helped Gorby install the gas line.

Today Gorby is out of the hospital and in hiding, in the federal witness-protection program. Thanks in part to Gorby's testimony, Drescher was convicted last December of first-degree murder in the St. Denis killing and was sentenced to life imprisonment. The trial lasted four days. A week later, in a separate trial, Daniel Reid pleaded guilty. He led the police to the body. Reid is in a West Virginia county jail. Drescher is in the West Virginia State Penitentiary awaiting extradition to California. He still claims he didn't kill St. Denis. He also insists he had nothing to do with the explosion at Gorby's house.

"Who am I, Lex Luthor, that I can blow somebody up from the county jail?" Drescher asks. "Gorby was cheating the gas company. He told me and a couple of people in the Krishna community he was bypassing his meter. He screwed up and didn't tighten the fittings down."

Drescher admits he knew Steve Bryant but swears he didn't kill him. "The Krishnas aren't idiots," Drescher says. "You think they wouldn't know that if this guy [Bryant] ended up killed, people would point the finger at them? I'm not going to get into the good graces of the Krishnas by embroiling them in the most scandalous controversy they've ever faced. So what's my motive?"

Investigators think Drescher's motive for killing Bryant was the same as it was for killing St. Denis – Kirtanananda Swami Bhaktipada, the New Vrindaban guru, wanted both men dead. "Drescher was an enforcer," says one investigator. "He would never have killed St. Denis or Bryant if the guru hadn't wanted it done."

Bhaktipada denies any connection with the Bryant or St. Denis murders. He dismisses Bryant as a spurned lover seeking revenge against his wife's benefactors. The guru asserts that Bryant's murder was probably Gorby's fault. "Gorby was always trying to incite everybody to do something," says Bhaktipada. Once, the guru recalls, Gorby warned a senior aide that

# Dial Om for Murder

PHOTOGRAPHS BY THANNGUNKI DERSKA

**AMERICAN TAJ MAHAL: Bhaktipada built the opulent Palace of Gold (left), high in the hills of West Virginia, to honor the church's founder, Prabhupada, a wax statue of whom can be found inside (below left).**

"you've got to do something, this guy's got to be killed." The aide threw Gorby out.

Bhaktipada claims that he never approved any payments to Drescher. He says he abhors violence. He derides the investigations of the Krishna church as the latter-day equivalent of the nineteenth-century persecution of utopian societies. The probes, he says, are an outgrowth of the inevitable antagonism between materialist Americans and spiritual Krishnas.

"We're eternally at loggerheads," the guru says.

THAT STEVE BRYANT WAS CONSIDERED SO DANGEROUS he had to be killed is a measure of the paranoia that wracks the Hare Krishna movement. Until two bullets ended Bryant's life, most people didn't consider him worth listening to, let alone killing.

The son of a career officer, Bryant was a typical army brat, living on bases around the world until he was eleven. Then his father retired and moved to Detroit to become a high-school mathematics teacher. Steve was an aimless, unhappy kid. His only extracurricular activity in high school was drugs. After graduation, he enrolled in a junior college but dropped out after the first semester. He laid carpet and did drugs, worked in construction and did drugs. He flirted with studying to be a masseur. Then in 1972 a Hare Krishna stopped him on the street and invited him to visit the ISKCON temple in Detroit. He went to lunch the next Sunday and was hooked.

"He told us he'd found the religion he'd been looking for," Steve's father, Jack Bryant, recalls. "We didn't see what he saw in it. But he was twenty, a grown

man, and we had no influence over his choice. He preached to us and tried to convert us. We got into arguments, mostly about meat. Don't eat meat, that was the big thing."

Across the country, thousands of youths were embracing the same message in one of the true religious revolutions of this century. It began in 1965, when an Indian guru, a retired pharmaceuticals executive named A.C. Bhaktivedanta and known as Swami Prabhupada, arrived in New York City and rented a dilapidated loft on the Bowery. Prabhupada didn't have a grand plan or detailed system; he simply began chanting and preaching on street corners, giving lectures out of a storefront, a curio shop called Matchless Gifts. His message was enticingly simple: by chanting Krishna's name hundreds of times a day and devoting one's labor to him, by eating no meat and living a pure life that included abstention from sex except for procreation, ordinary people could transcend material life and merge with God. When he died in 1977, at eighty-one, Prabhupada left behind a movement that had millions of followers in hundreds of temples all over the world.

"The fact that there is now in the West a vigorous, disciplined, and seemingly well organized [religious] movement — not merely a philosophical movement or a yoga or meditation movement . . . is a stunning accomplishment," wrote Harvey Cox, a professor of divinity at Harvard University, in his 1983 book Hare Krishna, Hare Krishna. "When I say [Prabhupada was] 'one in a million,' I think that is in some ways an underestimate. Perhaps he was one in a hundred million."

But Prabhupada's death led to an internecine war that has all but destroyed his legacy. He left few, if any, instructions on who should succeed him or how the Krishna church should be run. As a result, eleven gurus divided up the world like Mafia chieftains. Each became the godfather in his territory.

"The eleven members of the guru club started building their own empires," says Atreya Rishi, a graduate of the Berkeley temple and a member of the Governing Body Commission (GBC), the board of directors that in theory controls ISKCON. "They used their power to strengthen themselves instead of the movement. What was once a religion degenerated into a bunch of cults."

Soon the temples were at each other's throats. Their gurus disagreed on pivotal questions of doctrine and theory.

They competed for members and money. Membership began to decline as devotees, disenchanted by the factionalism, left the organized Krishna church. ISKCON still claims to have 1 million members in the United States and another 2 million around the world. But experts note that this roster includes names on mailing lists and temple guest registers. Hard-core

membership remains at about 10,000. One statistic, more than any other, shows how badly guru mismanagement has hurt the movement. According to Hinduism Today, an independent newspaper, only 500 of the 4000 devotees initiated by Prabhupada are still in ISKCON. Many of the disillusioned remain devout. The religion is pure, they insist. It is the gurus who are corrupt.

Even the Governing Body Commission, which is dominated by the gurus and works hard to protect them, has come to that conclusion. In the last six years, it has excommunicated six of the eleven gurus. Bhavananda (Charles Bacos), the Australian guru, was drummed out last year after being accused of homosexuality. Ramesvar (Robert Grant), the L.A. guru, was also kicked out last year because he seduced a teenage girl. Bhagavan (William Ehrlichman), the European guru, left his temple after he was discovered to be conducting a relationship with a woman despite a vow of chastity. Last December a GBC committee asked Bhaktipada to resign from the commission, according to Atreya Rishi, "because of his abuse of the philosophy and all his legal problems."

The Berkeley guru, Hansadutta, a.k.a. Hans Kary, a.k.a. Jack London, was booted out in 1983 because of his involvement with guns and drugs. One night, in a very black mood, Hansadutta shot up a liquor store and a Cadillac dealership in Berkeley. While he was still a guru, Hansadutta recorded several albums with songs such as "Guru, Guru, on the Wall" ("I once saw a guru just like you/New York Jew/Nothing new").

But the most bizarre guru was in London. In 1982, Jayatirtha (James Immel) was the first guru to be thrown out of ISKCON. Until then, Jayatirtha was considered unusually pure. His devotees worshiped him for his special relationship with Krishna. Often they sat at his feet, watching what they thought were spiritual journeys highlighted by direct conversations with Krishna. But these spiritual journeys were chemically fueled. The guru was an acid freak. While most of his followers lived in squalor, Jayatirtha and a select inner circle lived high in both senses of the word.

Steve Bryant lived in the London temple on and off for three years, from 1977 to 1980. A true believer, he managed to ignore the sex-and-drugs cult at the heart of the temple. He thought the movement was chaste because he so badly wanted it to be.

"Sulocana [Bryant's Krishna name, pronounced 'Su-low-chan'] was kind of innocent, kind of naive," says Yuvati Matusow, a close friend of Bryant's who was in the London temple at the same time. "He was really into the scriptures and worshiping the deities and was pretty oblivious to everything else. People used to make fun of him."

Bryant was lonely. He wanted to get married, not only within the faith but to a woman who, like him, had been initiated by the founder. The reason was that in Vedic culture, women must defer to men. A husband acts as his wife's spiritual master. If both spouses are initiated by the same guru, there is harmony, a clear line of authority. The guru tells the husband what to do, and he tells his wife. But if husband and wife have been initiated by different gurus, conflict is inherent. Inevitably the two gurus will give contrary advice. Further, the wife's guru undermines the [Cont. on 78]

## Dial Om for Murder

# Contrary to Krishna values, Bhaktipada equated opulence with devotion.

[*Cont. from 58*] husband's authority by assuming his spiritual role.

The problem was most of the women Prabhupada had initiated were already taken. So Bryant took on an eager novice who had been recommended by mutual friends. The woman was Jane Rangley, a twenty-year-old English woman whose boyfriend had just left her and their two-year-old son. Bryant wanted to gain a disciple almost as much as a wife, and Jane wanted to be a disciple.

"Friends asked me if I'd like to get married to Steve Bryant," Jane says. "I'd never met him, and when I did, I didn't like him. I didn't think liking him was important. I'd had a relationship before where I liked the person, and it didn't work out. I thought it would be a good opportunity to become a devotee. I felt I needed somebody to guide me."

Two weeks after they met in May 1979, the couple got married in a civil ceremony. The newlyweds had a two-year-old boy to support and not many friends. They had few skills and less money. To survive, they moved to Newcastle-upon-Tyne, working there in a broken-down, Krishna-owned incense factory. As soon as they had saved enough money, Bryant packed Jane and her son off to New Vrindaban.

"He was fond of the guru there [New Vrindaban] for a long time," his father recalls. "For a long time, he said that guru was the best of the eleven."

Bryant had a scheme. He bought a load of tape recorders and cameras and flew to India. There he sold the equipment, using the cash to buy cheap costume jewelry and paintings of Krishna deities. He returned to New Vrindaban and taught Jane how to make pendants, which he sold to devotees.

"He thought he was going to make a lot of money, but it didn't work out," Jane says. "His schemes hardly ever worked out. He was forever getting an idea, becoming completely fanatical about it and then letting it fizzle out."

But Bryant wasn't discouraged. A city boy, he loved the steep mountains and the deep forests that surrounded New Vrindaban. He thought he had a future in the 700-member commune. Bhaktipada had promised to make him the manager of the sect's hotel. Bryant believed he was about to become important, a senior aide to Bhaktipada.

Kirtanananda Swami Bhaktipada was born Keith Ham, the son of a Baptist minister in Peekskill, New York. A graduate student in the history of religion at Columbia University, Ham discovered Prabhupada on the Lower East Side of New York City and became one of the founder's first disciples. Since then, Bhaktipada has always claimed that he, and he alone, is the founder's true heir.

Bhaktipada conceived of the ornate Palace of Gold in West Virginia as Prabhupada's home away from home. It quickly became an obsession. Contrary to Prabhupada's teachings of simple living and high thoughts, Bhaktipada equated opulence with devotion. The domed roof and outside walls are coated with twenty-two-carat gold leaf, which shimmers in the afternoon sun. The palace boasts 200 tons of marble, imported from Italy and Canada, and stained-glass windows made from thousands of pieces of hand-shaped glass. The baseboards are gold, and gold-embroidered silken brocades hang from the walls. The entire palace, which Bhaktipada likes to call America's Taj Mahal, was built without blueprints by young devotees using do-it-yourself books.

The energy and money Bhaktipada lavished on the palace did not diminish after the death of the founder. It became a symbol of Bhaktipada's authority and still serves as tangible proof that he is the only true guru on the planet. The other gurus and their followers, Bhaktipada claims, are "in *maya*," living in sin.

For a year, Bryant and Jane lived like serfs in the shadow of the castle. Their apartment was a windowless basement in a friend's house. They had to insulate the dank walls with cardboard. Bryant and Jane made jewelry. Bryant also helped craft stained glass for the Palace of Gold. He was becoming increasingly bitter at the delay in his appointment as hotel manager. Jane kept house, but it was never clean enough for Bryant.

Bryant was an imperious husband who rode his wife unmercifully. He thought nothing of loading Jane, his stepson and his two baby boys into a van on the spur of the moment and moving cross-country. The thing Bryant liked best about Jane was he could dominate her. She says he beat her. He kept the pressure on, reminding his wife again and again she was his devotee. Therefore she had to do whatever he said.

When Bryant didn't get the hotel job, he went into a funk, mumbling that he wasn't appreciated. He began drinking and doing drugs. He stopped chanting and participating in daily devotional services. Finally, overcome with impatience, he fled back to India, leaving Jane and the children in New Vrindaban. It was a fateful decision.

Broke and alone with three small children, Jane decided the only man she could depend upon was Bhaktipada. He was paying her rent and giving her food. The guru kept telling her that he was the eternal man in her life, that her relationship with her husband was temporary and mundane. In her first independent act since her marriage, Jane asked Bhaktipada to initiate her. He agreed without seeking Bryant's approval, a violation of Krishna procedure.

When Bryant returned from India, he was furious. Jane no longer needed him. She had Bhaktipada. Eventually he badgered her into traveling to Redding, California, where they moved in with the couple who had introduced them in England. Jane was miserable. She missed Bhaktipada, New Vrindaban, her friends, the Krishna school the kids attended. After a year, Bryant agreed to return.

"Steve knew he could never have a relationship with Jane unless he went back," a friend says. "Jane was fixated on Bhaktipada. He'd brainwashed her."

Bryant stayed in New Vrindaban for eight unhappy months before flying off to India once again to buy jewelry and paintings. When he came back five months later, he immediately started making plans to go to Mexico. Supported by Bhaktipada, Jane refused to accompany him. She wanted to stay in New Vrindaban. And she wanted a divorce.

"I was tired of traveling and didn't really have any affection for Sulocana," Jane said in a recent interview at New Vrindaban, where she still lives. "I asked Bhaktipada if I could stay, and he said yes. Sulocana got really mad. He argued with Bhaktipada and started criticizing the community, saying, 'This place is just a tourist business to make money. There's no spiritual qualities left at all.' He was really devastated. I think he realized he was losing his only disciple."

Bryant still had his two sons, or so he thought. While Jane was sleeping one night, he packed his belongings, loaded his children into the camper and made his abortive attempt to flee with them.

After the kids were seized by Bhaktipada's devotees, Bryant continued on alone. He cursed Jane for leaving him. But chiefly he cursed Bhaktipada. It was his fault. The guru had turned Jane against him. Bhaktipada had split them up because he couldn't control Bryant. He wanted his followers to be sheep.

Disconsolate, Bryant traveled around the country. He kept calling Jane, trying to convince her [Cont. on 80]

GIORGIO BRUTINI

MEMBER **harbor** FOOTWEAR GROUP LTD.

## Le Sport.

Glove soft garment leather for your casual week-end pleasure. At your Giorgio Brutini footwear department or call 800-645-8305. In New York, 516-621-8400. Dept. RS-4
Giorgio Brutini® Member Harbor Footwear Group, Ltd.

# Bryant's mission was to overthrow the gurus and return the church to its origins.

[*Cont. from 79*] that Bhaktipada was evil. In some other conversations, though, he changed his tune, promising to reform, to return to the Krishna fold and become a devoted husband.

"I'll change, I'll change, you know I'll change," he says on a tape he made of one phone call to her. When that didn't work, he tried blackmail, threatening to "destroy New Vrindaban by media exposure."

One night, at 3:00 a.m., in Dallas, a frantic Bryant called Bhaktipada to confront him. He taped that conversation too.

"I have the only eternal relationship with her," the guru says. "There's only one thing you can do."

"What?" asks Bryant.

"You'll have to surrender to me," says the guru.

Bryant refuses. He says he cannot allow his sons to stay in New Vrindaban.

"All right, we'll fight for it," says the guru.

"You want to just go through with a fight, huh?" Bryant asks.

"Yeah!" says the guru.

Bryant decided to launch a two-pronged attack on Bhaktipada. First he would search Prabhupada's writings to show that Bhaktipada was a false prophet, that he had no right to initiate Jane without permission. Then he would interview alienated New Vrindaban devotees and collect evidence of the illegal activities of the commune. He would put everything in a book and circulate it throughout ISKCON. If that didn't force Bhaktipada to resign, Bryant would go public.

Bryant started in L.A., where a disaffected devotee gave him microfilm copies of 7000 of Prabhupada's letters. Reading through them, Bryant found his smoking gun. The founder did not trust the gurus who succeeded him. Most of all, he did not trust Bhaktipada. Prabhupada called Bhaktipada envious and said there would be nothing to lament if a thousand Bhaktipadas came and went.

Suddenly Bryant understood why Krishna had allowed Bhaktipada to break up his marriage. Krishna had given him a mission. He would expose all the bogus gurus — not just Bhaktipada but all those who had soiled the Krishna church. He would lead a revolution that would overthrow the gurus, purify the church and return it to the teachings of the founder. The penalty for false preaching was death. The gurus had to die.

**90** APRIL 9TH, 1987

In a state of ecstasy, Bryant bought a $495 Commodore computer and began to work on his manuscript. As soon as he finished one chapter, he boldly sent it to Bhaktipada. Then he called the commune, demanding that the swami debate him. Bhaktipada's lieutenants ignored his challenges. But Bryant did begin getting threats on his life.

The death threats only convinced him that he was striking a nerve. For the first time, somebody was taking him seriously. In September 1985, Bryant took his one-man crusade to the headquarters of the infidel. He called Sheriff Bordenkircher to ask if he could be placed in protective custody in the Moundsville jail. The sheriff, who recorded the conversation, asked him if he really believed his life was in danger.

"Without a doubt!" Bryant says with pride in his voice. "I've been living in a motor home for the last year, since Keith Ham would kill me in a second if he saw me."

Bryant spent a week in the jail, making phone calls to the press and demanding that the GBC, which was having its annual convention at New Vrindaban, expel Bhaktipada. Once again he was ignored. A month later, in October 1985, Bhaktipada was overseeing the construction of a brick road at New Vrindaban when Michael Shockman, a thirty-two-year-old devotee from North Dakota, sneaked up from behind and brained him with a three-foot steel pipe. Bhaktipada collapsed. He was rushed to a Pittsburgh hospital, where brain surgery was performed immediately. He remained in critical condition for weeks and has never fully recovered. The guru still needs two canes to walk and suffers from severe headaches. He is prone to memory lapses and is always accompanied by two attack-trained German shepherds.

Sheriff Bordenkircher arrested Shockman. A few days later Bryant called the sheriff to say, "Shockman shouldn't be in jail. He should be given a medal." Bryant and Shockman had never met. But to the devotees in New Vrindaban, the call was proof they were co-conspirators. After that, according to the sheriff, paranoia swept through the tightly knit commune. Once Bhaktipada was released from the hospital, he cleaned house, demoting senior aides who had previously possessed the authority to check his wilder impulses.

"New Vrindaban definitely thinks Sulocana's writings were responsible for

Shockman attacking Bhaktipada," says a Los Angeles devotee who has friends in the West Virginia commune. "A lot of us outsiders do too."

Convinced that Bhaktipada was ready to fall, Bryant went back to New Vrindaban one more time. In February 1986, Jane's new husband, who had been selected by Bhaktipada, called Sheriff Bordenkircher and told him Bryant had returned and was threatening to storm New Vrindaban with a band of Rambos and blow away the leaders of the commune. But when the sheriff found Bryant a few hours later, he was holed up in a cheap apartment five miles south of town, alone except for his .45 and LSD. He was arrested for carrying the gun and jailed.

"The first time Bryant was here, he's in fear of his life and screaming for protective custody," Sheriff Bordenkircher recalls. "The second time he's a new guy. He's full of bravado. He's got a gun. It's loaded, and he says he's got people helping him. He's now the hunter, not the hunted."

It was an act. Steve Bryant was alone. His swagger was a cover for growing despair and bone-rattling fear. He was in over his head, and he knew it.

"Sulocana knew they were going to get him, he knew it was just a question of time," says a close friend. "That's why he had a gun and was always on the run, driving here, driving there. He always said, 'They'll kill me, and they'll do it through the agency of Tirtha [Drescher].' "

A month after his arrest Bryant was released and immediately left for Michigan to visit his parents. It was their final meeting. "The last time he was home, he said, 'I think they might know I'm here,' " Bryant's mother, Helga, recalls. "He said, 'I'd better get going, or you'll be in danger.' "

Bryant was right. Drescher was down the block, tailing him. And Drescher says Randall Gorby was with him.

"After Bryant was released, Gorby came to my house and wanted me to go to Detroit with him and take some pictures of Bryant's parents' house," Drescher says. "I drove Gorby up there. He had a camera and took some pictures of the scene. We took a Snoopy bumper sticker and put it on Bryant's van."

With Drescher stalking him, Bryant had as much chance as a rat in a rattlesnake's cage. Bryant drove back to California, and several investigators think Drescher followed him. Drescher admits to taking two trips to California to tail him. Once, he says, he flew to L.A., rented a car and drove up to Berkeley, where Bryant was living in a small apartment. A few days before Bryant's murder Drescher flew back to L.A.

"Gorby gave me something like $4000 to go to Detroit and to California two different times," Drescher says.

"I was supposed to watch Bryant, to see where he went, what his contacts were, what he did next. I flew back east a couple of days before he was killed. My alibi is I was with the Krishnas at a festival in Columbus, Ohio, the day somebody killed Bryant."

The police in West Virginia say they have witnesses who will testify that Drescher told them he killed Bryant. One of them is Randall Gorby. Another is a former treasurer of New Vrindaban named Paul Ferry, who used to be married to Bryant's friend Yuvati Matusow.

"After I found out about the murder," Matusow recalls, "I called my former husband and said, 'So you guys finally got around to killing Sulocana.'

"My ex-husband said, 'Oh, Sulocana is dead?'

" 'Yeah,' I said. 'Tirtha came out here and shot him twice in the head.'

" 'I saw Tirtha a couple of weeks ago on the farm, and he told me that he was going to do that,' my husband said. 'He said he was going to go out to California and kill Sulocana.' "

What role, if any, Randall Gorby played in tracking down Bryant remains uncertain. Gorby declined requests for an interview. What seems clear is that Terry Sheldon, the Cleveland temple president who was arrested with Drescher, was in charge of the entire operation.

Sheldon took several trips to the West Coast. On one trip, Krishna sources say Sheldon offered a former member of the L.A. temple a contract to kill Bryant. The ex-Krishna refused it. Sheldon may also have solicited other help from within the L.A. temple. A few days before Bryant was killed, a member of the temple's security force was asking questions about Bryant's whereabouts. And the night Bryant was killed, two cars sped away from the murder scene.

"There were definitely people from Watseka Avenue [the site of the L.A. temple] watching Sulocana," says a temple member. "I heard they were on the scene and were communicating by walkie-talkie."

"A second car at the scene is now under investigation," says Sterling Norris, the Los Angeles County assistant district attorney who will prosecute Drescher.

When he was picked up with Drescher in Kent, Ohio, Sheldon was carrying a hooked-blade linoleum knife. The police charged him with carrying a concealed weapon and held him for three days, then released him. Sheldon immediately disappeared. He surfaced first in London, where he worked in the kitchen of a vegetarian restaurant owned by the Krishnas. Then, using an alias, he went to a small temple in Northern Ireland, where he was recognized by a devotee who had seen his picture in *The ISKCON* [*Cont. on 82*]

## Dial Om for Murder

# Life for women was hell at New Vrindaban. Police cite fifty reports of women being beaten.

[Cont. from 80] World Review, the Krishna newspaper.

"I confronted him, and he admitted he was Tapapunja [Sheldon] from New Vrindaban," says Peter Brinkman, the president of the Northern Ireland temple. "I asked him why he wasn't using his real name and said this must be in relation to the killing of Sulocana. He admitted he was involved. He said, 'I engineered it.'

"I was completely shocked," Brinkman continues. "I asked, 'How can you guys take the law into your own hands?' He said, 'Well, he was an offender.' I said, 'You'd better leave. I don't want anything to do with you guys from New Vrindaban.'" Sheldon flew to Bombay, apparently went on to Australia and is now thought to be in Ghana.

STEVE BRYANT'S MURDER HAS SPARKED investigations not only into his killing but also into New Vrindaban and the entire Krishna church. The state police are looking into allegations of widespread child abuse. State and federal authorities are investigating charges that the construction of the Palace of Gold was financed in part by trafficking in illegal drugs.

Federal and local investigators say there is evidence of at least two drug operations. One ring manufactured Quaalude-like drugs. The Marshall County Sheriff's Office says Drescher was involved, noting that Drescher had been arrested and convicted in 1979 of running a Quaalude factory in Columbus, Ohio. He was sentenced to nineteen months in prison and served a year.

A much larger and more lucrative drug operation, federal and local investigators say, was headed by Emil Sofsky, known as Adwaita, who smuggled cocaine from Colombia and hashish oil from Afghanistan. Based in New York, Sofsky periodically showed up at New Vrindaban carrying briefcases filled with cash, which he turned over to Bhaktipada, according to local investigators. The hash oil, the police say, was hidden in hollowed-out briquettes of incense. The cocaine was clandestinely transported in shipments of scarfs. Sofsky has fled and is currently being sought by U.S. marshals. "Adwaita was running a drug operation, it was a known fact [at New Vrindaban]," says Yuvati Matusow. "Everybody knew he was a drug dealer and was bringing the money to Bhaktipada. He was always running from the police."

Bhaktipada denies the charges. He says the construction of the Palace of Gold was funded entirely through voluntary donations from a worldwide network of supporters, as well as by panhandling and selling candles, incense and literature in airports.

"I find that very hard to believe," says one federal investigator who has studied the group's finances. "If you could raise that kind of money by panhandling, the Red Cross and the American Cancer Society would be out there mugging people."

Sergeant Thomas Westfall of the Marshall County Sheriff's Office says a slew of allegations of child neglect and child abuse at New Vrindaban are being probed. Several parents have claimed that church officials, in effect, kidnapped their children. At New Vrindaban, children are separated at the age of five from their parents. The children are required to live year-round in separate boys' and girls' boarding schools, sometimes called ashrams, on the estate. If the parents are "good," they are allowed a visit on Sunday afternoons. But if they are "bad," visits are barred. The children return home for four one-week vacations during the year.

"Recently a friend of mine went to Bhaktipada to ask if her five-year-old son could sleep at home instead of in the boys' ashram, where the atmosphere is very harsh," says Susan Hebel, a mother of four who lived at the commune from 1978 until last year. "Bhaktipada said, 'No. If you don't like it, leave, and I'll get your husband another wife.' That's always the pattern. He has a very low regard for the institution of marriage. He wants everyone to give up family life and just work hard to build the community."

In the summer of 1984, Charles St. Denis's five-year-old son and Daniel Reid's six-year-old son were found suffocated in an old refrigerator. A dead bunny was lodged between them. Last November, almost six months to the day after his father was murdered, Steve Bryant's three-year-old son drowned in a lake. Investigators say there is nothing at this point but coincidence to link the children's deaths.

"The deaths are typical of the neglect of children that goes on up there," says one investigator. "It's criminal. They leave kids alone all day long, or they'll put a ten-year-old or a pregnant girl in charge of them."

Child abuse and child molestation are also rampant in the boys' ashram, according to parents and the police. In a complaint filed with the Marshall County Sheriff's Office, Susan Hebel charged that over a three-year period, Larry Gardner, the headmaster of the school (known as the guru kula), and Frederick DiFrancisco, his assistant, molested her thirteen-year-old son on dozens of occasions. Hebel went to the police with her complaint after she told Bhaktipada what had happened and the guru refused to do anything.

"When I found out about it, I went to Bhaktipada and told him that people I've had trust in all these years had molested my child, and I started to cry," Hebel says. "He said, 'You stupid woman! Sex is sex. How much sex have you had?'

"He didn't see the difference between two consenting adults who are married and a child and a teacher," Hebel continues. "Later I found out he was planning to send Sri Galim [Gardner] to India to open another school. That really freaked me out."

(At press time, DiFrancisco had been arrested. Gardner, according to investigators, had fled, either to his home state of Texas or to India. Bhaktipada says he is unaware of Gardner's whereabouts.)

Bhaktipada denounces the child-abuse investigation as "harassment and persecution" and an attempt to pressure devotees into rebelling against their swami. He claims that Hebel is seeking revenge, trying to crucify him because he kicked her out of New Vrindaban for "immorality. She was more or less a prostitute." As soon as she told him that her son had been abused, Bhaktipada said he intervened, arranging for the two teachers to receive counseling. He also "gave" one of them "a new wife."

Bryant's charges about women being badly mistreated at New Vrindaban have also been corroborated. Most of the cases involve husbands beating wives, with Bhaktipada's approval.

"I got married a second time because Bhaktipada told me to," says one female ex-devotee. "My second husband was mentally and physically abusive, becoming violent when I wouldn't have sex and throwing me around the room. I told Bhaktipada, and he said, 'You just tolerate it.'"

To Bhaktipada, women were apparently little more than objects he could use to control male Krishnas. Before granting female devotees their weekly audience with him, he would, according to one former resident, "make comments like 'Get out the incense, boys, it's fish night.'"

An investigator elaborates on violence against women in the commune: "We've got fifty instances where women were beaten, and the guru's advice to them was always the same — 'Be submissive.'"

If life for women was hell in New Vrindaban, it was worse when they were on the road performing sankirtan — pan-handling, distributing literature and spreading the faith. According to Hebel, the women were given weekly quotas. If they didn't meet them or if they broke some minor rule, they were beaten, often with a rubber hose.

Instead of working airports for handouts and converts, once a common practice, many Krishnas now pursue other scams. For example, women devotees often identify themselves as schoolteachers collecting for an orphanage in West Virginia. The school is registered, but as one former devotee says, "If there are any orphans there, it is because Bhaktipada broke up the family."

During the pope's visit in 1979, some Krishna women represented themselves as members of the Catholic Youth Organization. And on Labor Day weekends, when the Jerry Lewis Telethon airs, they pretend to be collecting for muscular dystrophy. In return for some donations, devotees have been giving away counterfeit Snoopy bumper stickers as well as NFL and NCAA football emblems.

"We're the chosen of God," says one former Krishna official. "The rest of the people out there are Karmies [sinners]. If we don't take their money, they'll just use it for sense gratification. By taking their money any way possible, we're doing them a favor."

Several Krishnas say that while they were on the fund raising, they supported themselves by shoplifting and stealing. That was only right. Everything belongs to Krishna. So everything belongs to them.

Last January, a fifty-member task force composed of representatives of the FBI, the IRS and the West Virginia state and local police raided New Vrindaban, seizing records and alleged contraband. The raid grew out of a grand-jury investigation in Elkins, West Virginia, that last summer began looking into activities at the commune. A new grand jury will soon take up the matter. More raids are coming. So are more arrests.

"In the next twelve months, we're going to take a couple of high people at New Vrindaban down on conspiracy-to-murder charges," says one investigator. "We're very hopeful of getting Bhaktipada."

If he does land in jail, Bhaktipada says it will be Krishna's will. "I love it," he said in a telephone interview during a national speaking tour. "I'm using what is materially unfavorable circumstances for God's service. Then it becomes favorable. When we preach God's message, everything becomes perfect."

"It's like Christ being put on the cross," says Atreya Rishi, the former president of the Berkeley temple. "Even if Bhaktipada is put in jail, he will come out victorious because he's a martyr. The difference is, he's a martyr to a lie, and Steve Bryant is a martyr to the truth." ∎

# SRILA PRABHUPADA IS THE INITIATOR

Mukunda dasa 1993

I wrote the following article after reading The Guru Business.

Srila Prabhupada's transcendental books are his loud chanting of the holy name. Such loud chanting is giving the people of the world Harinama diksa. The ritvik acarya system should continue for the rest of the golden age to formalise such mass initiation. This is the verdict of Sadhu, Sastra and Guru

*"Regarding Sankirtana and book distribution, book distribution is also chanting. Anyone who reads the books that is also chanting and hearing. Why distinguish between chanting and book distribution?* **These books I have recorded and chanted, and they are transcribed. It is spoken kirtanas. So book distribution is also chanting. These are not ordinary books. It is recorded chanting. Anyone who reads, he is hearing.** *Book distribution must not be neglected." (S.P.L. to Rupanuga dasa, 19th October, 1974)*

*"When a devotee is perfectly qualified in chanting the transcendental vibration of the holy name, he is quite fit to become a spiritual master and to deliver all the people of the world. The chanting of the holy name is so powerful that it gradually establishes its supremacy above everything in the world. The devotee who chants it becomes transcendentally situated in ecstasy and sometimes laughs, cries and dances in his ecstasy. Sometimes the unintelligent put hindrances in the path of chanting this maha-mantra,* **but one who is situated on the platform of love of Godhead chants the holy name loudly for all concerned. As a result <u>everyone becomes initiated</u> in the chanting of the holy names--Hare Krishna, Hare**

*Krishna, Krishna Krishna, Hare Hare/ Hare Rama, Hare Rama, Rama Rama, Hare Hare."* (T.L.C. Chapter 18)

## SRILA PRABHUPADA'S BOOK DISRIBUTION: INITIATING THE WORLD WITH THE HOLY NAME.

In this article we will be examining book distribution through the eyes of sadhu, sastra and guru. In doing so we shall understand a little more deeply the purpose of distributing Srila Prabhupada'a original and authorized books, and there importance to the unity of Srila Prabhupada's society. The quotes we have presented analyse what is actually happening when a conditioned soul receives one of Srila Prabhupada books, and clearly defines that souls relationship to Srila Prabhupada. Before we present these quotes, let us hear from Srila Prabhupada on the importance of distributing his books.

*"Please try to popularize this book throughout England as much as possible.* ***Because if these books are read, there is no doubt that many sincere souls shall be attracted and will join you in your work for Krishna. So please try for selling these books, it shall be considered as the greatest service."*** *(S.P.L. to Gurudasa 1/12/68)*

*"One Krishna book sold means we go forward one step in our Krishna Consciousness.* ***We should always remember this."*** *(S.P.L. to Visnujana Maharaja 4th April 1971)*

*"But in my heart I want that KRISHNA book in small or large form, should be distributed in every home who are English-speaking people."* *(S.P.L. to Karandhara May 17th 1971)*

*"I am glad to hear that you are distributing nicely books and magazines.* ***The more we sell books, the more we advance in KC, and the more we help others to have solid information how they may take advantage of their human form of life and achieve the supreme perfection.*** *So I want that you should now increase very greatly this selling of books and literatures."* *(S.P.L. to Kulasekhara 20/1/72)*

*"I am very glad to hear all the good news, especially that you want to sell books more and more.* ***That is the best preaching work; each book sold means there is some practical effect of preaching, there is some tangible progress.*** *So try to sell books as many as possible in your country, and in this way, so long you remain active but not for your personal sense-gratification, so long you remain active only satisfying Krishna's senses, then this movement will be successful without any doubt. As soon as someone wants to satisfy his own senses, then he fails at everything."* *(S.P.L. to Kuruksetra 23/11/12)*

*"Actually producing and distributing books is our most important engagement, all other engagements* **culminate in this one end--distribution of books."** *(S.P.L. to Tamala Krishna 27th July 1973)*

*"I understand from Karandhara that you are one of the most staunch supporters and workers for distributing our books and* **I assure you that it is the highest service to my Guru Maharaja. Thank you very much."** *(S.P.L. to Trai dasa 8/12/73)*

**"So I am always emphasizing book distribution. It is the better kirtana. It is better than chanting.** *Of course chanting should not stop,* **but book distribution is the best kirtana."** *(S.P.L. to Srutadeva dasa 24/10/74)*

*"I am especially pleased at how you are distributing our books, particularly to the schools and universities. This program is so important and should be increased more and more.* **We want to flood the world over with our books. So go on in this way and Krishna will surely bless you."** *(S.P.L. to Sri Govinda 21/1/71)*

*"Actually this book production is most important, and you have pleased me very much.* **Just go on and flood the whole world with these Krishna books."** *(S.P.L. to Bali-mardana 8/873)*

*"So I am very pleased with your activities. Now continue and increase.* **Everyone will want our books. We will always have customers. This is Caitanya Mahaprabhu's mercy."** *(S.P.L. to Ghanasyama 20/11/75)*

*"Your report of the book distribution there is very encouraging. Make program to distribute our books all over the world. Our books are being appreciated by learned circles, so we should take advantage.* **Whatever progress we have made, it is simply to distributing these books. So go on, and do not divert your mind for a moment from this."** *(S.P.L. to Ramesvara dasa 11/10/74)*

**"So that is the real preaching, selling books. Who can speak better than the books?** *At least whoever buys, he will look over. If you have to sell books, do it by hook or by crook. The real preaching is selling books. You should know the tactic how to sell without irritating. What your lecture will do for three minutes,* **but if he reads one page his life may be turned."** *(S.P.L. to Bali Marden 30th September 1972)*

*"The results show that there is no limit to our book distribution.* **Our books are qualified to be distributed unlimitedly."** *(S.P.L. to Ramesvara dasa 18/1/76)*

*"The word kriyasu, meaning "by manual labor" or "by work," is important in this verse. One should engage in practical service to the Lord. In our Krishna consciousness movement,* **all our activities are concentrated upon distributing Krishna literature. This is very important.** *One may approach any person and*

*induce him to read Krishna literature **so that in the future he also may become a devotee.** Such activities are recommended in this verse. Kriyasu yas tvac-caranaravindayoh. Such activities will always remind the devotees of the Lord's lotus feet. **By fully concentrating on distributing books for Krishna, one is fully absorbed in Krishna. This is samadhi."** (S.B 10.2.37)*

*"These books are the life of human society. Others may be disturbed, but they cannot disturb this Srimad-Bhagavatam. Let any man come, but here they cannot touch. We are putting these books for deliberation before the topmost thinkers of human society. **Therefore, I have to see that in all languages all of our books are published.** If we strain, and if he takes one book home, some day people will come to understand what valuable knowledge they have received. It is transcendental literature. Nobody can challenge it. It is done so nicely, without any spot, the spotless Purana. **Please continue like this to print books in all the languages for the benefit of suffering, misdirected humanity."** (S.P.L. to Puranjana, 4th May, 1976)*

*"Please print as many books as possible, this is my real pleasure. **By printing these books of our Krishna Conscious philosophy in so many different languages we can actually inject our movement into the masses of persons all over the world,** especially there in the western countries and **we can literally turn whole nations into Krishna Conscious nations."** (S.P.L. to Hrdayananda Maharaja, 21st December, 1974)*

***"Anyway, print books, distribute profusely, and that will be the best preaching work.** What will your three minutes' preaching do?--**but if they buy one book, it may turn their life."** (S.P.L. to Bhagavan 5th November, 1972)*

*"Yes, that is a good proposal, **print many many books in African language and distribute widely, that is real preaching work.** If you sell a book to someone, that is better than your speaking to them--what will your three minutes' preaching do? **But if they read a book it may turn their life."** (S.P.L. to Brahmananda, 3rd November, 1972)*

Any devotee who has been fortunate enough to be an instrument in the hands of Srila Prabhupada, by distributing one of his books to a conditioned soul, will testify to a special taste in such a loving exchange. Let us try to understand such an exchange through the eyes of sastra.

*TRANSLATION: According to their karma, all living entities are wandering throughout the entire universe. Some of them are being elevated to the upper planetary systems, and some are going down into the lower planetary systems. Out of many millions of wandering living entities, one who is very fortunate gets an opportunity to associate with a bona fide spiritual master by the grace of Krishna. By the mercy of both Krishna and the spiritual master, such a person receives the seed of the creeper of devotional service.*

*PURPORT: When we speak of brahmanda, we refer to the whole universe, or to the cluster of many millions of universes. In all universes, there are innumerable planets and innumerable living entities upon those planets in the air and in the water. There are millions and trillions of living entities everywhere, and they are engaged by maya in suffering and enjoying the results of their fruitive activity life after life. This is the position of the materially conditioned living entities. **Out of many of these living entities, if one is actually fortunate (bhagyavan), he comes in contact with a bona fide spiritual master by Krishna's mercy.** Krishna is situated in everyone's heart, and if one desires something, Krishna fulfils one's desire. If the living entity by chance or fortune comes in contact with the Krishna consciousness movement and wishes to associate with that movement, Krishna, who is situated in everyone's heart, **gives him the chance to meet a bona fide spiritual master. This is called guru-Krishna-prasada. Krishna is prepared to bestow His mercy upon all living entities, and as soon as a living entity desires the Lord's mercy, the Lord immediately gives him an opportunity to meet a bona fide spiritual master.** Such a person is fortified by both Krishna and the spiritual master. He is helped from within by Krishna and from without by the spiritual master. Both are prepared to help the sincere living being become free from this material bondage. (C.C. Mad. 19.151.)*

Srila Prabhupada says "as soon as a living entity desires the Lords mercy, the Lord immediately gives him an opportunity to meet a bona-fide spiritual master."

*"There is no difference between the spiritual master's instructions and the spiritual master himself." (C.C. Adi. 1.35)*

The words of Srila Prabhupada are non-different than himself. Everyone who receives one of his books has received the mercy of the Lord, by meeting His bona-fide representative, His Divine Grace A.C. Bhaktivedanta Swami Prabhupada.

*TRANSLATION: Since one cannot visually experience the presence of the Supersoul, He appears before us as a liberated devotee. Such a spiritual master is no one other than Krishna Himself.*

*PURPORT: It is not possible for a conditioned soul to directly meet Krishna, the Supreme Personality of Godhead, but if one becomes a sincere devotee and seriously engages in devotional service, **Lord Krishna sends an instructing spiritual master to show him favour and invoke his dormant propensity for serving the Supreme. The preceptor appears before the external senses of the fortunate conditioned soul,** and at the same time the devotee is guided from within by the caittya-guru, Krishna, who is seated as the spiritual master within the heart of the living entity. (C.C. Adi 1.58)*

In the text to the above verse such a representative is described as siksa guru. Srila Prabhupada elaborates on this in the purport "Lord Krishna sends an instructing spiritual master to show him favour and invoke his dormant propensity for serving the Supreme. The perceptor appears before the external senses of the fortunate conditioned soul"

A conditioned soul has six senses including the mind, the perceptor can appear to any of these senses. He appears to give instructions and so appears predominantly to the sense of hearing. The picture of such a liberated devotee is also absolute and thus non-different than himself. Thus Srila Prabhupada can also appear to the external senses of a conditioned soul in the form of his picture, which he had placed on all his books.

*"There is no difference between me and my picture." (S.P.L. Jadurani, 4th September, 1972)*

The minute a conditioned soul contacts Srila Prabhupada in the form of his vani, he begins his eternal bond with him from that day.

***"The eternal bond between disciple and spiritual master begins from the first day he hears.*** *Just like my spiritual master. In 1922 he said in our first meeting, you are educated boys, why don't you preach this cult.* ***That was the beginning, now it is coming to fact. Therefore the relationship began from that day."*** *(S.P.L. to Jadurani, 4th September, 1972)*

How that relationship develops is described as follows:

*"The influence of a pure devotee is such that if someone comes to associate with him with a little faith, one gets the chance of hearing about the Lord from authoritative scriptures like Bhagavad-gita and Srimad-Bhagavatam. Thus, by the mercy of the Lord, who is situated in everyone's heart, one gradually develops his faith in the descriptions of such authoritative scriptures. This is the first stage of association with pure devotees.* ***In the second stage, after one becomes a little advanced and mature, he automatically offers to follow the principles of devotional service under the guidance of the pure devotee and*** <u>***accepts him as the spiritual master.***</u>*" (N.O.D. Chapter 19)*

One develops faith in Srila Prabhupada, automatically offers to follow the principles of devotional service and accepts Srila Prabhupada as diksa guru. This development is confirmed as follows:

*"It is the duty of the siksa-guru or diksa-guru to instruct the disciple in the right way, and it depends on the disciple to execute the process. According to sastric injunctions, there is no difference between siksa-guru and diksa-guru, and* ***generally the siksa-guru later on becomes the diksa-guru." (S.B. 4.12.32)***

*"Generally a spiritual master who constantly instructs a disciple in spiritual science* ***becomes his initiating spiritual master later on." (C.C. Adi, 1.35)***

This acceptance of Srila Prabhupada as the initiating spiritual master after hearing from him about the Lord, is the bona-fide process for accepting a guru.

*"Devotional service entails being initiated by a bona fide spiritual master and following his instruction in regard to hearing about the Lord. **Such a bona fide spiritual master is accepted by regularly hearing from him about the Lord."** (S.B. 3.5.42)*

*"My guru maharaja, my spiritual master, used to say that you have to **select a spiritual master not by seeing but by your ear, but by hearing.** And you don't select a spiritual master who has got a very good hair or beard or some very beautiful feature, "Oh, he is a very good, nice looking." **No. You must hear. Tad viddhi pranipatena. Sruti. The whole process is sruti. The Vedas are called sruti. The ear has to aural reception."** (B.G. 4.24.34 Lecture, N.Y. 2nd August, 1966)*

With this in mind, we can understand Srila Prabhupada's intense mood while begging us "please distribute book, distribute book, distribute book."

*"There is no comparison. There is no competition. Every word is for the good of the human society. Every word, each and every word. Therefore we stress so much in the book distribution. Somehow or other, if the book goes in one hand, he will be benefited. At least he will see, "Oh, they have taken so much price. Let me see what is there. **If he reads one sloka, his life will be successful. If one sloka, one word. This is such nice things. Therefore we are stressing so much, "Please distribute book, distribute book, distribute book."** A greater mrdanga. We are chanting, playing our mrdanga. It is heard within this room or little more. But this mrdanga will go home to home, country to country, community to community, this mrdanga." (S.B. Lec. 1.16.8., Los Angeles 5th January, 1974)*

Out of the nine items of devotional service, book distribution falls in the category of sravanam kirtanam.

*"Sravanam kirtanam is the beginning--to chant and hear. **Book distribution is under this category of sravanam kirtanam."** (S.P.L. to Satsvarupa, 19th January, 1975)*

*"Regarding Sankirtana and book distribution, book distribution is also chanting. **Anyone who reads the books that is also chanting and hearing.** Why distinguish between chanting and book distribution? **These books I have recorded and chanted, and they are transcribed. It is spoken kirtanas. So book distribution is also chanting. These are not ordinary books. It is recorded chanting. Anyone who reads, he is hearing.** Book distribution must not be neglected. If things deteriorate that is another thing, but it is not the fault of book distribution." (S.P.L. to Rupanuga dasa, 19th October, 1974)*

So more specifically book distribution falls into the category of the loud chanting of His Divine Grace Srila Prabhupada, and the hearing of the people of the world. The effects of such loud chanting on the conditioned souls of the world is described as follows:

*"When a devotee is perfectly qualified in chanting the transcendental vibration of the holy name, he is quite fit to become a spiritual master and to deliver all the people of the world. The chanting of the holy name is so powerful that it gradually establishes its supremacy above everything in the world. The devotee who chants it becomes transcendentally situated in ecstasy and sometimes laughs, cries and dances in his ecstasy. Sometimes the unintelligent put hindrances in the path of chanting this maha-mantra, but* **one who is situated on the platform of love of Godhead chants the holy name loudly for all concerned. As a result,** <u>**everyone**</u> **<u>becomes initiated</u> in the chanting of the holy names--Hare Krishna, Hare Krishna, Krishna Krishna, Hare Hare/ Hare Rama, Hare Rama, Rama Rama, Hare Hare."** *(T.L.C. Chapter 18)*

**"Such vedanta-vadis, or the bhakti-vedantas, are impartial in distributing the transcendental knowledge of devotional service.** *To them no one is enemy or friend; no one is educated or uneducated. No one is especially favourable, and no one is unfavourable. The bhakti-vedantas see that the people in general are wasting time in false sensuous things. Their business is to get the ignorant mass of people to re-establish their lost relationship with the Personality of Godhead.* **By such endeavour, even the most forgotten soul is roused up to the sense of spiritual life, and thus** <u>**being initiated**</u> **by the bhakti-vedantas, the people in general gradually progress on the path of transcendental realization."** *(S.B. 1.5.24)*

Srila Prabhupada's endeavour to get the mass of people to re-establish their lost relationship with the Lord, is through the mass distribution of his books.

*"I wish that all of our Krishna Consciousness literature's may be available to men of all languages throughout the world, so whatever assistance you can give in this connection is always appreciated."* (S.P.L. to Sivananda, 22nd July, 1969)

He wants that every conditioned soul throughout the world may have the opportunity of his association. This is described very nicely in this (S.B. 1.5.24) purport. "Bhaktivedantas are impartial in distributing the transcendental knowledge of devotional service. To them no one is enemy or friend, no one is educated or uneducated. No one is especially favourable and no one is unfavourable.... thus being **initiated by the Bhaktivedantas**, the people in general gradually progress on the path of transcendental realization."

*"Following in the footsteps of Lord Caitanya Mahaprabhu,* **the Krishna consciousness movement is distributing the Hare Krishna maha-mantra and inducing people all over the world to chant. We are giving people an immense**

*treasury of transcendental literature, translated into all the important languages of the world, and by the grace of Lord Sri Caitanya Mahaprabhu this literature is selling profusely, and people are chanting the Hare Krishna maha-mantra with great delight. This is the preaching process of the Caitanya cult. Since the Lord wanted this cult preached all over the world, the International Society of Krishna Consciousness is acting in a humble way so that the vision of Sri Caitanya Mahaprabhu may be fulfilled all over the world, especially in the western countries." (C.C. Adi 16.19)*

Srila Prabhupada's books are selling profusely and inducing people all over the world to chant with great delight, thus fulfilling the vision of Sri Caitanya Mahaprabhu that his name would be heard all over the world.

*"Srila Rupa Gosvami has described Sri Caitanya Mahaprabhu as maha-vadanya-avatara, the most munificent incarnation. Although Sri Caitanya Mahaprabhu is not physically present now, simply by chanting His holy name (sri-Krishna-caitanya prabhu nityananda sri-advaita gadadhara srivasadi-gaura-bhakta-vrnda) people throughout the world are becoming devotees. **This is due to the ecstatic chanting of the holy name of the Lord. It is said that a pure devotee can see the Lord every moment, and because of this he is empowered by the Lord.** This is confirmed in Brahma-samhita: premanjana-cchurita-bhakti-vilocanena santah sadaiva hrda yesu vilokayanti. Sri Caitanya Mahaprabhu appeared five hundred years ago, but it cannot be said that now the potency of the Hare Krishna maha-mantra is less powerful than it was in His presence. **By hearing Sri Caitanya Mahaprabhu through the parampara system, one can be purified.** Therefore in this verse it is said: tathapi tanra darsana-sravana-prabhave. It is not that everyone is able to see Krishna or Sri Krishna Caitanya Mahaprabhu physically, but **if one hears about Him through books like Sri Caitanya-caritamrta and through the parampara system of pure Vaisnavas, there is no difficulty in becoming a pure Vaisnava, free from mundane desires and personal motivations."* (C.C. Mad. 17.51)

Srila Prabhupada says "Although Sri Caitanya Mahaprabhu is not physically present now, simply by chanting his holy name people throughout the world are becoming devotees. This is due to the ecstatic chanting of the holy name of the Lord. It is said that a pure devotee can see the Lord at every moment and because of this he is empowered by the Lord......if one hears about him through books like Sri Caitanya Caritamrta and through the parampara system of pure Vaisnavas, there is no difficulty becoming a pure Vaisnava.free from mundane desires and personal motivations." By receiving the books of Srila Prabhupada the people of the world are hearing His ecstatic chanting of the holy name, and thus being initiated the people are becoming devotees of the Lord. Srila Prabhupada, the empowered devotee of the Lord is described more clearly as follows:

*"In this age of Kali, real religious propaganda should induce people to chant the Hare Krishna maha-mantra. This is possible for someone who is especially empowered by Krishna.* No one can do this without being especially favoured by

*Krishna. Srila Bhaktisiddhanta Sarasvati Thakura comments in this regard in his Anubhasya, wherein he quotes a verse from Narayana-samhita:*

*"In Dvapara-yuga, devotees of Lord Visnu and Krishna rendered devotional service according to the principles of pancaratrika in this age of Kali, the Supreme Personality of Godhead is worshipped simply by the chanting of His holy names.', Srila Bhaktisiddhanta Sarasvati Thakura then comments: "**Without being empowered by the direct potency of Lord Krishna to fulfil His desire and without being specifically favoured by he Lord, no human being can become the spiritual master of the whole world.** He certainly cannot succeed by mental concoction, which is not meant for devotees or religious people. **Only an empowered personality can distribute the holy name of the Lord and enjoin all fallen souls to worship Krishna. By distributing the holy name of the Lord, he cleanses the hearts of the most fallen people; therefore he extinguishes the blazing fire of the material world.** Not only that, he broadcasts the shining brightness of Krishna's effulgence throughout the world. Such an acarya, or spiritual master, should be considered non-different from Krishna--that is, he should be considered the incarnation of Lord Krishna's potency. Such a personality is Krishnalingita-vigraha--that is, he is always embraced by the Supreme Personality of Godhead, Krishna. Such a person is above the considerations of the varnasrama institution. He is the guru or spiritual master for the entire world, a devotee on the topmost platform, the maha-bhagavata stage, and a paramahamsa-thakura, a spiritual form only fit to be addressed as paramahamsa or thakura." (C.C. Mad 25.9)*

Only Srila Prabhupada, an empowered personality, can distribute the holy name of the Lord and enjoined all fallen souls to **worship Krishna.** This process is described in the sastra as follows:

*"It is the spiritual master who delivers the disciple from the clutches of maya by **initiating him** into the chanting of the Hare Krishna maha-mantra. in this way a sleeping human being can revive his consciousness by chanting Hare Krishna, Hare Krishna, Krishna Krishna, Hare Hare/ Hare Rama, Hare Rama, Rama Rama, Hare Hare. In other words, **the spiritual master awakens the sleeping living entity to his original consciousness so that he can worship Lord Visnu. This is the purpose of diksa, or initiation.** Initiation means receiving the pure knowledge of spiritual consciousness." (C.C. Mad 9.61)*

This initiation or awakening to pure consciousness performed by Srila Prabhupada's loud chanting (book distribution), should be given to all fallen souls.

*"Devotional service begins with sravana kirtana, hearing and chanting. When a man is sleeping, he can be awakened by sound vibration; therefore **every conditioned soul should be given the chance to hear the Hare Krishna mantra chanted by a pure Vaisnava.** One who hears the Hare Krishna mantra thus vibrated is awakened to spiritual consciousness, or Krishna consciousness." (C.C. Mad. 22-105)*

Srila Prabhupada is distributing the holy name and cleansing the hearts of the most fallen, therefore he is extinguishing the blazing fire of the material world.

*"So what is the guru? Guru has received the karunya. Karunya means just like the cloud has received water from the sea, similarly, a guru, spiritual master, receives the cloud of mercy from the ocean of kindness of Krishna. Ghanaghanatvam. And it is only the cloud that can extinguish the forest fire, samsara. No other watering system will be helpful. If there is fire in the forest, your fire brigade or buckets of water will not help. It is impossible. Neither you can go there; neither you can render any service by your fire brigade and bucket. Then how the fire can be extinguished? Now, ghanaghanatvam. If there is cloud in the sky and if there is rainfall, then the expansive forest fire can immediately be extinguished. **So that cloud is supposed to be the spiritual master. He pours water. He pours water. Sravana-kirtana-jale karaye secana. What is that water? The water is this sravana-kirtana.** Bhava-maha-davagni, the fire, the forest fire of material existence, is blazing continually. So you have to extinguish it by the rainfall from cloud, and that rainfall means sravana-kirtana. Sravana means hearing, and kirtana means chanting. This is the only way. Sravana-kirtana-jale karaye secana."* (S.B. Lecture 3.26.39, Bombay, 14th January, 1975)

So Srila Prabhupada is the cloud of mercy and his loud chanting (book distribution) is the rainfall, which is the only way to extinguish the blazing fire of material existence. This is confirmed as follows:

*"The spiritual master, **by his words**, can penetrate into the heart of the suffering person and inject knowledge transcendental, **which alone can extinguish the fire of material existence."** (S.B. 1.7.22)*

Srila Prabhupada is delivering all fallen souls through his transcendental sound vibration. This is the purpose of initiation, the deliverance of the disciple from the material existence.

*"The spiritual master **initiates the disciple to deliver him**, and if the disciple executes the order of the spiritual master and does not offend other Vaisnavas, his path is clear."* (C.C. Mad, 1.218)

*"It is the spiritual master who **delivers the disciple** from the clutches of maya **by initiating him** into the chanting of the Hare Krishna maha-mantra."* (C.C. Mad, 9.61)

By the association of Srila Prabhupada (sadhu sanga) the fortunate soul receives a process of spiritual activities, that is called bhajana kriya.

**"And if there is actually association of spiritually self-realized persons, then he will give you some process of spiritual activities. That is called bhajana-kriya.** Adau sraddha tatah sadhu-sangah atha bhajana-kriya tato anartha-nivrttih syat.

*And as you are more and more engaged in spiritual activities, so, proportionately, your material activities and affection for material activities will diminish. Counteraction. When you engage in the spiritual activities, your material activities diminishes." (B.G. Lec, 2.58-59, New York, 7th April, 1966)*

If we follow this process that is our initiation. By engaging in these spiritual activities our material activities diminish (anartha nirrtti). Thus devotees who haven't received formal initiation, but have been chanting and following the four regulative principles, are freeing themselves from gross and subtle anarthas. They have clearly received initiation from Srila Prabhupada, who is actually giving everyone this process (Bhajana Kriya) in his transcendental books.

Let us return to the Nectar of Devotion (page 150) "he automatically offers to follow the principles of devotional service under the guidance of the pure devotee and accepts him as the spiritual master." Srila Prabhupada describes how we can receive his guidance in the following lecture.

*"And the process is very simple. The process is very simple. We are recommending the followers of Krishna consciousness... Just now I received one letter from Jaipur. **They wanted my guidance. The guidance is not very difficult. It is very simple thing. First of all try to become sinless: no illicit sex life, no intoxication, no meat-eating, no gambling. Observe these four regulative principles and chant Hare Krishna mantra as far as possible, at least sixteen rounds. Then see how your life changes."** (S.B. Lecture 1.2.8, 22nd April, 1974)*

His guidance would amount to that process of spiritual activities described as Bhajana kriya (initiation), in the previous lecture (2.58.59 B.G. N.Y.) Srila Prabhupada's guidance to everyone is that process by which we awaken our transcendental knowledge, and vanquish all material contamination caused by our previous sinful activities. This is described in the sastra as follows.

*"Diksa is the process by which one can awaken his transcendental knowledge and vanquish all reactions caused by sinful activity. A person expert in the study of the revealed scriptures knows this process as diksa." (C.C. Mad., 15-108)*

*"Diksa actualy means initiating a disciple with transcendental knowledge by which he becomes freed from all material contamination." (C.C. Mad., 4-111)*

In the earlier lecture (S.B. 1.2.8) Srila Prabhupada says "observe these four regulative principles and chant Hare Krishna mantra as far as possible, at least sixteen rounds. Then see how your life changes." Again confirmation, that if we follow his guidance that is our initiation (Bhajana kriya) and as a result our life will change, or we will become free from material contamination (anartha nivritih).

If by chance one is fortunate enough to receive Srila Prabhupada's association through his transcendental books, the sastra advises:

*"As far as the time of diksa (initiation) is concerned, everything depends on the position of the guru. **As soon as a bona fide guru is received by chance or by a program, one should immediately take the opportunity to receive initiation.** in the book called Tattva-sagara, it is stated:*

*"If, by chance, one gets a sad-guru, **it doesn't matter whether one is in the temple or the forest. If the sad-guru, the bona fide spiritual master, agrees, one can be initiated immediately, without waiting for a suitable time or place."** (C.C. Mad., 24.331)*

We should take the opportunity to receive initiation regardless of where we are situated. If Srila Prabhupada agrees to accept us we should take his shelter.

**Reporter: *If I wanted to be initiated into your society, what would I have to do?***

**Srila Prabhupada:** *First of all, you'd have to give up illicit sex life.*

**Reporter:** *Does that include all sex life? What is illicit sex life?*

**Srila Prabhupada:** *Illicit sex is sex outside of marriage. Animals have sex with no restrictions, but in human society there are restrictions. In every country and in every religion, there is some system of restricting sex life. You would also have to give up all intoxicants, including tea, cigarettes, alcohol, marijuana--anything that intoxicates.*

**Reporter:** *Anything else?*

**Srila Prabhupada:** *You'd also have to give up eating meat, eggs, and fish. And you'd have to give up gambling as well. Unless you gave up these four sinful activities, you could not be initiated.*

**Reporter:** *Does "surrender" mean that someone would have to leave his family?*

**Srila Prabhupada:** *No.*

**Reporter: *But suppose I were to become an initiate. Wouldn't I have to come and live in the temple?***

**Srila Prabhupada:** *Not necessarily.*

**Reporter:** *I can stay at home?*

*Srila Prabhupada: Oh, yes.*

*Reporter: What about work? Would I have to give up my job?*

*Srila Prabhupada: No, you'd simply have to give up your bad habits and chant the Hare Krishna mantra on these beads--that's all.*

*(S.S.R. "Choosing a spiritual master")*

"You'd simply have to give up your bad habits and chant Hare Krishna mantra on these beads - That's All." That's what Srila Prabhupada asks of us if we want to become his initiated disciples.

*"Materialistic persons who are not inclined to give up their sinful activities like illicit sex, intoxication, gambling and meat-eating sometimes want to become our disciples, but, unlike professional spiritual masters who accept disciples regardless of their condition, Vaisnavas do not accept such cheap disciples. **One must at least agree to abide by the rules and regulations for a disciple before a Vaisnava acarya can accept him.**" (C.C. Adi., 12.50)*

*"**My advise is always chant 16 rounds minimum and follow the four regulative principles. All of my disciples must agree on this point otherwise they are not my disciples. Let one live anywhere, but stick to the principles.** Disagreements will continue in this material world. So one may live in a suitable place, but one must follow these five principles. **My disciples must follow these principles living either in heaven or hell.**" (Raja-Lakami-desi, 17th February, 1976)*

*TRANSLATION: "The hunter then said, `My dear sir, whatever you say I shall do.' Narada immediately ordered him, `First of all, break your bow. Then I shall tell you what is to be done.'*

*PURPORT: **This is the process of initiation.** The disciple must admit that he will no longer commit sinful activity--namely illicit sex, meat-eating, gambling and intoxication. He promises to execute the order of the spiritual master. **Then the spiritual master takes care of him and elevates him to spiritual emancipation.** (C.C. Mad., 24.256)*

The same is confirmed in all these quotes, and in the last Srila Prabhupada promises to take care of us and take us back to Godhead if we follow his guidance, such guidance is his causeless mercy. "Unless he's a sadhu he cannot be guru.....**Initiation means to accept the mercy of sadhu and spiritual master if you don't accept there is no other way.**" (C.C. Lecture) Who can deny the availability of Srila Prabhupada's mercy, if we take such mercy that is our initiation. There is no other way.

*"If you have understood this Krishna philosophy and if you have decided that you will take Krishna consciousness seriously and preach the philosophy to others. **That is your initiation, my touch is simply a formality. It is your determination that is initiation.**"* (B.T.G. Article "Search for the Divine")

Srila Prabhupada says his touch is a formality, our determination to follow the process is our real initiation.

**"The chanting Hare Krishna is our main business, that is real initiation. And as you are all following my instruction, in that matter, <u>the initiator is already there.</u> Now the next initiation will be performed as a ceremony officially,** *of course that ceremony has value because the name, Holy Name, will be delivered to the student from the disciplic succession, it has got value, but in spite of that, as you are going on chanting, please go on with this business sincerely and Krishna willing, I may be coming to you very soon."* (S.P.L. Tamal Krishna, 19th September, 1968)

Srila Prabhupada says that chanting Hare Krishna is the real initiation, and that because devotees were following his instructions in that matter (16 rounds, 4 regulations), he was already there as the initiator. In other words the initiation was already there and he had accepted them as his disciples. He then goes on to say the next initiation will be performed as a ceremony officially.

For 10,000 years, millions and millions of conditioned souls will be receiving Srila Prabhupada's association through his transcendental books, If they accept and agree to follow his instructions in regards to chanting the holy names, he will be with them all as the initiator and will accept them as disciples. The next initiation as an official ceremony must be performed on his behalf due to his physical absence, as acceptance of two diksa guru's is always forbidden in the sastra.

*"A devotee must have only one initiating spiritual master because in the scriptures acceptance of more than one is always forbidden."* (C.C. Adi., 1.35)

Due to illness and increasing demand for formal initiation, Srila Prabhupada established a system where ritvik priests accepted devotees as his initiated disciples by giving spiritual names. This system was in full operation, without Srila Prabhupada being physically involved for months before his departure in November, and should continue for the rest of the present golden age (10,000 years)

*"A disciple means one who is always following the orders of the spiritual master. So I instruct my disciples to refrain from four prohibitions, namely no eating of meat, fish or eggs, no illicit sex life, no taking of intoxication, including tea, coffee, cigarettes, etc., and no gambling. Besides that my students must chant sixteen rounds of japa-mala of Hare Krishna mantra daily. **So if you are able to follow these principles without fail, then you are as good as my disciple.** And*

*after you have practised these things for a few months' time, then we can see to your formal initiation." (S.P.L. to Suresh Chandra, 11th August, 1972)*

In this letter there is more confirmation that anyone following his instructions in regards to chanting the holy name, is as good as his disciple, even without formal initiation.

***"The eternal bond between disciple and spiritual master begins from the first day he hears.*** *Just like my spiritual master. In 1922 he said in our first meeting, you are educated boys, why don't you preach this cult. That was the beginning, now it is coming to fact. Therefore the relationship began from that day." (S.P.L. to Jadurani, 4th September, 1972)*

Srila Prabhupada says the relationship between the spiritual master and disciple begins from the first day the disciple hears from the guru, and he cites his own meeting with Srila Bhaktisiddanta Maharaja in 1922 as an example.

*"So anyway, from 1922 to 1933 practically I was not initiated but got the impression of preaching Caitanya Mahaprabhu's cult. That I was thinking.* ***And that was the initiation by my guru maharaja.*** *Then officially I was initiated in 1933 because in 1923 I left Calcutta." (Lecture, Diss. day Srila Bhaktisiddanta Hyderabad, 10th December, 1976)*

He describes such a meeting as the initiation by his Guru Maharaja. This is confirmed as follows.

*"So I was at that time a fool, but I opined like this.* ***And I accepted him as my spiritual master immediately. Not officially, but in my heart.*** *That was in 1922."* *(General Lecture, 1973)*

Any conditioned soul who is hearing from Srila Prabhupada after receiving his books and is accepting him in their heart as their spiritual master, that acceptance is their initiation. Srila Prabhupada was well aware that due to his books, such acceptance would take place in the hearts of sincere souls for 10,000 years. This is why he wanted the ritvik system to continue in his physical absence. The acarya Srila Prabhupada never deviates from the principles of sadhu, sastra and guru. Through this system all his disciples could formalize this acceptance and receive a spiritual name.

*TRANSLATION: My dear Sakara Mallika, from this day your names will be changed to Srila Rupa and Srila Sanatana. Now please abandon your humility, for My heart is breaking to see you so humble.*

*PURPORT: Actually this is Sri Caitanya Mahaprabhu's initiation of Dabira Khasa and Sakara Mallika. They approached the Lord with all humility, and the Lord accepted them as old servants, as eternal servants, and He changed their* *names. **It is to be understood from this that it is essential for a disciple to change his name after initiation.** (C.C. Mad., 1.208)*

In summary, book distribution or more specifically, Srila Prabhupada's loud chanting is giving all fallen souls his association. If they take this association seriously and follow his guidance, that is their initiation into the chanting of the holy name. To formalise such an initiation and thus give his disciples a spiritual name, he appointed eleven disciples (officiating acarya's) to conduct these initiation rites.

These initial eleven were placed in different locations of the world, and were to be added to accordingly, to meet increasing demands in those locations for formal initiations, due to the effects of the loud chanting of the Jagad Guru His Divine Grace A.C. Bhaktivedanta Swami Prabhupada.

*"That is Vaisnava behaviour. Vaisnavas, they are the best friend of the society, best friend, Vaisnava. Patitanam pavanebhyoh vaisnavebhyo namo namah. The Vaisnava is always thinking how to deliver these fallen souls who are so much captivated with this false philosophy of hedonism--"Eat, drink, be merry and enjoy." This is called hedonism. So they are always thinking how to deliver them. Advaita Prabhu did it. Therefore He is Isvara. Prahlada Maharaja did it. **Any Vaisnava who is actually feeling for the poor, conditioned souls, he must make arrangement for delivering these rascals from the death knell of ignorance."** (C.C. Adi. lila, Lecture 1.12.75)*

Srila Prabhupada's transcendental books are, very clearly, his arrangement for delivering the fallen souls of the world from the death knell of ignorance. Such is the potency of the Maha Bhagavata devotee Srila Prabhupada!

*"But now in your temple alone you are distributing so many, so this is very, very encouraging to me. It is the perfect form of preaching. Follow the line laid down by Prahlada Maharaja and **try to take every one back to home, back to Godhead. And this is done by distributing our literature.** I am so much pleased upon each and every one of you for helping me this way to push on this great movement." (S.P.L. to Vamanadeva 3/12/72)*

Srila Prabhupada in the form of his books (instructions) is taking everyone back to home, back to Godhead. This is the purpose of initiating a disciple, to deliver him.

*"The spiritual master **initiates the disciple to deliver him**, and if the disciple executes the order of the spiritual master and does not offend other Vaisnavas, his path is clear." (C.C. Mad, 1.218)*

*"It is the spiritual master who **delivers the disciple** from the clutches of maya **by initiating him** into the chanting of the Hare Krishna maha-mantra." (C.C. Mad, 9.61)*

*"If one is expert in Vedic literature and has full faith in the Supreme Lord, then he is an uttama-adhikari, a first-class Vaisnava, a topmost Vaisnava who **can deliver the whole world and turn everyone to Krishna consciousness.**" (C.C. Mad., 22.65)*

*"This example of Dhruva Maharaja's closing the holes of his personal body and thereby closing the breathing holes of the total universe clearly indicates that a devotee, by his personal devotional service, can influence all the people of the whole world to become devotees of the Lord. **If there is only one pure devotee in pure Krishna consciousness, he can change the total consciousness of the world into Krishna consciousness.** This is not very difficult to understand if we study the behaviour of Dhruva Maharaja." (S.B. 4.8.80)*

Srila Prabhupada is the initiating acarya for the golden age, the Jagad Guru. He is living still in sound and is most definitely spreading the holy name all around. All glories to you Srila Prabhupada!

*"After 80 years, no one can expect to live long. My life is almost ended. So you have to carry on, and **these books will do everything.**" (Room conversation, 18th February 1976)*

## SADHU, SASTRA & GURU
### Book distribution, Ritvik Acaryas, The Perfect Plan

While every devotee acknowledges the fact that Srila Prabhupada as the founder-acarya of the International Society for Krishna Consciousness, performed many unprecedented activities:

1. Harinama diksa given by mail

2. Brahminical initiation been given by tape recording

3. Ritvik's or deputies chanting on initiates beads

4. The performance of marriages by a sannyasi

5. Young unmarried women being allowed to live in the asrama as brahmacarinis

6. Initiates names being given at the time of Harinama diksa

Some souls challenge the ritvik system been used in Srila Prabhupada's physical absence, saying it is not supported by sadhu, sastra and guru. Therefore, it would not have been implemented by Srila Prabhupada and that it contradicts the law of disciplic succession.

*TRANSLATION:_Om namo bhagavate vasudevaya. This is the twelve-syllable mantra for worshipping Lord Krishna. One should install the physical forms of the Lord, and with the* **chanting of the mantra** *one should offer flowers and fruits and other varieties of foodstuffs exactly according to the rules and regulations prescribed by authorities.* **But this should be done in consideration of place, time, and attendant conveniences and inconveniences.**

*PURPORT: The prescribed rules, as stated here by Narada Muni, are that one should* **accept the mantra through a bona fide spiritual master and hear the mantra in the right ear.** *Not only should one chant or murmur the mantra, but in front of him he must have the Deity, or physical form of the Lord. Of course, when the Lord appears it is no longer a physical form.....The method of worship--* **chanting the mantra** *and preparing the forms of the Lord--* **is not stereotyped, nor is it exactly the same everywhere. It. is specifically mentioned in this verse that one should take consideration of the time, place and available conveniences.** *Our Krishna consciousness movement is going on throughout the entire world, and we also install Deities in different centers. Sometimes our Indian friends, puffed up with concocted notions, criticise, "This has not been done. That has not been done." But they forget this instruction of Narada Muni to one of the greatest Vaisnavas, Dhruva Maharaja.* **One has to consider the particular time, country and conveniences.** *What is convenient in India may not be convenient in the Western countries. Those who are not actually in the line of acaryas, or who personally have no knowledge of how to act in the role of acarya, necessarily criticise the activities of the ISKCON movement in countries outside of India. The fact is that such critics cannot do anything personally to spread Krishna consciousness. If someone does go and preach, taking all risks and allowing all considerations for time and place, it might be that there are changes in the manner of worship, but that is not at all faulty according to sastra.* **Srimad Viraraghava Acarya, an acarya in the disciplic succession of the Ramanuja-sampradaya, has remarked in his commentary that candalas, or conditioned souls who are born in lower than sudra families,** <u>**can also be initiated according to circumstances. The formalities may be slightly changed here and there to make them Vaisnavas.**</u> *(S.B. 4.8.54.)*

The system of ritviks (priests) chanting on beads, awarding spiritual names to new initiates on behalf of the acarya Srila Prabhupada, would fall into the category of an initiation formality. This is confirmed by the following quotes.

**"Initiation is a formality.** *I you are serious, that is real initiation.* **My touch is simply a formality.** *It is your determination. That is Initiation." (B.T.G. Search for the Divine)*

**Prabhupada:** *Well, initiation or no initiation, first thing is knowledge. (break) ...knowledge.* **Initiation is formality.** *Just like you go to a school for knowledge,* *and **admission is formality**. That is not very important thing. (Chandigarh 16th October, 1976)*

The essential principle of parampara is not the official formalities, but the revelation of transcendental knowledge by the process of submissive aural reception.

*"My guru maharaja used to say, "**Don't try to see a saintly person by your eyes. You see a saintly person by the ear.**" Because if you hear from the saintly person and if he is speaking from the experience which he has heard from the, another saintly person--**this is called guru-parampara**--then the knowledge is perfect."* *(S.B. lec 6.1.42, Los Angeles 8th June 1976)*

*"So we are gathering experience by hearing from the Supreme. Just like here Sukadeva Gosvami is narrating Srimad-Bhagavatam. He has heard it from his father, Vyasadeva. His father has heard it from Narada Muni, his spiritual master. Narada Muni has heard it from Brahma, the first living creature within this universe. And Brahma has heard it from Krishna. **This is called parampara system.**"* *(S.B. lec 6.1.32, San Francisco 17th July 1975)*

According to Sadhu (Narada Muni and Srimad Virarghava acarya), Sastra (Srimad Bhagavatam) and Guru (Srila Prabhupada) the performance of the formal ceremony may be changed to facilitate conditioned souls receiving initiation from the current link or spiritual master in the chain of disciplic succession.

Two important words in the text, kala and vibhaga-vit, are very interesting in understanding the process of adjusting the formalities of initiation. The word kala means time, which has three phases : past, present and future. The word vibhaga-vit means one who knows the divisions or attendant conveniences and inconveniences.

Knowing the past, present and future, Srila Prabhupada was well aware of the conveniences and inconveniences of linking conditioned souls to the disciplic succession. Taking these into consideration, he could adjust the formalities to facilitate this function taking according to kala or time.

Srila Prabhupada's loud chanting, initiating the fallen souls of Kali yuga into the chanting of the holy names, would be the unprecedented convenience. The small inconvenience, his physical absence from the initiation formalities. Considering these two factors, adjustments in the initiation rites would be required to formalise the linking of conditioned souls to the acarya Srila Prabhupada. Adjustments were already made by Srila Prabhupada during his physical presence, to facilitate initiation formalities being carried out (ritvik), thus linking conditioned souls to the parampara as his disciples. There is clear evidence that Srila Prabhupada desired this to continue in his absence.

*"Temple presidents may __henceforward__ send recommendation for first and second initiation to whichever of these eleven representatives are nearest their temple. After considering the recommendations, **these representatives may accept the devotee as an initiated disciple of Srila Prabhupada by giving a spiritual name.**"* *(Letter to G.B.C. and Temple presidents signed and approved by His Divine Grace. July 9th 1977.)*

To say Srila Prabhupada couldn't have established this system to continue in his absence, because it wouldn't have been supported by sadhu, sastra and guru is fallacious. Book distribution and ritvik acaryas is the perfect transcendental plan of His Divine Grace to continue the pure disciplic succession for the the golden age.

## SRILA PRABHUPADA IS THE INITIATOR

1. Srila Prabhupada's transcendental books are non-different than himself. They appear before the external senses of a fortunate conditioned soul, who was wandering aimlessly throughout the universe and plant the seed of devotional service in his heart (Bhakti lata bija) **THUS HE IS THE INITIATOR.**

2. Srila Prabhupada's transcendental books are his loud chanting of the holy name. Such loud chanting is giving the people of the world Harinama diksa (T.L.C. Chapter 18). **THUS HE IS THE INITIATOR**

3. Srila Prabhupada's transcendental books contain the nectarine words from his lotus mouth. Such words penetrate the hearts of the fallen souls, injecting transcendental knowledge, which alone can deliver them from material existence. This is the purpose of initiation. "The spiritual master initiates the disciple to deliver him." (C.C. Mad., 1.218) **THUS HE IS THE INITIATOR.**

4. Srila Prabhupada's transcendental books are non-different than himself, thus they give the conditioned souls his direct association (sadhu sanga). By such association they receive a process of spiritual activities (Bhajana kriya) (B.G. lec., 2-58-59, N.Y. 27th April, 1966). **THUS HE IS THE INITIATOR.**

5. Srila Prabhupada's transcendental books transmit transcendental knowledge which vanquish all material contamination caused by our previous sinful activities and thus bring us to pure love of God, where we can directly worship Krishna. This perfectly corresponds with sastric definitions of diksa. (C.C. Mad. lila, 15-108, 9-61, 4-111). **THUS HE IS THE INITIATOR**

6. Srila Prabhupada's transcendental books contain his instructions about chanting the holy name. If we accept such instruction and follow them, he is with us as the initiator. (S.P.L. Letter to Tamal Krishna, 19th September 1968) **THUS HE IS THE INITIATOR**

7. Srila Prabhupada in the form of his books (instructions) is taking everyone back to home, back to Godhead. This is the purpose of initiating a disciple, to deliver him."**The spiritual master initiates the disciple to deliver him**" (C.C. Mad, 1.218). **THUS HE IS THE INITIATOR**

*"In my books the philosophy of Krishna Consciousness is explained fully so if there is __anything which you do not understand, then you simply have to read again and again.__ By reading daily the __knowledge will be revealed to you__ and by this __process__ your spiritual life will develop."* (SPL to Bahuru-pa dasa, 22nd November, 1974)

The first point to note in this letter is that there is no need for a "living link" to understand Srila Prabhupada's books. If there is anything we do not understand, that thing will be understood by reading again and again. Srila Prabhupada describes our daily reading of His books, as a process of revealing or awakening transcendental knowledge. This process is described in the sastra as diksa.

*"**Diksa** is the **process** by which one can **awaken his transcendental knowledge** and vanquish all reactions caused by sinful activity. A person expert in the study of the revealed scriptures knows this **process as diksa.**" (C.C. Mad., 15-108)*

It is very clear from the evidence of sadhu, sastra and guru that the real initiation is being given by Srila Prabhupada through the mercy of his transcendental books. Thus, the question of successor doesn't arise.

**Reporter:** *Who will succeed you when you die?*

**Srila Prabhupada: I will never die!**

**Devotee's:** *Jaya! Haribol!*

**Srila Prabhupada: I will live forever from my books and __you will utilise.__**

*(Interview, Berkley, 1975)*

Here Srila Prabhupada is asked a question about his successor. Let us examine Srila Prabhupada's minimum words, maximum solution answer. The question has two key words [1] succeed and [2] die. Srila Prabhupada answers point [2] with "I will never die" and how is that "I will live forever from my books" and point [1] is answered with "and you will utilise". The word utilise is also described in the dictionary as, "use for a purpose". Thus Srila Prabhupada instructs us to use his books for the purpose of continuing the disciplic succession, by distributing them and thus giving the fallen souls of the world the opportunity of receiving his shelter as diksa guru.

The ritvik system should continue to formalise such mass Harinama diksa. Such a system is perfectly harmonious with Srila Prabhupadas loud chanting and part of his transcendental plan to deliver the world.

Let us not be small minded and say that the ritvik system continuing in the acaryas physical absence is unprecedented and therefore not bona-fide. It must be unprecedented (to our limited perceptions)or else how can it complement the unprecedented achievements of His Divine Grace A.C. Bhaktivedanta Swami Prabhupada. Never before has an acarya translated so many transcendental literatures into all the languages of the world and distributed such knowledge so mercifully and indiscriminately, making himself available as the eternal perceptor to the fallen souls. Srila Prabhupada was specifically chosen to deliver the whole world and thus fulfil the prediction of the Lord and the previous acaryas.

*"When Krishna appeared, He gave His orders, and when Krishna Himself appeared as a devotee, as Sri Caitanya Mahaprabhu, He showed us the path by which to cross the ocean of Kali-yuga. That is the path of the Hare Krishna movement. When Sri Caitanya Mahaprabhu appeared, He ushered in the era for the sankirtana movement. **It is also said that for ten thousand years this era will continue. This means that simply by accepting the sankirtana movement and chanting the Hare Krishna maha-mantra, the fallen souls of this Kali-yuga will be delivered**. After the Battle of Kuruksetra, at which Bhagavad-gita was spoken, Kali-yuga continues for 432,000 years, of which only 5,000 years have passed. Thus there is still a balance of 427,000 years to come. Of these 427,000 years, the **10,000 years of the sankirtana movement** inaugurated by Sri Caitanya Mahaprabhu 500 years ago provide the opportunity for the fallen souls of Kali-yuga to **take to the Krishna consciousness movement, chant the Hare Krishna maha-mantra and thus be delivered** from the clutches of material existence and return home, back to Godhead."* (S.B. 8.5.23)

*Prabhupada: Yes. Kalki, yes.*

*Allen Ginsberg: So He would come at the end of Kali-yuga to end the yuga.*

*Prabhupada: **Yes**. Then Satya-yuga will begin.*

*Allen Ginsberg: Then what begins?*

*Prabhupada: Satya-yuga.*

*Allen Ginsberg: Which is?*

*Prabhupada: Satya-yuga, the pious. Satya-yuga. People will be pious, truthful, long-living.*

*Allen Ginsberg: Are those people that remain or whatever new creation comes out of the destruction?*

*Prabhupada: Some of them will remain, some of them. It will not completely extinguish. Some of them will remain, pious. Paritranaya sadhunam vinasaya ca duskrtam. All miscreants will be killed, and out of them, there must be some pious... They remain.*

*Allen Ginsberg: Do you think of this in terms of a historical event that will occur in the lifetime of your disciples?*

*Prabhupada: No. This will happen at least 400,000's of years after, at least. So by that time...*

*Allen Ginsberg: They will go down, down, down for 400,000 years?*

**Prabhupada: Yes. So at that time my disciples will be with Krishna. (laughter)**

*Devotees: Haribol!*

**Prabhupada: And those who will not follow them, they will see the fun, how they are being killed. (laughter)**

*Allen Ginsberg: 400,000 years. Will people still be chanting Hare Krishna in 400,000...*

**Prabhupada: No. Hare Krishna will be finished within ten thousand years. There will be no more Hare Krishna.**

*(Room Conversation with Allen Ginsberg May 13, 1969, Columbus, Ohio.)*

# I AM THE SPIRITUAL MASTER OF THIS INSTITUTION, AND ALL THE MEMBERS OF THE SOCIETY, THEY'RE SUPPOSED TO BE MY DISCIPLES.

## "They follow the rules and regulations which I ask them to follow, and they are initiated by me spiritually."

*Interviewer: Now I just want to read one section here. I think you'll be able to...* "The International Society for Krishna Consciousness began when Swami Bhaktivedanta arrived from India with $2 on his person, a metal suitcase full of ancient-looking books and a cotton cloth robe, colored yellow, as a sign of the renounced order of life. In India, men of his order are completely dedicated to propagating the spiritual life of a mendicant wanderer. He had wandered across the sea upon the order issued to him by his guru who told him he should prepare to go to America to teach the principles taught in the Bhagavad-gita and to translate the sixty volumes of the Srimad-Bhagavatam into English." *Now, are you a guru?*

*Prabhupada:* **Yes, I am the spiritual master of this institution, and all the members of the society, they're supposed to be my disciples. They follow the rules and regulations which I ask them to follow, and they are initiated by me spiritually.** *So therefore the spiritual master is called guru. That is Sanskrit language.*

*(S.P. Radio Interview  March 12, 1968, San Francisco)*

Note: **All the members of ISKCON** [10,000 year transcendental preaching mission] they're supposed to be Srila Prabhupada's disciples. They follow his rules and regulations given in his lawbooks (mainly 16 rounds 4 regs.) and are thus initiated by him spiritually. To facilitate his disciples receiving spiritual names he established a ritvik system.

## One Should Be Careful About The Offense Of Maryada-Vyatikrama

One argument raised by people like Madhudvisa dasa from Krishna Org and Puranjana dasa (Tim Lee) from PADA, is that Srila Prabhupada may order one of us to be diksa guru when we are qualified.

*"For an honest reader of Srila Prabhupada's books it is impossible to come to any other conclusion than Srila Prabhupada desired his disciples to become qualified spiritual masters and accept disciples....However the ritviks DO NOT say Srila Prabhupada's disciples cannot become gurus at all. How could they say that? They simply say Srila Prabhupada established a ritvik initiation system for ISKCON and if Srila Prabhupada's disciples want to accept their own disciples*

*they should do it in their own preaching organization outside ISKCON."
(Madhudvisa dasa From Krishna.org)*

Note: In regards to Madhudvisa's claim that he may accept disciples outside of ISKCON in his own preaching organization, he should note the following:

*TRANSLATION: Sri Uddhava said: You may take lessons from the great learned sage Maitreya, who is nearby and who is worshipable for reception of transcendental knowledge. He was directly instructed by the Personality of Godhead while He was about to quit this mortal world.*

PURPORT: **Although one may be well versed in the transcendental science, one should be careful about the offense of maryada-vyatikrama, or impertinently surpassing a greater personality. According to scriptural injunction one should be very careful of transgressing the law of maryada-vyatikrama because by so doing one loses his duration of life, his opulence, fame and piety and the blessings of all the world. To be well versed in the transcendental science necessitates awareness of the techniques of spiritual science.** *Uddhava, being well aware of all these technicalities of transcendental science, advised Vidura to approach Maitreya Rsi to receive transcendental knowledge. Vidura wanted to accept Uddhava as his spiritual master, but Uddhava did not accept the post because Vidura was as old as Uddhava's father and therefore Uddhava could not accept him as his disciple,* **especially when Maitreya was present nearby. The rule is that in the presence of a higher personality one should not be very eager to impart instructions, even if one is competent and well versed.** *So Uddhava decided to send an elderly person like Vidura to Maitreya, another elderly person, but he was well versed also because he was directly instructed by the Lord while He was about to quit this mortal world. Since both Uddhava and Maitreya were directly instructed by the Lord, both had the authority to become the spiritual master of Vidura or anyone else, but Maitreya, being elderly, had the first claim to becoming the spiritual master, especially for Vidura, who was much older than Uddhava.* **One should not be eager to become a spiritual master cheaply for the sake of profit and fame, but should become a spiritual master only for the service of the Lord. The Lord never tolerates the impertinence of maryada-vyatikrama. One should never pass over the honor due to an elderly spiritual master in the interests of one's own personal gain and fame. Impertinence on the part of the pseudo spiritual master is very risky to progressive spiritual realization.** *(S.B. 3.4.26)*

Note: So if Madhudvisa was a pure devotee he would not impertinently surpass a greater personality like Srila Prabhupada who would be present nearby, everywhere in the universe initiating everyone in the form of his original books.

If Madhudvisa was actually pure in heart, Krishna would order him to bring all souls to Srila Prabhupada so they could accept him as Guru.

In regards to the various quotes in which Srila Prabhupada says his disciples should become guru, the following article from the first printing [1993] of ALL OF US SHOULD HEAR PRABHUPADA clears this up.

## KAMSA'S POLICY

The greatest danger to the propagation and development of the Krishna Consciousness movement is the adulteration of the pure message presented to us in disciplic succession from Srila Prabhupada's books. Srila Prabhupada comments on this as follows:

*"So if you read Bhagavad-gita as it is, that is mad-asrayah. But if you interpret Bhagavad-gita according to your rascal imagination, that is not Bhagavad-gita. Therefore it is called mad-asrayah, "under My protection, as I am tea..." We are therefore presenting Bhagavad-gita as it is. We do not change. **Why should you change? What right you have got to change?** If Bhagavad-gita is a book of authority and if I make my own interpretation, then where is the authority? Can you change the law book according to your interpretation? Then what is the meaning of that law book? That is not law book. **You cannot change. Similarly, if you accept Bhagavad-gita as the book of authority, you cannot change the meaning. That is not allowed. What right? If you have got some opinion, if you have got some philosophy, you can write in your own book. Why you are, I mean to say, killing others and yourself by interpreting Bhagavad-gita?** You give your own thesis in a different way. But these people, they take advantage of the popularity of Bhagavad-gita and interpret in a different way according to their own whims. Therefore people do not understand what is Krishna. That is the difficulty. And the purpose of Bhagavad-gita is to understand Krishna. And all the so-called scholars' and politicians' commentary is to banish Krishna or to kill Krishna--the Kamsa's policy. The Kamsa was always thinking of Krishna, how to kill Him. This is called demonic endeavour. So that will not help you."* (B.G. 7.1 Hyderabad, 27th April, 1974)

*"So Bhagavad-gita, the lessons of Bhagavad-gita, cannot be changed by the whims of rascals. This is not possible."* (S.B. 3.26.32, Bombay, 9th January, 1975)

Srila Prabhupada says that people change Bhagavad-gita to banish Krishna or kill Krishna, and thus minimise His position. He describes this as Kamsa's policy.

Let us examine the position of the G.B.C. and their changes of Srila Prabhupada's books. They write in the back of the Bhagavad Gita that by working with Srila Prabhupada's books for the last fifteen years, they are more familiar with his philosophy and language. With this newly accomplished scholarship, they claim to present a more accurate translation to that of the original standard translation, authorised by His Divine Grace. They achieved this by referencing the same sanskrit commentaries that Srila Prabhupada consulted when writing the Bhagavad

Gita as it is. They, of course, do not mention that they acquired their scholarship from an apa-sampradaya community in violation of Srila Prabhupada's instructions. Let us examine one of these scholarly changes and compare it to the original.

*TRANSLATION: Just try to learn the truth by approaching a spiritual master. Inquire from him submissively and render service unto him. The **self-realized souls** can impart knowledge unto you because they have seen the truth. (B.G. 4.34 Changed Version)*

*TRANSLATION: Just try to learn the truth by approaching a spiritual master. Inquire from him submissively and render service unto him. **The self-realized soul** can impart knowledge unto you because he has seen the truth. (B.G. 4.34 Original Version)*

The latter quote is from the original Bhagavad-gita in which Srila Prabhupada uses the word soul, whereas the scholarly version uses the plural souls. If we accept that this change is more true to the original Sanskrit manuscripts, then why did Srila Prabhupada himself never use the plural when quoting the verse in lectures? The following is an example illustrating how Srila Prabhupada would always present the verse:

*"And what is that submission? "Render service unto him." Try to please him by satisfying him, by service. Yasya prasadad bhagavat-prasadah, you singing. If he is pleased, then you know Krishna is pleased. And if he is displeased, then there is no other way. This is the process, submissive. "**The self-realized soul** can impart knowledge." And because you have to select spiritual master, a self-realized soul... Just like if you want to study particular subject matter, you have to approach a realized person, a perfect person. Then you get. "**The self-realized soul** can impart knowledge unto you because he has seen the truth." One who has not seen the truth, he cannot." (B.G. Lec., 4.34-9)*

Why didn't Srila Prabhupada himself instruct his disciples to change this so called mistake? Srila Prabhupada was very alert in making sure the correct translation was presented in his books. Here are a couple of examples:

**Nitai:** *"At the time of death, Ajamila saw three awkward persons, very fearsome in appearance, with ropes in their hands. They had twisted faces and deformed bodily features, and their hair stood on end. They had come to take Ajamila away to the shelter of Yamaraja. Ajamila became extremely bewildered when he saw them. His small child, Narayana, was playing a little distance off, and with tearful eyes and great anxiety, he called the name of his son very loudly three times, "Narayana, Narayana, Narayana!"*

**Prabhupada: Is there, "three times"?**

*Nitai: It said in the manuscript. The manuscript said, "three times."*

**Prabhupada: Who said in the manuscript? There is no three times. Not Narayana three times, one time. "Oh, Narayana," that's all. So did I say, "three times"? No, it is not said here. You should correct it. Once, "Oh, Narayana," that's all.** *There is no reason of calling three times. There is no mention here. Once is sufficient. (laughter) (S.B. Lec, 6.1.28, Philadelphia, 13th July, 1975)*

*Pusta Krishna: "My dear Prahlada, may you live a long time. One cannot appreciate or understand Me without pleasing Me, but one who has seen Me or pleased Me has nothing for which to lament for his own personal **self**."*

**Prabhupada:** *"His own personal **satisfaction**."*

*(S.B. Lec, 7.9.53, in Vrndvana, 8th April, 1976)*

The last quote is very significant as it appears to be a very minor fault. Nevertheless, Srila Prabhupada was very quick to correct Pusta Krishna by saying satisfaction.

*Madhu-dvisa: "Just try to learn the truth by approaching a spiritual master. Inquire from him submissively and render service unto him. The **self-realized soul** can impart knowledge unto you because he has seen the truth.*

**Prabhupada:** *This is the process of understanding spiritual knowledge. "Just try to learn the truth by approaching a spiritual master." (B.G. 4.34, Los Angeles, 12th January, 1969)*

Here we see Srila Prabhupada in the same situation as when with Pusta Krishna. He says nothing about the translation and particularly the word soul. Therefore this change by the G.B.C is the policy of Kamsa. By using the authority of the Bhagavad Gita, they are killing the spiritual lives of thousands of innocent readers by subtly indoctrinating them with their concocted philosophy. The self-realized soul "Srila Prabhupada" is now dead. Now we can approach sixty conditioned "souls". This type of change is made by persons outside the parampara.

*"But if you misinterpret, if you pollute it by your own interpretation, then you will not see. **These rascals, they are simply polluting. Because they are not coming in parampara system**, everyone is trying to (sic:) becoming a very learned scholar, very learned leader, but they are rascals. Actually they are rascals because they cannot see." (B.G. Lec., 16.8, 28th January, 1975)*

So rather than continuing the pure disciple succession, such Prabhupada killing policies are destroying the very basis of Vaisnava tradition.

*"But some way or other, if it is distorted at a certain point, then the knowledge is lost. As soon as any of the disciples in the succession distort the knowledge, then it is lost. That is being explained. Sa kalena mahata. The time is very powerful. It changes. That is the... Time means it changes, kills the original position. You have got experience. You purchase one anything. It is very fresh, new. But time will kill it. It will become shabby. It will be useless at a time, in due course of time. So time is fighting. This material time, it is called kala. Kala means death. Or kala means the black snake. So black snake destroys. As soon as touches anything, it is destroyed. Similarly, kala... This kala is also another form of Krishna. So kalena mahata. Therefore it is called mahata. It is very powerful. It is not ordinary thing. Mahata. Its business is to destroy. Sa kalena iha nasta. So by due course of time... Because how the kala can destroy? As soon as kala sees that you are distorting, then it will be lost. So don't try to understand Bhagavad-gita from persons who are under the influence of kala--past, present, future. Don't try to understand Bhagavad-gita from so-called rascal philosophers, commentators, and... They will write Bhagavad-gita in a distorted way. Somebody will say, "There was no Krishna." (B.G. Lec., 4.2., Bombay, 22nd March, 1974)*

Srila Prabhupada commented on this changing policy on the 22nd of June 1977, calling it whimsical and orders his disciples to reprint the books in the original way.

*Yasodanandana: Sometimes they (editors) appeal that 'We can make better English,' so they can change like that, just like in the case of the Isopanishads. There are over a hundred changes. So where is the need? Your words are sufficient. The potency is there. When they change, it is something else.*

*Svarupa-damodara: That's actually a very dangerous mentality.*

*Yasodanandana: What's it going to be in five years? It's going to be a different book.*

*Prabhupada: It is a very serious situation. You write one letter, 'Why you have made so many changes?' And whom to write to? Who will care? All rascals are there. Write to Satsvarupa that, 'This is the position. They are doing anything and everything at their whim.' The next printing should be (done) again the original way.*

Another dangerous philosophy presented by the GBC is in regards to the pure disciplic succession. They claim it can be contaminated, and that the acaryas, influenced by maya, may sometimes deviate from the instructions of the Lord.

*"One is therefore advised to study Bhagavad-gita, or any other scripture, under a bona fide spiritual master, with service and surrender. A bona fide spiritual master is in the disciplic succession from time eternal, and he does not deviate at all from the instructions of the Supreme Lord as they were imparted millions of*

*years ago to the sun-god, from whom the instructions of Bhagavad-gita have come down to the earthly kingdom.* **One should, therefore, follow the path of Bhagavad-gita as it is expressed in the Gita itself and beware of self-interested people after personal aggrandisement who deviate others from the actual path.***"* (B.G. 4.42)

A bona-fide spiritual master is in the disciplic succession from time eternal, and is never influenced by maya. He never deviates from the instructions of the Lord, anyone who does was never part of the strict chain of unalloyed acarya's. Thus the philosophy held by the G.B.C. is against the conclusion of sastra. Thus they must be considered apa sampradaya or "outside the sampradaya."

*"In the parampara system, the instructions taken from the bona fide spiritual master must also be based on revealed Vedic scriptures.* **There are many so-called followers of the Vaisnava cult in the line of Caitanya Mahaprabhu who do not scrupulously follow the conclusions of the sastras, and therefore they are considered to be apa-sampradaya, which means "outside of the sampradaya."** (C.C. Adi 7.48)

The major reason these apa-siddhantic conclusions have poisoned the society is due to the leaders disobediance of the following order given by His Divine Grace.

*"I am in due receipt of your letter dated September 3, 1975 with the enclosed statement about Bon Maharaja.* **So I have now issued orders that all my disciples should avoid all of my godbrothers.** *They should not have any* **dealings** *with them nor even* **correspondence***, nor should they give them any of* **my books** *or should they purchase any of* **their books***, neither should you visit any of* **their temples.** **Please avoid them.***" (S.P.L. to Visvakarma, 9th November, 1975)*

The first point to note is that in this letter to Visvakarma dasa, Srila Prabhupada is informing him that he has now issued orders to **all** his disciples to avoid **all** his Godbrothers. This is a very clear instruction, and no instructions to the contrary were given in writing or on tape after this. He specifically instructs us to have **no dealings** with them, not even **correspondance**, nor should we **give them** any of His books, nor **purchase theirs**,.neither should we **visit** any of their temples. He ends by strongly pleading with us: **"Please avoid them"**. The word avoid is used as it gives special stress to purposefully keeping away (dictionary definition).

We may say this instruction was given at a particular time, during certain circumstances and is no longer valid. What were these circumstances? The circumstances in question were, that Srila Prabhupada's neophyte Godbrothers, having disobeyed the instructions of Srila Bhaktisiddanta Sarasvati Thakura, had become useless or more precisely apa-sampradaya.

*"Bhaktisiddhanta Sarasvati Thakura, at the time of his departure, requested all his disciples to form a governing body and conduct missionary activities*

*cooperatively. He did not instruct a particular man to become the next acarya. But just after his passing away, his leading secretaries made plans, without authority, to occupy the post of acarya, and they split in two factions over who the next acarya would be. **Consequently, both factions were asara, or useless, because they had no authority, having disobeyed the order of the spiritual master.**" (C.C. Adi, 12-8)*

*"One who is in the line of disciplic succession **cannot manufacture his own way of behaviour.**" (C.C. Adi 7.48)*

Therefore to protect his innocent neophyte disciples and young but growing transcendental society from the contamination of apa-siddhantic philosophy, He ordered us to avoid association with them in any shape or form. Have these circumstances changed? **Of course not. Rather pots of poison become more potent with age.** This poison has completely infected the whole of Srila Prabhupada's society to such a degree, that our so called leaders are completely under the control of these offenders. These leaders have now become instruments in the hands of maya and through them this poison is being administered to all the members of the society. **Clearly the philosophical deviations remain within the Gaudiya Matha, therefore how can we possibly say Srila Prabhupada's order to avoid them does not?**

The order to avoid them is **clear!** It applies under the present circumstances, in fact, association with apa-sampradya communities is forbidden under **all circumstances**.

*"In order to **follow strictly** the disciplic succession of Lord Caitanya Mahaprabhu, **one should not associate with these apa-sampradaya communities.**" (C.C. Adi, 7.48)*

We cannot adjust this order according to our particular whim. **That is deviation**.

*"Any opinion different from the opinion of the spiritual master is useless. **One cannot infiltrate materially concocted ideas into spiritual advancement. That is deviation**. There is no scope for adjusting spiritual advancement to material ideas." (C.C. Adi 12-9)*

Such a deviation from the orders of Srila Prabhupada is an offence at his lotus feet, and the lotus feet of the Holy name. How can anyone claim to be acarya if he has not first become a disciple?

*"If someone blasphemes a Vaisnava, one should **stop him with arguments and higher reason.** If one is not expert enough to do this he should give up his life on the spot, and if he cannot do this, **he must go away.**" (C.C. Adi 7.50)*

If there were an acarya amongst us he would have spoken out about all this nonsense and blasphemy to His Divine Grace Srila Prabhupada. Any sincere disciple would at least completely disassociate himself from such offenders. What to speak of the acarya, the representative of the Lord, whose mission is to establish the principles of religion.

## Physical Spiritual Master

*"So Krishna, He is within our heart. Hrdy antah sthah. Therefore, as soon as we become a little inclined towards Krishna, then from within our heart He gives us favourable instruction so that we can gradually make progress, gradually. Krishna is the first spiritual master, and when we become more interested, then we have to go to a **physical spiritual master.**" (B.G. Lecture, 1966)*

***Prabhupada:** Therefore God is called caittya-guru, the spiritual master within the heart. And the physical spiritual master is God's mercy. If God sees that you are sincere, He will give you a spiritual master who can give you protection. He will help you from within and without, without in the **physical form of spiritual master**, and within as the spiritual master within the heart. (Car. Rome, 23rd May, 1974)*

These quotes are used by certain people to substantiate their claim that Srila Prabhupada is no longer accessible as an initiating spiritual master, and that we need to approach a "physically manifest guru". In the purport of S.B. 4.8.54 Srila Prabhupada says:

*"Not only should one chant or murmur the mantra, but in front of him he must have the Deity, **or physical form of the Lord**. Of course, when the Lord appears it is no longer a physical form. For example, when an iron rod is made red-hot in a fire, it is no longer iron; it is fire. Similarly, when we make a form of the Lord-- whether of wood or stone or metal or jewels or paint, or even a form within the mind--it is a bona fide, spiritual, transcendental form of the Lord." (S.B. 4.8.54)*

This is confirmed in a purport from Caitanya Caritamtra.

*"Thus in different places throughout the universe there are various Deities in temples bestowing Their causeless mercy upon the devotees. All these Deity forms are non-different from the murtis in the spiritual world of the Vaikunthas. Although the arca-murti, the worshipable Deity form of the Lord, appears to be made of material elements, it is as good as the spiritual forms found in the spiritual Vaikunthalokas. The Deity in the temple, however, is visible to the material eyes of the devotee. It is not possible for one in material conditional life to see the spiritual form of the Lord. To bestow causeless mercy upon us, the Lord appears as arca-murti so that we can see Him. It is forbidden to consider the arca-murti to be made of stone or wood. In the Padma Purana it is said:*

*arcye visnau sila-dhir gurusu nara-matir vaisnave jati-buddhir*
*visnor va vaisnavanam Kali-mala-mathane pada-tirthe'mbu-buddhih*
*sri-visnor namni mantre sakala-kalusa-he sabde-samanya-buddhir*
*visnau sarvesvarese tad-itara-sama-dhir yasya va naraki sah*

No one should consider the Deity in the temple to be made of stone or wood, nor should one consider the spiritual master an ordinary human being. No one should consider a Vaisnava to belong to a particular caste or creed, and no one should consider caranamrta or Ganges water to be like ordinary water. Nor should anyone consider the Hare Krishna maha-mantra to be a material vibration. **All these expansions of Krishna in the material world are simply demonstrations of the Lord's mercy and willingness to give facility to His devotees who are engaged in His devotional service within the material world.** *(C.C. Mad, 20 -217)*

"The Deity, the spiritual master, Ganges water and the holy name etc. are all completely spiritual. They are expansions of Krishna in the material world. They are simply demonstrations of the Lords mercy to fallen souls who cannot approach the spiritual form of the Lord in the conditioned state of material existence. In this way they can be called **physical**, or more clearly **manifest to the physical senses of the conditioned souls.**

The merciful Lord left behind Him the great teachings of the Bhagavad-gita so that one can take the instructions of the Lord even when He is not visible to material eyesight. Material senses cannot have any estimation of the Supreme Lord, but by His inconceivable power **the Lord can incarnate Himself to the sense perception of the conditioned souls in a suitable manner through the <u>agency of matter</u>, which is also another form of the Lord's manifested energy. Thus the Bhagavad-gita, or any authentic scriptural sound representation of the Lord, is also the incarnation of the Lord.** There is no difference between the sound representation of the Lord and the Lord Himself. One can derive the same benefit from the Bhagavad-gita as Arjuna did in the personal presence of the Lord." *(S.B. 1.15.27)*

Here we see Srila Prabhupada describing the Bhagavad Gita or any authentic scriptural sound representation of the Lord, as an incarnation of the Lord through the agency of matter, or in other words a "physical" form of the Lord.

"The Lord, out of His causeless mercy, touched His conchshell to Dhruva's forehead, and he was transcendentally inspired. This transcendental inspiration is called brahma-maya because when one is thus inspired, **the sound he produces exactly corresponds to the sound vibration of the Vedas.**" *(S.B. 4.9.4)*

The sound manifest by Dhurva Maharaja or more relevantly Srila Prabhupada exactly corresponds to the sound vibration of the Vedas. Thus it is an authentic spiritual sound.

So if we examine these quotes which describe the need to approach the physical spiritual master, we can conclude that we have to approach a spiritual master who is manifest to our physical senses, rather than thinking we can receive guidance from the Supersoul only, who is described as Adoksaja or beyond the material mind and senses.

Thus if we approach the transcendental vani of Srila Prabhupada, which is so mercifully manifest to our material senses, we have approached the "physical" spiritual master.

Using these quotes according to our whim, taking them out of context so we can support our deviant conclusions, is offensive! Srila Prabhupada repeatedly stressed we take shelter of a spiritual master's instructions, not his bodily presence.

Srila Prabhupada never contradicts himself! Contradictions manifest in the minds of persons who distort his teachings for personal interest.

*"To answer this argument, it is described here **that one has to associate with liberated persons not directly, physically, but by understanding, through philosophy and logic**, the problems of life."* (S.B. 3.31.48)

*"Such association with Krishna and the spiritual master should **be association by vibration, not physical presence. That is real association."** (Elevation to Krishna Consciousness Ch 4.)*

*"Physical presence is sometimes appreciable and sometimes not, but vani continues to exist eternally. **Therefore we must take advantage of the vani, not the physical presence."** (CC, Antya Chapter 5)*

### "Hence Forward" It's Very Clear!

This document has presented evidence for ritvik in absentia on the basis of pure and simple logic. Srila Prabhupada is very clearly present by his transcendental sound vibration and is still giving all fallen souls initiation into the holy name.

Thus the system he officially introduced on July 9th 1977 was to continue, any other conclusion would be illogical or more clearly madness.

*"Temple presidents may **henceforward** send recommendation for first and second initiation to whichever of these eleven representatives are nearest their temple. After considering the recommendations, **these representatives may accept the devotee as an initiated disciple of Srila Prabhupada by giving a spiritual name."** (Letter to G.B.C. and Temple presidents signed and approved by His Divine Grace. July 9th 1977.)*

This is a very clear instruction. Henceforward is defined in the dictionary as meaning from now into the future, indefinitely. Research showed that the word "henceforward" was used 81 times in the complete works of Srila Prabhupada. For example.

The Lord was also asked by Nityananda Prabhu to accept these repenting souls, and the Lord agreed to accept them on one condition, that they **henceforward** completely give up all their sinful activities and habits of debauchery. both the brothers agreed and promised to give up all their sinful habits, and the kind Lord accepted them and did not again refer to their past misdeeds. *(S.B. Introduction)*

In not one of these 81 occasions was the word used to indicate anything other than something that was unchangeable. Another very significant point is in regards to the person who wrote the letter, Tamal Krishna, he clearly knew what the word "henceforward" meant.

*Tamala Krishna: Prabhupada says, in future, **henceforward**, these people should not be allowed to hold lectures here. Strictly Caitanya Mahaprabhu's teaching forbids. Mayavadi haya krsne aparadhi. You tellthem, "You're Mayavadi. So this is a Krishna conscious temple. (S.P.C. Vrndavana, 1st November, 1977)*

Everyone recognises that a mayavadi will never be allowed to speak in our temples. Therefore, the word "henceforward" is clearly used to mean final and permanent. If due to the influence of the material energy he made a mistake when writing the letter, wouldn't Srila Prabhupada have told him to reword the letter, According to the dictionary definition and Srila Prabhupada's own use of the word, this letter would clearly indicate that these representatives would continue performing initiations on his behalf indefinitely. If this wasn't what Srila Prabhupada intended to happen, why didn't he have the letter re-worded and thus present his actual desires more clearly, Srila Prabhupada once told Ramesvara... "Krishna will speak to you directly. You will see him and hear him. **Every decision I make, Krishna is telling me to do it directly.**" (B.T.G. article).

Another important point is that if Tamal Krishna was well aware of the meaning and implications of the word "henceforward", why did he not use another word indicating a more temporary arrangement? Unless, he also understood that the ritviks where to continue performing initiations on Srila Prabhupada's behalf indefinitely.

In the following letter, which he wrote two days after the "henceforward" letter, he clearly reveals that he had in fact understood the permanence of the appointment.

*Tamal Krishna: A letter has been sent to all the temple presidents and GBC which you should be receiving soon **describing the process for initiation to be followed in the future.** Srila Prabhupada has appointed thus far eleven representatives who* *will initiate new devotees on his behalf. (Letter to Kirtananandana Maharaja, 11th July, 1977)*

This is confirmed by the following conversation which he had with Yasodanandana dasa as recorded in his diary on the 10th of July 1977.

*YND: "What does all this (officiating letter) mean?"*

*TKG: "Devotees have been writing to Prabhupada for initiations, and now Prabhupada has named eleven ritviks (priests) who can initiate on his behalf"...*

*YND: "And when Prabhupada <u>departs</u>?"*

*TKG: "They'll be ritviks, That's what Prabhupada said."*

And finally the following conversation took place on the 28th of May 1977, just prior to the official announcement on the 9th of July 1977.

*Satavarupa swami: Then our next question concerns initiations in the future, particularly at that time when you are no longer with us. We want to know how first and second initiations would be conducted.*

*Srila Prabhupada: Yes. I shall recommend some of you...I shall recommend some of you to act as officiating (guru) acarya.*

*Tamala Krishna swami: is that called ritvik-acarya (officiating-priest)?*

*Srila Prabhupada: Ritvik, yes.*

Tamala Krishna swami later on summarised his recollection of the above May 28th instructions:

*"If it had been anything more than that (a continuation of the ongoing ritvik--or officiating on behalf of Srila Prabhupada--priest system), you can bet your bottom dollar that Prabhupada would have spoken for days and hours and weeks--on end--about how to set this thing up with the gurus, but he did not, because he had already said it a million times. He said, 'My Guru Maharaja did not appoint anyone. It was by qualification.' We made a great mistake."*

*"Actually Prabhupada never appointed any gurus. He appointed eleven ritviks. He never appointed them gurus. <u>Myself and the other GBC have done the greatest disservice to this movement the last three years (1977-1980) because we interpreted the appointment of ritviks as the appointment of gurus.</u>"*

*"**You cannot show me anything on tape or in writing where Prabhupada says: 'I appoint these eleven as gurus.' It does not exist because he never appointed any gurus. This is a myth.**" (From Topanga Talks, December 3, 1980)*

Here we find clear confirmation that the appointment of gurus and their functioning in that capacity between 1977-1980, was in fact a concoction and disobedience of Srila Prabhupada's instructions for them to continue in their role as ritvik representatives. The following letter confirms Srila Prabhupada's continued status as the initiator.

*"**The GBC should all be the instructor gurus. I am the initiator guru**, and you should be the instructor guru by teaching what I am teaching and doing what I am doing. This is not a title, **but you must actually come to this platform**. This I want."* (SPL to Madhudvisa Swami, 4th August, 1975)

He says the devotees in the G.B.C. should all **become** the instructor gurus. The words **should** reveal that at that time nobody was actually on this platform. Srila Prabhupada says "you must actually come to this platform. This I want."

*"There are two kinds of instructing spiritual masters. **One is the liberated person fully absorbed in meditation in devotional service**, and the other is he who invokes the disciple's spiritual consciousness by means of relevant instructions."* (CC Adi, 1.47)

Here Srila Prabhupada describes the two kinds of instructor gurus. The second describes a person who gives instructions based on the revealed scriptures. The first describes the siksa guru Srila Prabhupada wants us all to become. On this platform we will be fully qualified to preach the glories of the Lord.

*"So this society is attempting to create a society of devotees all over the world, without any discrimination of caste, creed, colour. One must be a devotee of Krishna. Yei Krishna tattva vettha sei guru haya. **One must know the science of Krishna. Then he can preach to others. Sei guru haya. That is our purpose.**"* (N.O.D. Lec. 26th October, 1972)

Srila Prabhupada says that his society is trying to create devotees who are qualified to know the science of Krishna. Then they can preach to others.

*"This is complete liberated stage. In the previous verse it has been spoken, bhagavat-tattva-vijnanam mukta-sangasya jayate. **The science of God, bhagavat-tattva, the science of Absolute Truth, becomes manifest to the liberated soul**. We find sometimes that one man is posing to have very much advanced in spiritual understanding or a great devotee, but mukta-sanga, he's not mukta-sanga,"* (S.B. Lecture, Vrndavana, 1st November, 1972.)

Again confirmation of the qualifications of the siksa guru we all have to become. Therefore even when many devotees have reached such an advanced platform of devotional service, the position will remain:

"I AM THE INITIATOR GURU, AND YOU SHOULD BE THE INSTRUCTOR GURU BY TEACHING AND DOING WHAT I'M DOING."

## PRABHUPADA'S SUCCESSOR
## A COMPLETELY IRRELEVANT SUBJECT!!!

The basic argument presented by the envious dressed as devotees is that because Srila Prabhupada has physically departed therefore we need a successor to continue the disciplic succession. This argument is totally bogus and is not at all supported by the Vedic literature.

*TRANSLATION: This supreme science was thus received through the chain of disciplic succession, and the saintly kings understood it in that way.* **But in course of time the succession was broken, and therefore the science as it is appears to be lost.**

*PURPORT: It is clearly stated that the Gita was especially meant for the saintly kings because they were to execute its purpose in ruling over the citizens. Certainly Bhagavad-gita was never meant for the demonic persons, who would dissipate its value for no one's benefit and would devise all types of interpretations according to personal whims.* ***As soon as the original purpose was scattered by the motives of the unscrupulous commentators, there arose the need to reestablish the disciplic succession.*** *Five thousand years ago it was detected by the Lord Himself that the disciplic succession was broken, and therefore He declared that the purpose of the Gita appeared to be lost.* **In the same way, at the present moment also there are so many editions of the Gita (especially in English), but almost all of them are not according to authorized disciplic succession. There are innumerable interpretations rendered by different mundane scholars, but almost all of them do not accept the Supreme Personality of Godhead, Krishna, although they make a good business on the words of Sri Krishna. This spirit is demonic, because demons do not believe in God but simply enjoy the property of the Supreme. Since there is a great need of an edition of the Gita in English, as it is received by the parampara (disciplic succession) system, an attempt is made herewith to fulfill this great want.** *Bhagavad-gita--accepted as it is--is a great boon to humanity; but if it is accepted as a treatise of philosophical speculations, it is simply a waste of time. (Srila Prabhupada from Bhagavad-gita As It Is 4.2)*

Note: So when the purpose of the Bhagavad-gita is scattered or lost by the motives of unscrupulous commentators then there is a need to reestablish the disciplic succession. If the knowledge from the current acarya Srila Prabhupada is still present in human society in the form of the original Bhagavad-gita As It Is, then where is the need for the Lord to send another spiritual master or successor to reestablish it? THIS IS THE ESSENTIAL POINT!!!

Rest assured the demons understand to some degree that Prabhupada is very much present in the form of his original books as the current link in disciplic succession, delivering the people of the world back home back to Godhead. That is why they work so determinedly to change these books and make Prabhupada's message lost to the world!

*"As soon as any of the disciples in the succession distort the knowledge, then it is lost. That is being explained. Sa kalena mahata. The time is very powerful. It changes. That is the... Time means it changes, kills the original position. You have got experience. You purchase one anything. It is very fresh, new. But time will kill it. It will become shabby. It will be useless at a time, in due course of time. So time is fighting. This material time, it is called kala. Kala means death. Or kala means the black snake. So black snake destroys. As soon as touches anything, it is destroyed. Similarly, kala... This kala is also another form of Krishna. So kalena mahata. Therefore it is called mahata. It is very powerful. It is not ordinary thing. Mahata. Its business is to destroy. Sa kalena iha nasta. So by due course of time...*
**_Because how the kala can destroy? As soon as kala sees that you are distorting, then it will be lost._** *So don't try to understand Bhagavad-gita from persons who are under the influence of kala--past, present, future. Don't try to understand Bhagavad-gita from so-called rascal philosophers, commentators, and... They will write Bhagavad-gita in a distorted way. Somebody will say, "There was no Krishna. There was no Mahabharata." Somebody says, "Krishna stressed on this point," "Krishna stressed on that point." Somebody will say, "Krishna stressed on karma, karma-kanda." Somebody will say on jnana, and somebody will say yoga. There are so many editions of Bhagavad-gita."* (Srila Prabhupada from a Bhagavad-gita 4.2, Bombay, March 22, 1974)

Note: Prabhupada's knowledge will not be lost to the world and therefore he will remain The Initiator Guru for the 10,000 years of the golden age.

*"You have taken the right view of the importance of my books.* **Books will always remain**. *That was the view of my Guru Maharaja, and I also have taken it. Therefore I started my movement with my books. And we shall be able to maintain everything with the sales of the books. The temples will be maintained by the book sales, and* **if there are no more temples, then the books shall remain."** *(S.P.Letter to: Hansadutta: New Delhi 8 November, 1973)*

*Hanuman: One thing he's saying, this gentleman, and I would like to know, is your successor named or your successor will...*

*Prabhupada:* **_My success is always there_**. **Yes. Just like the sun is there always. It may come before your vision or not. The sun is there. But if you are fortunate, you come before the sun. Otherwise you remain in darkness.** *Sun is open to* *everyone. Our Krishna consciousness movement--Krishna is open to everyone. But if you are fortunate, you come to the light. If you are unfortunate, do not. That is your choice. (Srila Prabhupada Room Conversation with Sanskrit Professor, other Guests and Disciples, February 12, 1975, Mexico)*

*Reporter: Who will succeed you when you die?*

*Srila Prabhupada: **I will never die!***

*Devotees: Jaya! Haribol!*

*Srila Prabhupada: **I will live forever for my books and you will utilise.***

*(Interview, Berkley, 1975)*

His Divine Grace A. C. Bhaktivedanta Swami Prabhupada. Behind (left) is the chief culprit Tamal Krishna (aka Thomas Hertzig) who worked with other pseudo-Krishna cult leaders to poison Srila Prabhupada to "death". Note Srila Prabhupada's swollen hands and sun glasses [sensitive to light], the effects of the arsenic poisoning.

# THE HARE KRISHNA SAINT TORTURED AND POISONED "TO DEATH" BY HIS JUDAS DISCIPLES

Mukunda dasa 2001

His Divine Grace A.C. Bhaktivedanta Swami Prabhupada, the world-famous saint, cultural ambassador, scholar, social reformer and founder of the International Society for Krishna Consciousness (ISKCON), warned in a letter dated September 1970 that *"the great sinister movement is within our Society."* *(International Jewry)* In 1977 he was held in a small room and slowly tortured and poisoned "to death" by the leaders of this sinister movement, as the tape transcriptions in this pamphlet conclusively prove.

Srila Prabhupada continued translating his transcendental books up to the point of his death. Although he was personally being disturbed by these demons, still, he was merciful to the general people, who are suffering for want of Krishna consciousness. Even up to the point of death, Srila Prabhupada was trying to preach Krishna consciousness. In fact his only concern was that all the people of this planet should receive the highest perfection of life, namely Love of Krishna (God). So Srila Prabhupada truly manifested the symptoms of a Saint on the topmost level of self-realization. On one side he was tolerant of his own sufferings and on the other side he was merciful.

After Srila Prabhupada's physical departure, these Judas disciples immediately took complete control of ISKCON, its wealth and resources, which were intended for spreading love of Krishna. Whilst falsely declaring themselves Srila Prabhupada's successors, they and their followers performed countless atrocious acts, including child molestation. Those who stood against them were forced out or even murdered (Sulocana dasa).

This sinister movement masquerading as ISKCON are now threatened to be sued for $400,000,000 by some of their victims, who were subjected to child abuse whilst at schools originally set up by Srila Prabhupada to teach the children the message of pure love of God, as proclaimed in the Vedic scriptures. Evidence used in the court case is being distorted to divert the blame on to Srila Prabhupada both by the criminals (to avoid justice) and by the victim's lawyers (to gain the greatest financial rewards).

We have compiled this pamphlet in order to protect Srila Prabhupada's spotless character and to make it clear to the public that this cult is not the pure Hare Krishna movement founded by him, but rather a group of envious impostors in the dress of devotees. These impostors have completely neglected Srila Prabhupada's guidance on every level, particularly in regards to protecting children.

We are fighting to keep the Hare Krishna movement going on with Srila Prabhupada in the centre. We are printing his original transcendental books which are now being changed by the members of this cult, against Srila Prabhupada's order.

If you are interested in learning more about these issues and the genuine Hare Krishna movement then you are welcome to contact us on:

mukunda.dasa@prabhupada.org.uk

Please visit our website:
http://www.prabhupada.org.uk/    http://truth.prabhupada.org.uk

**You try to trace out the history of the world, you'll find always persons who are for Krishna or God, they have been persecuted**

*"You try to trace out the history of the world, you'll find always persons who are for Krishna or God, they have been persecuted. Lord Jesus Christ was crucified, Haridasa Thakura was caned in twenty-two market places, Prahlada Maharaja was tortured by his father. So there may be such things. Of course, Krishna will protect us. So don't be afraid. Don't be afraid if somebody tortures us, somebody teases us. We must go on with Krishna consciousness without any hesitation, and Krishna will give us protect." (Srila Prabhupada from a Srimad Bhagavatam Lecture, 7.9.8 Seattle, October 21, 1968)*

### It is a fact however that the great sinister movement is within our Society

*"Regarding the poisonous effect in our Society, it is a fact and I know where from this poison tree has sprung up and how it affected practically the whole Society in a very dangerous form. But it does not matter. Prahlada Maharaja was administered poison, but it did not act. Similarly Lord Krishna and the Pandavas were administered poison and it did not act. I think in the same parampara system that the poison administered to our Society will not act if some of our students are as good as Prahlada Maharaja. I have therefore given the administrative power to the Governing Body Commission. (GBC) ...You are also one of the members of the GBC, so you can think over very deeply how to save the situation. **It is a fact however that the great sinister movement is within our Society.**"* (Srila Prabhupada Letter to: Hansadutta, 2 September, 1970) Note: The sinister movement is International Jewry.

### And Lord Jesus Christ was killed. So they may kill me also

*Prabhupada: This is our position. Gradually they will show Hare Krishna movement. In India also, although India's... They will want to crush down this movement. So this will be up to Him. Krishna or Krishna's movement, the same thing. And Krishna was attempted to be killed by Kamsa class of men and his company, the demons. So it will be there; it is already there. Don't be disappointed, because that is the meaning that it is successful. Krishna's favor is there, because Krishna and Krishna's movement is not different, nondiff..., identical. So as Krishna was attempted to be killed, many, many years before He appeared... At eighth child, if the mother produces child yearly, still ten years, eight years before His birth, the mother was to be attempted to be killed. **So there may be attempt like that. And Lord Jesus Christ was killed. So they may kill me also.** (Prabhupada Room Conversation, May 3, 1976, Honolulu)* Note: Who killed Jesus? They are International Jewry!

### But I will be very glad to die if Krishna wants… But I am not afraid of death. That much strength I have got. Why shall I be afraid?

*Prabhupada: Yes. No, I am very much confident of this medicine because nobody is prepared to die, but I am prepared to die. That much strength I have got. Generally people do not like to die. But I will be very glad to die if Krishna wants. This is... And I shall stay with you. I have no objection either way. But I am not afraid of death. That much strength I have got. Why shall I be afraid? (Srila Prabhupada, May 28, 1977, Vrndavana)*

### Disaster will happen if you cannot manage it. Hm?

*Prabhupada: In this condition, even I cannot move my body on the bed. Only chance you should give me--let me die little peacefully, without any anxiety. I have given in writing everything, whatever you wanted--my will, my executive (?) power, everything.* **Disaster will happen if you cannot manage it. Hm?** *(S.P. Room Conversation October 2, 1977, Vrindavana)*

### For me, either live or die, I don't mind. But if you are trying for my life, try it very seriously. That is my formula. No negligence.

*Prabhupada: So far that... He said that "Life is finished, and you are simply still living by the grace of Krishna. And there is still life. Let us try it." Now he is coming. Ask him daily what...*
*Tamala Krishna: Yes. He speaks English. He spoke with me in English. I think he speaks some English, the kaviraja (doctor), a little bit. So you feel a little hopeful?*
*Prabhupada: Eh.* **For me, either live or die, I don't mind. But if you are trying for my life, try it very seriously. That is my formula. No negligence.** *Whatever he advises, that is good. (S.P. Room Conversation, October 3, 1977, Vrindavana)*

### Don't move me to the hospital. Better kill me here

*Bhavananda: We will never allow them to remove you to a hospital, Srila Prabhupada.*
*Prabhupada: You'll have to, gradually, according to his advice.*
*Bhavananda: Therefore we asked you yesterday for your guidance.*
*Prabhupada: No, I'll guide.* **Don't move me to the hospital. Better kill me here.**
*Svarupa Damodara: We won't, Srila Prabhupada.*
*Bhavananda: Never.*
*Prabhupada: But if you are disgusted, that is another thing.*
*(S.P. Room Conversation October 22, 1977, Vrindavana)*

### In this condition I do not wish to live...No, in this way to remain--not desirable. Every day, crisis...That I am thinking, that such a big society, the aims and object may be dismantled. I am thinking from that vision.

*Prabhupada: So this makara-dhvaja, (Medicine) I think not acting.*
*Tamala Krishna: It's not acting? How can you tell so soon?*
*Prabhupada: Hm?*
*Tamala Krishna: How can you tell so soon? How are you able to tell so soon after taking? Wouldn't it take a few days to feel the results?*
*Prabhupada:* **Things are deteriorating.**
*Tamala Krishna: You can feel that? You can feel things deteriorated? In what respect, Srila Prabhupada?*
*Prabhupada: Weakness.....*
*Tamala Krishna: Srila Prabhupada? You expected to immediately get some result by taking this makara-dhvaja?*
*Prabhupada: I am already puzzled? Mixed-up.(?)*

*Tamala Krishna: You said you're puzzled, Srila Prabhupada? You said you're puzzled?*

*Prabhupada: Atreya Rsi?*

*Atreya Rsi: Yes, Srila Prabhupada?*

*Prabhupada: I am puzzled.*

*Tamala Krishna: If you continue to desire to live, Srila Prabhupada... If you continue to desire to live, then Krishna will fulfill your desire.*

*Prabhupada:* **In this condition I do not wish to live.**

*Panca-dravida: The purpose of this medicine, though, Srila Prabhupada, is to cure the condition.*

*Prabhupada: Hm?....*

*Bhavananda: It is true, Srila Prabhupada, that if you lose your desire to remain here, then no medicine can be effective. But if you desire to remain, then the medicine can become effective.*

*Prabhupada: No, in this way to remain--not desirable. Every day, crisis.*

*Bhavananda: That is the crisis.*

*Tamala Krishna: That is the puzzlement. (break)*

*Bhavananda: ...we have to appraise that if Your Divine Grace leaves us, what will be the result both to ISKCON society, to each of you disciples individually, and to the entire planet.*

*Prabhupada:* **That I am thinking, that such a big society, the aims and object may be dismantled. I am thinking from that vision.** *(S.P. Room Con. October 26, 1977, Vrindavana)*

**That is my only request, that at the last stage don't torture me and put to death.**

*Prabhupada:* **That is my only request, that at the last stage don't torture me and put to death.** *So I am not eating anything, and if we chant, by batches chant, I'll hear. (S.P. Room Conversation November 3, 1977, Vrindavana)*

**Someone says that I've been poisoned. It is possible.**

*Prabhupada:* **Someone says that I've been poisoned. It is possible**

*Balaram Mishra (?): Hmm?*

*Kaviraja: (doctor) What is he saying?*

*Prabhupada:* **Someone says that someone has given poison.**

*Kaviraja: To whom?*

*Prabhupada:* **To me.**

*Kaviraja: Who said?*

*Prabhupada:* **These all friends.**

*Bhakticaru: Who said, Srila Prabhupada?*

*Tamal Krishna: Krishna das?*

*Kaviraja: Who would give you poison? Why would anyone do that?*

*Tamala Krishna: Who said that, Srila Prabhupada?*

*Prabhupada:* **I do not know, but it is said.**

*(S.P. Room Conversation November 9, 1977, Vrindavana)*

## Someone has poisoned me.

*Bhavananda: Prabhupada was complaining of mental distress this morning also.*
*Bhakti-caru: Srila Prabhupada?*
*Prabhupada: Hm?*
*Bhakti-caru: Srila Prabhupada?*
*Prabhupada: Hm?*
*Bhakti-caru: What was that all about mental distress?*
*Prabhupada: Hm, hm.*
*Kaviraja: (Doctor): Say it. Say it.*
*Prabhupada: That same thing … **that someone has poisoned me.***
*Kaviraja (Doctor): Look, this is the thing, that maybe some rakshasa (demon) gave him poison…*
*Bhakti-caru: **Someone gave him poison here.***
*Kaviraja (Doctor): Caru Swami, some rakshasa might have given it, maybe so. It's not impossible. Someone gave  poison to Sankaracharya for six months before he started to suffer. (The poisoner) ground glass, you know, bottle glass, and mixed it with his food. So what happened to him (the poisoner) as a result was that after twelve months, his entire body was covered with leprosy. So, you have to suffer the results of your actions. But whatever medicine I have given will, if it has an effect the poison will not be able to stay. That is guaranteed. Whatever it has affected, it will not be able to stay. But we cannot now catch the fellow who gave the poison. No matter what reason his kidneys are bad, whether from disease, planets or poison, my medicine will counteract it."*
*Tamala Krishna: Prabhupada was thinking that someone had poisoned him.*
*Adri-dharana: Yes.*
*Tamala Krishna: That was the mental distress.*
*Adri-dharana: Yes.*
*Kaviraja (Doctor): If he says that, they must definitely be some truth to it.*
*Tamala Krishna: What did Kavirāja just say?*
*Bhakti-caru: He said that when Srila Prabhupada was saying that, there must be some truth behind it.*
*Tamala Krishna: Tssh. (People all speaking at once)*
*Tamala Krishna: Srila Prabhupada, Sastriji (Doctor) says that there must be some truth to it if you say that. So who is it that has poisoned?*
*(13 seconds pause, Srila Prabhupada does not answer)*
*(S.P. Room Conversation November 10, 1977, Vrindavana)*

Note: Srila Prabhupada was silent because he agreed with what they had understood, as Bhakticaru immediately stated "Someone gave him poison here." Prabhupada says "If we remain silent, then whatever he says, that means we are accepting." (Discussion about Guru Maharaji August 13, 1973, Paris) Therefore, SRILA PRABHUPADA CONFIRMS AGAIN "SOMEONE HAS POISONED ME" BY REMAINING SILENT AND NOT ANSWERING TAMAL.

## Don't keep me locked up… All seriously
## consider this submission and let me go

*Prabhupada: I wish that you GBC manage very nicely and consider I am dead and let me try to travel all the térthasthäna (holy places)…. In the open air and bullock cart or during daytime, eh? Or you can say semi-suicide, although living what consider me dead for the time. You manage and nowadays there is in India ample sunshine. So during daytime I shall travel and night time you make a camp under a tree. In this way let me travel all the tirthas (holy places). I am thinking in this way. What is your opinion?..... So Lokanatha party has got some experience and let me go. In India the climate is now good. If I recover, it is very good. You know. So what is the wrong? If I die, then the body will be brought either in Vrindavana or Mayapura, that's all. And if I live, it will be a great end of a life. You are all experienced.*

*Jayapataka: As much as you have trained us, Srila Prabhupada, that is only how much we are experienced. We don't want that you be burdened any more with material management problems but…*

*Prabhupada: No, not from that point of view. What is the use of lying down here?*

*Jayapataka: The kaviraja (doctor) said…*

*Prabhupada: Kaviraja may say…*

*Jayapataka: …that even that your body is going to, is got a life of six to ten years but he said even a healthy cow, if it's kept locked up inside of a room, then it will deteriorate.*

*Prabhupada:* ***And therefore I say, (laughs) don't keep me locked up.…...All seriously consider this submission and let me go.*** *(S.P. Room Con. Nov. 10, 1977, Vrindavana)*

## And this is also suicidal…. The Ravana will kill
## and Rama will kill. Better to be killed by Rama. Eh?

*Jagadisa: Srila Prabhupada, can you tell us why you want to go on the parikrama? (travelling to visiting holy places)*

*Prabhupada: …good paddy.*

*Tamala Krishna: This seems like suicide, Srila Prabhupada, this program. It seems to some of us like it's suicidal.*

*Prabhupada:* ***And this is also suicidal.***

*Tamala Krishna: Hm. Prabhupada said, "And this is also suicide." Now you have to choose which suicide.*

*Prabhupada:* ***The Ravana (A great demon) will kill and Rama (God) will kill. Better to be killed by Rama.*** *Eh? That Marica--if he does not go to mislead Sita, he'll be killed by Ravana; and if he goes to be killed by Rama, then it is better. (S.P. Room Con. Nov. 10, 1977, Vrindavana)*

Note: Here Srila Prabhupada compares himself to Marica. His going to visit the holy places in weaken health would be like being kill by Rama (God) His staying in the room with his Judas disciples being forced to take their poison would be like being killed by Ravana (a great demon)

### This is sadhu. He is personally being disturbed by the demons, but still, he is merciful to the general people.

*"One who is devotee... That is explained in many sastras. Sadhavah sadhu-bhusanam. Sadhu-bhusanam. titiksavah karunikah suhrdah sarva-bhutanam ajata-satravah santah sadhavah sadhu-bhusanah This is the qualification of sadhu. Sadhu is titiksava, tolerates all kinds of miserable conditions. He is sadhu. Because this is a place of miserable condition. A sadhu learns how to tolerate. Sadhu is never disturbed. Yasmin sthito gurunapi duhkhena na vicalyate. A sadhu, who has got the shelter of Krishna, if he is placed in the severest type of dangerous condition, he is never disturbed. Just like Prahlada Maharaja, his father was putting him in so many dangerous conditions, even he was supplying with poison. He knew that "My father has given me poison to drink. All right, let me drink. If Krishna likes, He will save me. I am now put into such dangerous position. I have to drink. Father is giving poison. Who can check?" And such a big powerful Hiranyakasipu. The mother cried, requested... He forced the mother, Prahlada's mother, "Give your son this poison." So she begged so much, but he was a rascal demon. "No, you must give." So the mother knew, the son knew that the rascal father is giving this poison. What can he do, a small child? "All right, let me drink." Gurunapi duhkhena na vicalyate. He is not agitating. "All right, if Krishna likes, I will live." This is the position of sadhu. He is not disturbed. Titiksavah. In all circumstances, he is tolerant. That is sadhu. Sadhu does not become disturbed. Titiksavah. At the same time, karunikah. He is himself disturbed, but he is merciful to others. Just like Jesus Christ. He is being crucified, and still he is merciful: "God, these people do not know what they are doing. Please excuse them." This is sadhu. He is personally being disturbed by the demons, but still, he is merciful to the general people. They are suffering for want of Krishna consciousness. So even up to the point of death, he is trying to preach Krishna consciousness. "Let the people be benefited. Eh, what is this material body? Even if I am killed, I am not killed. This body is killed, that's all." This is sadhu. Titiksavah karunikah. In one side he is tolerant, and other side, merciful." (Prabhupada, Bhagavad-gita Lecture, 1.21-22 London, July 18, 1973)*

### Sometimes we see that a powerful preacher is killed

*"When something is arranged by the Supreme Personality of Godhead, one should not be disturbed by it, even if it appears to be a reverse according to one's calculations. For example, sometimes we see that a powerful preacher is killed, or sometimes he is put into difficulty, just as Haridasa Thakura was. He was a great devotee who came into this material world to execute the will of the Lord by preaching the Lord's glories. But Haridasa was punished at the hands of the Kazi by being beaten in twenty-two marketplaces. Similarly, Lord Jesus Christ was*

*crucified, and Prahlada Maharaja was put through so many tribulations. The Pandavas, who were direct friends of Krishna, lost their kingdom, their wife was insulted, and they had to undergo many severe tribulations.* **Seeing all these reverses affect devotees, one should not be disturbed; one should simply understand that in these matters there must be some plan of the Supreme Personality of Godhead.** *The Bhagavatam's conclusion is that a devotee is never disturbed by such reverses. He accepts even reverse conditions as the grace of the Lord. One who continues to serve the Lord even in reverse conditions is assured that he will go back to Godhead, back to the Vaikuntha planets." (Srila Prabhupada from Srimad Bhagavatam 3.16.37)*

### A devotee's attention is concentrated only upon the eternal loving service of the Lord, and therefore the power of death has no influence over him.

*"A devotee's attention is concentrated only upon the eternal loving service of the Lord, and therefore* **the power of death has no influence over him**. *In such a devotional state, a perfect yogi can attain the status of immortal knowledge and bliss." (Srila Prabhupada from Srimad Bhagavatam 3.27.30)*

### People with a poor fund of knowledge do not know the difference between the death of a devotee and the death of a nondevotee.

*"To take the passing away of a devotee and the passing away of a nondevotee as one and the same is completely misleading. While ascending the transcendental airplane, Dhruva Maharaja suddenly saw death personified before him, but he was not afraid. Instead of death's giving him trouble, Dhruva Maharaja took advantage of death's presence and put his feet on the head of death.* **People with a poor fund of knowledge do not know the difference between the death of a devotee and the death of a nondevotee.** *In this connection, an example can be given: a cat carries its kittens in its mouth, and it also catches a rat in its mouth. Superficially, the catching of the rat and the kitten appear to be one and the same, but actually they are not. When the cat catches the rat in its mouth it means death for the rat, whereas when the cat catches the kitten, the kitten enjoys it." (Srila Prabhupada from Srimad Bhagavatam 4.12.30)*

### Unfortunately, when the acarya disappears, rogues and nondevotees take advantage and immediately begin to introduce unauthorized principles

*"Whenever an acarya (spiritual master) comes, following the superior orders of the Supreme Personality of Godhead or His representative, he establishes the*

*principles of religion, as enunciated in Bhagavad-gita....* **Unfortunately, when the acarya disappears, rogues and nondevotees take advantage and immediately begin to introduce unauthorized principles** *in the name of so-called svamis, yogis, philanthropists, welfare workers and so on...The acarya, the authorized representative of the Supreme Lord, establishes these principles, but when he disappears, things once again become disordered. The perfect disciples of the acarya try to relieve the situation by sincerely following the instructions of the spiritual master...Similarly, a devoted disciple of the spiritual master would rather die with the spiritual master than fail to execute the spiritual master's mission."* (Srila Prabhupada from Srimad Bhagavatam 4.28.48,50,51)

## FORENSICALLY TESTED TAPES FIND SINISTER WHISPERS OF THE JUDAS DISCIPLES IN THE ACT OF POISONING SRILA PRABHUPADA

Conversations Vol. 36, page 373: After Srila Prabhupada says *"Hmmm. You make me flat"* is heard this whisper: *"Push real hard, it's going down him...(giggle) the poison's going down."* Con: 36.373: After Jayapataka says, *"follow the same treatment,"* a whisper: *"Is the poison in the milk? Um hum."* Con: 36.374: After Srila Prabhupada says, *"Daytime we expose...",* we hear the whisper, *"Do it now."* Then Srila Prabhupada drinks something. Con: 36.378: We hear the whispers, *"Jayadwaita... will you serve Srila Prabhupada poison Jayadwaita?",* then several negative responses followed by *"Nette, nette."* Con: 36.391: After Jayapataka says, *"Should there be kirtana?"* we hear a Bengali phrase, and then the whisper *"Poison ishvarya rasa."* Srila Prabhupada replies with *"To Me?",* then we hear, *"Take it easy, get ready to go,"* then a few seconds later, we hear what sounds like Jayapataka say *"You're taking it right now"* Srila Prabhupada then says *"How's this?"* Then someone says *"Let it go."* Then Hansadutta's kirtan (chanting) begins. On side A of the "poison tape", November 11, 1977, was found the following whispers: *"Going down" "Did it hurt?" "He's gonna die" "Listen, he's saying.... Going to die" "Yes, a heart attack time"*

**Mr. Jack Mitchell owner/engineer of "Commercial Audio/ Forensic Audio/ Computer Audio Engineering" Albuquerque, New Mexico.** (Sections of Mr. Mitchell's report on the 'poison whispers' are recorded above) "After a week, Jack Mitchell called Mahabuddhi and advised that we should be arranging for legal counsel, as it appeared that what he was analysing was a poison conspiracy, judging from what he had already found on the tape. Mr. Jack Mitchell (referring to Dr. Helen McCaffery): *"I sent her the report for her review and told her that if there was anything in there that she felt was incorrect she should tell me, she should change it. Or if she felt that anything needs to be added, then she should add it. She added nothing; she changed nothing. She actually submitted a document in which she says that she is in total agreement with the report, with the findings."*

**Mr. Tom Owen. OWL Investigations, Inc - Conclusion:** *"There is conversation about poison and the use of it. In my opinion there is certainly a basis for further investigation. Exhumation would settle the issue, although I am told that it is against religious beliefs. A forensic toxicologist and Homicide investigator should be consulted."* **Opinion:** *"Based on my training and experience, the word poison is clearly audible and intelligible in several instances."*

## 20 TIMES HIGHER THAN NORMAL ARSENIC LEVELS FOUND IN SRILA PRABHUPADA'S HAIR SAMPLES

**Dr. J. Stephen Morris (Ph.D.) Lauder, Nuclear Analysis Program. University of Missouri-Columbia**. *"The arsenic concentration found (in Srila Prabhupada's hair) was 2.6 micrograms arsenic per gram of hair (or 2.6 parts per million i.e. 2.6 ppm). The concentration is approximately 20 times higher than what I would consider a normal average for unexposed individuals living in the United States."*

**Richard. T. Callery. (M.D., F.C.A.P)** *"In my opinion, to a reasonable degree of medical certainty, that this individual, (Srila Prabhupada) with the history of multiple myocardial inferts (?) and non insulin dependent diabetes mellitus and considering his age would be an individual in frail health in which a chronic administration or exposure of arsenic leading to toxic levels would be expected to be a significant contributing condition to his death....." (Richard. T. Callery. M.D.,F.C.A.P. Chief Medical Examiner. Director, Forensic Sciences Laboratory. National Medical Services).*

## SRILA PRABHUPADA SPEAKS ABOUT CHANGING HIS BOOKS

### The next printing should be again to the original way....They cannot change anything

*Yasoda-nandana: Sometimes they appeal that "We can make better English," so they change like that, just like in the case of Isopanisad. There are over a hundred changes. So where is the need? Your words are sufficient. The potency is there. When they change, it is something else.*
*Svarupa Damodara: That's actually a very dangerous mentality.*
*Yasoda-nandana: What is it going to be in five years? It's going to be a different book.*
*Prabhupada: So you... What you are going... It is very serious situation. You write one letter that "Why you have made so many changes?" And whom to write? Who will care? All rascals are there. Write to Satsvarupa that "This is the position. They are doing anything and everything at their whim." **The next printing should be again to the original way**....So write them immediately that "The rascal editors, they are doing havoc, and they are being maintained by Ramesvara and party."....So you bring this to Satsvarupa. **They cannot change anything**... So on*

*the whole, these dangerous things are going on. How to check it?... So they are doing very freely and dangerously. And this rascal is always after change, Radha-vallabha. He's a great rascal. (S.P. Conversation, "Rascal Editors," June 22, 1977, Vrindavana)*

Note: Some rascals (Jay Israel or Purujit from Bliss Boys) claim that everyone can go to the manuscript and edit from that and then print. This makes Prabhupada's books open like a prostitute for anyone to misedit and print! *"The next printing should be **again** to the original way"* means to print the original first edition as authorized and approved by Prabhupada. The manuscript was never printed. You cannot **print again** something that was **never printed** in the first place!

### As soon as you change it, then the
### potency of the movement is lost.

*Faill: I'll look up some reference books on the history of the movement and that sort of thing.*
*Prabhupada: History, it is not a new movement. You have seen this book. You read that book thoroughly. You will get full knowledge. **This movement is very, very old and standard. It is never changed. As soon as you change it, then the potency of the movement is lost.***
*Faill: Sorry, what was that?*
*Prabhupada: Potency. Just like electricity. There is standard regulation: "This is negative; this is positive. You must act like this. You must fix like..." You cannot do whimsically: "No, why not this way? Why not that way?" Then it is lost. Then there will be no electricity. Similarly, there is standard method how to understand this philosophy, how to get it, I mean to say, what is called, authoritatively. Then it will act. (S.P. Room Conversation October 8, 1975, Durban)*

*Ganesa: Srila Prabhupada, if the knowledge was handed down by the saintly kings, evam parampara-praptam, how is it that the knowledge was lost?*
*Prabhupada: When it was not handed down. Simply understood by speculation. Or if it is not handed down as it is. **They might have made some changes. Or they did not hand it down. Suppose I handed it down to you, but if you do not do that, then it is lost.** Now the Krishna consciousness movement is going on in my presence. **Now after my departure, if you do not do this, then it is lost.** If you go on as you are doing now, then it will go on. But if you stop... (end) (S.P. Room Conversation, May 9, 1975, Perth)*

### SRILA PRABHUPADA SPEAKS ABOUT
### THE HARE KRISHNA CHILDREN

### The important matter is that the
### children are taken care of nicely.

*"**The important matter is that the children are taken care of nicely.** Bhavananda was talking with me that in New Vrindaban students were very much neglected.*

*Therefore they were immediately transferred to New York. Every parent wants to see that their children are taken care of very nicely. That is the first duty. If they are not healthy then how they can prosecute their education? If they are undernourished it is not good for their future activities. They must have sufficient quantity of milk and then dhal, capatis, vegetables, and a little fruit will keep them always fit. There is no need of luxurious fatty foods but milk is essential. A big building is also very good for the children's health. They can move freely and run and jump." (S.P. Letter to: Satsvarupa Nairobi 9 October, 1971)*

### These children are given to us by Krishna, they are Vaisnavas and we must be very careful to protect them.

*"My dear Arundhati, Please accept my blessings. I am in due receipt of your letter dated July 19, 1972, and I am simply surprised that you want to give up your child to some other persons, even they are also devotees. For you, child-worship is more important than deity-worship. If you cannot spend time with him, then stop the duties of pujari. At least you must take good care of your son until he is four years old, and if after that time you are unable any more to take care of him then I shall take care.* ***These children are given to us by Krishna, they are Vaisnavas and we must be very careful to protect them.*** *These are not ordinary children, they are Vaikuntha children, and we are very fortunate we can give them chance to advance further in Krishna Consciousness. That is very great responsibility, do not neglect it or be confused.* ***Your duty is very clear.*** *Hoping this will meet you in good health. Your ever well-wisher, A. C. Bhaktivedanta Swami." (S.P. Letter to: Arundhati Amsterdam 30 July, 1972)*

### Forcing will not make me agree. But if there is love, oh, I shall gladly do it. That is bhakti, that is Krishna Consciousness.

*"I am very glad to learn that the children at Gurukula school are making good progress in their Krishna Consciousness education, that is very good news. Yes, if we simply train them properly they will come out just to the highest standard of Vaisnava devotee. And what is that training? Simply they should be engaged in such a way that they are somehow or other remembering Krishna at every moment, that's all. It is not something mechanical process, if we force in such a way they will come out like this, no. We are persons, and Krishna is a Person, and our relationship with Krishna He leaves open as a voluntary agreement always, and that voluntary attitude--Yes, Krishna, I shall gladly co-operate whatever you say--that ready willingness to obey is only possible if there is love.* ***Forcing will not make me agree. But if there is love, oh, I shall gladly do it. That is bhakti, that is Krishna Consciousness.*** *So similarly, if we train children by developing and encouraging their propensity to love Krishna, then we shall be successful in educating them to the topmost standard. Then they shall always very happily agree to do whatever you ask them. So I have heard that there as been some*

*beating with sticks on the children. Of course I do not know, but that should not be. You may show the stick, threaten, but better art is to somehow or other, even by tricking them, avoid this matter of force and induce them to obey out of loving spirit. That is success of disciplinary method. Hoping this meets you in good health. Your ever well-wisher, A. C. Bhaktivedanta Swami." (S.P. Letter to: Rupa Vilasa Hyderabad 18 November, 1972)*

## If we want them to become great devotees, then we must educate the children with love, not in a negative way.

*"Regarding your question should force be used on children, no, there shall be no forcing the children to do anything. Child should not be forced. This is all nonsense. Who has devised these things?* **If we want them to become great devotees, then we must educate the children with love, not in a negative way.** *Of course, if they become naughty we may show the stick but we should never use it. Child is nonsense, so you can trick him to obey you by making some little story and the child will become cheated in the proper behavior. But never apply force, especially to his chanting and other matters of spiritual training. That will spoil him and in the future he will not like to do it if he forced." (S.P. Letter to: Brahmanya Tirtha Ahmedabad 10 December 1972)*

## Now the thing is, children should not be beaten at all, that I have told.

**"Now the thing is, children should not be beaten at all, that I have told.** *They should simply be shown the stick strongly. So if one cannot manage in that way then he is not fit as teacher. If a child is trained properly in Krishna Consciousness, he will never go away. That means he must have two things, love and education. So if there is beating of child, that will be difficult for him to accept in loving spirit, and when he is old enough he may want to go away--that is the danger. So why these things are going on _ marching and chanting japa, insufficient milk, too strict enforcement of time schedules, hitting the small children? Why these things are being imposed? Why they are inventing these such new things like marching and japa like army? What can I do from such a distant place? They should run and play when they are small children, not forced to chant japa, that is not the way. So I have given you the guiding principles, it is not that I must be consulted with every small detail, that is the business of the in-charge, but if no one is there who can manage in the right way, what can I do? Now if you have got the right idea how to do it, you may go there again and take some responsible post for correcting the situation, that will be your real duty, not that there is some disagreement and I go away disgusted, no. That is not Vaisnava standard. Standard should be that, never mind there is some difficulty, my spiritual master has ordered me to do like this, now let me do it, that's all." (S.P. Letter to: Bhanutanya Hyderabad 18 November, 1972)*

### These children are the future hope of our Society

*"Now I am concerned that the Gurukula experiment should come out nicely.* ***These children are the future hope of our Society****, so it is a very important matter how we are training them in Krishna consciousness from the very childhood. (S.P. Letter to: Satsvarupa, New York 11 April, 1973) Gurukula is our most important project. If the children are given a Krishna Conscious education from early childhood then there is great hope for the future of the world."* *(S.P. Letter to: Dayananda, Nandarani Calcutta 27 January, 1973)*

### The children of our devotees may live with their parents perpetually because you are all living in the temple and already engaged in devotional service.

*"So far your son leaving you, his parents, at 5 years, that is not necessary. Especially our Krishna Conscious children; they are already living in a asrama.* ***The children of our devotees may live with their parents perpetually because you are all living in the temple and already engaged in devotional service.*** *Other instructions are for those not engaged in Krishna Consciousness. Any family engaged in Krishna's service is living not in this material world. Such a home is considered as Vaikuntha. (the spiritual world) That is the verdict of Bhaktivinode Thakura."* *(S.P. Letter to: Indira London 15 August, 1971)*

# ISKCON LEADERS CHARGED WITH MURDERING SRILA PRABHUPADA

Sanat dasa (Stephen Voith) was the first person to go out and publically expose the poisoning of Srila Prabhupada. After reading Prabhupada's final conversations, he could clearly understand that Srila Prabhupada was saying that he was being killed by demons (Ravanas) dressed as devotees.

As a true follower of Sulocana prabhu, he has done so many of these protests at ISKCON Ratha Yatras at the risk of his life. Unfortunately, Sanat prabhu's great work has been suppressed and stolen by Puranjana dasa (Tim Lee) also known as PADA, who originally condemned his protests as "blasphemy of the gurus". Puranjana tries to present himself as the intimate friend and assistant of Sulocana prabhu. This is a complete lie that has being totally exposed in my new book called "Killing For Keith". Puranjana is a great offender of Srila Prabhupada and his perfect disciple Sulocana dasa.

**Sanat's Protest March 1997 New York Ratha Yatra.**

Sanat: So Ravindra what do you all say about Tamal's trying to poison Prabhupada and Bhakti Caru and all these other guys. *[Ravindra looks shocked, Bhakti Caru turns away looking fearful]* Poisoning Prabhupada in November.

Ravindra: Hey, peace brother.

Sanat: I know but what do you feel about that. What's your response?

Ravindra: Peace brother, peace.

Sanat: So you think it's alright that Prabhupada was poisoned by all these bogus gurus. You think that's ok? Now you want peace! Kill Guru kill self right? Kill Guru become guru.

Ravindra: There's nothing poison here but your little mind.

Sanat: Kill Guru become guru right? False worship, aggrandise Prabhupada's worship for yourself. *[Sanat starts to talk to Hariasva]* Hey Hariasva, Ravindra svarupa thinks it's good to be peaceful after his godbrothers poisoned Prabhupada in Vrndavana.

Hariasva: I like Ravindra svarupa.

Sanat: So you like the fact that he thinks it's a good thing be peaceful after his godbrothers tried to kill Prabhupada?

Hariasva: I like him, i like him alot. He takes care of me.

Sanat: Oh, so we're talking sense gratification here. *[Sanat to Ravindra again]* And what about all the children who were molested. And your cover up and your false reform Ravindra Svarupa, what do you have to say about that ah? Guru needs reform right? Jesus Chirst was fallen.Yes, two thousand kids molested "sweep them under the garbage, take the money take the position, who cares let it all go to hell" *[Sanat right up to Bhakti Caru's face]* Right Bhakti Caru! Yes, yes, we know your guilty, smirk all you want. I love them but i can't embrace a tiger. If a tiger's acting enviously you still have to deal with it cautiously. No philosophy, lets debated come on! Kill guru kill self right? So Prabhupada's crack because he said that, and I'm repeating it so I'm crazy right? Prabhupada said kill Guru kill self, so i repeat it but am crazy right Ravindra, right! Children were molested i repeat it am crazy. Nobody should say that we should just worship Ravindra Svarupa! We should forget about all the children that were raped right? Isn't that correct Ravindra Svarupa? We don't care about two thousand children molested by your godbrothers, let them go to hell and let's reform guru after all "He needs fixing, he's broken, guru falls down" No philosophy can't debate, character assassination. Kill guru kill self, kill your disciples, right? *[Ravindra bully boys start pushing Sanat]* I didn't make this philosophy up Prabhupada spoke it, read it! Kill guru kill self.[Ravindra bully boys pushing Sanat and Prabhupada's picture on sign]* That is perfection and as soon as he learns... *[Sanat turns to bully boys]*...that is Prabhupada why are you doing that!? As soon as he learns that Guru maharaja is dead now i am so advanced that i can kill my guru and i become guru.Prabhupada said that.Then he's finished.

ISKCON follower: *[starts complaining to Sanat about his protest]*

Sanat: I'm talking, I'm talking to the whole audience. This is brhat mrdanga *[big chanting, big face kicking. Sanat then addressing crowd]* It says right here, Prabhupada said "that is perfection and as soon as he learns that Guru maharaja is dead now i am so advanced that i can kill my guru and become guru!!"

Right."Then he's finished" Prabhupada said that. Is Prabhupada crazy? When don't you say it for the record Ravindra Svarupa. Prabhupada's crazy isn't he? He's crazy because he said that your not a guru, your a jerk.

ISKCON follower (2): Heh,don't push anybody, take it easy.

Sanat: I can't push a spirit soul. Right Ravindra? Prabhupada's crazy because he said your not a guru your a cockroach. Right? You look like a cockroach and a snake.

Ravindra: How's the slut Linda and your little bastard kids.

Sanat: So answer the question.

Ravindra: Why don't you follow the principles then you can talk to me.

Sanat: Follow the principles, of worshipping cockroaches, that's your only principle. You want people to worship cockroaches.You don't want to worship Prabhupada, you won't to kill guru and kill your disciples and send them to hell, right? And Prabhupada's crazy for saying that, that your not a guru. Right? He's crazy, say it! *[Ravindra pushes Sanat's camera]*

Sanat: Prabhupada's not following your principles!!

Ravindra: Get out of my face.

Sanat: Prabhupada's not following your principles, right? Prabhupada's not following..As soon as Prabhupada follows and worships you.

ISKCON follower (3): Can you stop

Sanat: As soon as Prabhupada worships you then he won't be crazy right? Right? *[Sanat singing, loudly]* Cockroach gurus can't take care of themselves. Cockroach gurus can't take care of themselves.

Police Officer: Get out of the parade.Out.

Sanat: Ok I'm out, I'm out. Ok thankyou officer, I'm out.

Police Officer: Good bye, good bye.

Sanat: Ok,ok where do you won't me to go?

Police Officer: That way,

Sanat: I'm i allowed to go backwards.

Police Officer: Yes you can go faster than that backwards. Keep going. All the way down, don't come back in.You understand.

Sanat: I'm I allowed to come back on the side walk?

Police Officer: Side walk, I don't won't to see you near the parade!

Sanat: Ok. Alright officer, thankyou we're having fun though,we're having a good time. I love you!

# GEORGE HARRISON (EX– BEATLE) SPEAKS ABOUT SRILA PRABHUPADA.

**George Harrison and Patti Boyd with Srila Prabhupada and a disciple at George's home in England, 1969.** Srila Prabhupada spoke of George as follows: *"I think George does not require to become my formal disciple because he is already more than my disciple…. Sriman George Harrison has certainly done an unique service by contributing $19,000 for publishing my Krsna book. When I was in London, he saw me four times and he was very submissive and devout and he was not at all proud of his very well-to-do material position. He has a reputation as a first class musician and he is considered to be rich or as they say one of the richest men in the world. Still he was not at all puffed up, but was humble, meek, polite, and devout. So all these qualities and his service to Krishna will certainly help him in his advancement of Krishna Consciousness….. this good boy George Harrison, we must give him all glories. We must be thankful to him that he has given us the facility, and Krsna will bless him more and more."*

### I realized later on that he was much more incredible than what you could see on the surface.

**Mukunda:** George, you and John Lennon met Srila Prabhupada together when he stayed at John's home, in September of 1969.

**George:** Yes, but when I met him at first, I underestimated him. I didn't realize it then, but I see now that because of him, the mantra has spread so far in the last sixteen years, more than it had in the last five centuries. Now that's pretty amazing, because he was getting older and older, yet he was writing his books all the time. I realized later on that he was much more incredible than what you could see on the surface.

**The thing that always stays is his saying, "I am the servant of the servant of the servant." I like that…. I liked Prabhupada's humbleness. I always liked his humility and his simplicity The servant of the servant of the servant is really what it is, you know. None of us are God--just His servants.**

**Mukunda:** What about him stands out the most in your mind?

**George:** The thing that always stays is his saying, "I am the servant of the servant of the servant." I like that. A lot of people say, "I'm it. I'm the divine incarnation. I'm here and let me hip you." You know what I mean? But Prabhupada was never like that. I liked Prabhupada's humbleness. I always liked his humility and his simplicity The servant of the servant of the servant is really what it is, you know. None of us are God--just His  servants. He just made me feel so comfortable. I always felt very relaxed with him, and I felt more like a friend. I felt that he was a good friend. Even though he was at the time seventy-nine years old, working practically all through the night, day after day, with very little sleep, he still didn't come through to me as though he was a very highly educated intellectual being, because he had a sort of childlike simplicity. Which is great, fantastic. Even though he was the greatest Sanskrit scholar and a saint, I appreciated the fact that he never made me feel uncomfortable. In fact, he always went out of his way to make me feel comfortable. I always thought of him as sort of a lovely friend, really, and now he's still a lovely friend.

**Mukunda:** In one of his books, Prabhupada said that your sincere service was better than some people who had delved more deeply into Krishna consciousness but could not maintain that level of commitment. How did you feel about this?

**George:** Very wonderful, really. I mean it really gave me hope, because as they say, even one moment in the company of a divine person, Krishna's pure devotee, can help a tremendous amount. And I think Prabhupada was really pleased at the idea that somebody from outside of the temple was helping to get the album made. Just the fact that he was pleased was encouraging to me. I knew he liked "The Hare Krishna Mantra" record, and he asked the devotees to play that song "Govinda." They still play it, don't they?

**That was the thing about Prabhupada, you see. He didn't just talk about loving Krishna and getting out of this place, but he was the perfect example…. He was a perfect example of everything he preached.**

**Mukunda:** Every temple has a recording of it, and we play it each morning when the devotees assemble before the altar, before kirtana. It's an ISKCON institution, you might say.

**George:** And if I didn't get feedback from Prabhupada on my songs about Krishna or the philosophy, I'd get it from the devotees. That's all the encouragement I needed really. It just seemed that anything spiritual I did, either through songs, or helping with publishing the books, or whatever, really pleased him. The song I wrote, "Living in the Material World," as I wrote in I, Me, Mine, was influenced by Srila Prabhupada. He's the one who explained to me how we're not these physical bodies. We just happen to be in them. Like I said in the song, this place's not really what's happening. We don't belong here, but in the spiritual sky: As I'm fated for the material world, Get frustrated in the material world, Senses never gratified, Only swelling like a tide, That could drown me in the material world. The whole point to being here, really, is to figure a way to get out. That was the thing about Prabhupada, you see. He didn't just talk about loving Krishna and getting out of this place, but he was the perfect example. He talked about always chanting, and he was always chanting. I think that that in itself was perhaps the most encouraging thing for me. It was enough to make me try harder, to be just a little bit better. He was a perfect example of everything he preached.

> **I think Prabhupada's accomplishments are very significant;
> they're huge. Even compared to someone like William
> Shakespeare, the amount of literature Prabhupada
> produced is truly amazing. It boggles the mind. He
> sometimes went for days with only a few hours sleep.**

**Mukunda:** How would you describe Srila Prabhupada's achievements?

**George:** I think Prabhupada's accomplishments are very significant; they're huge. Even compared to someone like William Shakespeare, the amount of literature Prabhupada produced is truly amazing. It boggles the mind. He sometimes went for days with only a few hours sleep. I mean even a youthful, athletic young person couldn't keep the pace he kept himself at seventy-nine years of age.

> **Srila Prabhupada has already had an amazing effect on
> the world. There's no way of measuring it. One day
> I just realized, "God, this man is amazing!"**

**George:** Srila Prabhupada has already had an amazing effect on the world. There's no way of measuring it. One day I just realized, "God, this man is amazing!" He would sit up all night translating Sanskrit into English, putting in glossaries to make sure everyone understands it, and yet he never came off as someone above you. He always had that childlike simplicity, and what's most amazing is the fact that he did all this translating in such a relatively short time--just a few years. And without having anything more than his own Krishna consciousness, he rounded up all these thousands of devotees, set the whole movement in motion, which became something so strong that it went on even after he left. And it's still escalating even now at an incredible rate. It will go on and on from the knowledge he gave. (Editiors note: Srila Prabhupada: "Even if they stop (the movement) externally, internally it will go on.") It can only grow and grow. The more people wake up spiritually, the more they'll begin to realize the depth of what Prabhupada was saying--how much he gave.

### His contribution has obviously been enormous from the literary point of view, because he's brought the Supreme Person, Krishna, more into focus.

**Mukunda:** Did you know that complete sets of Prabhupada's books are in all the major colleges and universities in the world, including Harvard, Yale, Princeton, Oxford, Cambridge, and the Sorbonne?

**George:** They should be! One of the greatest things I noticed about Prabhupada was the way he would be talking to you in English, and then all of a sudden he would say it to you in Sanskrit and then translate it back into English. It was clear that he really knew it well. His contribution has obviously been enormous from the literary point of view, because he's brought the Supreme Person, Krishna, more into focus. A lot of scholars and writers know the Gita, but only on an intellectual level. Even when they write "Krishna said...," they don't do it with the bhakti or love required. That's the secret, you know--Krishna is actually a person who is the Lord and who will also appear there in that book when there is that love, that bhakti. You can't understand the first thing about God     unless you love Him. These big so-called Vedic scholars--they don't necessarily love Krishna, so they can't understand Him and give Him to us. But Prabhupada was different.

### Well, Prabhupada's definitely affected the world in an absolute way. What he was giving us was the highest literature, the highest knowledge. I mean there just isn't anything higher.

**Mukunda:** The Vedic literatures predicted that after the advent of Lord Caitanya five hundred years ago, there would be a Golden Age of ten thousand years, when the chanting of the holy names of God would completely nullify all the degradations of the modern age, and real spiritual peace would come to this planet

**George:** Well, Prabhupada's definitely affected the world in an absolute way. What he was giving us was the highest literature, the highest knowledge. I mean there just isn't anything higher.

# MAYAVADI ATTACK

Mukunda dasa 2002

## SO AS SOON AS THERE IS MAYAVADI ATTACK, YOU MUST IMMEDIATELY DEFEAT THEM. THAT IS WANTED.

*"So you should not be simply chanting and dancing. Along with, you must know philosophy. There are so many Mayavadis; you have to defeat them. It is not that we are cowards. We are Krishna's soldiers. So as soon as there is Mayavadi attack, you must immediately defeat them. That is wanted. Therefore so many books are being written."* [Srimad-Bhagavatam Lecture, 2.3.20, Los Angeles, June 16, 1972]

Dear Prabhu's please accept my humble obeisances.

All glories to Srila Prabhupada.

Very recently there has been an attack on His Divine Grace A. C. Bhaktivedanta Swami Prabhupada and a fundamental principle of the Vaishnava philosophy, namely the constitutional position of the living entity. This attack has come in the form of a paper named "THE FINAL PROOF: THE JIVA DID NOT FALL FROM GOLOKA" This offensive paper is a transcript of a lecture given by the Mayavadi interpreter Narayana Maharaja.

So following the above order of Srila Prabhupada I have compiled this paper.

Your servant Mukunda dasa.

## CONTENTS

**1. Mayavadi Word Jugglery.**

**2. Mukhya-Vrtti ("The Direct Meaning") Gauna-Vrtti ("The Indirect Meaning")**

**3. Forgotten Krishna, We Fallen Souls.**

**4. The Constitutional Position Of The Living Entity.**

**5. Tatastha Sakti, Or Marginal Potency Of The Lord.**

**6. Independence And Falldown.**

**7. If He Desires, He Can Come Again. That Option Is Always There.**

## 1. Mayavadi Word Jugglery.

The following is taken from the offensive Mayavadi paper by Narayana Maharaja:

jivera 'svarupa' haya - krsnera 'nitya-dasa'
krsnera 'tatastha'sakti' 'bhedabheda-prakasa'
suryamsa-kirana, yaiche agni-jvala-caya
svabhavika krsnera tina-prakara 'sakti' haya

"It is the living entity's constitutional position to be an eternal servant of Krishna because he is the marginal energy of Krishna and a manifestation simultaneously one with and different from the Lord, like a molecular particle of sunshine or fire. Krishna has three varieties of energy." (Cc Madhya 20.108-109)

Krishna bhuli' sei jiva anadi-bahirmukha
ataeva maya tare deya samsara-duhkha

"Forgetting Krishna, the living entity has been attracted by the external feature from time immemorial. Therefore, the illusory energy (maya) gives him all kinds of misery in his material existence." (Cc Madhya 20.117)

[Narayana Maharaja]: We are eternally Krishna dasa, servants of Krishna, but now we are Krishna bhuli; we have forgotten Him. The words 'Krishna bhuli' are used here. It means 'the jiva forgets Krishna', but what does this actually mean? It seems to mean that the jiva was once engaged in Krishna's service, but now he has forgotten that service. Actually, this is not true. This is not the meaning. There is defect in worldly languages. They are not perfect, and therefore they cannot purely express what is the nature of our svarupa (constitutional form). To clarify the meaning of 'Krishna bhuli', Srila Krishnadasa Kaviraja Gosvami writes in the next line, "krsnera 'tatastha'sakti' 'bhedabheda-prakasa.'" ....They are all liberated. They don't know what is maya and what is this material world. Who knows? We know. We have come from tatastha-sakti, from a manifestation of Baladeva Prabhu called Karanabdisayi Visnu, who is situated on the marginal line, in the Karanabdhi (Causal Ocean). The jivas are not coming to this world from Goloka Vrndavana, nor are they coming from Vaikuntha. They are coming form the marginal line, from the glance of Karanabdhisayi Visnu. Among them, those who look towards Vaikuntha are liberated, and they go there at once without delay. Conversely, those who look toward this world will come here....Don't conclude that the jivas have come from Goloka. Although Srila Swami Maharaja never said that the jivas fell from Goloka, some of his disciples try to prove that he has said the opposite. But I know the truth. He has told me, and it is also in sastra. Srimati Syamarani dasi has collected so many of Srila Swami Maharaja words, confirming that he never accepted that the jivas came from Goloka Vrndavana.

na tad bhasayate suryo
na sasanko na pavakah
yad gatva na nivartante

tad dhama paramam mama

"That supreme abode of Mine is not illumined by the sun or moon, nor by fire or electricity. Those who reach it never return to this material world." (Bg 15.6)

[Narayana Maharaja]: Goloka is such a dhama that there is no maya. Rather, only Yogamaya is there. A person who is seriously chanting, remembering and following, passes through the stages of sraddha, nistha, ruci, asakti, and prema, after a long, long, long time. If he has gone to Goloka Vrndavana Dhama and is serving Krishna, there is no chance at all to fall down. There is no example at all in the Vedas, Upanisads, or any other scriptures....

It would be quite absurd to think that liberated souls in Goloka Vrndavana can ever be covered by maya. You should have strong faith that the jivas did not fall from there. They have come from the marginal point. They have come from Karanabdhisayi Visnu and from tatastha-sakti. Jiva himself is tatastha-sakti.

[Gokula dasa:] Actually, within ISKCON there was two or three. [Letters about originally being with Krishna]

[Srila Narayana Maharaja:] I know. I have read them. Srila Swami Maharaja sometimes gave baby food to babies. When I give a baby medicine like quinine, I tell him, "Baby, baby, it is very sweet." I'm telling him something that is not true so that I can give him the medicine. Similarly, Srila Swami Maharaja has written to someone who was very low in bhakti. A letter cannot always be proof. What Srila Swami Maharaja has written in Caitanya-caritamrta and in his Gita and Bhagavata explanation is authentic. These are proofs. He can write something else for a little baby, but it is not proof.

### 2. Mukhya-Vrtti ("The Direct Meaning")
### Gauna-Vrtti ("The Indirect Meaning")

In this section we will see very clearly that Narayana Maharaja has described the words 'Krishna bhuli' from Caitanya-caritamrta Madhya Lila verse 20.117 in terms of indirect meaning.

*"Upon this, the Lord spoke as follows: "My dear sir, I can understand the meaning of the sutras like janmady asya yatah, sastra-yonitvat, and athato brahma jijnasa of the Vedanta-sutra, but when you explain them in your own way it becomes difficult for Me to follow them. The purpose of the sutras is already explained in them, but your explanations are covering them with something else. You do not purposely take the direct meaning of the sutras but indirectly give your own interpretations." The Lord thus attacked all Vedantists who interpret the Vedanta-sutra fashionably, according to their limited power of thinking, to serve their own purpose. Such indirect interpretations of the authentic literatures like the Vedanta-sutra are hereby condemned by the Lord. The Lord*

*continued: "Srila Vyasadeva has summarized the direct meanings of the mantras in the Upanisads in the Vedanta-sutra. Unfortunately you do not take their direct meaning. You indirectly interpret them in a different way."* [S.B. Intro]

Note: Narayana Maharaja at first accepts the direct meaning of the words 'Krishna bhuli':

[Narayana Maharaja]: We are eternally Krishna dasa, servants of Krishna, but now we are Krishna bhuli; we have forgotten Him. The words 'Krishna bhuli' are used here. It means 'the jiva forgets Krishna',

Note: He then proceeds to give his indirect interpretation:

[Narayana Maharaja]: but what does this actually mean? It seems to mean that the jiva was once engaged in Krishna's service, but now he has forgotten that service. Actually, this is not true. This is not the meaning. There is defect in worldly languages. They are not perfect, and therefore they cannot purely express what is the nature of our svarupa (constitutional form). To clarify the meaning of 'Krishna bhuli', Srila Krishnadasa Kaviraja Gosvami writes in the next line, "krsnera 'tatastha'sakti' 'bhedabheda-prakasa.'"

Note: Such indirect interpretations of the authentic literatures like Caitanya-caritamrta is condemned by the Lord. Narayana Maharaja then makes the great offense of saying the Lords words are worldly or more clearly material and that the Lord is not able to express purely the nature of our svarupa (constitutional form). This is very nicely refuted as follows:

*Yogesvara: For them the word nirvana means an end but an end to this material existence and an entrance into the silence of the Absolute, onto a level that is real, whereas this one is false. This one is rejected.*
*Prabhupada: Why silence?*
*Yogesvara: He says the term "entering into silence" is a mystic term that means...*
*Prabhupada: **He cannot explain.** (break)*
*Yogesvara: ...**it is undescribable because it's something that's arrived at inside through meditation. You can't really describe it in words?***
*Prabhupada: **Why? You are describing so many thing in words and the ultimate goal you cannot describe.***
*Yogesvara: He says that many great masters like you from the East tend to smile at their explanations, but he...*
*Guru Gauranga: They tend to smile when this question is asked, "Who am I?" So what can I say compared to these masters?*
*Prabhupada: That means his knowledge is not perfect.*
*Guru Gauranga: His knowledge is not perfect, and like us, he is simply trying for perfect knowledge.*
*Prabhupada: **So unless you have got your goal perfectly known, how you can make progress?***
*[S.P. Room Conversation, with Rosicrucians, August 13, 1973, Paris]*

Note: The nature of our svarupa is very clearly described by Srila Prabhupada (See the section "The Constitutional Position Of The Living Entity")

Narayana Maharaja then finally becomes ludicrous and says "krsnera 'tatastha'sakti' 'bhedabheda-prakasa.'" is the next line of 'Krishna bhuli', when factually it is from a completely different sloka!!!

*TRANSLATION:* **"Sripada Sankaracarya has described all the Vedic literatures in terms of indirect meanings. One who hears such explanations is ruined.** *Sankaracarya is not at fault, for he has thus covered the real purpose of the Vedas under the order of the Supreme Personality of Godhead.*

*PURPORT:* **The Vedic literature is to be considered a source of real knowledge, but if one does not take it as it is, one will be misled.** *For example, the Bhagavad-gita is an important book of Vedic literature that has been taught for many years, but because it was commented upon by unscrupulous rascals, people derived no benefit from it, and no one came to the conclusion of Krishna consciousness. Since the purpose of the Bhagavad-gita is now being presented as it is, however, within four or five short years thousands of people all over the world have become Krishna conscious. That is the difference between direct and indirect explanations of the Vedic literature. Therefore Sri Caitanya Mahaprabhu said, mukhya-vrttye sei artha parama mahattva: "To teach the Vedic literature according to its direct meaning, without false commentary, is glorious." Unfortunately, Sri Sankaracarya, by the order of the Supreme Personality of Godhead, compromised between atheism and theism in order to cheat the atheists and bring them to theism, and to do so* **he gave up the direct method of Vedic knowledge and tried to present a meaning which is indirect.** *It is with this purpose that he wrote his Sariraka-bhasya commentary on the Vedanta-sutra.......* **Srila Bhaktisiddhanta Sarasvati Thakura comments that mukhya-vrtti ("the direct meaning") is abhidha-vrtti, or the meaning that one can understand immediately from the statements of dictionaries, whereas gauna-vrtti ("the indirect meaning") is a meaning that one imagines without consulting the dictionary.** *For example, one politician has said that Kuruksetra refers to the body, but in the dictionary there is no such definition.* **Therefore this imaginary meaning is gauna-vrtti, whereas the direct meaning found in the dictionary is mukhya-vrtti or abhidha-vrtti. This is the distinction between the two.** <u>**Sri Caitanya Mahaprabhu recommends that one understand the Vedic literature in terms of abhidha-vrtti, and the gauna-vrtti He rejects.**</u> *Sometimes, however, as a matter of necessity, the Vedic literature is described in terms of the laksana-vrtti or gauna-vrtti, but one should not accept such explanations as permanent truths.  The purpose of the discussions in the Upanisads and Vedanta-sutra is to philosophically establish the personal feature of the Absolute Truth.* **The impersonalists, however, in order to establish their philosophy, accept these discussions in terms of laksana-vrtti, or indirect meanings.** *(Caitanya-caritamrta Adi 7.109-110)*

Note: Narayana Maharaja has described Srila Prabhupada's books in terms of indirect meanings. One who hears such explanations is ruined. Srila Prabhupada's books are to be considered a source of real knowledge, but if one does not take it as it is, one will be misled. Narayana Maharaja gave up the direct method of Vedic knowledge and tried to present a meaning which is indirect. Srila Bhaktisiddhanta Sarasvati Thakura comments that mukhya-vrtti ("the direct meaning") is abhidha-vrtti, or the meaning that one can understand immediately from the statements of dictionaries, whereas gauna-vrtti ("the indirect meaning") is a meaning that one imagines without consulting the dictionary. For example, one politician has said that Kuruksetra refers to the body, but in the dictionary there is no such definition. Therefore this imaginary meaning is gauna-vrtti, whereas the direct meaning found in the dictionary is mukhya-vrtti or abhidha-vrtti. This is the distinction between the two. Sri Caitanya Mahaprabhu recommends that one understand the Vedic literature in terms of abhidha-vrtti, (Srila Prabhupada's direct purports) and the gauna-vrtti (the interpretations of Narayana Maharaja) He rejects. The impersonalists, (Narayana Maharaja and his followers) however, in order to establish their philosophy, accept these discussions in terms of laksana-vrtti, or indirect meanings.

TRANSLATION: *"You do not explain the direct meaning of the Brahma-sutras. Indeed, it appears that your business is to cover their real meaning."*

PURPORT: **This is typical of all Mayavadis or atheists who interpret the meaning of Vedic literature in their own imaginative way. The real purpose of such foolish people is to impose the impersonalist conclusion on all Vedic literature.** *The Mayavadi atheists also interpret the Bhagavad-gita. In every verse of Srimad Bhagavad-gita it is clearly stated that Krishna is the Supreme Personality of Godhead. In every verse Vyasadeva says, sri-bhagavan uvaca, "the Supreme Personality of Godhead said," or "the Blessed Lord said." It is clearly stated that the Blessed Lord is the Supreme Person, but Mayavadi atheists still try to prove that the Absolute Truth is impersonal.* **In order to present their false, imaginary meanings, they must adopt so much word jugglery and grammatical interpretation that they finally become ludicrous.** <u>**Therefore Sri Caitanya Mahaprabhu remarked that no one should hear the Mayavadi commentaries or purports to any Vedic literature.**</u> *(Caitanya-caritamrta Mad. 6.132)*

Note: Narayana Maharaja does not explain the direct meaning of Vedic literature like Srila Prabhupada's books. Indeed, it appears that his business is to cover their real meaning. This is typical of all Mayavadis or atheists who interpret the meaning of Vedic literature in their own imaginative way. The real purpose of such foolish people is to impose the impersonalist conclusion on all Vedic literature. In order to present their false, imaginary meanings, they must adopt so much word jugglery and grammatical interpretation that they finally become ludicrous. Therefore Sri Caitanya Mahaprabhu remarked that no one should hear the Mayavadi commentaries or purports such as those by Narayana Maharaja, to any Vedic literature.

*TRANSLATION "**For each sutra the direct meaning must be accepted without interpretation**. However, you simply abandon the direct meaning and proceed with your imaginative interpretation... Although there is other evidence, the evidence given in the Vedic version must be taken as foremost. **Vedic versions understood directly are first-class evidence.**"*

*PURPORT: Works that should be consulted are Srila Jiva Gosvami's Tattva-sandarbha (10-11), Srila Baladeva Vidyabhusana's commentary on that, and the following verses of the Brahma-sutra: sastra-yonitvat (1.1.3), tarkapratisthanat (2.1.11) and srutes tu sabda-mulatvat (2.1.27), as commented upon by Sri Ramanujacarya, Sri Madhvacarya, Sri Nimbarkacarya and Srila Baladeva Vidyabhusana. In his book Sarva-samvadini, Srila Jiva Gosvami has noted that although there are ten kinds of evidence--direct perception, the Vedic version, historical reference, hypothesis, and so on--and although they are all generally accepted as evidence, the person presenting a hypothesis, reading the Vedic version, perceiving or interpreting by his experience is certain to be imperfect in four ways. That is, he is subject to commiting mistakes, to becoming illusioned, to cheating and to having imperfect senses. Although the evidence may be correct, the person himself is in danger of being misled due to his material defects. Apart from the direct presentation, there is a chance that an interpretation may not be perfect. **Therefore the conclusion is that only a direct presentation can be considered evidence. An interpretation cannot be accepted as evidence, but may be considered proof of evidence**. In the Bhagavad-gita, at the very beginning it is stated:*

*dhrtarastra uvaca
dharma-ksetre kuru-ksetre
samaveta yuyutsavah
mamakah pandavas caiva
kim akurvata sanjaya*

*The statements of the Bhagavad-gita are themselves proof that there is a place of religious pilgrimage named Kuruksetra where the Pandavas and Kurus met to fight. After meeting there, what did they do? This was Dhrtarastra's inquiry to Sanjaya. **Although these statements are very clear, atheists try to interpret different meanings of the words dharma-ksetra and kuru-ksetra. Therefore Srila Jiva Gosvami has warned us not to depend on any kind of interpretation. It is better to take the verses as they are, without interpretation**. (Caitanya-caritamrta Mad. 6.134-35)*

Note: For each sutra the direct meaning must be accepted without interpretation. However, Narayana Maharaja simply abandons the direct meaning and proceeds with his imaginative interpretation. Therefore the conclusion is that only a direct presentation can be considered evidence. An interpretation cannot be accepted as evidence, but may be considered proof of evidence. Although the statements "Krishna bhuli' sei jiva anadi-bahirmukha - Forgetting Krishna, the living entity has been attracted by the external feature from time immemorial" are very clear, atheists like Narayana Maharaja try to interpret different meanings of the words Krishna bhuli. Therefore Srila Jiva Gosvami has warned us not to depend on any kind of interpretation. It is better to take the verses as they are, without interpretation.

* Another very important point in regards to evidence. You may recall the very offensive statement:

[Srila Narayana Maharaja:] I know. I have read them. Srila Swami Maharaja sometimes gave baby food to babies. When I give a baby medicine like quinine, I tell him, "Baby, baby, it is very sweet." I'm telling him something that is not true so that I can give him the medicine. Similarly, Srila Swami Maharaja has written to someone who was very low in bhakti. A letter cannot always be proof. What Srila Swami Maharaja has written in Caitanya-caritamrta and in his Gita and Bhagavata explanation is authentic. These are proofs. He can write something else for a little baby, but it is not proof.

Note: Here is one of those letters:

### Crow And Tal-Fruit Logic

*"We never had any occasion when we were separated from Krishna. Just like one man is dreaming and he forgets himself. In dream he creates himself in different forms: now I am the King discussing like that. This creation of himself is as seer and subject matter or seen, two things. But as soon as the dream is over, the "seen" disappears. But the seer remains. Now he is in his original position.*

*Our separation from Krishna is like that. We dream this body and so many relationships with other things. First the attachment comes to enjoy sense gratification. Even with Krishna desire for sense gratification is there. There is a dormant attitude for forgetting Krishna and creating an atmosphere for enjoying independently. Just like at the edge of the beach, sometimes the water covers, sometimes there is dry sand, coming and going. Our position is like that, sometimes covered, sometimes free, just like at the edge of the tide. As soon as we forget, immediately the illusion is there. Just like as soon as we sleep, dream is there.*

*We cannot say therefore that we are not with Krishna. As soon as we try to become Lord, immediately we are covered by Maya. Formerly we were with Krishna in His lila or sport. But this covering of Maya may be of very, very, very, very long duration, therefore many creations are coming and going. Due to this long period of time it is sometimes said that we are ever-conditioned. But his long duration of time becomes very insignificant when one actually comes to Krishna consciousness. Just like in a dream we are thinking very long time, but as soon as we awaken we look at our watch and see it has been a moment only. Just like with*

*Krishna's friends, they were kept asleep for one year by Brahma, but when they woke up and Krishna returned before them, they considered that only a moment had passed.*

*So this dreaming condition is called non-liberated life, and this is just like a dream. Although in this material calculation it is a long, long period, as soon as we come to Krishna consciousness then this period is considered as a second. For example, Jaya and Vijaya. They had their lila with Krishna, but they had to come down for their little mistake. They were given mukti, emerging into the Brahmasayujya after being killed three times as demons. This Brahmasayujya mukti is non-permanent. Every living entity wants pleasure, but Brahmasayujya is minus pleasure. There is eternal existence only. So when they do not find transcendental bliss, they fall down to make a compromise with material bliss. Just like Vivekananda founded so many schools and hospitals. So even Lord Brahma, he is still material and wants to lord it over. He may come down to become a germ, but then he may rise up to Krishna consciousness and go back to home, back to Godhead. This is the position.*

**So when I say Yes, there is eternal lila with Krishna, that means on the evidence of Jaya-Vijaya.** *Unless one develops full devotional service to Krishna, he goes up only up to Brahmasayujya but falls down. But after millions and millions of years of keeping oneself away from the lila of the Lord, when one comes to Krishna consciousness this period becomes insignificant, just like dreaming.* **_Because he falls down from Brahmasayujya, he thinks that may be his origin, but he does not remember that before that even he was with Krishna._** *So the conclusion is that whatever may be our past, let us come to Krishna consciousness and immediately join Krishna. Just like with a diseased man, it is a waste of time to try to find out how he has become diseased, better to spend time curing the disease.*

*On the top of the tree there is a nice tal-fruit. A crow went there and the fruit fell down, Some panditas, big big learned scholars saw this and discussed: the fruit fell due to the crow agitating the limb. No, the fruit fell simultaneously with the crow landing and frightened the crow so he flew away. No, the fruit was ripe and the weight of the crow landing broke it from the branch, and so on and so on. What is the use of such discussions? So whether you were in the Brahmasayujya or with Krishna in His lila, at the moment you are in neither, so the best policy is to develop your Krishna consciousness and go there, never mind what is your origin.*

**Brahmasayujya and Krishna lila--both may be possible, but when you are coming down from Brahmasayujya or when you are coming down from Krishna lila, that remains a mystery.** *But at the present moment we are in Maya's clutches, so at present our only hope is to become Krishna conscious and go back to Home, back to Godhead. The real position is servant of Krishna, and servant of Krishna means in Krishna lila. Directly or indirectly, always we are serving Krishna's lila. Even in dream. Just like we cannot go out of the sun when it is daytime, so where is the chance of going out of Krishna lila? The cloud may be there, it may become* *very gray and dim, but still the sunlight is there, everywhere, during the daytime. Because I am part and parcel of Krishna, I am always connected. My finger, even though it may be diseased, remains part and parcel of my body. Therefore, we try to treat it, cure it, because it is part and parcel. So Krishna comes Himself when we forget Him, or He sends His representative.*

*Awakening or dreaming, I am the same man. As soon as I awaken and see myself, I see Krishna. Cause and effect are both Krishna. Just like cotton becomes thread and thread becomes cloth, still, the original cause is cotton. Therefore, everything is Krishna in the ultimate sense. When we cannot contact Krishna personally, we contact His energies. So there is no chance to be outside Krishna's lila. But differences we see under different conditions. Just like in the pool of water and in the mirror the same me is reflecting, but in different reflections. One is shimmering, unsteady, one is clear and fixed. Except for being in Krishna consciousness, we cannot see our actual position rightly, therefore the learned man sees all living entities as the same parts and parcels of Krishna. Material existence is impersonal because my real personality is covered. But we should think that because I am now covered by this clay, I am diseased, and we should think that I must get to business to get myself uncovered, not wonder how I got this way. Now the fruit is there, take it and enjoy, that is your first business. God is not bound by cause. He can change, He is the Cause of all Causes. Now don't waste your time with this "Kaka taliya nyaya," crows and tal-fruit logic." (S.P. Letter to: Unknown, Unknown Place, Unknown Date)*

Note: Only a direct presentation can be considered evidence, therefore Narayana Maharaja's interpretation of the words 'Krishna bhuli' cannot be accepted as evidence, as they are indirect and oppose the principles of scripture.

*"To such a misguided interpreter we may reply, "Why should you suggest such fallacious logic?* **An interpretation is never accepted as evidence if it opposes the principles of scripture.***" (Caitanya-caritamrta Adi. 2.73)*

Note: We have to take the mukhya-vrtti ("the direct meaning"), or the meaning that one can understand immediately from the statements of dictionaries. The direct meaning of the words Krishna bhuli' is forgetting Krishna.

Therefore Srila Prabhupada's statements in the above letter, namely: [We never had any occasion when we were separated from Krishna. Just like one man is dreaming and he forgets himself... Even with Krishna desire for sense gratification is there. There is a dormant attitude for forgetting Krishna and creating an atmosphere for enjoying independently... We cannot say therefore that we are not with Krishna. As soon as we try to become Lord, immediately we are covered by Maya. Formerly we were with Krishna in His lila or sport.] are identical to the direct statement of the Lord in Caitanya-caritamrta "Krishna bhuli' sei jiva anadi-bahirmukha ataeva maya tare deya samsara-duhkha "Forgetting Krishna, the living entity has been attracted by the external feature from time immemorial. Therefore,

the illusory energy (maya) gives him all kinds of misery in his material existence."
*(Cc Madhya 20.117)*

The statement "Formerly we were with Krishna in His lila or sport." is also identical to the direct statement of the Lord in Caitanya-caritamrta "It is the living entity's constitutional position to be an eternal servant of Krishna because he is the marginal energy of Krishna and a manifestation simultaneously one with and different from the Lord" *(Cc Madhya 20.108-109)*

Therefore Srila Prabhupada's letters are DIRECT EVIDENCE and Narayana Maharaja's statements are extremely offensive!!!

### 3. Forgotten Krishna, We Fallen Souls.

In this section there are quotes about forgetting Krishna, I have only presented a few as there are too many to mention at this time.

*"So Srila Bhaktisiddhanta Sarasvati Thakura knew this art, how to turn our activities for the satisfaction of Krishna. This is Krishna consciousness movement. Therefore I... "Wonder thy ways to turn our face, adore they feet, Your Divine Grace. **Forgotten Krishna, we fallen souls.**" Why we are fallen? **Because we have forgotten. Our relationship with Krishna is eternal.** Unless it was eternal, how you Western peoples could be devotee of Krishna? Artificially you cannot be a devotee of Krishna. **The relationship is there eternally.** Nitya-siddha Krishna-bhakti. By the process it is now awakened. Sravanadi-suddha-citte karaye udaya. It is awakened. Love between young man and young (wo)man, it is not artificial. It is there. But by certain circumstantially, environment, the love becomes manifest. **Similarly, our love for Krishna, relationship with Krishna, is eternal.** Jivera svarupa haya nitya Krishna-dasa. But we have to create such situation--that eternal relation should be awakened. That is the art. That is wanted."* (His Divine Grace, Srila Bhaktisiddhanta Sarasvati Gosvami Prabhupada's, Disappearance Day, Lecture, Hyderabad, December 10, 1976)

*TRANSLATION: "**Forgetting Krishna, the living entity has been attracted by the external feature from time immemorial**. Therefore the illusory energy [maya] gives him all kinds of misery in his material existence.*

*PURPORT: When the living entity **forgets his constitutional position as an eternal servant of Krishna**, he is immediately entrapped by the illusory, external energy. The living entity is originally part and parcel of Krishna and is therefore the superior energy of Krishna. He is endowed with inconceivable minute energy that works inconceivably within the body. However, the living entity, forgetting his position, is situated in material energy. The living entity is called the marginal energy because by nature he is spiritual but by forgetfulness he is situated in the material energy. Thus he has the power to live either in the material energy or in* *the spiritual energy, and for this reason he is called marginal energy. He is sometimes attracted by the external illusory energy when he stays in the marginal position, and this is the beginning of his material life. When he enters the material energy, he is subjected to the threefold time measurement--past, present and future. Past, present and future belong only to the material world; they do not exist in the spiritual world. The living entity is eternal, and he existed before the creation of this material world.* **Unfortunately he has forgotten his relationship with Krishna.** *The living entity's forgetfulness is described herein as anadi, which indicates that it has existed since time immemorial. One should understand that due to his desire to enjoy himself in competition with Krishna, the living entity comes into material existence. (C.C. Mad. 20.117)*

Note: If we follow the spiritual authorities and take the mukhya-vrtti ("the direct meaning") of this verse, it is very clear that we have an eternal relationship with Krishna, but have now forgotten that constitutional position. If we try to present some indirect meaning of this verse, as Narayana Maharaja has done, then that is Mayavadi deviation!

*"The svarupa, or actual identification of the living entity, is described by Sri Caitanya Mahaprabhu as jivera 'svarupa' haya-krsnera 'nitya-dasa'.* **The conditioned soul has forgotten the real activities of his original position.** *However, this is not the case with Krishna. Krishna's name and His person are identical." [C.C. Mad. 17.132]*

*"Therefore Bhagavad-gita is best understood by a person who has qualities similar to Arjuna's. That is to say he must be a devotee in a direct relationship with the Lord. That is a very elaborate subject matter, but briefly it can be stated that a devotee is in a relationship with the Supreme Personality of Godhead in one of five different ways:*

*1. One may be a devotee in a passive state;*
*2. One may be a devotee in an active state;*
*3. One may be a devotee as a friend;*
*4. One may be a devotee as a parent;*
*5. One may be a devotee as a conjugal lover.*

*Arjuna was in a relationship with the Lord as friend. Of course there is a gulf of difference between this friendship and the friendship found in the material world. This is transcendental friendship which cannot be had by everyone.* ***Of course everyone has a particular relationship with the Lord, and that relationship is evoked by the perfection of devotional service. But in the present status of our life,*** ***we have not only forgotten the Supreme Lord, but we have forgotten our*** ***eternal relationship with the Lord.*** ***Every living being, out of many, many billions and trillions of living beings, has a particular relationship with the Lord eternally. That is called svarupa. By the process of devotional service, one can*** *revive that svarupa, and that stage is called svarupa-siddhi--perfection of one's constitutional position. So Arjuna was a devotee, and he was in touch with the Supreme Lord in friendship." [B.G. Intro]*

*"Because Caitanya Mahaprabhu says: jivera svarupa haya nitya-Krishna-dasa. Every living entity is eternal servant of Krishna. When he forgets Krishna he becomes servant of maya. That is our position. We have to serve. Therefore self-realization means to understand oneself that "I am dependent on Krishna. I am eternal servant of Krishna, let me engage myself to the service of the Lord." That is perfection of knowledge. Thank you very much." [Bhagavad-gita Lecture, 13.3, Paris, August 11, 1973]*

*"When a man in the material world takes more interest in the materialistic way of life than in Krishna consciousness, he is considered to be in a diseased condition. The normal condition is to remain an eternal servant of the Lord (jivera 'svarupa' haya--krsnera 'nitya-dasa'). This healthy condition is lost when the living entity forgets Krishna due to being attracted by the external features of Krishna's maya energy." [NOI 7]*

### 4. The Constitutional Position Of The Living Entity.

*"If the mind is purified by Krishna consciousness, one will naturally in the future get a body that is spiritual and full of Krishna consciousness. Such a body is our original form, as Sri Caitanya Mahaprabhu confirms, jivera 'svarupa' haya--krsnera 'nitya-dasa': "Every living entity is constitutionally an eternal servant of Krishna." [Srimad Bhagavatam 4.29.65]*

*"The rasas are exchanged between members of the same species. But as far as the spirit souls are concerned, they are one qualitatively with the Supreme Lord. Therefore, the rasas were originally exchanged between the spiritual living being and the spiritual whole, the Supreme Personality of Godhead. The spiritual exchange or rasa is fully exhibited in spiritual existence between living beings and the Supreme Lord. The Supreme Personality of Godhead is therefore described in the sruti-mantras, Vedic hymns, as "the fountainhead of all rasas." When one associates with the Supreme Lord and exchanges one's constitutional rasa with the Lord, then the living being is actually happy. These sruti-mantras indicate that every living being has its constitutional position, which is endowed with a particular type of rasa to be exchanged with the Personality of Godhead." [S.B. 1.1.3]*

*TRANSLATION: The merging of the living entity, along with his conditional living tendency, with the mystic lying down of the Maha-Visnu is called the winding up of the cosmic manifestation. Liberation is the permanent situation of the form of the living entity after he gives up the changeable gross and subtle material bodies.*

PURPORT: *As we have discussed several times, there are two types of living entities. Most of them are ever liberated, or nitya-muktas, while some of them are ever conditioned. The ever-conditioned souls are apt to develop a mentality of lording over the material nature, and therefore the material cosmic creation is manifested to give the ever-conditioned souls two kinds of facilities. One facility is that the conditioned soul can act according to his tendency to lord it over the cosmic manifestation, and the other facility gives the conditioned soul a chance to come back to Godhead. So after the winding up of the cosmic manifestation, most of the conditioned souls merge into the existence of the Maha-Visnu Personality of Godhead, lying in His mystic slumber, to be created again in the next creation. But some of the conditioned souls, who follow the transcendental sound in the form of Vedic literatures and* **are thus able to go back to Godhead,** __attain__ __spiritual and original bodies__ *after* **quitting the conditional gross and subtle material bodies.** *The material conditional bodies develop out of the living entities'* **forgetfulness of their relationship with Godhead,** *and during the course of the cosmic manifestation, the conditioned souls are given a chance to revive their original status of life with the help of revealed scriptures, so mercifully compiled by the Lord in His different incarnations. Reading or hearing of such transcendental literatures helps one become liberated even in the conditional state of material existence. All the Vedic literatures aim at devotional service to the Personality of Godhead, and as soon as one is fixed upon this point, he at once becomes liberated from conditional life. The material gross and subtle forms are simply due to the conditioned soul's ignorance and as soon as he is fixed in the devotional service of the Lord, he becomes eligible to be freed from the conditioned state. This devotional service is transcendental attraction for the Supreme on account of His being the source of all pleasing humors. Everyone is after some pleasure of humor for enjoyment, but does not know the supreme source of all attraction (raso vai sah rasam hy evayam labdhvanandi bhavati). The Vedic hymns inform everyone about the supreme source of all pleasure; the unlimited fountainhead of all pleasure is the Personality of Godhead, and one who is fortunate enough to get this information through transcendental literatures like Srimad-Bhagavatam becomes permanently liberated to occupy* **his proper place in the kingdom of God.** *[S.B. 2.10.6]*

*"Therefore the embodied soul, by his immemorial desire to avoid Krishna consciousness, causes his own bewilderment. Consequently, although* **he is constitutionally eternal, blissful and cognizant,** *due to the littleness of his existence he forgets his constitutional position of service to the Lord and is thus entrapped by nescience. And, under the spell of ignorance, the living entity claims that the Lord is responsible for his conditional existence."* *[B.G. 5.15]*

*"In the Srimad-Bhagavatam, real devotional liberation is defined as the reinstatement of the living entity in his own identity, his own constitutional position. The constitutional position is already explained: every living entity is the part and parcel fragmental portion of the Supreme Lord.* **Therefore his**

*constitutional position is to serve. After liberation, this service is never stopped. Actual liberation is getting free from misconceptions of life."* [B.G. 18.55]

TRANSLATION: *O friends, just think of His wives, whose hands He has accepted. How they must have undergone vows, baths, fire sacrifices and perfect worship of the Lord of the universe to constantly relish now the nectar from His lips [by kissing]. The damsels of Vrajabhumi would often faint just by expecting such favors.*

PURPORT: *Religious rites prescribed in the scriptures are meant to purify the mundane qualities of the conditioned souls to enable them to be gradually promoted to the stage of rendering transcendental service unto the Supreme Lord.* **Attainment of this stage of pure spiritual life is the highest perfection, and this stage is called svarupa, or** *the factual identity of the living being.* **Liberation means** *renovation of this stage of svarupa.* **In that perfect stage of svarupa, the living being is established in five phases of loving service, one of which is the stage of madhurya-rasa, or the humor of conjugal love.** *The Lord is always perfect in Himself, and thus He has no hankering for Himself. He, however, becomes a master, a friend, a son or a husband to fulfill the intense love of the devotee concerned. Herein two classes of devotees of the Lord are mentioned in the stage of conjugal love. One is svakiya, and the other is parakiya. Both of them are in conjugal love with the Personality of Godhead Krishna. The queens at Dvaraka were svakiya, or duly married wives, but the damsels of Vraja were young friends of the Lord while He was unmarried. The Lord stayed at Vrndavana till the age of sixteen, and His friendly relations with the neighboring girls were in terms of parakiya. These girls, as well as the queens, underwent severe penances by taking vows, bathing and offering sacrifices in the fire, as prescribed in the scriptures. The rites, as they are, are not an end in themselves, nor are fruitive action, culture of knowledge or perfection in mystic powers ends in themselves.* **They are all means to attain to the highest stage of svarupa, to render constitutional transcendental service to the Lord.** *Each and every living being has his individual position in one of the above-mentioned five different kinds of reciprocating means with the Lord, and in one's pure spiritual form of svarupa the relation becomes manifest without mundane affinity.* *The kissing of the Lord, either by His wives or His young girl friends who aspired to have the Lord as their fiance, is not of any mundane perverted quality. Had such things been mundane, a liberated soul like Sukadeva would not have taken the trouble to relish them, nor would Lord Sri Caitanya Mahaprabhu have been inclined to participate in those subjects after renouncing worldly life. The stage is earned after many lives of penance.* [S.B. 1.10.28]

TRANSLATION: *The living entities in this conditioned world are My eternal, fragmental parts. Due to conditioned life, they are struggling very hard with the six senses, which include the mind.*
PURPORT: **In this verse the identity of the living being is clearly given.** *The living entity is the fragmental part and parcel of the Supreme Lord--eternally. It is*

*not that he assumes individuality in his conditional life and in his liberated state becomes one with the Supreme Lord. He is eternally fragmented. It is clearly said, sanatanah. According to the Vedic version, the Supreme Lord manifests and expands Himself in innumerable expansions, of which the primary expansions are called visnu-tattva and the secondary expansions are called the living entities. In other words, the visnu-tattva is the personal expansion, and the living entities are separated expansions. By His personal expansion, He is manifested in various forms like Lord Rama, Nrsimhadeva, Visnumurti and all the predominating Deities in the Vaikuntha planets. **The separated expansions, the living entities, are eternally servitors.** The personal expansions of the Supreme Personality of Godhead, the individual identities of the Godhead, are always present. Similarly, the separated expansions of living entities have their identities. As fragmental parts and parcels of the Supreme Lord, the living entities have also fragmental qualities, of which independence is one. Every living entity has an individual soul, his personal individuality and a minute form of independence. By misuse of that independence, one becomes a conditioned soul, and by proper use of independence he is always liberated. In either case, he is qualitatively eternal, as the Supreme Lord is. In his liberated state he is freed from this material condition, and he is under the engagement of transcendental service unto the Lord; in his conditional life he is dominated by the material modes of nature, and he forgets the transcendental loving service of the Lord. As a result, he has to struggle very hard to maintain his existence in the material world...*

**It is stated here that when a living entity gives up this material embodiment and enters into the spiritual world, <u>he revives his spiritual body</u>, and in his spiritual body he can see the Supreme Personality of Godhead face to face.** *He can hear and speak to Him face to face, and he can understand the Supreme Personality as He is. In smrti also it is understood that in the spiritual planets everyone lives in bodies featured like the Supreme Personality of Godhead's. As far as bodily construction is concerned, there is no difference between the part and parcel living entities and the expansions of visnu-murti. In other words, at liberation the living entity gets a spiritual body by the grace of the Supreme Personality of Godhead.*

*The word mamaivamsah (fragmental parts and parcels of the Supreme Lord) is also very significant. The fragmental portion of the Supreme Lord is not like some material broken part. We have already understood in the Second Chapter that the spirit cannot be cut into pieces. This fragment is not materially conceived. It is not like matter, which can be cut into pieces and joined together again. That conception is not applicable here because the Sanskrit word sanatana (eternal) is used. The fragmental portion is eternal. It is also stated in the beginning of the Second Chapter that (dehino 'smin yatha) in each and every individual body, the fragmental portion of the Supreme Lord is present.* **That fragmental portion, when liberated from the bodily entanglement, <u>revives its original spiritual body in the spiritual sky in a spiritual planet and enjoys association with the Supreme Lord</u>.** *It is, however, understood here that the living entity, being the fragmental* *part and parcel of the Supreme Lord, is qualitatively one, just as the parts and parcels of gold are also gold. [Bhagavad-gita 15.7]*

*TRANSLATION: In this way the conditioned soul living within the body forgets his self-interest because he identifies himself with the body. Because the body is material, his natural tendency is to be attracted by the varieties of the material world. Thus the living entity suffers the miseries of material existence.*

*PURPORT: Everyone is trying to be happy because, as explained in the previous verse, sukham asyatmano rupam sarvehoparatis tanuh:* **when the living entity is in his original spiritual form,** *he is happy by nature. There is no question of miseries for the spiritual being. As Krishna is always happy, the living entities, who are His parts and parcels, are also happy by nature, but because of being put within this material world and* **forgetting their eternal relationship with Krishna, they have forgotten their real nature. Because every one of us is a part of Krishna, we have a very affectionate relationship with Him,** *but because we have* **forgotten our identities** *and are considering the body to be the self, we are afflicted by all the troubles of birth, death, old age and disease. This misconception in materialistic life continues unless and until one comes to understand his relationship with Krishna. The happiness sought by the conditioned soul is certainly only illusion, as explained in the next verse. [S.B. 7.13.28]*

*"Therefore, the Lord is rarely seen by them, but the inhabitants of Dvaraka, because of their being pure devotees without any tinge of the material contamination of fruitive activities and empiric philosophical speculation,* **can see Him face to face by the grace of the Lord. This is the original state of the living entities and can be attained by reviving our natural and constitutional state of life, which is discovered by devotional service only."** *[S.B. 1.11.8]*

*"In these four verses, Rsabhadeva tells His sons how they can be freed from the false identification arising from false ego and material conditional life. One gradually becomes liberated by practicing as mentioned above.* **All these prescribed methods enable one to give up the material body (lingam vyapohet) and be situated in his original spiritual body.** *First of all one has to accept a bona fide spiritual master. This is advocated by Srila Rupa Gosvami in his Bhakti-rasamrta-sindhu: sri-guru-padasrayah. To be freed from the entanglement of the material world, one has to approach a spiritual master." [S.B. 5.5.10-13]*

*TRANSLATION: Upon seeing the Visnudutas, Ajamila gave up his material body at Hardwar on the bank of the Ganges.* **He regained his original spiritual body, which was a body appropriate for an associate of the Lord.**
*PURPORT; The Lord says in Bhagavad-gita (4.9):*

*janma karma ca me divyam*
*evam yo vetti tattvatah*
*tyaktva deham punar janma*
*naiti mam eti so 'rjuna*

*"One who knows the transcendental nature of My appearance and activities does not, upon leaving the body, take his birth again in this material world, but attains My eternal abode, O Arjuna."* **The result of perfection in Krishna consciousness is that after giving up one's material body, one is immediately transferred to the spiritual world in <u>one's original spiritual body</u> to become an associate of the Supreme Personality of Godhead.** *Some devotees go to Vaikunthaloka, and others go to Goloka Vrndavana to become associates of Krishna. [S.B. 6.2.43]*

*Hrdayananda: (translating question) He says if we practice Krishna consciousness and develop a spiritual body, is there also a... Which spirit animates the spiritual body?*
*Prabhupada: Yes, we'll get spiritual body. <u>Spiritual body is already there; it is simply covered by material body</u>. You have to cure this material body. <u>Then you get your original, spiritual body</u>. It is curing process. Just like one has got fever. Fever is not permanent--temporary. But cure this fever; then you healthy. [Bhagavad-gita 2.14, Mexico, February 14, 1975]*

*"The constitutional position of a living entity, represented by Arjuna, is that he has to act according to the order of the Supreme Lord. He is meant for self-discipline.* **Sri Caitanya Mahaprabhu says that the actual position of the living entity is that of eternal servant of the Supreme Lord. Forgetting this principle, the living entity becomes conditioned by material nature, but in serving the Supreme Lord, he becomes the liberated servant of God. <u>The living entity's constitutional position is to be a servitor</u>; he has to serve either the illusory maya or the Supreme Lord. <u>If he serves the Supreme Lord, he is in his normal condition</u>, but if he prefers to serve the illusory external energy, then certainly he will be in bondage."** *[B.G. 18.73]*

### 5. Tatastha Sakti, Or Marginal Potency Of The Lord.

In this section it will be clearly understood that constitutionally every living entity, even if he is in the Vaikuntha Loka, has chance of falling down. Therefore the living entity is called marginal energy.

*"The answer to your question about the marginal energy is that* **<u>the jiva soul is always called marginal energy whether he is in the spiritual world or in the material world</u>. There are instances where marginal energy jiva souls have fallen from the spiritual world, just like Jaya and Vijaya. So the potency to fall under the influence of the lower energy is always there. And thus the individual**

*jiva soul is called as Krishna's marginal energy.*" *[S.P. Letter to: Rayarama, Los Angeles, 2 December, 1968]*

"*Regarding your question, in one sense both you and Mahapurusa are right. The fact is that after the dissolution of the Universe the living entities remain in slumber within Maha Visnu, and again when the creation takes place they are impregnated in their original position and they come out in different species of life. By gradual evolutionary process, when they come to the human form there is good chance of getting out of the repeated birth and death, and one can enter into the Spiritual Realm. But if one loses this chance he is again put into the cycle of birth and death. The conditioned souls are always within the Maha Visnu Form, whereas the liberated souls in Vaikuntha, they are engaged in the service of the Lord.* **Constitutionally every living entity, even if he is in the Vaikuntha Loka, has chance of falling down. Therefore the living entity is called marginal energy.** *But when the falldown has taken place for the conditioned soul is very difficult to ascertain. Therefore two classes are designated: eternally liberated and eternally conditioned. But for arguments sake, a living entity being marginal energy, he can't be eternally conditioned. The Time is so unlimited that the conditioned souls appear to be eternally so, but from the philosophical view he cannot be eternally conditioned. Since we cannot trace out when we have become conditioned, there is no use of arguing on this point. Better to take care first how we can get rid of this conditional existence; as much as a patient should take care for treating his disease more, and less waste his time in finding out the cause of his disease.*"*[S.P. Letter to: Upendra, Tittenhurst, 27 October, 1969]*

"**The living entities, who are residents of the spiritual as well as the material expansions, are His marginal energy (tatastha-sakti), and they are at liberty to live in either of the energies, external or internal.** *Those who live within the spiritual expansion of the Lord are called liberated souls, whereas the residents of the external expansion are called the conditioned souls. We can just make an estimate of the number of the residents of the internal expansions in comparison with the number of residents in the external energy and may easily conclude that the liberated souls are far more numerous than the conditioned souls.*" *[S.B. 2.6.17]*

TRANSLATION: *Kindly describe how the Supreme Lord, who is all-powerful, engages His different energies and different expansions in maintaining and again winding up the phenomenal world in the sporting spirit of a player.*

PURPORT: *In the Katha Upanisad (2.2.13) the Supreme Lord is described as the chief eternal being amongst all other eternal individual beings (nityo nityanam cetanas cetananam) and the one Supreme Lord who maintains innumerable other individual living beings (eko bahunam yo vidadhati kaman). So all living entities, both in the conditioned state and in the liberated state, are maintained by the*

*Almighty Supreme Lord. Such maintenance is effected by the Lord through His different expansions of Self and three principal energies, namely the internal, external and marginal energies.* **The living entities are His marginal energies,** *and some of them, in the confidence of the Lord, are entrusted with the work of creation also, as are Brahma, Marici, etc., and the acts of creation are inspired by the Lord unto them (tene brahma hrda). The external energy (maya) is also impregnated with the jivas, or conditioned souls.* **The unconditioned marginal** **potency acts in the spiritual kingdom,** *and the Lord, by His different plenary* **expansions, maintains them in** **different transcendental relations displayed in** **the spiritual sky.** *So the one Supreme Personality of Godhead manifests Himself in many (bahu syam), and thus all diversities are in Him, and He is in all diversities, although He is nevertheless different from all of them. That is the inconceivable mystic power of the Lord, and as such everything is simultaneously one with and different from Him by His inconceivable potencies (acintya-bhedabheda-tattva). [S.B. 2.4.7]*

*TRANSLATION: Also, Srutadeva, Uddhava and others, Nanda, Sunanda and other leaders of liberated souls who are constant companions of the Lord are protected by Lord Balarama and Krishna. Are they all doing well in their respective functions? Do they, who are all eternally bound in friendship with us, remember our welfare?*

*PURPORT: The constant companions of Lord Krishna, such as Uddhava, are all liberated souls, and they descended along with Lord Krishna to this material world to fulfill the mission of the Lord. The Pandavas are also liberated souls who descended along with Lord Krishna to serve Him in His transcendental pastimes on this earth. As stated in the Bhagavad-gita (4.8), the Lord and His eternal associates, who are also liberated souls like the Lord, come down on this earth at certain intervals.* **The Lord remembers them all, but His associates, although liberated souls,** **forget due to their being tatastha sakti, or marginal potency of** **the Lord.** *That is the difference between the visnu-tattva and jiva-tattva. The jiva-tattvas are infinitesimal potential particles of the Lord, and therefore they require the protection of the Lord at all times. And to the eternal servitors of the Lord, the Lord is pleased to give all protection at all times. The liberated souls never, therefore, think themselves as free as the Lord or as powerful as the Lord,* **but they always seek the protection of the Lord in all circumstances, both in the material world and in the spiritual world.** *This dependence of the liberated soul is constitutional, for the liberated souls are like sparks of a fire that are able to exhibit the glow of fire along with the fire and not independently. Independently the glow of the sparks is extinguished, although the quality of fire or the glowing is there. Thus those who give up the protection of the Lord and become so-called lords themselves, out of spiritual ignorance, come back again to this material world, even after prolonged tapasya of the severest type. That is the verdict of all Vedic literature. [S.B. 1.14.32-33]*

### 6. Independence And Falldown.

*"The Supreme Personality of Godhead expanded Himself into many for His ever-increasing spiritual bliss, **and the living entities are parts and parcels of this <u>spiritual bliss</u>**. They also have partial independence, **but by misuse of their independence, when the service attitude is transformed into the propensity for sense enjoyment, they come under the sway of lust."** [B.G. 3.37]*

*"The Lord is one without a second, and He expands Himself into many for His transcendental pleasure. All the expansions--the visnu-tattvas, the jiva-tattvas and the sakti-tattvas (the Personalities of Godhead, the living entities and the different potential energies)--are different offshoots from the same one Supreme Lord. The jiva-tattvas are separated expansions of the visnu-tattvas, and although there are potential differences between them, they are all meant for the transcendental sense gratification of the Supreme Lord. Some of the jivas, however, wanted to lord it over material nature in imitation of the lordship of the Personality of Godhead. **Regarding when and why such propensities overcame the pure living entities, it can only be explained that the jiva-tattvas have infinitesimal independence and that due to misuse of this independence some of the living entities have become implicated in the conditions of cosmic creation and are therefore called nitya-baddhas, or eternally conditioned souls.** The expansions of Vedic wisdom also give the nitya-baddhas, the conditioned living entities, a chance to improve, and those who take advantage of such transcendental knowledge gradually <u>regain their lost consciousness of rendering transcendental loving service to the Lord.</u>"* [S.B. 3.5.51]

*TRANSLATION: The material ego springs up from the mahat-tattva, which evolved from the Lord's own energy. The material ego is endowed predominantly with active power of three kinds--good, passionate and ignorant. It is from these three types of material ego that the mind, the senses of perception, the organs of action, and the gross elements evolve.*

*PURPORT: **In the beginning, from clear consciousness, or the pure state of Krishna consciousness, the first contamination sprang up.** This is called false ego, or identification of the body as self. **The living entity exists in the natural state of Krishna consciousness, but he has marginal independence, and this allows him to forget Krishna. Originally, pure Krishna consciousness exists, but because of misuse of marginal independence there is a chance of forgetting Krishna.** This is exhibited in actual life; there are many instances in which someone acting in Krishna consciousness suddenly changes. In the Upanisads it is stated, therefore, that the path of spiritual realization is just like the sharp edge of a razor. The example is very appropriate. One shaves his cheeks with a sharp razor very nicely, but as soon as his attention is diverted from the activity, he immediately     cuts     his     cheek     because     he     mishandles     the     razor.*

*Not only must one come to the stage of pure Krishna consciousness, but one must also be very careful. **Any inattentiveness or carelessness may cause*** *falldown. **This falldown is due to false ego.** <u>**From the status of pure consciousness, the false ego is born because of misuse of independence.**</u> **We cannot argue about why false ego arises from pure consciousness. Factually, there is always the chance that this will happen, and therefore one has to be very careful.*** False ego is the basic principle for all material activities, which are executed in the modes of material nature. As soon as one deviates from pure Krishna consciousness, he increases his entanglement in material reaction. The entanglement of materialism is the material mind, and from this material mind, the senses and material organs become manifest. [S.B. 3.26.23-24]*

"In the conditioned state the living entities of the marginal energy are a mixture of spiritual and material energies. The marginal energy is originally under the control of the spiritual energy, but, under the control of the material energy, the living entities have been wandering in forgetfulness within the material world since time immemorial.**The conditioned state is caused by misuse of the individual independence of the spiritual platform, for this separates the living entity from the association of the spiritual energy.** But when the living entity is enlightened by the grace of the Supreme Lord or His pure devotee and **becomes inclined to revive his original state of loving service,** he is on the most auspicious platform of eternal bliss and knowledge. **The marginal jiva, or living entity, misuses his independence and becomes averse to the eternal service attitude when he independently thinks he is not energy but the energetic.** This misconception of his own existence leads him to the attitude of lording it over material nature... When covered by the cloud of material energy, the living entity, who is also a spiritual energy of the Supreme Personality of Godhead, **forgets about the activities of the spiritual energy** and considers all that happens in the material manifestation to be wonderful... Deluded by material energy, the conditioned soul, enamored by these eighty-one varieties of manifestation, wants to lord it over material energy, just as a moth wants to enjoy a fire. <u>**This illusion is the net result of the conditioned soul's forgetfulness of his eternal relationship with the Supreme personality of Godhead**</u>. When conditioned, the soul is impelled by the material energy to engage in sense gratification, whereas one enlightened by the spiritual energy engages himself in the service of the Supreme Lord in his eternal relationship. Krishna is the original cause of the spiritual world, and He is the covered cause of the material manifestation. He is also the original cause of the marginal potency, the living entities. He is both the leader and maintainer of the living entities, who are called the marginal potency because they can act under the protection of the spiritual energy or under the cover of the material energy. With the help of the spiritual energy we can understand that independence is visible only in Krishna, who by His inconceivable energy is able to act in any way He likes. The Supreme Personality of Godhead is the Absolute Whole, and the living entities are parts of the Absolute Whole. **This relationship of the Supreme Personality of Godhead and the living entities is eternal**... The natural position of the living being is always as a subordinate of the Supreme Personality of Godhead. When one agrees to act in such a position, he attains perfection in life, *but if one rebels against this principle, he is in the conditioned state." [C.C. Adi 5.65-66]*

TRANSLATION: "Now that I have brought him here, I am asking him to leave. Now he can go wherever he likes, for I am no longer responsible for him."

PURPORT: *Kala Krishnadasa was influenced and allured by nomads or gypsies, who enticed him with women. Maya is so strong that Kala Krishnadasa left Sri Caitanya Mahaprabhu's company to join gypsy women.* **Even though a person may associate with Sri Caitanya Mahaprabhu, he can be allured by maya and leave the Lord's company due to his slight independence.** *Only one who is overwhelmed by maya can be so unfortunate as to leave Sri Caitanya Mahaprabhu's company, yet unless one is very conscientious, the influence of maya can drag one away, even though he be the personal assistant of Sri Caitanya Mahaprabhu. And what to speak of others? The Bhattatharis used to increase their numbers by using women to allure outsiders.* **This is factual evidence <u>showing that it is possible at any time to fall down from the Lord's association.</u> One need only misuse his little independence. Once fallen and separated from the Supreme Personality of Godhead's association, one becomes a candidate for suffering in the material world.** *Although rejected by Sri Caitanya Mahaprabhu, Kala Krishnadasa was given another chance, as the following verses relate. [C.C. Mad Lila 10.65]*

Karandhara: "Anjasa--completely. Translation: Sri Sukadeva Gosvami said: O King, unless one is influenced by the energy of the Supreme Personality of Godhead, there is no meaning to the relationship of the pure soul in pure consciousness with the material body. It is just like the dreamer seeing his own body working."
Prabhupada: So, purport?
Karandhara: "Purport. The question of Maharaja Pariksit is perfectly answered as to how a living entity began his material life, although he is apart from the material body and the mind."
Prabhupada: It is a very important question. Pariksit Maharaja inquired... Many people inquired that "How the living entity was with Krishna, he became fallen in this material world?" Is not done? This question is raised? So this question is answered here, that "How the living entity who was with Krishna became fallen down in contact with this material qualities?" So this is the answer. Read the translation.
Karandhara: "Sri Sukadeva Gosvami said: O king, unless one is influenced by the energy of the Supreme Personality of Godhead..."
Prabhupada: **It is simply the influence of the material energy, nothing. <u>Actually he has not fallen.</u> Another example given is given. Just like the moon is covered with scattered cloud, the passing cloud. You have seen. Everyone has experience. The cloud passes, and it appears that the moon is moving. Have you seen this?**

*Devotees: Yes.*

*Prabhupada: Actually the moon is not moving. It is a maya, illusion. It appears that the moon is moving. But similarly, the living entity, because he is spiritual spark of the Supreme, it has not fallen. It has not fallen. **But he is thinking, "I am fallen. I am material." That is the reason.** He is thinking, "I am this body." Actually the body has no connection with me. That is experienced, that the body has no connection with the soul. The body is changing, dying. But I am the same. The same example, the moon: The cloud is passing over in different way. The moon is far away from the cloud, and it has nothing to do with the cloud, but it appears the moon is moving. (break) Try to understand. Have questions and answer. It is very important thing. Atma-mayam rte rajan. Except atma-maya, the illusory energy... It is the maneuver or handling of the illusory energy of Krishna. This illusory energy develops **when we forget Krishna.** That's all. It is... In other words, this illusory identification of me with the body is simply due to my forgetfulness. We wanted to forget, we wanted to give up Krishna and wanted to enjoy this material world. Therefore Krishna is giving us. [Srimad-Bhagavatam 2.9.1, Tokyo, April 20, 1972]*

*"My Dear Uttama Sloka, Please accept my blessings. I am very glad to receive your letter (undated), and I have noted the contents that you had left the temple but now you have returned again. This is most encouraging, because it means that Krishna is very kind upon you. Although you left Him, He did not allow you to go away. It is His special favor upon you. As individuals there may be disagreement sometimes, but that is quite natural. Even in ordinary family affairs there is sometimes disagreement, but that does not mean immediately the disagreeing members shall leave the family. Similarly our Krishna Consciousness Movement means we are all gathering together in families of Krishna. **Actually we are eternal family members of the Lord, but due to our misuse of independence we have now forgotten our eternal relationship with Krishna, exactly like a man who is mad forgets his family relationship and loiters in the street. But when he is again in his normal mental condition, he remembers his family members and goes back to them.** Similarly this Krishna Consciousness Movement is a treatment for reviving the memory that we all belong to Krishna's family. So we are trying to establish a replica of Krishna's family in this material world wherein there is no material activities." [S.P. Letter to: Uttamasloka, New Vrindaban, 7 June, 1969]*

*"Regarding your questions concerning the spirit souls falling into Maya's influence, **it is not that those who have developed a passive relationship with Krishna are more likely to fall into nescient activities**. Usually anyone who has developed his relationship with Krishna does not fall down in any circumstance, **but because the independence is always there, the soul may fall down from any position or any relationship by misusing his independence**. But his relationship with Krishna is never lost, simply it is forgotten by the influence of Maya, so it may be regained or revived by the process of hearing the Holy Name of Krishna and then the devotee engages himself in the service of the Lord which is **his original or constitutional position**. The relationship of the living entity with*

*Krishna is eternal as both Krishna and the living entity are eternal; the process is one of revival only, <u>nothing new</u>."* [S.P. Letter to: Jagadisa, Los Angeles, 27 February, 1970]

"*Regarding your questions about how and from where did the conditioned souls fall, your first question if someone has a relationship with Lord Krishna on Krishnaloka, does he ever fall down? The souls are endowed with minute independence as part of their nature and this minute independence may be utilized rightly or wrongly at any time, **so there is always the chance of falling down by misuse of one's independence**. But those who are firmly fixed up in devotional service to Krishna are making proper use of their independence and so they do not fall down. Regarding your second question, have the conditioned souls ever seen Krishna? Were they with the Lord before being conditioned by the desire to lord it over material nature? **Yes, the conditioned souls are parts and parcels of the Lord and thus they were with Krishna before being conditioned.** Just as the child must have seen his father because the father places the child in the womb of the mother, similarly each soul has seen Krishna or the Supreme Father. But at that time the conditioned souls are resting in the condition called susupti which is exactly deep sleep without dream, or anesthetized state, therefore **they do not remember being with Krishna** when they wake up in the material world and become engaged in material affairs. I hope this will satisfy your questions."* [S.P. Letter to: Jagadisa, Los Angeles, 25 April, 1970]

*Cyavana: If God's energy is so perfect, then how does this ignorance come upon the living entity?*
*Prabhupada: That we have explained many times. You create your ignorance. Just like you cannot live without serving Krishna, but you create: "Why not independently?" That is your ignorance. By law, by nature's law, you cannot live without being subordinate to Krishna. But why you are thinking, "Why shall I be subordinate to Krishna?" Krishna is asking you, sarva-dharman parityajya mam ekam saranam. Why you are not doing that? Why you are not doing that? Krishna is personally asking, "You do this. I shall save you." Why you are not doing this? So you violate the laws of Krishna. You suffer. That's all.*
*Cyavana: But if that energy is perfect, how can it violate?*
*Prabhupada: **Then you do not know what is living being. Living being has got the, I mean to say, independence, little independence. He can obey; he can violate. In our society there are so many. Somebody is strictly obeying, somebody is willfully, voluntary..., not voluntarily, willfully violating. They must fall down.***
*Jnana: If God is perfect, why didn't He make us perfect?*
*Prabhupada: **He is made perfect, but He is not... You are not stone. God is not stone. You are living being. The same thing you are repeatedly asking. You have got little independence because you are part and parcel of God. So by misusing your independence, if you violate the orders of God, then you suffer. You are perfect because you have got independence, but you misuse that perfectness. That is your fault. You perfect. You become imperfect by misusing.***
*Jnana: Independence?*

Prabhupada: Yes. Everything is perfect. Purnasya purnam adaya purnam evavasisyate, purnat purnam udacyate. Because you are part and parcel of God, you are perfect, but willfully you become imperfect. Again you become perfect; then you become imperfect.

Jnana: Where does that will come from?

Prabhupada: Will is given to you. Living being means there is will--thinking, feeling and willing. Don't question if you do not know. Everything comes from God. What is the use of "Where will comes?" Janmadya asya yatah. Aham sarvasya prabhavo mattah sarvam... Everything is coming from Krishna. Krishna has got will; you have got will. Why do you ask? This is foolishness. Krishna has got independence; **you have got independence. You are a small Krishna**. A particle of gold is also gold. Everything is there. All chemical composition is there. It has come from Krishna. Why you are asking wherefrom it comes?

Jnana: All living beings are independent, but some choose to serve and some choose to disbelieve.

Prabhupada: **Yes. That is use of independence. Otherwise what is the meaning of independence? The meaning of independence is: "If I like, I can do. If I do not like, I do not do." That is independence. That means independence. If you are stereotyped, forced to do, that is not independence. Independence means if you like, you can do it, if not--you don't like--don't do it. That is independence. So misued independence means ignorance. He does not know that "If I infect this virus of this disease I'll suffer." But he does not know, ignorance. So he infects and he suffers.**

Devotee (6): Srila Prabhupada, I was noticing your Srimad-Bhagavatams the other day and Caitanya-caritamrta. So I would like to take my time this time and offer my obeisances for such perfected, exalted work from such an exalted personality. All glories to you.

Prabhupada: Hare Krishna. (devotees offer obeisances) Thank you very much.

Devotee (6): I haven't seen anything so beautiful, so transcendental.

Prabhupada: Try to understand. Make your life successful.

Devotee (6): I will with your mercy, with your grace. I need help.

Prabhupada: That is my endeavor. I am trying to put things how people will understand and they become perfect. That is my endeavor, humble endeavor. That's all.

Jnana: Thank you very much, Srila Prabhupada.

Prabhupada: Hare Krishna.

[S.P. Morning Walk, November 1, 1975, Nairobi]


### 7. If He Desires, He Can Come Again. That Option Is Always There.

One of the main arguments that Narayana Maharaja and his followers present to support their speculation that the living entities were never with Krishna in Goloka Vrndavana or the Vaikutha planets is as follows:

[Narayana Maharaja]: Srila Swami Maharaja never said that the jivas fell from Goloka, some of his disciples try to prove that he has said the opposite. But I know the truth. He has told me, and it is also in sastra. Srimati Syamarani dasi has collected so many of Srila Swami Maharaja words, confirming that he never accepted that the jivas came from Goloka Vrndavana.

na tad bhasayate suryo
na sasanko na pavakah
yad gatva na nivartante
tad dhama paramam mama

"That supreme abode of Mine is not illumined by the sun or moon, nor by fire or electricity. Those who reach it never return to this material world." (Bg 15.6)

[Narayana Maharaja]: Goloka is such a dhama that there is no maya. Rather, only Yogamaya is there. A person who is seriously chanting, remembering and following, passes through the stages of sraddha, nistha, ruci, asakti, and prema, after a long, long, long time. If he has gone to Goloka Vrndavana Dhama and is serving Krishna, there is no chance at all to fall down. There is no example at all in the Vedas, Upanisads, or any other scriptures.... It would be quite absurd to think that liberated souls in Goloka Vrndavana can ever be covered by maya. You should have strong faith that the jivas did not fall from there. They have come from the marginal point. They have come from Karanabdhisayi Visnu and from tatastha-sakti. Jiva himself is tatastha-sakti.

Note: These points will be shown to be completely false by the statements of Srila Prabhupada below. If we return to Goloka Vrndavana, we are not forced to return here again in the cycle of birth and death, neither will we fall like the impersonalists who are not tasting the bliss of personal variety. But we will retain our free will and if we desire, we can come again into the material world. That option is always there.

*Devotee (3): (break) You had said on a... **earlier on a morning walk, on a tape, that if one enters into the spiritual world that--you were asked that he will never have to return--and you said that if it's a desire, he can return to the material world.***
*Prabhupada: **So what is your objection?***
*Devotee (3): I was just wondering if the spirit soul being in the spiritual world is eternally liberated, how can he return. By desire?*
*Prabhupada: **Yes. If he desires, he can come again. That option is always there**. Just like I remain in India. I come here. And if I like, I may not come. It is my option.*
*Ambarisa: When we get to the spiritual sky, we'll always be able to remember how horrible it is down here? We'll always be able to remember how terrible it is in the material world?*
*Prabhupada: It is terrible.*
*Ambarisa: Yes, we will be able to remember that.*
*Prabhupada: That is intelligence. When one remembers that this world is duhkhalayam asasvatam, is a place of misery, then we can go. As long as we shall*

*think, "Oh, it is very nice place," we have to remain. Krishna is so kind, "All right, remain in this very nice place."*
*[S.P. Morning Walk, July 3, 1975, Denver]*

*Prabhupada: Yes, Caitanya Mahaprabhu. By mercy of spiritual master, the mercy of Krishna, he gets the seed of devotional service, and if he cultivates, then his life becomes successful. Otherwise he has to rotate, sometimes up, sometimes down. Sometimes this grass, sometimes lion.*
*Paramahamsa:* **But ultimately if we come to Krishna, there's no return. But nevertheless, Jagai, and..., the two gatekeepers, they returned?**
*Prabhupada:* **There is return, that is voluntary. Return there is.**
*Paramahamsa: If we want.*
*Prabhupada:* **Yes.**
*Paramahamsa:* **So we can come to the spiritual world and return?**
*Prabhupada:* **Yes.**
*Paramahamsa:* **Fall down?**
*Prabhupada:* **Yes. As soon as we try, "Oh, this material world is very nice," "Yes," Krishna says, "yes, you go."** *Just like nobody is interested in Krishna consciousness. Do you think everyone is interested? So. They want to enjoy this material world. Otherwise what is the meaning of free will? Every living entity has got a little free will. And Krishna is so kind, He gives him opportunity, "All right, you enjoy like this." Just like some of our students, Krishna conscious, sometimes go away, again come back.* **It is free will, not stereotyped.** *Just like one goes to the prisonhouse, not that government welcomes, "Come on. We have got prisonhouse. Come here, come here." He goes out of his free will; again comes out, again goes. Like that. Krishna-bahirmukha hana bhoga vancha kare, nikata-stha maya tare japatiya dhare. The police is there. Just like the police car was there. We have nothing to do with it. But if you do anything criminal, immediately you will be arrested, under police custody. The maya may be there, but maya captures him who is not a devotee of Krishna. That's all. Therefore, mam eva ye prapadyante mayam etam taranti te: "Anyone who surrenders unto Me, maya does not interfere anymore." [S.P. Morning Walk At Cheviot Hills Golf Course, May 13, 1973, Los Angeles]*

*Acyutananda: In Andhra, I said, "There's so much land where they're growing tobacco. You could grow food."* **But in the Gita, it says, "Once coming there, he never returns."**
*Prabhupada:* **But if he likes, he can return.**
*Acyutananda:* **He can return.**
*Prabhupada:* **That independence has to be accepted, little independence. We can misuse that. Krishna-bahirmukha hana bhoga vancha kare. That misuse is the cause of our falldown.**
*[S.P.Morning Walk, February 19, 1976, Mayapura]*

*Bhaktijana: Did Krishna create us for to serve Him?*
*Prabhupada: Eh?*
*Bhaktijana: Did Krishna create us to serve Him?*

*Prabhupada:* **Yes.**

*Bhaktijana: And to enjoy us?*

*Prabhupada:* **Yes. Very nice.** *So we should prepare ourselves to our healthy condition. That is our healthy condition. As soon as we understand that Krishna created us... Krishna created... There is no creation. Just like if I say that my hand is created, no, it is not created. As long as the body is there, the hand is there. Otherwise, there is no meaning of body. Similarly, we are not created. Krishna is always there; we are also always there. And there are millions and millions of liberated souls who are engaged in Krishna.* **They never misuse their independence. And we small quantity, we misused our independence. We wanted to enjoy separately. Therefore we are conditioned.**

*Bhaktijana: But there are, there are many...?*

*Prabhupada: ...liberated souls. They are never conditioned. They never become conditioned. Yes?*

*Devotee: You mean they never were conditioned at any time or...*

*Prabhupada: Eh?*

*Devotee: You said there were millions of souls...*

*Prabhupada: Yes. They were never conditioned. They were never conditioned, never conditioned. They are called nitya-mukta, eternally liberated. We are only simple few, this material world. Just like I have several times told you that the prison house. The population of prison house is nothing in comparison to the whole population. What is there? Suppose in New York there is a prison house. Oh, what may be the number? A few thousand maybe. But here, millions. Similarly, the liberated souls are millions; we are only few thousands, or hundreds...*

*Bhaktijana:* **How could we make a poor choice if we were part and parcel of Krishna? How could we have chosen the material world?**

*Prabhupada:* **Oh, because you have got independence.** *Don't you see so many students come. They go away again. Yesterday Kirtanananda went to call Ranchora. He said, "Oh, I have forgotten this!" So you can forget. There is another student. He was also our student, Wally. "Oh, you can go immediately!" Suppose if you... "Oh, I don't care for this Krishna consciousness Society. Who calls you? You can go." That independence is there. We can misuse.*

*Bhaktijana: But Krishna will always be there if we want to go back?*

*Prabhupada: Eh? Krishna is always prepared to accept you. He's always prepared. But because He has given us independence, we misuse it and we fall under the clutches of maya. That is our misfortune. We create this misfortune, and we can create our good fortune. "Man is the architect of his own fortune." So if you become Krishna conscious, it is to your good fortune. If you become maya conscious, it is to your bad fortune. You are the creator.*

*Bhaktijana:* **When the souls that were never conditioned at all..., do they also have the independence?**

*Prabhupada:* **Yes, but they have not misused. They know that "I am meant for Krishna's service," and they are happy in Krishna's service.**

*Bhaktijana:* <u>**Could they ever misuse it?**</u>

*Prabhupada:* <u>**Yes, they can misuse it also. That power is there. Yes?**</u>

*Devotee:* **Well, I believe you once said that once a conditioned soul becomes perfected and gets out of the material world and he goes to Krishnaloka, there's no possibility of falling back.**

*Prabhupada:* **No! There is possibility, but he does not come. Just like after putting your hand in the fire, you never put it again if you are really intelligent. So those who are going back to Godhead, they become intelligent.** *Why going back to Godhead? Just like we are in renounced order of life. So we have renounced our family life after thinking something. Now, if somebody comes, "Swamiji, you take thousand millions of dollars and marry again and become a family man," I'll never become, because I have got my bad experience. I'll never become. So if one is intelligent enough, if he has got actually the bitter taste of this material world, he'll never agree. He'll never agree. But those who have not advanced to such knowledge, oh, they think, "Oh, this material enjoyment is very nice. Let me taste it and let me do business in my sannyasi life, and stealthily and privately, let me enjoy." These things are going on. That means they have no taste. They come to hospital-making or this philanthropy. This come again. Sthanad bhrastad patanty adhah. Ye 'nye aravindaksa vimukta-maninah. "Those fools who are thinking that 'Simply by thinking myself, "I am God, I am Brahman, I have become liberated," ' " but ye 'nye 'ravindaksa vimukta-maninas tvayy asta-bhavat, "but there is no knowledge about You, Krishna," aruhya krcchrena param padam, "they, after performing so much austerity and penances, they rise up to the highest position, Brahman realization, but," patanty adhah, "they fall down." We have got so many instances. They take sannyasa. They say that brahma satyam jagan mithya: "This world is false. Brahman is truth." But after some days, they come to politics, they come to sociology, they come to hospital, they come to this and that. That's all. Finished. Brahman finished. Patanty adhah. They must fall down because they have no shelter in Krishna. Just like the sputnik goes very high, clap, hear clap. Uh, come down again. Where you'll go? Yes. Simply for the time being clapping, that's all. (laughs) But the fools, they are so nonsense, they are satisfied with that temporary clapping. That's all.*

*Bhaktijana: Has my soul ever been liberated?*

*Prabhupada: That you know. I do not know.*

*Bhaktijana: If I was once liberated...*

*Prabhupada:* **You are liberated. You are liberated. Simply just a cloud has covered you. Drive away the cloud. There is no question that you were ever. You are ever-liberated. That, the sky is always spiritual, but it is sometimes overcrowded with cloud, this maya. This is called maya. Actually, you are not conditioned. You are thinking.** *Just like in the dream you are thinking that tiger is eating you. You were never eaten by tiger. There is no tiger. So we have to get out of this dream. Don't you sometimes dream that tiger is eating you? Is there any tiger? You are simply thinking. So if you keep in Krishna consciousness, that nonsense thinking will go away. Therefore we have to keep ourself always in Krishna-thinking so that this dream will never come. If you are always awakened, then dream never comes. So keep yourself always awakened by Krishna consciousness. All right. Distribute prasadam. (end) [Sri Caitanya-caritamrta Lecture, Adi-lila 7.108, San Francisco, February 18, 1967]*

Syamasundara: But can we predict, can we tell in advance what there will be, what is the future?

Prabhupada: The future is to go back to home, back to Godhead. That is the ultimate future. But because he's not intelligent, he has to be kicked on his face very strongly by the (indistinct). That is the foolish man. And if one is intelligent, he can tell immediately, "Oh, my duty is to serve Krishna." That's all. "Why I am trying to serve my senses?" But to come to this platform, this understanding that "I am eternal servant of God. My business is to serve Krishna," it requires (indistinct); therefore the maya is there. Just like police force. The police force is there after the criminal, just to teach him that "You cannot (indistinct) the laws of the state. When you are under our supervision, and we shall simply kick on your face, that is our business." So maya is always kicking on the face, and (s)he is creating varieties, that's all. This is called conditional life.

Syamasundara: So that much is predictable, that for...

Prabhupada: You can see it is not predictable, it is actually happening. Everyone is trying to be happy, but he is being frustrated. Everyone can see. They are manufacturing different ways of material happiness but becoming frustrated. This is maya's kicking. There is no question of prediction. Any man who has got a little intelligence, he can see.

Syamasundara: So someone can understand, someone can know what the life force is going to do in the future, how it will manifest itself in the future?

Prabhupada: **The future, because he is eternally servant of God, so now he has forgotten. He wants to become master, and the material nature is kicking him, life after life. So one day he'll come to his senses and become again, renovate himself to become servant of God.**

Syamasundara: So we can predict that everyone will...

Prabhupada: Oh, yes. Everyone will be. Somebody sooner, somebody later.

Syamasundara: So that the purpose of the life force then is to eventually go back...

Prabhupada: Just like when a man becomes a prisoner, he will be freed, he'll be a free man at the end of his term, and within this term he is simply kicked by the police, so that he may not come back again to prison house.

Syamasundara: **But we can't predict that the process of punishment will have permanent effect, can we? Can we predict that? Many prisoners leave the prison, but some come back.**

Prabhupada: <u>**No, there is no permanent effect because we have got little independence. There is nothing as permanent. You can misuse your independence at any time**</u>.

Syamasundara: **And come back.**

Prabhupada: **Yes. <u>Otherwise there is no meaning of independence. Independence means you can do this, you can do that. "All right. Whatever you like."</u>**

Syamasundara: His conception of the soul, which he calls elan vital in French language, means the vital impulse.

Prabhupada: Yes. Vital..., this is living force, vital force. (indistinct), it is never addressed. God has (indistinct) for the mind, for the intelligence, for the body, God has (indistinct).

Syamasundara: Is it (indistinct) in the same quantity in every body, in every living body?

Prabhupada: Yes. Yes. Same quantity. The same measurement: one ten-thousandth part of the tip of the hair.

Syamasundara: I mean the energy, the amount of energy.

Prabhupada: Yes. Yes. That much, that spiritual energy is everywhere, in the ant or in the elephant.

Atreya Rsi: Prabhupada, you mentioned the size of the soul, and this size seems to connote a physical size. Now, my question is: in the spiritual world, size, it seems that it is a material concept, it is a relative thing, distance...

Prabhupada: Material size and spiritual size is not the same. Spiritual size is permanent; material size is changing.

Atreya Rsi: In other words, how could you measure the spiritual phenomenon with something like one-thousandth of the tip of the hair? Hair is material.

Prabhupada: No. Because you have no spiritual vision, therefore you have to be understood by material example.

Atreya Rsi: That's an example.

Prabhupada: Yes.

Atreya Rsi: And also Syamasundara Prabhu was asking about predicting about spiritual life. What is the qualification of the person who can make such predictions?

Prabhupada: He must be Krishna's representative, one who knows Krishna. That's all.

Atreya Rsi: No one else.

Prabhupada: No. If he does not know Krishna, how he can explain?

Devotee: That independence, if he exercises that independence from now on, forever, Krishna knows exactly how that independence is going to be used forever?

Prabhupada: Krishna?

Devotee: Well, the living entity has independence: now he may be liberated, then he may be conditioned, then he may be liberated, then he may be conditioned.

Prabhupada: No. Krishna has given you liberation. Now you misuse your liberation, you become entrapped.

Syamasundara: But it is that predictable?

Devotee: Is that known beforehand?

Syamasundara: Does Krishna know beforehand everything, before...?

Prabhupada: No. How Krishna can know? You can change your mind. So Krishna says "Surrender unto Me." If you don't surrender, then what Krishna can do? That much independence is there.

Syamasundara: So even God cannot predict?

Prabhupada: What is the use of prediction? Prediction is so much, that he will be kicked, kicked, kicked, and some day he will come.

Devotee: But the independence...

Prabhupada: Independence is there. Independence is always there. When he is being kicked, there is also independence.

Devotee: Then he is so many times falling down, again and again, **_eventually permanently he will come back_**.

*Prabhupada:* **No. There is no question of permanent. Because he has got independence, he can misuse his independence, he can fall down. That's why one man is released from the prison house, that does not mean permanently he... He can come back again.**

*Syamasundara: There's no guarantee.*

*Atreya Rsi: This concept of prediction, Prabhupada. You just said it's the duty of the material (indistinct) because he's (indistinct) material. Because he's not sure and...*

*Prabhupada: (indistinct) by experience (indistinct). Just like you can predict that four months after, there will be winter season. This prediction is like that. You have got experience that last year there was winter season, and again four months after there will be winter season. We call this prediction of experience, that's all.*

*Atreya Rsi: In the spiritual world everything is permanent.*

*Prabhupada: Yes.*

*Atreya Rsi: There is no need for making predictions all the time.*

*Prabhupada: No. Why there is? Prediction means when there is something wanting. There is no want at all.*

*Devotee:* **Once he's liberated, can he** *(indistinct)?*

*Prabhupada:* **Yes.**

*Devotee: (indistinct) Krishna conscious (indistinct)*

*Prabhupada:* **No. That is the general law. But if he likes, he can come back. Because otherwise, what is the meaning of independence? Just like one should become fit in the prison house, naturally he should not go again.** *But (indistinct) running again kicking, that's all.*

*Lilavati: So those eternally liberated souls in the spiritual sky will never come here because they choose not to. It's not that... (indistinct) they never choose to come here.*

*Prabhupada: Yes, yes. They never choose. They are very experienced. (laughter)*
*[Philosophy Discussions, Henri Bergson]*

Note: To say that the jiva soul cannot fall from Goloka or the Vaikuntha planets is to put the individual souls on the same level as Krishna as Acyuta (one who never falls down). This is impersonal philosophy.

*"Krishna's name is Acyuta. Acyuta means infallible, who never falls. That is the difference between... Krishna is Brahman. We are also Brahman, but we are not acyuta. We are cyuta. Cyuta means falling down. We have got the tendency of falling down. Krishna never falls down; therefore His name is Acyuta." (Prabhupada Lecture from Sri Caitanya-caritamrta, Madhya-lila 22.14-20, New York, January 10, 1967)*

# "THERE IS NO NEED TO READ ANY BOOKS BESIDES MY BOOKS"

Mukunda dasa 2007

"YOU SAY THAT YOU WOULD READ ONLY ONE
BOOK IF THAT WAS ALL THAT I HAD WRITTEN"

I am compiling this article to encourage those new souls who will be taking direct shelter of Srila Prabhupada as their initiating guru to develop the correct mood of total loyalty and chastity to His Divine Grace by reading his books and his books *[original books]* only! This is most pleasing to Srila Prabhupada and will lead to rapid advancement in Krishna Consciousness.

I also want to clear up this false notion presented by the sahajiya class *[those who take devotion to Krishna as something very cheap]* that Srila Prabhupada has authorized them to jump over him and thus attempt to directly read the books of the previous acaryas *[spiritual masters]*. Their self-interested and offensive interpretations of Srila Prabhupada's words cause general confusion and make his teachings appear contradictory. This should not be tolerated!

Of course this offensive cheating mentality of jumping over the guru and prostituting oneself around by hearing from different unauthorized sources and then trying to justify such material inclinations as spiritual and sanctioned by Prabhupada is totally abhorrent to the faithful chaste followers of Srila Prabhupada.

**You say that you would read only one book if that was all
that I had written, so you teach others to do like that.
You have very good determination**.

*"Regarding the Gaudiya Math books being circulated there, who is distributing?
Who is sending these books? The Gaudiya Math does not sell our books, why we
should sell their books. Who has introduced these books? Let me know. These
books should not at all be circulated in our Society. Bhakti Vilas Tirtha is very
much antagonistic to our society and he has no clear conception of devotional
service. He is contaminated. Anyway, who has introduced these books? **You say
that you would read only one book if that was all that I had written, so you teach
others to do like that. You have very good determination**."* [Srila Prabhupada
Letter to Sukadeva, 14 November, 1973)

Note: This quote can be divided into two sections. The first section consists of
many strong questions which reveal Srila Prabhupada's total displeasure at
unauthorized and contaminating "spiritual books" being circulated in his
movement. In the second section Srila Prabhupada clearly reveals his pleasure at
the correct chaste mood of his disciple Sukadeva dasa. Prabhupada tells him he
has good determination to read only one book, if that was the only book that
Prabhupada had written. He tells him to teach this to the others. So this instruction
is an OPEN INSTRUCTION TO ALL PRABHUPADA'S FOLLOWERS! The
prostitute class will try to write this off as a time and place instruction that doesn't
apply to them, this is nonsense. This letter with its clear message reveals the
danger of the unauthorized hearing process and also the correct mood of chastity
to the spiritual master by the bona-fide follower and hearer.

If this was a time, place and circumstance instruction *[which it clearly is not]*, then
the circumstances are far more serious now! The market place is now completely
flooded with these contaminated books and chastity and loyalty to Prabhupada is
rare to find. At this time the prostitution and philosophical deviations away from
the paramapara message of Prabhupada are massive in comparison to 1973!!!

**There is no need by any of my disciples to read any books
besides my books--in fact, such reading may be detrimental
to their advancement in Krishna Consciousness**.

*"**There is no need by any of my disciples to read any books besides my books--in
fact, such reading may be detrimental to their advancement in Krishna
Consciousness**. All reading of outside books, except in certain authorized cases
such as for example to read some philosopher like Plato to make an essay
comparing his philosophy with Krishna's philosophy--but otherwise **all such
outside reading should be stopped immediately**. It is simply another botheration.
If my students cannot even read my own books thoroughly, why they should read
others? **I have given you TLC, what need is there to read Caitanya Caritamrta
translated by someone else. You are right to stop such reading**."* [Srila
Prabhupada Letter to Sri Govinda, 20 January, 1972]

Note: There is no need by any of Prabhupada's disciples to read any books besides Prabhupada's books, in fact, such reading may be detrimental to their advancement in Krishna Consciousness. All such outside reading should be stopped immediately. What is the difficulty to understand this clear instruction? For the loyal and chaste follower of Prabhupada there is none. For the sahajiya class they will hear what they want to hear and disregard the rest.

In these times of disorder when the standard is to hear from anywhere and everywhere like a prostitute, presenting these simple truths of loyalty and devotion to Prabhupada is considered almost blasphemy.

### There is no need whatsoever for any outside instruction

*"Whatever is to be learned of the teachings of Srila Bhaktivinode Thakura **can be learned from our books**. **There is no need whatsoever for any outside instruction.**"* *[Srila Prabhupada Letter to Gurukrpa and Yasodanandana, 25/12/73]*

Note: Whatsoever is an intensive form of whatever. Whatever means no matter what: Do it, whatever happens. So no matter what, whatever happens we don't allow any outside instruction in Srila Prabhupada's movement or in our ears and hearts. Whatever *[meaning absolutely anything]* that is to be learned of the teachings of Srila Bhaktivinode Thakura can be learned from Srila Prabhupada's books.

### I request you to stop this practice.

*"Brahmananda Swami has read me your letter **regarding the students there reading other books. I request you to stop this practice**. Our students have no time to read our own books, but they have time to read other's books, and the money to purchase them? Why this mentality is there? You are a serious student, therefore you have correctly found out the defect in these books. **We don't want babaji class. We want active preachers.**"[Srila Prabhupada Letter to: Cyavana: Bombay 13 October, 1973]*

Note: Prabhupada again requests us to stop the prostitution and be loyal to him. He doesn't wants babaji class, he wants active preachers. In the next quote he GIVES THE CLEAR INSTRUCTION on what his followers are allowed to read to become those preachers.

### In our Krishna consciousness movement we have therefore limited our study of Vedic literatures to these four works

*TRANSLATION: "The twelfth item is to give up the company of nondevotees. (13) One should not accept an unlimited number of disciples. (14) One should not partially study many scriptures just to be able to give references and expand explanations.*

*PURPORT: Accepting an unlimited number of devotees or disciples is very risky for one who is not a preacher. According to Srila Jiva Gosvami, a preacher has to accept many disciples to expand the cult of Sri Caitanya Mahaprabhu. This is risky because when a spiritual master accepts a disciple, he naturally accepts the disciple's sinful activities and their reactions. Unless he is very powerful, he cannot assimilate all the sinful reactions of his disciples. Thus if he is not powerful, he has to suffer the consequences, for one is forbidden to accept many disciples. One should not partially study a book just to pose oneself as a great scholar by being able to refer to scriptures. In our Krishna consciousness movement we have therefore limited our study of Vedic literatures to Bhagavad-gita, Srimad-Bhagavatam, Caitanya-caritamrta and Bhakti-rasamrta-sindhu. These four works are sufficient for preaching purposes. They are adequate for the understanding of the philosophy and the spreading of missionary activities all over the world. If one studies a particular book, he must do so thoroughly. That is the principle. By thoroughly studying a limited number of books, one can understand the philosophy. [Srila Prabhupada from Sri Caitanya-caritamrta, Madhya-lila 22.118]*

Note: Unchaste people don't like to be limited because they do not understand or accept the unlimited nature of these four transcendental works coming in parampara from Srila Prabhupada. And the next quote which they use to support their offensive jumping over Prabhupada philosophy clearly reveals this.

## THE SAHAJIYA MISREPRESENTATION OF THE
## BRHAD-BHAGAVATAMRTA QUOTE

*"Sri Sanatana Gosvami Prabhu, the teacher of the science of devotional service, wrote several books, of which the Brhad-bhagavatamrta is very famous; anyone who wants to know about the subject matter of devotees, devotional service and Krishna must read this book." [Srila Prabhupada from Sri Caitanya-caritamrta, Adi-lila 5.203]*

Note: So it is clear, we should read Brhad-bhagavatamrta, the real question is HOW? In the Bhagavad-gita, Krishna says: "If one offers Me with love and devotion a leaf, a flower, fruit or water, I will accept it." The instruction appears simple but it requires more elaboration from Srila Prabhupada on how we offer these things to Krishna.

*Prabhupada: Yes, I'll chant. Hare Krishna. Oh, thank you very much. All should be offered there, Jagannatha. The etiquette is nice. **Everything should be offered to the, through the spiritual master. That is the etiquette. <u>No direct</u>.** [Srila Prabhupada Conversation, April 1, 1969, San Francisco]*

Note: So we shall use this example and apply the sahajiya philosophy to it. They would say that Krishna says we can offer him directly a leaf, a flower, fruit or water, and he will accept it. This of course is not the correct philosophy, we have to offer through the spiritual master this is the etiquette.

So let's read Brhad-bhagavatamrta by Sri Sanatana Gosvami Prabhu, this is what Srila Prabhupada has instructed. But we have to read it in the way he directs us.

### Or even if you read some books, you cannot
### understand unless you understand it from me.

*"This is called parampara system. The person who heard Bhagavad-gita directly from Krishna, whatever he says, that is to be accepted. You cannot interpret. This is the parampara system. So if you want to understand Bhagavad-gita, then we must understand in the same way as the person who directly heard from. This is called parampara system. **Suppose I have heard something from my spiritual master, so I speak to you the same thing. So this is parampara system. You cannot imagine what my spiritual master said. Or even if you read some books, you cannot understand unless you understand it from me. This is called parampara system. You cannot jump over to the superior guru, neglecting the next acarya, immediate next acarya.** Just like our, this Gau..., Caitanya Mahaprabhu's cult; we cannot understand Caitanya Mahaprabhu directly. It is not possible. We have to understand through the Gosvamis. Therefore you'll find in the Caitanya-caritamrta and at the end of every chapter, the writer says, sri-rupa-ragunatha-pade yara asacaitanya-caritamrta kahe krishna-dasa This is the process. He does not say that "I've understood Lord Caitanya Mahaprabhu directly." No. That is not understanding. That is foolishness. You cannot understand what is Caitanya Mahaprabhu. Therefore repeatedly he says, rupa-ragunatha-pade... "I am that Krishna dasa, Kaviraja, who is always under the subordination of the Gosvamis." This is parampara system. Similarly, Narottama dasa Thakura also says, ei chay gosai jar mui tar das, "I am servant of that person who has accepted this six Gosvamis as his master. I am not going to be servant of any other person who does not accept the way and means of..." Therefore we say or we offer our prayer to our spiritual master, rupanuga-varaya te, rupanuga-varaya te, because he follows Rupa Gosvami, therefore we accept, spiritual master. Not that one has become more than Rupa Gosvami or more than... No. Tandera carana-sebi-bhakta-sane vas. This is the parampara system."* [Srila Prabhupada from Srimad-Bhagavatam 1.15.30 Los Angeles, December 8, 1973]

Note: The sahajiyas have to stop jumping like monkeys. First they want to jump over Srila Prabhupada to Srimad Bhaktisiddhanta Sarasvati Goswami Maharaja now they are trying to jump over so many exalted Vaisnava's all the way back to

Sri Sanatana Gosvami prabhu. Let them meditate on the following: OR EVEN IF YOU READ SOME BOOKS, YOU CANNOT UNDERSTAND UNLESS YOU UNDERSTAND IT FROM ME. THIS IS CALLED PARAMPARA SYSTEM.

## YOU CANNOT JUMP OVER TO THE SUPERIOR GURU, NEGLECTING THE NEXT ACARYA, IMMEDIATE NEXT ACARYA!!!!

I will elaborate for you dear sahajiyas; the purport of all the previous Acaryas writings etc. can be found in Srila Prabhupada's books. So if you read Srila Prabhupada's books you are reading Brhad-bhagavatamrta by Sri Sanatana Gosvami Prabhu. EVAM PARAMPARA, ARE WE CLEAR YET???

*"Whatever is to be learned of the teachings of Srila Bhaktivinode Thakura* __can be learned from our books__*. There is no need whatsoever for any outside instruction."* (S.P.Letter to Gurukrpa and Yasodanandana, 25/12/73)

Whatever is to be learned of the teachings of Srila Bhaktivinode Thakura or Sri Sanatana Gosvami Prabhu can be learned from Srila Prabhupada's books. Any "follower" of Srila Prabhupada who is receiving and giving instruction of the teachings of Srila Bhaktivinode Thakur or the other previous Acaryas outside of Srila Prabhupada's books is disobeying Srila Prabhupada's order. Such offensive personalities cannot make any advancement in chanting Hare Krishna, everything is finished for them in the beginning. Such rascals cannot be siksa-guru or anything else.

*"First offense is guror avajna, defying the authority of guru. This is the first offense.* **So one who is offensive, how he can make advance in chanting? He cannot make. Then everything is finished in the beginning.** *Guror avajna. Everything is there.* **If one is disobeying the spiritual master, he cannot remain in the pure status of life.** __He cannot be siksa-guru or anything else.__*" (Bhagavad-gita, lecture 17.1-3 Honolulu, July 4, 1974)*

### You are giving us the essence of all the previous acaryas' books in your books.

*Paramahamsa: Srila Prabhupada, I remember once I heard a tape where you told us that we should not try to read the books of previous acaryas.*
*Prabhupada: Hmm?*
*Amogha: That we should not try to read Bhaktivinoda's books or earlier books of other, all acaryas. So I was just wondering...*
*Prabhupada: I never said that.*
*Amogha: You didn't say that? Oh.*
*Prabhupada: How is that?*
*Amogha: I thought you said that we should not read the previous acaryas' books.*
*Prabhupada: No, you should read.*
*Amogha: We should.*
*Prabhupada: It is misunderstanding.*
*Paramahamsa: I think maybe he was thinking that there was some things about some of the Gaudiya Matha books.*

*Prabhupada: Maybe.*

*Paramahamsa: And sometimes you said that better not to..., better to read your books.*

*Amogha: When the devotees went to India this year, they said that Acyutananda Swami very..., chastised them that "You should never... If I catch any of you buying Bhaktisiddhanta's books from Gaudiya Matha then I will take it away," something like this.*

*Paramahamsa: Yeah, that was, the reason was because of, he didn't want the devotees going to Gaudiya Matha. But there's nothing wrong with the idea of studying the previous acaryas' books.*

*Prabhupada: No. Who said? That is wrong.* **We are following previous acaryas.** *I never said that.*

*Paramahamsa:* **All of your commentaries are coming from the previous acaryas.**

*Prabhupada:* **Yes.**

*Jayadharma: But that wouldn't mean that we should keep all the previous acaryas' books and only read them.*

*Prabhupada:* **That is already there.** *You first of all assimilate what you have got. You simply pile up books and do not read--what is the use?*

*Jayadharma: First of all we must read all your books.*

*Prabhupada:* **Yes.**

*Paramahamsa:* **Practically speaking, Srila Prabhupada, you are giving us the essence of all the previous acaryas' books in your books.**

*Prabhupada:* **Yes. Yes.**

*[Srila Prabhupada Morning Walk, May 13, 1975, Perth]*

Note: THAT IS ALREADY THERE. This is the clear instruction. The essence of all the previous acaryas books are already there in Srila Prabhupada's books. "YES YES" His Divine Grace says.

So when Srila Prabhupada says "No, you should read. *[the previous acaryas books]* It is misunderstanding." There is no contradiction. The misunderstanding is only that people think they can read the previous acaryas books translated by completely unauthorized persons from the Iskcon or Gaudiya matha cults rather than reading them in disciplic succession from the liberated soul Srila Prabhupada [his books].

Reading Srila Prabhupada's books **only** is the correct mood to approach the previous acaryas. WE CANNOT JUMP OVER. We have to go through Srila Prabhupada who is the servant, servant, servant, then we can become advanced, this is the process, the law of parampara. And if we think that we have now become master, and can jump over to the previous acaryas we are going to hell.

## You cannot jump over. You must go through the
## parampara system. You have to approach through
## your spiritual master to the Gosvamis

*You cannot jump over Krishna consciousness without going through the mercy of Sri Caitanya Mahaprabhu. And to go through Sri Caitanya Mahaprabhu means to go through the six Gosvamis. This is parampara system. Therefore Narottama dasa Thakura says, ei chay gosai jar--tar mui das ta-sabara pada-renu mora panca-gras This is parampara system.* **You cannot jump over. You must go through the parampara system. You have to approach through your spiritual master to the Gosvamis, and through the Gosvamis you will have to approach Sri Caitanya Mahaprabhu, and through Sri Caitanya Mahaprabhu you have to approach Krishna. This is the way.** *Therefore Narottama dasa Thakura said, ei chay gosai jar--tar mui das. We are servant of servant. That is Caitanya Mahaprabhu's instruction, gopi-bhartuh pada-kamalayor dasa-dasanudasah.* **The more you become servant of the servant, the more you are perfect. And if you all of a sudden want to become master, then you go to hell. That's all. Don't do that. This is the teaching of Sri Caitanya Mahaprabhu. If you go through the servant, servant, servant, then you are advanced. And if you think that you have now become master, then you are going to hell. This is the process. Dasa-dasanudasah.** *Caitanya Mahaprabhu said. So servant, servant, servant, a hundred times servant now, that means he is advanced. He is advanced. And one who is becoming directly master, then he is in the hell. So anarpita-carim cirat. So we should always remember the instruction of Srila Rupa Gosvami. Therefore we pray, sri-caitanya-mano-'bhistam sthapitam yena bhu-tale. Our mission is to establish the desire of Sri Caitanya Mahaprabhu. That is our business. Sri-caitanya-mano-'bhistam sthapitam yena bhu-tale. Srila Rupa Gosvami did it. He has given us so many books, especially Bhakti-rasamrta-sindhu, which we have translated into English as Nectar of Devotion, to understand the science of devotional service. This is the greatest contribution of Srila Rupa Gosvami, how to become a devotee. How to become a devotee. It is not sentiment; it is science. This Krishna consciousness movement is a great science. Yad vijnana-samanvitam. Jnanam me paramam guhyam yad vijnana-samanvitam. It is not sentiment. If you take it as sentiment, then you will create disturbance. (Srila Prabhupada from a Sri Caitanya-caritamrta, Lecture, Adi-lila 1.4 Mayapur, March 28, 1975)*

## One has to understand the writings of the previous acaryas
## not directly but through the medium of the current link
## in disciplic succession Srila Prabhupada.

*TRANSLATION: By the mercy of Vyasa, I have heard these most confidential talks directly from the master of all mysticism, Krishna, who was speaking personally to Arjuna.*

*PURPORT: Vyasa was the spiritual master of Sanjaya, and Sanjaya admits that it was by his mercy that he could understand the Supreme Personality of Godhead.* **This means that one has to understand Krishna not directly but through the** *medium of the spiritual master. The spiritual master is the transparent medium, although it is true that the experience is direct. This is the mystery of the disciplic succession. When the spiritual master is bona fide, then one can hear Bhagavad-gita directly, as Arjuna heard it.* (Note: This means that one has to understand the writings of the previous acaryas not directly but through the medium of the current link in disciplic succession Srila Prabhupada. His Divine Grace is the transparent medium, although it is true that the experience is direct. Because Srila Prabhupada is bona-fide then we can hear the previous acaryas directly) *There are many mystics and yogis all over the world, but Krishna is the master of all yoga systems. Krishna's instruction is explicitly stated in Bhagavad-gita--surrender unto Krishna. One who does so is the topmost yogi. This is confirmed in the last verse of the Sixth Chapter. Yoginam api sarvesam. Narada is the direct disciple of Krishna and the spiritual master of Vyasa. Therefore Vyasa is as bona fide as Arjuna because he comes in the disciplic succession, and Sanjaya is the direct disciple of Vyasa. Therefore by the grace of Vyasa, his senses were purified, and he could see and hear Krishna directly. One who directly hears Krishna can understand this confidential knowledge.* **If one does not come to the disciplic succession, he cannot hear Krishna; therefore his knowledge is always imperfect, at least as far as understanding Bhagavad-gita is concerned.** (Note: If one does not come to the current link in disciplic succession Srila Prabhupada, he cannot hear the message of the previous acaryas; therefore his knowledge is always imperfect, at least as far as understanding the various books of the previous acaryas is concerned) *In Bhagavad-gita, all the yoga systems, karma-yoga, jnana-yoga and bhakti-yoga, are explained. Krishna is the master of all such mysticism. It is to be understood, however, that as Arjuna was fortunate enough to understand Krishna directly, similarly, by the grace of Vyasa, Sanjaya was also able to hear Krishna directly.* **Actually there is no difference between hearing directly from Krishna or hearing directly from Krishna via a bona fide spiritual master like Vyasa.** (Note: Actually there is no difference between hearing directly from the previous acaryas or hearing directly from previous acaryas via their bona fide representative Srila Prabhupada) *The spiritual master is the representative of Vyasadeva also.* (Note: Here's the confirmation of the previous note) *According to the Vedic system, on the birthday of the spiritual master, the disciples conduct the ceremony called Vyasa-puja.* [B.G. 18 Chapter TEXT 75] (authorized version 1972 by Srila Prabhupada)

### These two, three books, that's all.... You haven't got to learn so many huge volumes of books

*Journalist: You go for a prescribed course of study?*

*Prabhupada:* **Yes, prescribed course of study, these two, three books, that's all. Anyone can read. Bhagavad-gita and Srimad-Bhagavatam or Caitanya-caritamrta. You'll learn everything. You haven't got to learn so many huge volumes of books.** *Because Bhagavad-gita is such nice book, if you can understand one line, you advance hundred years. You see? So, I mean to say, meaningful and so solid. Therefore we have published this Bhagavad-gita As It Is.*

*Let your people read it, let them question, and try to understand what is this movement. [Press Interview, December 30, 1968, Los Angeles]*

**Yes you can print one copy... Not for distribution....**
**They are not devotees... Liberated for going to hell.**

*Prabhupada:* **My Guru Maharaja wanted to publish Govinda-lilamrta. He asked permission of Bhaktivinoda Thakura. So first of all Bhaktivinoda Thakura, "I'll tell you some day." And when he reminded, he said, "Yes you can print one copy. If you are so much anxious to print it, print one copy. You'll read and you will see that you have printed. <u>Not for distribution</u>." So we are printing all these books for understanding properly.** *Not that "Here is Radha-kunda. Let us go." Jump over like monkey. "Here is rasa-lila. Immediately..."*
*Acyutananda: Even in Krishna book rasa-lila should not be told in public.*
*Prabhupada: No, why? Krishna book must be there, in the book must be there.*
*Acyutananda: But in public...*
*Prabhupada: But you should go gradually. You should go gradually. You first of all understand Krishna, then Krishna-lila. If you have not understood Krishna, then you'll think Krishna's rasa-lila is just like we mix with young women. And that becomes as polluted. Because they do not understand Krishna. Manusyanam sahasresu kascid yatati siddhaye yatatam api siddhanam. Krishna understanding so easy? If you do not understand Krishna how can you go to the Krishna's confidential activities?*
*Acyutananda: Some of the devotees, they said that it is for liberated souls. So they said, "Well, we are all liberated."*
*Prabhupada:* **Yes. Liberated for going to hell.**
*Devotee: In your Krishna book, Srila Prabhupada, you've given such clear explanations along with the stories of Krishna that it's very difficult to misinterpret, because you use such clear explanation.*
*Prabhupada: No, you read all the books first of all. Then you'll be able to understand.*
*Yasomatinandana: Even theoretical understanding that Krishna is transcendental will not help unless one...*
*Prabhupada: Because Krishna will lift, samaste, Krishna lifted the hill. Now how you can become equal with Krishna?*
*Devotee: Srila Prabhupada, what about if some devotees, I know they want to come to Vrndavana...*
*Prabhupada: Every devotee, they must follow the rules and regulations, that's all.*
*Devotee: And engage in practical service to Krishna.*
*Prabhupada:* **Yes. Guru-mukha-padma-vakya cittete kariya aikya ara na kariha mane asa. Has he taken order from Guru Maharaja that "I am going to jump over Radha-kunda"? Why does he go? Daily singing, guru-mukha-padma-vakya cittete, ara na kariha. Why should he desire like that?**
*Gopala Krishna: There are some devotees who always want...*
*Prabhupada:* **They are not devotees. Rascals. Don't say "some devotees." Devotees will hear: guru-mukha-padma-vakya cittete kariya aikya ara na kariha mane.** *[Srila Prabhupada Room Conversation, August 16, 1976, Bombay]*

## There is no need to read such a high
## standard of transcendental literature

*"Sri Bhaktisiddhanta Sarasvati Thakura comments in this connection that such feelings of separation as Lord Caitanya Mahaprabhu enjoyed **from the books of Vidyapati, Candidasa and Jayadeva** are especially reserved for persons like Sri Ramananda Raya and Svarupa Damodara, who were paramahamsas, men of the topmost perfection, because of their advanced spiritual consciousness. Such topics are not to be discussed by ordinary persons imitating the activities of Lord Caitanya Mahaprabhu. For critical students of mundane poetry and literary men without God consciousness who are after bodily sense gratification, there is no need to read such a high standard of transcendental literature. Persons who are after sense gratification should not try to imitate raganuga devotional service. In their songs, Candidasa, Vidyapati and Jayadeva have described the transcendental activities of the Supreme Personality of Godhead. Mundane reviewers of the songs of Vidyapati, Jayadeva and Candidasa simply help people in general become debauchees, and this leads only to social scandals and atheism in the world. One should not misunderstand the pastimes of Radha and Krishna to be the activities of a mundane young boy and girl. The mundane sexual activities of young boys and girls are most abominable. Therefore, those who are in bodily consciousness and who desire sense gratification are forbidden to indulge in discussions of the transcendental pastimes of Sri Radha and Krishna."* [Srila Prabhupada from Sri Caitanya-caritamrta, Adi-lila 13.42]


## WHO ARE THE PEOPLE JUMPING OVER AND DIRECTLY
## TRANSLATING THE "PREVIOUS ACARYAS BOOKS"?

*Tamala Krishna.: Pradyumna. Pradyumna is carrying out a single-handed investigation. Pradyumna has become an investigator. He goes around everywhere (laughs) investigating the sahajiyas. I hope he doesn't become won over.*
*Prabhupada: He was.*
*Tamala Krishna:. Yes, I know, that's why he's doing it. He was once like that.*
*Prabhupada: He was smarta.*
*Ramesvara: Pandita, you used to call him pandita.*
*Tamala Krishna: Sometimes Prabhupada would tell him he was a smarta.*
*Ramesvara: He's always carrying an armful of books.*
*Prabhupada: Smarta is also counted amongst the sahajiyas.*
*Tamala Krishna: He was really.... **That's another problem, Prabhupada. All of these boys that take part in this Sanskrit-Bengali translation department, they all become like this, because they read these other books. As soon as they learn Bengali and Sanskrit, they start reading so many books.***
*Prabhupada: **Aula baula, karttabhaja, neda, daravesa, sani sahajiya, sakhibheki, smarta, jata-gosani. They are all counted in one group.***
*Tamala Krishna: One thing I've noticed, Srila Prabhupada, and I see it as a direct link, that most of these people who get involved like this, they're not engaged in*

*active preaching work, and because of it, their mind has time to create these*
*fantasies and get attracted. Someone who's engaged in forcefully preaching...*
*Ramesvara: He has to be more practical.*
*Tamala Krishna: Yes. Practical and purified by the activity. Have you noticed*
*that? That these people who are engaged, they're all in the Press, or all day*
*writing, or something like this.*

*[Srila Prabhupada from a Morning Walk, June 7, 1976, Los Angeles]*

Note: They are in one group that is called apa-sampradaya [outside the
parampara]. Yet the prostitute class like to hear from them. These sahijiyas who
"translate" have no access to the books of the previous acaryas. They are
offensively licking the bottle only, not tasting the sweet juice in the bottle. Most of
the translators of these books don't even understand the basic philosophy that
Prabhupada gives about the diksa process and how his Divine Grace is still present
in sound giving the process. There are so many basic things they don't understand
like origin of the soul etc. etc. Prabhupada instructs us to avoid their association,
not hear from them and thus support their offensive jumping over.

## One should not associate with these
## apa-sampradaya communities.

*"In the parampara system, the instructions taken from the bona fide spiritual*
*master must also be based on revealed Vedic scriptures. One who is in the line of*
*disciplic succession cannot manufacture his own way of behavior.* **There are**
**many so-called followers of the Vaisnava cult in the line of Caitanya**
**Mahaprabhu who do not scrupulously follow the conclusions of the sastras, and**
**therefore they are considered to be apa-sampradaya, which means "outside of**
**the sampradaya."** *Some of these groups are known as aula, baula, kartabhaja,*
*neda, daravesa, sani sahajiya, sakhibheki, smarta, jata-gosani, ativadi, cudadhari*
*and gauranga-nagari.* **In order to follow strictly the disciplic succession of Lord**
**Caitanya Mahaprabhu, one should not associate with these apa-sampradaya**
**communities."** *[Srila Prabhupada from Sri Caitanya-caritamrta, Adi-lila 7.48]*

Note: By avoiding these apa-sampradaya communities who are flooding the
market place with their offensive translations of the "previous acaryas books" and
thus titillating the mind and senses of the prostitute class, we can then be engaged
in various important preaching projects for Prabhupada. Sulocana prabhu made it
clear we need to categorize Srila Prabhupada's complete works and then print
them in smaller books so the general public who may not have time to read the
complete works can get quick and direct access to the particular subjects they are
interested in. The 7,000 personal letters that Prabhupada wrote also need to be
indexed and printed. Why not work to support these projects and thus flood the
world with the bone-fide parampara books of the messiah Srila Prabhupada? Why
be a prostitute and thus support the proliferation of these offensive apa-siddhantic
books in human society?

### No learned man should be willing to hear a person
### who does not represent the original acarya

*TRANSLATION: On hearing Suta Gosvami speak thus, Saunaka Muni, who was the elderly, learned leader of all the rsis engaged in that prolonged sacrificial ceremony, congratulated Suta Gosvami by addressing him as follows.*

*PURPORT: In a meeting of learned men, when there are congratulations or addresses for the speaker, the qualifications of the congratulator should be as follows. He must be the leader of the house and an elderly man. He must be vastly learned also. Sri Saunaka Rsi had all these qualifications, and thus he stood up to congratulate Sri Suta Gosvami when he expressed his desire to present Srimad-Bhagavatam exactly as he heard it from Sukadeva Gosvami and also realized it personally. Personal realization does not mean that one should, out of vanity, attempt to show one's own learning by trying to surpass the previous acarya. He must have full confidence in the previous acarya, and at the same time he must realize the subject matter so nicely that he can present the matter for the particular circumstances in a suitable manner. The original purpose of the text must be maintained. No obscure meaning should be screwed out of it, yet it should be presented in an interesting manner for the understanding of the audience. This is called realization. The leader of the assembly, Saunaka, could estimate the value of the speaker, Sri Suta Gosvami, simply by his uttering yathadhitam and yatha-mati, and therefore he was very glad to congratulate him in ecstasy. __No learned man should be willing to hear a person who does not represent the original acarya.__ So the speaker and the audience were bona fide in this meeting where Bhagavatam was being recited for the second time. That should be the standard of recitation of Bhagavatam, so that the real purpose can be served without difficulty. Unless this situation is created, Bhagavatam recitation for extraneous purposes is useless labor both for the speaker and for the audience. [Srila Prabhupada from Srimad Bhagavatam 1.4.1]*

Note: We hear from Srila Prabhupada because he represents the original acarya but how can these sahajiya babajis be considered to be representatives of Prabhupada? They are rather in the camp of the enemies of Prabhupada. No learned man will hear their offensive translations of the "previous acaryas books", only foolish prostitutes!

## OTHER COMMENTS

**Sanat dasa prabhu:** So, yes, also Srila Prabhupada has stated that "everything is there in My Books" And "I have already answered all your questions in My Books," like that.

If it's not in Prabhupada's Books, we take it as illicit, and prostitution, offensive to Srila Prabhupada. We have no right to jump over the Spiritual Master, bona fide Guru Acarya Who sacrificed everything just to save us from nirvisesa and sunyavadi. We had nothing bona fide prior to Srila Prabhupada's most munificent appearance in our wasted lives, now we should very much be grateful to His Divine Grace, chaste to Him and adhere strictly ONLY to His transcendental Teachings, which are all-inclusive. Otherwise it's accepting another 'guru' by jumping over, prostituting oneself.

Personally I'd be very embarrassed to even be seen opening one such unauthorized book; can't imagine offending Srila Prabhupada by leaving aside His unlimited Spiritual Library of Books - which can't even be read and fathomed by me in a 100 lifetimes - for one syllable of some non-essential non-Prabhupadized book written by either an unscrupulous person or one whom I'm unable to approach due to my servitorship to Srila Prabhupada Maharaja.

**Locanananda dasa prabhu:** His Divine Grace said that he included all we needed to know to go back to Godhead in the three volumes of the First Canto. He also said that we could become fully Krishna conscious by reading the Bhagavad-gita, the Srimad Bhagavatam, the Nectar of Devotion and the Teachings of Lord Caitanya. In his books, there are hundreds upon hundreds of references to the writings of the previous acaryas, and by extracting the essence of their teachings, Srila Prabhupada has given the most confidential knowledge to the entire world.

One need not go beyond what has been presented by the spiritual master, but rather one should become expert in presenting the same message.

*"It is important that we preach the message of Krishna consciousness EXACTLY as we have heard it from OUR spiritual master. The same philosophy and spirit must be there." (Letter to Sivananda dated 1-23-69)*

# ARE YOU A SUPPORTER OF SISUPALA ISKCON?

Mukunda dasa 2006

*"Just as a lion does not care when a flock of jackals howl, Lord Krsna **remained silent** and **unprovoked**. Krsna did not reply to even a single accusation made by Sisupala, but all the members present in the meeting, **except a few who agreed with Sisupala**, became very agitated because it is the duty of any respectable person not to tolerate blasphemy against God or His devotee. Some of them, who thought that they could not properly take action against Sisupala, left the assembly in protest, covering their ears with their hands in order not to hear further accusations. Thus they left the meeting condemning the action of Sisupala. It is the Vedic injunction that whenever there is blasphemy of the Supreme Personality of Godhead, one must immediately leave. If he does not do so, he becomes bereft of his pious activities and is degraded to the lower condition of life. All the kings present, belonging to the Kuru dynasty, Matsya dynasty, Kekaya dynasty and Srnjaya dynasty, became very angry and immediately took up their swords and shields to kill Sisupala."*

*(KRSNA BOOK CHAPTER SEVENTY-FOUR The Deliverance of Sisupala)*

Note: If we draw the parallel of the Rajasuya arena and ISKCON, then we can see that as Sisupala could not tolerate Krishna being glorified and thus blasphemed him, in the same way these envious souls dressed as devotees cannot tolerate Prabhupada being exclusively glorified as the Guru of Iskcon. Therefore they poisoned him, usurped his movement, changed his books and presented him as the leader of their child molesting cult, to the world.

It is the duty of any respectable person not to tolerate this blasphemy against Srila Prabhupada!!! Anyone who cannot properly take action against this cult of offenders, must at least leave this demoniac society in protest for good, never again to return! It is the **Vedic injunction** that whenever there is blasphemy of a pure devotee like Srila Prabhupada, one must immediately leave that place. If he does not do so, he becomes bereft of his pious activities and is degraded to the lower condition of life.

*"If someone blasphemes a Vaisnava, one should stop him with arguments and higher reason. If one is not expert enough to do this he should give up his life on the spot, and if he cannot do this, **he must go away**." (C.C. Adi 7.50)*

Note: Go away for good never to return, never to associate again, this is the Vedic injunction!!!

As those who agreed with Sisupala were silent, *[Prabhupada makes this same point also "If we remain silent, then whatever he says, that means we are accepting." (Discussion about Guru Maharaji August 13, 1973, Paris)]* those who visit or associate with this cult in anyway and don't take proper action *[as described in the above quote]* against their blasphemous activities but are simply silent in the face of them, such persons are ultimately supporters of these blasphemies and will equally share the result of these extremely sinful actions!!!

## AFTER DEATH THE RESULT OF AN ACTION IS EQUALLY SHARED BY IT'S DOER, IT'S DIRECTOR AND IT'S SUPPORTER

*"I request all the pure-hearted demigods, forefathers and saintly persons to support my proposal, for **after death the result of an action is equally shared by its doer, its director and its <u>supporter</u>."** (S.B. 4.21.26)*

Note: So visit a Sisupala Iskcon temple at your own peril!!!

**Those sinful people who blaspheme Vaisnavas, who are all great souls, are subjected very severely to the punishment offered by Yamaraja.**

*TRANSLATION: "If the man who blasphemed Sri Caitanya Mahaprabhu is killed, his sinful action may be atoned."*

*PURPORT: The Hari-bhakti-vilasa cites the following quotation from Skanda Purana concerning the blaspheming of a Vaisnava... In this conversation between Markandeya and Bhagiratha, it is said: "My dear King, if one derides an exalted devotee, he loses the results of his pious activities, his opulence, his reputation and his sons. Vaisnavas are all great souls. **Whoever blasphemes them falls down to the hell known as Maharaurava. He is also accompanied by his forefathers. Whoever <u>kills</u> or blasphemes a Vaisnava and whoever is envious of a Vaisnava or angry with him, or whoever does not offer him obeisances or feel joy upon seeing a Vaisnava, certainly falls into a hellish condition."***

*The Hari-bhakti-vilasa (10.314) also gives the following quotation from Dvaraka-mahatmya... In a conversation between Prahlada Maharaja and Bali Maharaja, it is said, "**Those sinful people who blaspheme Vaisnavas, who are all great souls, are subjected very severely to the punishment offered by Yamaraja.**"*

*In the Bhakti-sandarbha (313) there is a statement concerning the blaspheming of Lord Visnu. "One who criticizes Lord Visnu and His devotees loses all the benefits accrued in a hundred pious births. **Such a person rots in the Kumbhipaka hell and is bitten by worms as long as the sun and moon exist. One should therefore***

*not even see the face of a person who blasphemes Lord Visnu and His devotees.*
*Never try to associate with such persons."*

*In his Bhakti-sandarbha (265), Jiva Gosvami further quotes from Srimad-*
*Bhagavatam (10.74.40): "If one does not immediately leave upon hearing the Lord*
*or the Lord's devotee blasphemed, he falls down from devotional service."*
*Similarly, Lord Siva's wife Sati states in Srimad-Bhagavatam (4.4.17): "If one*
*hears an irresponsible person blaspheme the master and controller of religion, he*
*should block his ears and go away if unable to punish him. But if one is able to*
*kill, then one should by force cut out the blasphemer's tongue and kill the offender,*
*and after that he should give up his own life." (C.C. Madya Lila 15.261)*

Note: It does appear that even seeing these various blasphemers is so polluting
what to speak of giving them any type of support. This is why Prabhupada called
such violators of religious principles the most dangerous elements in human
society [Isopanisad mantra 12]. By associating with them one will also be thrown
into the darkest regions of hell, the most obnoxious place in the universe. A man is
known by his company... birds of a feather..... is it not?

Never try to associate with the Sisupala Iskcon group, the Iskcon Reform [not
neglect] the Prabhupada Killers movement [IRM], the PADA work with the
Turley blasphemers group, or the Sisupala Gaudiya Matha sahajiya party that is
the CLEAR WARNING! Prabhupada tells us to completely neglect all association
with such jealous persons in the dress of Vaisnavas.

*"A mundane person in the dress of a Vaisnava should not be respected but*
*rejected. This is enjoined in the sastra (upeksa). The word upeksa means neglect.*
*One should neglect an envious person. A preacher's duty is to love the Supreme*
*Personality of Godhead, make friendships with Vaisnavas, show mercy to the*
*innocent and reject or neglect those who are envious or jealous. There are many*
*jealous people in the dress of Vaisnavas in this Krsna consciousness movement,*
*and they should be completely neglected. There is no need to serve a jealous*
*person who is in the dress of a Vaisnava. When Narottama dasa Thakura says*
*chadiya vaisnava seva nistara payeche keba, he is indicating an actual Vaisnava,*
*not an envious or jealous person in the dress of a Vaisnava." (C.C. Madhya Lila*
*1.218)*

Note: Again the same Vedic Injunction is stressed by Srila Prabhupada. Leave
[reject, completely neglect] that place where jealous persons in the dress of
vaisnavas blaspheme the pure devotee. His Grace Sulocana Prabhu, commenting
on the following Prabhupada letter: "*Regarding the poisonous effect in our*
*Society, it is a fact and I know where from this poison tree has sprung up and how*
*it affected practically the whole Society in a very dangerous form... It is a fact*
*however that the great sinister movement is within our Society. (Hansadutta,*
*9/2/70)*" has said "*This exact same sinister movement is still there, but it is no*
*longer within the Society, it has become the Society and everyone else has fled*
*for their lives*"

Devotees have fled for their lives because they know that to stay in a place or society where Prabhupada is blasphemed is spiritual suicide. Those who hang around are the parasites of the most obnoxious, abominable characters in the universe.

An interesting point in regards to Prabhupada's assets like the temples, they are now stolen property. If anyone visits these usurped temples even unknowingly, he will be subjected to the reactions of stealing the topmost brahmana's property.

*"At this time, Lord Krsna was present among His relatives who were members of the ksatriya class. To teach them through the exemplary character of King Nrga, He said: "Even though a ksatriya king may be as powerful as fire, it is not possible for him to usurp the property of a brahmana and utilize it for his own purpose. If this is so, how can ordinary kings, who falsely think of themselves the most powerful beings within the material world, usurp a brahmana's property? I do not think that taking poison is as dangerous as taking a brahmana's property. For ordinary poison there is treatment--one can be relieved from its effects; but if one drinks the poison of taking a brahmana's property, there is no remedy for the mistake. The perfect example was King Nrga. He was very powerful and very pious, but due to the small mistake of unknowingly usurping a brahmana's cow, he was condemned to the abominable life of a lizard. Ordinary poison affects only those who drink it, and ordinary fire can be extinguished simply by pouring water on it; but the arani fire ignited by the spiritual potency of a brahmana can burn to ashes the whole family of a person who provokes such brahmana." (Formerly, the brahmanas used to ignite the fire of sacrifice not with matches or any other external fire but with their powerful mantras, called arani.) "If someone even touches a brahmana's property, he is ruined for three generations. However, if a brahmana's property is forcibly taken away, the taker's family for ten generations before him and for ten generations after him will be subject to ruination. On the other hand, if someone becomes a Vaisnava or devotee of the Lord, ten generations of his family before his birth and ten generations after will become liberated."*

*Lord Krsna continued: "If some foolish king who is puffed up by his wealth, prestige and power wants to usurp a brahmana's property, it should be understood that such a king is clearing his path to hell; he does not know how much he has to suffer for such unwise action. If someone takes away the property of a very liberal brahmana who is encumbered by a large dependent family, then such a usurper is put into the hell known as Kumbhipaka; not only is he put into this hell, but his family members also have to accept such a miserable condition of life. A person who takes away property which has either been awarded to a brahmana or given away by him is condemned to live for at least 60,000 years as miserably as an insect in stool. Therefore I instruct you, all My boys and relatives present here, do not, even by mistake, take the possession of a brahmana and thereby pollute your whole family. If someone even wishes to possess such property, let alone attempts to take it away by force, the duration of his life will be reduced. He will be defeated by his enemies, and after being bereft of his royal position, when he gives up his body he will become a serpent. A serpant gives trouble to all other living entities. My dear boys and relatives, I therefore advise you that even if a brahmana becomes angry with you and calls you by ill names or cuts you, still you should not retaliate. On the contrary, you should smile, tolerate him and offer your respects to the brahmana. You know very well that even I Myself offer My obeisances to the brahmanas with great respect three times daily. You should therefore follow My instruction and example.* **I shall not forgive anyone who does not follow them, and I shall punish him. You should learn from the example of King Nrga that even if someone <u>unknowingly</u> usurps the property of a brahmana, he is put into a miserable condition of life.***"*

*Thus Lord Krsna, who is always engaged in purifying the conditioned living entities, gave instruction not only to His family members and the inhabitants of Dvaraka, but to all the members of human society. After this the Lord entered His palace.*" (*Prabhupada From Krishna Book - Sixty-fourth Chapter "The Story of King Nrga"*)

Note: Someone may say that: "But some of the people in Sispala Iskcon are doing good things like putting Prabhupada's film footage on DVD etc.... or transcribing his conversations into book form." Of course this is wonderful service for the people involved and all those souls reading etc. But still these projects also benefit the cult and allow it to continue. And for each "good" thing they may do there are many bad. For example by purchasing the conversation set from the cult one also supports the printing of many offensive unauthorised changed books. The Vedabase is another example, a wonderful facility but full of changed books, so it is like sweet rice mixed with a little sand. All these projects should be done properly by devotees who are completely independent of the cult and it's influence. Otherwise these thieves are simply getting full facility to exploit Prabhupada's assets and followers for their own demoniac ends.

Another view is that if one makes a mistake in the beginning of a maths calculation then whatever one does after that will be an expansion of that original mistake, or in other words an expansion of the offense to Prabhupada. Even if it is not viewed as an expansion of the original mistake one will still be subject to getting a reaction for both his good and bad actions, as was King Nrga. Just because one may do something apparently as service to Prabhupada that doesn't mean he is free from equally sharing the reactions of all the blasphemous offenses to Prabhupada, as a supporter.

And it doesn't mean that because we perceive with our imperfect senses some expansion of that original mistake as service to Prabhupada, or because the Deity and Prabhupada's Murti in the cult are transcendentally situated, we can again mix with the cult on the plea of going to see the Deities and think we are also transcendental and above contamination by association. No we are not transcendental; we **will** be subject to reactions of blasphemy. We are not above the Vedic injunctions. We **must** leave that place where offenses to Prabhupada are taking place unless we wish to commit spiritual suicide.

Nor should one think that because a few original books are printed 27 years after Prabhupada demanded it, or because these jealous persons suddenly accept the formal rtvik system of initiation that that wipes the slate clean... "now i'm free to enjoy in the vipers nest without a reaction." NO!!!

**CONCLUSION**: Anyone claiming to be a sincere follower of Srila Prabhupada MUST completely neglect all association with Sisupala Iskcon and those who support it. This is not a question of opinion, it is a Vedic Injunction. If one violates this injunction, he is committing spiritual suicide.

## IF THE OFFENSE IS VERY SERIOUS, THEN
## ONE'S ATTACHMENT BECOMES ALMOST NIL

*"As attachment can be invoked by the association of pure devotees, so attachment can also be extinguished by offenses committed at the lotus feet of pure devotees. To be more clear, by the association of pure devotees attachment for Krishna can be aroused, but if one commits offenses at the lotus feet of a devotee, one's shadow attachment or para attachment can be extinguished. This extinguishing is like the waning of the full moon, which gradually decreases and at last becomes dark. One should therefore be very careful while associating with pure devotees to guard against committing an offense at their lotus feet.*

*Transcendental attachment, either shadow or para, can be nullified by different degrees of offenses at the lotus feet of pure devotees. **If the offense is very serious, then one's attachment becomes almost nil**, and if the offense is not very serious, one's attachment can become second class or third class."*

*(N.O.D. Chapter 18)*

Note: This is also a very important consideration. If we are serving under the ISKCON leadership, who have committed extremely serious offenses to Srila Prabhupada, then how can we develop our attachment to Krishna? We are associating and rendering service to offenders who have almost no attachment to Krishna. By their association we will also lose our attachment to Srila Prabhupada and Krishna.

The 1976 Dodge van in which Sulocana prabhu wrote his epic Guru Business.

# DRAWINGS OF SULOCANA

By Radharani Devi Dasi - Age 6

By Tulsi Devi Dasi - Age 6

# OTHER BOOKS AVAILABLE

Śrīla Prabhupāda
Līlāmṛta As It Is

The Pastimes of His Divine Grace
A.C. Bhaktivedanta Swami Prabhupada

**Prabhupada's Authorized Autobiography**

**SRILA PRABHUPADA LILAMRTA AS IT IS - Mukunda dasa**

**The Pastimes of His Divine Grace**

**A.C. Bhaktivedanta Swami Prabhupada**

First Printing 2001

"Srila Prabhupada speaks out. He speaks for himself about himself. Truly a work of pure love and devotion. Fully utilizing all the space on every page to print the actual words spoken by Srila Prabhupada himself about the mission of his life to spread Krsna-consciousness all over the world." Krsna dasa, India.

Hear the life story of His Divine Grace A.C. Bhaktivedanta Swami Prabhupada directly from his own lotus mouth that is authentic!

*"If you want to know me, then you must know about me from me. You can not speculate about me." [Srila Prabhupada Room Conversation with Reporter June 4, 1976, Los Angeles] "So that means, anyway, if you want to know about me, then you must know from me. That is authentic. That is authentic." [Srila Prabhupada from a Bhagavad-gita Lecture, 3.17-20, New York, May 27, 1966]*

**ALL OF US SHOULD HEAR PRABHUPADA - Mukunda dasa**

First Printing 1993 - Second Printing 1999.

This book is a compilation of quotes from the teachings of HIS DIVINE GRACE A.C. BHAKTIVEDANTA SWAMI PRABHUPADA on the importance of hearing from the self realized soul. The simple practice of hearing Srila Prabhupada lecture twice daily in association puts His Divine Grace practically in the center of all our lives. By hearing from Srila Prabhupada all misconceptions will be cleansed from our hearts. Then we can unite and spread the Sankirtana Movement in every town and village in the world.

*"Every devotee who follows Prabhupada's teachings should have this book!" - Rukmini Devi Dasi (USA)*

400

NEW PRINTING!!! "Henry Doktorski's recent book called Killing For Krishna, The Danger Of Deranged Devotion, falls in the same category as ISKCON's biography of Srila Prabhupada. It is an offensive book of poisonous slander that is nicely sugar coated with false glorification, so that the foolish will swallow it and thus commit spiritual suicide. The only difference between the two books is that Killing For Krishna lacks any of the subtleness of ISKCON's biography. Doktorski's slander of Sulocana is totally gross and in your face, unlike Satsvarupa's slander of Prabhupada which has a more covert nature. The amazing thing is that so many "devotees" claiming to be Prabhupada followers praise this offensive book that slanders Sulocana on page after page!" (Mukunda dasa - Killing For Keith, Chapter One)

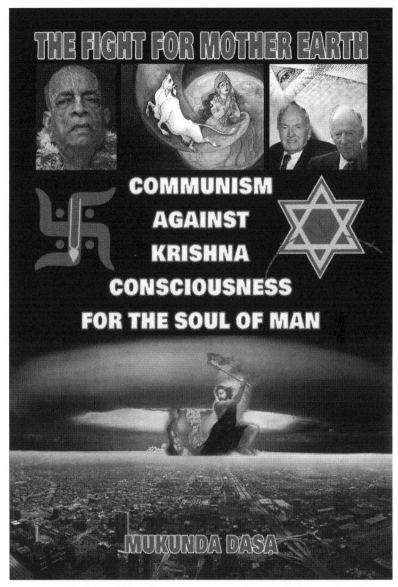

THIS BOOK WILL BE AVAILABLE SOON!!! "The fight
between the Lord, the Supreme Personality of Godhead, and the
demon is compared to a fight between bulls for the sake of a
cow. The earth planet is also called go, or cow. As bulls fight
between themselves to ascertain who will have union with a cow,
there is always a constant fight between the demons and the
Supreme Lord or His representative for supremacy over the
earth." (Srila Prabhupada from Srimad Bhagavatam 3.18.20)

ALL THESE BOOKS CAN BE PURCHASED FROM
PRABHUPADA STORE ON THE FOLLOWING LINK:
https://www.gokula-incense.co.uk/
prabhupada-original-books-107-c.asp

# ACKNOWLEDGEMENTS

I would like to thank my wife Gauri Devi Dasi and my son Nitai-Gaura Dasa for patiently helping me with all the editing that had to be done to produce this book. Hare Krishna. Jaya Prabhupada. Jaya Sulocana Prabhu.

Mukunda dasa

Monday the 3<sup>rd</sup> of August, 2020. Lord Balarama's Appearance Day.

"Anyone who has read The Guru Business will have at once felt the powerful and illuminating clarity in the words of Sulocana prabhu. The way in which he has strung Prabhupada's words together, like pearls on the thread of his own amazing realizations, came from his total surrender to the instruction of Srila Prabhupada. Sulocana prabhu was prepared to die rather than not execute Prabhupada's mission properly. Because of this faith not only did the Lord manifest Prabhupada's previously hidden letters to Sulocana but he revealed their purport in his heart."

Mukunda dasa from Killing For Keith, Chapter Seven.

Printed in Great Britain
by Amazon

47289112R10246